D0078339

About Island Press

Since 1984, the nonprofit Island Press has been stimulating, shaping, and communicating the ideas that are essential for solving environmental problems worldwide. With more than 800 titles in print and some 40 new releases each year, we are the nation's leading publisher on environmental issues. We identify innovative thinkers and emerging trends in the environmental field. We work with world-renowned experts and authors to develop cross-disciplinary solutions to environmental challenges.

Island Press designs and implements coordinated book publication campaigns in order to communicate our critical messages in print, in person, and online using the latest technologies, programs, and the media. Our goal: to reach targeted audiences—scientists, policymakers, environmental advocates, the media, and concerned citizens—who can and will take action to protect the plants and animals that enrich our world, the ecosystems we need to survive, the water we drink, and the air we breathe.

Island Press gratefully acknowledges the support of its work by the Agua Fund, Inc., Annenberg Foundation, The Christensen Fund, The Nathan Cummings Foundation, The Geraldine R. Dodge Foundation, Doris Duke Charitable Foundation, The Educational Foundation of America, Betsy and Jesse Fink Foundation, The William and Flora Hewlett Foundation, The Kendeda Fund, The Forrest and Frances Lattner Foundation, The Andrew W. Mellon Foundation, The Curtis and Edith Munson Foundation, Oak Foundation, The Overbrook Foundation, the David and Lucile Packard Foundation, The Summit Fund of Washington, Trust for Architectural Easements, Wallace Global Fund, The Winslow Foundation, and other generous donors.

Ecotourism and Sustainable Development
Second Edition

Ecotourism and Sustainable Development

Second Edition

Who Owns Paradise?

Martha Honey

Washington • Covelo • London

Honey, Martha.
Ecotourism and sustainable development : who owns paradise? / Martha Honey. — 2nd ed.
p. cm.
Includes index.
ISBN-13: 978-1-59726-125-8 (cloth : alk. paper)
ISBN-10: 1-59726-125-4 (cloth : alk. paper)
ISBN-13: 978-1-59726-126-5 (pbk. : alk. paper)
ISBN-10: 1-59726-126-2 (pbk. : alk. paper)
1. Ecotourism. 2. Ecotourism—Latin America. 3. Ecotourism—Africa. 4. Sustainable development—Latin America. 5. Sustainable development—Africa. I. Title.
G156.5.E26H66 2008
338.4'791—dc22q 2007045269

Printed on recycled, acid-free paper 

Manufactured in the United States of America

10 9 8 7 6 5 4 3 2 1

Keywords: travel, tourism, tour operators, economic development, parks and protected areas, conservation, environment, nature, indigenous peoples, Galapagos Islands, Costa Rica, Tanzania, Zanzibar, Kenya, South Africa, sustainable tourism, ecotourism, sustainable development

Contents

Acknowledgments

This new edition has had a long birthing process. Beginning, I believe, in 2003, my editor at Island Press, Todd Baldwin, began nudging me to take the time to do an updated version. I was gratified to see how widely the first edition has been used in university courses, by ecotourism practitioners and professionals, and by interested travelers. Because I was working full time, I didn't have the time to carry out in-depth, on-the-ground research in all the countries, as I had done for the first volume. So instead, I assembled a small army of researchers in the United States and around the world who have worked with me to update each chapter, as well as to create the new addition, a chapter on ecotourism in the United States. In roughly chronological order, these researchers included Zoe Chafe, Emy Rodriguez, Mollie Chapman, Roselyn Cameron, Audrey Davenport, Kamweti Mutu, Judy Kepher-Gona, Fred Nelson, Anna Spenceley, Duna Biggs, Christopher Lupoli, Cabeto Lopez, Amos Bien, and Katrina Shum. I am deeply indebted to these people for their invaluable assistance in creating this volume.

The original book grew out of my years living in East Africa and Central America, where my curiosity was piqued about whether nature tourism and later ecotourism could really contribute to sustainable economic development, particularly for rural communities. I was struck by the destructiveness of so many economic activities geared toward earning foreign exchange, from conventional mass tourism, to mining, logging, and industrial agriculture. And I was impressed by how the countries where I had lived (Tanzania and Costa Rica) had, with foresight and sacrifice, established extensive systems of national parks and other protected areas, totaling, in each case, close to a quarter of their territory. One of my unfinished projects from the decades abroad was to look closely and systematically at ecotourism, to trace its origins, and to critically examine how it fit into the development strategies of a number of countries. I arrived back in the United States in the early 1990s on the crest of the ecotourism wave, as environmental organizations, aid agencies, and the travel industry were all heralding ecotourism as a win-win proposition for Third World countries, conservation, and the traveling public.

I embarked on my quest into ecotourism with a belief that I was going to find little more than marketing hype, to discover, as Sierra Club's Carl Pope said to me, "no there there." What I found was, thankfully, a much more rich and varied panorama with many countries and communities attempting to apply the principles and best practices of ecotourism to create businesses that would benefit both conservation and host communities. I became convinced that ecotourism was possible, was being practiced to varying degrees, in scores of places around the world.

Since completing the first edition, I have moved from doing ecotourism research in my off hours to working full time in the field, with The International Ecotourism Society (TIES; which I directed from 2003 through 2006) and the Center on Ecotourism and Sustainable Development (CESD), which I have codirected since its founding in 2003. Fortunately, my ecotourism work has taken me to ecodestinations, field projects, conferences, and meetings around the world, and this has enabled me to keep abreast of developments and trends.

This new edition is, in many sections, markedly different from the original text. This is a tribute to how, over the last decade, ecotourism has grown both in terms of its geographical reach and its practical innovations. Watershed events have included the UN's International Year of Ecotourism in 2002 and the first ever conference on ecotourism in the United States in 2005 (which was organized by TIES while I was director). In addition, a number of new concepts and tools are helping to deepen the meaning of ecotourism. These include the growth of "green" certification programs. In 2000, I organized, together with Abigail Rome, the first ever international workshop on ecotourism and sustainable tourism certification programs, held at the Mohonk Mountain House outside New York City. Now, in 2008, we are on the cusp of launching the Sustainable Tourism Stewardship Council (STSC), the first global accreditation body that will assess "green" certification programs against a set of common criteria. This marks a major step forward in setting environmental and social standards for the tourism industry, and much of the credit for success goes to Ronald Sanabria and the Rainforest Alliance, which has carried out the broadly participatory process over the last decade.

In addition to the primary researchers, many others contributed to specific subjects, by reading sections of the manuscript, and by helping to ensure its accuracy. They include for the three first chapters, Iain Christie, Santiago Soler, Michael Conroy, Juan Luna, Roberta Hilbruner, Carol Hansen, Emma Stewart; Kurt Kutay, Eileen Gutierrez, Ronald Sanabria, and Pam Wight; for the Galapagos, Bill Durham; for Costa Rica, Karen Lewis, Glenn Jampol, Tamara Budowski, Andrea

Holbrook, Beatrice Blake, Beatriz Gamez, Andrea Bonilla, Jim Damalas, Dan Janzen, Pedro Leon, Eduardo Villafranca, Alex Khajavi, Alexi Huntley, and former president Rodrigo Carazo; for East Africa, Abdul Sheriff, Fatma Alloo, David (Jonah) Western, Ian Bryceson, Kjersti Thorkildsen, Sibylle Riedmiller, Helen Peeks, Hitesh Mehta, Stefan Gossling, and Paul Oliver; for South Africa, Les Carlisle, Hilton Loon, Hector Magome, and P. J. Massyn; and for the United States, Bill Bryan, Roger Lang, Barbara Richman, Chris Seek, Jestena Boughton, and Rod Erdmann. I could not have done this new edition without the support of my colleagues at the Center on Ecotourism and Sustainable Development (CESD) who provided time and resources for me to do the writing and editing. I owe special thanks to CESD's codirector Bill Durham (my counterpart at Stanford) and David Krantz, the Washington coordinator who picked up various balls that I dropped. In addition, CESD staff Whitney Cooper and Laura Driscoll willingly helped with bits and pieces of research and copyediting.

I want to pay special tribute and give thanks to two dear colleagues who have suffered personal tragedies. Tom Horton, a leading innovator in sustainable design of larger tourism projects, was recently paralyzed in a freak fall. In the past couple of years, Tom has generously worked to assist CESD and has taught me a great deal about transforming the broader tourism industry. Eddie Koch, a widely respected journalist, scholar, activist, and ecotourism expert in South Africa, suffered a debilitating heart attack and has not been able to continue working full time. Over the years, Eddie taught me a great deal about efforts in his country to use ecotourism to help empower and benefit local communities.

I am enormously grateful to Island Press, and most especially to Todd Baldwin, who encouraged me to undertake this new edition, provided some much needed financial support, and competently edited the manuscript. In addition, I want to thank production editor Katherine Macdonald, who has overseen the final stages of this book.

And finally, I want to thank, once again, my family for providing the critical "enabling environment" of quiet space, good meals, and emotional support and encouragement. My husband Tony (dubbed a saint by my parents) put up with all the weird hours and angst in preparing this book. My father John used his professorial skills to do fine copyediting on a number of the chapters, while my mother Mary and mother-in-law Fran have continued to take an interest in my progress. My brother Tim helped me with the South African chapter while he was living in Cape Town. And my now grown children, Shanti, Jody, and Deta, all of whom helped with the first edition, have continued to give me insights from their travels, new readings, and their steadfast support. I am grateful to you all!

Part 1
What Is Ecotourism?

1

In Search of the Golden Toad

In 1987, Costa Rican Giovanni Bello and other investigators counted more than 1,500 adult golden toads in the Monteverde Cloud Forest Reserve. The next year, scientists and naturalist guides found just ten. In 1989, they found only one. Later that same year, there were two unconfirmed sightings of others. Since then no golden toads have been found. Many scientists concluded that the brilliant orange-colored toad, which was thought to exist only in Costa Rica's Monteverde Reserve, had become extinct. At the same time, scientists around the world began noticing a dramatic drop in numbers of other species of toads and frogs. There are many theories to explain why. Some speculate a connection with volcanic eruptions, the warming El Niño winds and currents, acid rain, depletion of the ozone layer, chemical pollution, habitat destruction, or disease caused by a lethal, single-celled protozoan.[1] Others warn that frogs, like canaries carried down a coal mine shaft, are giving a biological signal that conditions for survival are horribly out of balance and catastrophe is close at hand. Most recently, a type of fungus, known as the *chytrid fungus*, has been found to be driving amphibian extinctions worldwide, including in Central America.[2]

Bello and other Costa Rican naturalists continue to hope that the golden toads are simply in hiding, buried deep under the reserve's rich, moist biomass, and that one spring day they will again emerge, hopping from fern to vine to root. Such hopes may be maintained by the fact that another amphibian, the harlequin frog, had also disappeared in Costa Rica, but in 2003, a Yale scientist rediscovered it.[3] Nowadays, visitors to Monteverde see the golden toad only on postcards and on the

Researchers Chris Lupoli and Emy Rodriguez researched and updated this chapter.

entrance sign to one of the reserve's most popular tourist lodges, El Sapo Dorado.

In Monteverde, the disappearance of the golden toad has coincided with the phenomenal growth of tourism, in particular a relatively new "species" known as ecotourism. Although often equated with nature tourism, ecotourism, properly understood, goes further, striving to respect and benefit protected areas as well as the people living around or on these lands. The history of the golden toad and that of ecotourism are intertwined, and some speculate that an ecotourist (or perhaps a scientist) may have carried into Monteverde's rain forest an alien organism that caused a plague among the reserve's toad population.[4] If true, it is ironic, since Monteverde scientists and residents have consciously used conservation grants and ecotourism profits to protect the habitat of the golden toad and other exotic, endangered species, including the Resplendent Quetzal, one of the world's most majestic birds. Monteverde's farming community and conservation organizations began buying and incorporating surrounding land so that by 2005, more than ten thousand hectares (some twenty-six thousand acres) had been incorporated into this privately owned park, which is managed by a nonprofit scientific organization.[5] Initially, the reserve attracted only scientists, some students, visiting friends and family (known in tourism lingo as VFFs), and a trickle of hardy travelers. But beginning in the mid-1980s—on the eve of the golden toad's disappearance—the worldwide growth of ecotourism brought a flood of visitors and a tidal wave of change to this small community. Tourist numbers grew from just over 450 in 1974, to 3,100 in 1980, 17,500 in 1989, 50,000 in 1993, to about 200,000 by 2005.[6] Most of Monteverde's hotels have been built since 1990, and ecotourism has surpassed dairy farming as the community's main source of income.

Around the world, ecotourism has been hailed as a panacea: a way to fund conservation and scientific research, protect fragile and pristine ecosystems, benefit rural communities, promote development in poor countries, enhance ecological and cultural sensitivity, instill environmental awareness and a social conscience in the travel industry, satisfy and educate the discriminating tourist, and, some claim, build world peace.[7] Although "green" travel is being aggressively marketed as a win-win solution for the Third World, the environment, the tourist, and the travel industry, close examination shows a much more complex reality.

This book is about the search for ecotourism. Although nearly all countries in the world, including the United States, Canada, Germany, Australia, and other developed countries, are now engaged in ecotourism, perhaps its most exciting potential is in its use as a tool for economic development and environmental protection in developing countries. I lived in East Africa and Central America for nearly twenty years, first as a graduate student and then as a journalist covering liberation struggles, civil and cold war–inspired conflicts, natural and human-made disasters, popular protests, and a variety of economic development strategies spanning the political spectrum. Although tourism was only occasionally a central focus of my reporting, I was fascinated by its complexities and contradictions as they played out on the ground in East and southern Africa, Latin America, and the Caribbean.

During my decades abroad I had found that for many economically poor countries with rich, unique, and largely unspoiled national parks and natural wonders, tourism offered a possible means for earning foreign exchange. But the infrastructure costs of conventional tourism are high, its adverse social effects are often great, and the economic benefits frequently meager, since most of the profits did not stay in the host countries. In the 1970s, I witnessed a lively and contentious political debate over tourism between socialist Tanzania and capitalist Kenya, which shared between them some of the world's finest game parks. By the early 1990s, these countries and the island of Zanzibar were all aggressively promoting nature tourism and ecotourism, with historically marginalized rural communities demanding a slice of the tourism pie. When I lived in Costa Rica during the 1980s, I saw the country transform itself from a low-key outpost for nature lovers into the most popular ecotourism destination in the Americas. Beginning in the 1990s, there were alarming reports that the Galapagos Islands—a unique ecosystem and one of the world's most fragile, often cited as the place where ecotourism began—was being permanently altered by an uncontrolled influx of tourists, immigrants, and commercial fishermen. And, during this same decade, I was intrigued to see that both South Africa and Cuba, two countries that for very different political reasons had been considered international pariahs, were promoting tourism (and ecotourism) as the engine for economic growth and reintegration into the worldwide free-market system. By 2005, ecotourism was booming in South Africa. With Fidel Castro's retirement, however, Cuba's future direction was very much up for grabs. Cuba's early ecotourism innovations did not expand into wider government-backed eco-projects. Instead, its development model appeared increasingly to be based on classic Caribbean-style resort tourism.[8] Given these uncertainties and the difficulties of conducting research in Cuba, I decided to shift gears and add to this edition a chapter on the relatively unexplored topic of ecotourism in the United States. Prior to 2005, when The International Ecotourism Society (TIES) organized the first-ever conference on ecotourism in the United States,[9] little attention had been paid to its growth here in the American heartland. Today ecotourism is taking off, informed both by lessons and experiences from abroad and by our own history, most importantly our tradition of environmentalism and our well-developed national parks system.

In looking closely at Costa Rica, the Galapagos Islands, Tanzania, Zanzibar, Kenya, South Africa, and the United States, I have assessed whether ecotourism is succeeding in its objectives of protecting the environment and benefiting local people and developing countries. I came to realize that to make such an assessment, it is necessary to examine the growth of ecotourism within each country's tourism strategy, its political system, and its changing economic policies. Just as scientists have come, over the past thirty years, to realize that individual species cannot be studied in isolation but must be analyzed within their ecosystems, so, too, must tourism and ecotourism be placed within a country's overall development strategy, as well as within the context of a global economy that is systematically eliminating trade barriers and facilitating the penetration of foreign capital.

Research for this book involved journeys to all these countries, briefer forays to other destinations and international conferences, and the contributions of numerous researchers who have helped to revise, add valuable information, and update the case studies. What I found in the search for ecotourism was a mixture of hype and experimentation, superficiality and creativity, juxtaposing industry promises before international forums and "green" imaging in slick brochures with in-the-field struggles over the uses of parks and other protected areas between tour operators, government officials, and some of the world's poorest and most marginalized peoples. At its worst, when not practiced with the utmost care, ecotourism threatens the very ecosystems on which it depends. At its best, ecotourism offers a set of principles and practices that have the potential to fundamentally transform the way the tourism industry operates. In the early years of the new millennium, the scorecard is very mixed: genuine ecotourism is hard to find but, unlike the golden toad, it is far from extinct.

The Contemporary Context

In 1990, The International Ecotourism Society (TIES), the world's first ecotourism organization,[10] coined what has become the most popular and succinct, yet encompassing, definition of ecotourism: "Responsible travel to natural areas that conserves the environment and improves the well-being of local people."[11] Ecotourism is often claimed to be the most rapidly expanding sector of the tourism industry,[12] but when its growth is measured, ecotourism is often lumped together with nature, wildlife, and adventure tourism. In fact, ecotourism should be viewed as distinct from these other categories. Nature tourism involves travel to unspoiled places to experience and enjoy nature. It usually involves moderate and safe forms of exercise such as hiking, biking, sailing, and camping. Wildlife tourism involves travel to observe animals, birds, and fish in their native habitats. Adventure tourism is nature tourism with a kick: it requires physical skill and endurance (rope climbing, deep-sea diving, bicycling, or kayaking) and involves a degree of risk taking, often in little-charted terrain. Whereas nature, wildlife, and adventure tourism are defined solely by the recreational activities of the tourist, ecotourism is defined as well by a set of principles that include its benefits to both conservation and people in the host country.

"Real ecotourism," writes tour operator Kurt Kutay, "is more than travel to enjoy or appreciate nature."[13] It also includes minimization of environmental and cultural consequences, contributions to conservation and community projects in developing countries, and environmental education and political consciousness-raising, such as the establishment of codes of conduct for travelers as well as a wide variety of certification programs for components of the travel industry.

Within the tourism industry, it is difficult to calculate the size of the ecotourism sector. Unfortunately, there has been little systematic effort to gather data worldwide on ecotourism as a category distinct from nature, wildlife, and adventure tourism. However, there is a range of estimates. During the 1990s, the annual growth in demand for ecotourism was said to range from 10 to 34 percent,[14] while in 2004, the UN's World Tourism Organization (UNWTO) estimated that ecotourism and nature tourism were growing three times faster than the tourism industry as a whole.[15] In 2005, The Tourism Network also rated ecotourism as one of the fastest-growing sectors in the tourism industry, with an annual growth rate of 5 percent worldwide, representing 6 percent of the world gross domestic product and 11.4 percent of all consumer spending.[16]

Looking ahead, broadly defined, ecotourism is expected to grow in the coming years, while some types of traditional tourism have reached a saturation point. According to a 2001 UNWTO analysis, sun-and-sand resort tourism, for decades the staple of Caribbean tourism, has now "matured as a market" and its growth is projected to remain flat. In contrast, both cruise tourism and "experiential" tourism (which encompasses ecotourism, nature, heritage, cultural, soft adventure tourism, rural and community tourism) were among the sectors expected to grow most quickly during the coming two decades.[17]

The projected growth is not surprising. Ecotourism, or at least a revamped version of nature and wildlife tourism, is at the core of many

Third World nations' economic development strategies and conservation efforts. Nearly every developing country is now promoting some brand of ecotourism. At international conferences and in the travel and environmental literature, the choice of countries seems endless: Dominica, Bolivia, Belize, Mongolia, Vietnam, Cambodia, Bhutan, Fiji, Indonesia, Peru, Senegal, Namibia, Madagascar, Thailand, Uganda, Australia, New Zealand, and Canada are, in addition to the ones profiled here, among the countries worldwide actively marketing themselves as ecotourism destinations. In May 2002, over a thousand delegates from 132 countries gathered in Quebec City for the World Ecotourism Summit. The event culminated in the drafting of the Quebec Declaration on Ecotourism, a comprehensive and visionary proclamation on behalf of all involved parties that "ecotourism embraces the principles of sustainable tourism, concerning the economic, social and environmental impacts of tourism." The Declaration focused on the establishment of small and locally run enterprises, emphasized the use of local materials and products, encouraged the establishment of legal mechanisms to promote such activities, and encouraged international finance institutions to direct their resources toward promoting small and medium-sized ecotourism firms.[18]

Major international conservation organizations have initiated ecotourism-linked departments, programs, studies, and field projects, and many are conducting nature tours, adventure tours, or ecotours for their members. International lending and aid agencies, under the banner of sustainable rural development, local income generation, biodiversity, institutional capacity building, poverty alleviation, and infrastructure development, pump billions of dollars into projects with tourism components; most of these are described as ecotourism or sustainable tourism projects. According to a 2005 analysis, twelve international donor agencies, including the World Bank, US Agency for International Development (USAID), UN Development Program (UNDP), and Inter-American Development Bank (IDB), were giving almost $10 billion to some 370 tourism-related projects.[19] The major travel industry organizations have set up programs, developed definitions and guidelines, and held dozens of conferences on ecotourism.[20] Simultaneously, many of the leading mass tourism players have tried to "green" their operations.[21] In the United States alone, there are scores of magazines, consultants, public relations firms, and university programs specializing in ecotourism. Globally, a growing number of nationally based and regional ecotourism societies have emerged in countries and regions such as Kenya, Zanzibar, Laos, Pakistan, Australia, Italy, France, Japan, Ecuador, Mexico, Indonesia, Sri Lanka, Belize, Brazil, and the Caribbean.[22]

And all this has happened in just three decades.

The Historical Context

The word tourism—describing travel as a leisure activity—first appeared in the Oxford English Dictionary in 1811. But the concept goes back as far as the ancient Greeks and Romans, whose wealthy citizens vacationed at thermal baths and explored exotic places around Europe and the Mediterranean region. A French monk, Aimeri de Picaud, is credited with writing the first tour guide. His book, published in 1130, was intended for pilgrims traveling to Spain. Early travel was often combined with religious pilgrimages, scientific investigation, geographic exploration, cultural and anthropological study, human and resource exploitation, or conquest, but from the beginning travelers have also sought out places of natural beauty for exploration and relaxation. Until the second half of the twentieth century, the number of travelers was small and their pace was slow. They traversed the globe by foot, sailing boat, horse, mule, and camel and, more recently, by ship, train, car, and plane.

In the eighteenth and nineteenth centuries, European aristocrats, British gentry, and, gradually, wealthy Americans took leisurely "grand tours" of the Continent's natural and cultural features.[23] With the industrial revolution, the first paid holidays and cheaper travel by railroad combined to create an annual mass exodus to seaside resorts in Europe. In 1841, Thomas Cook organized the first tourist excursion, a train ride through the English Midlands taking groups to temperance rallies, and by the mid-1850s, he was offering railway tours of the Continent. About the same time, in the United States, the American Express Company introduced traveler's checks and money orders.

Nothing, however, has altered tourism as profoundly as the airplane. Air travel for pleasure dates from 1948, when Pan American World Airways introduced tourist class. Mass international tourism really took off with the opening of commercial airplane routes between the United States and Europe, and in 1957, jet engines made air travel more accessible to the public. Not until the 1970s, with the advent of wide-bodied, high-speed airplanes, did Third World destinations come within reach of many people. In the mid-1970s, 8 percent of all vacationers traveled from developed to developing countries; by the mid-1980s, the number had jumped to 17 percent, by the mid-1990s it had climbed to 20 percent, and after 2000, Asia, Africa, and the Americas continued to grow more rapidly than mature markets in Europe. Between 1992 and 2004, the number of international tourists worldwide grew from 463 million to 763 million,[24] and according to the UNWTO, by 2020, will reach 1.56 billion.[25] In addition, four to five times as many people travel domestically, within their own countries.

Changing work patterns, like improved modes of transportation, have also altered how and where people spend their leisure time. Leisure time and paid vacations have been increasingly recognized by the International Labor Organization (ILO) and other bodies as a basic human right. The ILO's first convention on holidays with pay, passed in 1936, provided for merely one week's leave per year; a 1970 convention expanded holidays to a minimum of three weeks with pay for all workers.[26] With paid vacation time, shorter hours of work, less physically taxing jobs, and better education, vacationers began to demand personal development as well as relaxation and entertainment. By 2005, the length of paid vacations ranged from an average of twelve paid vacation days in the United States, to a minimum of four weeks for European Union countries. Finland and Italy topped the list with 37.5 and 37 days, respectively.[27]

The result of these trends is that, by the 1990s, tourism vied with oil as the world's largest legitimate business. In 2006, international tourism receipts (including transport) generated $8.8 trillion and was the world's largest employer, accounting for 200 million jobs or one in every twelve worldwide.[28] The United States is the world's biggest generator and beneficiary of tourism, accounting for about 15 percent of total spending, but tourism also plays a major role in the economies of 125 of the world's 170 countries.[29]

For economy and convenience, and, particularly after the 9/11 terrorist attacks, for security, many vacationers opt for prepaid packages on cruise ships and to a lesser (in fact declining) extent, at beach resorts. Over the past four decades, mass tourism has become synonymous with the "four S's," sun, sea, sand, and sex, and has given rise to derogatory—and often accurate—stereotypes of the typical tourist.[30] Host countries, as well as tourists, began growing disappointed with this type of tourism. Although mass tourism was originally embraced by many countries as a "smokeless" (nonpolluting) industry that could increase employment and the gross national product, evidence quickly grew that its economic benefits were marginal and its social and environmental costs high. Much of the money did not stay in the host country, and often the only benefit to the local community was found in low-paying service-level employment as maids, waiters, and drivers. Mass tourism often brought overdevelopment and uneven development, environmental pollution, and invasion by culturally insensitive and economically disruptive foreigners. In 1980, popular opposition within developing countries crystallized into a strongly worded statement drawn up at a conference in Manila convened by religious leaders. The Manila Declaration on World Tourism stated unequivocally that "tourism does more harm than good to people and to societies in the Third World." The Ecumenical Coalition on Third World Tourism, founded at this meeting,[31] became a leader in the fight against sex tourism and other forms of exploitation and in calls for a new type of tourism.

In many cases, popular vacation spots were becoming degraded as a result of human activities linked to industrialization. In the Adriatic Sea, algae blooms have made the water unappealing to swimmers. Beaches have been closed in England because of radioactivity, in New Jersey because of hospital waste, and in Haiti because of sewage. In Canada, acid rain has depleted salmon stocks, threatening the closure of six hundred fishing lodges. In some instances, such damage is caused by uncontrolled mass tourism; in others, by industrialization, overexploitation of natural resources, consumerism, and other forms of "unsustainable development that characterizes contemporary Western civilization," according to Héctor Ceballos-Lascuráin, an ecotourism expert with the International Union for the Conservation of Nature and Natural Resources (IUCN, now known as the World Conservation Union).[32] In recent years, with increasing frequency, disasters linked at least in part to global warming—from hurricanes and typhoons to coral bleaching, rising sea levels, and melting glaciers and snow caps—are disrupting tourism in many parts of the world.

Yet at the same time that a wide variety of natural wonders were being threatened and degraded, there was a trend toward vacations with nature-based activities. A 1998 survey of 3,342 U.S. households found that nearly half (48.1 percent) had included nature-based activities in their last vacation, and 14.5 percent stated that they had planned their most recent trip so that nature-based activities would account for the majority of the time on vacation.[33] Nature had become a key ingredient in the tour industry, and ecotourism developed in part in response to demand for the kind of authentic experience that nature can provide.

The Evolution of Ecotourism

In the United States, regularly organized nature tourism—that is, travel to pristine places, usually involving physical activity—probably started with the Sierra Club Outing program. Known as the High Trips, these annual expeditions first began in 1901 and involved some one hundred hikers (plus Chinese chefs as well as pack mules and wagons) who trekked to the backcountry wilderness of the Sierra Nevada. Although their purpose was "to take Club members into the Sierra to show them the natural wonders so that those persons could become active workers for 'the preservation of the forests and other natural features of the

Sierra Nevada Mountains,'" these enormous caravans, which grew to an average of 115 to 125 people, were "anything but 'eco'" in terms of their effects on the environment, said Charles Hardy, a director of Sierra Club Outings.[34] High Trips continued until 1972 when growing environmental concern about the human "impact on the fragile High Sierra landscape,"[35] led the Sierra Club's Outing Committee to stop conducting the High Trip and shift to smaller trips, usually for twelve to fifteen people. These have featured backpacking, biking, river rafting, and mountain climbing trips to a variety of U.S. locations and, beginning in 1964, overseas.

The rapid growth of nature tourism within the United States and overseas has been facilitated in recent years by the same ease and accessibility of modern transport that has fueled the rise in conventional tourism. The increasing number of people to whom these formerly remote natural areas are now available has resulted in serious damage to some of the most popular destinations. Visitors to the National Park System in the United States, one of the world's oldest and best-maintained park systems, rose by nearly 30 percent between 1980 and 2000, from about 220 million to more than 285 million.[36] During the peak months of July and August, popular parks such as Yellowstone and Yosemite are anything but restful. Traffic jams resemble urban gridlock, exhaust fumes and loud music permeate the air, and the millions of visitors leave behind tons of garbage. The Grand Canyon, the second most visited U.S. national park, attracts 4.4 million tourists per year,[37] and the sheer number of visitors is having a negative effect on the canyon's ecosystem. By the mid-1990s, negative impacts were evident. According to a press report, "Park rangers are killing off more than two dozen mule deer that have become hooked on . . . snack food and candy handed out at Phantom Ranch, the hotel located on the floor of the Canyon. The deer were reportedly losing their natural ability to digest vegetation. David Haskell, chief of resource management for Grand Canyon National Park, called junk food the "crack cocaine of the deer world."[38] Fortunately, the Park Service stepped in, launching a successful campaign to stop the hotel and tourists from feeding deer and other wild animals.[39]

Turned off by overcrowded, unpleasant conditions and spurred by relatively affordable and plentiful airline routes, increasing numbers of nature lovers began seeking serenity and pristine beauty. Between the late 1970s and mid-1980s, a new field known as ecotourism gradually took shape. The definition has often been vague: the travel industry typically classifies ecotourism with nature or adventure tourism; it is frequently referred to as "responsible," "sustainable," "green," or "low-impact" tourism[40] and, by 2000, new terms such as "pro-poor tourism" and "geotourism" were complicating the picture and confusing the public.[41] The confusion over the definition of ecotourism is partly due to its historical roots, which, broadly stated, can be traced to four sources: (1) scientific, conservation, and nongovernmental organizations (NGOs); (2) multilateral aid institutions; (3) developing countries; and (4) the travel industry and traveling public. Almost simultaneously but for different reasons, the principles and practices of ecotourism began taking shape within these four areas, and by the early 1990s, the concept had coalesced into a hot new genre of environmentally and socially responsible travel.

Conservation Organizations: Better Protection of Natural Areas

Most typically, ecotourism involves visits to areas that are under some form of environmental protection by governments, conservation or scientific organizations, or private owners or entrepreneurs. Around the world, many protected areas have been modeled after the U.S. National Parks System, which was created in the late nineteenth century by drawing boundaries around specific areas to preserve them in their natural state and free them of direct use. The United States Congress decreed that these national parks would serve as "pleasure grounds" for visitors, thus linking national parks to tourism from their inception. Other countries followed, setting aside land for national parks: Australia (1879), Mexico (1898), Argentina (1903), and Sweden (1909).[42] Since the 1970s, the decade that saw the rise of a global environmental movement, more protected areas have been established worldwide than during all preceding periods. By 1992, about forty-eight thousand sites, totaling about 12.3 million square kilometers, had been established worldwide.[43] Then by the Fifth World Parks Congress, held in Durban, South Africa in 2003, it was announced that there were over a hundred thousand protected areas, encompassing 17 million square kilometers (about 6.5 million square miles), and representing 11.5 percent of the earth's total land surface.[44]

However, there is a downside to this impressive achievement. Some were merely "paper parks" existing in name only, many were underfunded, and it was gradually recognized that most were guided by an antiquated philosophy of park management. As early as the late 1960s, environmentalists, scientists, and community organizers in Latin America and Africa began to reach two related conclusions. In Africa, they began to realize that "preservationist" conservation methods of separating (often forcibly) people and parks were not working. Most national parks and reserves in Africa were originally established for hunters, scientists, or tourists, with little or no regard for the local people. Park management emphasized policing—fences, fines and firepower—which forcibly evicted and kept out local community members, who were often politically and ethnically marginalized rural poor. These people, who received little or no benefit from either the parks or tourism, deeply resented being excluded from lands of religious and economic value and being restricted to increasingly unsustainable areas around the parks. Poaching, degradation of resources, and local hostility toward the parks and tourism were on the increase. The "preservationist approach," one study concluded, "requires an essentially militaristic defense strategy and will almost always heighten conflict."[45]

Some scientists, conservationists, park officials, and environmental organizations concerned about this clash between parks and people began to rethink the protectionist philosophy guiding park management. They began to argue that protected species, areas, and ecosystems would survive only if those people living nearest them benefited financially from both the parks and tourism. As David Western, director of the Kenya Wildlife Service (KWS) between 1994 and 1998 and first president of TIES, wrote, these "conscientious concerns for nature were soon extended to local (usually indigenous) peoples. Implicit in the term [ecotourism] is the assumption that local communities living with nature can and should benefit from tourism and will save nature in the process."[46] It was in Kenya that Africa's first official experiments with this new approach began. In the early 1970s, the government agreed to put several reserves, including Masai Mara Game Reserve and Amboseli National Park, under the control of local county councils, which began receiving revenue from both park entrance fees and hotels and other tourism facilities. This "stakeholders" theory—that people will protect what they receive value from—has dovetailed with economic development theories holding that the road out of poverty must begin at, not simply trickle down to, the local community level. In the mid-1980s, as the concept of ecotourism began to take hold in East and southern Africa, the stakeholders theory was broadened to encompass environmentally sensitive, low-impact, culturally sensitive tourism that also helped educate visitors and local community members.

Parallel to this trend, scientists and environmental activists in Latin America were becoming increasingly alarmed that illegal logging, ranching, oil drilling, mining, and human settlement were destroying much of the world's remaining tropical forests. These rain forests are vital as the homes of many indigenous communities, reservoirs of biological diversity, and suppliers of oxygen necessary to maintain a balance in the earth's atmosphere. Initially, Latin Americans, from Mexico to Chile, tended to view ecotourism narrowly, as a conservation tool that could provide an economic alternative to these more invasive and extractive activities, promote public awareness of environmental issues, and increase funds for conservation. In a groundbreaking 1976 article, Gerardo Budowski, a Costa Rica–based conservationist, argued that the relationship between tourism and conservation can be variously one of conflict, coexistence, or symbiosis. He also outlined ways in which tourism can be used to support conservation.[47] Mexican Ceballos-Lascuráin defined ecotourism as travel "to relatively undisturbed or uncontaminated natural areas with the specific object of studying, admiring, and enjoying the scenery of its wild plants and animals, as well as any existing cultural aspects found in these areas." He argued that "the person who practices ecotourism will eventually acquire a consciousness that will convert him into somebody keenly interested in conservation issues." These Latin American scholars put the emphasis on building an activist constituency among the traveling public committed to environmental protection.[48]

In what may well be Costa Rica's earliest ecotourism-related news report, an October 1980 article in the weekly, English-language *Tico Times* hailed tour operator Michael Kaye's "new recipe" of "wilderness adventure" that was "being tossed into the traditional blend of museums, churches and 'pueblos típicos.'" It described Kaye's recently formed company, Costa Rica Expeditions, which specialized in whitewater rafting, as "the chief, if not only, alternative to traditional tourism" and quoted Kaye as saying, "Tourism should contribute to, rather than exploit (the land). . . . It should be active rather than passive, emphasizing cultural exchange rather than mere sightseeing."[49] These were pioneering words. Over the years, Kaye moved on to build one of Costa Rica's most successful ecotourism companies.

Thus, the notion of ecotourism emerged almost simultaneously, although for somewhat different reasons, in Latin America and Africa. Quickly, however, there began to be a cross-fertilization of these concepts such that today ecotourism is usually seen as a tool for benefiting fragile ecosystems and local communities. The concept of integrating conservation, local communities, and tourism may have first been articulated in Kenton Miller's 1978 work on national park planning in Latin America. Miller, a distinguished American conservationist, argued that development must integrate biological considerations with economic, social, and political factors to meet both environmental and human needs. He contended that the potential for national parks to contribute to "ecodevelopment" had grown during the 1970s as greater numbers of well-trained personnel were able to work with larger budgets on more parklands. Miller's concepts of ecodevelopment via tourism quickly entered the debate on sustainable development.[50] However, Ceballos-Lascuráin, an architect and avid birder, claims to have first coined the term "ecotourism" in 1983. As president of PRONATURA, Ceballos-Lascuráin argued that increasing numbers of tourists could facilitate the conservation of the wetlands in Mexico's northern Yucatán, the breeding and feeding habitat of the American flamingo.[51]

In 1980, the IUCN issued the World Conservation Strategy, which reflected the views of a growing number of organizations in stressing that protected area management must be linked with the economic activities of local communities. In 1982, conservationists at the IUCN's World Congress on National Parks in Bali endorsed this concept, arguing that conservation programs need to be community friendly and promote economic development.[52] A decade later, at its Fourth World Congress on National Parks and Protected Areas in Caracas, Venezuela, the IUCN expanded on these concepts, making a policy recommendation that "in developing greater cooperation between the tourism industry and protected areas the primary consideration must be the conservation of the natural environment and the quality of life of local communities."[53]

At this 1992 World Congress, the IUCN set up a small Ecotourism Consultancy Program, headed by Ceballos-Lascuráin, to offer IUCN members "technical consultation support service and a range of advice" for planning ecotourism developments.[54] In 1996, the Ecotourism Consultancy Program was expanded into the Task Force on Tourism and Protected Areas, with a broader mandate to collect data on protected area tourism, develop case studies and tourism management guidelines for protected areas, and provide advice to the World Commission on Protected Areas (WCPA), a global network of more than one thousand protected area managers and specialists that is supported by the IUCN. At IUCN's 2003 World Parks Congress, held in Durban, South Africa, tourism was not an official "stream" or theme, but an impressive number of sessions, side events, and speakers, beginning with former South Africa President Nelson Mandela's opening speech, described ecotourism as part of the solution for both sustainable management of protected areas and poverty reduction for surrounding rural communities. At the same time, a small group of mainly indigenous representatives protested that they had not been consulted by the Task Force on Tourism and, more broadly, expressed strong concerns that industry and major NGOs were using ecotourism to exploit their lands and cultures.[55]

For more than a century, NGOs have led the drive to set aside significant parks of the globe for both biodiversity protection and recreation. While the achievements have been enormous, the tensions between indigenous people and parks have continued (as discussed in other chapters), with NGOs playing a mixed role, some continuing to promote an orthodox preservationist approach to conservation, while others arguing that parks will only survive over the long haul if the people living on their perimeters support them.

Multilateral Aid Institutions: Responding to Environmentalism and the Debt Crisis

With the rise of both the environmental movement and Third World debt in the late 1970s, international aid and lending institutions also took a fresh look at tourism as a development tool and support for conservation. The trendsetter for the multilateral institutions was the International Bank for Reconstruction and Development, or the World Bank, created following World War II.

The bank's first tourism development loan agreement with governments was in 1966 with Morocco and Tunisia, and during this decade, tourism lending was estimated at only 2.8 percent of the bank's total portfolio. In 1969, the bank created the Tourism Projects Department and, although tourism continued to represent only a small part of its overall portfolio, during the 1970s, the World Bank became a major source of public finance for tourism-related projects. The first tourism-related loan by the International Finance Corporation (IFC),[56] the arm of the World Bank Group that both invests in and lends for private sector projects (rather than lending to governments) was in 1967. This was for a hotel in Kenya that was partly owned by the Inter-Continental Hotel Corporation, which was then a subsidiary of the now-defunct Pan American Airways. More recently, the Multilateral Investment Guarantee Agency (MIGA), a third arm of the World Bank Group, has entered the picture, issuing investment guarantees for tourism projects around the world and providing advice on investment promotion.[57]

Between 1969 and 1979, the World Bank's Tourism Projects Department invested in conventional tourism as a strategy for encouraging foreign investment and earning foreign exchange, often in regions deemed to have few other economic options. Tourism, as an export industry, was seen as a source of growth and economic diversification and as a means of redistributing wealth from rich nations to poor. During this period, the World Bank loaned about $450 million directly to governments for twenty-four tourism projects—referred to as "tourist plants"—in eighteen developing countries.[58] These loans, for infrastructure, training, and lines of credit for hotel development, helped create what are today internationally recognized destinations such as Bali (Indonesia), Zihuatanejo (Mexico), and Puerto Plata (the Dominican Republic). However, as competition for bank funding grew, there were increasing concerns that the bank should be investing in low-cost housing and other poverty-reduction programs, and not in luxury hotels and large infrastructure projects to support international tourism and the private sector. These concerns, coupled with a string of financially and environmentally disastrous projects in such countries as Egypt, South Korea, and Morocco, led the World Bank to close its Tourism Projects Department in 1979.[59]

By the 1980s, failed tourism projects were not all that sullied the World Bank's reputation. The bank was under attack around the globe for its environmentally destructive big dams and other megaprojects that uprooted hundreds of thousands of people as well as for a pattern of lending that seemed in some instances to favor repressive regimes. Beginning in the 1980s, the bank linked its loans to crippling structural adjustment policies that forced poor countries to cut spending and social programs, privatize, and open their economies to foreign investment and trade. This also drew increasingly critical attention to bank practices. As Third World nations' foreign debt continued to climb, the bank looked for new directions. By the mid-1980s, the institution was once again contemplating tourism as part of its export promotion and debt repayment strategy. As Clark University professor Cynthia Enloe wrote in 1990, "The international politics of debt and the international pursuit of pleasure have become tightly knotted together."[60]

By the late 1980s, the bank's rhetoric shifted to include sustainable development and environmental protection. In 1986, the bank issued its first official statement regarding protection of wildlands defined as natural habitats relatively untouched by human activities within development plans. Its guidelines, initiated more as an encouragement than as a "will-do" policy, stated that the World Bank "promotes and supports" protection of wildlands and improved land use in its projects, which increasingly included tourism. They emphasized the need "to include local people in the planning and benefits" of wildland management projects and noted that "rural development investments that provide farmers and villagers in the vicinity [of wildland management areas with] an alternative to further encroachment" can also help protect parks and reserves.[61]

In 1990, the World Bank, together with two United Nations agencies (UNEP and the United Nations Development Program, or UNDP)[62] set up the Global Environment Facility (GEF), first as a pilot project and then, in 1994, as a permanent mechanism. The GEF's purpose is to facilitate and fund the integration of environmental concerns into development projects and to help implement the global environmental conventions agreed to at the 1992 United Nations Conference on Environment and Development (UNCED), known as the Earth Summit. One of the GEF's four focal areas is protecting biodiversity through, among other means, development of environmentally sustainable nature-based tourism and participatory schemes for sustainable natural resource management, including local communities, indigenous groups, and other sectors of society.[63]

By the mid-1990s, the World Bank was once again contemplating tourism in a limited way as part of its programs focusing on growth and export development. Although the bank did not reconstitute a centralized, specialized tourism unit, during the 1990s, it undertook a large number of tourism studies and invested in a variety of multimillion-dollar tourism-linked loans under categories such as infrastructure, environment and biodiversity, rural development, and technical assistance. In Africa, for instance, these included planning for tourism development (Madagascar, Mauritius, Mozambique, and Senegal), infrastructure and management reform in national parks and protected areas (Tanzania, Kenya, and Zambia), and support for community-based and small enterprise development. In addition, the IFC's Tourism Unit, which was never closed, began adding more variety to its portfolio beyond large city hotels, although it has funded only a handful of ecotourism projects (see chapter 3).[64] By 2005, the World Bank had extended $407.4 billion in loans to governments and public sector agencies for over six thousand economic and development projects in its 184 member countries.[65] By 2006, the three components of the World Bank Group had a portfolio of 114 tourism projects, including both free-standing tourism projects and projects having tourism components, with lending at a level of about $3 billion.[66]

The World Bank has not been the only player in the tourism game. By the turn of the millennium, the World Bank, Inter-American Development Bank (IDB), Asian Development Bank, African Development Bank, Caribbean Development Bank, Organization of American States (OAS), U.S. Agency for International Development (USAID), various UN agencies, and other international assistance agencies were supporting a variety of tourism programs and projects, including ecotourism. According to a 2005 study, of the approximately $9.4 billion currently invested by some dozen major international donor agencies in tourism and tourism-related projects worldwide, 25 percent originated from the UNDP/GEF, 22 percent from the World Bank, 12 percent from USAID, and 10 percent from the IDB.[67]

USAID, the U.S. government's main tool for providing bilateral development assistance to poor countries, has since the 1980s been actively involved in nature tourism and ecotourism activities to help meet a shifting set of policy objectives. Initially ecotourism fit within two of the agency's four broad objectives—promoting national economic growth and conserving biodiversity—and this facilitated the inclusion of ecotourism in many projects. In 1985, USAID began its support for ecotourism activities (loosely defined by the agency as nature-based tourism) by funding some twenty conservation and development projects in developing countries carried out by the World Wide Fund for Nature (WWF, known as the World Wildlife Fund in the United States and Canada);[68] in 1989, the agency initiated its Parks in Peril project to improve management as well as recreational and educational use of twenty parks in Latin America and the Caribbean;[69] and in 1992, it began funneling assistance for biodiversity projects in Asia and the Pacific region through a consortium of U.S. conservation NGOs. As a 1992 USAID study summarized, "AID's central environmental objective is to promote environmentally and socially sound, long-term economic growth. . . . At the same time, AID has placed high priority on stimulating private investment, free markets, and free enterprise. Many officials within AID view nature-based tourism as well-suited for simultaneously meeting both objectives. As a result, there has been an increasing level of activity related to ecotourism within the agency."[70]

By the mid-1990s, USAID had 105 projects with ecotourism components, totaling more than $2 billion in funding. Of these, fifty-two involved the private sector, thirty-seven involved community participation, forty-six involved government capacity building, and forty-seven involved nongovernmental capacity building.[71] They were in countries such as Belize, Costa Rica, Ecuador, Nepal, Kenya, Zaire, Madagascar, Jamaica, and Thailand. In 1993, USAID and World Wildlife Fund helped newly independent Namibia to enact legislation that allowed communities to register as conservancies and adopt game management practices. This has fostered an increase in previously depleted wildlife numbers, and many communities can now derive income from handicraft sales, trophy-hunting contracts, and game meat distributions. More than eighty communal area conservancies are up and running or in various stages of formation, and wildlife tourism has now become Namibia's third-highest contributor to GDP.[72]

In the first five years of the new millennium, USAID implemented ninety-eight projects in seventy-two countries "that specifically relate[d] to the tourism sector or employ[ed] tourism as a component to achieve other, broader objectives" of natural resources management, biodiversity conservation, and economic development.[73] Some USAID projects are being implemented "through a cluster-based competitiveness approach" under which USAID targets several industries within a country, "with tourism increasingly selected as an area of focus."[74] USAID's first large-scale cluster-based competitiveness project, begun in Lebanon in 1998, focused on agriculture and tourism.

In some areas, USAID has focused on transnational natural resource management, recognizing the importance of ecosystem-wide conservation. For example, USAID is working on a program to promote regional conservation approaches between the Democratic Republic of the Congo, Rwanda, and Uganda to protect mountain gorilla populations. USAID funding has contributed to the establishment of the Tayna Gorilla Reserve in eastern Democratic Republic of the Congo, which has become a tourist destination managed by local communities. USAID has also been instrumental in incorporating its goals of gender equity, education, and health into its tourism projects. A USAID project in Tanzania has trained village women to establish their own enterprises and increase handicraft sales to tourists. In Botswana, conservation-based education has been implemented in primary schools, and at Madagascar's Andasibe-Matadia National Park, tourism revenues have enabled schools and health clinics to be constructed on the park's periphery.[75] Many of these USAID-funded tourism projects have emphasized local empowerment, capacity-building, and the integration of tourism development into broader development objectives.

These projects notwithstanding, a USAID consultant contracted to evaluate the agency's ecotourism projects in the mid-1990s concluded that not infrequently its personnel failed to understand the full dimensions and complexities of implementing such projects. The consultant found that despite USAID's stated goal of fostering community-based development, in practice USAID showed a preference for working with the private sector and U.S. NGOs. In addition, she stated, "There's increasing pressure from Congress to get the money to come back to the U.S., not keep aid money in-country." The consultant concluded that many USAID functionaries are not "aware of all the complexities involved in ecotourism. AID is very linear in its thinking. There was a lot of enthusiasm at first, but now people are starting to see it's harder to implement on the ground than on paper. It's a great idea but hard to turn into a success."[76]

In 2006, the Bush administration merged USAID into the State Department, a move widely viewed as diminishing the agency's independence and importance. A 2005 White Paper described the agency's main goals as supporting geo-strategic interests, strengthening fragile states, and providing humanitarian relief, with almost no focus on environmental issues with the exception of water. In 2006, a new Sustainable Tourism Global Development Alliance strategy was launched, which set out a new model that is less dependent on USAID funding and leadership and looks instead to partnering with key tourism agencies and organizations and the private sector.[77]

Another key institution in the Americas is the Inter-American Development Bank (IDB). Established in 1959, the IDB is the main source of multilateral financing and technical cooperation for economic, social, and institutional development in Latin America and the Caribbean. In 1971, the IDB began providing financing for infrastructure, hotels, and cultural attractions, including for mega-developments such as Cancún and the Bay of Huatulco in Mexico, and the Cuzco area in Peru. In 1977, the IDB adopted its first tourism policies, and also began financing national credit institutions in Latin America, thereby permitting local banks to finance smaller tourism infrastructure development. However, at the end of the 1970s, the IDB, like the World Bank, halted funding for tourism because of growing concerns that mass tourism projects were not a good development tool.[78]

In the 1990s, the IDB resumed funding for tourism, typically under the umbrella of sustainable tourism or ecotourism. In 1994, it revamped its tourism lending policies, prioritizing investments that, according to an internal analysis, "equally favor the local population and tourist population, value the natural and cultural patrimony, improve the institutional capacity for the planning of tourism development, support small and medium size enterprises to increase their competitiveness, and enable the local population to participate in the process of tourism development."[79] This 2006 internal document states that the IDB's lending policies in the field of tourism emphasize privatization, environmental protection, and social impacts. Since the 1970s, the IDB has approved twenty-nine tourism loans totaling over $1.5 billion in total aid, with 43 percent of all money going to Brazil, and 30 percent to Mexico. In 2005, IDB's loans for tourism totaled $284 million, of which $251 million was going to Brazil. A range of smaller tourism-related grants have been awarded to other countries for technical assistance and regional studies.[80]

Like the World Bank, the IDB does not have a central tourism unit. Tourism projects are handled by various regions and departments, and coordinated informally through a sporadically functioning tourism working group and several tourism specialists.[81] In recent years, the IDB's private sector wing, the Multilateral Investment Fund (MIF), has moved most aggressively and innovatively into tourism projects. The MIF has undertaken a 'cluster strategy' of building links among its tourism projects. A MIF report describes this as "pertinent because it allows projects to share the same goal and similar technical approaches making it possible to manage and supervise them as a group."[82] It adds, "The purpose of this cluster is to finance projects supporting the sustainable development of tourism by improving marketing functioning and the capacities and competitiveness of the SMEs [small- and medium-size enterprises]."[83] By 2006, the MIF was funding fourteen different projects, including a four-country, multi-year certification project spearheaded by the Rainforest Alliance; the development of a national "green" certification program in Brazil; rural tourism in Colombia and Costa Rica; and improving small tourism business competitiveness in Belize. In 2007, it approved a $6 million technical assistance grant to "market sustainable tourism" in seven Latin American countries.[84] Today, this handful of international development agencies are important sources of funding for sustainable tourism projects, infrastructure, and marketing. However, they still lack clear guidelines for what constitutes sustainable development and they tend to support larger NGOs and companies, which can make it difficult for newer, grassroots, and more innovative projects to win approval.

Developing Countries: Seeking Foreign Exchange and Sustainable Development

The third key set of actors in the development of ecotourism is the host country governments. During the mid- to late 1980s, many Third World countries turned to ecotourism as a foreign exchange earner that was potentially less destructive than alternatives such as logging, oil extraction, cattle, bananas, commercial fishing, or conventional mass tourism. They viewed ecotourism as minimizing negative effects through its emphasis on low-impact construction, controlled visitor numbers, and care in interacting with the local flora, fauna, and human population. Further, it could, in some instances, be more profitable. Studies in various countries have found that ecotourism and related economic activities may be a better form of land use than cattle ranching or agriculture, especially in arid and semiarid areas. A study in South Africa found that net income from wildlife tourism was almost eleven times more than that from cattle ranching, and job generation was fifteen times greater.[85] In Kenya, it is estimated that one lion is worth $7,000 per year in income from tourism, and an elephant herd is valued at $610,000 annually.[86] A 2001 study found that in the Turks and Caicos Islands, spiny lobsters are prized by recreational divers, and therefore may actually be more valuable in the water, for ecotourists, than trapped for the dinner table.[87] A study in Iceland found that the economic value of whale watching worldwide is $1 billion, far more than any financial gain that would come from hunting should Iceland resume commercial whaling.[88]

By the early 1990s, nearly every nonindustrialized country was promoting ecotourism as part of its development strategy. In several countries, nature-based tourism mushroomed into the largest, or one of the largest, foreign exchange earners, surpassing bananas in Costa Rica, coffee in Tanzania and Kenya, and textiles and jewelry in India. Namibia, which gained independence in 1990, purportedly became the first developing country to include what has been dubbed an "ecotourism plank" in its new constitution, pledging to protect "ecosystems, essential ecological processes and biological diversity . . . on a sustainable basis."[89] In 1994, Australia's government committed $10 million over a ten-year period to develop a national ecotourism strategy.[90] In 1997, Brazil announced it was launching a new $200 million program to develop ecotourism in its nine Amazonian states.[91] In 2003, the southern African country of Malawi was facing an acute food crisis and announced that it planned to "jumpstart the economy with ecotourism."[92] Even places such as Zanzibar and Burma, which once were leery of tourism, the former Soviet Union, Eastern Europe, China, and Vietnam, which once tightly controlled tourism, and one-time international outcasts such as South Africa and Cuba are now on the ecotourism bandwagon. In 1991 Montenegro, then part of the former Yugoslavia, declared in its new constitution that it would be an "ecological state" and a decade later it adopted "sustainable tourism" as the main engine of growth for the northern and central mountain region. Tourism thus became one of three priority industries, along with timber and energy, that the government pledged to "green." Some entire countries, such as Costa Rica, Belize, and Dominica, are billed as ecotourism destinations. Elsewhere, pockets are promoted: Zanzibar, Mount Kilimanjaro, and the game parks in Tanzania; Amazonia, the highlands and the Galapagos Islands in Ecuador; the habitat of the mountain gorillas in Uganda and Rwanda, and around Petra in southern Jordan. In 1998, the UNWTO predicted that developing countries would continue to gain from the tourism boom and that international travelers would remain "interested in visiting and maintaining environmentally sound destinations."[93]

Throughout most of the world, the rise of ecotourism has coincided with the promotion of free markets and economic globalization, with the private sector hailed as the main engine for development. Nearly everywhere, state-run enterprises, including those in the tourism industry, are being sold off or shut down. The push toward privatization has been propelled by the international lending and aid agencies and major corporate players and is justified by the collapse of communism. Also popular are "private-public partnerships," a term that often turns out to be a euphemism for state-provided subsidies and services for the private sector. State-run tourism operations (hotels, travel bureaus, and transportation services) have often—but not always—been overly bureaucratic and unresponsive to the standards of service that international tourists demand. So beginning in the early 1990s, from Tanzania and Mozambique in Africa to Russia and its former states in eastern Europe and Central Asia, to former socialist outposts like Nicaragua, Vietnam, Laos, Albania, Croatia,[94] Bosnia, Serbia, and Montenegro, the sale of government-owned tourism assets, often to foreign investors and brand-name chains, became a stepping stone to integration into the global tourism market. Even Cuba opened up to foreign ownership and management agreements beginning with the "Special Period" of economic crisis in the early 1990s.[95] China is also beginning to privatize much of its natural patrimony, and a 2001 report revealed that many of China's monuments, parks, temples, and scenic and cultural areas had been privatized.[96]

One of the most unique examples is the tiny Himalayan kingdom of Bhutan, whose government ran and tightly regulated international tourism. It limited numbers and charged a hefty daily tariff to those fortunate enough to be granted entry visas. However, in 1991, the state-owned Bhutan Tourism Corporation was privatized,[97] and by 2006, there were at least 180 private tour operators in Bhutan.[98] In spite of this privatization, the government still continues to strictly regulate entry visas to about fifteen thousand a year and charge daily tariffs of between $165 and $200 (depending on the season).[99] Tourism is estimated to bring Bhutan between $10.5 million and $14 million a year, constituting 15 to 20 percent of the total value of exports.[100] While privatization of accommodations and services might satisfy the demands of foreign visitors, it may prove costly. If unregulated and undertaxed, privatization can mean an influx of foreign companies, with most of the profits flowing out of the host country.

The Travel Industry: Tapping the Public's "Green" Sentiments

Although the travel industry did not originate the concept of ecotourism, it quickly adopted it, popularized it, mainstreamed it—and watered it down. The tourism industry, including the travel press, has come to view "green travel" as a marketing tool to attract the growing number of environmentally and socially conscious travelers seeking alternatives to conventional "mass tourism." The growing public concern with the environment and interest in outdoor-oriented travel, coupled with the growing dissatisfaction with conventional mass tourism, showed the tourism industry that there was a sizable market for ecotourism. As early as 1982, the UNWTO, together with the United Nations Environment Programme (UNEP), declared: "The satisfaction of tourism requirements must not be prejudicial to the social and economic interests of the population in the tourist areas, to the environment, or above all to natural resources which are fundamental attractions of tourism."[101]

A 2005 analysis of dozens of recent surveys by the Center on Ecotourism and Sustainable Development (CESD) found that more than two-thirds of U.S. and Australian travelers, and 90 percent of British tourists, consider active protection of the environment, including the support of local communities, to be part of a hotel's responsibility.[102] Further, more than 75 percent of U.S. travelers and 87 percent of British travelers felt that it is important for their visits to not damage the environment; over one-third of both British and U.S. travelers said they were willing to pay more to travel companies committed to environmental protection. And, by 2001, half of all British tour operators said that their companies had developed some type of responsible tourism policy.[103] In response to the growing "green sentiments" of today's travelers, numerous associations have been formed, including the Green Hotels Association in the United States and the Tour Operators Initiative based in Europe, with the purpose of providing information to travelers, hotels, and other providers of tourism services, in order to promote more environmentally sustainable and culturally sensitive travel.

Since the late 1980s, ecotourism has been endorsed, to various degrees, by the major tourism associations. The World Travel & Tourism Council (WTTC), based in London and Brussels and made up of some seventy chief executive officers of major airlines, hotel chains, catering companies, and cruise lines, is dedicated to raising awareness about the importance of tourism and realizing "sustainable benefits for everyone involved."[104] The Travel Industry Association of America (TIA),[105] based in Washington, D.C., represents over 2,200 travel-related businesses promoting travel to and within the United States. TIA has collaborated with National Geographic's Sustainable Destinations Resource Center to carry out several innovative surveys of consumer demand for "geotourism" and other aspects of socially and environmentally responsible travel.[106] In addition, at the UN, the World Tourism Organization (UNWTO) has a Sustainable Development of Tourism Department. UNWTO, whose members include government tourism ministries, private enterprises, academic institutions, and NGOs,[107] acts as a center for compiling industry statistics and market trends and studying and monitoring the industry. Together with the United Nations Environment Programme (UNEP), which also has a Sustainable Tourism Department,[108] the UNWTO sponsored the UN's 2002 International Year of Ecotourism.

But travel industry adoption of ecotourism has often been more form than substance. The largest travel trade association in the world is the American Society of Travel Agents (ASTA),[109] headquartered in Alexandria, Virginia, and representing twenty thousand travel professionals in 140 countries. ASTA, to which virtually every travel agent in the United States belongs, is potentially a strong mechanism for educating travel agents, developing ecotourism standards, and helping to monitor implementation. As one analyst puts it, travel agents need to "clearly assess and evaluate the environmental practices and responsibilities of the tourist suppliers they work with. Only then will they be able to satisfy environmental tourists by booking them with companies that are truly 'green.'"[110] In 1991, ASTA set up an Environmental Committee, which, according to committee member Marie Walters, demonstrated that "the travel industry is really moving in a good direction to help preserve the environment." The Environmental Committee's two main programs—the "Ten Commandments on Eco-Tourism" and its two annual environmental awards, one with Smithsonian Magazine and the other with British Airways—were more public relations than substance. In reality, its ecotourism efforts were modest; then, after several years, the committee folded, and the awards were transferred to other sponsors. Currently ASTA handles any ecotourism and environmental issues on an ad hoc basis through its Special Projects committee.[111]

Because the tourism industry, more than any other, depends on a healthy environment, it has had to embrace the principles of ecotourism as a means of survival. The 1992 Earth Summit, held in Rio de Janeiro, resulted in the Rio Declaration on Environment and Development and Agenda 21, which together make up an environmental blueprint for the future. It calls on industry, including travel and tourism, to develop a strategy for sustainable development.[112] The tourism industry responded with *Agenda 21 for the Travel and Tourism Industry*, a lengthy document published in 1995 by the WTTC, the UNWTO, and the Costa Rica–based Earth Council, which is supposed to be overseeing implementation of Earth Summit directives. The report states, "The product that Travel & Tourism packages and sells ultimately relies on clean seas, pristine mountain slopes, unpolluted water, litter-free streets, well-preserved buildings and archaeological sites, and diverse cultural traditions." It contends that the industry has both a "vested interest" and a "moral responsibility to take the lead in making the transition to sustainable development"[113] and lists ten priority areas for action by travel companies, including energy efficiency, wastewater management, and sustainable design.[114] The United Nations' International Year of Ecotourism in 2002 came a decade after the Rio Earth Summit and marked the first time that ecotourism was elevated to global significance.

But without a uniform definition, clear standards, and globally recognized certification programs, ecotourism, writes tour operator Kurt Kutay, "is used indiscriminately to describe anything related to nature or unrelated to conventional tourism."[115] Beginning in the early 1990s and growing into the new millennium, ecotourism became a hot new topic in the travel and environmental press and gradually even in the mainstream media. As former KWS director David Western puts it, ecotourism "emerged like a phoenix from terms like nature tourism and wildlife tourism to become a universal conservation catchword, an exemplar of sustainable use. The reassuring prefix gave nature tourism the legitimacy and recognition it lacked. Few words have been adopted so quickly by a movement predisposed to catchwords or have offered so much promise. Ecotourism and biodiversity were popularized by a media hungry for a new, evocative and consoling jargon."[116]

Definition: How to Know Ecotourism When You See It

Over the last few years, other terms have been added to the ecotourism vernacular, and added to the confusion. They include pro-poor tourism, geotourism, responsible tourism, sustainable tourism, and the list goes on. Competing terms and lack of precise definition, combined with ecotourism's diverse roots and multiple actors, have helped produce what are today two conflicting crosscurrents within ecotourism: one, genuine ecotourism, toward putting into practice the multiple principles of ecotourism, often within a single accommodation, tour company, park, or destination; and the other, ecotourism lite, toward adopting only its facade, without making fundamental changes to mass tourism practices. Ultimately, the goal must be to move ecotourism beyond simply a new niche within nature travel. It must become a vehicle for significantly transforming the way tourism itself is carried out, for "greening," not merely "greenwashing," the entire industry.

The first trajectory, ecotourism proper, is encapsulated in TIES's definition of ecotourism, given earlier in this chapter, as "responsible travel to natural areas that conserves the environment and improves the welfare of local people."[117] Costas Christ, one of the founders of TIES, recalled when, in 1991, he, David Western, and other tourism and conservation experts from around the world got together and came up with this working definition. "Afterward," Christ said in a 1998 interview, "we looked around at each other and said, 'Okay, who among us is really doing what we have just defined?' No one spoke up." Properly understood, the emphasis in ecotourism is on a set of principles and how to put them into practice: on what ecotourism stands for and how these standards are being implemented. "We were all achieving various aspects of the definition," said Christ, "but none among us (and we were the committed of the committed!) was hitting in our practices all that ecotourism means."

Ecotourism so described is a relative fledgling, but it has unleashed a great deal of experimentation and creativity among tour operators, travel agencies, hotel builders and owners, park and tourism officials, scientists, environmentalists, NGOs, and community activists. It has led to experimentation, to a pushing of the parameters of the concept through, for instance, environmentally sensitive lodge construction, well-trained nature guides, and a variety of ownership schemes between local communities and NGOs or the private sector. It has also generated, in the wake of the Rio Earth Summit, dozens of "green" certification programs designed to measure the environmental and social impact of tourism businesses. Building on these sound initiatives, it is possible to expand TIES's bare-bones definition and broaden it into a multi-layered definition that forms the backdrop for this book. Real ecotourism, then, has the following seven characteristics:

- *Involves travel to natural destinations.* These destinations are often remote areas, whether inhabited or uninhabited, and are usually under some kind of environmental protection at the national, international, communal, or private level.
- *Minimizes impact.* Tourism causes damage. Ecotourism strives to minimize the adverse effects of hotels, trails, and other infrastructure by using either recycled or plentifully available local building materials, renewable sources of energy, recycling and safe disposal of waste and garbage, and environmentally and culturally sensitive architectural design. Minimization of impact also requires that the numbers and mode of behavior of tourists be regulated to ensure limited damage to the ecosystem. Ecotourism is generally classified as a nonextractive or nonconsumptive industry, but it can also include such enterprises as Zimbabwe's innovative CAMPFIRE program of community-run safari hunting, begun in the 1980s, as long as they are sustainable industries based on renewable resources.[118] Similarly, one of the first self-described eco-lodges in the United

States, Papoose Creek/Sun Ranch in Montana, offers hunting packages for its visitors, in which a limited amount of big game can be taken (one elk per person).[119]

- *Builds environmental awareness.* Ecotourism means education, for both tourists and residents of nearby communities. Well before the tour begins, tour operators should supply travelers with reading material about the country, environment, and local people, as well as a code of conduct for both the traveler and the industry itself. This information helps prepare the tourist, as TIES's guidelines state, "to learn about the places and people to be visited" and "to minimize their negative impacts while visiting sensitive environments and cultures."[120] Essential to good ecotourism are well-trained, multilingual naturalist guides with skills in natural and cultural history, environmental interpretation, ethical principles, and effective communication. Ecotourism projects should also help educate members of surrounding communities, schoolchildren, and the broader public in the host country. To do so, they must offer greatly reduced entrance and lodge fees for nationals and free educational trips for local students and those living near the tourist attraction.
- *Provides direct financial benefits for conservation.* Ecotourism helps raise funds for environmental protection, research, and education through a variety of mechanisms, including park entrance fees; tour company, hotel, airline, and airport taxes; and voluntary contributions. Many national park systems were first created to protect the land, facilitate scientific research, and, in Africa, promote sport hunting. Only later did parks open access to the public, and only recently have they begun to be viewed as potential sources of funding for scientific investigation and conservation.
- *Provides financial benefits and empowerment for local people.* Ecotourism holds that national parks and other conservation areas will survive only if, as Costa Rica–based ecologist Daniel Janzen puts it, there are "happy people" around the perimeters. The local community must be involved with and receive income and other tangible benefits (potable water, roads, health clinics, etc.) from the conservation area and its tourist facilities. Campsites, lodges, guide services, restaurants, and other concessions should be run by or in partnership with communities surrounding national parks or other tourist destinations. Ecotourism further promotes the use of tour and car rental agencies, hotels, airlines, and other related businesses owned by host country nationals, so that profits are more likely to stay in the developing countries. More important, if ecotourism is to be viewed as a tool for rural development, it must also help to shift economic and political control to the local community, village, coop-

erative, or entrepreneur. This, as the case studies in part 2 of this book show, is the most difficult and time-consuming principle in the ecotourism equation, the one that foreign operators and "partners" most often let fall through the cracks or that they follow only partially or formally.

- *Respects local culture.* Ecotourism is not only "greener" but also less culturally intrusive and exploitative than conventional tourism. Whereas prostitution, black markets, and drugs often are by-products of mass tourism, ecotourism strives to be culturally respectful and have a minimal effect on both the natural environment and the human population of a host country. This is not easy, especially since ecotourism often involves travel to remote areas where small and isolated communities have had little experience in interacting with foreigners. And like conventional tourism, ecotourism involves an unequal relationship of power between the visitor and the host and a commodification of the relationship through exchange of money. Part of being a responsible ecotourist is learning beforehand about the local customs, respecting dress codes and other social norms, and not intruding on the community unless invited, either individually or as part of well-organized tours.
- *Supports human rights and democratic movements.* The United Nations–sponsored World Tourism Organization proclaims that tourism contributes to "international understanding, peace, prosperity, and universal respect for and observance of human rights and fundamental freedoms for all."[121] Such sentiments, however, are little reflected in conventional mass tourism. Although tourism often is glibly hailed as a tool for building international understanding and world peace, this does not happen automatically; frequently, in fact, tourism bolsters the economies of repressive and undemocratic states. Mass tourism typically pays scant attention to the political system of the host country or struggles within it, unless civil unrest spills over into attacks on tourists.

Ecotourism demands a more holistic approach to travel, one in which participants strive to respect, learn about, and benefit both the environment and local communities. Although not explicitly part of The International Ecotourism Society's definition, giving economic benefits and showing cultural sensitivity to local communities cannot be separated from understanding their political circumstances. In many developing countries, rural populations living around national parks and other ecotourism attractions are locked in contests with the national government and multinational corporations for control of the assets and their benefits.

Ecotourists therefore need to be sensitive to the host country's political environment and social climate and need to consider the merits of international boycotts called by those supporting democratic reforms, majority rule, and human rights. The campaign by the African National Congress (ANC) to isolate South Africa through a boycott of investment, trade, sports, and tourism helped bring down apartheid. In recent years, similar boycotts have been called for by those fighting for democracy in Nigeria, Burma, and Tibet. For many Americans, the toughest political choice is in our own backyard: Cuba. Although the U.S. government, under pressure from Cuban exiles, has spent more than four decades barring most travel and other trade to Cuba, growing numbers of Americans had concluded that contact, not isolation, was more likely to strengthen the democratic forces within the island as well as build fuller understanding in the United States of the nature of the Cuban Revolution. By 2005, an estimated fifty to one hundred thousand U.S. citizens were traveling to Cuba annually, many without permission and in defiance of the U.S. government blockade.[122]

Determining whether to boycott or visit a country is not always easy. As then–Executive Director of Amnesty International William F. Schulz pointed out in 1997, only one country—Iceland—has never been cited for a serious human rights abuse. Schulz argued that when considering travel to a country, among the questions to ask are, "Does economic growth fueled by tourism really improve the chances of human rights being respected? In some cases, like Singapore, a booming economy and tourist trade has not been enough to guarantee respect for individual liberty. Will boycotting a country harm already impoverished workers more than it will corporate or government titans? Or are the short-term economic penalties more than offset by the ultimate benefits of change?" Schulz added that "if one visits a repressive state like China or Indonesia, Peru or Syria, it is possible to make the trip rewarding both personally and politically" by consciously learning about the country beforehand, meeting with dissidents and average folks, as well as government officials, while there, and speaking about the political climate, not just the weather, after returning.[123] Responsible travelers must carefully assess the consequences of travel both on a country's ecosystem and cultural norms and on movements for social and political democratization and human rights. In recent years, for instance, responsible travelers, companies, and organizations have debated whether or not to travel to Burma whose military government ousted and put under house arrest the democratically elected leader and Nobel laureate, Aung San Suu Kyi.[124]

This is the range of tenets and considerations that helps to provide a broad definition of ecotourism. Properly defined, then, *ecotourism is travel to fragile, pristine, and usually protected areas that strives to be low impact and (often) small scale. It helps educate the traveler, provides funds for conservation, directly benefits the economic development and political empowerment of local communities, and fosters respect for different cultures and for human rights.*

The long-term challenge is to find ways to maintain the rigor and multidimensional qualities of ecotourism while widening it beyond individual projects and making it integral to the concept of tourism in general. How can the principles of ecotourism be used to restructure conventional tourism and bring fundamental, not superficial, changes to the way mass tourism functions? In many quarters, the opposite trend is dominant: the principles underlying ecotourism are being "greenwashed" by superficial, feel-good rhetoric and minor cost-saving modifications that do not transform tourism into a tool that protects the environment, benefits local communities, and educates the tourist.

Some experts have pronounced ecotourism dead, passé, or hopelessly diluted. However, amid the superficiality, hype, and marketing, I found some excellent examples in the field, lots of dedicated people, vibrant grassroots movements and struggles, much creativity and experimentation, and some early models and standards. In my assessment, although ecotourism is indeed rare, often misdefined, and frequently imperfect, it is still in its adolescence, not on its deathbed. Whether ecotourism matures into adulthood in the twenty-first century, whether it gains permanence and becomes the predominant way in which we travel and interact with our physical and cultural environment, depends on myriad factors. One step toward ensuring ecotourism's survival is helping to build a more discriminating and informed traveling public. Ecotourism travelers, practitioners, professionals, educators, and proponents need to understand the major problems and challenges confronting ecotourism, as well as how ecotourism fits within the tourism industry and within a country's development strategy.

2

The World Travel Industry: Going "Green"?

Tourism, like other global industries, has been affected by both free trade and globalization and by the antiglobalization or "fair trade" movement. While not as clearly articulated as in other sectors, there are contradictions and divisions within the tourism industry. Chain hotels, airlines, and other multinational tourism companies, even when they support environmental protection and sustainable development, generally favor open borders and free trade. In contrast, one of the tenets of ecotourism is the support of locally owned businesses, local hiring, and local purchasing, all practices that are circumscribed under the growing number of international trade agreements and organizations.

One of the early indications of the contradictions among proponents of sustainable tourism was *Agenda 21 for the Travel and Tourism Industry*, the travel industry's response to the 1992 Earth Summit Declaration on Environment and Development. This document, which was endorsed by a number of the large international corporations, made it clear that the industry coupled sustainable development and environmental protection with free trade, privatization, and government deregulation. Two of the twelve guiding principles in the document state that "nations should cooperate to promote an open economic system in which international trade in Travel & Tourism services can take place" and "protectionism in trade in Travel & Tourism services should be halted or reversed."[1]

At first glance, the emphasis on free trade principles might seem

Chris Lupoli provided the updates and helped with editing this chapter. Mollie Chapman and Emy Rodriguez assisted with the initial updates.

strange. But because tourism today is a global industry regulated by international trade agreements, just like steel or wheat or automobiles, its actions must be understood in the context of larger debates around trade and governance. In the 1990s, international agreements for opening borders for trade and investment accelerated the penetration of multinational corporations into developing countries, and sometimes into previously regulated markets, and are often directly at odds with local efforts to participate in and benefit from tourism. Economic globalization and the growing trend toward free trade were facilitated by creation in 1995 of the World Trade Organization (WTO) as a successor to the General Agreement on Tariffs and Trade, which was established in the wake of World War II to govern barriers to trade in goods. The WTO is a more powerful global institution intended to set the global rules for trade, investment, and capital flows.[2] As Renato Ruggiero, the first director-general of the WTO, observed in 1995, "We are no longer writing the rules of interaction among separate national economies. We are writing the constitution of a single global economy."[3]

In addition, a growing number of regional and bilateral agreements with the United States, such as NAFTA (North American Free Trade Agreement), are designed to increase the power of foreign investors in developing countries and to promote liberalized trade in services such as tourism. The WTO and regional agreements often weaken fledgling domestic industries and businesses, override laws protecting the environment, and undermine efforts at environmental auditing and public scrutiny of these projects.[4] Of particular importance for tourism is the GATS (General Agreement on Trade in Services) which opens up WTO member countries to foreign investment in services and disallows government policies that favor national over foreign providers. While current trade law is less restrictive on trade in services than in goods, and there have been, to date, few test cases relating to tourism, law professor Barton Thompson cautions, "Future liberalization of trade in services poses perhaps the greatest risk to sustainable tourism."[5] Anita Pleumarom, an early and outspoken critic of "greenwashing" under the guise of ecotourism, goes further, warning that GATS "will edge out small, independent enterprises as transnational corporations and their affiliates, with the advantage of financial resources and technology, muscle their way in to control the tourist trade in countries in the South."[6]

In the wake of the 1992 Earth Summit in Rio de Janeiro, international tourism organizations also promoted self-regulation, including voluntary certification programs, rather than international or government directives. The World Travel & Tourism Council's (WTTC) "Environmental Guidelines," for example, were a clear call for preemptive action to stave off outside regulation: "Travel and Tourism companies should seek to implement sound environmental principles through self-regulation, recognizing that national and international regulation may be inevitable and that preparation is vital."[7] Despite the tourism industry's antiregulation stance, by the new millennium, global consciousness of the negative impacts of free trade and the imperative of sustainable tourism was on the rise.

Recognition of this imperative was driven by a host of nongovernmental and intergovernmental organizations, intent on setting a new international agenda for tourism. The UN's 2002 International Year of Ecotourism (IYE) was sponsored by the UN Environment Programme (UNEP) and the UN World Tourism Organization (UNWTO) and included eighteen preparatory meetings around the world, which generated heated debates. Spearheaded by indigenous rights activists in the Americas and Southeast Asia, critics of IYE accused the UNEP and UNWTO of doing the bidding of big businesses. These businesses were charged with using ecotourism to open new areas, trample on indigenous lands and rights, exploit workers, and destroy the environment. They expressed "grave concerns that the event [would] result in misconceived and inflationary ecotourism or more correctly 'mass nature tourism' . . . "[8]

Yet in the end, the World Ecotourism Summit took place in May 2002 in Quebec City, Canada, without the activist street clashes that characterized World Bank and G-8 meetings from Seattle to Washington, D.C., Davos, Singapore, and elsewhere. The tone and content of speeches and the final proclamation of this three-day Ecotourism Summit were crucial to this outcome: they reflected the growing global skepticism about the benefits of unfettered free trade. The summit, which brought together over one thousand delegates from 132 countries, culminated in the *Quebec Declaration on Ecotourism*. This comprehensive and visionary document does not contain any of the free-market language of the Earth Summit era, but rather focuses on the establishment of small and locally run enterprises, the use of local materials and products, and the establishment of legal mechanisms to promote such activities. It calls on international finance institutions and governments at all levels to direct their resources toward promoting small and medium-sized ecotourism firms. More importantly, it insists that tourism "contribute[s] actively to the conservation of natural and cultural heritage; Includes local and indigenous communities in its planning, development and operation, and contribute[s] to their well-being; Interprets the natural and cultural heritages of the destination to visitors; [and] Lends itself better to independent travelers, as well as to organized tours for small size groups."[9]

Did the industry get the message? Somewhat, perhaps. At least the rhetoric has been toned down. The *Blueprint for New Tourism*, issued in 2003 by the WTTC, puts far less emphasis on trade liberalization and more on "building New Tourism to bring new benefits to the wider world." The WTTC, which is made up of CEOs from mainstream tourism, calls in its *Blueprint* for "liberalizing trade, transport and communications and easing barriers to travel and to investment." But the document couples this with a call for "a new vision" that includes "business balancing economics with people, culture and environment."[10] While there have been no major legal challenges that have pitted ecotourism against big international tourism companies, the push toward opening borders, particularly in coastal areas for resorts, vacation homes, and cruise tourism, continues to expand. So despite some softening of language and some "greening" initiatives of mass tourism businesses, the international tourism industry continues to be located within the free trade camp.

Structure of the Tourism Industry

The tourism industry that funnels travelers to developing countries is a complex, multi-layered maze. In the country of departure, it includes travel agencies (retailers), tour operators (wholesalers), airlines, cruise lines, car rental agencies, credit card companies, public relations firms, advertising companies, tourism bureaus, and the media. In the host country, it includes inbound tour operators, ground transporters, guides, accommodation facilities, national tourism bureaus, national and private parks and other recreational sites, cultural and craft centers, and special concessions such as providers of balloon, camel, and boat rides. The international travel industry is supported by government policies and regulations, infrastructure projects, and, frequently, direct subsidies, as well as by a wide array of commercial banks and international financial and aid institutions. Ecotourism receives support from conservation organizations and other NGOs, most of which are based in the United States and other developed countries but operate primarily in developing countries. Given the realities of overseas travel, "much of the trip cost, and thus the economic benefit," writes ecotourism expert Kreg Lindberg, "remains with outbound operators and source country airlines. To some extent this simply is due to the nature of the tourism industry; substantial funds are spent on marketing, commissions, and transport before tourists even reach the destination."[11] One of the tenets of ecotourism is, of course, to put a larger portion of the tourism dollars into host countries and communities.

The Big Players

The tourism industry is dominated by transnational corporations that are, on one hand, becoming increasingly interlinked and consolidated and, on the other, spreading around the world and penetrating new markets. Since the 1960s, there has been a simultaneous and accelerating process of vertical and horizontal integration. In his analysis of the tourism industry from the global South perspective, Thanh-Dam Truong, a Vietnamese professor with the Institute of Social Studies at The Hague, explains, "When expanding into developing countries, the industry has required mass production and the standardization of services and quality. Given their late entry into the field, many developing countries have limited possibilities to develop their own stock of knowledge and control over the business. They have had to adopt the established standards and therefore must rely on foreign firms to run major sectors of the industry."[12]

Multinational institutions such as the World Bank, the International Monetary Fund (IMF), and the U.S. Agency for International Development (USAID) have facilitated economic globalization and free trade. A proliferating number of U.S.-backed international trade agreements, particularly in the Americas, are seeking removal of barriers, including investment regulations, labor standards, and environmental protection. Nevertheless, the American international travel industry, and especially the private airline companies, has always depended heavily on government subsidies and support. After World War II, the U.S. government used its surplus of military aircraft to subsidize the aerospace industry. It created financial institutions, such as the Export-Import Bank of the United States, that gave low-interest loans to corporations for purchase of U.S.-made aircraft and equipment. U.S. assistance programs constructed and enlarged airports overseas, improved long-haul navigation, and financed development of long-range and wide-body aircraft. More recently, federal funds and powerful financial institutions also have underwritten research, development, and application of computer technology for the booking of airline reservations, hotel rooms, and car rentals. This, coupled with airline deregulation policies, has enabled the integration and consolidation of the travel industry. Pan American World Airways, which was founded in 1927, and went out of business in 1991,[13] was among the first to develop an integrated global reservation system, in which British Airways worked with Holiday Inn. Other airlines quickly followed.

Nontourism companies in industrialized countries have also assumed a significant role in the industry as it has globalized. Major banks, along with firms specializing in brewing, food processing, gambling, media, telecommunications, shipping, and real estate, have bought shares in airlines and hotel chains. ITT Corporation, for instance, bought 100 percent of the Sheraton hotel chain in 1968. Midland Bank bought 78 percent of the Thomas Cook Group's shareholdings, and the Rothschild Group purchased a sizable slice Club Méditerranée (Club Med). As Thanh-Dam Truong wrote in 1990:

> The general trend in integration in international tourism is that firms from industrialized countries tend to dominate the market through control of knowledge about the market, control of the means of distribution (travel agents, banks, department stores, business travel centers, etc.), and control over the advertising industry which, to a large extent, shapes and determines demand. This entails a division of labor according to which Third World countries, with few exceptions, merely provide the social infrastructure and facilities with little or no control over the process of production and distribution of the tourist-related services at an international level.[14]

This trend has continued. As Andrey Shlevkov, an official with the World Tourism Organization, stated in a 2004 speech, "There is a clear trend for globalization, concentration and consolidation in the world tourism industry [that is] competing hard for tourist euros and dollars. Just four global distribution systems dominate electronic reservations, while five global air alliances control 60 percent of international air traffic. In major European generating countries, a handful of tour operators dominate a lion's share of the market, and their clout may sometimes contribute to making or breaking a destination."[15]

What Truong called "the four main economic agents in international tourism"—airlines, hotels, tour operators, and travel agents—have all become increasingly integrated in terms of their services, financing, management, research, and development. Take, for instance, the American Express Company, whose tourism-related activities were traditionally confined to banking, that is, the sale of traveler's checks. In the 1960s, American Express moved beyond traveler's checks, buying shares in tour operations, tourism financing companies, and computerized reservation systems. In 1971, it bought into CITEL, an electronic reservation system for hotel rooms, allowing it to provide reservation services for a half million rooms and some five thousand car rental agencies in fifty countries. Today, American Express is the largest travel agency in the United States with offices in every important city around the globe and revenues of $29.1 billion in 2004. Worldwide spending on American Express cards in 2004 reached an all-time high of $416 billion, an 18 percent increase from the previous year.[16] American Express now handles many other travel-related services, including hotel reservations and airline, cruise, and ground travel; traveler's checks and credit cards; financial and small business advice; computer services; guidebooks; passport-processing assistance; and real estate services. American Express has been an industry trendsetter in modernizing, consolidating, and integrating various branches of the travel industry. These companies can and do respond to public opinion. AmEx, for example, has taken some steps to build its "green" profile, offering environmental grants to conservation projects, introducing recycling and energy-saving procedures, and partnering with groups like the World Monument Fund and the Caribbean Alliance for Sustainable Tourism.

Airlines

The biggest-ticket item in an overseas holiday has traditionally gone to the airlines, the part of the industry (along with cruise ships and car rental companies) least infused with ecotourism principles or practices. Although the percentage varies with distance, size of group, carrier, and season, 61 percent of total U.S. travel agency sales went for airline tickets in 1995, with 14 percent going to cruise lines, 10 percent to hotels, 7 percent for car rentals, and 8 percent for other sales.[17] However, by 2005, the percentage of travel agent sales going for airline tickets had fallen to about 25 percent, according to the American Society of Travel Agents (ASTA).[18] The main reason has been the rapid growth of the Internet: Americans using the Internet to plan or book travel jumped 25 percent between 2001 and 2002, and by 2002, airline tickets accounted for 77 percent of all online purchases.[19] According to hospitality marketing expert Peter Yesawich, in 2006, 56 percent of leisure travelers say they go to the Internet exclusively to plan a vacation and 51 percent of travelers who book a hotel or airfare check the price online beforehand.[20] Despite this shift from travel agents to the Internet, airline tickets remained the largest component of most international travel.

For most developing countries and newly independent colonies, setting up a national airline that carried the country's flag, and was fully or partially owned by the government, was an important symbol of sovereignty. Back in the 1950s, the founder of Hilton Hotels Corporation, which pioneered investments in developing countries, quipped, "No new nation has got it going until it has a seat in the United Nations, a national airline, and a Hilton Hotel."[21] Today, the United Nations membership remains, Hilton Hotels and other international hotel chains have probably multiplied, but the national airlines may well be gone.

Although they were symbolically important, these new national airlines—sometimes with a fleet of only two or three planes—were involved in a David and Goliath contest. Many bought jet aircraft, navigation equipment, and services from the Boeing Company and other U.S. corporations. These deals were frequently financed by the Export-Import Bank, which both made direct loans to foreign carriers and guaranteed loans made by commercial lenders. Other foreign airlines leased their planes and/or had management contracts with international commercial carriers such as Pan American, Compagnie Nationale Air France, and British Airways. As these nascent companies struggled to get a toehold in the international market, the big airlines from developed countries were acquiring wide-body aircraft with increased carrying capacity and decreased operating costs and were rapidly linking up with international hotel chains, travel agencies, tour operators, and car rental agencies for sales and promotional purposes and to offer discount tour packages. Inclusive tour packages offered by air charter companies also undercut the market for the new national airlines.[22] Whereas the national airlines offered travelers from overseas a bit of the flavor of the destination, thus becoming part of the holiday experience, today's big carriers provide increasingly homogenized and nondescript service.

In the 1990s, as economic liberalization and deregulation took hold, international carriers, with hefty marketing budgets, name recognition, and hookups with other sectors of the tourism industry, entered the most lucrative foreign markets in developing countries. During this decade, Costa Rica's flagship airline, LACSA, a small but well-run operation, was gradually sold to foreign conglomerates. In the Caribbean, BWIA International Airways and Air Jamaica were privatized in 1995, Air Aruba ceased functioning in 2000, while Bahamasair and LIAT (based in Antigua) developed code-shares with other airlines.[23] Without protective trade barriers to keep out competition and control fares, computer systems and other technological innovations, and integration with hotel chains, car rental agents, and tour operators, many small national airlines could not compete and were sold to foreign carriers.

In 1997, six of the top international carriers, led by US Airways and United, formed the Star Alliance, which they called "the first truly global airline network in the world." The carriers agreed to meld their frequent flier mileage programs, ground services, and airport lounge services and to simplify ticketing and link schedules "to provide seamless service on every continent."[24] By 2006, Star Alliance included eighteen airlines serving 842 destinations in 152 countries and offering travelers a choice of fifteen different frequent flyer programs in which to earn mileage points. A few national carriers were part of the Alliance, but this did not necessarily stem financial troubles: in 2006, Varig, once considered Latin America's premier airline, declared bankruptcy and was up for sale.[25] Meanwhile, American and United airlines have gained "an insurmountable edge over their Latin counterparts" because of their "vast international networks" and their "virtual lock on travel within North America," the destination of 75 percent of Latin Americans traveling outside the region. This, combined with high operating costs, forced more Latin American airlines to privatize, merge, or close.[26] This phenomenon is not limited to U.S. and Latin American airlines. In Europe, the integration of Swiss International into the German-owned Lufthansa was announced in 2005, and the same year in Asia, China Eastern Airlines announced that it would consolidate with Yunnan Airlines and China Northwest Airlines. So even if conscientious ecotravelers or tour operators try to patronize a national or regional airline, they may find that in reality, many so-called national airlines are owned by a larger foreign corporation.

With the rise of environmentalism and ecotourism, a number of the international carriers have given a nod to conservation by adopting some "green" practices, often in the form of fuel efficiency, which also saved on the corporate bottom line. One of the newer airline startups in the United States, JetBlue, took steps to reduce consumption and decrease emissions by acquiring planes that burn up to 50 percent less fuel than older models. Japan Airlines established a set of Environmental Action Guidelines and by 2004 it had a recycling program (for aluminum cans, tickets, uniforms, and cargo packing sheets); was purchasing more fuel-efficient airplanes, had reduced use of hazardous chemicals, and had wastewater treatment systems.[27] Of the international carriers, British Airways has long been hailed as the environmental leader. Together with the WTTC, British Airways ran the annual "Tourism for Tomorrow Awards" between 1992 and 2003, and has since continued as a sponsor. The airline company has also made efforts to improve fuel efficiency, reduce noise pollution and waste, and improve local air quality.[28]

Aircraft manufacturers, governments, and various agencies have also responded to rising fuel prices and environmental awareness by implementing new technologies, policies, and international agreements. General Electric has been developing a new aircraft engine, the GEnx, which is designed to deliver 15 percent better fuel consumption and reduce emissions to 94 percent below 2008 regulatory limits—while launching a huge advertising campaign hailing its "green" practices.[29] Manufacturers such as Boeing and Airbus continue to design newer and more fuel-efficient aircraft, such as the Boeing 787 Dreamliner and the Airbus A320. The International Air Transportation Association (IATA), whose mission it is to "represent, lead and serve the airline industry,"[30] is composed of approximately 265 of the world's largest airlines or 94 percent of all international scheduled air traffic. In order to reduce fuel consumption, which is the second-largest cost item after employee wages, IATA has published a fuel and emissions checklist of industry "best practices," created training programs, and worked on initiatives to reduce flight time, improve airport traffic flows, and adopt more efficient operating procedures designed to help airlines reduce fuel consumption on a scale that saved several billion dollars per year.[31] In 2005, the Federal Aviation Administration (FAA) in the United States implemented a new procedure allowing more planes to fly preferred altitudes and routes, thereby saving an estimated $5.3 billion in fuel costs over the next decade.[32] In 2004, the European Parliament approved a set of four regulations that compose the Single European Sky initiative, designed to optimize flight paths, reduce flight times, improve fuel efficiency, and modernize air traffic management.[33]

Despite these environmental initiatives, there has been growing awareness of the impact of air transportation on climate change. Air transport is estimated to be the fastest-growing source of greenhouse gases, contributing between 4 to 10 percent of carbon dioxide emissions by all types of transport.[34] Although the world's aircraft fleet has improved its fuel efficiency by 70 percent in the past forty years, global air traffic has quadrupled since 1970, from 350 billion passenger miles a year to 1,500 billion passenger miles a year.[35] This led some to question whether long-haul ecotourism is just too costly for the planet. As writer Joanna Walter commented at the time of the 2002 World Ecotourism Summit, "Travel industry leaders will argue the toss on whether 'eco' and 'tourism' can ever live happily together, but there will be shockingly little debate on whether there is any point in having the greenest of "green" eco-resorts in deepest Peru if all the wealthy, sandalled 'ecotourists' each burn six tonnes of carbon dioxide getting there and back."[36]

This is, however, hardly the solution, given that ecotourism is an increasingly important development tool for poor countries and communities as well as for biodiversity conservation. Global warming needs to be addressed on a wide range of levels, including traveling "smarter"—by, when possible, bus and train rather than car and plane—and working in a variety of ways to reduce greenhouse gas emissions. By 2005, a growing number of carbon-offset programs were offering airline passengers and companies ways to calculate the amount and cost of greenhouse gas emissions produced during a flight and offset the emission by contributing to renewable or alternative energy projects. British Airways began a program to encourage its customers to "neutralize" their travel emissions by contributing to Carbon Care, which funds sustainable energy projects around the world.[37] In 2006, Virgin Airlines CEO Sir Richard Branson captured headlines with his announcement to commit $3 billion over the next ten years to combat global warming. Branson pledged "to invest 100 percent of all future proceeds to the Virgin Group from . . . both our trains and airline businesses, into tackling global warming."[38] Later that same year, NatureAir, a regional airline based in Costa Rica, announced that the company itself would contribute to carbon-offset programs for all its flights, thus becoming the "world's first and only emission-neutral airline."[39] Other companies began to join the carbon-offset bandwagon. Online travel sites Expedia and Travelocity developed programs to encourage travelers to purchase carbon offsets as they bought their tickets.[40] And shoe mogul Nike set out to reduce its CO_2 footprint. Through its "Eco-Class Program," Nike teamed up with Delta Airlines and Hertz to offset airplane and auto emissions from business trips by Nike's employees.[41]

Hotel Chains and Resorts

In the 1950s, Hilton, InterContinental, and Holiday Inn were among the first specialized hotel chains to invest abroad, before significant economic alliances were forged with air carriers and tour operators. Over the next half century, more international chains expanded into developing countries, attracted by new investment opportunities for their excess capital, by low wages, and, increasingly, by the potential offered through integration with other sectors of the tourism industry. By 1995, nineteen of the twenty largest hotel conglomerates were based in developed countries (the other was based in Hong Kong) and twelve of the top twenty operators were American multinational corporations.[42] These large hotel conglomerates have operations around the globe: ninety countries (Accor and InterContinental); eighty-three countries (Best Western); eighty-one countries (Starwood); seventy-three countries (Hilton); and sixty-seven countries (Marriott). By 2002, the Cendant Corporation, a U.S.-based hotel franchiser, was the largest hotel group in the world, with 6,513 hotels and approximately 536,000 hotel rooms. The other largest chains included InterContinental (515,000 hotel rooms); Marriott (463,000); Accor (440,000); Choice Hotels International (373,000); and Hilton Hotels (337,000).[43]

International hotel chains typically use one of five different forms of investment in developing countries, most of which minimize their risks and maximize their ability to muscle aside small, locally owned hotels, lodges, and resorts. The types of investment used by multinationals are: (1) ownership or equity investment; (2) management contracts; (3) hotel leasing agreements, whereby the multinational pays the hotel owner a percentage of the profits; (4) franchise agreements, whereby the owner uses the multinational's corporate name, services, and trademarks for a fee while maintaining certain operating standards; and (5) technical service agreements, whereby the multinational provides the local hotel with a consultant for management, marketing, and technology.

Most of the large chains no longer seek to own property, preferring "lighter" structures that require less financial commitment and reduce risk for the operator. The use of leases, management contracts, and franchises also allows for a more rapid rate of expansion. Growth has to be the cornerstone of any branded chain's strategy. The more flags that can be planted around a country and around the world, the more a hotel chain can benefit from key customer agreements with large multinationals or tour operators to guarantee a steady flow of business. The more widespread a chain's properties, the more completely the group can serve large corporate customers by guaranteeing the same standard of accommodation (and security) anywhere their hotels may be located in the world. Most common are the management contracts, which allow for control of a property with a minimum of financing and risk. Developing countries have long paid a premium for such contracts. Whereas hotel management fees in industrialized countries range from 6 to 15 percent and average 12 percent, in developing countries they average 17 percent and can be as much as 23 percent. In addition, the international firm extracts additional fees for advertising and sales services, computerized reservation facilities, and routine inspections and consultations.

While affiliation with an international chain may be costly, it is frequently viewed as imperative in giving local investors a competitive edge over locally owned hotels—particularly in marketing, reservations, technology, training, and service standards, as well as access to goods at lower marginal costs. By increasing its geographical coverage, a hotel chain can help maintain a steady flow of business while guaranteeing customers the same standard of accommodation and security around the world. Whereas only about 2 percent of the hotels in Western Europe are linked to multinational corporations through management contracts, in developing countries the proportion has approached, or well exceeded, 50 percent: 75 percent in the Middle East, 72 percent in Africa, 60 percent in Asia, and 47 percent in Latin America.[44]

Beginning in the 1990s, several prominent hotel chains—InterContinental Hotels and Resorts, Holiday Inn Worldwide, and Fairmont

Hotels & Resorts—began taking steps to "green" parts of their operations. Typically, this involved reducing water and energy consumption, measures that were good for the environment while also saving money. In 1992, Hilton International and other hotel groups founded the International Hotels Environment Initiative (IHEI) "to increase general environmental awareness and to establish valid guidelines within the global hotel industry." IHEI, which grew to represent over sixty-eight brands and 11,200 hotels on five continents, was absorbed by the London-based International Tourism Partnership, the tourism program of The Prince of Wales International Business Leaders Forum.[45] Similarly, the Green Hotel Initiative (GHI) is a program developed by CERES, a U.S.-based network of investment funds, environmental organizations, and other public interest groups. The GHI is designed to increase and demonstrate market demand for environmentally responsible hotel services, focusing on educating the purchasers of hotel services, creating vehicles for these purchasers to express their demands, and providing mechanisms for hotels to communicate their environmental performance. It focuses particularly on getting large corporations to use "green" hotels for business travel and conferences.[46]

Yet there are still no clear standards for social and environmental performance. Absent these, mass tourism resorts have been using the "eco" label, some with little or no substance. In the early 1990s, for instance, there was the advertisement for The Enchanted Garden in a special ecotourism magazine published for travel agents. The photo featured a towel-draped female tourist lying on a massage table in the middle of a palm-shrouded garden. She was being rubbed down by a uniformed Jamaican woman, and the caption read, "As Nature Intended . . . " But the Enchanted Garden is no eco-resort; it's a 112-room luxury spa complex managed by DHC Hotels & Resorts, a major international hotel chain. Typical of such places, most bookings are made in the United States, most profits flow back to the corporate headquarters, and Jamaicans receive scant benefits other than menial hotel jobs.[47]

Eco-labels, backed by measurable criteria, are one way to help counter this problem. Over the last fifteen years, a number of voluntary tourism certification programs have been launched, designed to measure the environmental, social, and economic impacts of hotels. Today there are some sixty to eighty tourism certification programs, most for hotels and most located in Europe, and several dozen others under development. However, there are a growing number of programs in Latin America and elsewhere, some of which target larger hotels.[48]

Certification is, in fact, an old and well-entrenched concept within the tourism industry. Beginning in 1900, Michelin, the French tire company, published its first guidebook measuring and rating hotels and restaurants.[49] Shortly afterward, the American Automobile Association or AAA, made up of U.S. automobile clubs, also began producing motorist handbooks that ranked businesses using one to five stars.[50] Today most countries use a variant of this five-star quality and safety rating system for accommodations. Much newer are the "green" tourism certification programs designed to measure sustainability, most of which were launched in the wake of the UN's 1992 Rio Earth Summit.

As discussed in the next chapter, there are a variety of different types of "green" certification programs within the tourism industry. Most common for large resorts and hotel chains are programs using an environment management system (EMS), including ISO 14001 (International Organization for Standardization).[51] Certification to ISO standards is "process-based," that is, it requires having an acceptable process for developing and revising the EMS; it is not based on implementation of the EMS. Today ISO 14001 and other types of EMS have been used to certify a few hotel chains and a scattering of individual hotels around the world. The advantage of ISO 14001 is that it is internationally recognized, can operate globally and across tourism sectors, and has standards tailored to the needs of the individual business. The drawbacks are, however, considerable: it is costly (setting up an EMS can cost twenty to forty thousand dollars for a medium-sized company, and far more for a large hotel) and it is complicated and heavily engineering oriented, with the focus on internal operating systems, not a company's social and economic impacts on the surrounding area. Given these limitations, a number of the newer "green" certification programs include performance criteria to measure the impacts of a hotel or other businesses and involve far less cost to implement.

Today, Green Globe 21 is the only significant international certification program that covers the whole industry, and the whole globe. It has participants in over forty countries and works with consumers, companies, and communities. Unfortunately, Green Globe has made little headway so far. Less than one hundred hotels and resorts have earned certification. Almost all are in tourist destinations, with, by early 2008, fifty-seven in the Caribbean. Europe plays a major role in eco-labeling for tourism accommodations, as 80 percent of eco-label programs are based in or operate in Europe. There are several examples of regional eco-labeling schemes. The European Flower, an initiative financed by the EU, represents an attempt to create one unified eco-label for eighteen European countries.[52] The Blue Swallow, established in Germany in 1990 as a private initiative, targets spas, hotels and conference centers in Austria, Finland, Greenland, Germany, France, Portugal, and Switzerland.[53] Accommodations must comply with a list of criteria that assess the sustainability of food and beverage operations, transport, energy, water, waste, cleaning products, and gardens. In return for a small annual fee, members have their properties featured in a large trade magazine and promoted at a dozen different trade fairs in Germany. The Nordic Swan operates in Scandinavia, where it has a high level of public recognition.[54] This certification program, which receives government financial support, has also been considered as a benchmark for a Europe-wide standard. A number of other programs have emerged, especially in the Americas (see chapters 3 and 10), and, by late 2007, efforts spearheaded by the Rainforest Alliance were moving rapidly toward creating a global accreditation body, the Sustainable Tourism Stewardship Council (STSC).[55]

Cruise Ships

Cruise ship vacations are the fastest-growing sector of the leisure travel industry—with ship size and numbers, passengers, ports, and profits all on the rise. Since 1970, the number of people taking cruises has jumped 1,000 percent; between 1990 and 2005, the number tripled, and it continues to grow. In 2004, there were 13.2 million passengers; by 2010, this number is projected to double.[56] Ship size has increased from 500 to 800 passengers in the 1970s to newer ships, so-called floating cities, which accommodate 2,600 to 3,800, with crews of a thousand or more.[57] Nearly 90 percent of cruise ships ply the waters in just six regions: the Caribbean (50 percent), Mediterranean (15 percent), Alaska (6.7 percent), Mexican Riviera (6.6 percent), Western and Northern Europe (5 percent), and Asia/Pacific (5 percent).[58] Following the 9/11 terrorist attacks, cruise lines pulled ships out of the Mediterranean and redeployed them in the Caribbean. Capitalizing on the region's image as a safe, terror-free travel destination, the cruise lines offered discounts to attract a wider clientele, opened new departure ports in the United States, and expanded the ports of call in Mexico and the Caribbean. In 2002, as much of the tourism industry was reeling from 9/11, the SARS virus, and economic recession, the cruise industry recorded record profits of $14.3 billion; in 2004, they reached $16.5 billion.[59] Most of this was reaped by the three mega-lines—Carnival, Royal Caribbean, and Norwegian Star Cruises—which control 90 percent of the North American market and account for almost 75 percent of total capacity deployed in the Caribbean.[60]

The Cruise Lines International Association (CLIA), founded by the major companies in 1976, works closely with travel agents to promote cruises as less expensive and more glamorous alternatives to land-based Caribbean hotels. Cruise line sales have become a bread-and-butter business for U.S. travel agents, generating earnings of close to $600 million in commissions each year. Airlines also earn more than $650 million in ticket sales to cruise passengers flying to major cruise ports such as Miami, Florida. But almost all the money is spent either before the cruise begins or on board; as discussed below, cruise passengers buy relatively little onshore, and port taxes and other cruise line fees are low. In 1998, ASTA President Joe Galloway announced that agency cruise sales totaled an estimated $8 billion and were expected to grow to $54 billion by 2003.[61] For travel agents, cruises represent 29 percent of domestic sales and 22 percent of international sales, although more than half of the respondents said their estimates included some other components, such as airline tickets and hotels, according to *Travel Weekly*'s 2005 Travel Industry Survey.[62] CLIA has nineteen member cruise lines that represent over 95 percent of the North American cruise industry. With 90 percent of cruise business generated through travel agents, CLIA claims that its primary objective is to assist its nearly seventeen thousand member agencies in maximizing benefits from the booming and profitable cruise market.[63]

Cruise tourism, probably more than any other sector of the mass tourism industry, is anathema to the concepts and practices of ecotourism. These high-volume, prepaid, packaged holidays—with their celebration of sun-and-fun, overconsumption, self-indulgence, and brief ports of call to allow tourists to buy local souvenirs or duty-free First World luxuries—are the mirror opposite of the small-scale, locally owned, culturally sensitive, environmentally low-impact, and educational precepts of ecotourism. While ecotourism seeks to deepen the traveler's understanding of the world, cruise tourism builds on fantasy, on board and off. Take, for instance, Royal Caribbean's port of call in Haiti, the Caribbean's poorest, most war-torn country. Several times a month, Royal Caribbean ships drop off thousands of passengers at "a stunning stretch of white sand between turquoise water and lush rolling hills" where they frolic on the beach, ride on Jet Skis, shop at a tourist craft market, and eat food prepared on board the ship. The cruise's itinerary used to list the location as "Hispaniola," until Haitian officials complained. But passengers still don't see the reality of Haiti: "rail-thin children, the mounds of garbage and open sewage dumps or the heavily armed peacekeeping troops struggling to keep a lid on the sprawling urban slums." And at least some passengers don't want a reality tour: "I don't want to see poverty," one told the *New York Times*. "I'm on vacation. I don't want to think that these people don't have enough to eat."[64]

In other ways as well, cruise ships and their passengers typically violate ecotourism principles. Even though tourism is the Caribbean's main industry, and unemployment on many of the islands tops 20 percent, most of the fifty thousand-plus employees on cruise ships plying the waters between the United States and the Caribbean are neither West Indians nor Americans. Many of these low-wage workers are recruited by specialized labor contractors from depressed markets such as those in Eastern Europe and Asia, and many work for only tips or commissions. Most of the ships are foreign owned and registered in tax havens such as Liberia and Panama. Because they are foreign registered and travel mainly in international waters, they are largely unregulated and untaxed. According to a Mintel study, "Even though their ships carry U.S. passengers and are based or call at U.S. ports, these cruise companies are largely exempt from U.S. labor regulations, profit and income taxes, safety standards, sales tax, and environmental standards. Similarly, they are exempt from most taxes and laws of the twenty-odd island countries, colonies, and dependencies in the Caribbean."[65] As journalist James Anderson noted, "The [cruise] industry's profitability comes in part from a global pool of cheap workers and foreign ships registries that let operators avoid American union wages and the U.S. income tax."[66]

And then there's the practice of dumping. In the 1980s, garbage from cruise ships started washing up on Florida beaches and the Gulf of Mexico coastline. In the early 1990s, Greenpeace "eco-warriors" secretly trailed a cruise ship and videotaped illegal dumps. In 1993, Princess Cruises was fined five hundred thousand dollars after a couple on the cruise videotaped crew dumping overboard twenty plastic bags off the Florida Keys. This led to more surveillance, by passengers, the U.S. Coast Guard, and others, and to more fines. Between 1998 and 2002, the cruise industry paid more than $50 million in fines and three cruise lines were placed on five-year felony probation by the U.S. Department of Justice. But the problem, according to NGO experts and activists, goes beyond illegal dumps. Currently luxury liners can dump sewage once they are three miles offshore, and can release other wastewater almost anywhere except in Alaskan waters. Ships carrying upwards of three thousand passengers and crew each produce about thirty thousand gallons of raw sewage a day—as much as a small city. In one year, it is estimated that the North American cruise industry generates fifty thousand tons of food waste and a hundred thousand tons *each* of glass, tin, and burnable waste.[67] And, as Teri Shore of Bluewater Network writes, "Inadequate and poorly enforced U.S. federal laws allow cruise ships to legally dump treated sewage and dirty water from laundries into ports, harbors, and coastal waters. Raw sewage, food wastes, and garbage can be dumped off-shore at three miles or more, depending on the size and type of waste. . . . Only plastics and oil are clearly forbidden from overboard disposal."[68]

Bad press, government fines, and NGO campaigns have led the cruise lines to take a series of steps to try to clean up their practices and image. In 2003, the International Council of Cruise Lines (ICCL), a trade association of fifteen leading cruise companies, teamed up with Conservation International's Center for Environmental Leadership in Business (CELB) to form the Ocean Conservation and Tourism Alliance. The Alliance, funded by ICCL and CI, convened a science panel "tasked with determining best practices for cruise ship wastewater management, identifying ways of accelerating the development of advanced wastewater purification systems, and subsequently encouraging their adoption on board cruise ships." In 2006, ICCL was absorbed by CLIA and a new "joint initiative" was announced with Conservation International.[69] This partnership raised some eyebrows among some NGOs; others, however, recognized that insider discussions and negotiations with the cruise industry are a critical component in any successful reform campaign.

While the environmental issues around waste management and dumping—both legal and illegal—are actively studied, debated, and corrected, much less attention has been paid to the social and economic impacts of mass cruise tourism on poor coastal and island communities. Cruise line associations—CLIA and the Florida-Caribbean Cruise Association—regularly publish industry-generated statistics on how much money the cruise industry puts into the U.S. and other local economies.[70] Less independent study has been done on the complex social, economic, and environmental impacts of cruise tourism on communities. From Alaska and Hawaii to Mexico, Honduras, Dominica, Belize, Costa Rica, and beyond, host communities and governments are grappling with the promise of rapid economic development via cruise tourism. The allure can be great. Take, for instance, the *Washington Post* profile of the tiny native village of Hoonah, on an island in southeastern Alaska, which was suddenly "swimming in cash."[71] With more than five hundred cruises a summer carrying more than 750,000 passengers, it is no surprise that cruise ships generate $595 million a year in spending in Alaska, according to industry reports.[72] For Hoonah, the newly arrived cruise industry had appeared as a savior in the wake of sharp declines in logging jobs and salmon fishing. Yet lessons from other communities elsewhere in Alaska are sobering. The Yakutat, for instance, have argued they have a territorial right to protect their subsistence resources and levy taxes on the cruise ship industry, while the Central Council of the Tlingit and Haida Indian Tribes filed a legal protest against cruise ship dumping. Juneau, Sitka, Haines, and other Alaskan towns have met arriving cruise ships with protests.[73] In 2006, these concerns coalesced when a board coalition gathered twenty-seven thousand signatures to put a Cruise Ship Ballot Initiative (CSBI) up for popular vote.[74] In August 2006, the cruise industry suffered financially and politically when "Alaska voters imposed new measures, including a $50 per passenger tax, environmental monitoring and enforcement of a rule that requires cruise lines to disclose commissions they receive from shore-based tour operators and stores advertised on ships."[75]

In Central America and parts of the Caribbean cruise tourism is going toe-to-toe with "stayover" ecotourism. In the Caribbean, the total number of cruise ship passenger and stayover arrivals is currently about equal—some 15 million each[76]—and the markets for both are dynamic and growing. The UNWTO ranks "experiential" tourism—which encompasses ecotourism, nature, heritage, cultural, and soft adventure tourism—as among the sectors expected to grow most quickly over the next two decades. It also predicts that cruise tourism will continue to be a top product worldwide.[77]

In a study of Caribbean tourism, the WTTC found that, despite its impressive arrival numbers, the economic contribution of cruise tourism is "negligible," accounting for only 8 to 10 percent of total international tourism receipts; 90 percent or more still comes from stayover tourism.[78] Similarly, the Caribbean Tourism Organization (CTO) estimates that for nineteen Caribbean countries, stayover tourism generated $7.3 billion in 2003, while cruise tourism produced only $1.1 billion—despite the parity in arrivals for each category. Stayover passengers spent an average of $994 in a destination, while cruise passengers spent only $77 per port, a difference of nearly thirteen to one. In terms of taxes, the CTO estimated that on average a cruise passenger paid $17 in taxes per port of call, while stayover visitors paid $133 on average, a difference of nearly eight to one.[79] The notable exception is Bermuda, which imposes a head tax of sixty dollars on each cruise passenger, requests that the cruise lines give each embarking passenger a voucher worth thirty dollars for purchases in port, and requires that the lines contribute $1.5 million toward training young Bermudans. In spite of these regulations, cruise passenger arrival numbers jumped 20 percent between 2004 and 2005, an indication that the cruise industry continues to consider Bermuda a popular and profitable port of call.[80]

But for most countries, balancing cruise and stayover tourism has proved an enormous challenge. In Belize, for example, there are fears, as the *Los Angeles Times* wrote, that "Belize is killing its golden goose" of ecotourism with far too many cruise passenger "day trippers." Between 2000 and 2005, Belize was the fastest-growing cruise market in Central America or the Caribbean, and by 2005, over 3.5 times more cruise passengers arrived than stayover tourists. Yet cruise tourists spend an average of just $44 per visit, while stayovers spend on average $653 per visit. The Belize government's strategic vision for the new millennium calls for promoting "responsible tourism" that encourages "a strong eco-ethic to ensure environmental and socio-cultural sustainability."[81] Yet, policy has not coincided with practice: in Belize, the "tendency of cruise operators is to consolidate, through vertical integration, their control of shore-side businesses and to maximize spending onboard through controlling shore visits and expanding onboard offerings. There is, therefore, an inherent tension between the objectives of the cruise industry and those of Belize and other host countries."[82]

In terms of alternatives, several studies urge collective bargaining—that countries in the Caribbean and Central America adopt a common position and negotiate as a block contracts with cruise lines to address multiple concerns including cruise passenger fees (known as the head tax), port operations, carrying capacity, and infrastructure development.[83]

Outbound Travel Agents

Although the functions of tour operators and travel agents often blur and overlap, travel agents are generally retailers who sell airline tickets and prepackaged trips put together by tour operators and wholesalers. These packages are featured in brochures and distributed through the national network of travel agencies.[84] The bulk of the retail trade consists of package tours. A package usually includes airfare, ground and domestic air transportation, accommodations, some or all meals, transfers from airports to hotels, visa and other fees and taxes, park entrance fees, and excursions such as white-water rafting, mountain climbing, and balloon rides—in short, all but incidentals, souvenirs, and tips. A package has a fixed departure date, length, itinerary, cost, and minimum (and often maximum) number of tourists. Generally, the travel agent earns between 8 and 12 percent of the cost of any package tour, though this has been decreasing in recent years.[85] In Costa Rica, for example, packages put together by tour operators normally include a 20 to 30 percent markup, of which 10 to 12 percent may go to travel agents selling the packages (in the United States, for instance), and the remaining profit stays with the tour operator.[86] In addition, large travel agencies and tour operators can make significant commissions from airlines and hotels by selling large blocks of tickets.[87]

In 1998, an estimated 75 to 80 percent of U.S. air travel and 95 percent of cruises were booked through travel agents.[88] However, this trend has clearly changed with the boom of the Internet in recent years. By 2006, the tenth "anniversary" of the Internet revolution, travelers were booking 70 percent of their airline tickets and 50 percent of hotel reservations online.[89] In Costa Rica, for example, it is estimated that more than half of all international tourists now arrive independently, rather than booking through travel agencies. By way of the Internet, travelers now have access to a wealth of information about the hotels, restaurants, transportation, lodges, tour-guiding services, and customs of the countries that they visit. While their control of such information used to give a clear advantage to travel agents selling packaged tours, travelers who are increasingly using the Internet see travel agents as an unnecessary added expense. Therefore, many travel agents have had to shift their focus to offer more value-added services, such as health and safety insurance, specialty tours, and specific destinations to supplement their inventory of packaged tours.[90] In response to travelers' demands for outdoor, nature-based holidays, some mass-market travel agents have started to sell ecotours or conventional tours that include "eco-experiences"—a cruise that includes a day's hike in a rainforest and incorporates the lingo of "green" travel—and others are selling packages from a few select ecotourism wholesalers. For instance, Belize, aiming to harness its growth as a cruise destination, offered passengers a wide variety of nature and cultural/archeological tours rather than the usual fare of duty-free shopping. Cruise passengers have responded, with 85 percent disembarking in Belize, the highest rate in the Caribbean. Unfortunately, Belize's motto—"Nature's Best Kept Secret"—and its strategic vision of promoting "responsible tourism" that encourages "a strong 'eco-ethic'" no longer seemed appropriate.[91]

In 1991, the *New York Times* reported that there were nearly five hundred U.S. "tour companies" (agents and operators) offering trips with environmental themes, mostly to developing countries.[92] Five years later, Marie Walters, a member of ASTA's Environmental Committee (which no longer exists), stated that "all travel agents these days handle ecotourism," including prepackaged nature and adventure travel or "eco-" add-ons to conventional tours, although she conceded that "some are more professional than others." Indeed, the reality is that most travel agencies lack the time, expertise, and training to sell ecotourism packages, which have been largely handled, as described below, by tour operators. In a 1997 *Washington Post* survey of D.C.-area travel agents, only one, Green Earth Travel, listed ecotourism among its specialties. Today, Green Earth Travel specializes in vegetarian holidays, while Washington, D.C.–based Solimar Travel provides customized service and promotes companies committed to sustainable travel.[93]

There are about twenty thousand authorized travel agencies in the United States and a potentially large, but unrecorded, number of home-based agents.[94] Most are members of ASTA. They vary widely in quality due to weak training and licensing procedures. The only regulatory bodies are the Airline Reporting Corporation (ARC) and the International Airlines Travel Agent Network (IATAN) through which travel agencies are licensed to write airline tickets. The Institute of Certified Travel Agents, for example, offers professional travel counselor degrees; however, only a small percentage of agents are certified through this program.

Outbound and Inbound Tour Operators

Tour operators are classified as wholesalers, although they sell both to travel agents and directly to the public. Those sending tourists abroad sell their own exclusive package tours and/or resell packages put together by tour operators in the host countries. Known as outbound tour operators or outfitters, they package the trips, oversee the creation of itineraries, select and contract with inbound tour operators in the host countries, arrange airline tickets, and handle travel and liability insurance. They sell tour packages to the general public through travel agents or special-interest organizations such as environmental groups, alumni associations, and museums. Some operators market directly through magazine or newspaper advertisements or through catalogs, brochures, videotapes, CD-ROMs, and the Internet. Tour operators charge a markup of 15 to 40 percent, depending on how customized the tour is. Since competition is very stiff, many tour operators try to entice travel agents to carry their packages by offering higher commissions, incentive programs, glossy advertising, news articles, contests, and free or reduced-rate trips.[95]

Standards, however, are lacking: no accrediting body or licensing procedure exists for tour operators, and because little capital is required to get started, virtually anyone can hang out a shingle. The United States Tour Operators Association (USTOA), with membership restricted to well-established operators, requires the posting of a $1 million bond, which is applied to a consumer protection plan for tourists and travel agents using these companies. However, the USTOA evaluates tour operators primarily on the basis of their financial worthiness and references obtained from travel industry organizations or other members, and not specifically on whether they are promoting high-quality or socially and environmentally responsible travel.[96]

In 2001, the World Tourism Organization (UNWTO) carried out an insightful comparative study of tour operators in the main ecotourism-generating markets in Europe and North America—France, Germany, Spain, Italy, the United Kingdom, Canada, and the United States. The researchers interviewed tour operators in these seven countries to determine current volume and market share for ecotourism, products and price range, distribution channels, market trends, destinations, and specific travel behavior and characteristics. The study found that ecotour operators "are small companies with smaller advertising budgets" who rely on word-of-mouth referrals and targeted promotion channels such as affinity groups (universities, conservation organizations, etc.) and specialized travel shows and magazines. Internet bookings were "increasing tremendously" while travel agents were considered a "less successful way of selling." They reported that while ecotourism is currently "a small niche market," it was expected to continue to grow in the future. According to this study, the German Travel Agency and Tour Operator Association (DRV) reported at least 122 tour operators, or 6 to 8 percent of all operators, specialized in ecotourism, in Spain, 5 to 6 percent of outbound operators specialized in nature or eco-tours, and in the United States, 62, or 5 percent of the 1200 tour operators listed by the National Tour Association (NTA), offered ecotours.[97]

Outbound operators usually subcontract with inbound operators in host countries, who meet the travelers at the airport (or port or border); provide transportation throughout the trip; select local businesses to patronize; hire staff; and arrange accommodations (lodges, tented camps, inns, etc.), visits to parks, and other specialty activities. As geography professor and ecotourism specialist Bryan Higgins put it, inbound operators are the essential link, making "upstream connections to industrialized countries" and "downstream economic ties to 'local' businesses within a particular country."[98] These companies are located in key urban centers, usually the capital city or the gateway town (Arusha, Tanzania, for example) to the main ecotourism attractions. With the exception of Cuba, where inbound tour companies are run by the government, in most countries nowadays they are private or in the process of being privatized. They range from multinational companies, such as Abercrombie & Kent and CC Africa, that also own lodges and sometimes vehicles, to nationally based operators such as Horizontes Nature Tours in Costa Rica, to low-budget mom-and-pop shops with little more than a desk, a telephone, and a couple of employees.

The Travel Industry Press

When planning a vacation, many travelers rely on guidebooks, specialty travel magazines, travel supplements in newspapers, television documentaries, nature programs or travelogues, and, increasingly, the Internet. In recent years, there has been an explosion of magazines, TV and radio programs, guidebook series, and Web sites specializing in travel. In the United States and Canada, a database search revealed there were 2,417 print and broadcast travel media outlets in early 2007. The general public often looks to the travel media for even-handed and insightful assessments of prospective destinations. In contrast, destinations, from specific hotels or restaurants to entire countries, view the press more as an in-house public relations arm of the industry that, properly cared for, can provide valuable, low-cost advertising. Over the years, several factors have worked to pull travel journalists into alliance with others in the industry.

The principal vehicle for wooing the writers, photographers, and television journalists who cover tourism and travel has been what are known as "fam" trips. *Fam* stands for *familiarization*; these are all-expenses-paid or highly subsidized trips to tourist destinations that are underwritten by national or local tourist boards, airlines, resorts, inns and lodges, hotel chains, restaurants, and overseas tour operators. Fam trips are usually organized by tourism offices or public relations firms in the United States hired by the destination. They are intended to garner good press in return for a good time.[99] An article in *Adventure Travel Business*, a monthly magazine that bills itself as "the voice of the adventure travel industry," is explicit about how to use the press: "Press trips are an important part of a public relations program as there is no substitute for the in-depth coverage that is generated by a media visit. It is the best 'advertisement' you can buy." The article goes on to give guidelines on how to "entice a journalist to cover your story" and "increase the chances that you'll get a return on the cost of hosting a journalist, in the form of a long, flattering article." It adds, "The most important part . . . is to have a good time."[100] For the travel press, especially its large stable of freelance writers and photographers, fam trips are standard operating procedure. "Unless you're writing for *National Geographic* [which pays well, besides covering expenses], you can't travel and survive without subsidized trips," says Diann Stutz, a public relations official who has been organizing fam trips since the late 1970s. Freelance writers are normally paid a pittance for travel articles and guidebooks: newspapers generally pay only a few hundred dollars for a supplement piece, and publishers typically pay a flat fee of ten to fifteen thousand dollars for writing a guidebook from scratch, a project that could take a year or more to complete.[101]

Given these realities, fam trips are imperative, but the obvious danger is of travel writers losing their independence. They may become—as is the intent of fam trips—a public relations arm for the travel industry rather than a watchdog for the public. As a *Washington Post* exposé on freebies given to guidebook writers put it, "Perhaps the biggest misconception about guidebooks is that they offer truly objective critiques of restaurants and hotels. . . . In reality, the objectivity of many guidebooks is undercut by 'comps'—free meals, lodging and entertainment accepted by the guidebook writer while on assignment." Edie Jarolim, who has written Fodor's and Frommer's guidebooks, calls fam trips and other comps "the dirty little secret of the industry."[102] Of the dozen-odd fam trip veterans I interviewed for this book, only one flatly denied that free trips influence what she writes. Others admitted that they find it awkward to write critically about a destination that has graciously hosted them. "It's difficult not to be influenced. I feel hesitant to lambaste [a place]," said one seasoned writer. Most said they simply opt not to write anything about a place that is bad.[103] Due to the difficulty of selling a critical travel story, travel writer Kim Lisagor admits to posting a critical review of a bad experience on the Web site tripadvisor.com and sometimes writing to the management of the hotel or other business with suggestions rather than trying to get it published in a magazine.[104]

The issue of fam trips and comps has long been debated by travel writers and editors. Many of the largest-circulation newspapers and magazines have officially stopped accepting articles by writers taking subsidized trips. These include the *New York Times*, the *Washington Post*, the *Los Angeles Times*, the *Philadelphia Inquirer*, the *Miami Herald*, and *Newsday*. In its exposé on comps given to guidebook writers, the *Washington Post* included the comment—twice—that it "does not permit contributors to accept any complimentary or discounted accommodations or meals, and our reporters usually travel incognito." The *Post* added, "We pay our writers' expenses or they pay their own."[105] *Newsday* goes as far as to require writers to turn in receipts showing that they have paid for the trip themselves. And some publications say they require their writers to travel incognito and show up unannounced to prevent their being given the red carpet treatment. But writers say that in practice, the policy is often "don't ask, don't tell": many editors and publishers will turn a blind eye if they like the writer or the article. *Condé Nast Traveler*, started in 1987 by former journalists with the motto "Truth in travel," was one of the first travel magazines to ban articles written on the basis of subsidized trips. They contract with writers and photographers to do particular stories, pay all expenses, and do not insist on only positive stories.[106] As writer Brook Wilkinson, who oversees *Condé Nast Traveler*'s "Green List" (see below), explains, "It is our policy not to take FAM or media trips. Our writers and editors always travel incognito and pay the going rate. Sadly, not all travel journalism outlets have the same policy. It's no secret that a writer who takes a press trip is expected to write a mostly favorable review of the places."[107] Much of the travel media would argue it cannot afford to underwrite all the travel expenses incurred by its journalists. However, one easy alternative would be to require travel articles, documentaries, radio reports, and books to state clearly all companies who provided free or discounted services. This "buyer beware" disclosure would at least let the public know what companies underwrote the information.

Travel writers say it is through advertising, as well as fam trips, that the travel industry works to keep the travel press tepid. Travel advertisements are vital in underwriting the cost of publications. Some guidebooks go so far as to require destinations to pay a fee to be listed, sometimes letting the proprietor write the copy, and some magazines refuse to list establishments that don't advertise.[108] The travel press has therefore taken on a role as the "good news" branch of journalism, a genre that helps people escape from the cares and woes of the real world. As one writer put it, they are "more cheerleaders than critics."[109] Although travel sections in the *Washington Post*, the *New York Times*, and other major newspapers do carry travel advice, including articles warning, for instance, about airport luggage theft, the dangers of traveling to certain parts of the world, and even the effect of fam trips on the accuracy of guidebooks, they rarely pan specific companies, tourist attractions, restaurants, or lodgings. Writers say that some criticism is permitted if it is "balanced" with positive comments. "Horror stories do not fit the genre," explained one. He went on to say that he'd once received a stack of documents outlining severe health and sanitary violations on a number of cruise ships. He never pursued the story. "Who's going to run it? Certainly not a travel section." Why? "Because of the advertisers."[110]

Another travel industry institution—the professional association—also helps keep travel writing light and in line. The most important of these in the United States is the Society of American Travel Writers (SATW), with 1,300 members, including nearly half who are freelance writers; the rest are public relations officials employed by resorts, tourism boards, airlines, and other parts of the tourism industry. Rather than promoting the independence of the press and its right and duty to critically examine the industry, the society helps create a cozy relationship between its travel press and industry public relations flacks. Admission requirements are rigorous, and membership is restricted and relatively expensive. Applicants must be nominated by two current members (who in turn are permitted to nominate only two members per year) and must either be staff travel writers or have published at least twelve different major travel articles or one original travel book within the past year.[111] One writer described SATW as "a closed shop"; another said, "It's designed to keep people out" because it is often through SATW that journalists secure fam trips. For example, a public relations officer for a city in Virginia explained that before issuing invitations to a press event, she first checks to see whether particular writers are SATW members and then checks their reputation with her public relations colleagues.

Although SATW's "Code of Ethics" states that "no member shall deliberately misrepresent his or her participation in a press trip in order to secure an editorial assignment" and "no member shall accept payment or courtesies in exchange for an agreement to produce favorable material about a travel destination," there is no enforcement.[112] These rules are routinely bent, travel writers say. In a 2006 interview, SATW past president Edwin Malone said that the society has become more stringent in encouraging its journalists to write honest pieces and resist bias toward tourism businesses or destinations that supported their travel. He said that SATW is opposed to journalists promising favorable coverage in return for a subsidized trip, and that SATW is considering revising its Code of Ethics to bar any writers found to be accepting subsidized trips in return for a promise of positive publicity.[113]

And what if the story a travel writer unearths is a negative one? It typically appears not in the travel supplement but in the "hard news" sections of a newspaper. For instance, in 2003, *Washington Post* travel section staff writer Steve Hendrix was sent to Burma, a country run by a brutal military junta that had seized power from the democratically elected leader (and Nobel laureate) Aung San Suu Kyi.[114] Hendrix's sensitive and balanced travel piece described not only the country's "tourist loop" of ancient temples, floating villages, lovely lakes, and beach resorts, but also the pros and cons of travel to what he termed "Asia's most controversial destination." Just days after Hendrix's piece was published, the junta ambushed Suu Kyi's motorcade, rearrested her, and killed and detained a number of her supporters. Two weeks later, Hendrix wrote another Burma piece in which he explained "The attack on Suu Kyi's traveling party makes me look back at my visit as a sort of Potemkin postcard. Behind the pretty scenery, democracy wasn't just stalled. It was being destroyed." He concluded, "Suu Kyi has implied that she will drop her call for a tourism boycott as soon as the time is right. Clearly—tragically—the clock has stopped. She says don't come. This time, I'm listening."[115] And this time, the *Post* ran Hendrix's piece in its Sunday "Opinion" section. The message of "don't travel" apparently just didn't fit in the Travel section.[116]

Nonetheless, this story is one of a number of signs that there are some winds of change wafting through the travel media. In principle, a number of writers, editors, and producers believe that the travel industry, including the branch known as ecotourism, needs to be scrutinized by a probing, investigative press, just as it is done in other powerful industries—oil, armaments, automobile, and so on. In the last few years I have been pleased to find a growing cadre of rigorous, often younger journalists committed to covering the various facets of ecotourism and socially and environmentally responsible travel, as well as, at least on occasion, to shedding light on some of the major problems and scandals within the tourism industry.

Critical commentaries are also growing from the grassroots, with the proliferation of travel blogs, Web logs, and online forums where writers, unencumbered by advertising dollars or editors, detail their personal experiences and lay out their heartfelt impressions. According to the *Wall Street Journal*, "Travel blogs are a valuable resource because they are based on people's experiences . . . blogs are timely, idiosyncratic and full of detail. They often contain subtle hints not found in guides."[117] Lonely Planet, for one, has responded by taking its guidebook concept online through The Thorn Tree,[118] a web forum where travelers can post messages and engage in organized discussions. In Europe, the European Travel Commission has launched a new travel portal, www.visiteurope.com, which provides links to worldwide travel networks such as TravelDailyNews International, TravelMole.com, and TravelPress.com, as well as sites featuring ecotourism, such as ECOTRANS.

Tourism Marketing

Although tourism executives recognize that the health, sustainability, and profitability of their industry depend in large part on protecting the environment, marketing techniques often allow the travel industry to appear "green" without making fundamental or costly reforms. Marketing is one of the most important components of the travel industry, and many tourism companies have strategies to obtain free or inexpensive media coverage through the Internet, fam trips, press releases, awards programs, and public relations gimmicks. Promotional materials for nature tourism and ecotourism have long been a marketing staple, and they have developed a distinct style designed to sell "experiences," not simply products.[119] Through effective advertising, one tourism consultant writes, "a destination can literally be created in the traveler's mind."[120] Although travel brochures draw on imagery and language found in historical travel writing, they carefully weave adventure with safety, the unknown with the familiar, the primitive with the modern, ruggedness with comfort.

In his doctoral dissertation, which analyzed promotional brochures from fifteen educational tour companies conducting nature and cultural trips to Latin America, Ronnie Casella found tourists depicted as "time-travelers."[121] Voyagers International's brochure for the Galapagos Islands, for instance, promised, "Where we travel, it's a little piece of Eden—the world as it should be, at peace with itself and with you." The California Academy of Sciences' brochure for its trip to Panama included a photograph of tourists landing on an isolated island beach with the caption, "Zodiacs give us the freedom to land virtually anywhere at will." The text explained, "The Kuna live in autonomous island communities, keeping their traditional lifestyle essentially intact. Adorned in their colorful embroidered fabrics, they invariably turn out to greet us when our Zodiacs arrive at one of their villages." This is well-managed time-travel, the "discovery" of a far-off culture aboard First World Zodiacs and the assurance of a warm welcome by Indians whose friendliness has been previously tested.

The Cruise Company of Greenwich also offered a visit to unknown lands, in this case in one of Costa Rica's largest national parks: "The Corcovado area is so remote, inaccessible, and undisturbed that even most Costa Ricans have never visited." The notion that cruise ship passengers will machete their way through Corcovado's dense, steep, and rain-drenched tropical forest is ludicrous, but the image is appealing. Equally absurd is an Overseas Adventure Travel brochure's "special invitation to join us on [a seventeen-day safari to] Unexplored Serengeti," Tanzania's most famous game park, which is visited by tens of thousands of tourists each year. Casella found that these travel brochures promised, as well, a combination of both physical and intellectual rigor, often with tours led by a biologist guide, boats equipped with "onboard laboratories," and a clientele that includes environmental organizations, universities, and NGOs.[122]

In marketing materials, mainstream ecotourism, or "ecotourism lite," is often described with catchy phrases such as "treading lightly on the earth" and "taking only photos, leaving only footprints." The advertisements, brochures, and eco-publications contain buzzwords such as *quiet, rain forest, clean air, pure, lush, unspoiled, nature, breathtaking, bio-*, and, of course, *eco-* and *green*. In recent years, much of the mass tourism industry has adopted "green" language or even established environmental departments, but it has made only superficial changes in conventional tour packages, such as offering a brief walk in the rain forest or not changing guests' sheets and towels each day. In a 1999 press release headlined "Keep Your Towels—and Help Save the World!" British Airways' hotel division and International Hotels urged their hotels to "think green" by installing energy-saving showers and by laundering towels only when guests signal that they want them changed. These are sensible moves, but ones whose most significant impact was to save hotels on their laundry bills.[123] Today nearly every hotel chain has signs in guest rooms, giving similar "options" to not launder sheets and towels and often promising exaggerated "green" benefits. In one of his early "Frommer's World" columns in *Travel Holiday* magazine, Arthur Frommer, certainly no ecotourism extremist, summed up the dichotomy between what many environmentally conscious travelers desire and what the industry is delivering. He wrote, "In a frantic rush to board the bandwagon, travel-related companies all over the world are proclaiming that they support—and practice—the principles of ecotourism. In many cases, they really don't. The evidence they cite includes such trivial steps as using recycled-paper menus and stationery or putting biodegradable soap in guest bedrooms. These sometimes exaggerated half truths mislead an increasingly large number of travelers who are fervently determined to preserve the fragile and finite natural resources of the earth."[124]

The major U.S. nature tour and ecotourism operators have traditionally relied heavily on glossy brochures with colorful photographs, advertisements in tourism publications and travel supplements, and the Specialty Travel Index and other in-house trade publications. They also use direct mail to consumers, appearances at tourism trade shows and travel markets, and newspaper advertisements.[125] Advertising and brochures are expensive, and many tour operators today are doing more targeted mailings while putting a premium on free or more cost-effective strategies to market their product. The large California-based company Mountain Travel-Sobek has been spending $350,000 per year on its catalog and brochures, which it regularly sends to a large database of previous and potential customers. In order to maximize more cost-effective marketing techniques, they are constantly increasing their Internet presence via their website, presenting slide shows at various travel events across the United States, and using small-space advertising in travel publications. However, their number-one source for new customers continues to be word of mouth.[126] Overseas Adventure Travel (OAT), based in Massachusetts, which caters to American travelers over the age of fifty, states that 70 percent of their client base comes from repeat travelers, and 98 percent of their advertising budget is used to send mailings to their database of previous customers. With forty-three thousand active travelers, OAT has a very successful referral program, and also depends very much on word of mouth to acquire new customers. In light of the high costs of advertising and brochures, the company says that this more "lean and mean" approach can be very beneficial.[127]

With travelers turning to online platforms to share candid travel experiences, some marketing and public relations companies are using these sites to post flattering comments about their client companies. As one study reveals, "Most commonly referred to as 'undercover marketing,' 'buzz marketing,' or 'guerilla marketing,' these practices consist of companies posing as objective consumers or members of a movement or fan base. These companies tout their products and services in a manner that would not lead consumers to suspect that the company itself is behind the message."[128] Another report found that some company executives are "blogging for the same reasons they do public speaking, to build credibility for themselves and their companies. Blogging has become a new . . . less time consuming and less expensive way to reach potential and current customers."[129]

Awards

There are, as well, a growing number of ecotourism awards that receive considerable press coverage and are used by the winning companies for marketing on their Web sites and in their promotional materials. In the 1990s, most were shoe-string operations, based on self-nominations, vague criteria, and no independent onsite inspections. At their best, these awards helped give publicity and recognition to lesser-known but highly worthwhile projects. For instance, in 1997, *Condé Nast Traveler*'s annual Ecotourism Award went to Clive Stockil, founder of an innovative CAMPFIRE program (Communal Area Management Programme for Indigenous Resources) in Gonarezhou National Park, in the southeastern corner of Zimbabwe. Stockil helped negotiate an agreement between the local Shangaan people and Zimbabwe Sun hoteliers to build a luxury ecotourism lodge, Mahenye.[130] However, many of the recipients of the various ecotourism awards in the 1990s were either industry giants or already-popular ecotourism projects; a few of the winners were actually involved in scandals. The same names kept popping up, and there was, particularly in the early years, a revolving cycle of corporations giving awards to one another. Between 1991 and 1996, for instance, those honored in the ASTA/*Smithsonian Magazine* Environmental Award included seven airlines, two cruise lines, and two international hotel chains. Among the winners were British Airways, Inter-Continental Hotels and Resorts, Princess Cruises, American Airlines, and Canadian Pacific Hotels & Resorts. British Airways has also received awards for "environmental commitment" from the WTTC and the Pacific Asia Travel Association (PATA). British Airways' own Tourism for Tomorrow Awards (run at the time in association with ASTA, PATA, and two British travel associations) went, in turn, to Inter-Continental Hotel and Carnival Cruises. It also went the Mnemba Club, on a small island off Zanzibar which at the time was Italian owned and embroiled in controversy. During this same period, the Mnemba Club won an award for ecotourism excellence from the WTTC's Green Globe program. Had these eco-award programs done site visits, they would have learned of Mnemba's conflictive relationship with the neighboring village (see chapter 8).

One of the more blatant examples of "greenwashing" was the 1996 decision by ASTA and *Smithsonian Magazine* to give their Environmental Award to Princess Cruises for its "strong corporate commitment towards protecting the environment to which they bring passengers and guests." In 1993, Princess Cruises was fined five hundred thousand dollars after passengers aboard the Regal Princess witnessed crew members illegally dumping, in the dead of night, twenty trash-filled bags, five miles off the Florida Keys. Princess Cruises paid the fine and then went on the offensive to repair its reputation. ASTA's Environment Committee newsletter claimed that Princess Cruises "has chosen to make the incident a learning experience" through Planet Princess program, begun in 1993 and described as "a comprehensive initiative developed by the line to preserve the areas currently visited by its passengers." In addition, through its "Princess standard" for management of pollution prevention efforts, each ship was said to be "regularly inspected for compliance with strict environmental guidelines." The company launched, in effect, a public relations campaign targeting its customers. In announcing the award, ASTA praised Princess Cruises' "environmental protection practices," including "model waste recycling programs." No mention was made of its environmental fines for dumping waste in the ocean.[131] The *Smithsonian Magazine* subsequently left this annual Environmental Award program which, under ASTA's sponsorship, became very weak. In 2005, for instance, applicants simply submitted "175 words or less" describing their "environmental efforts," and a five-person committee of ASTA members made the selection. There is no on-site verification.[132]

Over the years, the number of eco-awards has grown, and many programs have changed names, sponsors, award categories, and criteria.

ASTA aside, there has been, overall, a gradual move toward making eco-awards more rigorous and reputable. I have been a judge for several of the best-known programs and have been heartened to see the criteria and judging procedures strengthened. For instance, as one of nine judges for *Condé Nast Traveler*'s "World Savers Awards" (formerly called "EcoTourism" and "Green List") I am asked to score applicants from one to one hundred on three categories: environmental initiatives, local contributions, and the guest experience. The application itself is elaborate, containing a list of questions asking about construction and land use planning, presentation of native surroundings, energy systems, waste disposal, employee benefits, contributions to the local community, problems encountered, and future plans. In 2006, over eighty candidates applied, representing a "smorgasbord" of choices from every continent, and some submitting applications of thirty pages or more.[133] *Condé Nast Traveler* announces the winners in its September issue. The list includes the twelve hotels, tour operators, and destinations receiving the highest average scores. In recent years, *Condé Nast*'s Green List/World Savers awards have gone to a number of smaller and less well-known lodges and tour operators, including the Casa Mojanda Mountainside Inn & Farm in Ecuador, the Papoose Creek Lodge in Montana, Jungle Bay in Dominica, and the Hoopoe Safaris tours in Tanzania. The judging process, criteria, and quantity of good applicants have improved significantly. According to Klara Glowczewska, the magazine's editor in chief:

> *Condé Nast Traveler* turned its attention to the rise of ecotourism back in 1994, and gave out its first such awards a year later. We at the magazine are pleased to see more coverage of the environmental and social impacts of tourism, as this benefits all conscientious travelers. But increased media attention only increases the temptation among travel companies to "greenwash" their operations, and few awards or articles include a rigorous screening process like ours, which starts with a 50-question application. As for on-site inspections, since 2003 we have visited at least one of each year's finalists—incognito and paid for by the magazine—after the judging but before publication of the winners.[134]

A number of other awards programs help to raise the profile of ecotourism. Of the newer eco-awards, the First Choice Responsible Tourism Awards in Britain, which started in 2004, has grown most rapidly and gained a solid reputation. By 2006, Responsible Tourism Awards claimed to be the "largest of their kind in the world." The awards are organized by the online travel agent responsibletravel.com, in association with UK media partners the *Times* (London) and *Geographical Magazine,* and supporters include Conservation International and The World Travel Market. The awards are given in ten categories including Best Tour Operator, Best Hotel, Best Mode of Transport or Initiative, Best in a Mountain Environment, and Best for Poverty Reduction. The Web site states, "The central tenet of the Awards is that all types of tourism, from niche to mainstream, can and should be operated in a way that respects and benefits destinations and local people." Unlike the other awards, nominations must come from the public (in 2006, there were 1,200 nominations) and are reviewed by the organizers, who send detailed questionnaires to those under consideration. Opinions are also solicited independently from independent references, and then a panel of thirteen international judges meets at the Royal Geographical Society to pick the final winner in each category. Winners have included The Calabash Trust in Port Elizabeth, South Africa; Chumbe Island Coral Park in Zanzibar; and Ol Malo Lodge, Il N'gwesi Community Lodge, and Basecamp Mara, all in Kenya. According to Harold Goodwin, professor of Responsible Tourism Management at Leeds University, the large number of nominations "demonstrates increasing awareness of responsible tourism among travelers and the advances being made by those at the forefront of responsible tourism. Competition for the awards is stronger every year. Raising awareness about the principles and what it means in practice contributes to ensuring that the Responsible Tourism movement is not undermined."[135]

In November 2005, Lapa Rios Ecolodge in Costa Rica, already a recipient of a number of eco-awards, received yet another from a prestigious but unlikely place. In the ornate top floor reception room at the U.S. State Department overlooking Washington's granite monuments and Potomac River, U.S. Secretary of State Condoleezza Rice gave the 2005 Award for Corporate Excellent to Lapa Rios, a sixteen-room ecolodge nestled in a private rainforest reserve on the Osa Peninsula in southern Costa Rica. Secretary Rice described Lapa Rios as "a model of environmental stewardship and enlightened corporate leadership" and praised its American owners, Karen and John Lewis, for understanding "that the best way to do well is to do good." In accepting the honor and the trophy—a clear glass globe perched on a pedestal—Karen Lewis graciously thanked the lodge's staff and explained, "The Award validates not only our 15-year effort but also the concept of ecotourism. It verifies that ecotourism, when built on sound environmental and social principles, can be a successful business." Indeed, ecotourism had never before received such high-level praise from the U.S. government.[136] Secretary Rice, chief diplomat for Washington's "war on terror," had never before revealed an interest in ecotourism, and Karen and John

Lewis are hardly Washington insiders, having spent years deep inside Costa Rica's remote Osa Peninsula. But somehow the "good news" of ecotourism had percolated upward, from the Osa, to the U.S. Embassy in San José, to the top echelons in Washington. It seemed somewhat ironic that the U.S. government chose to honor ecotourism in tiny Costa Rica rather than within the United States. But the reality is that in the United States, ecotourism is just beginning to take root and grow quickly as a conscious movement, built, in part, on lessons learned from Costa Rica and other countries around the world.

The Dangers of Ecotourism Lite

While over the last decade there has been considerable progress in deepening the practices of ecotourism, expanding its breadth, "greening" mainstream tourism, and setting more solid standards, ecotourism "lite" still remains far too common. Much of what is marketed as ecotourism is simply conventional mass tourism wrapped in a thin veneer of "green." Ecotourism lite is propelled by travel agents, tour operators, airlines and cruise lines, large hotel and resort chains, and international tourism organizations, which promote quick, superficially "green" visits within conventional packages. In the mid-1990s, Diane Kelsay, a coordinator of the annual World Congress on Tourism for the Environment, warned, "We've seen ecotourism used to mean all nature, adventure, and cultural travel. Someone even published a definition that includes Sunday afternoon drives. A lot of travel companies used it to call attention to anything they were selling."[137] In 2002, at the time of the International Year of Ecotourism, Patricia Barnett, Director of the UK-based organization Tourism Concern, voiced similar reservations: "Ecotourism can be whatever anyone wants," She added, "The mass tourism operators have learnt the language of sustainable tourism. . . . But little has really changed."[138]

Perhaps more than any other big player in the tourism industry, the Walt Disney Company has tried to cash in on the traveling public's desire to "go green" with an ecotourism lite theme park, Animal Kingdom. Disney spent $800 million to transform five hundred acres of central Florida cow pasture into an African savannah, with fake wide-trunk baobab trees, a Zulu village, and some 1,700 animals representing 250 species. This largest of Disney's theme parks is designed to let the American public "go on safari" without leaving the shores of the United States. Animal Kingdom opened in 1998 on Earth Day amid protests from animal rights groups and an investigation by the U.S. Department of Agriculture into the deaths of some dozen animals, including representatives of endangered species. Within one year of opening, four cheetah cubs died from consuming a chemical found in antifreeze, one rhino died while in a routine examination, a rare black rhino died from ingesting wood, a hippo died from foot and back infections, two otters died from ingesting toxic seeds, and two West African crowned cranes were run over by tour vehicles.[139] Despite the rocky start and initial bad press, Animal Kingdom won praise from zoo-industry officials and quickly brought in the crowds, who dubbed the African Savannah ride the "Kilimanjaro 500" because the jeeps rarely slow down long enough to allow a good picture. One of the theme park's most popular newer attractions is "the highest peak in Disney's Florida mountain range—Expedition EVEREST. This new mountain addition at Disney's Animal Kingdom's land of Asia rises from the mists nearly 200 feet!"[140]

A sizable segment of the traveling public wants this type of tourism. In recent years, there has been a gradual trend for many travelers to ecotourism destinations to be less intellectually curious, socially responsible, environmentally concerned, and politically aware than in the past. Increasing numbers of older, wealthier, and "softer" travelers have begun opting for comfort over conservation. Once, some of the world's oldest and most prized nature destinations, including the Galapagos Islands, Nepal, the game parks in Tanzania and Kenya, and even Monteverde in Costa Rica, were visited by only the most physically rugged and intellectually curious. Now, however, with improved air and ground transportation, better accommodations, and extensive publicity, these destinations are being marketed to a mass audience. Ecotourism lite travelers are, as David Western, former Kenya Wildlife Service Director, puts it, "entertained by nature, but not unduly concerned with its preservation."[141]

When poorly planned, unregulated, and overhyped, ecotourism lite, like mass tourism or even traditional nature tourism, can bring only marginal financial benefits but serious environmental and social consequences. Nepal, for instance, was visited through the 1960s by only a robust subset of adventure travelers, numbering fewer than ten thousand per year. Between 1980 and 1991, the number of trekkers increased by 255 percent. The impact on this Himalayan kingdom's fragile environment has been tremendous. Careless trekkers wander off trails, destroy vegetation and leave behind tin cans, packaging, and other litter. According to the World Wide Fund for Nature, wood demanded by lodge operators for construction and by trekking groups for cooking, heating, and bathing has pushed back the timberline several hundred feet and forced local Nepalese to go long distances in search of firewood. Ridges once covered with rhododendrons are now barren, and deforestation is destroying the natural habitat of the rare snow leopard and red panda.[142] By the mid-1990s, "the explosion of trekking tourism has upset the delicate ecological balance and contributed significantly to the loss of cultural integrity in the Annapurna region," reported Chandra Gurung of the Annapurna Conservation Area Project.[143] Some visitors were reaching mountain summits via what is marketed as "ecotourism of the future"—and their only step upward is into a helicopter. "Helicopter treks" fly visitors to high mountain peaks, where they get out, stretch their legs, take photographs, and then fly back.[144] Today scores of companies can be found on the Internet offering these high-priced tours, which do nothing for conservation or local economic development.

The travel industry's efforts to water down ecotourism, to sell ecotourism lite in exchange for short-term profits, led some travel experts to drop the word *ecotourism* and dismiss the concept as simply a fad. As tourism expert Bob Harvey declared, "The word *ecotourism* became a buzz-word in the early 1990s, but so many people used it in so many different ways that it has become virtually meaningless."[145] A decade-plus later, ecotourism was competing with a host of other, similar terms: pro-poor tourism, geotourism, responsible tourism, and sustainable tourism. Yet to abandon the concept because of its misuse or confusion is a classic case of throwing out the baby with the bathwater. What is most important is to view ecotourism as a set of principles and to monitor and measure them in practice. Viewed this way, ecotourism is still in its infancy. "We've only just scratched the surface in realizing the potentials of ecotourism," says Daniel Janzen, a University of Pennsylvania biologist who has worked in Costa Rica for several decades. In identifying what is ecotourism lite and determining where genuine ecotourism is being practiced today, we need also to discover how authentic ecotourism—even if it goes under a different name—can go from being viewed as a niche market to being a broad set of principles and practices that transforms the ways we travel and how the tourism industry functions. Despite the enormous challenges, movement has clearly begun, as the case studies in this volume demonstrate, toward using ecotourism to benefit conservation and communities while providing visitors with enjoyable and educational travel experiences.

3

Ecotourism Today

Throughout the international tourism chain, entrepreneurs are marketing themselves as being involved in ecotourism. Strictly defined, everyone in ecotourism should practice the principles of low-impact, educational, and ecologically and culturally sensitive travel that benefits local communities and the host country. But the conscientious traveler can have a difficult time sifting tourism's wheat from the chaff to find genuine ecotourism projects. Guidebooks, brochures, press reports, and ecotourism awards are not always accurate. While the growing number of third party ecotourism and sustainable tourism certification programs are often more reliable, they still cover only a tiny fraction of the tourism industry. Frequently, it is only by going to a destination and spending vacation time and personal savings that the discerning traveler discovers that what is marketed as ecotourism is missing several key pillars of the definition.

Maho Bay: Some Missing Pillars or True Ecotourism?

Maho Bay, located in St. John, U.S. Virgin Islands, is a resort consisting of four unique and environmentally conscious developments, ranging from rustic tents to more luxurious condominiums. They are situated on private lands surrounded by and adjacent to Virgin Islands National Park, which has been leased by the owner and developer, Stanley Selengut. Maho Bay has succeeded in building a worldwide reputation as one of the best-known and -publicized ecotourism destinations. It has

Chris Lupoli provided updates and helped with the editing and fact-checking for this chapter.

done so largely on the strength of its loyal and large clientele, international awards, press coverage, and the personal appeal of Stanley Selengut. Selengut claims that his advertising budget is zero, yet Maho Bay operates at nearly 90 percent occupancy during the high season. He has achieved this primarily by means of word-of-mouth referrals, repeat customers, and by garnering more good media coverage and awards than most other ecotourism ventures. Maho Bay's promotional material includes a two-inch-thick packet of laudatory press coverage, and it has been the recipient of numerous recent awards.

The appeal of Maho Bay is enhanced by its setting. Unlike the heavily developed islands of St. Thomas and St. Croix, two-thirds of the approximately fifteen-by-eight-kilometer (nine-by-five-mile) St. John is preserved in Virgin Islands National Park, thanks to philanthropist Laurance Rockefeller, who, in 1956, donated the land for conservation purposes. In 1976, Selengut signed a thirty-five year lease for 5.7 hectares (14 acres) of hillside on private land surrounded by the national park, just above secluded Little Maho Bay. He has since built four distinct resort complexes on St. John. The oldest is Maho Bay Camps, which consists of 114 platformed tent-cottages hidden in deep foliage overlooking the turquoise-blue bay. The wood-frame, canvas, and mosquito-net tents are set on posts, and nearly five kilometers (three miles) of elevated wooden walkways connect them to the beach.

Above the tents, on about one hectare (two and a half acres) of land adjacent to Virgin Islands National Park, stands Selengut's second development, Harmony Resort, which consists of a dozen upscale and innovative eco-condos. These newer luxury villas were constructed using primarily recycled materials, and feature solar panels, solar water heaters, wind-powered cooling, and rainwater-capture systems for guest use. Elevated walkways connect the dwellings, and were designed to reduce soil erosion and protect nearby coral. Each villa has its own computer, which keeps track of how much electricity and water guests have used and warns when they might run out (as I did). Selengut decided to build Harmony after the National Park Service and the Virgin Islands Energy Office hosted a workshop in 1991 on sustainable design at Maho Bay Camps. The Park Service subsequently produced a how-to manual on sustainable design,[1] and Selengut put these principles into practice. He received help from the Energy Office, which provided the computers, and the U.S. Department of Energy's Sandia National Laboratories, which supplied experimental products such as solar ovens, solar ice-making machines, and biodegradable detergents. "Harmony proves," says Selengut, "a delightful solution to comfortable living within a fragile environment." Harmony cost $70,000 per unit to build and rents for between $120 and $230 double occupancy per night, making it impossible for Selengut to recoup the investment quickly.

Across the island on a dry, barren, and hot hillside, in sharp counterpoint to the lushness of Maho Bay Camps and Harmony Resort, are Selengut's other two properties. The newest project, started in the early 1990s, is the Concordia Eco-tents, perched on stilts overlooking Salt Pond Bay and a rough stretch of the Caribbean Sea. Each of the twenty-five eco-tents consists of a low-impact wooden structure with mesh screens framing a full apartment that features solar- and wind-generated electricity, energy-efficient kitchen appliances, composting toilets, and space to sleep six. The eco-tents blend the best features of Maho Bay Camps' close encounter with nature and Harmony Resort's environmentally sensitive construction and upscale living; they were named the world's best lodge with alternative energy sources in 2002 by the Discovery Channel. In addition, four of these eco-tents were made accessible for wheelchairs and individuals with disabilities. The eco-tents rent for between $95 and $155 per night ($175 for premium eco-tents). Next to the eco-tents is Selengut's Estate Concordia, which consists of nine luxury condominiums with passive solar design, fully equipped kitchens, a hillside swimming pool, and large open-air rooms. These condominiums rent for between $95 and $140 per night (for standard condos) and between $150 and $215 per night (for loft duplexes). In 2007, Selengut undertook an expansion of Concordia, using eco-friendly design in the new units.

By 1993, Maho Bay Camps was taking in $3 million per year and its net income was close to $750,000. "It's almost like stealing," Selengut told *Forbes* magazine,[2] and by all indications Selengut's resorts continue to be hugely successful. While the Maho Bay tents are billed as appealing to "vacationers of a Sierra Club bent," *Travel Weekly* rates Harmony as the world's top "ecosensitive honeymoon resort."[3] Selengut himself is the chief salesman for his eco-projects; "the travel industry's green guru"[4] is what United Airlines' in-flight magazine called him. An engaging and affable New Yorker with a Bronx accent and signature white golf cap, white sport shirt, and white beard, Selengut has become a popular speaker at ecotourism conferences and forums. "Ecotourism is a kind of theater, and I'm doing the choreography," Selengut is fond of saying. Or, as he sometimes more bluntly puts it, "A lot of what we do [here] is show business."[5] Selengut is also fond of saying that good ecotourism is good business. His tents at Maho Bay Camps cost only about $7,500 each to put up, and renting for between $75 and $130 double occupancy per night, they earned back the investment in the first year. The tents can hold up to four people, which makes for an affordable vacation, something that many of the newer and more high-end eco-lodges are not.

Selengut's resorts appear to be a model of ecotourism development. But appearances can be deceiving. When Selengut hosted The International Ecotourism Society's International Eco-lodge Development Forum and Field Seminar in October 1994, Maho Bay came under close scrutiny by ecotourism experts from around the world. Virtually everyone in attendance praised Selengut for effectively and creatively pushing the perimeters of eco-lodge design in a blend of low-impact construction, recycled materials, and renewable energy sources. However, a number of experts interviewed at the conference were disturbed to discover that Maho Bay Camps and Selengut's other properties paid little heed to other ecotourism principles involving the local community, conservation, and tourist education. "I would give Maho Bay a mixed evaluation," said Ray Ashton, executive director of Ashton, Ashton, & Associates, a Florida consulting firm specializing in sustainable tourism program development for governments, private entrepreneurs, international agencies, and conservation organizations. In summing up his assessment, another expert concluded, "These are "green" lodges, not real eco-tourism." Joshua Reichert, managing director of the Pew Charitable Trusts' environmental program, argued that sound ecotourism should meet four criteria: (1) it should be designed, built, and operated so that it leaves a "soft imprint"; (2) it should contribute money to the local economy and local community services; (3) it should contribute financially to environmental protection; and (4) it should educate visitors and members of the local community. Reichert concluded that under scrutiny, the Maho Bay properties, like much else that is advertised as ecotourism, falls short on a number of counts.

Maho Bay Camps and Selengut's other properties, for instance, employ very few local West Indians. Even though the Maho Bay tents have been around for two decades, the vast majority of Selengut's staff members are North Americans—mostly young and single—working for no wages as part of a work exchange program. This work exchange staff—averaging about twenty-five volunteers at any given time—is required to work four hours per day in exchange for a tent, a deep discount on food at the restaurant, and a stint in the tropics. In 2006, there were only eight full-time, paid staff, and only half of them were native West Indians.[6] On a nine-day visit family vacation in June 2006, Barbara Richman, Managing Editor of *Environment* magazine, said she only saw two islanders working at Maho Bay. "We were quite surprised by that. We have vacationed in the Caribbean several times, staying mostly on St. Thomas, and we've always seen lots of locals working at the resorts," Richman commented. "My family and I always like to talk to the local residents, because that adds to our 'sense of place'."[7]

Selengut has long argued that he hires "off-island" because the Virgin Islands have no unemployment. However, according to the U.S. Virgin Islands Department of Labor, unemployment averaged between 3.5 and 5.9 percent between 1992 and 1997, and as of 2007, had risen to 7.5 percent for the "leisure & hospitality" sector.[8] Although unemployment is not high, islanders I interviewed say that local people are seeking work in tourism establishments. Employees, including senior staff members, at other resorts and tented camps on St. John are almost all West Indian. Islanders say that Selengut does not attract West Indian workers because he pays less than other hotel owners and requires employees to live in tents on-site.[9]

Selengut preaches that an eco-resort is far more profitable than a traditional resort. "What makes sense from an environmental and conservation point of view also saves money," he tells his audiences. Certainly, collecting rainwater and recycling wastewater at Harmony make environmental and financial sense, but as Ray Ashton warns, "There's a thin line between what's ecologically sound and what cuts overhead." He argues that although the Maho Bay tents "could use solar power to heat the showers and light the walkways," such upgrades may not be cost-effective because the property is leased. "If you're an ecologist you should go above and beyond and do more than just a cheap tented camp if you want to be touted as a model," says Ashton.[10] Guests at Maho Bay Camps are encouraged to use biodegradable dish and laundry soaps, which are provided, as well as to use dishwater to water nearby foliage. Recycling bins for glass and plastic are also provided, and much of the collected materials are used in a "Trash for Treasure"[11] craft-making program, in which glass-blowing, pottery-making, and textile-recycling studios are run and classes are offered by staff and visiting guest artists. The program turns a significant amount of the resort's waste, especially glass bottles, into jewelry, ornaments, and other souvenirs.

Despite this innovative Trash to Treasures project, Maho Bay has done little to stimulate local artisanship. While commendable in reducing waste, the products can hardly be deemed as local, since the artists working in the studio are not islanders. Selengut contends that St. John has few crafts and that those available are too expensive to display and sell. But other gift shops on the island are full of locally produced baskets, pottery, and paintings, offered at a range of prices. American professor Bernard Kemp, who has studied the local arts and crafts, said that "Selengut has made no effort to utilize, display, or promote them to Maho Bay visitors."[12]

While Maho Bay lacks several key pillars of ecotourism, Selengut himself and his tented camp nestled within the national park have successfully built a loyal and large clientele sensitized to the joys of living close to nature and light on the land. With the property's lease due to expire in 2012, it appears likely that the current owners of the land will sell, Maho Bay Camps will be closed, and the land will be sold to a higher-end developer. Selengut hopes to put together a package to preserve the place, but the stars may not line up. "Nothing good lasts forever," laments one writer just back from her family holiday at the tented camp. "When Maho Bay Camps disappears, it will be the Brigadoon of ecotourism, remembered forever as a place that seemed too good to be true," writes Colette Bachand-Wood. She reminds us that Brigadoon is the story of a man who stumbles upon and falls in love with a village lost in time. Nevertheless, he must eventually leave. When he wants to return, he discovers that the village does not exist on any map and he cannot return. When Maho Bay's tents close, writes Wood, "those of us who have fallen in love with it will feel like he did—left wondering if such a magical green vacation was a figment of our imagination."[13]

Tracking True Ecotourism

As Maho Bay illustrates, the difference between good ecotourism and ecotourism lite or even "green" tourism projects may be difficult to discern. Throughout the entire ecotourism chain, in fact, there is frequently a blurring of the boundaries between nature tourism and the more multidimensional concept of ecotourism. This lack of precision makes it difficult, for instance, to quantify, with scientific certainty, the growth in the number of ecotourists. By 2005, it was estimated that about 13 percent of all U.S. outbound leisure travelers could be considered ecotourists.[14] In 2004, ecotourism and nature tourism were estimated to be growing globally three times faster than the tourism industry as a whole.[15] While these statistics are imprecise because they lump together nature travel, ecotourism lite, and real ecotourism, they do demonstrate a growing public commitment to this type of travel.

Who are these ecotourists? Since no universally accepted definition exists, there is considerable overlap with nature, adventure, and cultural tourism. According to Canadian ecotourism researcher Pamela Wight:

> The oft-asked question, 'Who are the eco-tourists?' has no definitive answer for many reasons, including the limited studies of markets, poor definitional understanding, and the fact that ecotourist markets are not homogenous. Despite the large body of literature on

> ecotourism, market studies are limited to destination area markets, to tour operator perceptions, or to more general studies of nature or adventure-based tourists.[16]

Nevertheless, experts say that ecotourists in the United States fit a broad profile. Most are between thirty-five and fifty-four years of age,[17] but there are also a considerable number of "mature" adults (older than fifty-five). While they are equally divided by gender, most are physically active. They tend to be better-educated professionals or businesspeople, with college degrees and a genuine interest in learning about nature and culture. They often come from dual-income families.[18] Tour operator Kurt Kutay says that ecotourists fall roughly into two main categories: "DINCs" (dual income, no children) and "empty nesters" (couples with grown children).[19] They are discriminating, they recognize quality, and they are willing to pay for it. Many are from the some 30 million Americans who belong to environmental organizations or profess an interest in conservation.[20] Many are also socially minded and interested in the culture, history, and people in developing countries. In the new millennium, Kutay notes a strong emergence of two other segments: families, often three generations traveling together, and single professionals, most of whom are women. Kutay says that for all these categories "a big part of ecotourism for them is a real connection to the local people in the countries they're visiting, even more than the environmental contribution."[21]

Geographically, "the ecotourism market exists in virtually every major metropolitan area in North America," concludes Wight, from her survey in the United States and Canada of "experienced ecotourists"[22] and global companies offering nature, adventure, and cultural tours. In Europe, 20 to 30 percent of travelers are aware of the needs and values of sustainable tourism, 10 to 20 percent say they look for "green" options, and 5 to 10 percent say they demand "green" holidays.[23] In Germany, 65 percent (39 million) of travelers expect environmental quality and 42 percent (25 million) "think that it is particularly important to find environmentally-friendly accommodation."[24] Nearly half of those surveyed in Britain said they would be more likely to go with a "company that had a written code to guarantee good working conditions, protect the environment and support local charities in the tourist destination. . . . [E]thical tourism will rightly be a big issue in the new millennium."[25] In the United Kingdom, 87 percent say their "holiday should not damage the environment"; 39 percent said they were prepared to pay 5 percent extra for ethical guarantees.[26]

In general, Pamela Wight finds that ecotourists are better informed, more experienced, and more adventuresome travelers than the conventional tourist. They tend to seek wide-ranging activities and multi-destination vacations and tend to prefer modest, intimate accommodations.[27] Some other product preferences of North American ecotourists include tourist facilities that profess conservation goals, offer remote settings and wildlife viewing, and provide opportunities to visit national parks or protected areas.[28] Many are former backpackers and are knowledgeable about the logistics of travel, developing countries, and conservation. In comparison with general consumers, ecotourists exhibit a much greater propensity to belong to nature-oriented organizations, such as the Sierra Club.[29] According to one survey of travelers, more than two-thirds had previous experience with overseas travel, and one-third were repeat customers.[30] Rather than consulting travel agents, ecotourists tend either to travel individually and independently ("foreign independent travelers," or FITs, in the industry jargon) or to use nature tour operators (known also as outfitters, wholesalers, or suppliers) to find an appropriate fixed-itinerary tour. By going directly to the tour operator, ecotourists may save some money, but their primary motive is to customize their tour or find a more ecologically sensitive package. They have a similar profile in Europe. European ecotourists are experienced travelers, highly educated, fall into a higher income bracket, and are "opinion leaders" who ask and tell their friends and colleagues about their trips.[31]

Ecotourism Structures in the United States

In planning an eco-holiday, there are a variety of companies, organizations, publications, and online services that can help to put the trip together. Many are located in the United States; others are found in the destination country.

Outbound Ecotour Operators

True ecotourists, in contrast to conventional vacationers, often plan their own trips or seek specialized nature tour operators rather than general travel agents. These operators are usually located in the same country as the tourist, but they often have an intimate knowledge of the destination country and firsthand experience, having lived or traveled there frequently. These operators are therefore the ecotraveler's most important source of expertise and information; the choice of an outbound ecotour operator can make or break a vacation. As part of their oversight responsibility, outbound operators are supposed to ensure that ecotourism objectives and practices are followed. According to The International Ecotourism Society (TIES), "This may require extensive work with their in-bound operators to insure that guiding, business and conservation practices, as well as relations with local communities, are in line with ecotourism guidelines."[32] In 1994, *Condé Nast Traveler* paid tribute for the first time to ecotourism by selecting outstanding eco-companies and outlining "seven golden rules" to guide travelers in choosing a tour operator and destination. Ideally, eco-operators should (1) link commercial tourism with local conservation programs; (2) provide money and other tangible support for development of parks and management of natural resources; (3) support indigenous businesses by buying local goods and services; (4) arrange and promote meaningful contact between travelers and local people; (5) promote ecological research programs; (6) develop sustainable tourist facilities that minimize environmental damage; and (7) help to repair the damage done by others (such as the Sierra Club's trail cleanup trips).[33]

An increasing number of specialized tour operators involved in ecotourism are acting as both travel agents and packagers, selling fixed-itinerary trips as well as customized trips to fit the interests, schedules, and budgets of particular groups or individual travelers. A number of outbound tour operators are also inbound ground operators, such as Abercrombie & Kent, which has its own ground transport system and hotels at some destinations. Because of the time and added expense involved, outbound tour operators tend to charge 25 to 40 percent more for individually designed tours.

During the 1990s, the number of nature and adventure tour operators in the United States has been growing by 10 to 20 percent per year, according to Canadian ecotourism consultant Carolyn Wild.[34] In 1901, there was just one, the Sierra Club, and in 1970, there were only nine.[35] By 1996, the Specialty Travel Index (STI) listed 219 U.S. tour operators offering ecotours to developing countries,[36] while the 2006 edition of STI found that 92 U.S. firms were involved in nature tourism to developing countries. However, editor Steen Hansen stated that this latter number represents only the number within "the STI universe" and he estimated that that total number of nature/ecotourism operators was "around 300." The number of clients handled by each of the ninety-two operators listed in STI ranged from twenty to three thousand per year. The 2006 edition stated that 76 percent of nature-oriented tours were to developing countries; the most popular destinations were Ecuador, Costa Rica, Tanzania, Chile, and Mexico. The most popular activities, in descending order, were trekking and hiking, wildlife safaris, fishing, river rafting, nature photography, canoeing, kayaking, bird-watching, camping, mountain climbing, and botanical study.[37] Their tours are generally small, usually including no more than twenty persons. They are designed to minimize adverse impact on the resources and maximize the tourists' interaction with the natural environment, foreign culture, and tour leader, guide, and other experts. In an interview, ecotourism expert Carolyn Wild explained that tour leaders are "very important in giving interpretation and making tracks come alive. Most are trained biologists, ecologists, or some other -ologists, and the tour companies are very proud of them and feature them in their literature. They are the ones who sell the next trip—that make the ecotourist want to return next year and recommend the trip to a friend."

In her pioneering 1989 study for Conservation International, Karen Ziffer suggested that ecotour operators fall into one or more of four categories: (1) those "selling nature," who are trying to maximize profits from a lucrative market; (2) members of the "sensitive group," who try to design trips that are low impact and culturally respectful; (3) "donors," who give a portion of their revenues to local environmental or community projects; and (4) "doers," who take an active role in conserving or improving the areas they visit.[38] Nearly two decades later, these categories still ring true and all have undoubtedly grown. The "donors" and the "doers," in particular, are beginning to coalesce under the umbrellas of Travelers' Philanthropy and Voluntourism (see below). Kurt Kutay states that "a more substantive contribution to ecotourism these days, beyond financial contributions, is community development/community-based tourism. Developing partnerships (formal business or informal itinerary planning) with local communities is a more supportive and lasting way to create real ecotourism."[39]

Small Ecotour Operators

Many ecotour operators are small companies, often run by the founder. They range in size from tiny firms that specialize in a few countries and customize all their tours, to larger firms that offer a variety of packaged trips and customized tours. They may specialize in particular activities, such as wildlife safaris, cultural heritage tours, bird-watching, mountain climbing, hiking, rafting, or biking. However, what these companies share in common is a social, environmental, and political sensitivity; an operating ethic, including hands-on involvement with their customers; and a personal, in-depth knowledge of the destinations they visit. They personally select the best overseas operators, guides, and accommodations and carefully put together trip itineraries that reflect their clients' specific interests.

For instance, Tamu Safaris is based in the United States and run largely via the Internet. Founded in 1987 by Sally and Costas Christ,

Tamu Safaris offers small (two- to fifteen-person), customized nature and cultural tours to eastern and southern Africa, as well as to Belize. "Our philosophy has always been to stay small and effective, both in offering personalized high-quality tours and in terms of making contributions to local communities where we operate and keeping any negative environmental impacts to a minimum," Sally Christ explained. As part of its ecotourism ethic, Tamu Safaris supports small-scale community development and conservation projects. In Southern Africa, for instance, Tamu supports Children in the Wilderness, a program in partnership with Wilderness Safaris that offers disadvantaged African schoolchildren an opportunity to visit national parks and learn firsthand about nature. In Belize, Tamu Safaris raised funds for Friends of Nature to establish and manage a new marine national park.

Sally and Costas Christ's commitment to responsible tourism grew out of years of living and working in East Africa, first as wildlife researchers and anthropologists, then as directors of U.S. college study abroad programs, and finally as private tour guides. Today, they are well known in international ecotourism circles. In addition to organizing trips for small groups of friends and family who like to travel together, their client roster has included celebrities such as Diane Sawyer of ABC News and Eddie Vedder of the band Pearl Jam. Everything they recommend they know firsthand and have assessed according to ecotourism principles, blending learning and adventure into personally tailored itineraries.

Tamu Safaris advertises selectively, and after nearly two decades in business most of their business comes via word of mouth. At an Ecolodge Forum at Maho Bay in the U.S. Virgin Islands, I heard Costas give a thoughtful lecture about ecotourism developments in Africa. When I first called Tamu Safaris, Sally began by listening—to my needs and desires, my timeframe and my budget. Over the course of two months, Sally helped me identify the most important ecotourism destinations and put together an increasingly refined and detailed itinerary. She prepared a packet of suggested reading and general travel tips and graciously and efficiently handled numerous last-minute changes. There were no glossy brochures, no off-the-rack packages; everything was personalized and tailored to our needs.[40]

Large Ecotour Operators

G.A.P (Great Adventure People) Adventures was founded in 1990 by Canadian entrepreneur Bruce Poon Tip.[41] Over nearly two decades, it has become a world leader at providing small group experiences, with a strong focus on culture, nature, and active travel, on all seven continents, to more than forty thousand travelers per year. G.A.P Adventures offers a thousand different trips in one hundred countries, making it the world's largest adventure travel company.[42] According to its mission statement, G.A.P fosters "traveling while respecting the land and her people. While others focus on attractions and creating a western environment, our vision is face to face travel at a grassroots level."[43] The company pledges to follow sustainable tourism practices, which it defines as minimizing environmental impact, respecting local people and cultures, offering economic benefit to local businesses and communities, and providing memorable experiences for travelers.

Despite its enormous growth, G.A.P Adventures continues to offer customized service and small group tours (twelve to sixteen people), as well as varied forms of local transportation, rustic or simple accommodations, and regional cuisine. Their packages are generally not all-inclusive, providing some freedom to the traveler to explore local activities, attractions, and restaurants. According to G.A.P Adventures, "By using small-scale lodging, local transportation, supporting locally owned businesses, and incorporating community-based ecotourism projects into our tours, we demonstrate our commitment to tour operations that are environmentally, socially, and culturally responsible."[44] Despite their focus on smallscale, owner Bruce Poon Tip has worked to dispel what he terms the "myth" that ecotourism businesses must themselves be small-scale. He also rejects the notion that ecotourism means "leave only footprints." Tip argues that "we've got to get those 10,000 people off the cruise ships and into 200 small groups. I think that tourists can leave behind a huge impact."[45]

One way that G.A.P Adventures is endeavoring to make an impact is through creating its own nonprofit foundation, Planeterra, to provide financial and material support to local organizations and community projects in the destinations it visits.[46] These include a range of projects in Latin America, including a children's educational center in Chiapas, Mexico; a short-term loan program for Honduran families affected by Hurricane Mitch in 1998; a women's weaving project in Peru; and an environmental NGO in Cuba that promotes school gardens. G.A.P Adventures covers all of Planeterra's administration costs, matches each donation made by its guests dollar-for-dollar, and delivers financial and material resources on an annual basis to the projects it supports. G.A.P also supports three international charities and has started an endowment to ensure long-term support of its community development and conservation projects.[47]

G.A.P Adventures has received numerous awards and recognition for its exemplary practices. In 2006, *Condé Nast Traveler* named G.A.P

Adventures to its Green List, praising it and several other tour operators, as well as lodges and destinations, for demonstrating "the best ways to preserve the environments and cultures that make this planet worth exploring."[48]

Mid-size Ecotour Operators

Nestled between G.A.P Adventures and Tamu Safaris are mid-sized tour operators such as Seattle-based Wildland Adventures. It has ten employees, handles more than 1,500 tourists per year, and grosses about $4 million annually conducting tours to Central America, the Andes, East and southern Africa, Morocco, Turkey, Egypt, Jordan, New Zealand, and Alaska. The company's president, Kurt Kutay, says that Wildland Adventures offers three types of tours: (1) private tours with custom-made itineraries for couples, families, or small groups (50 percent of the company's business); (2) exclusive tours put together by the company itself (30 percent); and (3) fixed-itinerary tours that Wildland represents for reputable overseas ecotourism operators (20 percent).

Kutay once worked for Costa Rica's national park service and holds a master's degree in natural resource management; he entered into ecotourism as a conservationist, not a businessman. In 1980, just as ecotourism was getting started, Kutay and a friend began informally putting together and leading tours to Central America and Nepal. "Our style was to take friends to countries we loved," says Kutay. Gradually, through word of mouth and limited advertising, they put together a small company specializing in "authentic cultural and natural history explorations for active and inquisitive travelers." In 1986, the young entrepreneurs created the Traveler's Conservation Trust, a nonprofit corporation affiliated with their for-profit business that contributes a portion of Wildland Adventures' earnings to community-level projects and conservation organizations in the developing countries they visit. Wildland Adventures routinely asks its clients to make voluntary contributions of twenty-five dollars or more to the trust, and Kutay estimates that "95 percent contribute." Projects supported by the trust include conservation and community development projects in Costa Rica; the Charles Darwin Research Station on the Galapagos Islands; African Wildlife Foundation projects; and native Maasai communities in Africa. "For our 'Travelers as Conservationists' program, we seek local organizations to support with English-language newsletters," Kutay explains:

> We send the contributions and list of names to the local organizations and our clients automatically receive the newsletter from the country

> where they recently traveled for a year following their trip. Hopefully, they continue to make contributions. The November 2007 issue of *National Geographic Adventure* magazine released results of the 'Best Adventure Travel Companies on Earth,' an extensive survey of hundreds of travel companies worldwide and Wildland Adventures scored 94.3% putting us 4th overall as a 'Do-it-All' outfitter.[49]

Tour Operator Collectives

In 2000, a small group of mainly European-based tour operators joined to form a voluntary alliance known as the Tour Operators Initiative for Sustainable Tourism Development (TOI). It was created based on the idea that while most tour operators recognize that a clean and safe environment is critical to their success, few have the management tools or experience to be able to design and conduct tours that minimize their negative environmental, social, and economic impacts. By 2006, TOI had twenty members, most based in Europe but some operators in Brazil, Pakistan, the United States, and Morocco as well. TOI's mission is twofold: to advance the sustainable development and management of tourism, and to encourage tour operators to make a corporate commitment to sustainable development. In 2004, together with Conservation International, TOI produced a manual of guidelines for developing a sustainable supply chain, and in 2005, it developed a management guide for tour operators to integrate sustainability into their business practices.[50]

Another initiative, the Adventure Collection, brought together leading U.S. and Canadian tour operators in the adventure travel industry to better collaborate in marketing and branding their upscale tours and develop stronger and more uniform standards. Created in 2000, the Adventure Collection had by 2007 ten member companies,[51] together offering over five hundred trips ranging from wildlife safaris to bicycle tours, rafting, fly-fishing, heli-skiing, and cultural exploration. In 2005, it boasted a combined revenue of $270.4 million, an increase of 23.1 percent over 2004. The members put together a common set of "Strategic Principles of Responsible Travel," which include supporting specific projects, accountability in their offices and in the communities where their trips take place, responsible travel education guidelines, and a systematic review of their corporate performance regarding responsible travel.[52] (See chapter 10.)

In order to join the Adventure Collection, a prospective company must demonstrate that it has a substantial track record, excellent trip leaders, high-quality travel experiences, expertise in the activities offered, high safety and operating standards, and leadership in conservation and environmental practices. Adventure Collection is funded through the yearly dues of its members. Larry Mogelonsky, the executive director of Adventure Collection, states, "The adventure travel market's continued growth reflects that accelerated demand by 'baby boomers' for experiential travel: a combination of culture, learning and testing new horizons. . . . With this demographic segment moving into retirement over the next 5–10 years, we expect continued strengthening in demand as leisure time increases."[53]

Ecotours Sponsored by Nonprofit Organizations

A number of environmental, educational, and scientific organizations also offer nature, adventure, study, and service tours to their members. Usually, these travel programs contract with international or inbound tour operators in the host countries.[54] In the United States, the best known of these organizations include the Smithsonian Institution, The Nature Conservancy, the Audubon Society, the World Wildlife Fund, the Earthwatch Institute, American Museum of Natural History, and the Sierra Club. Increasingly, these travel programs are incorporating ecotourism principles, although they tend to use the larger, best-advertised U.S. nature tour operators and overseas ground operators, which are not always the most innovative and responsible ecotourism outfits. The main purposes of these trips are to promote the education and professional development of members, showcase the organizations' projects in other countries, provide entertainment and relaxation for travelers, and raise revenue for the organization while allowing participants to write off a portion as a tax-deductible contribution.

Many U.S. universities and colleges also offer study tours, taking alumni and "friends of the university" to a variety of natural and cultural destinations. Stanford University is one of the leaders in this regard, featuring "Travel/Study Trips" with lectures by faculty whose research and teaching interests bear on the carefully chosen destinations. Among the innovative formats in the Stanford program are Field Seminars that bring together alumni and undergraduates in a combination of classroom and travel experience focused on Galapagos, the Amazon, Costa Rica, and other destinations. Stanford anthropologist William Durham, who regularly leads Field Seminars, says they are an especially effective format for nonprofit ecotourism: "Combining the youthful enthusiasm of the undergraduates with the worldly and wise perspectives of the alumni makes this an unforgettable learning experience for everyone."[55]

Of the environmental organizations offering ecotours, The Nature Conservancy (TNC) had one of the best-known overseas tour programs, at one time offering some two dozen trips per year to twelve to fifteen destinations in Latin America, the Caribbean, Canada, and the Asia/Pacific region. These trips, available to all TNC members, were education-based natural and cultural history tours with a conservation theme. In 2002, their International Member Trip Program ended as part of a TNC-wide organizational streamlining and restructuring. At present, the Conservation Journeys Program's structure and concept are the result of a successful evolution in pursuit of their increasing conservation and fundraising objectives. Currently, they run about twenty to twenty-five trips per year, averaging about ten participants per trip, to a handful of international destinations where TNC has programs. While their previous travel program was open to all TNC members and the general public,[56] the majority of their current trips are not; most are now designed for past or prospective major donors to showcase TNC's efforts firsthand and provide a unique educational experience that encourages support and increased involvement in their mission. TNC staff and experts serve as guides on the trips. Together with TNC's Ecotourism Department, the Conservation Journeys Program has developed a set of "Green Guidelines" for all their tour operators. Such guidelines include demonstrating a strong interest in TNC's mission, offering financial contributions to conservation, supporting community-based tourism, promoting and implementing environmental best practices, promoting responsible visitor behavior, monitoring impacts, and reporting policy compliance.[57]

The World Wildlife Fund (WWF—known as the World Wide Fund for Nature outside North America) also runs a travel program for its members, offering trips to over twenty destinations in Africa, Asia, North America, and Latin America and using the revenue to support their conservation efforts worldwide. Initiated in 1983, the WWF travel program now runs thirty-five to forty trips per year for its members, and handles over four hundred travelers. The trips focus on wildlife observation, while some also visit WWF project sites. All trips are run by U.S. tour operators, who in turn hire local operators and guides in the host countries; WWF staff also accompany many groups.[58] Some, but not all, of WWF's member trips are run in partnership with Natural Habitat Adventures, a U.S.-based adventure travel company that pledges, according to its Web site, "to practice responsible tourism by selecting the most responsible local guides and operators, by attempting to ensure our activities have a minimal impact on the areas we visit, and by supporting local conservation, education and research projects."[59]

Most of these organizations—museums, zoos, universities, and NGOs—keep abreast of travel trends and changes in the Internal Revenue Service's standards and regulations for tax exempt organizations by attending an annual Educational Travel Conference (formerly "Nonprofits in Travel") run by Travel Learning Connections of Montana.[60] Under the rules guiding nonprofit organizations, these trips themselves cannot be money-making or fund-raising activities. However, according to one study, such travel targets "the 'upscale market' [and] a key implicit objective is to win favor with present or potential donors and benefactors."[61] Some organizations, such as TNC, now successfully support many of their ecotourism and conservation projects by taking donors to project sites as part of the membership travel program.[62] According to Jill Bernier, the senior manager of TNC's Conservation Journeys program, "Designing customized journeys to explore, immerse, and engage our supporters in our mission creates a high level of trust in the quality of our work and provides an opportunity for us to direct even more well-intentioned support to critical conservation efforts throughout the globe."[63]

Ecotourism Structures in Developing Countries

When viewed as a tool for sustainable development in poorer countries, ecotourism means, in the main, the movement of travelers from the North to the South: from developed to developing countries. As Héctor Ceballos-Lascuráin writes, "Tourist travel is still very much the privilege of people of the industrialized world. . . . Nevertheless, the shift in favored tourism destinations—from developed to developing countries—indicates that international tourism could become a means of redistributing wealth 'from north to south.'"[64] Although Europe and North America remain the top destinations in international travel, representing about 65 percent of all international tourist arrivals, Latin America, Africa, Asia, and the Pacific are growing rapidly. In particular, Asia, Central America, and South America are growing far faster than the global rate,[65] with China on the cusp of becoming the world's powerhouse in tourism.

Today both international and domestic tourism in China are experiencing exceptional growth, with over 20 million international arrivals in 2005 and far higher numbers of domestic tourists.[66] The UN World Tourism Organization (UNWTO) predicts that by 2020, China will become the world's largest tourism destination.[67] Concern, even alarm, has also grown that without sufficient management and controls, the sheer number of vacationers will overwhelm China's natural and cultural attractions, from the Wolong Giant Panda Nature Reserve to the Great Wall of China. In response, a number of ecotourism projects have begun in China,[68] particularly in and around protected areas and culturally rich areas such as Tibet.[69] In 2006, China's first "planned ecotourism destination" was completed by an international team of architects and builders, in consultation with a rural community. The Crosswaters Ecolodge in the Nankun Mountain Reserve in South China is constructed from bamboo, the region's traditional building material, with a respect for local cultural and spiritual feng shui values and beliefs.[70] A growing number of tour operators are promoting ecotourism holidays in China.[71] Meanwhile, China's growing middle class is no longer staying within its national borders: outbound travelers from China reached an estimated 35 million in 2006, a 13 percent increase over 2005. According to one estimate, 150 million Chinese are already affluent enough to take holidays abroad and, by 2020, it is estimated that Chinese traveling outside the country will reach 100 million.[72]

Inbound Tour Operators

Despite the growth in tourism numbers in developing countries, benefits will only come if host countries are able to retain the tourism dollars and stop the leakage of profits from the South back to the North. Tourists, travel agents, tour operators, and conservation organizations can help maximize the benefits to developing countries by utilizing, as much as possible, environmentally sensitive, socially responsible, and locally based companies and facilities in developing countries. Outbound tour operators and nonprofit organizations contract with inbound tour and ground operators in the host country, and it is these companies that are the most important component in ensuring high-quality ecotourism. Inbound operators are responsible for arranging all details of the trip, including assembling a network of lodges close to or within the attractions. Ecotourism facilities run the spectrum from basic backpacker tents and cabins to small, exclusive, high-end luxury resorts, as well as eco-lodges that fall in the intermediate price range. Inbound ecotour operators also select locally owned restaurants featuring authentic cuisine and the best artisans and cooperatives selling local crafts or displaying local culture. In recent years, the growth of the "slow food movement" and growing popularity of organics has increased links between ecotourism and local farms and regional cuisine, and spawned a whole movement known as "agritourism."[73]

Many inbound operators involved in ecotourism are, like their counterparts in the United States, owned by their founders, who are either nationals or longtime foreign residents who keep most of the profits within the country; many see themselves contributing to poverty alleviation and as actors for social justice. Costa Rica, more than most host countries, has a wide range of high-quality inbound operators. Virtually all handle some nature tourism, but about a dozen are known for specializing almost exclusively in ecotourism. As early as 1992, a survey by researcher Ana Báez collected data on eighteen tour operators and revealed that they had a high degree of environmental and social consciousness. Yet a 2003 study of several rural Costa Rican communities adjacent to ecotourism destinations found evidence that ecotourism operators in Costa Rica were not significant players in raising environmental awareness among such communities, and that legal restrictions were more influential than tourism in reducing deforestation and illegal hunting. The authors concluded that ecotourism will stand a greater chance of positively influencing conservation and development in Costa Rica "if tourism operators demonstrate a firm commitment to seriously embrace and advance conservation strategies and ensure meaningful local involvement."[74] This has begun to happen. In September 2006, the Costa Rican government launched a "green" certification program for inbound tour operators and certified eight operators. One of those certified, Horizontes Nature Tours, received top ranking—five "green" leaves—under the rigorous Certification for Sustainable Tourism (CST) program.[75] (See chapter 5.)

Although a number of companies have prospered with Costa Rica's ecotourism boom, many smaller inbound operators in other countries have faced challenges breaking into the international market, even with tourism expanding. In Tanzania in the mid-1990s, for instance, Unique Safaris, an inbound tour operator owned by two longtime and highly qualified Tanzanian guides, had only two vehicles. It was therefore unable to meet the demands and secure contracts with international tour operators such as Overseas Adventure Travel.[76] However, with Tanzania's recent ecotourism expansion, Unique Safaris has managed to grow substantially. By 2006, it had a hundred employees, and was operating some of the best luxury mobile camping on the northern circuit. The company continues to be all-Tanzanian owned and operated, and to include cultural, educational, and social issues in its itineraries. The company also helps to support a number of village projects.[77] Not all inbound tour operators were so successful, as local banks in Tanzania had been charging up to 30 to 40 percent interest for loans, making it difficult for small companies to access funds to grow.[78]

Given the lack of ecotourism standards and regulation in many places, outbound operators have difficulty assessing ground operators, especially if these firms are skillfully marketed. Although some of the best outbound and inbound operators consciously place long-term benefits ahead of short-term profits, many do not. There is a need for more regulation and independent evaluation of international tour operators, as well as local service providers, lodges, and other in-country businesses, to ensure adherence to the principles of ecotourism. Some donor agencies, including the European Union, World Bank, and Britain's Department of International Development (DFID), through its pro-poor tourism initiative, are focusing on capacity building for tour operators in developing country destinations.[79]

The Conservation NGOs

In a study of ecotourism in Latin America, Michele Zebich-Knos found that "few instances of grassroots ecotourism development occurred without the insertion of nongovernmental organizations (NGOs) into the mix." She contends that "NGOs can provide training and management skills needed to organize tourism infrastructure, marketing and other essentials for successfully bargaining with sophisticated outsiders."[80] Today, almost all of the major U.S.-based international conservation organizations, including the World Wildlife Fund (WWF), National Geographic, World Resources Institute (WRI), The Nature Conservancy (TNC), Conservation International (CI), African Wildlife Foundation (AWF), Environmental Defense, RARE Center for Tropical Conservation, and the Rainforest Alliance, among others, are involved in ecotourism at some level, from issuing sets of principles and policy statements to establishing departments, providing technical assistance and public education, operating projects in developing countries, and conducting travel programs. They have received hundreds of millions of dollars in funding from the U.S. Agency for International Development (USAID), the Inter-American Development Bank (IDB), World Bank, and UN agencies,[81] among others. Much of their funding has also come from the Ford, Packard, Moore, Rockefeller, and other philanthropic foundations to implement scores of programs, projects, and studies in Africa, Latin America, the Caribbean, and Asia.

These programs are typically aimed at protecting threatened ecosystems and conserving biodiversity. Ecotourism is being hailed as a means of "giving nature value" and achieving sustainable development.[82] Many in the sponsoring organizations view ecotourism as a way to promote small-scale private enterprise linked to free trade and economic liberalization, and they recognize the need for a business plan as well as environmental and social development plans. The WWF, WRI, and TNC, as well as USAID and the World Bank, view ecotourism as one of a variety of "enterprise-based approaches to conservation"[83] that champion the marketplace and the private sector and reorient the role of government to catalyze growth and investment, in addition to providing needed public services and infrastructure. They often choose to enter into partnerships with private organizations, reserves, and parks. A recent trend is to develop programs to strengthen and support financially strapped national park systems in Mozambique, Zambia, Gabon, and other developing countries.[84]

As early as 1985, USAID began providing assistance to WWF's Wildlife and Human Needs Program, which included some twenty pilot projects in developing countries aimed at combining conservation and development.[85] One of the initial successes was the Annapurna Conservation Area Project in Nepal, which began to curb the adverse environmental effects of trekkers and to increase local income from ecotourism. By the mid-1990s, the Annapurna project had trained seven hundred local people to work in lodges used by ecotourists, built a visitors' education center, and instituted a conservation fee of twelve dollars per person, which was generating more than $1 million annually for local conservation and development activities, including tree planting and trail maintenance.[86] Similar initiatives were subsequently replicated in the Mt. Everest National Park and Chitwan National Park in Nepal. However, Nepal's growing political unrest after 2000, which included a Maoist insurgency and prodemocracy movement led by students and intellectuals, caused a 50 percent drop in tourism numbers. Then in April 2006, King Gyanendra ended his direct rule and relinquished power to the parliament, and in November, peace accords were signed, bringing a formal end to the Maoist Peoples War and denying the King all political rights. The tourism industry began to reflect the new optimism, as arrivals had increased a modest 7 percent by late 2006. Then in 2007, international arrivals soared 27.1 percent. The Nepal Tourism Board attributed this "inspiring growth" to the ongoing peace process and political stability and to the nine new international airlines that began flying to Nepal.[87]

Although WWF did not have a sustainable tourism program until 2008, the organization undertook in 1990 the first major analysis of ecotourism in a two-volume study of five Latin American and Caribbean countries.[88] WWF has also had many projects around the world that include ecotourism components. WWF has, for instance, a variety of ecotourism-linked projects in the tiny Central American country of Belize (population two hundred thousand). Belize is an important ecotourism destination, with 36 percent of its land under some form of protection and the world's second largest barrier reef. WWF helped institute a $3.75 conservation fee, which is added to the airport departure tax charged to all foreign tourists and placed in a fund that can be used for activities related to biodiversity, cultural heritage preservation, and community-based ecotourism ventures. Viewed as a model for other developing countries, the fund is administered by the Protected Area Conservation Trust (PACT), made up of government officials and representatives from the tourism industry, village councils, and Belize NGOs.

In 2002, WWF and seven other international and local NGOs helped to establish eleven new Marine Protected Areas along the Belizean coast. The following year, WWF began working with the Central American Organization of the Fisheries and Aquaculture Sector, in an effort to improve the management of the marine protected areas. Together with the Coral Reef Alliance,[89] WWF has worked to establish marine recreation standards and improve tourism planning in the coral zones of Belize, in cooperation with the government, local communities, and industry, including hotel owners, cruise ship lines, and tour operators.[90] WWF has been involved in ecotourism projects in Africa and Asia as well. In Europe, WWF has partnered with a Dutch leisure company, Molecaten, to found PAN (Protected Area Network) Parks. PAN Parks is a certification program designed to promote conservation management and sustainable development of Europe's protected areas and their neighboring communities through ecotourism and other sustainable economic activities.[91]

The Nature Conservancy (TNC) is involved in a number of ecotourism projects, mainly in South America. Its small Ecotourism Program works with governments, protected areas, and local conservation organizations to promote tourism as a tool for conservation. TNC supports efforts at the national policy level to generate tourism income and investment for conservation and local communities, and to reduce threats posed to natural areas by visitation. For example, TNC worked with the Bolivian park system to establish for the first time park entrance fees at the Eduardo Avaroa National Andean Fauna Reserve, the country's most visited park. By 2006, park entrance fees were bringing in about two hundred thousand dollars per year "to an extremely hard-pressed protected area system," said Andy Drumm, director of the Ecotourism Program. He explained that the successful entrance fee system is being extended to all Bolivian parks and "we anticipate it will generate U.S. $1.5 million per year." TNC has also conducted studies in Ecuador and Peru to measure the value of protected area tourism and proposed policies to increase the flow of tourist spending into conservation and local communities. It has also created training manuals and other publications in various languages designed to help park staff and conservation managers improve tourism management in national parks.[92]

Conservation International (CI), the newest of the major U.S. organizations (founded in 1987), created a relatively large Ecotourism Program at its Washington, D.C. headquarters and with its regional offices and partners in the field. CI has been involved in dozens of ecotourism projects in biodiversity "hotspots"—areas of high biodiversity but under great threat—in Latin America, Africa, and Asia. "CI is addressing the difficult challenge of effectively linking local ecotourism projects in developing countries with the international ecotourism market. The program helps to develop and market local ecotourism facilities—lodges, trail systems, and concessions—as part of a larger effort to provide sustainable livelihoods and support biodiversity conservation efforts," explained Eileen Gutierrez, who worked until 2007 in CI's ecotourism program. But Gutierrez said that CI has gradually moved away from a concentration on product development such as specific ecotourism lodges and toward developing policy criteria, which strengthens the capacity of local partners to engage in ecotourism development and partner with the private sector. As part of its efforts to promote ecotourism, CI has created an ecotourism Web site with profiles of CI-affiliated destinations, tour operators, and lodges.[93]

CI also has a Travel and Leisure Program which focuses on reducing the environmental footprint of major players in tourism[94] in partnership with and through funding from the industry. This program's cruise ship initiative is "engaging cruise companies to integrate biodiversity conservation practices into their management systems and become a positive force for biodiversity conservation in the destinations that they visit."[95] It has drawn considerable criticism from other NGOs. In 2004, a coalition of thirty environmental groups charged that a joint initiative between CI and the International Council of Cruise Lines (ICCL) to address the problem of cruise ship pollution "lacks substance and specific commitments."[96]

Multilateral Lending and Aid Institutions

Following the 1992 United Nations Conference on Environment and Development (UNCED), known as the Earth Summit, the World Bank heightened its emphasis on environmentally sustainable development. A 1995 press release titled "Greening of the World Bank" noted that since the Earth Summit, the bank had become "the world's leading financier of environmental projects in the developing world," including $10 billion in project loans in sixty-two countries and another $20 billion per year for "greening" its own operations.[97] For instance, the GEF (Global Environment Facility) and USAID committed $4 million to set up a trust fund for conservation of the Bwindi Impenetrable Forest Gorilla Reserve, a biologically important tropical forest in Uganda, which contains about half (some three hundred) of the remaining population of mountain gorillas. The trust fund, jointly managed by representatives of Uganda's government, local and international NGOs, and the fifty local communities touching the reserve's boundaries, set aside 60 percent of its net income for community development that is compatible with conservation. In addition, Uganda National Parks and a consortium made up of the AWF, WWF, and other international NGOs developed ecologically sound tourism, which, by the mid-1990s, was permitting twelve tourists at a time to visit the two groups of gorillas that have become accustomed to the presence of people. Despite the steep cost—about $145 per person for a one-hour viewing—"gorilla tourism" has been running at near capacity. It earns about four hundred thousand dollars annually, making Bwindi the highest revenue earner among Uganda's parks. Uganda National Parks also set aside revenues for community development, designating 10 to 20 percent of the combined earnings from gorilla viewing and accommodations for local community projects.

Although initial problems diminished local support for the Bwindi Reserve, by 2000 new programs had been implemented to beef up benefits to communities and to raise their sense of responsibility for protecting the forest. In addition to the trust fund established by GEF, a proportion of income from tourism at Bwindi was being used for development projects in communities adjacent to the park, amounting to about 170,000 people. Agreements with the communities also permitted limited harvesting of medicinal plants, honey, and other natural resources within the park. Surveys of community attitudes conducted by CARE show increasing numbers of people in favor of the park; in addition, the study found that deliberate burning has ceased, and local interest in gorillas has increased.[98]

The World Bank's International Finance Corporation (IFC) invests in tourism and other private sector projects both as a shareholder and as a lender. From its founding in 1956 through 2005, the IFC has committed more than $49 billion of its own funds and arranged $24 billion in syndications for 3,319 companies in 140 developing countries. With lending totaling $4.8 billion in 2004 and $5.4 billion in 2005, the IFC is the largest source of financing for private sector projects in developing countries. Like the World Bank, the IFC has had its share of socially and environmentally destructive megatourism ventures, in places such as Cancún, Mexico. However, unlike the Bank, which closed its Tourism Projects Department in 1979 and only resumed tourism lending in the 1990s under the rubric of sustainable or ecotourism, the IFC never stopped funding tourism projects. In fact, its portfolio has been growing: until 1987, IFC's Tourism Unit financed one to three new projects per year, while between 1990 and 1994, it averaged thirteen to sixteen new tourism projects annually. As of June 2002, the IFC held $461 million in the tourism sector, with investments in scores of developing countries in Asia, Latin America, and most importantly, Africa.[99] Most IFC tourism loans have been for hotels, often city center hotels. The IFC, together with the World Bank, works closely with the World Bank's Multilateral Investment Guarantee Agency (MIGA), established in 1988, which sells insurance against risks such as war or nationalization to private operators, including those in the tourism business in developing countries. In 1994, MIGA invested in its first ecotourism project, the Rain Forest Aerial Tram in Costa Rica, which quickly became a highly popular attraction.[100] (See chapter 5.)

The IFC has made some efforts to integrate sustainable tourism criteria into its lending criteria and adopt an institution-wide strategy. However, its overall lending for tourism remains relatively modest. Over the long term, about 3 to 4 percent of IFC loans have been for tourism projects. Most of the IFC projects listed as involving "ecotourism" focus on infrastructure development, particularly construction of accommodations, in areas that are tied to preserving ecologically sensitive land. Like the World Bank, the IFC conducts environmental impact and safeguard studies for its projects, including those in national parks and other fragile areas. Together with the private sector, NGOs, and other bilateral donors, the IFC has created a department for environmentally driven private sector projects and set up a $25 to $30 million fund to support biodiversity, conservation, and sustainable use "through a convergence of private profit and conservation objectives."[101]

The IFC requires a bankable business plan and often a recognized operator as partner; too often in the past this has resulted in financing only large, well-established, usually foreign-owned tourism projects. IFC officials indicate that tourism projects are time-consuming to design, implement, and coordinate; that finding suitable local investors with an established track record is difficult; and that most ecotourism projects fall below its investment threshold. Typically, the IFC finances projects ranging from $5 million to $150 million, while support for preparing small projects is provided through regional Project Development Facilities (PDFs).[102] In the case of nature-based tourism projects, IFC's investments have tended to be with well-established eco-friendly operators such as Abercrombie & Kent and Conservation Corporation of Africa.

In recent years, IFC support for smaller businesses (up to $1 million) has been growing rapidly, and it has also financed "linkage" projects, that is, loans for the outsourcing of services to local businesses. For instance, the IFC helped the Mandarin Oriental in Peru to develop a relationship with a fish supplier for the hotel. In Tanzania, the World Bank, in partnership with IFC, launched a Private Sector Development project that includes assistance for SMEs (small and medium enterprises) and micro enterprises, including those in tourism. Many of the leading tour operators have formed alliances with Tanzanian firms to represent them for ground services—a trend that is fast developing in many destinations as there is recognition of the gap between the international outbound tour operators and local suppliers.[103] In another initiative, in 2003, the IFC commissioned a study on the environmental, social, and economic sustainability of nature-based lodges and eco-lodges, and the key factors leading to their success. This study was the beginnings of an effort to set some standards and clearer policies for IFC lending in the field of ecotourism.[104]

The United Nations Environment Programme (UNEP), based in Nairobi, has over the past two decades developed a sustainable tourism strategy aimed at safeguarding the environment, benefiting host communities, and protecting cultures. By the mid-1990s, UNEP's Tourism Sector, which operates out of Paris, declared that its mandate was working directly with the big players in the tourism industry as well as governments, with the aim of implementing voluntary "green" reforms.[105] The primary objectives of UNEP's current tourism strategy are to integrate sustainability into tourism development policies, to promote sustainable production and consumption patterns in the tourism industry, and to create and encourage demand for sustainable tourism services. UNEP's main tools and activities include providing advisory services to assist national tourism and environmental agencies, capacity building, field projects, management tools for protected and fragile areas, communication and information, technical and scientific support, and partnerships with other international organizations, development agencies, and NGOs.[106]

Ecotourism's Promise—and Pitfalls

By the opening of the new millennium, ecotourism had taken on global significance. International funding organizations, NGO's, governments, and tour operators of all sizes began turning to ecotourism. It was no longer a "specialty" industry with little global impact. It had become a significant economic activity, especially in developing countries, and was being used as a tool for conservation and community development. In addition, the principles and good practices of ecotourism were beginning to impact—and change—the broader, mainstream tourism industry. "Green" hotels, sustainable ski slopes, Blue Flag beaches and "committed to G" golf courses were signs that tourism as we had known it was beginning to change. By 2006, it seemed clear that ecotourism was being propelled forward by a rejuvenated and rapidly rising environmental consciousness. As *Condé Nast Traveler* wrote in announcing the winners of its 2006 Green List of outstanding ecotourism businesses, "The Green movement has arrived. Want proof? Americans buy organic, locally grown produce. We drive hybrids. We spend $10 to watch not a Hollywood superhero but a politician with a PowerPoint presentation [i.e., Al Gore's *An Inconvenient Truth*]. And travelers are increasingly looking for options that keep the earth and its occupants in mind: More than 75 percent of *Condé Nast Traveler* readers recently surveyed deemed it important for hotels near impoverished areas to help local people obtain education, clean water, food, and health care."[107]

While there is clearly much to celebrate, the path toward a more planet-friendly tourism, toward genuine ecotourism, is lined with pitfalls. Ecotourism is not a panacea; at present, it is a set of interconnected principles whose full implementation presents multilayered problems and challenges. A number of pressing issues surround ecotourism that are crying out for deeper investigation, more rigorous analysis, and more careful theoretical work. A discussion of the most important of these issues follows.

Indigenous People, Protected Areas, and Ecotourism

In his keynote speech to the IUCN's 2003 World Parks Congress in Durban, South Africa, former president Nelson Mandela noted that while national parks like Kruger are a source of pride, "Unfortunately a great many South Africans do not see it as such, and for very understandable reasons." He went on, "Many of Africa's beautiful protected areas have their origins in the colonial past, and have a legacy of being 'set aside,' thus alienating local people who viewed them as meaningless or even costly."[108] Mandela did not mention that the colonial tradition of creating national parks by forcibly seizing lands and evicting the local people has continued, in some countries, up to today.

In the early 1960s, on the cusp of the end of colonialism, there were about 1,000 protected areas in the world. Today there are 108,000, a hundredfold increase in the last four decades. This equals more than 12 percent of all land, and exceeds the IUCN's target of protecting 10 percent of the earth, as was proudly announced at the 2003 World Parks Congress. "At first glance, so much protected land seems undeniably positive, an enormous achievement by good people doing the right thing for our suffering planet," writes investigative journalist and Berkeley professor Mark Dowie. "But," he cautions, "the record is less impressive when we consider the impact of setting aside large tracts of land upon millions of displaced indigenous people."[109] These displaced people have created a new class of "conservation refugees" found on every continent but Antarctica. They are largely invisible, often live in squalid conditions around protected areas, and are roughly estimated to number between 5 million and tens of millions of human beings. One of the largest forced removals, which attracted international attention, occurred in the central African country of Chad. While the total protected area was increased from 1 percent to 9.1 percent in the 1990s, an estimated six hundred thousand people were evicted from their lands.[110]

Many of the world's approximately 350 million indigenous people live in spectacularly beautiful parts of the globe, areas increasingly penetrated by tourism, frequently in the name of ecotourism.[111] Indeed, often the most vibrant and militant rural social movements in developing countries center on national parks, local people, and tourism. As one study of ecotourism and economic liberalization puts it, "a new grassroot environmentalism gained strength worldwide in the 1990s [and] became connected to issues of social justice and the concept of environmental justice."[112] These struggles have pitted local communities and indigenous people against their own governments, international development agencies like the World Bank and USAID, and, not infrequently, against the agendas of international conservation organizations. Mac Chapin, in his 2004 critique of the relationship between local communities and large conservation organizations, the so-called BINGOS (Big International NGOs),[113] claimed that "cooperation by the large conservationist NGOs, both among themselves and with other, smaller groups, including indigenous and traditional peoples, has lost ground over the past decade, only to be replaced by often intense competition, largely over money."[114] Fundamentally, these struggles are over who owns and controls the land's scarce and valuable resources. As Clark University professor Cynthia Enloe reminds us, "Tourism is not just about escaping work and drizzle; it is about power, increasingly internationalized power."[115]

In many places, these movements were for decades held in check by colonialism, military regimes, or one-party states that prohibited local organizing. Resistance took the form of individual or group acts of sabotage, poaching, fires, or cutting of trees or bush inside protected areas. However, since the mid-1980s, a number of factors have coalesced in Latin America and Africa to heighten the ability of rural people to organize. These factors include the economic and political liberalizations of the 1980s, the growth of local and international environmental movements, the decline of military dictatorships in Latin America, an end to white rule in southern Africa, moves toward multiparty elections in many countries, and an increasing realization that sustainable development, even though supported by national and international programs and funds, must be carried out by empowering, educating, and providing tools and infrastructure to local communities.

In Tanzania, for instance, the Maasai living around Serengeti National Park and Ngorongoro Conservation Area have organized to demand a sizable slice of the tourism pie and the return of their rights to use land and water within the parks. In Zimbabwe and South Africa, rural people anticipated that with majority rule, national park lands would be returned to them. When this did not happen, they organized, often in alliance with local environmental and rural development groups, to win a stake in running the parks and tourism facilities. In Zimbabwe, CAMPFIRE (Communal Area Management Programme for Indigenous Resources), a loosely organized nationwide network of communities that conducts hunting and camera safaris, became, in the 1990s, internationally acclaimed as a model of rural development through ecotourism. Even though the CAMPFIRE program provided income and inputs for community development projects, the majority of rural Africans involved were guides, porters, trackers, artisans, and waiters; rarely were they managers.[116] In Ecuador's Amazon basin, indigenous groups, occasionally with support from Quito-based or international environmental organizations, militantly resisted oil-drilling operations and have set up alternative, environmentally respectful economic activities in the rain forest.

In these places as elsewhere, those living around or in parks, reserves, and other protected or fragile ecosystems have increasingly come to see ecotourism as an economic activity with the potential—if done well—to provide both environmental protection and financial and material resources. In addition to securing employment as hotel workers, guides, drivers, and game scouts, people in many rural communities are negotiating or demanding the right to sustainable use of lands appropriated for national parks, rent or lease agreements with hotel and tour operators to use their traditional lands, and a percentage of park entrance fees or hotel profits. They are also demanding sole ownership of or joint partnership in campsites, cultural and handicraft centers, restaurants, lodges, and concessions such as those offering horseback riding, hiking, and fishing. Despite the rhetoric of incorporating people and parks and the democratic developments in a number of countries, old ways and power relationships die hard. A 1992 study of various ecotourism projects concluded that "the results [of participation] thus far have been disappointing, to say the least,"[117] and although there are some wonderful and exciting exceptions, this still appears to be the norm. As Peruvian activist and scholar Miguel Hilario writes, "Although indigenous peoples are considered key subjects in the ecotourism development model, they have not yet assumed roles as primary actors." Hilario points out that while indigenous peoples are typically listed as stakeholders in ecotourism, "not all stakeholders are equal." As he elaborates, "[I]ndigenous communities seem to have a comparative disadvantage in ecotourism ventures. They often lack the know-how, the market information, and most importantly, the cash to sustain any serious ecotourism business. Furthermore, they lack political and economic power to negotiate freely and evenly with governments, private entities, and international institutions. Consequently, at the end of what can be a long road of negotiations, the agreed-upon deal is generally not favorable to indigenous interests."[118]

In recent years there were instances in Namibia, Botswana, South Africa, Rwanda, and Uganda of rural people being expelled from their land to create new parks and ecotourism projects. Many people resisted moving from their traditional lands, even when they were offered compensation. As one elderly South African in the Kosi Bay area put it, "Where do these people take the right to make money out of our land? We don't want compensation, we want our land. . . . They say they want to protect nature. But aren't people also part of God's nature?"[119] Although the ultimate outcome of many of these disputes remains unclear, the terms of discourse and forms of organizing have changed: environmental protection and the land and economic rights of rural people are now part of the debate. In these struggles, rural communities and indigenous people are building national and sometimes international alliances to demand an equitable slice of the economic pie, which now frequently includes ecotourism.

The UN's designation of 2002 as "International Year of Ecotourism" (IYE) raised, as never before, debates over the rights of host communities to control of their lands and to specify fair and equitable terms for participation in ecotourism. Evolving ground rules for this relationship are the subject of a wide range of codes of conduct written by the UN, national governments, international financial and development agencies, NGOs, tour operators, eco-lodges, indigenous rights groups, and porters' associations. Many of these codes recognize in some manner the basic rights of indigenous peoples to self-determination, to chart their own economic, social, and cultural development priorities, to prior informed consent, and to say "no" to tourism projects in the first place.[120]

Gradually the "fortress conservation" philosophy of parks management is changing. In the 1990s, for example, South Africa's post-apartheid government set up a process by which communities could petition to get back their lands within protected areas. (See chapter 9.) During the same period, the IUCN supported resolutions allowing indigenous people to comanage protected areas. The IUCN created an important new task force, the Commission on Environmental, Economic, and Social Policy (CEESP) to promote two unique types of protected areas, Community Conservation Areas and Indigenous Reserves. This set up a mechanism under which indigenous people can ask the government to declare their homeland a biological reserve and thereby bar outside interests, including miners, loggers, and oil drillers.[121] Then in late 2006, the San (or Bushmen) from the Kalahari desert won a historic court case against the Botswana government for forcibly removing them four years earlier from their land within a national reserve. The San brought the case after about a thousand people were evicted and resettled in "functional but bleak settlements outside the Kalahari game reserve," ostensibly so that the government could provide them social services, including schools and health clinics. The government repeatedly denied the allegations that they had expelled the San to make way for diamond mining in the reserve. The case brought by the San, the oldest people in Sub-Saharan Africa, was widely seen as a test of whether governments can legally remove people from their ancestral lands.[122]

Effects on Local and Indigenous Cultures

Closely linked with the above discussion of local people and parks are complex issues of the impact of ecotourism on local cultures. By definition, ecotourism often involves seeking out the most pristine, uncharted, and unpenetrated areas on earth. Often, these are home to isolated and fragile human civilizations. In some areas, ecotourism is the front line of foreign encroachment, and can accelerate the pace of social and environmental degradation and lead to a new form of outside penetration and domination of the last remaining "untouched" parts of the world.[123] Take, for instance, the voyeuristic "First Contact" tours offered by American tour operator Kelly Woolford in West Papua, Indonesia. According to *Outside* magazine, Woolford's Papua Adventures offers three-week, eight-thousand-dollar treks into the jungle "in search of uncontacted native tribes who have never seen outsiders—and who aren't supposed to mind tourists barging into their lives."[124]

Ecotourism, as opposed to conventional tourism, holds out the twin promise of educating the visitor and respecting the local culture. Proponents say ecotourism has the potential to confront stereotypes of "exotic remnant" populations and offer visitors a fuller understanding of both cultural differences and the ongoing struggles of indigenous peoples. But without real standards and rules, ecotourism itself can be invasive and exploitative. People in Zanzibar, for instance, complain that backpackers who live in cheap guest houses or with families and try to learn from the locals are often the most intrusive of visitors (see chapter 8). "Authenticity" is a current buzzword within the field of ecotourism, but we are still struggling to find models for authentic cultural exchange that respect the rights of the hosts and satisfy the curiosity of the visitors. Without clear ground rules reached through democratic and transparent discussions with host communities, the danger remains that ecotourism may destroy the culture and lifestyles it is seeking to protect.

Free Trade versus Local Control

Ecotourism promotes locally owned enterprises, but in today's era of globalization and free trade, weak national capital often cannot compete with strong foreign companies. The lowering of trade barriers and opening up to unfettered foreign investment is again and again undermining the sustainability of smaller and locally owned ecotourism ventures in developing countries. Beginning in the 1990s, economic liberalism made "a robust comeback" with the backing of many national governments.[125] The UNWTO, and particularly the General Agreements on Trade in Services (GATS), plus a growing number of regional and bilateral agreements such as NAFTA (North American Free Trade Agreement) and CAFTA (Central American Free Trade Agreement) are promoting liberal international trade, not only in import/export products, but in services such as tourism. While CAFTA was quickly ratified by the governments in El Salvador, Guatemala, Honduras, Nicaragua, and the Dominican Republic, in Costa Rica, opposition led to heated public debate. In October 2007, the country held an historic public referendum—the first ever public vote on a free trade agreement. CAFTA, which was aggressively supported by the Costa Rican and U.S. administrations, was narrowly approved. The strength of the "No" campaign, particularly in the Guanacaste region, reflected growing concerns about the impacts of globalization and unrestricted foreign investment in tourism and other sectors.[126] Over the last fifteen to twenty years, the complexion of Costa Rica's tourism industry has shifted significantly, as independent hotels have been bought by international chains, beachfront property has been purchased for foreign hotels and vacation homes, and the number of foreign-owned ecotourism lodges and boutique inns has grown on top of the country's traditional foundation of locally owned accommodations. (See chapter 5.) As one study of one small Costa Rican coastal town found, "Although the USA and Costa Rican governments boast about increased job opportunities and economic growth, the experience of Costa Ricans living in small and impoverished towns, like Tarcoles, reveals another reality. . . . While a few tourists are attracted to Tarcoles due to its lush natural beauty—its mangroves, its rare species of scarlet macaws, and its crocodiles—most only see a blur of the town as they speed down the newly paved highway toward the famous beaches and surfing resorts of the south."[127]

Yet in the 1990s, such on-the-ground realities were often glossed over by the major tourism industry organizations and international lending and development agencies. Typically, in their promotion of ecotourism they fail to acknowledge a central contradiction: they continue to advocate both community-based ecotourism and open trade and investment markets as if the two fit seamlessly together. In recent years, however, a growing number of studies warn of the mixed impacts of economic liberalizations on sustainable tourism, particularly in developing countries.[128] UN trade official David Diaz Benavides perceptively notes that the liberalization and globalization of tourism has "led to high concentration of new international firms in key sectors, including organized travel, international booking, marketing and sales of tourism and related activities [that] creates market power and the potential for the abuse of dominance by large international firms." Benavides adds, "This creates further challenges for those developing countries that want [to] open their economies to investment and trade in tourism while ensuring that the unequal power relations between large firms and small countries do not further marginalize them and increase poverty." Benavides calls on developing countries to help counter this trend by taking an active and "coordinated approach to trade in tourism" including collectively participating "in the GATS rule-making process," in order to both maximize the economic benefits and create "an adequate framework for the environmental sustainability of tourism and preservations of the domestic cultural heritage."[129]

The Marketing of Ecotourism

Ineffective or insufficient marketing is probably the primary reason why worthy ecotourism ventures in developing countries fail to attract visitors. Throughout Latin America, Asia, and Africa, promising locally owned or run lodges, hotels, bed and breakfasts, ground operators, handicraft and cultural centers, and other attractions flounder for lack of know-how, financial resources, or government and industry assistance in carrying out proper marketing. In areas frequented by low-budget travelers, many rural communities have had success opening their houses for "family homestays," which can be a very viable source of income for families who otherwise would not have the financial capital to build larger tourism establishments. Even this type of tourism, though, often requires some marketing ability or middlemen, as many such rural areas are cut off from the principal tourism paths, and need strategies to attract tourists away from the usual tourism meccas.[130] For this reason, the focus of small or community-run ecotourism ventures has become more and more centered on successful marketing, linkages to markets, and the role of middlemen.

Although ecotourism strives to empower and benefit local residents and rural communities, community and rural projects tend to lack the knowledge, business skills, and resources required to market their products, and thus often require outside support from either the government or intermediaries in order to be successful. Government tourism agencies can play a key role in promoting and marketing locally owned ecotourism projects, as, for instance, the Belize Tourism Board has successfully done in providing international marketing as well as infrastructure to assist Mayan communities involved in ecotourism in Toledo District, Belize.[131] But positive examples like this are far too rare: often government agencies are underfunded and under pressure to promote large resorts.

Intermediaries to help with marketing can be NGOs, private companies, or international aid and development agencies. According to one marketing study, "intermediary institutions have different areas of expertise . . . in terms of capacity-building, marketing know-how, financial resources and overall livelihood impacts."[132] Over the last two decades, NGOs, particularly those located in developing countries, have become critical as intermediaries providing capacity building and market access to small, indigenous or community-based tourism businesses. For instance, in South Africa, the NGO Mafisa Research and Planning Agency works with communities to raise their skill levels in various aspects of ecotourism so that they can better negotiate with private companies and parks authorities.[133]

Scores of instances have also occurred in which private companies and local communities have formed partnerships, with the companies providing capital, infrastructure, quality control and business skills, and market access. In Peru, Posada Amazonas is one of the longest-running ecotourism experiments involving a partnership between a private tour operator and an indigenous community, with the goal of eventually turning over ownership completely to the local community. This is a joint venture between the local Ese'eja indigenous community and Rainforest Expeditions, one of the country's leading ecotourism operators. Rainforest Expeditions splits the profits from the thirty-room Posada Amazonas lodge forty/sixty with the four-hundred-member Ese'eja community. Rainforest Expeditions is committed to gradually turning ownership and management over to the community.[134]

In addition, the major international development agencies, including the World Bank, IDB, USAID, and various UN agencies, have funded community-based ecotourism projects. Probably no agency has grappled more systematically with the complexity of issues around creating viable community ecotourism projects than the Small Grants Program of the United Nations Development Program (UNDP).[135] In Costa Rica, for instance, the UNDP has worked with Cooprena,[136] a local NGO, to create a network of rural tourism projects and provide them with marketing, including an attractive guidebook in both English and Spanish. The guidebook, entitled *The Real Costa Rica: Rural Community Tourism Guide*, first published in 2002 for the International Year of Ecotourism, is regularly updated and includes information on lodges, homestays, tours, and handicrafts. In recent years, similar webs of community-based ecotourism projects have become increasingly important tools for marketing small ecotourism businesses. From Montenegro in Central Europe[137] to the MesoAmerican Ecotourism Alliance[138] in Central America to the World Hotel Link that is attempting to cover the globe, [139] community ecotourism businesses are being collectively marketed on the Web.

Role of the State

Sound ecotourism, if it is to move beyond small individual projects and become a set of principles and practices on which tourism is based, will require careful planning and implementation. Within developing countries, for instance, ecotourism must become part of the country's overall development strategy. Although most countries have adopted national tourism plans, these often entail little more than sales promotion. In addition, planning is often carried out by a tourism department, without proper integration with agencies overseeing local development, conservation and the environment, and national planning. As ecotourism consultant and writer Katrina Brandon writes, "A strategy or overall plan for nature-based tourism, even in countries where the revenues from such tourism are high, is usually nonexistent."[140]

Whereas in the past, governments in socialist and communist countries such as the Soviet Union, eastern and central Europe, China, Vietnam, Tanzania, and Cuba owned, operated, and profited from their tourism industries, today the state is typically consigned to activities that do not generate income: setting broad tourism policies; carrying out overseas marketing and promotion; educating and training a workforce for the tourism sector (guides, interpreters, hotel staff and managers, drivers, etc.); establishing and maintaining the natural attractions (national parks and reserves, marine areas, waterfalls, mountaintops, forests, and other resources) on which tourism is based; putting in infrastructure such as airports, roads, electricity, ports, and waste and sewage treatment systems; and facilitating the entry of private, often foreign, capital, often by offering generous tax breaks and other enticements.

Government revenue is generated mainly through tourism-related taxes, including hotel, restaurant, entertainment, sales, and, increasingly, airport departure taxes. The level and types of taxes impact both government coffers and policies. In addition, governments are frequently faced with having to choose among different types of tourism and to decide how much support to provide in areas such as infrastructure, training, permits, taxes, and incentives. In recent years, the cruise industry has grown enormously, moving into a number of countries where ecotourism has been dominant (as discussed in chapter 2 in the case of Belize).

Another area where governments have had to make critical policy decisions is around park entrance fees. Over the last two decades, a growing number of countries have moved to implement tiered park entrance schemes, which charge nonresidents considerably higher fees for visiting national parks and reserves. While raising park fees for foreign visitors has often increased revenue, there has been a push to keep more tourism dollars at the local level in order to better protect the most popular parks and channel a percentage of revenues to nearby communities. By the late 1990s, Kenya, Rwanda, Nepal, Thailand, Mexico, Ecuador, and Costa Rica were all generating substantial foreign exchange from tiered park entrance fees. Several parks—Amboseli National Park in Kenya, Annapurna Conservation Area in Nepal,

Monarch Butterfly Overwintering Reserves in Mexico, and the Ranomafana National Park in Madagascar—were sharing a proportion of the gate fees with local people. Ranomafana, in fact, began giving half of its revenues for local community development.[141] After a hard-fought contest, the Ecuadorian government finally passed the Special Law for the Galapagos, which agreed to retain 30 percent of entrance fees to the islands for the local town councils and 40 percent for the Galapagos National Parks Service. (See chapter 4.)

Within the field of ecotourism there is much facile talk about a "public-private partnership," but finding an equitable balance between the public and private sectors remains one of the unsolved challenges. In many countries, the market, not the state, is the main vehicle for redistribution of tourism profits. The private sector, including businesses involved in ecotourism, typically opposes new and higher taxes and seeks less regulation, yet it demands that the government provide well-trained workers, good infrastructure, and pristine, well-run national parks.

Even where tourism and ecotourism have grown enormously, the percentage of profits going into central government treasuries has frequently diminished as states have divested their ownership in tourism facilities and more tax revenue is retained locally. This has contributed to cutbacks in funding for national parks, public education and health care, and other environmentally and socially vital development programs. In addition, many international organizations and aid agencies have shifted their funding toward the private sector, including to private parks and reserves. Taken together, these factors mean that national governments in developing countries typically have less authority and resources for careful planning of their tourism-related economic activities and development strategies.

Leakage

One of the promises held out by ecotourism proponents is that the portion of the profits retained within the Third World will be substantially greater, and the environmental and social consequences will be far less, than with conventional tourism. For mass tourism in developing countries—prepaid tours, cruises, and all-inclusive resorts—most money generated by tourism flows out of the host country, or never even enters it. Major outflows of foreign exchange come from payments for imported goods, management fees, administrative costs, expatriate salaries, tax breaks, and import content on local purchases. The local and national economies benefit through job creation; taxes on imported goods; park entrance fees; airport, hotel, and other user taxes;

use of local hotels, transport companies, restaurants, tour operators and concessions; and the domestic content on local purchases.

However, even as ecotourism was growing rapidly in the early 1990s, economic globalization, free trade, and privatization were proving to be strong countervailing forces to the philosophy and promise of ecotourism. In Costa Rica, which by the early 1990s was the number-one overseas ecotourism destination for United States travelers, half of every tourist dollar never left the United States, and only twenty cents actually went into the local economy, according to a USAID official.[142] According to a 2001 study, the average leakage from tourism in most small developing countries was between 40 and 50 percent of gross tourism earnings, while it is only between 10 and 20 percent for most advanced and diversified developing countries.[143] The study found that much of this leakage occurs through payments to foreign-owned tour operators, airlines, and hotels, and when locally owned operators purchase imported food, drinks, and other supplies.[144] Some studies estimate this leakage to be as high as 80 to 90 percent.[145]

Mexican ecotourism expert Héctor Ceballos-Lascuráin notes that the size and style of tourism affects the amount of leakage. A study in the island of Antigua found that leakage was greater from large hotels than small ones, while another study in Bolivia found that the economic impact of unorganized "rucksack tourists" is "more than three times that of organized [or packaged group] tourists."[146] While backpackers spend less per day, they stay longer and are more likely to patronize small, locally owned facilities. Ceballos-Lascuráin concludes that such comparative analyses "could be very useful in exploring whether the economic benefits of nature-based tourism, which typically involves small-scale facilities, are greater than those of resort-based tourism."[147]

Visitors: How Many and What Kind?

Ecotourism typically implies small-scale projects and small groups of tourists, yet developing countries need to earn large amounts of foreign exchange. The fine balance between conservation and tourism development comes into question when analyzing the ecological footprint of the tourism industry. The notion of recreational "carrying capacity" was used to try and determine the number of visitors a protected area could sustainably accommodate.[148] However, the carrying capacity framework was designed to measure the biological capability of resources to sustain a given number of animals, and soon proved to be an imperfect model for measuring impacts of tourism. Although efforts have been made to limit visitor numbers in many places, including the Galápagos Islands and Costa Rica's Manuel Antonio National Park and Monteverde Cloud Forest Reserve, many scientists came to realize that the very concept of setting fixed visitor numbers is flawed. As scientist Craig MacFarland, former president of the Charles Darwin Foundation, argues, "Pure numbers are not the answer." MacFarland says that park officials and scientists in the United States, Canada, Australia, and South Africa "have all independently found the same thing: that about 90 percent of visitor management is not controlling numbers per se, it's controlling what behaviors, activities, and equipment you allow and the time of day or time of year you allow them in a particular place."[149]

In response to the shortcoming of the carrying capacity concept, George Stanky, Robert Lewis, and Frissell Sidney developed the concept of Limits of Acceptable Change (LAC) to evaluate and plan for managing recreational use in national protected areas.[150] Unlike carrying capacity, LAC differentiates between types of tourists, and sets limits based on both scientific research of the ecosystems and multistakeholder discussions and consensus about the desired goals and objectives. As ecotourism and natural resources expert John Shores writes, "A minimum-impact trekker does not have the same impact as an off-road 4WD recreationist. So we set thresholds (limits) for the amount of change a given ecosystem or habitat can absorb (acceptable change) . . . management of the ecosystems and the tourist impacts [is designed] to try to stay within those limits."[151] Today there are a number of variants on this LAC model, all designed to measure the impact of tourism. They include: Visitor Impact Management (VIM), Visitor Experience and Resource Protection (VERP), Tourism Organization Management Model (TOMM), and Recreation Opportunity Spectrum (ROS).[152]

Coupled with these different tools for measuring visitor impacts is the tension between international and domestic tourism. Many developing countries put most of their tourism resources into attracting foreign visitors, but it is increasingly apparent that domestic tourism is important for numerous reasons, including the need to build a constituency that appreciates and wants to protect national parks, local culture, and fragile ecosystems. In 1992, just after peace accords ended the decades-long civil war in El Salvador, the Salvadoran Tourism Institute began a very popular government-subsidized program of "social tourism" to enable low-income Salvadorans to visit different tourist centers in national parks.[153] In other countries, such as South Africa, where most visitors to national parks have historically been nationals, domestic tourism can be an important source of income. A central challenge, however, since the end of apartheid, is to open South Africa's parks, long the playgrounds of the white minority, to all nationals. (See chapter 9.) In addition, domestic tourism provides a cushion when, for reasons beyond a country's control, international tourism suddenly drops off, as happened during Peru's conflict with the Shining Path guerrilla movement in the 1980s, Mexico's Zapatista uprising in the 1990s, and Haiti's ongoing political and socioeconomic chaos.

Domestic tourism flourishes in many developed, "first world" countries. Japan's strong domestic tourism market—totaling 255 million overnight stays per year—is becoming a potential driving force for implementation of community-based ecotourism programs. According to a recent study, the growing Japanese domestic tourism market is seeing an increasing consumer demand for ecotourism, in part because of the recent designation of several UNESCO World Heritage Sites, as well as a growing concern about damage to cultural and natural sites. In May 2006, Japan's Ministry of the Environment launched the Ramsar Site Ecotourism Project as a means to promote public awareness of conservation and wise use of Ramsar Sites.[154] The growing numbers of Japanese visiting national parks has also led to overcrowding and a call to control tourism numbers in protected areas.

Boom and Bust

Tourism is a skittish and fickle industry: one place will be "in" for a number of years, and then another will rise to the top of the charts. Ecotourism, like tourism, frequently suffers from extraneous factors beyond its control: tsunamis, hurricanes, and other natural disasters; AIDS, malaria, and other diseases; civil wars; the volatile stock market; terrorism, hijackings, high levels of crime, and adverse media coverage. Wildlife tourism in Kenya soared after Hollywood released *Out of Africa* in the late 1980s, and then plummeted in the wake of the 1990–1991 Persian Gulf War, the embassy bombing and terrorist attack at the end of the decade, and 2007 election violence. Similarly, a murder on a golf course on St. Croix hurt tourism for a decade, and then, just as the numbers were starting to pick up, a hurricane devastated the island's port, preventing cruise ships from docking. Tourists can also become easy targets in broader political struggles, as illustrated by the killing of tourists in Egypt or their kidnapping in Colombia and Guatemala. The 9/11 terrorist attacks on the World Trade Center, together with Hurricane Katrina, crippled tourism in the United States. According to the Travel Industry Association of America (TIA), the U.S. share of worldwide travel market dropped 20 percent between 2000 and 2006, amounting to 58 million fewer visitors, 194,000 lost jobs, $94 billion in lost spending, and $15.6 billion in lost tax revenue.[155] In 2005, following the tsunami, the Thailand Tourism Council reported occupancy rates between 10 and 15 percent, down from 60 to 70 percent in the same period a year earlier.[156]

Locally based ecotourism can be less susceptible to the whims of the outside world if the communities maintain other forms of economic activity. Some of the most successful ecotourism projects are tied to scientific research stations, working farms, or fishing communities where there are several sources of income. Likewise, domestic tourism can cushion fall-offs in international visitor numbers. Moreover, some experts argue that, worldwide, tourism is more stable over the long term than are many other foreign exchange earners. Ceballos-Lascuráin contends, for instance, that "compared with other industries, which are prone to abrupt fluctuations and frequent sharp declines, tourism has seldom fallen into a serious long-term down-turn, making it seem a near recession-proof industry at the global level."[157] He finds further grounds for optimism in the fact that tourism to developing countries is growing. According to a report from the Worldwatch Institute, tourism is a principal export (foreign exchange earner) for 83 percent of developing countries, and the leading export for a third of the world's poorest countries.[158] What this broad picture misses, however, are the sharp rises and falls that can occur among Third World countries, whose economies have little cushion to withstand the shortfalls.

Travelers' Philanthropy and Voluntourism: A New Type of Development

On the positive side of the ledger has been the growth of corporate social responsibility initiatives within the tourism industry, spearheaded in many instances by ecotourism companies. A growing number of civic-minded ecotourism businesses and tourists are now part of the Travelers' Philanthropy program (run by CESD) and other projects that are providing tangible financial and material contributions to development and conservation projects in host communities where tourism occurs. These voluntary donations come from corporate earnings, visitor donations, or a combination of both. Like much else in the field of ecotourism, such giving of "time, talent or treasure" has grown from the ground up, with individual lodges and tour operators working on their own to provide resources for urgent health, educational, or environmental needs in communities around the globe. I first came upon a number of these initiatives in places as far flung as Fiji and Australia, East Africa and South Africa, Ecuador, and Costa Rica as I worked, in the late 1990s, on the first edition of this book. I was struck that many owners or managers of ecotourism companies said they began supporting local schools, health clinics, libraries, orphanages, and other community services because of their ethical beliefs. Rather than describing this as "charity" work, I think it is more accurately viewed as industry and visitor *pay back*[159] or *give back* to the often very poor communities and environments in which much tourism takes place.

Intrepid Travel, the popular Australian tour operator, has from the outset pledged 10 percent of its after-tax profit to a range of NGOs and local projects. Responsible Travel Coordinator Jane Crouch explains that the company created the Intrepid Foundation to manage and grow their support for a wide range of local NGOs and community projects involving health care, education, human rights, child welfare, and environmental and wildlife protection. These include a school for the blind in Tibet, a women's project in East Timor, and caring for domesticated and wild elephants in Thailand. All donations to the Intrepid Foundation are matched by Intrepid Travel dollar for dollar.[160] Dennis Pinto, managing director of Micato Safaris,[161] described how his family in Kenya, as the owners of this high-end East African tour company, had quietly started supporting local orphanages for children whose parents had died of AIDS. Gradually they realized that many of their guests were interested in learning about and contributing to this project, so they set up a nonprofit division, America Share,[162] which supports over a thousand children in orphanages close to Nairobi. They have also created a special travel program, "Lend a Helping Hand on Safari," which enables their travelers to spend a few days visiting Micato-sponsored homes, schools, or orphanages, and also to contribute their time working with the children in the orphanage.[163]

Tourism executive Sven Lindblad, whose company has a highly developed guest donation program supporting conservation efforts in the Galápagos and Baja California, notes that one of their "unintended" benefits is increased staff pride and commitment in the company. Lindblad Expeditions receives an average of $250 per guest in the Galápagos and has raised several million dollars for local conservation programs. This trend is borne out in survey statistics that indicate support for corporate and traveler payback. According to one survey, 46 million U.S. travelers say they prefer to choose companies that "donate part of their proceeds to charities," and another found that 31 percent of American tourists believe that companies should support the local community.[164] It is clear that Travelers' Philanthropy and similar programs constitute a new, important, and growing—but largely unrecorded—development tool that is putting probably hundreds of millions of tourism dollars into community projects in Asia, Africa, and the Americas.

But at a 2004 conference hosted by the Center on Ecotourism and Sustainable Development (CESD), David Abernethy, Stanford Professor Emeritus in Political Science, noted that there can be unintended "bad consequences" from "doing good." Abernethy suggested criteria that travel companies undertaking charitable work should consider, such as partnering with well-established local NGOs. In an effort to provide support for ecotourism businesses involved in community projects, CESD's Travelers' Philanthropy program helps raise awareness and funds via a special Web site, and is hosting another major conference in Tanzania in 2008.[165]

While Travelers' Philanthropy is focused on the support of community-based projects in and around tourism destinations, many travelers also desire to take holidays that go one step further: to donate their own time, effort, and hard work as volunteers. This movement is known as Voluntourism, and is defined by Sustainable Travel International as "a seamlessly integrated combination of voluntary service to a destination, and the best, traditional elements of travel—arts, culture, geography, history and recreation—in that destination.[166] Voluntourism vacations enable travelers to combine leisure travel with community or volunteer service and to directly interact with local residents. A California-based nonprofit, VolunTourism,[167] was created to facilitate "the unification and alignment between the world's two largest economic and social engines—respectively, the tourism industry and the nonprofit sector." VolunTourism specializes in providing information to travelers interested in incorporating various types of volunteer service into their travel plans, as well as providing guidelines and resources for tour operators, suppliers, and destinations so that they can better serve the growing demand for service-oriented travel trips.

Standards, Monitoring, and Evaluation: Growth of "Green" Certification

It is widely recognized that if ecotourism is going to move from a good concept to good practices, it must be measured against clear standards. Today the topic of setting standards and measuring impacts is one of the most fertile within ecotourism circles. The 1992 Rio Earth Summit provided impetus for a variety of efforts to set environmental standards through voluntary compliance, governmental regulation, and international agreements and treaties. In this mix of reforms and regulations, certification is increasingly viewed as an important tool for ensuring sustainability. In the decade between the Earth Summit and the International Year of Ecotourism, there was a "flowering" of "green" tourism certification programs. Today (as discussed in chapters 2 and 10), there are some 60 to 80 "green" tourism certification programs, with more in development. A few are global, most importantly Green Globe, but most cover one country or region. This makes sense since tourism is typically organized and marketed on a national basis.

Certification—as voluntary, third-party, multi-stakeholder programs that award logos based on environmental, economic, and social criteria—is a tool uniquely suited to our times. As academics Gary Gereffi, Ronie Garcia-Johnson, and Erika Sasser argue, "While certification will never replace the state, it is quickly becoming a powerful tool for promoting worker [host country, and local community] rights and protecting the environment in an era of free trade." They conclude that certification programs, as a "voluntary governance mechanism," are "transforming traditional power relationships in the global arena."[168] And as Michael Conroy writes in *Branded!*, in which he traces the history of certification initiatives in a range of industries: "The certification revolution has shown remarkable success in creating the conditions that help transform corporate practices towards greater social and environmental accountability."[169] The 2002 Quebec Declaration on Ecotourism acknowledged the importance of certification, calling on governments to "use internationally approved and reviewed guidelines to develop certification schemes, eco-labels and other voluntary initiatives geared towards sustainability in ecotourism."[170]

While there is much room for optimism, much needs to be done to build "green" tourism certification into a real tool for environmental and social protection. One question of concern has been whether, under the UN World Trade Organization and other international trade agreements, certification would be viewed as a barrier to trade and therefore ruled illegal. Stanford University law professor Barton (Buzz) Thompson undertook to study this question and, after reviewing various legal cases brought in connection with the WTO, GATT, GATS, NAFTA, and CAFTA, he concluded that voluntary tourism certification is not likely to violate trade agreements. His findings suggest that as long as certification programs are internationally recognized or comply with generally accepted international criteria, there are unlikely to be serious problems. The areas where tourism certification programs might have difficulty are where there are government incentives for local purchasing, hiring, or ownership of businesses seeking certification. As long as all businesses seeking certification are treated equally, Thompson concluded that certification programs do not violate trade agreements.

Another major challenge has been to standardize "green" tourism certification programs so that, as tourists move from one country to another, they can be sure that the eco-labels conform to common standards. The current crop of tourism certification programs is spread unevenly around the world, with some areas—Europe—having too many programs while large stretches of Africa and Asia have no "green" tourism certification programs. In addition, these programs do not conform to a uniform set of criteria or protocols. It is widely recognized that "green" tourism certification needs to become as widespread and standardized as the five-star quality and service certification programs. This requires creating a global accreditation body or "stewardship council" for tourism to, as the Rainforest Alliance explains, "assess and help standardize" sustainable tourism certification programs and to help with "functions such as marketing, training and development."[171] This process began in 2000, when forty-five tourism certification experts from twenty countries met at Mohonk Mountain House outside New York City and drew up "The Mohonk Agreement," a document that contained a proposed framework for sustainable and ecotourism certification programs.[172] This workshop also endorsed a proposal that the Rainforest Alliance take the lead in carrying out a feasibility study for a global accreditation body. The Rainforest Alliance's tourism department, headed by Ronald Sanabria and based in Costa Rica, undertook a multi-year project to hammer out answers to a range of issues and to develop a business plan for creating a new accreditation system. By 2008, this enormous effort to launch the Sustainable Tourism Stewardship Council was on the cusp of reality.[173]

Ecotourism in Its National Context

As I have investigated ecotourism and grappled with the foregoing issues and others, as well as the twin trajectories of real ecotourism and ecotourism lite, it became clear that these phenomena must be examined within their particular national settings and historical contexts. For this reason, I decided to study the growth of ecotourism on a country-by-country basis in order to fully understand the constraints on it and its possibilities of success. Just as conservationists and biologists have come to believe that individual species must be studied within their ecosystems, ecotourism must not be analyzed as an isolated phenomenon. Rather, it must be seen as part of the political economy and development strategy of each particular country. As Desmond de Sousa, former executive secretary of the Ecumenical Coalition on Third World Tourism, put it, "Tourism development is not isolated from, but rather an aspect of, the development process. So the tourism debate has to be situated within the development debate itself."[174]

My search for ecotourism entailed journeys through developing countries in the Americas and Africa as well as briefer forays to many other countries and international conferences. Since 2003, I have been running NGOs dedicated to strengthening the principles and practices of ecotourism and have had an opportunity to visit many parts of the world. The countries I examine here—Costa Rica, Ecuador's Galapagos Islands, Kenya, South Africa, and Tanzania and Zanzibar—are all promoting ecotourism as a key component of their development strategies. In the first edition of this book, I also examined Cuba, a country with a small and fascinating ecotourism sector and a vigorous but not very visible debate about whether tourism was a sound development tool in the post-Soviet era. As I began preparing this edition, Cuba had become highly unstable: Fidel Castro was beginning to step down, and the island's future economic and political course was uncertain. It did not seem possible at this time to do a credible evaluation of ecotourism. Indeed, my colleague Emma Stewart had a very challenging time completing research for her thesis on sustainable tourism in Cuba. So I decided to drop Cuba and to add instead a chapter on ecotourism in the United States. In September 2005, I and others at TIES organized the first-ever conference on ecotourism in the United States. Held in Bar Harbor, Maine, it brought together three hundred people from across the country to examine various aspects of ecotourism. We collected case studies, issued the Bar Harbor Declaration, and pledged to hold the North American ecotourism conference (to include Canada), held in September 2007 in Madison, Wisconsin.

The chapters that follow examine how the principles underlying ecotourism are being played out in these seven locations and propose an "ecotourism scorecard" for each. Each of the countries included here followed different routes toward ecotourism. Until the mid-1980s, the socialist governments in Tanzania and Zanzibar—like Cuba under Fidel—largely financed and conducted tourism with the aim of using the profits for social programs. At the other end of the political spectrum, the apartheid government in South Africa had created parks and subsidized tourism for the benefit of its privileged white minority and a trickle of white foreigners. Postcolonial Kenya has had a roughshod brand of capitalism, laced with corruption and political patronage. Costa Rica and Ecuador (including the Galapagos Islands) have outstanding national park systems and mixed economies, with the governments playing an active but diminishing role in regulating their economies and social welfare programs. Costa Rica, the Galapagos Islands, Tanzania and Kenya are among the most popular ecotourism destinations in the world. Postapartheid South Africa—like post-Soviet Cuba—has pushed international tourism as a main engine of growth and integration into the global economy, and has used nature-based tourism as a tool for poverty alleviation. The United States, while ranking first globally in international tourist receipts and third in international tourist arrivals,[175] has never been known as an ecotourism destination. Ecotourism began on our periphery—in Alaska, Hawaii, and the Virgin Islands—and only recently is it taking off in the lower forty-eight. Since little has been written on ecotourism within the United States, it seemed appropriate to give it a serious look and dedicate the final chapter in the volume to the state of ecotourism in this country.

Part 2
Nation Studies

4

The Galapagos Islands: Test Site for Theories of Evolution and Ecotourism

Standing on top of a sand dune, naturalist guide Jorge Marino gives his spiel to a small group of tourists. Sea lions lounge like huge gray rocks on the powder-white beach. On a branch of a low-flowering shrub, a yellow warbler sings; just three feet away, several people snap its photograph. Like all creatures on the Galapagos Islands, the warbler and the sea lions seem oblivious to the human spectators. Here, as nowhere else in the world, people can get within feet, sometimes inches, of sea lions, marine iguanas, giant tortoises, tropical penguins, songbirds, and unique birds such as the blue-footed booby, the flightless cormorant, the waved albatross, and thirteen kinds of Darwin's finches.

The Galapagos, originally known as the Enchanted Isles,[1] is often cited as the place where ecotourism originated. As one leading guidebook puts it, "Tourists from Europe started coming to [Ecuador's] Galapagos Islands more than 150 years ago. They may have called themselves sailors, scientists or adventurers, but in many ways they walked like, talked like, and looked like ecotourists."[2] This archipelago is universally viewed as one of the most unusual and precious ecosystems on earth.[3] Half the birds, half of the insects, a third of the plants, and all the reptiles are endemic to Galapagos and are found nowhere else on the planet.[4]

Since the 1960s, scientific research, sound park management, well-trained naturalist guides, and a fairly well-regulated and responsible nature tourism industry have helped ensure that the wildlife of the Galapagos has been little disturbed by the steep rise in visitors. But

Roslyn Cameron, development manager at the Charles Darwin Research Station (CDRS) in the Galapagos, supplied updates for this chapter.

since the late 1980s, the Galapagos Islands have had to cope with a variety of complex problems—new immigrants, introduced species, industrial fishing, unemployment, and conflicts between development interests and park management—that have come in the wake of the ecotourism boom. Despite passage in 1998 of the Special Law for the Galapagos, an historic piece of environmental legislation hammered out through years of contentious debate, the number of people living in the Galapagos and tourism visitation rates have more than doubled over the last ten years. New immigrants also reinforce a frontier mentality, bringing a culture based on resource extraction, low awareness about the Galapagos ecosystem, and strong external alliances. Commercial fishing, while legally restricted to fewer than a thousand local artisanal fishers, continues to grow, with serious environmental consequences.

In this fragile natural and political environment, ecotourism is widely recognized as the only viable commercial activity capable of both protecting the resource base and providing sustainable livelihoods. Yet ecotourism has also brought in its wake a complex set of crosscurrents. Ecotourism earnings can support conservation efforts, scientific research, and park management. Ecotourism educates visitors and builds national awareness of the significance of the archipelago. On the other hand, ecotourism has also precipitated immigration, increased pressures on the ecosystem and civic infrastructures, and raised the risk of introduced alien species, a principle threat to endemic species. The influx of capital from ecotourism transformed the Galapagos economy and complicated efforts at regulation.[5] Today there are sobering signs that the Galapagos is losing its reputation as the world's oldest and finest ecotourism destination.

History

Located some six hundred miles off Ecuador's coast, the Galapagos Islands are a cluster of some 120 volcanic islands. Their biological significance was first recognized in 1835, when Charles Darwin, a young British aristocrat with a love of biology, stopped there while sailing around the world on the HMS *Beagle* as part of a five-year British expedition. Darwin spent just five weeks on the islands, but his observations there changed the course of Western scientific thought. Darwin noted two important phenomena: that the wildlife, with no natural predators, were unusually "tame," and that many of the islands had developed their own unique species of animals, birds, and plants. As Darwin recorded in his journal:

> [B]y far the most remarkable feature in the natural history of this archipelago . . . is that the different islands to a considerable extent are inhabited by a different set of beings. . . . I never dreamed that islands, about fifty or sixty miles apart, and most of them in sight of each other, formed of precisely the same rocks, placed under a quite similar climate, rising to a nearly equal height, would have been differently tenanted . . . [with] their own species of the tortoise, mocking-thrush, finches, and numerous plants.[6]

It is an irony of history that these idyllic islands, frequently described as a "Garden of Eden" or "peaceable kingdom," became the fountainhead for creationism's most serious challenge: the theory of evolution. In *On the Origin of Species by Means of Natural Selection*, published in 1859, Darwin outlined his theory of evolution by natural selection—that all living creatures adapt to and evolve in accordance with their environment—based in significant part on observations made in the Galapagos.

Darwin's work put the Galapagos Islands on the map. As writer Kurt Vonnegut noted in his science fiction novel, *Galapagos*, "Darwin did not change the islands, only people's opinion of them."[7] For several centuries, a trickle of adventurers, naturalists, utopia seekers, aristocratic travelers, pirates, shipwrecked sailors, and ne'er-do-wells had sailed through and sometimes settled on the islands. By the beginning of the nineteenth century, the archipelago, in particular Floreana Island (also known as Santa María Island or Charles Island) with its freshwater and its plentiful supply of tortoises, had become a favorite resting spot for passing whaling ships. Floreana also became the site of South America's first post office, a wooden barrel just off the beach (still functioning today) where crews on outbound whalers, whose voyages lasted as long as two years, would drop mail in the barrel; sailors on homebound ships would collect the letters and, eventually, deliver them.

By the time Darwin arrived, the islands had in fact already begun experiencing the negative effects of human presence. Passing ships and the tiny permanent settlements on several islands had introduced into the archipelago rats, cats, pigs, goats, and other animals highly destructive to the local flora and fauna. Whaling vessels collected for fresh meat hundreds of thousands of Galapagos giant tortoises, which they piled upside down (alive) in the holds of their ships. The whalers had decimated the tortoise population before the 1860s, when (fortuitously for both whales and tortoises) the bottom fell out of the whaling industry. However, much damage had already been done, and one species of tortoise, the endemic Floreana species (*Geochelone galapagoensis*), was extinct by the turn of the twentieth century.

Only gradually were steps taken toward conservation and rehabilitation, and the destructive trends were slowly reversed. In 1935, to mark the centennial of Darwin's visit, the Ecuadorian government passed legislation to protect the islands' wildlife and declared several uninhabited islands as protected areas.[8] But the legislation was not enforced and serious conservation efforts did not begin until the 1950s, when scientists investigating the islands for the International Union for the Conservation of Nature (IUCN) and UNESCO recommended "the setting aside of nearly all undeveloped land as an inviolate nature sanctuary . . . and establishing an international science station to study the wildlife."[9] In 1959, to commemorate the hundredth anniversary of the publication of Darwin's *Origin of Species*, Ecuador declared 97 percent of the islands a national park and restricted human habitation to the remaining 3 percent of the islands where settlements were already established. By then, scientists say, most of the twenty endemic species and subspecies of reptiles, mammals, and plants known to have disappeared since people first arrived in the archipelago had already become extinct.[10]

In 1959, the Charles Darwin Foundation for the Galapagos Islands (CDF) was created under the auspices of UNESCO and the IUCN and by 1964, the CDF's operational arm, the Charles Darwin Research Station (CDRS), was built and began carrying out research in the islands. In 1979, the landmass of the islands was designated a UNESCO World Heritage Site, and in 1986, the Ecuadorian government declared approximately seventy thousand square kilometers (twenty-seven thousand square miles) of ocean a marine reserve intended to protect the waters within the archipelago and a zone of fifteen nautical miles around the islands. Then, in 1998, a piece of environmental legislation known as the Special Law extended the marine reserve to cover all waters within forty miles of the coast of the Galapagos Islands. In 2001, UNESCO granted World Heritage status to this gigantic marine reserve, which covers 138,000 square kilometers or 53,200 square miles.[11] But despite these positive steps at setting a legal framework for protection, the Galapagos remains at risk. In June 2007, UNESCO added the Galapagos to the list of "World Heritage in Danger" sites, noting specifically the negative effects brought by the sizeable growth of tourism, which had grown from 41,000 in 1990 to 145,000 in 2006.[12]

Over the decades, the government-run Galapagos National Park Service (GNPS) and internationally funded CDRS, located next to each other on Santa Cruz Island just outside the main town, Puerto Ayora, have maintained a symbiotic relationship in scientific research, protection, and educational programs. The breeding of captive endangered tortoises and land iguanas and reintroduction to their native islands has aided in the recovery of species on the brink of extinction. The extraordinary biodiversity of the islands is highly susceptible to a number of forces, including introduced species, overharvesting of limited resources, natural and manmade disasters, and climate change. To date, biodiversity in the Galapagos has survived well, but the long-term future of the biodiversity of the islands may well depend on decisions about sustainable development that are made during the next few years.

The Ecotourism Boom

Until recently, the islands' remoteness helped preserve the Galapagos as a unique living laboratory for observing evolution. Before the 1970s, the only "public" transportation to the islands was aboard infrequent and uncomfortable cargo ships from Ecuador's main port, Guayaquil. David Balfour, honorary British counsel and director of Metropolitan Touring's operations office on the Galapagos, recalls that when he first arrived, in 1969, "Tourism had not really started. Cargo ships were coming every three months or so, bringing groups of visitors." Numbers grew only after an old U.S. military base on the island of Baltra[13] was refurbished and regular commercial air links were established. Gradually, a tourism infrastructure within the islands began to be built.

Organized ecotourism began in the late 1960s, when two Ecuadorian companies headquartered in Quito, Metropolitan Touring and Turismundial, joined with a New York company, Lindblad Travel (later taken over by Lindblad Expeditions, which was a division of Lindblad Travel). The first cruise ship, the *Lina A*, which could carry fifty-eight passengers, arrived in the islands in 1969, marking the official start of organized ecotourism.[14] Balfour says that Metropolitan Touring began by doing "a feasibility study, especially from the point of view of conservation. Tourism was done in close conjunction with the CDRS and the new national park service. It was pioneering work. The notes that we still publish and hand out to passengers about how they should conduct themselves were put out right at the start of our operations. So there was a close link between tour operations, scientists, and the national park."

During the early 1970s, tourism facilities grew slowly: about five small boats occasionally carried tourists on day trips, and Puerto Ayora had one "luxury" hotel with green, shaded lawns and individual bungalows, three other smaller hotels, and a few restaurants. Then, between 1974 and 1980, tourism picked up (see table 4.1), and the number of vessels increased from thirteen to forty-two. As the industry expanded, ownership shifted: in the early and mid-1970s, with the exception of Metropolitan Touring's two boats, the "floating hotels" were owned by long-term island residents, most of whom lacked the capital and the foreign-language and marketing skills required to do business on an international scale. Adding to this obstacle was the lack of basic banking and telecommunications facilities on the islands. However, by 1982, about six tour agents from mainland Ecuador wholly or partially owned more than a dozen intermediate-size vessels catering to foreigners, but only Metropolitan maintained a full-time operations office on the Galapagos.

During the 1980s, as the ecotourism explosion began to bring world attention and new funds to the Galapagos, it also strained the islands' ecosystem and their resident human population. As one study put it, "Tourism . . . is the driving force which, directly and indirectly, dictates the pace and types of changes that are occurring in the islands."[15] Since 1979, the number of tourists has increased more than tenfold, facilitated by a second airport on San Cristóbal Island and extra flights daily to Baltra Island. Since the late 1980s, there have been worrisome tendencies toward both poorly done ecotourism and expansion of conventional tourism, as well as uncontrolled immigration and commercial fishing. In the Galapagos, more than almost anywhere else in the world, the only viable commercial activity is high-quality, limited, and carefully monitored ecotourism. This, combined with the key components of the 1998 Special Law, which aims to carefully regulate immigration and fishing, holds out a possibility of protecting the fragile environment and striking an equilibrium with the local population. However, if ecotourism and the collateral problems it has spawned, such as increased immigration and introduced species, are not carefully managed, the ecosystem of the Galapagos will be pushed to the point of no return. Finding the right balance is difficult. As Graham Watkins, executive director of the Charles Darwin Foundation, told the *New York Times* in early 2008, "What we have here is an unsustainable model of development."[16]

Current Tourism Trends in the Galapagos

Gradually, two competing tendencies developed in the Galapagos's nature-based tourism industry: toward low-budget, higher-volume, conventional sun-, beach-, and land-based tourism via on-land hotels and day boats; and toward upscale, lower-density ecotourism aboard comfortable tour boats or floating hotels, which have, at least in principle, less direct effect on the ecosystem. Whereas the first type of

Table 4.1.
The Galapagos Islands' Tourism Growth: Visitors to Galapagos National Park (in Thousands)

Year	*1972*	*1975*	*1979*	*1985*	*1990*	*1993*	*1996*	*2000*	*2004*	*2005*
Foreigners	6.7	7	10	12	26	37	46	54	75	86
Nationals	0.1	0	2	6	15	10	16	14	33	35
Total	6.8	7	12	18	41	47	62	68	108	121

Source: Bruce Epler, *An Economic and Social Analysis of Tourism in the Galapagos Islands* (Providence: University of Rhode Island, Coastal Resources Center, 1991), 3, 15; "Tabla 1: Visitantes al Parque Nacional Galapagos entre 1979 y 2004," obtained from the Charles Darwin Foundation; José Rodriguez Rojas, "Las islas Galapagos: Estructura geográfica y propuesta de gestión territorial," (Cayambe, Ecuador: Talleres Abya-Yala, 1993), 107; George Wallace, "Visitor Management in Galapagos National Park," draft (Fort Collins, Colo.: College of Natural Resources, Colorado State University, January 1992), 1; Telephone conversation with Katty Gallardo, Tourism Department, Galapagos National Park, September 27, 2006.

tourism is dominated by local Galapagos residents, and serves primarily Ecuadorians, the second is controlled primarily by foreigners and wealthy Ecuadorians, and caters mainly to foreigners. Each type—the day boats and floating hotels—"brings in its wake a different set of direct and indirect environmental and social impacts and produces important economic effects that require significant management investment by local and national authorities and other institutions," says Conservation International's Scott Henderson.[17]

As Ecuador adopted free-market and structural adjustment polices in the mid-1980s and ecotourism became the latest buzzword within the travel industry, there was a flurry of tourism investment, producing new vessels, companies, and hotels in the archipelago. There has been talk, but fortunately no action, about building casinos and high-rise hotels. According to University of Rhode Island professor Bruce Epler, by the early 1990s, the islands' tourism industry was dominated by two mainland-based, vertically integrated inbound tour operators, Metropolitan Touring and Ecoventura, both offering high-quality ecotourism. These companies own several floating hotels, and they also conduct tours to other regions of Ecuador as well as to the Galapagos.[18] The owners of Ecoventura were also part owner of an Ecuadorian airline, SAN/Saeta, which served the islands until 2000. Ecoventura was launched in the late 1980s by Roberto Dunn after he obtained landing permission in the Galapagos for the SAN airline. Already facing competition from U.S. carriers on Miami, Quito, and Cuenca routes, Dunn concluded that he could gain a competitive advantage by diversifying into flights and tour boats in the Galapagos.[19] Over the last decade, the dominance of these original companies has been challenged by the growth of other reputable ecotourism operators, including, in addition to Lindblad Expeditions, other U.S.-based companies such as Adventure Life Journeys, Holbrook Travel, Mountain Travel Sobek, International Expeditions, and Wilderness Travel; Ecuador-based companies such as Quasar Nautica, Klein Tours, Ocean Adventures, Ecuadorian Tours, and Galamazonas; and some owned by Galapagos families, including Daphne Cruises, Enchanted Expeditions, and Angermeyer Cruises (also known as Andando Tours). By the late 1990s and into the new millennium, the islands had eighty to ninety registered yachts, motor cruisers, cruise ships, and day boats. Between 1981 and 2006, the number of tourism boats increased from 40 to 80, and their capacity grew from 597 to 1805 passengers. In 2007, eighty-four tourism boats were registered with the GNPS: seventy-nine live-aboard boats ("floating hotels") and five day-tour vessels; about 40 percent are locally owned.[20]

In recent years, tour companies and boat owners have responded to the growing international market by offering more comfort and safety, better sanitation, air-conditioning, higher-quality meals, and better-trained crews. Safety regulations were improved and annual inspections and rescue courses were instituted following the 1990 *Bartolomé* disaster. Faulty electrical wiring caused a fire and explosion aboard this tour boat, which sank, killing five passengers.[21] Several subsequent accidents prompted a group of socially and environmentally conscious foreign tour operators to create the International Galapagos Tour Operators Association (IGTOA) to work for high professional, safety, and service standards, as well as protection of the Galapagos's unique natural environment and heritage.[22]

The Galapagos has, however, continued to be plagued by occasional disasters, some linked to ecotourism. In January 2001, the Ecuadorian-flagged fuel tanker *Jessica*, carrying some 234,000 gallons of diesel and "bunker" fuel, ran aground off the town of Puerto Baquerizo Moreno on San Cristóbal Island. Within days, leaked fuel was reported to have spread across approximately one hundred square miles of water and to have reached the bays of three islands in the archipelago. The spill made news around the world, Ecuador declared a state of emergency, and hundreds of volunteers joined rescue crews struggling to stop further leakage from the vessel, clean up the spill, and save birds, iguanas, sea lions, and other wildlife. Jonathan Weiner, author of a Galapagos bird book, warned that the Galapagos "can be damaged incredibly easily—like spilling a cup of coffee on the 'Mona Lisa.'"[23] After several frantic days, fortuitous winds and strong currents shifted the direction of the spilled diesel to the northwest, where there were no major islands.

While rapid response and favorable conditions averted a major ecological disaster, the immediate costs, estimated at five hundred thousand dollars a day, and long-term financial burden to the local conservation groups was debilitating. There were also concerns that the escaped fuel would sink, destroying algae that is vital to the food chain.[24]

Fortunately, subsequent studies detected no clear effects from the oil spill, indicating that impacts on shore seaweeds, marine invertebrates, and fishes were probably slight. But the incident proved embarrassing for a leading ecotourism company and a recently initiated certification program. The bunker oil was destined for the hundred-passenger *Explorer II*, one of the largest tourism vessels and the only vessel in the archipelago using this type of cheap, heavy fuel.[25] This luxury floating hotel was owned by Canodros, a well-known Ecuadorian company and owner of the Kapawi Ecolodge, a pioneering experiment in community-based ecotourism in the Ecuadorian Amazon.[26] Built in 1990, the *Explorer II* is described by a travel trade publication as one of the finest cruise ships in the Galapagos and "its operations are adapted to ecotourism, providing superior environmental education and interpretation on the Galapagos."[27] The *Explorer II* was also one of the five original vessels granted a seal of approval under the Smart Voyager certification program, described below.[28]

In the wake of this near disaster, conservation organizations called for regulations to effectively implement the Special Law, which prohibits the transport of bunker and other toxic or high-risk materials in the marine reserve.[29] In addition, in 2005, the GNPS began implementing a new management plan that united the terrestrial and marine protected areas. The plan was based on adopting social and eco-systematic managerial concepts, with the capacity for technical and financial self-management, as outlined in the international quality certification system ISO 9000. In contrast with Smart Voyager and other "green" certification programs (discussed below), the 9000 series of ISO (International Standards Organization) contains quality management systems that lay out key objectives aimed at achieving continual improvements in environmental performance.[30]

Local residents usually do not have the capital to buy or build luxury boats; however, under the Special Law, foreign investors are required to be in partnership with permanent residents. Using existing licenses, new and bigger floating hotels are appearing every year, replacing many locally owned fishing boats.[31] Enhanced banking facilities and modern telecommunications systems in the islands now enable local operators to make direct partnerships with international travel agencies, and this has improved the local owner/operators' ability to be competitive in the international market. Under the Special Law, tour companies are required to hire locally unless they can prove that the skills they require are not available in the islands. Some companies have also financed hotel management training, including language training and service courses. When stopping at islands with human settlements, many tour boat companies now arrange for passengers to visit restaurants, private farms, and local schools. By 2006, there were 114 restaurants and bars in the Galapagos, up from just 20 in 1982.[32] Larger vessels are required to visit two ports during an eight-day/seven-night tour, and this has stimulated new ecotourism income for the communities. Tourist dollars also flow to the growing number of souvenir stores in Puerto Ayora, although many prefer to support the kiosk at the Charles Darwin Research Station, whose profits go to support Galapagos scholarships and conservation programs.

The Galapagos also attracts a sizeable number of domestic visitors, a positive development that both boosts the economy and builds national support for conservation of the archipelago. Whereas elsewhere in the world, the percentage of domestic tourists has tended to decline in relation to international tourism, on the Galapagos the number of Ecuadorian visitors increased from less than 15 percent in the late 1970s to 40 percent by 1985 and has since stabilized at 25 to 30 percent. Local currency devaluations in the 1980s made the Galapagos affordable for many Ecuadorians, and, much earlier than in other countries, nationals began receiving deep discounts on airline flights, park entrance fees, and day-tour boats. On the mainland, nationals are offered special discount packages to visit the Galapagos. National tourists pay a park entrance fee of just six dollars, compared to one hundred dollars for foreigners, and airline tickets costs less than a third for Galapagos residents and about half for mainland residents compared with international visitors.[33] Most Ecuadorian visitors stay in land-based hotels in Puerto Ayora or Puerto Baquerizo Moreno (the archipelago's political capital, located on San Cristóbal), and use day boats to visit national park sites on other islands. Between 1982 and 2006, the number of on-land hotels increased from 18 to 65, and their capacity grew from 214 to 1,668 rooms; they in fact increased much faster (nearly 8-fold) than the number of berths in floating hotels.[34] As these facilities have grown and improved, a new, higher-end foreign visitor, often only staying a weekend, is starting to appear.[35] A 2000 study found that foreigners were spending on average 3.5 times more than Ecuadorians ($3,676 and $932 per person, respectively) to tour the Galapagos, but that a far greater percentage of the money spent by nationals stays in the local economy. While foreign visitors outnumber domestic tourists almost four to one (fifty-four thousand compared to fourteen thousand in

2000), the study found that just 15.1 percent of the foreign expenditures stayed in the Galapagos local economy, compared to 95.2 percent of the money spent by Ecuadorians.[36]

The reason for this is that the day boats are locally constructed of wood, locally owned and crewed by island residents, and supplied mainly with local provisions. Day boats are closely linked to the on-land hotels, which also are usually locally owned; it is common for a tour operator to own both a hotel and a day boat.[37] However, the number of day boats has been shrinking. While there were sixteen in 1991 capable of accommodating two hundred passengers, by 2007, there were only five that could accommodate ninety-two passengers.[38]

Many old hotels are being torn down and replaced by large multi-story hotels.[39] Campaigns to encourage national visitors have been designed to increase the occupation rate, which has hovered around 30 percent, compared to over 80 percent of the floating hotels.[40] After 1993, Santa Cruz placed a moratorium on new hotel construction, and the 1998 Special Law prohibited the further development of hotels on all islands except Isabela. Despite this, housing and other commercial developments, including hotel renovation and expansion, have continued at an unrelenting pace, with urban areas now zoned for commercial, multi-story buildings, and suburban areas expanding to the very borders of the park. Epler concluded that "if the social well-being of the local population is a consideration, day boats and small hotels produce a wider stream of benefits to a poorer segment of society."[41] Once considered by mainland Ecuadorians as a place of hardship and deprivation, the islands now have a reputation as an area of privilege and relatively easy living, with higher incomes and better social services than other provinces.[42]

Although domestic tourism to the Galapagos can be important in putting money into the local economy and helping to build a national constituency committed to conservation and protection of the islands, it has a downside. One problem, notes David Blanton, the long-time head of IGTOA, is safety. "Some smaller operators cut corners, or simply do not follow proper safety procedures," says Blanton. "This has resulted in boats sinking, some with loss of life. This poses a more serious risk for the budget traveler, who often books the least-expensive boat, not knowing that safety or health is being compromised. Although the boats in this category are few, little has been done by the government control unsafe practices or to sanction violators."[43]

Tourism services—both boat and on-land—provide an estimated 71 percent of the "gross island product" and generate one-third of all tourism revenues earned by the Ecuadorian government. The islands raise more money from tourism than any other place in Ecuador,[44] and in recent years there has been much debate over how to keep more of the profits on the islands for the benefit of both the park and the local community. Both airlines and floating hotel vessels spend very little on the islands; most of the profits go off-island. The inequalities in distribution were apparent as early as 1993, when a study by Epler found that roughly 85 percent ($27.5 million) was paid to vessels and airlines and a mere 3 percent each went for on-land hotels and park entrance fees. Epler also found that 92 percent of the tourist dollar was spent on floating hotels, and only 8 percent on day boats and land-based hotels. Further, the multiplier effect of this money was found to be "exceptionally low" because "market linkages" between local farmers, cattle ranchers, fishers, and the floating hotels are "virtually nonexistent": most food and other supplies are imported, and families of crew members live on the mainland.[45] Though the amount and steady supply of produce required by the floating hotels is often difficult for local producers to meet, several companies, such as Lindblad Expeditions, buy from fishers and farmers, as well as products from a cooperative run by the wives of fishermen.[46] Overall, however, agriculture in the islands has experienced a recession and farm area declined between 1986 and 2000, as farming is no longer able to compete with earnings from other occupations.[47]

The 1998 Special Law for the Galapagos: A Victory for Conservation and the Community

"If there's one place in the world where we should draw a line in the sand, it's the Galapagos," a U.S. scientist told *Time* magazine in late 1995.[48] In February 1994, Ecuadorian television had showed shocking footage of large, clandestine encampments of *pepineros* (sea cucumber fishers, derived from *pepino*, the Spanish word for cucumber) on Isabela and Fernandina islands. Scores of Ecuadorian fishers were diving into the shallow waters and collecting tens of thousands of sea cucumbers per day. It was an industrial-style operation that involved cooking and drying the foot-long, light brown, sea cucumbers. Garbage and empty cans littered the site, and the fishers were shown bringing fresh food and other products onshore. They were also cutting for firewood the tall mangrove forests, which, according to a study by the Charles Darwin Foundation, provide "the only habitat for the rarest species of Darwin's finch, the tool-using Mangrove Finch. Cutting those heretofore undisturbed forests directly endangers that bird species."[49] Denouncing "these types of 'gold rush' fisheries," the foundation reported that by 1995, every suitable beach and cove—more than five hundred separate localities—had been used by illegal fishers.[50] From the Galapagos, the dried sea cucumbers and some sea horses were being clandestinely exported to Asian markets, sometimes via the United States.

Most often, it is the naturalist guides, tour boat operators, scientists, and park officials who discover the illegal encampments. Dive guides reported finding longlines and nets with dead sharks, sea lions, and turtles attached to them, as well as live, but dying, sharks, including whale sharks, without their dorsal fins on the beaches and in shallow waters. This, in turn, has led fishing interests to launch verbal and physical attacks on the central government, park service, and research station. In the mid-1990s, one of the original instigators of the illegal sea cucumber trade was Puerto Ayora businessman Luis Copiano, manager of the Coca-Cola distributorship on the Galapagos. Copiano admitted he had been involved in collecting and exporting sea cucumbers, and he blamed the antifishers bias of the central government, park service, research station, and scientists for the closure of his fishing camps: "I don't know why they are against fishermen here in the Galapagos. They have no right to come here from nowhere, giving orders from a desk, from Quito, to the people living here, born here. I believe that's crazy." Copiano was, in fact, a recent arrival from the port city of Guayaquil, where he was linked to illegal commercial fishing operations tied to the Asian market.[51]

Shortly after the illegal camps were exposed, park guards and tour guides discovered the carcasses of eighty-one butchered giant tortoises at five sites on Isabela Island.[52] Fishers were widely suspected to have been behind the slaughter. In another incident, in April 1994, an enormous fire started on Isabela, probably accidentally when a campfire was not properly extinguished.[53] It burned for months, destroying more than 4,500 hectares (11,100 acres).[54] Personnel from the research station and park officials mounted a rescue mission, using two Ecuadorian army helicopters to airlift ten tortoises from the fire areas to a breeding center in Puerto Villamil, on Isabela.[55]

Meanwhile the Ecuadorian government was divided over how to handle the sea cucumber situation, with the Ministry of Industry and Fisheries and the Galapagos Islands member of Congress, Eduardo Véliz, favoring, and the GNPS and Ministry of Agriculture (together with the tourism industry, scientists, and research station) opposing, commercial collection. Eventually, a compromise was struck: it was agreed that for a three-month period, beginning October 15, 1994, fishers could harvest no more than 550,000 sea cucumbers. The experiment was disastrous. No effective controls or enforcement were put in place; even before the trial period had elapsed, the Charles Darwin Foundation estimated that 6 to 10 million sea cucumbers, along with a wide variety of other valuable species, including sea horses, were harvested. According to *Time* magazine, there were also reports "that boats coming to collect the sea cucumbers arrive with prostitutes and drugs from the mainland, and some prostitutes are said to be paid in bags of sea cucumbers, which they later trade for cash."[56]

When the government announced it was closing the fishing season in December 1994, a month early, the conflict quickly escalated. On the morning of January 3, 1995, a group of *pepineros*, some masked and wielding machetes and clubs, blockaded the road to the national park headquarters and research station outside Puerto Ayora. For four days, forty or more *pepineros* occupied the park and blockaded the research station headquarters, harassing scientists, threatening to kill the tortoises, and forcing staff members to stay inside the buildings. "In effect," the Charles Darwin Foundation announced in an emergency bulletin, "the two institutions, their staffs, the facilities, and the breeding groups of tortoises and land iguanas are being held hostage."[57] The siege ended after the government flew in military troops and representatives of the fisheries authority to negotiate.

Next, congressman Véliz managed to push through the National Congress in Quito a law giving the islands near-autonomy in setting the rules for tourism and development. The populist bill had something for everyone: it doubled the salaries of public employees, required charter boat itineraries to include one night in a shore hotel, and put the national park under the control of a new bureaucracy, a provincial council. In September 1995, when Ecuador's president vetoed the legislation, Véliz led a militant three-week strike during which dozens of protestors blockaded and closed down the airport on San Cristóbal, blocked off the road from the main Baltra airport, and again occupied the GNPS buildings and Charles Darwin Research Station. The then-Station director Chantal Blanton hid out in the bush one night, while San Cristóbal Mayor Milton Aguas, with an aggressive but relatively small portion of the Galapagos population, numbering a few hundred, threatened over the radio "to kidnap tourists and if necessary burn any area of the national park."[58]

Needless to say, tourists on the Galapagos fled, and many others canceled their reservations. IGTOA estimated that reservations dropped by 15 percent, thus making, according to tour operator Andy Drumm, "a bad year even worse."[59] In response, local people organized another group, the Committee for Peace and Well-being in the Galapagos, and the strike was finally called off in exchange for the president's pledge to set up a commission, including local residents, to draft a new Special Law for the conservation of the Galapagos. In March 1997, after sea cucumber harvesters who were illegally encamped on Isabela shot and severely wounded a park guard and masked men again attacked park headquarters and held officials hostage, more than three hundred people from the local fishing cooperatives, labor unions, municipality, civic organizations, tour boat companies, and research station marched through Puerto Ayora in a show of solidarity with the GNPS and a protest against violence and vandalism.[60]

The international community also weighed in with its concern over the political turmoil and deteriorating environmental conditions on the Galapagos. In December 1996, UNESCO's World Heritage Committee warned that the Galapagos would be designated a "World Heritage Site in Danger" if the Ecuadorian government did not adopt effective conservation measures. The government and the Galapagos Islands' tourism sector vigorously opposed this classification, fearing it would hurt Ecuador's international image and tourism industry. As Ximena Flores, leader of a group of Galapagos women working in tourism, put it, "Such a classification would have a direct repercussion on the economic prospects of our families, the islands, and the entire country."[61] At the same time, the government recognized that if it appeared recalcitrant, international organizations were likely to withhold funding for the Galapagos.

In April 1997, the president of Ecuador at last signed the Galapagos Decree, recognizing conservation of the archipelago as a national priority and listing a number of intended government reforms for controlling immigration, fishing, and introduced species. In May, the government set up for the first time a process of consultation and negotiation led by the Permanent Galapagos Commission and assisted by trained facilitators. The commission was composed of representatives from conservation groups, the tourism industry, and various social sectors, including industrialists, environmental authorities, and representatives from national and international organizations.

But while what was dubbed the Galapagos Consensus was evolving on the islands, opponents of the law were busy lobbying the central government in Quito. In mid-November 1997, a vote was blocked by influential politicians, businessmen, and representatives of the Ecuadorian industrial fishing industry who wanted local control, open access to the marine reserve, and more liberal residence policies.[62] In January 1998, Ecuador's single-chamber Congress countered by passing the law, but in March, Ecuador's interim president issued a partial veto and proposed an alternative clause that would permit some industrial fishing within the marine reserve. The momentum, however, was shifting toward conservation. In early March 1998, while demonstrators dressed in black carried coffins through the streets on the Galapagos in a "march to mourn the archipelago," Congress again approved "The Special Law for the Conservation and Sustainable Development of Galapagos Province" (known simply as the Special Law), thereby overturning the presidential veto.[63]

The Special Law, a complex set of some eighty articles, was a strong piece of environmental legislation that also provided support for residents of the Galapagos. It sought to stabilize the islands' population by stipulating that only those who have lived on the Galapagos for more than five years will be eligible for legal residency. Everyone else was declared a temporary resident with a temporary but renewable work permit tied to an employment contract. The rest could be deported. INGALA (National Galapagos Institute, created in 1980, which is responsible for coordinating policies and planning throughout the Galapagos), with support from the environmental police, deported an average of ninety-four people each month during 2000.[64] Effective enforcement, however, has remained a long-term challenge. In addition, the Charles Darwin Foundation noted a significant loophole: the law granted unlimited residence rights to all future descendants of Galapagos residents, whether or not they have ever lived in the archipelago, and this created a sizable pool of potential immigrants. Recognizing future pressures from the local community, the law also set aside another 2 percent of the park area on the inhabited islands for use by INGALA for projects (excluding residential development) required to support the community.[65]

The Special Law also officially established the Galapagos Marine Reserve, making it the world's second-largest marine reserve. It covers all the area within forty miles from the baseline coast of all the Galapagos Islands, for a total of 138,000 km^2 (53,000 square miles) and is managed and administered by the GNPS. A unique participatory management system involves key stakeholders—tour operators, guides, fishers, scientists, and park and government officials—in the decision-making process about the use and conservation of the marine reserve. The recommendations and decisions of this body are formalized by the Inter-Institutional Management Authority (IMA), the highest authority for the Galapagos Marine Reserve, composed of four ministries and three stakeholder groups: tourism, fisheries, and a scientific and educational group. Milestone achievements of this system included a consensus-based coastal zoning plan for the Galapagos Marine Reserve, with regulations such as a five-year fisheries calendar that sets the legal harvest of commercially important marine species, as well as the establishment of participatory fisheries monitoring programs for the two principle fishing resources: spiny lobster and sea cucumbers.

The legislation divided the reserve into different use and protection zones. The permanent-resident artisanal fishers were given the exclusive right to fish within the marine reserve, while industrial-level fishing was banned completely. Local fishers became part of the Participatory Management Board, which decides at a local level the fishing calendar, quotas, and locations for catching lobsters, sea cucumbers, and specified types of fish. Although key issues remained to be negotiated—the precise definition of artisanal fishing and what measures should be taken to reduce overexploitation of the islands' resources—the Charles Darwin Foundation concluded that in passing the law, the Ecuadorian Congress had bucked the industrial fishing lobby and "took a bold decision to opt for something close to the Galapagos consensus. . . . [T]he law provides an excellent framework for conservation of the marine reserve."[66] In an effort to control alien species, the legislation enacted and provided limited funding for the development of a quarantine inspection system and a regional management plan.[67] In terms of revenue, the law distributes park entrance fees by carefully balancing the needs of conservation and the local community, with 95 percent of the total remaining in the Galapagos—a fast improvement over the previous decade. The law stipulates that 40 percent of the entrance fees go to the GNPS; 20 percent to the town council; 10 percent to the Galapagos provincial council; 5 percent each to the marine reserve, navy, quarantine programs, and INEFAN (Ecuadorian Institute of Forestry, Natural Areas, and Wildlife); and the final 10 percent to INGALA.[68]

The Special Law also sought to keep the revenue and employment benefits from tourism in the Galapagos. While it grandfathered in existing tourism businesses, including international and mainland companies, it stipulated that all new permits go to permanent residents only. The law states that permits for construction of new tourism facilities, as well as preferential credits for tourism businesses, must generate local profits. The Special Law, however, said little about the regulation of tourism numbers, and no ceiling was set on the maximum number of tourists per year.[69]

The Special Law negotiating process and the legislation itself were remarkable pieces of effective and consultative government action aimed at promoting sustainable development and ensuring local benefits. Its lofty goals—including to control immigration and to increase local benefits from tourism—have, sadly, not been met. In this process, ecotourism, as the archipelago's primary revenue generator, has played a central and complex role.

The Ecotourism Industry's Role in Conservation Efforts

The ecotourism boom has brought expanded resources for the GNPS, which counts on its portion of the park entrance fee to fund many of its activities. The entrance fee also provides core funds for other government institutions, such as INGALA and the navy. Alongside the GNPS, they are charged with implementing the components of the 1998 Special Law. In the early 1990s, the park entrance fee, paid at the airport and covering the entire stay, was low—forty dollars for foreigners and only sixty cents for Ecuadorians. This generated about $1 million in government revenues,[70] but only 10 to 20 percent went to support the Galapagos National Park and the rest was distributed to support other Ecuadorian parks. In April 1993, park entrance fees were raised to eighty dollars for foreign visitors, with the national park retaining a higher percentage of the intake. By 2001, tourism had become, at $430 million, Ecuador's third-largest foreign exchange earner, after petroleum and bananas. Tourism to the Galapagos accounted for one-third of Ecuador's total tourism revenue.[71] The 1998 Special Law raised park entrance fees to one hundred dollars for foreigners, of which forty dollars was earmarked for the GNPS. In 2004, the entrance fee generated more than $7.6 million, or about $3 million for the GNPS.[72]

The ecotourism sector, particularly the tour operators and floating hotels catering mainly to foreigners, represents the island's largest legal commercial activity and a powerful economic and political force on the islands. Direct taxation on hotels and boats has increased significantly over the years with several of the taxes required by the national park, navy, and local municipality built into the annual operating permit requirements; there are also taxes associated with wages and insurance. In 2005, the Santa Cruz municipality tourism department received forty-two thousand dollars from local hotel operations.[73] Floating hotels pay an annual tax per berth, ranging from $150 to $250 per passenger, depending on the number of passengers they are authorized to carry, the quality of services offered, and the type of itinerary. Day tours pay either $50 or $150 per passenger per year.[74] The government has been wise to levy a small "percent tax on the intake of the tourism industry, including hotels, restaurants, boats, and tour agencies," rather than "simply raising the park entrance fee over and over again," say experts such as Craig MacFarland, who ran the Charles Darwin Research Station in the 1970s and was president of the Charles Darwin Foundation from 1985 to 1996. He laments, however, that this has been opposed by the tourism industry for what MacFarland labels "knee jerk, short-sighted reasons that it will hurt their numbers."[75]

Nevertheless, the ecotourism industry's contribution to conservation efforts on the Galapagos has, on the whole, been positive, because the industry recognizes that its long-term success is based on a healthy and well-protected environment. A number of tour boat operators and guides work closely with the park service and research station to patrol for illegal fishing activities and help in monitoring key species. Often, tour boat operators are the first to discover, photograph, and report illegal encampments and fishing activities on the outer islands. There have been several efforts to organize parts of the Ecuadorian tourism industry to more systematically support ecotourism principles and practices. The Ecuadorian Ecotourism Association (ASEC), headquartered in Quito and founded in 1991, was one of the first national ecotourism organizations in the world. In early 2008, ASEC had sixty-seven members (seven of which operate in the Galapagos) representing all the social actors of ecotourism in Ecuador: indigenous and local communities, private tour operators, NGOs, universities, local governments, the Ministry of Tourism, clean energy companies, and private persons. Together, these members manage approximately 75 percent of the incoming tourism in Ecuador.[76]

The government-recognized Association of Galapagos Tour Operators (ASOGAL), founded in 1992, is more specifically oriented to Galapagos, and has been much more involved in Galapagos tourism than ASEC. ASOGAL was created by a group of Galapagos tour operators and has ten members, including some large, Quito-based companies as well as local Galapagos operators. Many of these are Ecuadorian companies dedicated to raising the environmental, educational, and safety standards of tour boats and working for long-term environmental protection of the archipelago. ASOGAL has actively promoted a certification pilot project that combines ISO quality standards and ISM (International Safety Management Certification).[77] In addition to this joint certification effort, ASOGAL has contributed to other noteworthy activities, including the collection of used oil, vigilance of the marine reserve and national park, trash collection, environmental education, and a training program for tour guides and boat crews.

In the Galapagos, small local operators, predominantly family-owned and -run companies, have worked together for more than fifteen years to protect their interests and develop the small-scale tourism industry. In 2003, this group legalized their initiative into the Asociación de Armadores Turísticos (Association of Tourism Providers; or ADATUR) to provide a local voice on issues affecting small local operators. "We give back to the community, we are the local community" says Rocio Malo, owner and operator of family-run Daphne Cruises. "We live here, we buy our supplies here, hire local people, and it is us that the community turns to when there is a social need," such as a sick child or other family emergency.[78]

The larger tour operators from both Ecuador and outside the islands also have a dynamic nonprofit organization. Founded in 1995, the International Galapagos Tour Operators Association (IGTOA) was formed to lobby the Ecuadorian Congress for passage of the new comprehensive legislation on the Galapagos (what became the 1998 Special Law), to raise professional and safety standards of boat operators, and to raise funds for local conservation efforts. Since then, IGTOA has continued to grow, with over fifty members, including twelve Ecuadorian companies, twenty-five international full members, and fourteen international associate members. Their stated mission is to "preserve the Galapagos Islands as a unique and priceless world heritage that will provide enjoyment, education, adventure and inspiration to present and future generations of travelers."[79] IGTOA has become a collective voice to petition the government of Ecuador for proper funding, management, and legal enforcement.

Another large and important organization is CAPTURGAL, a nonprofit organization founded in 1996 and based in the archipelago to promote sound ecotourism. Its nearly 250 members include a wide range of local tourism-related businesses such as hotels, restaurants, tour boats, floating hotels, yachts, travel agencies, discos, and small bars on the four inhabited islands. CAPTURGAL provides its members with a range of services such as legal advice, technical assistance, and arbitration, with a special emphasis on marketing, quality and security certifications, and training. It works closely with the GNPS and also maintains a close relationship with various international organizations.[80] In 2005, CAPTURGAL spearheaded the creation of the "Sustainable Development of the Galapagos Productive Sectors" project, a "green" certification program for local products in the tourism, fishing, and agriculture sectors.[81]

This is but one of several certification programs being used in the Galapagos to help measure quality and service as well as environmental and social impacts of tourism companies. Larger companies such as Metropolitan Touring and Galamazonas, as well as the Galapagos National Parks Service, have opted to pursue ISO certification.[82] In 2001 Smart Voyager, a new environmental certification program for boats in the Galapagos, was launched. It was created and sponsored by Conservación y Desarrollo (Conservation and Development, C&D), an Ecuadorian nonprofit organization based in Quito, and the Rainforest

Alliance, a nonprofit specializing in "green" certification. (Rainforest Alliance's sustainable tourism program is based in Costa Rica.) Smart Voyager is designed to measure and minimize the environmental and social impact of tour boats in the Galapagos through on-site, independent auditing and the issuing of logos to companies that conform to its standard. Smart Voyager's certification criteria are organized into twelve principles including conservation of natural ecosystems, lowering the risk of introduction and dispersal of exotic species, just and proper treatment of workers, safety, community relations, and local welfare. Achieving certification is not easy. Boat operators that are certified may use the Smart Voyager logo. This seal gives travelers the assurance that they are supporting operators who care about the environment, wildlife conservation, and the well-being of workers and local communities.[83]

Ecoventura and Canodros, two of the larger, mainland-based companies, were the first to be certified under Smart Voyager. For several years, Ecoventura's fleet of four boats and the large cruise ship run by Canodros (*Explorer II*) were the only members. "From the onset, we have taken measures to provide tourists with the finest personal services while simultaneously protecting the environment," says Santiago Dunn, president of Ecoventura. "Now, for the first time, a 'green seal of approval' acknowledges our efforts and underscores their importance. The Smart Voyager seal sends a message to our clients, our peers, and our staff, that we uphold the highest environmental standards in the Galapagos Archipelago."[84]

Smart Voyager gained momentum slowly. Early on, the *Jessica* oil spill also cast some doubts on the validity of program because the bunker fuel carried by the vessel was destined for the Smart Voyager certified *Explorer II*. The launch of Smart Voyager also coincided with the government decision to make the ISM (International Safety Management) certification obligatory for all tourism vessels operating in the Galapagos. This was a costly and time-consuming process for the tour companies and few companies were in a position to invest in the changes needed to meet the Smart Voyager requirements as well. The owner of a small, family-run company explained that he would be very interested in Smart Voyager if it were not for "the upfront costs needed for investment in the boat."[85] In contrast, another local company, Daphne Cruises, chose to obtain Smart Voyager certification with the belief that the initial high cost would bring results over the long term. "The tourist wants to know that the operator behaves in a certain way and the 'green seal' recognizes that we protect the environment and give good service at the same time," said owner Rocio Malo.[86] Gradually, however, Smart Voyager has increased both the professionalism of its operations and the number of certified boats. By 2007, Smart Voyager had certified eight boats and also moved into certification of hotels and other accommodations throughout other parts of Ecuador.[87]

In addition, a growing number of tour operators in the Galapagos are involved in projects aimed at providing assistance to the national parks, the CDRS, and local conservation projects. This voluntary movement, known as Travel Philanthropy, is becoming a force in the support of community development, biodiversity conservation, and other environmental, sociocultural, and economic improvements in the Galapagos Islands. One of the leaders in this movement has been Lindblad Expeditions, which in 1997 created the Galapagos Conservation Fund (GCF) to develop a link between its visitors, the tourism industry, and local conservation institutions. "The guests that we bring here year-round represent more than tourists to a threatened environment," explains the company's president, Sven Lindblad. "They are a genuine constituency of people who are eager to participate in and care about the long-term preservation and social development of the Galapagos. If every operator in the Galapagos had similar programs, then tourism could be a major contributor to the long-term stewardship of these islands." The primary tool of the Galapagos Conservation Fund is an on-board conservation communication strategy to inspire visitors to actively support prioritized conservation projects in Galapagos. Nearly all comply, and this highly successful program is raising an average of four hundred thousand dollars per year from visitors on Lindblad's two ships based in the islands. One hundred percent of the on-board donations go to the projects, with Lindblad Expeditions absorbing all administration costs.

Over the last decade, a number of other tourism businesses have established their own conservation, environmental education, and training initiatives. IGTOA, for instance, has raised funds from its members to support two types of projects: (1) conservation projects that directly impact issues like introduced species, patrol of the park, and scientific research; and (2) professional standards projects that promote boat safety; passenger care; training and treatment of captains and crew members; guide training; and other issues relating to health, safety, and the enrichment of both travelers and tourist industry personnel. Over the years, IGTOA has given in excess of one hundred thousand dollars for such projects.[88] Many of these tourism operators view Travelers' Philanthropy not as charity but as an important part of responsible business practices. "It's good business," contends Sven Lindblad, pointing out that it deepens the visitor experience, increases the pride of his staff in their company, and improves the company's stature with the community in the Galapagos.[89]

Visitors' Effects on the National Park

Despite a nearly twenty-fold increase in visitors since 1970, the GNPS has maintained extremely strict rules, and tourists still seem to have had little effect on the animals.[90] About two-thirds of the foreign visitors are from the United States, and surveys invariably find that most tourists come away impressed. "I'm so astounded at what I've seen and the ambience of the islands. The whole environment, I would say, is as near as one could get to paradise on earth as is possible," mused Glenn Brisley of Norwich, England, as he boarded a plane to fly home. "One thing that's been most striking to me is that for all the people who come here, there's very little mark left on the land. It's really nice to see what the earth looks like without man's imprint," commented Ben Mejia of Seattle, Washington. "I was very pleasantly surprised to discover that the sites we visited do not appear to have changed at all; the wildlife is as abundant, curious, and tame as it was at my first visit in 1992, the boobies still nest on the path at Española, the sea lions still enjoy teasing the swimmers at the snorkeling sites, the iguanas still lie in huge heaps on the rocks," commented Gillian Key after a 2005 trip with Lindblad Expeditions.[91]

Keeping footprints off the Galapagos means carefully controlling all visitors. Tourists visiting any of the seventy designated land sites and sixty-two marine sites must be accompanied by naturalist guides; about a dozen sites are the most visited, and the vast majority of the islands are off limits to tourists. Although the guides work for the tour companies, they are trained and authorized by the GNPS and must renew their license each year. In order to obtain a guide license, they must now also be a permanent resident, since under the Special Law of 1998, permanent residents are the only people automatically permitted to live and work in the islands. Nonresident guides who held licenses prior to 1998 are able to continue to work in the islands if they meet the INGALA temporary residency permit conditions. There is a great variety in the background of current guides, and while many hold degrees in biology or natural sciences and speak several languages, others (as explained below) do not. They function as both educators and park wardens. The guides make sure people comply with the park rules, stay on the marked trails, don't touch or take anything, don't take food onto the islands, don't litter, and don't disturb the animals. Before leaving an island, everyone carefully washes off so as not to transport anything, even grains of sand, from one island to another.

This hasn't always been the case. In the first years after the park was established, there were no rules for visitors. In 1965 the Ecuadorian government sought guidance from a team of British park planners to recommend "the best means of exploiting its economic potential through tourism."[92] Since the introduction of well-trained guides in 1975, marked trails, and strict rules,[93] scientists report that through regular monitoring, they have found little impact on animal behavior. As MacFarland found in a 2000 analysis of tourism in the Galapagos, "Long-term studies on impacts on key indicator species . . . have shown no detectable impacts on reproductive success over several decades."[94] However, some park officials, tour operators, and scientists say that since the tourism boom, they are beginning to detect adverse environmental effects on the most-visited islands, including some trail erosion, loss of vegetation, and, perhaps, some change in behavior of certain animals. The GNPS regularly monitors the visitor sites to assess impact, and if necessary may close a site to enable it to recover. Since 2000, the GNPS has established new monitoring techniques that include defining the base line for each indicator, such as congestion or erosion, and defining the acceptable ranges of impact. Management strategies are based on the findings of surveys that serve to establish the impact of tourism activities on the islands' ecosystem.[95] On a few beaches, male sea lions are reported to have become more aggressive, possibly due to the presence of too many tourists or tourists not respecting the animals' territory. However, no behavioral change has been detected among other animals or nesting birds, which live in high concentrations along the coast. "The system is getting a little weak here and there, but overall, it works," concludes MacFarland.[96]

Some tourists, scientists, and boat owners complain that even though the GNPS must authorize schedules for all tour boats, some boats ignore the requirement or fail to file itineraries, so the most visited sites are sometimes overcrowded. "You are having to wait behind perhaps ninety people, and that changes the whole flavor of your trip," complained one long-time tour operator. In the early 1990s, the government tried to set a limit on the number of tourists admitted each year, but the ceiling kept being raised. According to the Galapagos Global Tourism Management of 1991, the number of visitors permitted was calculated by the "carrying capacity" of the islands, based upon the number of passengers each boat was permitted to carry times the total number of boats. In 1994, the GNPS permitted the smaller boats to upgrade their capacity to carry sixteen passengers. "Definitely, more boats and larger boats are arriving," said David Balfour, who manages the Metropolitan Touring logistical operations in the islands. During the mid-1990s, many small vessels began to fuse their tourism permits into single permits, thus permitting larger boats with a capacity for more passengers. These are usually owned and operated by companies outside of the Galapagos. This process has been gradually eliminating some of the local operators, and has certain negative consequences, including an increased pressure on the most popular visitor sites.

Most controversial was the decision in early 1994 by GNPS to permit, for the first time, the entry into the Galapagos of two cruise ships, with a combined total of more than 1,200 passengers. At eighty dollars per passenger (then the entrance fee), this brought in considerable income. But many, including members the Permanent Galapagos Commission (appointed by Ecuador's president), local tour operators, and scientists, disapproved. Marta Lucia Burneo, an official with the commission, argued that the archipelago's tourism industry was moving in the wrong direction: "We should not have mass tourism, people who go traveling around the world in big comfortable ships with swimming pools and so on. We need to develop ecotourism."[97] The GNPS subsequently announced a moratorium on visits by foreign cruise ships, admitting that the islands could not sustain such large numbers, and that such visits would undercut local boat operators.

However, the cruise ship controversy resurfaced in 2005 with a new initiative aimed at bringing more tourism to one community whose facilities were underutilized. The government ruled that one five-hundred-passenger ship per month would be permitted to visit Puerto Baqueriz Moreno on San Cristóbal Island.[98] In 2006, Discovery World Cruises, owned by the London-based company Voyages of Discovery,[99] began arriving in the Galapagos. The environmental regulations were strict and the ship was inspected from top to bottom to prevent the introduction of invasive species. After each visit, a survey and audit were conducted on customer satisfaction, benefits to the community, and environmental impacts, in order to assess the feasibility of continuing with the activity. The ships were not allowed to travel around the islands; rather, passengers were transferred to smaller boats and could visit the islands only with a park department guide and fixed itinerary.[100] According to Mark Flager, vice president of marketing and sales for Discovery World Cruises, their five-hundred-passenger cruise trips have been well received by the local community. He stated that due to high population growth and recent restrictions on fishing, unemployment has increased, and this initiative is a way of generating much-needed employment on the island. During the two and a half days that their ship is anchored on San Cristóbal, local operators, boat owners, fishers, and other local businesses are used to provide land and marine excursions for cruise ship passengers.[101] In 2007, another cruise line, Classic International Cruises, announced it had scheduled a 2008 visit to the islands.

However, cruise ship tourism in the Galapagos also has strong opponents. Felipe Cruz, the technical director of the Charles Darwin

Foundation, states, "We don't want cruise ships in the Galapagos—we don't think it's sustainable." Cruz argues that the cruise ships bring their own food with them and don't deal with the local people, so the tourist money doesn't filter into the economy.[102] Other critiques of cruise tourism contend that they increase the chances of introduced species and disease and leave dirty laundry water and sewage waste in their wake, and the large number of visitors have "Disneyfied" the experience, that is, made it less reflective and respectful of the surroundings. In late 2007, the government bowed to the critics and halted visits by larger cruise ships.[103]

At the other end of the spectrum from the larger, more luxurious cruises, another recent innovation is raising some eyebrows. In mid-2006, a U.S.-based adventure tourism company, ROW International, began leading sea kayaking and island camping trips that it bills as "the first of its kind offered in this tropical archipelago, allowing you to see the wonderful wildlife of these islands 'up close and personal' from behind the paddle of a sea kayak . . . "[104] Groups are kept small and no permanent structures, equipment, or generators are allowed to be used in the campsites.[105] A glowing article in the *Washington Post* described the experience: "The feeling . . . of being able to paddle around, pull up your kayak, wander around a bit and set up camp—just hang out—was completely new. It was like being in the Louvre after everyone else had gone home, pondering the 'Mona Lisa' alone and hearing the echo of your footsteps down the hallways."[106] While kayaking and camping may appear to be low-impact and environmentally sensitive, it has raised concerns with the GNPS, CDRS, and others about both its limits and its long-term effects. After a violent altercation between the Air Force (which had granted a camping permit) and the GNPS on Baltra, ROW International modified its itinerary and said it was operating with all the necessary permits.[107] As of now, no other companies had been granted permission to camp on the islands, but if the popularity of this unique experience increases, other operations will certainly pressure for permission.

Decline in Quality of Ecotours

With the soaring tourist numbers to the Galapagos Islands since the early 1990s, the guide "pool" has been forced to expand rapidly and to certify a new classification of "auxiliary" guides. These are most commonly local residents who know a great deal about the islands but often lack a depth of formal scientific training and knowledge, and frequently speak only Spanish. The current guide categorization system contains three levels: the lowest, category one, is auxiliary guides, and categories two and three are Ecuadorian and foreign guides with science backgrounds and the ability to speak more than one language. Training courses are occasionally offered for guides, and those who score well in the courses can move to a higher category. A maximum of thirty candidates are accepted for training, and all new guides must be Galapagos permanent residents.[108]

Despite these restrictions, some express concern that the auxiliary guides are lowering the overall quality of Galapagos guides, long considered among the most highly qualified in the world. David Blanton, the executive director of IGTOA, contends, "In addition to a lowering of the quality of information, enthusiasm, and interpretive skill, tour operators inside and outside of Ecuador complain about the lack of professional and social skills of many new guides. There have been serious breaches of safety procedures by some guides, such as leaving people behind on the trail and not supervising swimmers and snorkelers in the strong ocean currents. Some guides do not have experience or skill handling diverse groups, and, especially with local guides, there is often a wide social and cultural gap between guides and visitors. Little or nothing is being done by the government to correct this."[109]

In addition, as the number of ecotourists has expanded, it has also been diluted by less serious and less curious travelers. Tour boat operator Georgina Martin de Cruz describes many of the newer tourists as "softer," more concerned with comfort than conservation and with "ticking off a destination rather than having dreamt and saved up for it." In an informal survey of tourists I took during a sailing cruise, I found that none had read Darwin, few seemed aware of the scientific importance of the Galapagos Islands, and many were "savvy" travelers who had toured much of the rest of the world. Asked why she came, one Florida housewife said, "Well, we did Africa last year. We've done more luxurious cruising in the Mediterranean, to Greek Islands, around the world, so the Galapagos seemed like a good place to come." In 1993, Temptress Cruises (now called Temptress Adventure Cruises), which was already well established in marketing ecotourism "lite" in Costa Rica, began operating around the Galapagos, offering passengers a choice between "a soft tour or hard-core natural history."[110] Many similar groups now regularly visit the islands, including Celebrity Cruises, Abercrombie & Kent, and Overseas Adventure Travel. These tours visit the same sites and offer similar activities as most other tours, and do not necessarily market their packages as "soft tours," but they do tend to offer more luxuries to their passengers. David Blanton of IGTOA noted a worrisome trend toward "larger and more luxurious boats. Marketing by larger companies often emphasizes comfort, food, and accommodation, with natural history getting less emphasis."[111] Some of the most qualified naturalist guides complain that many tourists today are not interested in detailed information about the islands and their habitat. While many of the most professional guides are leaving the profession, some, like Ivonne Torres, a naturalist guide since 1989, sees opportunity and challenge as the profile of visitors is shifting: "A naturalist that prides himself on being a good naturalist will always strive to give the best experience to the passengers. Even when a group is not interested, a good guide can still try to impart a conservation message."[112]

As tourist numbers have grown and competition has increased, companies have taken cost-saving shortcuts that negatively affect the marine reserve. Until recently, one of the most common practices was for boats to discharge their sewage and organic kitchen wastes into the ocean. However, new regulations appear to be effectively controlling this practice. The GNPS now requires all boats, in order to renew their operating licenses, to subscribe to oil and solid waste recycling programs, and to obtain a fumigation certificate to prevent introduction of alien species.[113] Boats must also be fitted with holding tanks for waste water that is then collected in ports by local councils.[114] A used oil recycling program, RELUGAL, initiated by a local fisherman in 1999, had recycled 120,000 gallons by 2005, equivalent to 75 percent of the total oil used in the islands.[115] The GNPS can review licenses of suspected violators and may even bring legal proceedings. However, as of 2006, no sanctions had been imposed and all tourism vessels were said to be complying.[116]

Some efforts to diversify the tourism product have also posed threats to the marine reserve. In the late 1990s, the government, under pressure from some dive boat operators and private Ecuadorian yacht owners, authorized "tag-and-release" sport fishing. Supporters argued that this type of sport fishing offered a viable alternative to commercial fishing. Opponents, including a number of tour operators, tour boat owners, and scientists, contended that with overfishing already a pressing problem, sport fishing could not be properly policed and would only lead to further exploitation. Jack Grove, author of the definitive book on the fish of the Galapagos and activist for marine conservation in the Galapagos, calls this tag-and-release fishing "a facade" because "billfish such as marlin and sailfish are already showing up in the market in San Cristóbal. It's a sign of what is to come. . . . The Galapagos Islands are the only place in the world where divers can approach big fish. It's analogous to getting close to the 'big five' game in the Serengeti," referring to the five African wildlife—lion, buffalo, rhino, leopard, and elephant—traditionally most prized by safari hunters. According to Grove, sport fishing "is contradictory to selling ecotourism trips. It will attract a new type of clientele who do not come to learn about the flora and fauna, but to capture it."[117] While tag-and-release was authorized under the 1998 Special Law, it remained illegal because no rules or administrative machinery were created to regulate it.

In 2005, the Inter-Institutional Management Authority (IMA) approved an alternative approach to sport fishing, referred to as *pesca vivencial* (experiential fishing). Based on collaboration between the Charles Darwin Foundation, local fishers, guides, the local tourism sector, and the GNPS, this new activity is intended to allow local fishers to provide services to tourists without the fishers losing their rights to fish in the Galapagos Marine Reserve. The primary objective of this activity is to showcase fishing culture, including the way fishers work, the resources they use to do their work, and their family life, and to help visitors to better understand the fishing community in Galapagos. The activity will also reduce fishing pressures because the numbers of fish harvested during these trips will be limited and the fishers will generate revenue from the visitor rather than from fishing.[118]

Threats from Introduced Species

One of the most worrisome environmental threats to the Galapagos Islands has been the introduction of nonnative species, whose numbers have accelerated in the wake of the ecotourism and migration booms, endangering the survival of fragile and endemic species. At the top of the conservation agenda for scientists and park officials is eliminating introduced species—plants, animals, insects, fungi, bacteria—that are brought in by boat or plane. Scientists monitoring invasive species had by 2007 identified introductions of 36 species of vertebrates (including donkeys, cattle, goats, dogs), 540 species of invertebrates (various ants, wasps, flies), and 740 plant species,[119] and the numbers continue to rise. Scientists say that plant species constitute the biggest management problem. Most were brought in deliberately as food crops and ornamental plants, and some, such as blackberry and guava, are now prolific and abundant, and probably impossible to eradicate.

Many of the exotic species are capable of outcompeting the unique native species of the Galapagos.[120] The worst species transform native habitat as well as invertebrate fauna, altering the food chain and nesting sites. According to biologist Gillian Key, coordinating the invasive species total control plan for the Galapagos, "At a global level the problem of invasive species has been recognized as the biggest threat to biodiversity, together with habitat loss. Over the past few decades, the transfer of species both within and among regions has increased with the growth of tourism, trade, and general travel around the world. The Galapagos is not immune. With a human population now around upwards of 25,000 and nearly 150,000 tourists visiting the islands each year, the risk of accidental and deliberate introductions of new and potentially damaging exotic species is higher than ever before."[121]

In 1989, scientists working on the Galapagos drew up a comprehensive quarantine plan, including inspection and fumigation of cargo and people arriving by boat and plane. But it was inadequately enforced during the 1990s, making establishment of a quarantine service a priority under the Special Law. With the fledgling quarantine and control system now in place to try to stop introductions, the GNPS has concentrated on eradication. Through coordinated research and management between the Charles Darwin Research Station and the GNPS, successful control and eradication campaigns have been carried out against rats, goats, cats, a wide variety of plants, and other alien species. On some islands, certain species of tortoise came close to extinction because feral goats have eaten the vegetation they feed on and rats have eaten their eggs. On Isabela Island, home of more than one-third of the Galapagos giant tortoises, as many as seventy-five thousand feral goats and burros, brought in by people living on the island's southern tip, were causing massive erosion, threatened the tortoises' habitat, and trampled their nests. This forced the GNPS to close Alcedo Volcano as a visitor site and initiate a massive eradication campaign. As of 2006, feral goats were finally considered to be eradicated on northern Isabela and Santiago Islands—and this complex and costly eradication campaign was hailed as achieving "the impossible."[122] More broadly, the GNPS and CDRS have adopted a multifaceted campaign to remove the threat of invasive species and restore several island ecosystems, while maintaining efforts to boost low populations of key species through captive breeding, fencing, seed banks, and reintroduction of native plants.[123]

Immigration and Colonization

Even more worrisome and, for political reasons, difficult to control has been the rapid acceleration in human arrivals, including colonists, fishers, poachers, and job and fortune seekers. Historically, the tiny population of early colonists consisted of subsistence farmers and fishers; since the 1960s, some have worked for the Charles Darwin Research Station or the GNPS. By the late 1980s, as word spread on the mainland that ecotourism was a *mina de oro* (gold mine) for the Galapagos, new arrivals began pouring in, lured by stories of plentiful jobs and high salaries.[124] However, the cost of living on the islands is also significantly higher than on the mainland,[125] driven up by the cost of food and other imported commodities, a housing market inflated by the tourism industry, and the 5 percent limit of land for settlements. Employees are legally entitled to an increase of 75 percent on the basic Ecuadorian wage paid on the mainland,[126] but this does not always fully compensate for the cost of living, especially for the poorer segment of the population. It is estimated that some 12 percent of the population of the Galapagos lives in poverty.[127]

Until the Special Law, Ecuadorian citizens had the legal right to move freely to the Galapagos, as they could to any of Ecuador's twenty-one provinces. During the 1990s, the Galapagos Islands were the fastest-growing region in Ecuador and one of the fastest-growing areas in the world, with a population that was increasing at a wholly unsustainable rate of 6 to 10 percent per year. The islands' permanent population leaped from a few hundred in the 1960s, to 6,200 in 1982, to 15,000 to 20,000 by the late 1990s, and to an estimated 25,000 in 2007.[128] While the 1998 Special Law set rules for limiting migration, controlling the illegal flow of immigrants remained a major concern.[129] The population was also increased by the presence of temporary residents who arrived with work contracts previously authorized by INGALA.[130] By 2002, INGALA had issued residency cards to 15,035 registered permanent residents and 811 temporary residents.[131] Most of these immigrants gravitated toward the main tourist hub, Puerto Ayora, on the island of Santa Cruz. Lyjia Ayove is typical of the migration during the early 1990s. She found work in one of the town's small outdoor restaurants. In a few short years, she and fourteen members of her family had moved to the Galapagos from their home in the crowded port city of Guayaquil. Ayove says, "Back then it was easier to find work here than on the continent."[132] Today, reality is much harsher: non-residents no longer have the right to live and work in the islands, jobs are hard to find, and the high cost of living and unemployment have created a marginalized class of transients.[133]

Geographically, the Galapagos are an anomaly: whereas elsewhere national parks are surrounded by human communities, here the tiny patches on five islands designated for human habitat are encircled by the national park and marine reserve. Government officials and island residents say the new arrivals are straining limited resources such as freshwater, electricity, telephone service, and schools; are increasing the need for more fuel for electricity, water desalination, cars, boats, and garbage and sewage disposal; and are demanding more fishing rights, timber, and parkland for houses and farms. Equally worrisome, while long-term residents have been taught from childhood to respect the animals and conserve supplies, many immigrants don't arrive with a similar respect for the islands' fragility. Tour boat owner and teacher Georgina Martin de Cruz says, "Obviously, the children, when they go to school, are taught about the Galapagos Islands and why we mustn't hit the iguanas over the head with rocks or let our dogs run loose. But the adult people who come here have no idea, and a lot of damage is being done that way."[134]

Fishing and the Marine Reserve: Conflicts between People and Parks

It is, however, around the issue of commercial fishing within the marine reserve that the most serious conflicts have crystallized. Fishing activity began in the 1940s, when "whitefish" (grouper and sea bass) were first dried, salted, and exported to the mainland for the Lenten season and sold locally on the Baltra military base. By the late 1980s, the annual whitefish catch had decreased 80 percent, suggesting that these species had been overfished. In October 1986, the government took a positive step by declaring the Galapagos Marine Resources Reserve and, with passage of the 1998 Special Law, the marine reserve was placed under the primary control of the GNPS and more funds were appropriated for its protection. But this followed years of serious exploitation by illegal commercial fishing interests.

Despite the 1998 Special Law, described above, commercial fishing, both legal and illegal, has continued to take a toll. "The sea cucumber population in the Galapagos has declined dramatically over the last 6 years as a result of agreeing to fishing quotas that are not correlated with the results of biological studies," Graham Watkins, executive director of the Charles Darwin Foundation (CDF), reported to a 2005 meeting of the Inter-Institutional Management Authority (IMA) for the Galapagos Marine Reserve.[135] In 2004, with the sea cucumber and lobster industries on the verge of collapse, the fishing sector lobbied strongly that long-lining be permitted in the marine reserve. In 2005, the IMA, citing pilot studies on long-lining carried out between 1994 and 2003,[136] responded by announcing a prohibition on the use of surface long lines (at depths less than sixty meters) within the reserve, and then, in December, completely banning long-lining.

By 2005, it was widely recognized that the Galapagos' marine resources were under excessive pressure from illegal industrial fishing, and efforts to reduce the pressure continued. There have been attempts, for instance, to develop various small-scale business alternatives, to improve sales of fish to the local tourism industry, and to move fishers into tourism as dive guides and fishing instructors.

Worrisome Trends in Ecotourism

In June 2007, the World Heritage Committee, based on the recommendations of a joint IUCN and UNESCO monitoring mission, finally carried out the threat first made a decade earlier: they added the Galapagos Islands to the list of World Heritage sites "in danger." In outlining the reasons, David Sheppard, head of the IUCN delegation, said, "The main problems associated with the Galapagos Islands relate to the impact of tourism growth, which is driving immigration and overfishing. Adding the islands to the danger list is a positive way of raising the profile of these threats and highlighting the need for international action."[137] The Minister of Tourism pledged to consider limiting tourist numbers, activities, and new permits.[138]

Today the Galapagos is no longer the isolated archipelago that Darwin helped put on the map. It is a must-see ecotourism icon, with crowded ports, bustling airports, expanding government, and increasing economic clout. As Durham perceptively concludes: "Galapagos now suffers from globalization and all that globalization brings with it, including the rapid build-up of tourism. . . . In many ways, the circumstances of Galapagos today are rather emblematic of globalization and the long reach of capitalism."[139]

One of the clearest indications that globalization, and not the core principles of ecotourism, appears to be winning is that, despite phenomenal economic growth, the lot of the average person in the Galapagos has not improved. In a sobering analysis, researchers from the University of California at Davis found that, while tourism drove the GDP in the Galapagos up an impressive 78 percent between 1999 and 2005—giving the islands one of the fastest-growing economies in the world—per-capita income increased only 1.8 percent annually. In fact, the study concludes, "In real terms, income per capita almost certainly declined." The study also found that a higher percentage of tourism dollars spent by foreigners are never reaching the Galapagos. In comparing 1998 and 2005, surveys reveal that although the average cost of international tour packages had increased 12 percent (from $1,271 in 1998 to $2,098 in 2005), over half (50.2 percent) of the money was being spent abroad, up from 34.6 percent in 1998.[140] A study completed in 2006 by the Charles Darwin Foundation reached similar conclusions: "there is a shift toward multinational investors and operators away from local ownership," and, it concluded, "At present, Galapagos tourism represents a total value of $418M, of which an estimated $63M enters the local economy."[141]

Although virtually all of the economic growth in the islands depends on the health of the natural environment, the rapid expansion and unrestricted levels of ecotourism, as along with commercial fishing and immigration, are threatening the natural areas on which these activities depend. According to IGTOA, the group of activist tour operators, ecotourism in the Galapagos has been a double-edged sword:

> Ecotourism has brought great economic benefit to Ecuador, and remains the only practical way of supporting the Galapagos National Park. The model of low-impact tourism developed in the Galapagos has served the islands well. Yet there are unwanted by-products from the tourist industry—contamination from boat paint and engines, oil spills, overused sites, a drain on the fresh water supply, and introduction of plants and animals from the mainland. All of these must be addressed for ecotourism to work. Tourism also needs to be kept to sustainable levels. This means a limit to the number of tourists, restriction on the type of tourism development, and close monitoring of tourist impacts.[142]

Reflecting on the growth in numbers and types of tourism, the Charles Darwin Foundation wrote in its November 2005 newsletter that

> the recent focus on additional tourism growth through new modalities (sport fishing, large cruise ships, community-based tourism, day tours, and diving tours) is a cause for concern. Development initiatives should consider the environmental, economic, social and cultural impacts of this growth and recognize the need to first resolve the inequity issues that plague existing development in the islands. The tourism model in the islands requires detailed consideration and change before developing new approaches to tourism: Galapagos should first have in place the regulatory controls that will ensure long term sustainability in tourism.[143]

Indeed, while ecotourism has brought both financial benefits and international recognition to the Galapagos, the archipelago is continuing to suffer from a range of problems, including industrial fishing, immigration, introduced species, and some unsustainable types of tourism. This has begun to take a toll on its international reputation. A 2004 global survey by *National Geographic Traveler* magazine asked expert panelists to evaluate 115 of the world's best-known vacation destinations based on criteria pertaining to their cultural, environmental, and aesthetic integrity. In that survey the Galapagos ranked slightly above average.[144] In a follow-up survey done in 2006, the Galapagos dropped twenty-three points—farther than any other destination, moving it into the "serious trouble" category.[145]

The Galapagos Islands' Ecotourism Scorecard

The Galapagos Islands, with their geographic remoteness, well-run national park and biological research station, coterie of scientists and naturalist guides, and low-impact floating hotels and environmentally aware tourists, have been heralded as a model, a beacon light on the road to sustainable and sound ecotourism. However, in the latter half of the 1990s, headlines from the islands told of mysterious fires, slaughter of tortoises, illegal fishing camps, angry marchers with machetes, and other troubles in paradise. The Galapagos suddenly appeared to have become a warning light signaling the dangers of ecotourism that expands too rapidly without sufficient planning, government control, community benefits and involvement, tourism sector responsibility, and international concern. Then, just as the archipelago's fragile ecosystem seemed to have reached the point of no return, the Ecuadorian government did the right thing: it yielded to the Galapagos Consensus and passed the Special Law in 1998. This, however, did not fully stem the slide. A decade later, the Galapagos Islands remain at a crossroads, an appropriate point to take stock of their ecotourism record and to evaluate how they stand up to the seven characteristics of real ecotourism.

Involves Travel to Natural Destinations

Nature is the allure of the Galapagos. This midocean moonscape of stark lava rock and scrub brush remains one of the world's most precious ecosystems. It offers ecotravelers both clues to understanding evolution and chances for close encounters with exotic as well as familiar creatures.

Minimizes Impact

Over the last several decades, ecotour operators, naturalist guides, national park officials, and research station scientists in the Galapagos have worked together to create a model for low-impact, high-quality ecotourism. However, the 2007 decision to include the Galapagos on the list of endangered World Heritage sites indicates that tourism numbers have become too high for the islands' capacity. There are signs of erosion at visitor sites, a slippage in the quality of guiding and enforcement of regulations, and occasional incidents of tour boats dumping organic and inorganic waste within the marine reserve. "Tag-and-release" sportfishing, special types of spearfishing, and kayaking and camping tours are inappropriately (and sometimes illegally) marketed as part of the ecotourism mix. The most popular visitor sites are often overcrowded; occasionally, cruise ships are permitted to discharge too many passengers on some of the other islands; and many day boats and on-land hotels are marketing a more conventional type of "sun-and-sand" tourism.

The archipelago's land and sea parks are now divided into zones. However, no effective system has ever been introduced to limit the number of either tour boats or tourists, and many scientists now believe it is sounder to analyze impacts of specific sites rather than setting broad-brushed carrying capacity numbers for the archipelago. In summing up the effect of ecotourism on the parks, Tom Fritts, a wildlife biologist with the Smithsonian Institution's National Museum of Natural History, states, "The bottom line is that . . . the Galapagos still have about 95 percent of their native [species of] flora and fauna. . . . They're disturbed but not destroyed."[146]

Far more serious than this litany of minor problems are three other phenomena that have accelerated in the wake of the ecotourism boom: introduced species, immigration, and commercial fishing. This trio is threatening both the marine and land parks, as well as areas designated for human habitation and economic activity, and has led to repeated clashes between commercial fishing interests and those involved in environmental protection and ecotourism.

Builds Environmental Awareness

Again, ecotourism has made a largely positive contribution to the broadening environmental awareness about the importance of these islands. Although Darwin's *Origin of the Species* put the Galapagos on the map as a laboratory for the study of evolution, over the subsequent century, the islands' significance was the concern of only a rather small and elite club of scientists. The growth of the environmental movement and of ecotourism has helped to expand the world's understanding of the islands' uniqueness and fragility. But as visitor numbers have grown, there has been a gradual watering down of environmental education. Naturalist guides, many of whom are scientists, have long provided high-quality educational tours to tourists traveling via the floating hotels. In recent years, this guide pool has been expanded to include auxiliary guides, who are less academically qualified and often speak only Spanish. Although this has provided an opportunity for a number of local people to move into guiding, it has meant that the most experienced guides command higher salaries and tend to work on the more luxurious and exclusive cruises.

Simultaneously, many of today's international ecotourists are requesting less-rigorous physical and intellectual experiences, and this, too, has served to water down the level of learning. While the government and the travel industry have taken positive steps to promote domestic tourism by offering deep discounts to Ecuadorians, many nationals stay in less expensive land-based hotels and take day trips, which give them only a cursory view of the most popular islands. The environmental understanding of the resident population has also been diluted by an influx of new immigrants who are seeking quick money and do not have a long-term commitment to the islands. The Special Law recognizes this latter problem and contains provisions for promoting environmental education in schools and for new immigrants.

Provides Direct Financial Benefits for Conservation

The Galapagos Islands are Ecuador's biggest tourism destination, bringing in one-third of the government's revenue from tourism.[147] The rise in visitor numbers, the steep hike in park entrance fees for foreigners, and the increase in the percentage of gate fees kept by the national parks service have greatly increased the amount of funds for environmental protection, allowing the GNPS to hire more staff and purchase badly needed equipment. This is a solid victory for conservation, but it comes at a time when the islands and marine reserve are facing greater environmental assaults than ever before, most linked directly or indirectly to the growth of ecotourism. In addition, the floating hotels, tour agencies, and other private businesses within the tourism sector continue to contribute only modestly to the national park system and conservation efforts.

Provides Financial Benefits and Empowerment for Local People

Ecotourism has done both. Since the late 1980s, the standard of living and job opportunities on the islands have grown, as have the political militancy of the local population. The Special Law dictates a fairly even distribution of park entrance fee revenues. Moreover, it outlines measures to strengthen economic capacity and opportunities, educational level, technical skills, and social services of the resident community while attempting to curb its unsustainable level of growth. This is a clear victory for the islanders.

But the island community is a divided community. As Emory University law professor Marc Miller and Stanford University President and environmental science professor Donald Kennedy cautioned in the mid-1990s, "This is not the familiar story of poor locals whose need for economic development is being fought by affluent outside conservationists."[148] Rather, the struggle on the Galapagos has been and continues to be largely between, on the one hand, newer immigrants who are aligned with international fishing interests and are pushing for political autonomy and, on the other hand, national park officials, research station and resident scientists, ecotourism operators, and many long-term Galápagueños who have traditionally relied on subsistence fishing and agriculture and, more recently, ecotourism. Although the Special Law offered the best opportunity yet for building a stable and prosperous community centered on ecotourism, unless its provisions are enforced, it seems that these two broad factions will continue to engage in political and economic wrestling matches. There is still much to be done to fulfill the Special Law's pledge to make ecotourism benefits flow to the local population.

Respects Local Culture

This is not a significant issue in the Galapagos, since much of the local community is imported. Planes arriving from the mainland often carry Otavalo market women bringing hand-woven tapestries, thick sweaters, and woolen shawls from Ecuador's highland regions, but their culture is as alien as their woolen wares are inappropriate to life on the islands. The few Galápagueños who trace their roots to nineteenth-century sailors, prisoners, adventurers, and settlers do believe that they have a distinct culture, which includes both a spirit of independence and a deep understanding of and respect for the fragility of the islands, as well as a code of conduct for protecting them. By aiming to strengthen the environmental education of schoolchildren and newcomers, the Special Law attempts to transfer some of these cultural and environmental norms to future generations. In addition, the high-quality naturalist guides, scientists, and park officials do a superb job in educating tourists about the archipelago's ecological and cultural uniqueness.

Supports Human Rights and Democratic Movements

For a long time, elected representatives from the Galapagos couched their populist campaigns in terms of local control and political autonomy. But they were primarily representing the interests of the fishing industry and newly arrived immigrants who worked, often illegally, for these international operations. Over the last decade, a much broader and more representative movement has developed that pushed for participatory democracy on the islands and passage of the Special Law by the national government in Quito. This highly significant development is in line with the principles and goals of ecotourism.

On the Galapagos, ecotourism operators can and must play a more active role in promoting conservation and providing financial benefits for the local population. But ultimately it is the Ecuadorian government and, most importantly, the GNPS, not enlightened ecotourism operators or NGOs such as the Charles Darwin Foundation, that must be given the authority and resources to provide stewardship for the islands. Ecotourism concessions and NGOs could obviously provide an important complement to park management, writes George Wallace, a specialist in ecotourism and environmental resources at Colorado State University. They should not, however, supersede or replace park administrators, rangers, or interpreters as those primarily responsible for the management of protected areas. There is no substitute for the long-term security, and the ecological and egalitarian management of the Galapagos. As Wallace concludes, "Protected areas like Galapagos are worth fighting for and protecting for all people, for their own sake, for all time. It is an achievable goal."[149]

Wallace's sound thesis is that the GNPS should be viewed as primary among the various stakeholders in providing for the long-term health and protection of the archipelago. A recent but important caveat to this thesis is the need to strengthen the democratic participation of other local stakeholders who contributed to development of the Galapagos Consensus. When the Special Law was passed in 1998, there was cautious optimism that the goal of finding an equilibrium between ecotourism, parks, and local people on the Galapagos Islands could be achieved. In the years since, sound and careful implementation and enforcement has proved difficult. While ecotourism is at an all-time high, the decision to classify the Galapagos as a "World Heritage Site in Danger" is a clear signal that much more aggressive enforcement is needed to balance tourism, immigration, fishing, and conservation. Once again, there are headlines asking, "Can Darwin's Lab Survive Success?"

5

Costa Rica: On the Beaten Path

Costa Rica is ecotourism's poster child. Beginning in the mid-1980s, this tiny Central American country was transformed from a staging ground for the covert U.S. war against Nicaragua and a testing ground for USAID's free-trade and privatization policies[1] into a laboratory for "green" tourism. More than any other event, President Oscar Arias Sanchez's 1987 receipt of the Nobel Peace Prize propelled Costa Rica onto the world stage, securing its image as a peaceful country and marking the start of the ecotourism boom. In the 1990s, Costa Rica jumped in popularity to the front of the ecotourism queue, ahead of older nature travel destinations such as the Galapagos Islands, Kenya, and Nepal. In 1992, the U.S. Adventure Travel Society dubbed Costa Rica the "number one ecotourism destination in the world," and a survey conducted by Costa Rica's government showed that most tourists were entering Costa Rica for ecotourism-related reasons.[2] In 1996, the Costa Rican Tourism Institute (ICT) initiated a highly successful advertising campaign using the slogan, "Costa Rica: No artificial ingredients."[3] By the time Oscar Arias was again elected president in 2006, the country was perceived internationally as the world's prime ecotourism destination.

Costa Rica's natural wonders, encapsulated in the statistic that the country contains 5 percent of the world's biodiversity within just 0.035 percent of the earth's surface, were once a well-kept secret. When my family and I first moved to Costa Rica in the early 1980s, the country was not yet on the radar screen of most U.S. travel agencies and tour

Research for this chapter was done by eco-lodge owner and ecotourism consultant Amos Bien and by naturalist guide and consultant Carlos Alberto (Cabeto) López.

operators. In Costa Rica itself, environmentalism was confined to a small cadre of scientists and national park offices. When we left, a decade later, ecotourism and environmental ethics had become part of Costa Rica's national consciousness. "Ecotourism has helped create the self-image of Costa Ricans. It's now their self-identity," says writer and activist Chris Wille, who works with the Rainforest Alliance in San José. "That's tremendously important. There's a lexicon of environmentalism here, right up to the president." Indeed, in 2007, President Oscar Arias launched the Peace with Nature Initiative, an ambitious plan that brings together the country's core values of nonmilitarism and environmentalism. Among its goals, Arias declared, are to plant some 5 million trees per year, to make the country "carbon neutral" by 2023, and "ensure that our proud tradition of environmental stewardship grows ever stronger."[4]

Costa Rica has the right stuff, the proper building blocks, for ecotourism. As is the case in many developing countries, Costa Rica's ecotourism industry is built on its national park system. Here, however, it is complemented by other ingredients lacking in many developing countries: a well-functioning democracy, political stability, the abolition of its army, respect for human rights, and a (generally) welcoming attitude toward foreigners, particularly the gringo variety. Costa Rica has one of the highest standards of living, and the highest literacy rate, in Latin America. It also has a large middle class, a first-rate public health care system, universal public education, and excellent government-supported universities. The country has produced an outstanding coterie of scientists and conservationists, and more than a hundred local and international environmental NGOs have branches in the country. Costa Rica is physically compact and easy to get around in, with paved roads, telephones, electricity, and a pleasant climate—and it is just a few hours' flight from the United States.

Pure and simple ecotourism, however, is only part of the mix of tourist attractions that draw people to Costa Rica. Although 61 percent of visitors in 2005 visited national parks and 66 percent observed flora and fauna, over 77 percent went to the beach. Other activities include visiting volcanoes (50 percent), canopy ziplines (41 percent), snorkeling (23 percent), rafting (9 percent), and surfing (18 percent). Traditional activities such as sportfishing have held at about 12 percent, while newer activities, such as visits to rural communities (13 percent) and spas (12 percent), are growing rapidly. (In contrast, only 3 percent of visitors play golf while in Costa Rica.)[5] In 2007, the tourism ministry announced it would officially promote four types of tourism—eco-, adventure, sun/sand/beach, and rural community based. This mix of offerings is one of the great attractions of the country, but many ecotourism operators report that visitors increasingly demand more luxurious accommodations, while their knowledge and interest in nature are increasingly casual. "Sustainable tourism," which can apply to any type and scale of tourism, rather than small-scale ecotourism, is the new theme of the Costa Rican tourist industry.

Government Policies and the Rise of Ecotourism

In the 1960s and 1970s, many tourist resorts, clubs, and parks were developed by Costa Rican entrepreneurs especially for the country's middle and upper classes. Domestic tourism was substantial, and most foreign tourists were from other Central American countries. By 1980, tourism was the country's third-largest foreign exchange earner (see table 5.1) and the largest source since 1993, holding at about 20 percent of all foreign exchange earnings since 2000.[6] In the 1980s, the government began for the first time to invest seriously in tourism, reorganizing and beefing up funding (in part through hotel and airfare taxes) for the country's tourism ministry, the Costa Rican Tourism Institute (ICT). The ICT's operating budget comes from a 3 percent hotel room tax and an 8 percent airline ticket tax.[7]

Beginning in the mid-1980s, the visitor pattern began to shift: the number of tourists from North America and Europe grew while both the percentage of domestic tourism and the proportion of visitors from other Central American countries declined. Investment patterns also changed. In the 1980s, assistance from USAID, the World Bank, and the International Monetary Fund (IMF) mushroomed and helped engineer the shift toward overseas, particularly U.S., investment. This flow of dollars came with strings attached, including the requirement that Costa Rica quietly support the U.S. war against Nicaragua and adhere to wide-ranging structural adjustment policies such as privatization of government businesses and industries, promotion of exports and foreign investment, and cutting of funds for national parks, the ICT, and other public institutions.[8]

In 1984, the government of Costa Rica passed legislation to provide investment incentives for hotels, air and sea transportation companies, car rental agencies, and travel agencies. Most of the shares of LACSA, Costa Rica's national airline since the mid-1940s, were gradually sold to Japanese and Salvadoran investors, and the government's share shrank to a mere 3 percent. With passage of the Tourism Development Incentives Law in 1985, tourism projects became eligible for ICT-

Table 5.1.
Costa Rica's Tourism Growth

Year	*1976*	*1982*	*1986*	*1990*	*1995*	*2000*	*2005*
Arrivals (thousands)	299	372	261	435	792	1,088	1,659
Gross receipts (millions $)	57	131	133	275	718	1,229	1,570
% of foreign exchange						21	22

Source : ICT, "Anuario estadístico", 1998, 2000, 2005.

administered incentives and tax breaks. These included exemptions from property taxes and from import duties for construction and remodeling materials, as well as for vehicles such as vans and cars, fishing and pleasure boats, jet skis, dune buggies, and golf carts. To qualify, however, facilities needed to have more than twenty rooms and had to conform to strict standards on use of space and furnishings. "These restrictions often preclude local people from qualifying for incentives," wrote Carole Hill, a professor of anthropology and geography, in 1990.[9] The 1985 tourism incentives provided hotel developers, car rental agencies, and tour operators with a twelve-year moratorium on taxes in return for investments in new tourism projects. Between 1985 and 1995, the number of hotel rooms nearly tripled, growing from 4,866 to some 12,000; by 2005, there were 16,696 officially registered rooms, with perhaps as many or more not officially registered with the ICT.[10]

In 1987, the ICT kicked off a campaign to attract foreign investment in luxury tourism resorts, and ICT officials later signed a tourism incentives agreement with CINDE (Coalition for Development Initiatives, subsequently renamed Costa Rican Investment and Trade Development Board), an institute created and financed by USAID for the purpose of bringing in overseas investment. The agency began making tourism loans to U.S., as well as to some Costa Rican investors and developers, via private Costa Rican banks that had earlier been created as part of USAID's structural adjustment program. By 2001, nearly all of the tax incentives originally offered to tourism projects were gradually eliminated. Still in place is a tax exemption for the import and purchase of the goods necessary for building a new hotel, which favors large businesses that can afford the onerous legal work necessary to qualify for this exemption.[11]

By 1993, tourism had become Costa Rica's number-one foreign exchange earner, surpassing coffee, bananas, and the rest of Costa Rica's increasingly diversified economy. (In the late 1990s, microchip manufacturing briefly exceeded tourism.) Today tourism accounts for about

20 to 22 percent of Costa Rica's foreign exchange earnings and 7 to 8 percent of its GDP.[12] However, while Costa Rica's international reputation as the leading ecotourism destination rose, the government pursued a two-track policy supporting both ecotourism projects and large conventional urban hotels, beach resorts, and cruise ships.

Beginning in the 1990s, large international chains moved in. Most of the medium to large hotels in the capital, San José, have been acquired by international chains since 1990. These include Best Western, Barceló, Sol Melia, Marriott, Hilton (Hampton Inn), the Salvadoran Camino Real, and the European Occidental chain. Some of the foreign-owned chain hotels have been involved in environmental controversies. Spanish-owned Barceló first completed a long-abandoned half-built hotel in San José without proper permitting, and used this model of ignoring local legislation when they built their first beach hotel at Playa Tambor on Costa Rica's Pacific coast. This led to a controversy that lasted many years and seriously damaged the image of both the hotel owners and the Costa Rican government. Tourism Minister Luis Manuel Chacón, under President Rafael Angel Calderón Fournier (1990–1994), received the unflattering "Green Devil" award from German environmentalists for his role in the development of Hotel Tambor. Opponents charged that in the hotel construction, the company had destroyed mangroves, burned out the homes of the original residents who refused to be bought out, and ignored coastal regulations. The government's position was that the hotel was largely in compliance, and court cases remained inconclusive. The final result was that the local community lost in their attempts to require environmental restitution, but won some minor monetary compensation.

Coastal Resorts: The "Other" Tourism Model

Despite the success of Costa Rica's ecotourism and sustainable tourism model, along its coasts and particularly in Guanacaste, a radically different tourism model of large resort and vacation home developments has increasingly become the norm. As early as 1990, an ICT document warned that along Costa Rica's coastlines, U.S., Canadian, Taiwanese, and Japanese investors were buying beachfront property for hotels, condominiums, and vacation homes at an astonishing pace, equal to the rate of all foreign property investment over the previous two to three decades. Experts estimated that by the early 1990s, 80 percent of the country's beachfront property had been purchased by foreigners.

Alarmed by this trend, congressman Gerardo Rudín asked the ICT to investigate this "privatization of the coasts."[13]

President Jose Maria Figueres (1994–1998), touted ecotourism as one of the best business opportunities in Costa Rica. He offered a variety of incentives to tourism investors, and launched a $15 million publicity campaign to attract U.S. and Canadian eco-travelers. But despite his high-profile environmental agenda, Figueres decided in mid-1995 to give a green light to Papagayo, a $3 billion mega-resort project—the largest in Central America—that was the antithesis of "green" development. Papagayo has been dubbed Costa Rica's Cancún: a giant conventional resort complex of luxury hotels, vacation homes, shopping centers, restaurants, golf courses, and marinas strung around seventeen beaches on the Gulf of Papagayo. When all three phases are complete, it will have twenty-five to thirty thousand rooms—twice as many as the thirteen thousand hotel rooms in all of Costa Rica in 1994.

With few exceptions, Papagayo and most other large beach resorts in Costa Rica make little claim of being involved in ecotourism. (The large developer at Papagayo is, however, called Eco-Desarrollo (Ecodevelopment) Papagayo, and its Four Seasons hotel has been certified under Costa Rica's "green" certification program and its golf course includes a few environmental features.) Some large hotels, in fact, have been built in violation of the maritime zone, an imaginary 200-meter strip (approximately 656-foot) of land running along Costa Rica's coastline above the high-tide mark and intended to control beachfront construction. The zone is divided into a 50-meter (164-foot) strip closest to the shore, where no development is allowed. In the remaining 150 meters (492 feet), land can be leased from local municipalities, and construction is permitted so long as zoning, taxation, and ownership guidelines are followed. Concessions are awarded by the local municipality, upon submission of a management plan that must be approved by the ICT. Forested areas and wildlife refuges are subject to the jurisdiction of the Ministry of the Environment (MINAE). Often, these guidelines are not followed. Foreigners, for instance, cannot obtain a concession for beachfront property unless they have resided in Costa Rica for at least five years, and foreign-based or foreign-owned companies do not qualify. Many foreigners get around this by applying for concessions in the names of Costa Rican partners.

However, even though they are being built, these resorts do not always have an easy road to approval. Some have been opposed by local groups, environmental activists, and the scientific community. The struggles over Hotel Playa Tambor and Papagayo, though losses for the cause of ecotourism, helped build Costa Rica's environmental movement and stimulate public debate over mega versus modest tourism projects. One of the flash points became the Pacific coast's Playa Grande, which is considered an important nesting beach for leatherback turtles. In 1995, an Iranian firm announced it was building a $50 million, "green luxury" beach resort with a range of "environmental considerations" that would protect the turtles. It turned out the environmental claims were bogus, a "greenwashing" scam that ignited public protests and succeeded in stopping this project. The government then took the positive step of declaring Las Baulas National Marine Park, which protected the fifty-meter public beach zone. This in turn helped to turn poachers (who had been illegally gathering turtle eggs) into turtle-viewing guides and park guards, and poaching dropped to almost zero. But, sadly, numbers of leatherbacks nesting each season continued, according to the *Tico Times*, in "a veritable freefall," dropping from 1,367 turtles in 1989 to just 125 in 2006. Environmentalists and a number of scientists argued that an additional seventy-five meters of terrestrial portion above the public beach, much of it privately owned, also needed to be incorporated to protect the nesting areas.[14] Although the long-term protection of leatherback nesting is not guaranteed, Playa Grande and Las Baulas National Marine Park represent a victory of sorts, especially compared with the high-profile but unsuccessful battles fought against the Playa Tambor and Papagayo megaresorts.

But even unsuccessful battles have had positive consequences. In recent years, a handful of resorts have adopted some modest environmental reforms. In 2007, for example, a major resort project took up the "green" gauntlet: at a high-profile press conference, together with President Arias, billionaire entrepreneur Steve Case, co-founder of AOL and Chairman of Revolution Places, announced the launch of Cacique, "a first-of-its-kind 650-acre luxury resort community" near Papagayo in Guanacaste. According to the press release, the $800 million beach resort project, which includes a golf course, tennis and fitness center, spa, and low-density, high-value vacation homes, is scheduled to open in 2010. Despite these generic ingredients, the corporation's press release described the resort as "a new authentic vacation experience that retains the local environment and culture" and incorporates "a full complement of sustainability principles and community involvement." Specifically, Revolution Places announced it would invest in a series of community initiatives in Costa Rica, including donation of 1 million trees, several computer learning centers, and $1 million for local nonprofit projects.[15]

Despite such nods to sustainable development, the pace of development up and down Costa Rica's coasts is accelerating, while enforcement of regulations is often lax or nil. "Until the early 1980s, the beaches were ours," bemoaned Ottón Solís, a former planning minister who in 2000 founded the Citizens' Action Party (PAC), which nearly won the 2006 presidential election. "Now all the best ones are American and Canadian owned. Costa Rican families can't go anymore. It's too expensive, and it's an alien culture. The signs and talk are all in English." In a detailed 1996 survey of hotel ownership along most of Costa Rica's Pacific beaches, ecotourism analyst and writer Anne Becher found that the majority (57 percent) of hotels and resorts were foreign owned. Foreign investment is most dominant, Becher says, along "the most famous and ritzy" beaches, whereas Costa Rican–owned hotels (and those most frequented by Costa Ricans) are along the least desirable beaches.[16] By 2002, Becher's partner, Beatrice Blake, found that foreign, particularly U.S., ownership dominated in higher-price coastal hotels, particularly in Guanacaste's Nicoya Peninsula.[17] In 2006 there were over 6 million square meters of new construction, mostly for coastal hotels and condominiums (64 percent more than in 2005, and this was expected to increase another 20 percent in 2007).[18]

True Ecotourism Developments

Ecotourism projects run a wide gamut in Costa Rica. Whereas many developing countries have only a handful of really fine ecotourism experiments, Costa Rica offers a cornucopia of choices, ranging from rustic to luxurious, from counterculture to indigenous culture, from spiritual to scientific, from purely Costa Rican to undeniably North American or European to eclectic, cross-cultural blends. The numberof accommodations has increased over eightfold, from about 300 in 1990 to 2,500 in 2007. The average size is a modest sixteen rooms—an indication that small-scale ecotourism remains dominant in much of the country.[19] And ecotourism has spilled over to the wider tourism market, with a number of urban, chain, and resort hotels adopting some socially and environmentally sound practices. Many of the best of these have received eco-labels under Costa Rica's CST (Certification for Sustainable Tourism), which by 2007 had certified sixty-one hotels.

Punta Islita

Among the few beach resorts that do uphold key components of ecotourism is Hotel Punta Islita, located on the relatively remote southern stretch of the Nicoya Peninsula, nearly five hours drive or a half-hour flight from San José. Built in the early 1990s, the hotel's whitewashed adobe villas, manicured gardens and lawns, elegant open-air bar and restaurant, and crystal clear "infinity" pool, all set into a hillside overlooking the Pacific Ocean, appear typical of members of Small Luxury Hotels. Punta Islita was, in fact, invited to join this exclusive association back in 1996.

But the Costa Rican owners say they are most proud of the bevy of eco-awards the hotel has won in recent years, including, in 2006, the WTTC's Tourism for Tomorrow award in the "Investor in People" category. In an interview, hotel vice president Eduardo Villafranca described the hotel's philosophy as the antithesis of the "enclave business model" of all-inclusive resorts.[20] He said Punta Islita is consciously seeking to bring economic development and environmental stewardship to residents in the neighboring coastal towns. These towns have been characterized by poverty, environmental degradation, lack of basic services, and outward migration of people. In 2002, Villafranca and his partner Harry Zurcher (who is the hotel's owner) created a foundation and embarked on a deliberate initiative to make Punta Islita "a paradigm for community development through tourism."[21] The flagship project has been the creation of what Villafranca says is Latin America's first Outdoor Museum of Contemporary Art. Several of Costa Rica's leading artists have teamed up with local residents and some international craftspeople to turn the tiny, dusty, rundown ranching town of Punta Islita into a brightly adorned and thriving center, with a remodeled church, community center, primary school, and health clinic and new day care center, artists' studio, and several stores. Today nearly every whitewashed wall is covered with brightly colored murals depicting local folklore and history. Sculptures and art displays are scattered around in nontraditional places: four carved wooden totem poles stand near the soccer field, the *malinche* tree across from the store is decorated with mirrors and other materials, while a tree next to the church is "clothed" in wool of colors used by the Chorotega Indians who used to live in this region. A walking tour of the town quickly demonstrates the pride people feel in its transformation. As one local resident puts it, "This used to be the ugliest town in Costa Rica. Now it's the most beautiful."

This newfound pride has been bolstered with new employment opportunities. The Punta Islita hotel and foundation have helped to start three artisan workshops, using local materials and traditions: a group of women makes jewelry, clothing, and small purses with shells and local clothes; a group of men makes lamps, mirrors, and furniture from drift wood; and a youth group creates paintings on wood and makes sand candles. Tourists can visit these workshops and purchase handicrafts signed by the individual artists.

In addition, the hotel hires 85 percent of its staff locally and tries to outsource many of its purchases of goods and services. The foundation has provided loans and training to create a range of locally owned microenterprises that service the hotel. These include small businesses for local produce, processing seafood, and furniture making, a grocery store, restaurants and a café, a taxi service, and a pair of local musicians. Together with MINAE (the Ministry of Energy and Natural Resources), the hotel trains guards and guides to protect the turtle-nesting beach of Camaronal from both developers and poachers. The hotel and foundation also created the area's first recycling center, have set up a credit union, participate in reforestation projects, and provide a range of educational opportunities and scholarships to local residents. Between 2004 and 2006, the hotel and its foundation injected $857,000 into the local communities through local purchases and loans to the microenterprises.[22] For the first time in decades, there is now an inward migration of people moving to the Punta Islita area.[23]

National Parks and Protected Areas

In 1502, when Christopher Columbus came ashore south of present-day Limón, he named the land Costa Rica (Rich Coast) under the mistaken belief that the country was full of precious minerals.[24] Only in the past few decades has this misnomer seemed appropriate as scientists, conservationists, and tourists discovered Costa Rica's vast ecological richness. As part of the narrow isthmus joining North America and South America, Costa Rica has flora and fauna from both continents as well as its own endemic species. This country, a little larger than Denmark, boasts more bird species (850) than are found in the United States and Canada combined and more varieties of butterflies than in all of Africa. It has more than 6,000 kinds of flowering plants (including 1,500 varieties of orchids), 208 species of mammals, 200 species of reptiles, and more than 35,000 species of insects. A long spine of volcanic mountains runs down the center of Costa Rica and the country contains twelve distinct ecosystems, ranging from cloud-covered mountain peaks some 3,840 meters (12,600 feet) high, down to white- and black-sand beaches along the Pacific and Caribbean coasts. Costa Rica is, as former minister of natural resources Alvaro Umaña put it, a biological "superpower."[25]

Today, more than 25 percent of Costa Rica's territory, with an estimated land value of $2 billion, is under some form of protection. Costa Rica has a long tradition of environmental protection, but it wasn't until 1969 that its first national park was officially created. By 2006, the country had 160 different protected areas, falling into eight categories, ranging from completely protected biological reserves, to national parks where tourism, research, and infrastructure are allowed (but nothing can be extracted), to refuges where controlled development and extraction are permitted.[26] In recent years, the country has been divided into ten regional conservation areas, each financed autonomously and headed by a director who is responsible for both management and community outreach.

In creating parks and protected areas, Costa Rica's government pledged to buy out, rather than forcibly remove, those living within the boundaries of national parks and biological reserves. Although this is a more humane approach, it has proved costly and time-consuming, with landowners often waiting years for payment and the park service legally unable to stop logging, farming, and grazing until land is completely acquired. By 2005, an estimated 10 percent of national park land still needed to be purchased. Private inholdings with restricted activities—including ecotourism—are permitted, and sometimes encouraged, in wildlife refuges, forest reserves, and protected zones.

Costa Rica's world-renowned system of national parks and protected areas has in fact served as the springboard for ecotourism, with many eco-lodges located around protected areas. By the early 1990s, 63 percent of foreign visitors to Costa Rica went to at least one park, according to ICT statistics, and this figure has remained relatively constant since then. Between 1990 and 2005, the number of foreigners visiting parks doubled (from 511,233 to 1,066,821).[27]

Yet ironically, while tourism was becoming Costa Rica's largest foreign-exchange earner and many private entrepreneurs were turning handsome profits from tourism in protected areas, the national park service itself was falling into crisis. The parks are plagued by insufficient funds, personnel, and infrastructure; incursions by loggers, gold miners, and homesteaders; and uneven usage, with some parks inaccessible to all but the hardiest backpackers and others overrun with visitors. With few exceptions—Poás Volcano, Irazú Volcano, and Santa Rosa National Parks—national parks do not have visitor centers, roads, restaurants, or other facilities. There are campsites and hiking trails, but no hotels and often no trained naturalist guides. At the same time, the number of privately owned reserves has grown dramatically, and increasing numbers of tourists are spending their time and money in these reserves. To resolve this problem, in 2005 the government of Costa Rica requested a loan of $20 million from the Inter-American Development Bank (IDB) for developing infrastructure in and bordering the national parks, as well as training park personnel in financial and tourism management skills.[28] At the same time, private initiatives in support of the national parks, such as the Pro Parks Association[29] and the Osa Campaign,[30] have grown since 2005, with substantial support from the Costa Rican tourist industry.

Although Costa Rica's economic crisis subsided by the mid-1980s, the park system continued to face financial problems, partly because new protected areas continued to be created and partly because the IMF, the World Bank, and USAID forced the government to cut park funding and staff. In the late 1980s, Alvaro Umaña, the first Arias government's capable Minister of Natural Resources, Energy, and Mines (MINAE), succeeded in raising about $45 million in local currency for the park system through five debt-for-nature swaps, complex transactions involving international lending banks, Costa Rica's Central Bank, conservation organizations, and foreign governments. In these swaps, lending countries or institutions forgave part of Costa Rica's foreign debt in exchange for conservation projects including land purchases, reforestation projects, environmental education programs, and job creation for those living in buffer-zone areas.[31]

Following this period, however, Costa Rica became ineligible for foreign aid because of its relatively high standard of living and relatively well-protected system of national parks. When donations for national parks began to fade and the government entered a fiscal crisis, it turned for the first time to tourism to provide substantial funding for the parks. In 1994, the government announced a steep rise in park entrance fees for nonresident foreigners: $15 at the gate, $10 for advance purchases, and about $5.25 for bulk purchases by travel agents.[32] Until then, foreign and Costa Rican tourists had paid the same modest entrance fee (about one dollar), with an equally modest annual yield of less than $1 million. The result of the fee hike was swift and dramatic. Despite a 20 percent drop in the number of foreigners visiting national parks in 1994 and 1995, entrance fees netted $3.78 million during the first nine months of 1995, four times more than in all of 1994. Yet these additional funds from entrance fees were not sufficient to fully offset the shortfall in government funds and external donations to the national parks.

Although the concept of a two-tiered park entrance fee—a low rate for local residents and a higher one for foreign visitors—is widely accepted around the world,[33] members of Costa Rica's tourism industry strongly criticized the fee formula. Some tour operators stopped offering day tours to parks such as Poás Volcano and Irazú Volcano National Park, which tourists visited for only a few hours, or to parks without trail systems, guides, or other facilities offered in private reserves. In 1996, fees for foreigners were lowered to six dollars at all parks. This compromise seemed to quell criticism while still guaranteeing increased income for the national park service. This formula held through 2002, when a market study indicated that the more popular parks could charge more, and the least-used parks, much less. Fees have since then been adjusted to fifteen dollars for Manuel Antonio, ten dollars for Carara, and six dollars for the less popular parks.[34] Under the plan for park fees, 75 percent of park entrance fees were to go into the operating budget of the administrative region of the park that generated the fees and 25 percent to support conservation areas where tourism and income are low. In practice, the central government withheld a varying percentage of funds, the administrative region used much of the remaining amount, and only a small portion was actually reinvested in the national parks themselves.

As the government was on an austerity budget from 1998 until 2005, in a successful effort to reduce the national deficit, funds for national parks (and all other government departments) were highly restricted. Unlike other departments, however, the parks generated more income than they consumed, and this surplus was taken by the central government for deficit reduction. Only since 2006 have adequate funds been released; this, combined with the $20 million IDB loan and campaigns like Pro Parques[35] is likely to put the parks back on a sound financial footing, if well administered.

Parks, Rural Poor, and Ecotourism

Costa Rica's national park system has received minimal benefit and new problems from the ecotourism boom. Several small Pacific Coast parks, such as Manuel Antonio National Park, Cabo Blanco Wildlife Reserve, and Carara Biological Reserve, have suffered environmental decay and loss of wildlife from far too many visitors. Tiny Manuel Antonio, whose curved, white-sand beaches and mountain backdrop have made it Costa Rica's most famous national park, received a staggering 216,000 visitors in 2005. The rapid, uncontrolled growth of more than a hundred mostly small hotels, as well as restaurants, bars, nightclubs, casinos, and other tourist concessions, along the road leading to Manuel Antonio is proof that small can also be ugly and destructive. The area around the park and the nearby town of Quepos both lack sewage systems, so refuse is dumped directly into the sea. Former park director Alvaro Ugalde calls Manuel Antonio "a red alert" signaling that government regulation, stricter zoning laws and enforcement, and environmental impact studies are needed for all tourism development, not just the large resorts. Starting in the mid-1990s, the park service closed Manuel Antonio National Park on Mondays and set limits on the number of visitors permitted inside the park at any one time. At the other end of the spectrum, a number of Costa Rica's largest parks, including Braulio Carrillo National Park, just fifteen minutes from San José, are rarely visited because they lack even basic infrastructure. Although they remain undamaged by visitors, they earn virtually nothing from tourism.

Parallel to these debates over how to finance and manage the parks in the wake of the ecotourism boom have been ongoing conflicts with rural poor people living around the parks. Costa Rican park officials and scientists did not initially view these protected areas as sources of income and employment for those living around their boundaries. Rather, as is the case in Africa, they adhered to a preservationist philosophy that sought to isolate the parks and prevent any outside encroachment. Costa Rica's conservationists had good reason for concern because, outside the parks, environmental destruction has continued at an alarming pace. By the 1980s, Costa Rica had, outside its parks, the highest rate of deforestation in all of Latin America; in many areas, squatters and homesteaders have also felled forests and cleared land inside parks for grazing and agriculture. However, with the enactment of a forestry law in 1995 that made clear-cutting a felony, and the simultaneous drop in cattle prices and the rise of tourism, deforestation dropped 98 percent in ten years.[36] As ecotourism has grown, forested land in tourist areas is worth far more than cleared land, the reverse of Costa Rica's historical pattern. A study of Lapa Rios Eco-lodge on the Osa Peninsula, for instance, revealed that in 1987, before the lodge was built, the property "had less forest cover than the peninsula as a whole," while by 2000, "the Lapa Rios property had the highest forest coverage of all." The study concludes that "Lapa Rios is clearly a leader among the communities studied here in rate of *reforestation,* showing almost 9 times the peninsula average increase in forest cover over the interval."[37]

Corcovado National Park

Lapa Rios is located near Corcovado National Park, which is recognized by scientists as one of the richest tropical areas on earth and widely considered "the jewel in the crown" of Costa Rica's park system.[38] Corcovado has also been the scene of the most volatile, intractable, and long-running conflict between rural people and parks. It is a conflict centered around gold, not trees. In the early 1980s, large, well-financed mining companies consolidated control outside the park, driving hundreds of small gold panners (*oreros*) into the park, where they killed fish and wild animals for food and silted and poisoned the rivers with the mercury they used in panning. Over the years, the Rural

Guard (rural police) and park authorities periodically rounded up and expelled the fortune seekers, only to have them return on their release. On occasion, scientists were forced to abandon their research inside Corcovado and tourism camps were closed down. Even though tourism in Corcovado National Park was earning an estimated $1 million per year, twice as much as gold mining was netting, the perception was that mining was potentially more lucrative, especially for the region's poor.

In 1985, parks director Alvaro Ugalde asked University of Pennsylvania biologist Daniel Janzen, who had worked since 1972 in Santa Rosa National Park in Guanacaste province, to study the adverse environmental effects of the Corcovado gold miners and propose a way to get them out of the park. Janzen's findings were shocking—some 1,400 miners and hangers-on were living inside the park, game animals had been "practically eliminated," and most of the rivers had become "canals, sterile and full of sediment." The report predicted that the park's ecosystem would recover only after most of the miners were removed, but it said that police action was no long-term solution. Rather, Janzen proposed that to stop such invasions, "the [park service] should involve itself deeply with neighboring communities and other planning agencies to show the benefits of the park."[39] This early articulation of one of ecotourism's precepts proved, of course, much easier to propose than to implement. The miners showed little fear of arrest; the government itself was wary of confrontation because Costa Rica has traditionally tolerated peasant land invasions. Eventually, the park service decided to permit low-level incursions of as many as two hundred *oreros* inside the park. They were not removed until years later, when the government paid compensation to all the former gold panners.[40]

At the same time, the park has suffered recurrent financial crises, in spite of being a major tourist attraction for the region. From sixty-three park rangers in 1990, the numbers plunged to only ten in 2002.[41] As a result, hunting of peccaries (wild pigs) became a problem, also affecting the population of jaguars. A campaign by the Corcovado Foundation, Regenwald Der Österriecher, Lapa Rios, Hotel La Paloma, The Nature Conservancy, and other entities has allowed more guards to be hired and hunting to be greatly reduced. These sorts of problems have occurred on a cyclical basis since the establishment of the park.

In the meantime, the area surrounding Corcovado National Park has become an ecotourism pole in Costa Rica. Dozens of lodges adjoin the park, Golfo Dulce Bay, or the Atlantic side of the Osa Peninsula. Some of them are small, rustic lodges, and especially around the former gold-mining town of Puerto Jimenez, some are run or staffed by former gold miners. Others are luxury eco-lodges catering to clients who pay up to $250 per night. Numbers are kept down because most tourists arrive aboard small planes to Puerto Jimenez; a smaller number arrive by road—a five- to eight-hour drive from San José. A proposal by the government to build an international airport and marina for pleasure boats,[42] together with a proposed development plan financed by the Japanese development agency (JICA),[43] have created fears that the Osa region might see rapid, uncontrolled coastal real estate and mass tourism development of the sort that has lined the Pacific coast of Guanacaste.[44]

Lapa Rios Eco-lodge

The type of tourist development that has been seen as a model for ecotourism and the antidote for mass tourism is Lapa Rios, the best known eco-lodge in Costa Rica, and arguably in all of the Americas. With just sixteen bungalows strung along a remote hillside overlooking the Pacific Ocean's Golfo Dulce (Sweet Gulf), Lapa Rios has won an impressive list of eco-awards including, in three consecutive years, from *Condé Nast Traveler* (2003, 2004, and 2005),[45] and has gained high recognition in *Fodor's*, *Lonely Planet*, and other leading travel guides. In 2003, Lapa Rios became the first hotel in the country to earn "5 'green' leaves," the top rating in the rigorous CST "green" certification program (see below). And in 2005, Lapa Rios was selected from a pool of sixty "compelling nominations" of U.S. businesses around the world for the Secretary of State's "Award for Corporate Excellence"—the only eco-lodge to ever receive this honor. In presenting the award, Secretary of State Condoleezza Rice said, "More than a hotel, Lapa Rios is a model of environmental stewardship and enlightened corporate leadership." She praised its owners, Karen and John Lewis, for understanding "that the best way to do well, is to do good."[46]

The Lapa Rios story began in 1990, when the Lewises gave up their suburban lifestyles and careers as a music teacher and a lawyer in Minneapolis, liquidated their assets and retirement funds, took out loans from family and friends, and moved to Costa Rica. They had been Peace Corps volunteers in Kenya in the 1960s, become avid amateur birders, and, by the late 1980s, decided to find a new project. They didn't yet know the word *ecotourism,* but they knew they wanted to contribute to both rainforest conservation and local rural communities. After three months of looking at properties around Costa Rica, they purchased 389 hectares (about 1,000 acres) on the Osa Peninsula from a local Costa Rican for $400,000. Bucking the advice of "everyone," Karen Lewis says they decided to buy this tract of 82 hectares of degraded cattle pasture and 307 hectares of stunningly beautiful primary rainforest, located in a remote and impoverished backwater of the country—twelve miles south of Puerto Jimenez, on a dirt road that narrowed into a rutted cart track, without bridges for crossing the numerous rivers and streams.

The Lewises defined their mission as demonstrating that "a rain forest left standing is more valuable than one cut down." They envisioned that a small "above rustic" eco-lodge built in the already-cleared pasture could provide resources to protect the primary forest in a private reserve, while also providing employment for the local community. However, when they consulted their neighbors on the Osa, they were told of their wish to have a primary school for the area children. Therefore, Karen and John Lewis undertook both, building the Carbonera School (the first in that region) together with the Lapa Rios Eco-lodge. The bright-blue, two-classroom cement school is a "puro Tico" (typically Costa Rican) structure, while the lodge is a cultural blend: designed by a well-known Minneapolis architect, David Andersen, its construction was overseen by a *ranchero*, a master craftsman from the Osa who incorporated native and largely renewable materials and local building techniques and styles into the structure. The simple-yet-elegant lodge, with its thatched bungalows, vaulted dining room and reception area, and spiral staircase to a treetop observation platform, was opened in 1993, and from the outset it captured attention: its first guests included the minister of tourism and David Rockefeller.

Vacationers trade typical hotel amenities such as television, air conditioning, telephones, Internet, and elevators for deck viewing of monkeys, macaws, and toucans; up to 175 hillside steps connecting the bungalows and other buildings; miles of guide-interpreted hiking trails in the reserve; early morning and sunset bird tours; night walks and jungle overnights; naturalist excursions by boat, on shore, and in the rainforest; and sea kayaking, fishing, surfing, and swimming. There are excursions to botanical gardens, horseback riding through the forest or along the beach, and a stunning pool, yoga, massage, and world-class cuisine that mixes organics and local Costa Rican delicacies.

Also offered is a "sustainability tour" of the lodge's eco-friendly practices, from biodegradable soap and shampoos to biogas produced by the lodge's pigs and, most recently, biodiesel for electricity generation and to run the lodge's vehicles. Guests can also visit the Carbonera School, which has continued to be supported, through an education foundation, by the lodge and its guests. (The Lapa Rios Web site contains a year-by-year description of lodge-financed school activities, as well as a "wish list" for guests to consider supporting with donations, as part of the Travelers' Philanthropy initiative.)[47] The lodge has contributed to other community projects, including the library, Red Cross, a local preschool, conservation campaign, and a recycling initiative. Lapa Rios has also helped to provide salaries for Corcovado National

Park guards and to develop a Blue Flag certification program for the local beach. In an agreement with The Nature Conservancy and CEDARENA (a Costa Rican land trust organization), Lapa Rios has agreed to preserve 920 acres in perpetuity as a biological reserve.

While the "driver" has been responsible environmental protection and practices, Lapa Rios has also excelled in implementing the community benefits "leg" of ecotourism. The lodge has an affirmative action plan to hire and train locals: all but two of its sixty-five permanent staff are from the peninsula. Continual staff training and skills improvement (including English lessons and job promotion) are part of the daily routine, and many staff members have worked at the lodge for more than ten years. According to one recent study, Lapa Rios "provides good stable income and high quality training in the necessary skills" and "better income than other economic activities in the area. . . ."[48] In addition, the researchers found that, unlike many other lodges in the Osa, Lapa Rios "is making a deliberate effort to support local producers and local stores."[49]

Through hard work and attention to detail, Lapa Rios has evolved into a well-functioning, finely crafted, and highly profitable ecotourism operation that has put into practice the best principles of environmental, social, and economic sustainability. The owners and staff have remained continually open to change and have not been afraid of outside scrutiny—via the CST certification, a steady stream of media, and a range of ecotourism experts, consultants, and academic researchers. Beginning in 1999, the Lewises sought to take a break from the day-to-day operations and to further professionalize performance by hiring Cayuga Sustainable Hospitality, the only Costa Rican–based management company committed to ensuring environmental, social, and financial best practices while ensuring guest satisfaction.[50] By 2007, the Lewises were deeply embroiled in what may be their most challenging task: selling Lapa Rios to "the right" buyers who will continue to run the lodge with a similar vision.[51] They are not alone. The question of how to ensure that sound practices continue as the property moves from one owner to the next is among the challenging issues facing a number of the older ecotourism businesses.

Guanacaste Conservation Area

On a national level, the *oreros* crisis with the gold miners in Corcovado did force a number of Costa Rica's leading conservationists to rethink the way the national parks are run. "The concept of a national park," Janzen explained in an interview, "as a place that you set aside, administer with staff sent by the central office, and guard with a gun is dying here very, very rapidly, and we're trying to make it die as fast as possible."

In 1987, Janzen abandoned this fortress conservation philosophy and adopted new principles that incorporated local people in expanding Santa Rosa from a small, unsustainable 10,000-hectare (24,710-acre) park into the 120,000-hectare (296,500-acre) Guanacaste Conservation Area, making it the largest protected dry tropical forest in Central America or Mexico. The new park, financed through Costa Rica's first debt-for-nature swap, incorporated both biologically unique, unspoiled land and what Janzen describes as "trashed old pastures, land that had very little economic value and still had some people living on it here and there."

The plan was twofold: restoration of pastureland to its original dry tropical forest condition and incorporation of the people. Janzen argued, "If you threw them out you'd have had a social problem. We decided wherever there were people we were buying out who wanted employment in the conservation area, we'd employ them. This very quickly evolved into a new kind of administration." A number of farmers have been retrained to be caretakers, firefighters, research assistants, and guides, and their cattle remained in the park and have helped spread seeds to rejuvenate the original dry tropical forest. Although there was some resistance from middle-management park officials, the plan has worked: the land recovered and there are, as Janzen puts it, "happy people" living around and working in the park. The Guanacaste Conservation Area has become a center of innovation in park management and applied conservation research. Because it runs its own endowment fund, it has been spared many of the budgetary limitations of the other protected areas.

Community-based Tourism on the Caribbean Coast

On much of the Caribbean coast, the levels of community integration have not matched that of the Osa Peninsula or Guanacaste Conservation Area on the Pacific coast. Costa Rica's Caribbean coast has its own distinct culture. A third of its people are Afro-Caribbean, and English dialects, Protestant denominations, and reggae music predominate over Spanish, Catholicism, and salsa. In recent years, Nicaraguan immigrants, many of whom are Miskito-Afro-Caribbeans from Nicaragua's Caribbean coast, have settled here as well. Historically, most of the region's economic activities have involved exploitation of resources for sale to the international market. Yet until recently, this coastal region was an isolated and economically depressed backwater. Its population rose and fell with the boom and bust of exports: lumber; cacao; bananas; and turtle shells, meat, eggs, and calipee, a substance found under the lower shell and used to make soap.

From the main port of Limón southward to the Panama border are several protected areas and Caribbean towns, all scenes in recent years of conflicts between local people and outsiders for control of land, natural resources, and the tourism market. Cahuita National Park was established in 1970 without compensating the original landowners until more than twenty years later. Farther south, toward Puerto Viejo and the Gandoca-Manzanillo Wildlife Refuge, the original Afro-Caribbean land owners were partially displaced in the mid-1980s by Spanish speakers from the central highlands when cacao production collapsed. This area, the Talamanca region, has now become a center of small- and medium-scale tourism development, much of it run by Costa Ricans and Europeans and centered on the beach. Some are community-run tourist enterprises on indigenous-owned land.

Tortuguero

Today, the turtle-nesting hamlet of Tortuguero, along the canals running northward from Limón and completely surrounded by Tortuguero National Park, is most frequently cited as the place where a national park and ecotourism have worked together to benefit both the cause of conservation and the economic well-being of the community. Besides its remoteness, it is protected by other conditions that make it unsuitable for resort tourism: the weather is almost always cloudy and rainy, the beach is composed of black, silty sand, the surf is rough, there are sharks, and the national park backs up to the beach, thereby reducing the land available for hotels. Although Puerto Viejo, Cahuita, Talamanca, and other spots along Costa Rica's Caribbean coast are promoted as ecotourism destinations, it is Tortuguero that has been most fully identified with sound conservation and small-scale ecotourism on the Caribbean coast.

As tour-boat owner Modesto Watson maneuvers his awning-covered launch, *Riverboat Francesca* (named for his wife and partner, Fran, a former Peace Corps volunteer), up the 80-kilometer (50-mile) coastal canal linking Limón to Tortuguero, he points out sea turtles, crocodiles, sloths, monkeys, parrots, toucans, and iridescent blue morpho butterflies. Along the canals, ecotravelers pass homesteads and tiny hamlets where the wooden houses are built on stilts. "We're not just taking you from point A to point Z," Watson tells his mostly foreign clientele. "Traveling is like music: the pause between each musical note is what makes it beautiful. You should also enjoy the pause between where you're leaving from and where you're going to." Watson, a Nicaraguan who opposed both the Sandinistas and U.S. interventionism in the

1980s, is part of the new breed of entrepreneurs riding Tortuguero's ecotourism wave. "Ecotourism has brought a 100 percent improvement to people in Tortuguero, and I've seen a change in mentality as well," he proclaims. "People now see that through conservation they realize more income." A closer examination shows, however, that although ecotourism has spawned both entrepreneurship and environmentalism, its effects on the local population are more mixed.

In the mid-1950s, American herpetologist Archie Carr founded the Caribbean Conservation Corporation's (CCC's) Green Turtle Research Station in Tortuguero, which has conducted widely acclaimed research, tagged and tracked some twenty-six thousand green turtles, and played an active role in conservation efforts. By the 1970s, the turtle trade had declined, and in 1975, largely as a result of the CCC's work, Tortuguero National Park was established to protect most of the green turtles' nesting beach and nearly twenty thousand hectares (forty-nine thousand acres) of lowland tropical forest and rivers.[52] Some *campesinos* with farms within the forested park were bought out by the national park service, and in the late 1980s, the park was extended to create a corridor linking it with Barra del Colorado National Wildlife Reserve to the north. The creation of the park meant that turtling and forestry were no longer allowed near Tortuguero. Prohibition of the use of natural resources profoundly changed the ecology—after thirty years of protection, there has been a large increase in the number of turtles that come to nest every year—[53]as well as the economy of the village. Tortuguero residents had little option but to turn to the new economic activity just getting started—tourism.

Many tourists come to Tortuguero to visit the largest nesting beach in the Caribbean for green sea turtles and smaller numbers of leatherbacks (March to June), hawksbills, and loggerheads, which nest during the rainy season between July and September. Larger numbers of visitors arrive during the country's high season (December through April) when there are few turtles; nevertheless, according to naturalist guide Cabeto Lopez, Tortuguero is the best place in Costa Rica to observe a number of other kinds of wildlife.

The basic transportation is by boat—river taxis for tourists and wealthier Costa Ricans and dugout canoes, known as *cayucos*, for local residents. There is no official transport service to Tortuguero, although a local boatman known as Bananero offers daily boat service that connects with public buses for residents and budget travelers. A small landing strip in Tortuguero receives at least two flights a day by Costa Rica's domestic airline companies, Sansa and NatureAir, as well as several charters. So far, no roads lead to Tortuguero, and this has helped stave off mass tourism, although increasing numbers of cruise passengers who arrive in the port of Limón have been taking tours up the canal. In recent years, the number of flights and the size of boat engines have increased substantially, and this has increased both noise pollution and tourism numbers.

Tortuguero has grown in population and visitation from a village of some thirty inhabitants in the 1970s. In 1986, less than 20 percent of Tortuguero's tiny population made a living from tourism. By 1991, approximately 70 percent worked directly or indirectly in tourism, including with the park and the CCC. During this same period, average income doubled, and new migrants brought the local population up to about five hundred.[54] By 2006, nearly all of the population in Tortuguero was working in tourism. In fact there are scant other job opportunities, since there are no other services or public offices in town, and virtually no fishing, as the traditional hunting of lobsters has suffered from overexploitation.

The original dwellers have always had a foot in their ancestral homes in Limón or Nicaragua, and some have emigrated there or to the United States. The CCC has also designed, and the town has adopted, a zoning plan based on the needs of the turtles—purportedly the first such plan in Central America. Nevertheless, land tenure in Tortuguero is a monumental problem as virtually all land is within the restricted maritime zone. More recently, a group of squatters, mostly from Guapiles, invaded the land at the base of Cerro Tortuguero. The number of squatters is now estimated to be much larger than the original Tortuguero settler population. Local park rangers are stretched thin in their efforts to deal with increased poaching, as well as illegal drugs and other social problems.

The growth of the population is closely tied to the explosive growth in tourism in the 1990s. The number of tourists visiting Tortuguero National Park rose 28-fold, from 2,000 in 1986 (1,032 foreign visitors and 972 domestic) to 56,000 in 2005. In 1988, there were five tour boats carrying passengers from Limón and only two or three hotels. By 1995, there were forty-two boats and seventeen hotels, lodges, and small pensions in Tortuguero. Ten years later, there were over four hundred rooms available in the village and an unknown number of boats. Every lodge, even the smallest, has a few tour boats; two large hotels, with more than a hundred rooms each, have at least ten boats capable of transporting up to thirty passengers. Most of the transportation to and from Tortuguero is offered as part of a package deal that includes accommodation, meals, and usually tours.

In addition to the noise and pollution from tourism transportation, there have been other problems related to viewing nesting turtles and other wildlife. When the number of visitors permitted on the nesting beaches was raised to four hundred per night, crowding became excessive. Large numbers of people were walking up and down the beach and gathering chaotically around any female turtle laying eggs. The problem was resolved when the CCC and the park service implemented a good system of beach trails, and authorized only a small number of trackers with radios to walk the beach and indicate to the guides where nesting was taking place.

In the early 1980s, night tours to see other animals—using bright lights to illuminate them from boats—became popular and, scientists found, this was threatening to wildlife. Waterfowl, such as kingfishers and herons, safely perch near the banks during twilight, when they can still see. Night tours on the canals disturb these birds, forcing them to relocate after dark, when they are more likely to be eaten by caimans. With weak protocols for wildlife viewing, lodges began using ever more powerful spotlights on their boats to illuminate wildlife. Then in 1996, the park service banned all night tours, over protests from many lodge owners. Some, including Michael Kaye, owner of Costa Rica Expeditions and Tortuga Lodge, have tried to reinstate night tours, but the park service has held firm on the ban.

In socioeconomic aspects, surveys of ownership of Tortuguero's tourism infrastructure reveal a complicated and sobering reality: the rapid pace of tourism expansion has worked against local entrepreneurs, who need time to gather sufficient skills and capital.[55] The economic gap has widened between the few locals who own tourism businesses and other Tortuguero residents who are either salaried employees in tourism businesses or are outside the tourism sector.[56] In addition, although the majority of tourism dollars generated in Tortuguero at least stays within Costa Rica, most profits from the lucrative package tours do not remain in the community. As early as the mid-1990s Randy Leavitt, the then-director of the CCC's research station, estimated that only 5 to 10 percent of tourists were visiting the area independently, using local hotels, restaurants, boats, and guides.

The ability of Tortuguero residents to benefit from ecotourism has been hindered since the outset by a lack of organization and by weak kinship, community, and institutional ties. Community cohesiveness and participation have been impeded by "powerful internal and external obstacles . . . from factionalism within the village to state policies that promote centralized planning and the accumulation of capital among large . . . tourist facilities," wrote geographer Susan Place in 1995.[57] By 2007, of seven small pensions in the town itself catering to the budget crowd, only one was owned by a long-term local resident. Other pensions are owned by newcomers, while the larger and more expensive hotels are all owned by people from San José or from other countries.

Rather, education and training of guides and hotel employees may be a surer way to give local residents the necessary skills for upward mobility. The CCC, the park service, and the Canadian-financed Cabo Palma Biological Station have played a positive role both in training local turtle guides and in organizing a guides' cooperative, which has become a model for good turtle protection and viewing.

Although its effects on the local community have been mixed, ecotourism has been largely good for conservation. "Because Tortuguero is really a little enclave and all around it is a national park, I can see the turtles surviving and Tortuguero being a good example of how ecotourism can be successful forever," says former CCC ecologist Bob Carlson. Most local people now do see economic value in protecting the turtles and their eggs as well as other threatened species, such as the West Indian manatee and the macaw.

Private Nature Reserves

Costa Rica's history of private reserves and refuges is even older than its national park system. By the mid-1950s, the country was already home to a number of foreign conservationists and scientists, including ornithologist Alexander Skutch, forester Leslie Holdridge, and herpetologist Archie Carr, who were interested in preserving particular types of land, flora, or fauna. From the 1960s until the late 1980s, the number of private reserves grew modestly. Most were intimately connected to scientific research and had a close relationship with the national parks. Since the 1980s, the number of private reserves and refuges has grown rapidly, totaling several hundred by 1996 and equal to an estimated 2 to 5 percent of Costa Rica's territory. Most are forested areas belonging to Costa Rican middle-class families and farmers; some have been bought by foreigners or international conservation organizations; and an estimated one hundred are involved in ecotourism, ranging in size from ten hectares to twelve thousand hectares (approximately twenty-five acres to thirty thousand acres). Private reserves do not need to register with the government, but if they do, they receive a package of benefits including exemption from real estate tax, guaranteed expulsion of squatters within three days, and the possibility of receiving payments for environmental services.[58]

In 1995, the Costa Rican Network of Private Nature Reserves (Red Costarricense de Reservas Naturales) was established, and by 2007 there were seventy-seven private reserves, comprising about 1 percent of the national territory.[59] Nearly half of the private reserves belonging to the association have ecotourism activities and/or lodges. The

Network became a major force in lobbying the government to consider the reserves as a private-sector force for conservation, in counterpoint to the wood industry.

Although most ecotourists are drawn to Costa Rica by the international reputation of its large, well-protected national park system, increasingly these visitors spend their time and money in private reserves, which offer accommodations, more infrastructure, and higher-quality interpretation.

Monteverde Cloud Forest Reserve: Quakers and Quetzals

Costa Rica's best-known private reserve is Monteverde. This Cloud Forest Reserve is located in the Tilarán Mountains, several hours' drive up a bone-jarring, muffler-mashing, switchback dirt road off the Pan-American Highway. It is the most famous of Costa Rica's private reserves and the country's leading ecotourism destination. It is closely linked geographically to two other large private reserves, the Children's Rainforest and the Santa Elena community's Cloud Forest Reserve, as well as many small ones belonging to tourist enterprises and farmers. Internationally acclaimed for its sound conservation and ecotourism strategies, Monteverde is blessed by its relative inaccessibility, careful monitoring by scientists, well-trained guides, the Resplendent Quetzal and other outstanding birdlife, and a socially responsible local community. Since the late 1980s, however, as the tourism explosion has brought world attention and new funds to Monteverde, it has also put strain on its ecosystem and nearby population.

Monteverde, a bucolic, misty mountaintop on Costa Rica's continental divide, was "discovered" in 1951 by a small band of North American pacifists, twelve Quaker farming families who moved to Costa Rica to protest the military draft in the United States. (Costa Rica had abolished its army in 1948.) The Quaker immigrants bought 1,200 hectares (3,000 acres) at the top of the mountain from a local land company, began dairy farming, and set up a milk and cheese factory as a profit-sharing cooperative that quickly became the economic hub of the area. The factory is run democratically by its five hundred shareholders (who must be area residents, and none can own more than 5 percent of the business) and has from the outset been actively involved in community affairs. "In one way or another, we always participated in the community, with education, health, roads, and general services," explained José Luis Vargas, a former general manager of the cheese factory. In recent years, the factory has been restructured more along vertical corporate lines and tourism has surpassed it as Monteverde's main source of employment. But the factory remains deeply involved in the community and an influential economic driver over a wide geographical area, while its cheese is sold throughout the country.

According to longtime Monteverde residents John Trostle and Wilford "Wolf" Guindon, the Quakers who settled here did not initially have a strong environmental ethic. Guindon said he had arrived as a "chainsaw expert," and his "vision of development was clearing pastures and building roads and schools," until he began working with biologist George Powell and got "converted to a philosophy of protection."

Moreover, when the Quaker immigrants arrived, they found that environmental destruction was already moving up the slopes toward Monteverde: Costa Rican loggers, agriculturalists, and cattle ranchers were rapidly clear-cutting the forest in an agrarian settlement program supported by the government. The Quakers themselves started to clear-cut the cloud forest at the top of the mountain for dairy cattle, but discovered that this caused their water supply to dry up. As a result, they decided to conserve 554 hectares (1,370 acres) of virgin cloud forest from their original 1,200 hectare purchase. Known as the Monteverde Cloud Forest Reserve, they set aside this land to protect their watershed and buffer the force of wind on their pastures. This became the centerpiece of Monteverde's ecotourism industry. In the early 1970s, George Powell, a biologist working in Monteverde, proposed that this area and another 328 hectares, or 810 acres (for which he raised funds to purchase), be joined in order to protect the primary breeding area of Monteverde's rare endemic golden toad. (Sadly, however, the Quakers' conservation efforts did not save the golden toad, which now appears to be extinct; see chapter 1.)

The Monteverde community granted a ninety-nine-year lease and management of the reserve to the San José–based Tropical Science Center (TSC), a nonprofit scientific research and educational organization. The TSC built a field station at the entrance to the reserve, and increasing numbers of biologists, students, and bird-watchers came to study the cloud forest's flora and fauna. Through land purchases largely financed by U.S. conservation organizations and private individuals, the reserve has grown to 10,522 hectares (26,000 acres), encompassing eight ecological zones.

Originally, the Monteverde Cloud Forest Reserve was intended for research and protection, not tourism. The twenty-five-mile trek from the Pan-American Highway up a steep, frequently impassable dirt road meant that only the most hardy travelers made the journey during the early decades. Even so, as Monteverde and TSC's Cloud Forest Reserve became a center for biological research in the 1970s and 1980s, the area became populated by a growing number of English-speaking scientists and conservationists. At the same time, ecotourism was becoming an important source of employment for the Costa Rican farmers who lived in and around the neighboring village of Santa Elena. As land prices rose with the tourism boom, more and more small dairy farmers sold their land, often to conservationists; then, after spending the windfall, many often sought employment in tourism businesses. At the same time, new immigrants moved in, lured by Monteverde's image as an ecotourism mecca.

Even before the ecotourism boom, deforestation for dairy farming was threatening much of the surrounding forest. In response, a group of resident conservationists formed the Monteverde Conservation League as a membership organization in 1986 and began a campaign to purchase forested land and conserve it in another private reserve. Schoolchildren in Sweden became aware of this project and began to raise money for what became known as "The Children's Rainforest." Eventually six hundred schools in forty-four countries contributed to the effort, and, by 2007, the reserve was 22,500 hectares (55,600 acres), making it the largest private reserve in Costa Rica. Part of the purchases were financed, as well, through a $540,000 debt-for-nature swap involving the Rainforest Alliance and several other conservation organizations.[60]

Several smaller private reserves have been opened adjacent to the Monteverde Cloud Forest Reserve and the Children's Rainforest. The most innovative is the 314-hectare (775-acre) Santa Elena Cloud Forest Reserve, officially opened in 1992. It is leased and run by the local high school, together with Youth Challenge International, a Canadian-based NGO, with the aim of using ecotourism to benefit community development in Monteverde. One of the country's first community-administered reserves, the entrance fees are used for the protection of the Reserve and to provide higher quality education for the local schools.[61] Many other small private reserves are scattered throughout the area, often associated with hotels or other tourist projects.

Tourism grew slowly in the beginning, then accelerated rapidly in the 1980s. The first pension, Irma's, opened in 1952, and additional dormitory space in the reserve's field station adequately accommodated visiting friends, students, and scientists until the mid-1970s. In 1974, when the reserve first opened, Monteverde had a mere 471 visitors. In 1980, there were 3,257 visitors; in 1983, there were 6,786; and in 1985, there were 11,762. By 2004, the number had reached 74,000, and seems to have stabilized or dropped slightly.[62]

The ecotourism boom has brought expanded resources for conservation, as well as for the community. However, as tourist numbers climbed, reserve officials began to foresee problems from overuse of trails and diminished quality of experience from crowding. In response, the Tropical Science Center limited visitors in 1991 to 100 at a time (later raised to 160), restricted most tourists to well-marked trails through only about 2 percent of the reserve, hired and trained more naturalist guides, and sharply increased entrance fees for foreigners to thirteen dollars for an entrance ticket or twenty-eight dollars if a natural history guided walk is included, in hopes of curbing the number of visitors, particularly those on package tours. Fees for Costa Ricans are $3.50 for adults ($2 for students). Limits on the number of visitors who can be on the trails at any given time have been set, and a well-organized system of guided excursions in the morning, led by well-trained naturalists, has helped alleviate the crowds at the entrance of the Reserve.

Today, the Monteverde Cloud Forest Reserve brings in over $1 million per year. Ninety percent of this money goes to the reserve's operating costs, an endowment fund, and a fund for scientific research; the rest is used to help finance scientific research and other private reserves around Costa Rica.

Scientists monitoring visitor impacts on Monteverde's wildlife have found some species more sensitive than others. Quetzals, for example, seem to tolerate human presence quite well, whereas other species avoid the proximity of trails and noise—although this does not necessarily affect population size and health. The Cloud Forest managers made a prudent decision to "sacrifice" a small part of the park for intensive ecotourism use, and this income in turn finances the entire conservation effort. Less than 2 percent of the Cloud Forest Reserve is used for trails. Undoubtedly this causes impact on soils and mating practices of birds and perhaps other species, but the overall impact is negligible. In the villages of Monteverde and Santa Elena, tourist facilities have proliferated and improved in quality. The two pensions that existed in 1977 have given way to more than sixty-five officially recognized ecolodges and hotels in 2007, most of them along the road from Santa Elena to the reserve.[63] Tourism-linked employment steadily increased as well. By 1992, there were some seventy services related to ecotourism in the Monteverde area, including souvenir and crafts stores, horseback riding, art galleries, restaurants, transportation services, and a discotheque-bar, employing a total of 231 people.[64] This number has no doubt doubled or tripled in recent years, but there is no recent census. Longtime resident Richard LaVal has indicated that the real number of visitors to Monteverde might be far higher than the number who enter the Cloud Forest Reserve, because there are so many other opportunities and activities now available.[65]

Visitors to Monteverde now are far more diverse in their interests and tastes than the original rugged breed of scientists, bird-watchers, and ecotourists. Many tourists seek more amenities at lower cost, and the hotel owners have sought to satisfy their demands. Many businesses have moved from the original concept of ecotourism, with its contemplation and interpretation of the natural environment, toward adventure tourism. For instance, canopy ziplines have become ubiquitous in Costa Rica, with over two hundred in operation all over the country. This trend started commercially in Monteverde in 1994, in the backyard of a small lodge owned by one of the oldest local families, the Valverdes. According to Mario Solano, owner of Selvatura Park Canopy Tour, people are still primarily attracted by the history of the area and the natural history of the Monteverde Cloud Forest Reserve, yet they want to do other activities; the ziplines provide an adrenaline rush but offer little or no environmental interpretation.

Although most hotels and restaurants around Monteverde are small and owned by local families, several of the biggest (with up to one hundred rooms) are owned by outsiders, and, as in Tortuguero, increasing numbers of visitors arrive on prepaid package tours. However, the business practices of many tour operators have changed for the better. Rather than "importing" goods and services, they are now able to use the many high-quality, locally owned tourism auxiliary businesses—from naturalist and cultural guides, lecturers, massage and yoga experts, and beauticians to locally owned transportation, restaurants, craft centers, horse rentals, and butterfly farms—that have grown with the ecotourism boom. Some newer owners appear motivated purely by profit, whereas Monteverde's original business owners were often guided by strong environmental and social principles.

The makeup of the population today is very diverse, as economic success has attracted Costa Rican and international investors, construction laborers, and skilled and unskilled tourism workers. English-speaking naturalists, scientists, and other professionals such as doctors, lawyers, and teachers, have migrated to Monteverde since the mid-1970s, attracted by its bilingual culture and the beauty of the region. This has forced up the cost of living, led to housing shortages, and put pressure on schools, the health clinic, and electrical, water, and other services. Land value has also been driven up by purchases for hotels or conservation. Long-term Monteverdians Nery Gomez and Jim Wolf believe that there are now far too many people in Monteverde—both residents and visitors.[66] Although this means more cash circulates in the economy, it has also brought growing pains, as Monteverde and Santa Elena have evolved from pristine mountain villages into small modern cities, with traffic, petty crime, and alcohol and drug abuse, particularly by young people.

Growth has also made it possible for Monteverde to have its own local government. In the past it was administered by the distant municipal council in the port city of Puntarenas. Mario Solano, Selvatura Park owner as well as president of the Monteverde Chamber of Tourism, welcomes this local control, but says there is a need to establish more effective zoning regulations that will control haphazard growth. As is the case elsewhere in Costa Rica, land-use planning and zoning laws in Monteverde are not adequately enforced in the construction of hotels, restaurants, and other tourist facilities. Solano believes that although growth has been uncontrolled until now, most of the established businesses want to move toward "quality tourism." He notes that most owners of tourism-related businesses are not expanding their size, but rather are improving their quality and services. "We certainly do not want to replicate the experience of other very popular destinations in Costa Rica that have become too massive," says Solano.

Ecotourism as a Monocrop

Some in Monteverde worry that the area has become too dependent on its ecotourism "monocrop." It is estimated that 65 to 70 percent of the area's income now comes from tourism—up from just 10 percent in the late 1980s. Many local residents have entered into ecotourism activities, some more successfully than others. Near Monteverde's hotels, for instance, Jorge Rodriguez rented a farm with abundant wildlife but terrain so steep that his cattle kept falling into ravines and breaking their necks. With the absentee owner's permission, Rodriguez put in trails and a parking lot and changed the property's name to Ecological Farm (*Finca Ecologica*). "For the first time," said Rodriguez in 1994, "the farm is making a little profit, just enough to maintain the paths and sustain my family." Ten years later, however, Rodriguez, an intelligent entrepreneur who developed the original idea, had lost control of the project. He says another member of the community saw an opportunity and collaborated with the absentee owner from the United States to evict Rodriquez and take over what had become a very popular business. The new management has invested in additional services, including a restaurant and a gift shop.

Four miles down the road, fifteen farmers in the hamlet of Los Olivos have also had a hard time growing a successful ecotourism business. They borrowed fifty thousand dollars, built a rustic lodge and cabins overlooking a pond, and put in nature trails. But their Eco Verde Lodge suffered from poor marketing, a hard-to-find location, and stiff competition from dozens of ecohotels in Monteverde. By 1997, occupancy was less than 4 percent. "It's easy to talk about ecotourism and sustainable development, but the reality is very difficult," says Huber Barquero, a farmer and Eco Verde's main investor. Like many other community-based ecotourism initiatives in Costa Rica, Eco Verde, though sponsored by a large international environmental organization, failed to take into account such basics as quality infrastructure and good management, marketing, accounting, interpretation, and language skills. By early 2008, Eco Verde, though still marketing on the Internet, was also up for sale.[67]

While building and running accommodations catering to the international market takes know-how and capital that is often beyond the capacity of local entrepreneurs, ecotourism has brought a range of benefits to the area. Ecotourism income has helped to expand and improve the educational system, permitting the children of poor subsistence farmers to become guides, business owners, and even university graduates. Quality education and sophisticated technical training have become widely available, where once it was a rarity for children to stay in school beyond sixth grade. And today, virtually everyone in the Monteverde region is aware of the social and economic value of environmental conservation. Although Monteverde is still a leading example of sensitive tourism in Costa Rica, many of its original concepts have changed, some for the better, others not.

One of the clearest beneficiaries of the ecotourism wave has been CASEM (Comité de Artesanías Santa Elena–Monteverde), a women's handicraft cooperative. Since its founding in 1982, it has grown from eight to some ninety members (including three men)[68] and has greatly improved the quality, variety, and marketing of its embroidery, hand-painted stationery and clothing, T-shirts, jewelry, wooden crafts, ceramics, and other products. With the help of a few outside experts, the members of the cooperative, most of whom had never before earned an income, "created a handicraft environment that didn't exist before," explained Monteverde resident Sue Trostle, who worked with CASEM in the beginning. "CASEM has been a wonderful way for women to feel empowered, to gain self-esteem, and to build a sense of sisterhood to address family problems such as alcoholism and domestic violence."

However, in the last few years, there has been some disaffection, and some members have left CASEM. Several of the women who left have found that there are stores and hotels where they can sell their products directly, without following the strict practices of the cooperative. According to Nery Gomez, CASEM's director, the organization is still very strongly attached to its original goals and is committed to education, empowerment, and raising living standards in the community. However, CASEM faces competition from several newer handicraft cooperatives. One, Women of the Cloud Forest, is a Fair Trade project with seventy members who make hand-embroidered bags and jewelry from rainforest seeds.[69]

While ecotourism has brought more income and opportunities, it has also increased social and economic inequality. "You have people with capital who can afford to build the hotels and people who come in and work as chambermaids and cooks," says Nathaniel Scrimshaw, former codirector of the Monteverde Institute. "Yes, it benefits the whole community, but it's creating increasing differences in wealth as well." Beginning in the 1990s, the price of land has shot up, and Carlos Vargas, a Costa Rican Quaker who managed the Santa Elena banking cooperative, worried that too many people were abandoning dairy farming, either selling their land to outsiders or converting their farms into pensions, hostels, and restaurants. "Now we say we can sell what we have, but we cannot afford to buy. We are losing the properties that we have had," says Vargas.

The Monteverde way of doing things is symbolized by the community's decision to grade but not pave the road. (A paved road would bring even more tourists; the dirt-and-stone road keeps down the number of visitors and ensures that they must spend at least one night in Monteverde, and this is good for the local economy.) Over the years, the community consensus, as voiced through town meetings, has repeatedly reaffirmed the decision that the main road to Monteverde should not be paved. But the rapid growth from ecotourism has taken a toll on the community's social fabric, as Scrimshaw describes: "In the past, there was a lot of moral force that acted to shape whether something happened or somebody did something. And that is simply no longer true. Now there's no time, and it's too diverse. And that has been pulling at the texture of the traditional town meeting that used to run everything." Many of the new economic immigrants don't understand or appreciate Monteverde's community activism and participatory, town-meeting style of governance.

Ecotourism has changed Monteverde forever. The community is no longer a tiny and remote utopian experiment. Monteverde is sharing its wealth with the world, not only through ecotourism but also through scientific and educational programs and through interaction with the surrounding Costa Rican communities. The results have been both positive and negative. As Nathaniel Scrimshaw reflects, "Monteverde is doing all the right things, and making all the mistakes. It is dealing with the ecotourism boom as best as any community can, and it's also having all the disappointments of overdevelopment."

Villablanca Hotel and Cloud Forest Reserve

Jim Damalas says he "sells" his Villablanca Hotel and Los Angeles Cloud Forest Reserve, together with the neighboring town of San Ramon, as an alternative destination to Monteverde. Villablanca Hotel,[70] just a two-hour drive north of San José, was built in the mid-1990s by former Costa Rican president Rodrigo Carazo and his wife, Dona Estella, on the family's dairy farm, which has an adjacent two-thousand-acre private reserve. Carazo is an avid proponent of ecotourism. "There's no other way for Costa Rica to earn the foreign exchange and protect its national parks and protected areas," he explained in the late 1990s as he showed me around this beautiful mountaintop eco-lodge. Villablanca's food, furnishings, and whitewashed adobe cottages with their blue trim and red tile roofs—the colors of the Costa Rican flag—were *puro Tico.* However, when I returned with my family a few years later, I was saddened to see this idyllic lodge looking tired and worn down, with few guests. Basically the Carazos, who were both in their seventies, did not have sufficient resources or energy for proper upkeep.

In 2003, a happy solution was found: Jim Damalas, owner of Green Hotels, which includes the well-known luxury eco-lodge Si Como No,[71] at Manuel Antonio, bought Villablanca. Damalas, a former Hollywood director, had known the Carazos for twenty-five years and, he says, they were "concerned that we respect the virgin cloud forest and respect the cultural integrity of the hotel." Damalas spent a year overhauling, upgrading, and "greening" the facilities. "Hollywood Jim," as Damalas is known, also added a small, multimedia theater and other conference facilities. He recounts, "I felt a great responsibility as a gringo, buying from an ex-President. We enhanced but did not change Villablanca." He says he was relieved when Dona Estrella told him at the opening of the newly renovated lodge, "I don't feel like we've lost a daughter. I feel like we've gained a rich son-in-law."

Damalas also strives to promote San Ramon, which is not yet a tourist hub but, he believes, offers outstanding attractions and opportunities for high-quality ecotourism. Ninety-five percent of employees are from the local area, the hotel strives to buy locally, and it encourages local businesses to provide local nature, cultural, and historic tours for their guests. Damalas explains, "Our big thing is getting the word out that San Ramon is an alternative to Monteverde."[72] Visitors readily notice that staff pride in the lodge and in San Ramon is high.[73] As one of the managers showed me around, he explained how, in 2005, the staff created a Green Team and set out, with the help of certification experts from Rainforest Alliance's Sustainable Tourism project, to earn a top rating from the CST certification program. After a year's work, Villablanca was audited and, in 2006, became only the third hotel in the country to receive five "green" leaves—along with Lapa Rios and Finca Rosa Blanca.

Private Reserves of the Organization of Tropical Studies

In contrast with the amenities adjacent to the Monteverde and Los Angeles cloud forests, more modest and controlled ecotourism—lodging, meals, and guide services—is offered at facilities run by the Organization for Tropical Studies (OTS) at its two private reserves and at facilities inside a national park. OTS is a consortium of sixty-three research institutions and universities in the United States, Puerto Rico, Costa Rica, Mexico, Peru, Australia, and South Africa that offers scientific courses at its Costa Rican field stations in areas such as tropical biology, ecology, plant systems, agriculture, and tropical forestry. With its headquarters at Duke University and an office in San José, OTS was founded in 1963 by the National Science Foundation (NSF) in Washington, D.C., and U.S. biologists who wanted to learn more about the tropics. "In terms of science, the tropics were as unknown as the far side of the moon," says Chuck Schnell, a lanky biologist with an MBA degree who became OTS's associate director in the mid-1990s. Schnell explained that OTS's three ecologically distinct field stations are used to support its courses, and have become involved in ecotourism.

The oldest and best known of OTS's private reserves is La Selva Biological Station, a 1,538-hectare (3,800-acre) tract of humid lowland rain forest along the Sarapiquí River's watershed in northern Costa Rica. In 1968, when OTS acquired the core of the reserve, a 619-hectare (1,530-acre) cacao farm, from American forester Leslie Holdridge, the area was extraordinarily rich in wildlife and was part of a much larger unbroken forest. OTS registered La Selva as a natural forest reserve in order to protect it from cutting and to avoid problems with squatters who might claim it as unused land. However, OTS soon found that registration was not enough to ensure the survival of a piece of pristine land. Over the next fifteen years, roads, settlers, farmers, and loggers cut into the region. By the early 1980s, only a two-mile-wide, nine-mile-long neck connected La Selva to the 31,768-hectare (78,500-acre) Braulio Carrillo National Park, which had been created in 1978.

The alarming rate of deforestation forced OTS to rethink its preservationist conservation philosophy and strategy. Since small islands of habitat tend to lose much of their biodiversity, expanding the size of La Selva and linking it to the enormous Braulio Carrillo National Park became vital to its survival. The government did not have the $2.2 million necessary to buy the corridor, so OTS helped raise the money from private U.S. foundations and conservation organizations and bought up enough land to double the reserve's original size. A 1986 presidential decree officially added this corridor to Braulio Carrillo and, in the process, saved La Selva.

OTS staff members also came to realize that since successful conservation means contented neighbors, La Selva must provide benefits to its surrounding community. As Gary Hartshorn, a former OTS student who went on to become a vice president of the World Wildlife Fund and then director of OTS, put it, "There are some 10,000 families of colonists in an area going two-thirds the way around La Selva and on 50,000 hectares of land. If La Selva doesn't deliver useful outreach [to them]—whether tree seedlings, environmental education, or community services—the reserve won't survive."[74] La Selva employs more than a hundred local people and runs a variety of programs, including training naturalist tour guides, technicians, and research assistants; and offering environmental education programs such as tours, seminars, and classes for schoolchildren, teachers, and parents.

Down near the Panama border, with a pleasant mountain climate, is the OTS's Las Cruces Biological Station, 146 hectares (360 acres) of tropical rain forest and cultivated plantings that includes the 8.1-hectare (20-acre) Wilson Botanical Garden, a diverse and beautifully landscaped nursery of tropical and subtropical plants. The botanical garden, established in 1960 by Florida horticulturalists Robert and Catherine Wilson, contains ferns, bromeliads, gingers, and 680 species of palms—the world's second-largest collection. The OTS's third field station and accommodation facility is located within a national park, Palo Verde Biological Station, a dry forest area in Guanacaste Province. Thanks to OTS, this is one of the few national parks and reserves where it is possible to spend the night in relative comfort.

While OTS's main mission is scientific research, it also provides unique and educational experiences for tourists who are interested in Costa Rica's natural habitat. All three field stations have branched out into ecotourism, providing reasonably priced full-board accommodations including guides, and thereby providing "unique and educational experiences for tourists who are interested in Costa Rican nature."[75] As Schnell contends, "In some sense, we're a scientific travel agency, and I would say that OTS is one of the reasons that Costa Rica has the privileged position in the ecotourism market." Indeed, a study published back in 1987 revealed that visits by family and friends of OTS researchers, as well as return visits of former students, were the principal source of the growth of nature-oriented tourism in Costa Rica at that time.[76] Ecotourists to these three field stations are accommodated only when space is available, so as not to interfere with OTS's research and teaching functions, and this serves to keep the numbers low. Schnell explained that the research stations charge "a pretty penny," in part to offset OTS's free programs for the local community. The price is, in fact, relatively moderate—under a hundred dollars per person—at the three stations for dormitory accommodation, full board with family-style meals, and naturalist guides.

OTS's role in promoting ecotourism is broader than simply hosting tourists at its research stations. "Many of the interesting little stories about organisms and natural history have grown out of OTS [work]," Schnell says, "and former OTS people are now working all over the country." He lists, for instance, Daniel Janzen, who first came to Costa Rica with OTS in the 1960s; Donald Perry, who established the Rainforest Aerial Tram; Amos Bien, owner of Rara Avis; many of the biologists now at Monteverde; and a number of Costa Rican scientists, professors, resource management experts, and national park officials.

The Rise of Sarapiquí

The Sarapiquí region has become known as one of the five ecotourism "poles" in Costa Rica, along with Tortuguero, Monteverde, the Osa Peninsula, and the Cerro de la Muerte region. Sarapiquí's ecotourism development stems directly and indirectly from the establishment of the OTS's La Selva Biological Station. Over the last twenty-five years, a number of ecotourism facilities, including Rara Avis Rainforest Lodge, Selva Verde Lodge, Hotel La Quinta, and the Rainforest Aerial Tram, were established in Sarapiquí by entrepreneurs with a direct relationship with La Selva, as staff or as users.

Ecotourism enterprises in Sarapiquí date back to 1983, but they have proliferated dramatically since about 1999. At present, the zone offers a wide range of tourism products, all related in some way to nature or adventure, or provision of complementary services. These include eco-lodges, canopy ziplines, horseback riding, butterfly houses, yoga centers, spas, restaurants, a cultural museum, and private reserves, as well as a range of river-related activities, such as kayaking, white-water rafting, and boat tours. Now the largest tourist operations in the region are Sueño Azul, with fifty-seven rooms, Selva Verde Lodge, and Hacienda Pozo Azul, each offering a variety of activities. Sueño Azul has a yoga center and spa, horseback riding, a visitor center for cruise tourists next to a jungle waterfall, a butterfly house, and rainforest trails. Pozo Azul features canopy ziplines, horseback riding, river tubing, and a butterfly house, all in a natural setting. Selva Verde Lodge, one of Costa Rica's original eco-lodges, offers nature walks in its private reserve, low-key conference facilities, and lectures on the rain forest. In 1993, as one of the earliest examples of Travelers' Philanthropy, Selva Verde started the Sarapiquí Conservation Learning Center (SCLC), whose mission is "linking communities and conservation through ecotourism and education." Located on the lodge grounds, SCLC staff and volunteers provide community services such as environmental education, after-school programs, educational scholarships, and English language training for residents in the surrounding rural towns. Financed by the lodge and its parent company, Holbrook Travel (based in Florida), SCLC also has a gift shop with local handicrafts, dance and music classes, and other cultural activities for the local community and lodge guests.[77]

Another regional organization, the Sarapiquí Chamber of Tourism (CATUSA), has become an important element in cementing good and mutually supportive relationships among tourist enterprises in the zone. These businesses perceive that their strength is in unity, in presenting the region as a whole ecotourism attraction, and in offering a range of complementary activities. Nearly all of the businesses refer clients to other members of CATUSA, and the group engages in numerous joint marketing and lobbying activities. In 2005, nearly all its members, as well as the municipal government, signed a pledge to purchase only certified wood products for all future construction. In addition, Sarapiquí ecotourism operators played early leadership roles in Costa Rica's national ecotourism society, CANAECO (see below).

Rara Avis Rainforest Lodge and Nature Reserve

Amos Bien wears a beard, tall rubber boots, a brimmed canvas hat, and a machete strapped to his waist as he briskly strides into the rain forest. He's followed by a small band of hikers. Bien knows how to read the rain forest, and he's also a good storyteller. He weaves together what we're seeing in one small patch of forest: a black-and-white butterfly, a passionflower, white dots on the leaves, a caterpillar, and a fruit called a granadilla. "A good guide," Bien contends, "without using a single scientific name or technical word, will explain how the forest works, will build up whole concepts based on interesting natural history stories."

Amos Bien's name and attire conjure up the image of a Pennsylvania Dutch farmer, but he is a transplanted New Yorker who has lost most of his city accent and become *puro Tico*, with deep roots in his adopted country. In many ways, Bien is the pioneer of ecotourism in Costa Rica. Whereas Monteverde and OTS backed into ecotourism, Bien intentionally set out to build his lodge and private reserve, Rara Avis (Latin for rare bird), in accordance with what are now viewed as sound ecotourism principles. Bien first came to Costa Rica in 1977 to take an OTS biology course at La Selva. There he spent a lot of time talking with farmers who had cut out small homesteads on the reserve's periphery. "When I sat down and did the math with them about how much money they hoped to make and how much they really could make from cattle," Bien says, "the two things were widely different." He was convinced he could demonstrate that rain forest left intact could be more profitable than clear-cut land. "The rain forest is becoming scarce, and because of that scarcity, people are going to want to come as tourists and see it," Bien explains.

In 1983, Bien spent six months backpacking around Costa Rica and finally found 607 hectares (1,500 acres) of virgin rain forest in Sarapiquí on the Caribbean side of the country. It is adjacent to Braulio Carrillo National Park and has a good climate, four spectacular waterfalls, and an old jungle prison colony, El Plastico, which became Rara Avis's first lodge. Bien recounts that he initially approached the World Bank's private sector branch, the International Finance Corporation (IFC), for funding, "and they said if I could find a way of doing it for $4 or $5 million they would finance it, but if it was less, they weren't interested." Bien instead talked some friends and relatives into becoming stockholders and took out a modest loan from a Costa Rican bank. "We were the very first project to get local bank financing for ecotourism. It was considered totally radical, and the banks thought they were taking a substantial risk. But in the end, they were happy because we paid back all our loans, and they have gone on to finance other ecotourism projects." Community involvement was also vital to Rara Avis's success. The townspeople of Las Horquetas helped Bien find the land, build the dirt road (often consisting of deep mud and slippery clay), construct small bridges, repair the prison camp, and rescue stranded vehicles and people. "I felt that if the surrounding community of Las Horquetas—the potential chainsaw wielders—were not part of the project, then it would never work," Bien explains.

Initially, Rara Avis was based at the very rudimentary prison colony's dormitory; today, this is used by visiting scientists and students. Tourists stay in either the eight-room Waterfall Lodge; Las Cabinas, designed especially for bird-watchers; or a treetop cabin that is reached by climbing a rope (accompanied by a guide). Accommodations are fairly basic: there's no electricity, but there are excellent communal meals, bathtubs, and hot showers. The main activity is the guided hikes along narrow forest trails, where coatimundis, anteaters, and tapirs are common and jaguar and other cat tracks are often seen. As the name of the reserve implies, the bird-watching is unparalleled. More than 380 species have been identified, including the great green macaw, the slaty-tailed trogon, the snow-capped hummingbird, and other unusual species.

Nearly all of Rara Avis's employees, including guides, are from the nearby town, and the lodge buys most of its supplies locally. Employees have received English-language instruction, and training in cooking, guiding, and other skills. Those who have been with the company for two years become stockholders, and there is also a profit-sharing scheme for lower-level employees. The community is involved in other ways as well. Rara Avis gives free tours to elementary and secondary school groups and has made in-kind donations to the local clinic and schools. Bien calculates that Rara Avis generates about eighty thousand dollars annually for the local community, making it one of the most important sources of income and employment.[78]

Bien says that Rara Avis has successfully demonstrated to people in the area that "the rain forest offers a higher income-producing potential for ecotourism than for any other use." Rara Avis's Web site describes it as "a fascinating project in commercial rainforest conservation—using ecotourism to make the rainforest profitable without destroying it, and using publicity to teach others to do the same." However, like Daniel Janzen, Bien sees ecotourism as just one of the "products" that can be harvested from protected lands. Rara Avis has, over the years, grown tree seedlings for reforestation programs in Costa Rica and raised and exported butterfly chrysalises and the endemic "stained glass window" palm, which makes a lovely ornamental plant. Rara Avis also plans to collect seeds from dozens of species of orchids and package them in test tubes for the overseas market.

Until a few years ago, Rara Avis's most famous "product" was the "mechanical web," a mobile perch that permits scientists to move horizontally and vertically through the forest canopy. OTS biologist Don Perry built this engine-powered cable car over Rara Avis's main waterfall and some twenty acres of forest. However, Rara Avis lost the mechanical web when Perry moved operations to another, more accessible site, where he and other investors established the Rain Forest Aerial Tram, a large, commercial ecotourism venture. This loss, combined with a growing competition among ecotourism facilities and a shift toward "softer" ecotourists who don't want to spend hours on Rara Avis's awful "road" before reaching the lodge, have all hurt business. The number of visitors to Rara Avis dropped from 1996 to 2003 and then leveled off, even as the number of visitors to the country grew. Bien observes that current visitors to Costa Rica desire more luxury and are less interested in hard-core immersion in nature. Rara Avis is not, Bien readily admits, for everyone. "After we tell people they have to wear boots, take a difficult tractor ride, [and] slough around in the mud, the people who come here are the right sort." Over the years, more than ten thousand of the "right sort" have made the journey to Rara Avis, which remains Costa Rica's most authentic ecotourism experiment.

La Quinta Sarapiquí Country Inn—A Cautionary Tale

La Quinta, located just down the road from La Selva, is owned by a Costa Rican couple, Leonardo Jenkins and Beatriz Gamez, who describe it as their "life project."[79] It is one of the finest examples of how Costa Ricans, though of modest means, have used hard work, tourism expertise, ingenuity, and collaboration with the local community to create an eco-lodge that showcases Costa Rica's natural and cultural beauties. Gamez says she learned about ecotourism by working, first, in the late 1980s for Horizontes Nature Tours, the country's most respected tour operator; then with OTS; and finally, together with Leonardo, as partner and manager of a hotel in Puerto Viejo, Limón. After four years at this hotel, they sold their shares and "left not only with plenty of experience, but also enough capital to start our own project." They chose Sarapiquí and initially considered finding a piece of remote forested land, but ultimately decided that while remote was "romantic" it "would not put dinner on the table." Instead, they bought a large orange plantation with "access to essential services," including main roads, electricity, and water. They remodeled the small buildings already on the land and built an additional twenty rooms. In their first year, 1992, occupancy was a paltry 6 percent. Gamez says that when, two years later, things were still not improving, they were about to give up. But then their luck turned: the representative of a large U.S.-based outbound tour operator, Overseas Adventure Travel (OAT), came and offered La Quinta its "first real business."

Gamez says, "It took us about five years to consolidate a product that could be considered competitive in this field. We see ecotourism as an activity through which we can preserve or even restore our cultural and natural heritage," she states. "It is very important for us that 99 percent of our employees come from the immediate community. We buy all our fruits, vegetables, eggs and meat from local producers. We also have trained farmers to provide various services, such as transportation, for our clientele. So lodges like ours are not only for the leisure and enjoyment of foreigners who visit us, but are going to have an impact in the lives of people around us." In addition to white-water rafting, visits to OTS's La Selva, and rainforest walks, La Quinta offers several specialized tours, including a "Cocktail Tour" that includes a visit to a local school, a pineapple plantation, a chocolate (cacao) tour, a tree planting, and a cooking class.[80] At La Quinta itself, activities include birdwatching, a butterfly house, a reforestation project, frog walks along the river, a gallery with exhibits of local insects and archeological artifacts, and a garden featuring heart of palm, yucca, papaya, and other typical Costa Rican food crops.

While La Quinta has become financially viable and has also earned three "green" leaves under Costa Rica's rigorous CST eco-labeling program, Gamez says that in recent years they have had to struggle to "comply with tour operator demands for comfort and luxury that simply do not match La Quinta's simplicity and commitment to the surroundings. Unfortunately, we are witnessing less support and interest in community projects as an important component of sensitive travel." She says that while La Quinta has played an active role in both the community and the Sarapiquí Chamber of Tourism, some of the larger and newer resorts are not interested in working collaboratively and supporting community businesses. Instead, they seem only concerned with "making more money by bringing in larger volumes of people, at higher prices, with more sophisticated services that are not sensitive to ecotourism." She explains further, "In contrast, because we are trying to stimulate the participation of the community, most of our services are contracted outside La Quinta, and when it comes to negotiations, we do not have control over the prices and cannot lower them at our will, as large operators do."

Rain Forest Aerial Tram

Also near Sarapiquí is one of the most successful private reserves and nature tourism attractions: the Rain Forest Aerial Tram, a $2 million, state-of-the-art "soft" ecotourism project designed by biologist Don Perry as an upscale version of his original Rara Avis mechanical web. Opened in 1994 and just a fifty-minute drive from San José, the Tram quickly became one of the country's most popular tourism attractions; by 2007, it was catering particularly to cruise passengers on day visits to Costa Rica. The Tram carries visitors and their naturalist guides in green cable cars through nearly a mile of treetop canopy, giving them a spectacular bird's-eye view of the rain forest.

The 450-hectare (1,000-acre) private reserve is adjacent to the magnificent Braulio Carrillo National Park, which is one hundred times bigger but largely inaccessible. Many of the Tram's workers are former ranch hands and banana workers and the Tram is now the area's largest employer. Perry calls his project "the school of the treetops," and each year the tram offers free trips for several thousand Costa Rican schoolchildren. Tourists pay $49.50 for park entrance or a hefty $78.50 for a full day, including transportation and a meal, while Costa Ricans pay between $20 to $49 for the same services. The Aerial Tram meets important ecotourism criteria: it's educational, accessible to elderly and handicapped tourists, ecologically quite sensitive, and, apparently, beneficial to the surrounding community. A major drawback, however, is that although the tram's rich canopy comes from its proximity to a vast national park, the park itself receives no direct benefit from this ecotourism project. Aerial Tram officials say they provide no support to the national park, and instead use their profits to purchase and create other private reserves.

Two Faces of Private Reserves

The proliferation of private reserves that protect unspoiled land and promote ecotourism is widely endorsed by Costa Rican government and national park officials; members of the tourism industry; officials of conservation organizations, the World Bank, and other lending agencies; academics; and scientists.[81] They argue that private reserves conserve land that the government cannot afford to buy and therefore are the most expedient way to expand Costa Rica's protected areas. Private reserves also provide facilities for ecotourism that the national parks cannot finance or do not want to provide. Private reserves bypass government bureaucracy and red tape, are often more efficiently run than national parks, can respond quickly to conservation and ecotourism needs, offer an opportunity for community-run conservation and ecotourism, and provide resources to support other activities such as scientific research, organic farming, and sustainable harvesting from the forest.

Several studies have concluded that private reserves are, overall, enormously beneficial.[82] However, in studying private reserves in Costa Rica (and then in Africa), I became convinced of a number of pitfalls and problems that need to be addressed. What happens, for instance, to the rural poor who are displaced when private reserves are created by foreigners or wealthy Costa Ricans? Whereas Costa Rica's national parks are, at least in principle and on paper, committed to paying a fair price for land that is incorporated into parks, there is no such requirement for private reserve owners. The backbone of Costa Rica's economic and social stability has been the yeoman farmer, but in recent years increasing numbers of small landowners have sold out, often too cheaply, and joined the ranks of rural or urban laborers. Environmentalist and former legislator Guillermo Barquero says, "In the name of ecotourism, our poor peasants are giving away their land for pennies." Not only are there few restrictions on foreigners owning land, but also, in a break with its historic support for squatters (*precaristas*),[83] the Costa Rican government now pledges to quickly remove squatters from private reserves.

Although private reserves are often praised as a low-cost means to help governments establish protected areas, they may not include the most ecologically important land. In Costa Rica, many are too small or too remote to fit into the country's system of megaparks. Further, Costa Rica's main problem is financing and preserving the existing park system. Private reserves are siphoning off NGO funds, scientists, and tourists from the national parks. International conservation organizations that in the past would donate funds and experts to the national parks are today investing in private reserves, where they find more flexibility and fewer bureaucratic hassles. Increasing numbers of ecotourists are visiting private reserves, which, though much more expensive than the national parks, offer more amenities.

A number of private reserves do voluntarily work closely with neighboring publicly protected areas by training guards and guides or lending buildings for park meetings. Private reserve owners could, however, be required to contribute more systematically to national conservation efforts through, for instance, a visitors' tax, educational programs, lower entrance fees for Costa Ricans, hiring and training of employees from the surrounding area, and cooperation in scientific research with Costa Rica's universities and national parks. If the popularity and profitability gap between private reserves and public parks continues to widen, pressure will surely mount, as it is in the United States, to privatize national parks. This would be a tragic mistake: Costa Rica's megaparks are an important part of the national patrimony, and their long-term protection is best ensured by the government, not private owners, who increasingly are not Costa Ricans.

Setting and Measuring Sustainable Tourism Standards

In April 1996, ICT official Bary Roberts stood up in the audience during a conference on "Ecotourism, Measuring the Impacts" at Yale University's School of Forestry and the Environment. From the floor, he announced that the government of Costa Rica was about to become the first in the world to create a certification program to rate the environmental and socioeconomic sustainability of hotels. This announcement took the speaker, Beatrice Blake, by surprise since she had been invited to Yale to explain a pioneering "green" rating system for eco-lodges that since 1992 had been included in editions of her popular guidebook, *The New Key to Costa Rica.*

Throughout much of the 1990s, the *New Key* women had set out to identify and evaluate all lodges in Costa Rica that claimed to be involved in ecotourism. They traversed the country, spending hours at each location interviewing lodge owners, employees, and community representatives. Those lodges that passed muster, usually around sixty-five, received a rating of one to three "suns"; those that failed were not listed in the *New Key*'s "Sustainable Tourism Rating."[84] The survey findings were kept confidential but Blake's partner Anne Becher wrote long reports to all the lodge managers, outlining the results and suggesting areas for improvement.

This homegrown, low-budget, labor-intensive project was a creative pioneer in the field of ecotourism certification. The small team doing the audits knew Costa Rica well and, in keeping with sound ecotourism principles, they gave weight to locally owned lodges, to ones that offered "a true experience of nature," had their own reserve or made use of a national park, tried "to use sustainable practices," and were actively involved in the community and in environmental initiatives and struggles. They had a good marketing tool through Costa Rica's oldest guidebook. But over time, Beatrice Blake says, the model proved difficult to sustain. The problems were several-fold: the publishers of *New Key* were not willing to invest sufficient resources to fund the survey; other guidebooks on Costa Rica became more popular;[85] and the eco-rating system was heavily dependent on Becher and Blake, both of whom moved away from Costa Rica. The Green Rating in the 2006 edition listed seventy-two businesses, but a number of lodge owners said they had not had a recent site visit by *New Key*.[86]

Certification for Sustainable Tourism (CST)

By the mid-1990s, two young ICT officials, Marco Picado and Rodolfo Lizano, proposed that the government create and run the Certification for Sustainable Tourism (CST) program. The idea was quickly accepted within the agency.[87] Lizano, who was a student at INCAE (Central American Institute for Business Administration), a business school connected with Harvard University, then spent more than a year developing the concept. In 1997, the first edition of CST for hotels and lodges was released, and the following year, the first hotels were certified.[88] While stimulated by the New Key program, CST did not draw heavily on this model and explicitly sought to cover a larger swath of the market than simply ecotourism. Lizano felt strongly that tourism in Costa Rica was moving beyond small eco-lodges and that if the country were to remain competitive internationally, the newer, larger, more conventional, and often more luxurious hotels also needed to abide by responsible environmental and social principles. According to INCAE professor Lawrence Pratt, who is a member of the National Accreditation Commission, CST addresses environmental, social, and community variables, but CST "is not an ecotourism seal per se. It is applicable to all types of hotels—city, country, eco, beach. That is its principal strength."[89]

However, like the *New Key* eco-rating, Lizano and others behind the CST were similarly motivated by the belief that a solid certification program was vital to protect Costa Rica's tourism reputation and weed out "greenwashing." As Lizano wrote, "This program directly attacks the practices of some businesses which operate as 'greenwashers' (businesses which abuse the concept of 'eco' or 'sustainable') because it will offer reliable information about which businesses really make an effort to offer a sustainable tourism product and which don't."[90] According to an early evaluation of CST, many of the 104 hotels that initially signed up to be assessed described themselves as "eco-friendly," "sensitive to the environment" and as resentful of other facilities that "also use such terminology but do not really put into practice basic environmental principles or contribute to the quality of life in their communities."[91]

The CST measures sustainability along three axes: environmental, social, and economic, using a checklist of 153 yes/no performance-based questions in four general categories: (1) physical-biological environment, (2) hotel facilities, (3) guest services, and (4) socioeconomic environment. These questions can be relatively easily answered first by the hotel management and then by the onsite auditor. "For this reason," writes engineer and certification expert Robert Toth in evaluating CST, "there is little need for the intensive training, consultants, and other service providers typical of sectors which apply generic (environment management systems) standards."[92] The total points received in each category are then tallied and a formula is used to calculate the final score for each of the four general areas. The *lowest* final score received for any of these four categories determines the sustainability category obtained by the hotel. Lizano, the architect of this unusual and seemingly harsh scoring system, says it is designed to encourage improvement. "We don't use an average because businesses could then work harder only in the areas easiest for them. We want them to advance in all four areas equally, to give all equal importance," he explains.[93]

In a system that mirrors the five-star rating, certified hotels receive between one and five "green" leaves. To achieve level five, a hotel must score 94 percent or above in each of the four rating areas; by 2007, only three accommodations—Lapa Rios Rainforest Eco-lodge, Finca Rosa Blanca Country Inn, and Villablanca Cloud Forest Hotel—had earned five leaves. Andrea Bonilla, who as Lapa Rios manager, oversaw the lodge's certification process, says, "The process of going through the certification steps is very positive for the staff. CST evaluators came here for several days and then gave us feedback and a due date. They said they would come back and see if we have made the changes. This gave us a lot of ideas and also was a way to confirm that we were doing most things right. We'd developed these things sort of seat of the pants, on our own, and this helped confirm we were doing well."[94]

Beatrice Blake, however, argues that the CST has set the bar too low by requiring only 20 to 39 percent "yes" answers to get one "green" leaf. "It doesn't take much to get that score—which would be an F in school," she notes.[95] In contrast, Glenn Jampol, owner of Finca Rosa Blanca, a high-end country inn outside San José that became the second hotel to earn five "green" leaves, contends, "While many of us are doing it out of a desire to do the right thing, there's a need to get others on the bus, to give them a leaf for doing minimal things, and then have them move up slowly."[96]

CST's eco-award program is run and financed by the government, and, at least through its first decade, has been free to businesses seeking certification. The program is voluntary, in contract with the five-star quality rating that the government requires hotels to be part of in order to be licensed.[97] Clearly if the CST program were also mandatory, it would have grown much more quickly. It has also been hampered because government funding has been relatively modest, and this has limited the number of auditors, created a backlog of hotels wanting to be audited or reaudited, and allowed for almost no marketing. The main marketing tool has been an uninspired Web site, which posts the survey results in Spanish and English (this is positive)[98] and sorts certified hotels by level (number of leaves), province, and type (city, mountain, or beach), but otherwise fails to delineate the type of tourist experience offered by different accommodations. For instance, level-three ratings include the Hotel San José Palacio, a 254-room, five-star center city chain hotel, and Rara Avis, a rustic, rugged eight-room lodge with a private reserve that specializes in nature hikes. "It mixes apples and oranges and it waters down the real ecotourism places," says one ecotourism expert who has studied the Web site. Because of this, a number of ecotourism operators and experts have pushed the CST to establish a version specifically for ecotourism (CST-eco) that would recognize the unique conservation and community roles these smaller lodges are playing.

By mid-2000, 171 of the estimated 400 hotels in Costa Rica suitable for certification had signed up, but only 37 had been certified; the rest were on the long waiting list. By 2002, the program had stagnated, as interest in it by both the ICT and the industry waned, and bureaucratic problems associated with budget cutbacks and internal politics appeared to have doomed the program. Ironically, CST's reputation outside Costa Rica remained strong, and its principals and criteria were used in creating certification programs in many other countries.

Then, in 2005, an abrupt change for the better occurred. When the International Organization for Standardization (ISO) established a committee on tourism standardization, Costa Rica set up a mirror committee representing all sectors of the tourism industry, as well as government and academia. One of the first actions of the committee members was to pressure the government to give fresh resources and support to CST. Shortly thereafter, CST for Tour Operators (CST-TO) was implemented and seven tour operators, including industry leaders such as Horizontes Nature Tours, Swiss Travel, and Camino Travel, were certified. These tour operators, in turn, announced that they would gradually begin to only use certified hotels. Hotels once again started clamoring for certification and recertification. CST returned with vigor, and from 2004 to 2007, the number of certified hotels grew from thirty-seven to sixty-one.

The reasons for the about-face are several. There's a growing realization that Costa Rica is losing its comparative advantage as an ecotourism destination, as countries such as Ecuador, Panama, and Nicaragua become more powerful competitors. In addition, as both resort tourism along the coasts and urban tourism including chain hotels, casinos, and night clubs expanded, Costa Rica's ecotourism image was tarnished, although, as the periodic airport survey shows, nature tourism remains the principle reason why tourists come the country. International tourists and tour operators had begun to complain that Costa Rica was not demonstrating a commitment to environmental practices outside of the national parks.[99] European tour operators, in fact, began requiring sustainability policies from their suppliers.[100] Strengthening the CST program became an important tool for showing the government's and the tourism industry's commitment to sustainable tourism. As hotelier Jampol puts it, "The CST is an extraordinarily important concept. Today tourists talk about five stars like it's an adjective. We need them to do the same with CST's five 'green' leaves."[101]

Community-based Rural Tourism and Best Management Practices

Another development that has strengthened ecotourism in Costa Rica has been the efforts by several organizations to train small and medium ecotourism businesses in good environmental and management practices. An analysis of surveys completed since 2000 in the United States and Europe shows that an increasing number of tourists are looking for genuine cultural experiences.[102] This is reflected in Costa Rica's airport exit surveys, which found that 12 percent of tourists visited rural communities in 2005, and this rose to 15 percent in 2006.[103]

However, as demand grew, it became increasingly clear that many small, community-based lodges and attractions suffered from poor quality of services, lack of marketing, and scant attention to environmental issues. Beginning in the mid-1990s, several international agencies, including the United Nations Development Program (UNDP) and the Dutch government, began assisting several Costa Rican organizations that specialized in capacity building and training for community-based ecotourism businesses. In addition, the *New Key to Costa Rica* began highlighting community-owned eco-lodges both in its guide and on its Web site.[104] By 2005, Rainforest Alliance's Sustainable Tourism office in San José had established a program to teach good practices to dozens of small tourist enterprises in Costa Rica, Guatemala, Belize, and Ecuador. The program was coupled with an important marketing effort to promote these businesses on the internet and at international trade shows.[105] External audits of these programs have shown that many of the positive changes have lasted long after the end of the training programs.[106]

Three Costa Rican organizations, Cooprena, Actuar, and ACEPESA, have played a key role in helping communities to develop and market small, community-owned ecotourism businesses. The oldest is Cooprena,[107] a membership organization of eighteen tourism cooperatives that run lodges and activities.[108] Under the leadership of a dynamic Costa Rican lawyer Leyla Solano, Cooprena started developing and marketing community-based rural ecotourism in 1994. It is based around the principles of local management, women's participation, protection of natural resources, recuperation of local traditions, equitable income distribution, and using community-based tourism to support rural development.[109] Cooprena has successfully promoted ecotourism at its member cooperatives, while training and motivating them in better management and environmental practices. It also operates Simbiosis Tours, specializing in rural community-based tourism.[110]

ACEPESA is an association that was created in 2000 to help small tourism businesses in Central America implement good management practices,[111] as part of a project called the "Route of the Corn Cultures" ("*La Ruta de las Culturas de Maíz*"). In Costa Rica, ACEPESA's projects have included training local guides in Barra Honda National Park, helping farming communities in San Carlos create homestay programs, supporting a local community-based tour operator, JAZÓN (Young Farmers of the Northern Zone), and providing technical skills to the "Daughters of Guanacaste," a group of women who own small tourism businesses.[112]

A third organization, ACTUAR, was established in 2001[113] as the Costa Rican Community-based Rural Tourism Association, with funding from the UNDP's Small Grants program. Comprising over twenty rural tourism enterprises, ACTUAR describes itself as "a network of community associations that have developed local tourism businesses to generate alternative income sources and initiatives for environmental conservation purposes."[114] A number of the lodges are owned and operated by indigenous communities in the Talamanca region. It operates an online reservations center and a booking office in downtown San José.

These three organizations have collaborated with the UNDP in assembling a popular guidebook on community-based tourism, published in Spanish and English and called *The Real Costa Rica: Your Community-based Tourism Guide*.[115] In addition, they run an annual trade show for the Costa Rican domestic tourism market that promotes community-based tourism. In 2007, they convinced the ICT to promote community-based rural tourism and establish special regulations to support it. All three organizations have also run programs in other countries in Central America to assist local community organizations in establishing solid, good-quality, community-based tourism businesses.

Ecotourism Organizations: CANAECO

A final positive trend has been the formation, in 2005, of CANAECO, the Costa Rican National Chamber of Ecotourism.[116] Given Costa Rica's global international reputation and the leadership role a number of Costa Rican businesses and consultants play in ecotourism, it is surprising that it took so long to form a national association. However, once formed, CANAECO quickly grew to include about one hundred of the leading ecotourism companies and experts and became an important national voice of ecotourism businesses within the tourist industry lobby and with the ICT. It has been active in promoting the reactivation of the CST certification program, as well as providing a national forum for ecotourism in workshops and biennial congresses.[117] In addition, CANAECO members have served on the board and as staff for The International Ecotourism Society (TIES), and CANAECO has played a significant role in global gatherings.[118]

Many CANAECO members, as well, support projects in their host communities as part of the growing Travelers' Philanthropy movement to promote corporate social responsibility within the tourism industry. Among the many examples are, as mentioned earlier, Lapa Rios, which supports a local primary school; Selva Verde, which runs a community center; and Punta Islita, which is promoting arts, crafts, and microenterprises in the surrounding towns. Initially several of the CANAECO officers came from Sarapiquí, one of the up-and-coming ecotourism hubs in Costa Rica. In 2007, CANAECO elected a new leadership team headed by Glenn Jampol (owner of Finca Rosa Blanca[119] and Arenas del Mar, a new beachfront lodge and nature preserve at Manuel Antonio) and undertook a major reorganization and revitalization. Under the umbrella of the Arias government's Peace with Nature Initiative, CANAECO embarked on a campaign to address climate change and work to make Costa Rica the world's first "carbon neutral" ecotourism destination. In 2004, the Costa Rican regional airline Nature Air became the world's first "carbon neutral" airline when its owners made the decision that the company would pay to offset the greenhouse gas emissions from all its flights and donate these funds for protection of forests in the Osa Peninsula.[120] Other CANAECO members, including Horizontes Nature Tours and Lapa Rios, also implemented carbon offset and alternative energy programs.

Costa Rica's Ecotourism Scorecard

From 1990 through 2005, the number of tourist arrivals to Costa Rica grew by a vigorous 28 percent per year,[121] tourism became the country's top dollar earner, and Costa Rica's international image was transformed from that of a Central American banana republic to an ecotourism mecca. This tiny country has become the second most frequented tourist destination in Latin America, following Mexico. Although this transformation has not been without problems and drawbacks, particularly along the Pacific coast where the model of large resort complexes and vacation homes is increasingly dominant, Costa Rica has, in much of the rest of the country, high-quality nature tourism. On a number of fronts, the country has fulfilled the seven main criteria for sound ecotourism.

Involves Travel to Natural Destinations

It is Costa Rica's fine national park system and its growing number of outstanding private parks and reserves that draw most international visitors to the country.

Minimizes Impact

While the majority of hotels are small, in recent years the fastest-growing tourism sector has been resorts by big international hotel chains, according to the Costa Rican Chamber of Hotels.[122] Even though this development has been around, rather than in, the national parks, and much of the development within the private reserves is environmentally sensitive, the steep rise in numbers of tourists has caused environmental decay in some of the most popular parks. It is, however, along Costa Rica's coasts that the negative effects of mass tourism are most apparent and sound ecotourism—with some notable exceptions—most rare. There has been serious overdevelopment of lodges and hotels, as well as growing complexes of vacation homes and other tourism-related facilities and businesses in areas such as Manuel Antonio National Park, Montezuma, Tamarindo, and Jacó. In several controversial projects, Papagayo and Hotel Playa Tambor, for instance, government officials, from ministers to municipal functionaries, were accused of taking bribes in return for granting licenses for environmentally inappropriate construction. In other areas, most notably Manuel Antonio, lack of enforceable zoning has led to uncontrolled growth of small tourism establishments.

Scant official attention is paid to the need for low-impact construction. Without enforceable zoning regulations and environmentally strict construction standards, few of Costa Rica's hotels have been built with an overall rigor intended to limit impact. A number of eco-lodges, however, have some ecological features, such as solar-heated water, natural ventilation or ceiling fans instead of air conditioning, and use of thatch and other local construction materials.

Environmental impact can be minimized through enforceable regulations, coordination among various ministries and municipalities, and better land-use planning. In her pioneering 1990 ecotourism study, Elizabeth Boo wrote that "concrete governmental actions . . . and coordinating efforts of the National Park Service and the Costa Rican Tourism Institute, still must be taken"[123] if ecotourism in Costa Rica is to improve. Nearly twenty years later, little had changed. Costa Rica's tourism planning has been fragmented, characterized by a lack of coordination and overlapping responsibilities among the different government agencies and an absence of (or at least an absence of enforcement of) regulations.

Builds Environmental Awareness

Ecotourism has clearly helped to build environmental awareness among both visitors and Costa Ricans. There are scores of Costa Rican and international environmental organizations, environmental classes are now taught in many schools, and several universities offer courses or a degree in ecotourism. And initially the *New Key*'s "sustainable tourism rating" and more recently the CST's "green" certification program have been useful in helping to raise standards and inform choices by tourists and intermediaries such as tour operators, guide books, and the media.

Traditionally, Costa Ricans have vacationed along their beaches, but with the rise of ecotourism, increasing numbers are visiting parks and reserves. Local visitors can enter the national parks for a very modest fee, and some private reserves also have reduced entrance fees for local visitors. Guanacaste Conservation Area, in particular, has developed nature programs for schoolchildren, and the privately owned Rain Forest Aerial Tram admits free of charge a limited number of local school groups. All of this is helping to build a solid national base of support for both conservation and ecotourism.

In terms of tourist education, most tour companies and private parks have well-qualified, bilingual naturalist guides who are also knowledgeable about the country's history and culture. The national parks, however, frequently are understaffed, and their best guides are often drawn away to better-paying jobs in the private sector. In addition, many tourists themselves are demanding vacations that are less rigorous both physically and intellectually. Thus, some of the best ecotourism companies have been forced to water down their programs, and conventional tour operators have moved in to offer ecotourism lite experiences that include only quick overviews of both nature and the country, such as a visit to a volcano or a botanical garden.[124]

Provides Direct Financial Benefits for Conservation

The growth of ecotourism in Costa Rica has helped support conservation efforts and scientific research, particularly in the older private reserves, such as Monteverde, La Selva, and Corcovado, and this has undoubtedly helped slow the rate of deforestation. But although Costa Rica's national parks system remains among the world's finest and, with the hike in entrance fees for foreigners, is earning more from ecotourism, it is far from self-supporting. Greater effort needs to be made to open parts of the larger national parks to visitors, with better limits on tourism numbers in the smaller, most popular parks. Because most national parks offer little in terms of naturalist guides, trails, lodging, and restaurants, many visitors are choosing to go to private reserves, which typically provide better services and attract more foreign visitors. The government needs to ensure that the private parks, which benefit from the international reputation and often the boundaries of the national parks, make appropriate economic and educational contributions to conservation and community development efforts. Currently, Pro Parques is seeking to create an endowment for the national parks system as well as raise sufficient funds to, at last, buy out the remaining landholdings within the national park system.

Provides Financial Benefits and Empowerment for Local People

More than in many other developing countries, a sizable number of local people have managed to benefit from Costa Rica's ecotourism boom.

On average, Costa Rica in 2005 was earning two times more per tourist than it was in 1987, when the ecotourism boom was just getting started. This shows that ecotourism has, overall, brought benefits to the country. And even Costa Ricans of modest means have managed to move into the ecotourism market by operating concessions (handicrafts, horseback riding, tour boats, white-water rafting, butterfly farms, trout fishing, bird-watching, orchid and organic farms, etc.); building a few tourist cabins and hiking trails on their *fincas* (farms); and opening small restaurants serving *comida típica* (local food).

Costa Rica's countryside is now dotted with locally owned tourism enterprises, many of them wisely combined with other economic activities, such as farming. Increasing numbers of Costa Ricans have also been trained as naturalist guides, park rangers, hotel managers, tour drivers, chefs, or multilingual tour operators. Parallel with the growth of locally owned or managed eco-lodges, small hotels, restaurants, and bed and breakfasts has been a proliferation of Costa Rica–based travel agencies and tour operators, which have grown to about three hundred today. Almost all of them handle nature tourism, and about a dozen specialize in high-quality ecotourism.[125]

But there is a downside as well. The demands of Costa Rica's rural poor for land and for access to the parks for hunting, logging, farming, and gold mining have been only partially and often temporarily addressed. Under pressure from foreign investors, the government has become less tolerant of squatters who move onto private lands set aside for tourism or other economic activities. In addition, the cost of land and the cost of living have skyrocketed in ecotourism havens such as Monteverde as well as in mass tourism resorts along the beaches, making it impossible for Costa Ricans with modest resources to cash in on the ecotourism boom without borrowing heavily and at high interest rates. Unlike the situation in many other developing countries where there is capital flight, in Costa Rica, overall political stability has meant that most of the profits from locally owned tourism projects are kept in the country. There has been, however, a sharp rise in the number of tourists who arrive on prepaid packages, charter flights, and cruises, from which Costa Ricans receive only minimal benefit.

Respects Local Culture

This is somewhat more difficult to measure, in part because on the surface the country appears to lack a strong national character and culture. Costa Ricans often refer to themselves as more pro–United States than any other Latin Americans, and middle- and upper-class Costa

Rican values are linked to those of the United States via music and movies, vacations at Disney World, and shopping in Miami. Simultaneous with the ecotourism boom has been an expansion of U.S.-style fast-food chains and shopping malls, as well as transactions in dollars and signs in English, all of which have further diluted Costa Rica's culture. On the other hand, ecotourism has helped stimulate and improve local crafts, increased interest in folkloric dancing, music, theater, and museums, and stimulated pride in and protection of regional cultures such as those of the Afro-Caribbeans along the Caribbean coast, the pockets of indigenous Indians, and the Guanacaste cattle ranchers and cowboys. The number of guidebooks and historical and cultural books about Costa Rica has grown enormously since the 1980s. One tiny gem, *Costa Rica: A Traveler's Literary Companion*, compiles English translations of some of Costa Rica's finest literature, arranged geographically to give visitors a flavor of regional distinctions.[126] And despite the tourism onslaught, Costa Ricans continue in various ways to hold on to strong cultural traditions such as a commitment to the extended family, a respect for the elderly and a loving indulgence of children, a pride in Costa Rica's pacific and democratic traditions, and an adherence to religious holidays. At both Easter and Christmas, for instance, the country literally shuts down and goes on holiday, despite pressure from the tourism industry to keep stores and banks open.

Supports Human Rights and Democratic Movements

Costa Rica has the oldest democracy in Latin America, a strong tradition of respect for human rights, and an absence of both a military force and armed guerrilla groups. These favorable social and political conditions, together with the country's parks and reserves, have provided a solid foundation for the growth of ecotourism. Many people attribute the start of the ecotourism boom to President Oscar Arias's receipt of the 1987 Nobel Peace Prize, which helped the world to distinguish Costa Rica from its war-torn and largely undemocratic neighbors. Ecotourism has helped expand international awareness of Costa Rica's pacific and democratic traditions and has probably increased Costa Ricans' pride in their fine national heritage. The principles of ecotourism have helped stimulate government actions to expand and better protect the national parks and to promote other environmental programs, to strengthen NGOs, and to create some concrete projects to improve the political rights and economic conditions of the rural poor, Afro-Caribbeans, and indigenous Indians living around the parks and reserves and along the beaches. On the other hand, the simultaneous growth of conventional tourism has worked to undermine the rights of local people to ownership of land, particularly beach-front property, and has increased government removal of squatters.

Regrettably, Costa Rica continues to pursue a risky, two-track policy of heavily marketing its parks and ecotourism while trying to increase visitor numbers by means of cruise tourism, prepaid air charter tours, large beach resorts, and urban hotels owned by international chains. While all of tiny Costa Rica is being marketed as an ecotourism destination, the reality is that ecotourism exists only in certain areas. There is concern that the rapidly expanding mass tourism is tarnishing and undermining Costa Rica's well-deserved international reputation for high-quality ecotourism. Unless effective control is exerted to ensure sustainable development, particularly in the coastal areas, Costa Rica risks losing its reputation as the world's leading ecotourism "superpower."

6

Tanzania:

Whose Eden Is It?

For nearly five years, Kambi ya Tembo—Swahili for "Camp of the Elephants"—earned its name well. Kambi ya Tembo was found in Sinya village, which consists of about 150,000 acres of savannah lying approximately ten miles west of Mount Kilimanjaro and adjacent to the Tanzania-Kenya border. Just across the border in Kenya, Amboseli National Park provides a refuge for wildlife that range far and wide, particularly during the rainy season, into surrounding areas of Kenya and northern Tanzania. Foremost among these are Amboseli's famous population of elephants—numbering about 1,200 animals today—which migrate regularly into Sinya, feeding on the thick groves of *Acacia* fever trees found in the area. A number of old Amboseli bull elephants, gray and creased animals with some of the largest tusks found in East Africa, took up residence in Sinya in the late 1990s.

It was chiefly these elephants that piqued the interest of Tanzanian tour operators in using Sinya village as an ecotourism destination. Beginning in about 2000, a few operators began bringing tourists to Sinya for camping, walking in the bush, and viewing the area's famous elephants and other wildlife such as giraffe, zebra, wildebeest, eland, and gazelles. Sinya's resident community of about three thousand Maasai pastoralists, who had always lived relatively harmoniously with the area's wildlife but never knew these "wild cattle" to be of any value to them, soon became the recipients of income and employment from ecotourism. Following models established by a handful of leading

Fred Nelson did a great deal of field research and substantial updates for this chapter. Fred has lived in Arusha, Tanzania, for much of the time since 1998, working first as the Tanzania program director for the Sand County Foundation Community-Based Conservation Network and then as a private consultant with CESD.

operators a few years earlier for conducting ecotourism in community lands, these investors in Sinya paid fees directly to the village for their clients' rights to enter the area, usually about ten or twenty dollars per person for each night spent in Sinya. One of these tourism companies, Kibo Safaris,[1] came to a more formal contractual agreement in 2001 with the village for exclusive use of the main area of wildlife-rich woodlands, for which Sinya would receive a minimum of Tanzania Shillings (TShs) 30 million, or roughly thirty thousand dollars, each year based on a per-tourist payment of twenty dollars each night. Kibo built a small tented camp (ten two-bed tents) for high-paying clients looking for a relatively isolated and unique bush experience, and named it after the bull elephants that would lurk in the ribbons of *Acacia* woodland around the camp. Some of these elephants, long since habituated to people through contact with tourists in Amboseli, became so bold as to enter the camp and take food from the dining tent, often from rather startled tourists.[2] Despite the trespassing of elephants in the camp—or perhaps because of it—Sinya's Kambi ya Tembo quickly proved a great success for both the tour operator and the host village.

By 2004, tourism payments to the village amounted to about forty thousand dollars for the year.[3] Money had been invested in the village primary school, which had tripled in size from five years earlier. New classrooms and dormitories were constructed with these funds as well as additional donations by tourists visiting the camp. Wildlife had become a source of village income and value for the local people, who had always lived beside it but never knew its potential benefits. Species like elephants, giraffe, and zebra increased in number in the woodlands around the village, and predators like lion and cheetah became more frequently sighted in the area.

But today one would be hard-pressed to find the idyllic grove of *Acacias* where Kambi ya Tembo was situated. The camp in Sinya is gone without a trace, save a few gravel paths where tourists used to walk between their sleeping tents and the main dining area. Gone too is most of the income that Sinya village earned from its tourism agreement, and the additional benefits from employment and crafts sales that many individual men and women in Sinya had earned. Starting in 2001, the government's Wildlife Division decided that Sinya should not be used for tourism carried out under the sanction of the local village, and instead determined that it could only be used as a government-managed safari hunting concession where it deemed ecotourism (with cameras rather than guns) would not be permitted. The village has had no acknowledged legal right to even determine who hunts there, and is not permitted by the government to engage in tourism on the community's traditional lands.[4]

Tourism in Sinya was a victim of conflicts of interest—battles over power and money—which go far beyond the scope of this single village, but have come to define the ups and downs of ecotourism in Tanzania.

Tanzania's Ecotourism Potential

Tanzania is one of the poorest countries in the world. But it is arguably the richest in wildlife, with just about more elephants, lions, zebras, antelopes, and many other large mammals than any other country in Africa. Its fourteen national parks include the 14,763-square-kilometer (5,700-square-mile) Serengeti, which contains some 3 million animals, giving it the greatest concentration of wildlife in the world. Just outside the entrance to Serengeti is the famous archaeological site known as Olduvai Gorge. Other world-famous parks include Kilimanjaro National Park, containing the snow-capped, 5,895-meter (19,341-foot) Mount Kilimanjaro, Africa's highest peak, and Lake Manyara National Park, a compact lakeside park renowned for its flamingos and its lions, which lounge in the trees. There are also about twenty-five game reserves where licensed hunting by tourists is permitted. Among these is Selous Game Reserve, the biggest wildlife area in Africa and home to some of the continent's largest herds of elephants. Finally, there is the Ngorongoro Conservation Area, housing Ngorongoro Crater, a wildlife-filled caldera 300 square kilometers (100 square miles) in area and 610 meters (2,000 feet) deep that is often called one of the natural wonders of the world. Altogether, the government estimates, over 25 percent of Tanzania is under some form of protected area status.[5] Four conservation areas—Serengeti, Ngorongoro Crater, Mount Kilimanjaro, and Selous—have been designated World Heritage Sites by the United Nations because of their "outstanding universal value."

For much of the past forty years, and in the past decade more than ever, many have predicted that wildlife tourism will help to pull Tanzania out of poverty. The president of Tanzania from 1995 to 2005, Benjamin Mkapa, called for tapping this potential in a 2002 speech with "a heightened onslaught on poverty, using the weapon of tourism."[6]

Since the late 1980s, the Northern Safari Circuit, which includes places like Serengeti, Lake Manyara, Kilimanjaro, and Ngorongoro Crater, has been undergoing an enormous boom. This part of the country has seen the rise of new hotels and tented camps, dozens of new tour companies, and an exponential rise in the numbers of tourists. From virtually nothing twenty years ago, tourism now accounts for about 15 percent of the total value of Tanzania's economy, placing it second only to agriculture in overall national economic importance.

Tanzania's national parks are marketed under the umbrella of nature and adventure tourism, both of which are frequently described as ecotourism. As Tanzania's then-director of tourism, Hassan Kibelloh, put it in a 1995 interview, "What we have now is basically ecotourism, and we think this is the line we're going to take. We're revising our policy whereby ecotourism will feature very high, including community development and involvement."[7]

Tanzania is increasingly successful at marketing ecotourism, and in the past two decades has established itself as one of Africa's premier nature travel destinations. A British travel brochure promises that visitors to Tanzania will discover "a vast Garden of Eden," and adds, "Its game viewing experiences are widely regarded as the best in Africa." Africa Travel Resource, a Web site that markets holidays throughout Africa, writes, "Tanzania is our favourite country. It not only contains more of Africa's crown jewels than any other country . . . Serengeti, Ngorongoro, Kilimanjaro, Zanzibar . . . but also a host of lesser known but equally fantastic locations . . . Serengeti is the mother of all parks."[8] I agree. Despite its fame and a reputation to the contrary, Serengeti remains remarkably remote and undisturbed once you get off the main safari routes. I still find the Serengeti, in fact all of the Northern Safari Circuit, to be among the most awe-inspiring and thrilling game parks I know. And for an increasing number of Americans and Europeans, northern Tanzania has gradually established itself as *the* African safari experience, a unique spectacle of wildlife in today's world.

But the serene vistas of Tanzania's parks and wildlife areas belie an increasingly tense debate over the use and management of these valuable resources. Today in Tanzania, the national parks and protected areas not only are at the heart of the tourism boom but also are center stage for rural social movements, legal contests, and political struggles. Ecotourism is flourishing, but the rapid rise in the tourism values of this "African Eden" creates winners and losers in the scramble to cash in. Tourism is beginning to live up to its potential to bring increased economic growth to Tanzania and dollars for funding wildlife protection, but it also continues to lead—as happened under colonialism—to rural communities being pushed to the fringes and their lands taken away. This history of wildlife, local people, and the land provides the backdrop to ecotourism's boom in modern Tanzania.

"Conservation without Representation" in Colonial Tanganyika

The traditions of wildlife conservation in Tanzania, including the establishment of places like the Serengeti National Park, are traceable back to early colonial times. The first international conservation treaty, the Convention for the Preservation of Animals, Birds and Fish in Africa, which was signed in London in 1900 by all the continent's colonial powers—Britain, Germany, France, Italy, Portugal, Spain, and Belgium—laid the foundation for the top-down, preservationist style of management[9] that came to characterize African conservation policies. Under the treaty, only a few animals, including the giraffe, the gorilla, and the chimpanzee, were accorded complete protection.[10] Big game hunting, a favorite sport of the European aristocracy, was permitted for all other species and was even encouraged for lions, leopards, wild dogs, and other animals considered threats to settler farming. Hunting required a license, something Africans could not obtain or afford; further, the colonial governments did not permit Africans to own rifles. Historically, Africans had killed wild animals only for food, ritual use, or self-protection, never for sport or pleasure. But now, these traditional practices were largely banned, and writes Ray Bonner in *At the Hand of Man*, "Africans who shot wild animals for meat . . . or to protect their livestock became, ipso facto, poachers."[11] The 1900 treaty became the basis for most subsequent legislation that demarcated game reserves and subsequently national parks without consideration of traditional land-use systems or the consent of those living in or around the protected areas.[12]

The colonialists' premise was that Africans, left to their own devices, were wiping out the continent's wildlife. But, by 1900, the record had already proved it was the white interlopers, not the indigenous peoples, who were most swiftly and systematically killing off Africa's wildlife. Not covered by the treaty, for instance, was the Cape Colony in South Africa, because the European settlers had already slaughtered all the big game there. This mistaken belief—that parks and the surrounding people must be separated in order to ensure wildlife's survival—guided nearly a century of colonial and postcolonial conservationist policy in Africa.

By 1912, the German colonial rulers had declared thirteen game reserves, covering 30,000 square kilometers (11,583 square miles), and mapped Ngorongoro Crater in German East Africa (later known as Tanganyika and then Tanzania).[13] Following Germany's defeat in World War I, the League of Nations gave Tanganyika to Great Britain to rule as a "mandated territory" or protectorate. From the outset of British rule, Tanganyika was viewed as a prime piece of real estate by international conservationists, big game hunters, and wildlife adventurers. In ordinances passed between 1940 and 1951, the Serengeti was upgraded to a national park, the first in East Africa. No other national parks were declared in Tanganyika until 1960, when Arusha and Lake Manyara National Parks were gazetted. Another eleven parks have been declared since independence, including new ones on the coast at Saadani and on the Kitulo Plateau created in the last few years, for a total of fourteen today (excluding Zanzibar).

The original colonial law declaring Serengeti a national park did, however, contain a provision that the resident Maasai could continue to live there. But it was a promise that didn't hold for long. From the outset, conservation organizations in Europe and the United States weighed in to build an increasingly powerful lobby to expel the Maasai, arguing that the Serengeti's soil was too fragile and its water too scarce to support both humans and wildlife. Among the most influential was British paleontologist Louis Leakey, who, with his wife, Mary, excavated in the Serengeti's Olduvai Gorge, a sand-swept canyon that turned out to be a gold mine for the origins of humankind. While his wife dug, Leakey lectured, arguing that the Maasai should have no legal right to remain in the Serengeti.[14] Even more influential was Bernhard Grzimek, director of the prestigious Frankfurt Zoo, who, together with his son, studied the park's wildlife migration patterns. His 1960 book *The Serengeti Shall Not Die* made an impassioned plea for expelling the Maasai and maintaining Ngorongoro Crater and the Serengeti as a single national park.[15] The Maasai, marginalized politically, resorted to "everyday" forms of confrontation born of necessity, including illegal hunting, fires, grazing, and collection of fuelwood.[16]

Then, on the eve of independence, a compromise was struck. Under the amended National Park Ordinance, passed in 1959, the Maasai and other Africans were excluded from the western Serengeti, while the Ngorongoro Crater and surrounding highlands were removed from the park and reconstituted as a separate management unit known as the Ngorongoro Conservation Area (NCA), where Maasai pastoralists were permitted to live.[17] In concluding this agreement, British colonial officials convinced a group of twelve Maasai elders to sign off on these new boundaries, putting their marks on a document that stated, "We understand that as a result of this renunciation we shall not be entitled henceforth in the years to come to cross this line which will become the boundary of the new Serengeti National Park. We agree to move ourselves, our possessions, our cattle and all our other animals out of this land by the end of the next short rains."[18] National park officials breathed a sigh of relief: with the removal of the Maasai from most of the Serengeti, they were successfully "eliminating the biggest problem" they faced.[19]

The Maasai, however, continued to be haunted by this agreement. More than thirty years later, Ray Bonner tracked down one of the dozen elders, Tendemo Ole Kisaka, who revealed, "We were told to sign. It was not explained to us." None of the signers, he said, knew how to read or write. The elderly Maasai recalled how, shortly after they had put their marks on the paper, six large trucks arrived and moved the Maasai and their few possessions outside the park. "You white people are very tough," Ole Kisaka told Bonner.[20]

Tanzanian Socialism and State-run Tourism

Despite the end of the colonial era in 1961, the loss of Serengeti to wildlife conservation and foreign tourism was an experience the Maasai and other local people in Tanzania were fated to repeat many times over. Just as Serengeti National Park blends seamlessly with Masai Mara National Reserve to the north across Tanzania's boundary with Kenya, Tanganyika's colonial conservation policy made a transition virtually unaltered in ideology and, at least initially, in personnel into postcolonial Tanzania. It was a transition carefully scripted by the major international conservation organizations, which, in the early 1960s, feared that the end of colonialism would mean the end of Africa's wildlife. "We felt that under the new African governments, all prospects for conservation of nature would be ended," related E. M. Nicholson, the first head of the World Wide Fund for Nature–International (WWF).[21] In September 1961, WWF and the International Union for the Conservation of Nature and Natural Resources (IUCN, now the World Conservation Union) summoned the newly independent African leaders to a meeting in Arusha to discuss what they described as a state of emergency facing Africa's wildlife. Julius Nyerere, as the titular host of the meeting and the first prime minister of Tanganyika, delivered the brief opening address. These three paragraphs, known as the Arusha Manifesto, have often been quoted over the years by Western environmental organizations:

> The survival of our wildlife is a matter of grave concern to all of us in Africa. These wild creatures amid the wild places they inhabit are not only important as a source of wonder and inspiration but are an integral part of our natural resources and our future livelihood and well being.
>
> In accepting the trusteeship of our wildlife we solemnly declare that we will do everything in our power to make sure that our children's grand-children will be able to enjoy this rich and precious inheritance.
>
> The conservation of wildlife and wild places calls for specialist knowledge, trained manpower, and money, and we look to other nations to co-operate with us in this important task—the success or

failure of which not only affects the continent of Africa but the rest of the world as well.[22]

Nyerere, though a gifted writer and orator, did not draft this proclamation. Nicholson and several others from WWF wrote it in order to commit Africa's new rulers to both wildlife protection and a continued reliance on European and American expertise. With its expansive and rich natural reserves, Tanzania (as the new country became after its 1964 union with Zanzibar) quickly became a central focus for international conservation organizations. The IUCN-WWF gathering in Arusha kicked off an intense effort by the major international environmental NGOs to funnel money, technical support, and management training into Tanzania's park system. Under British colonialism, African participation in wildlife conservation had been limited to jobs as trackers, gun bearers, cooks, game scouts, and reserve guards rather than positions of management or authority. Tanzania's tiny white population, made up of retired soldiers, civil servants, farmers, big game hunters, and adventurers with little formal wildlife training, played a disproportionate role in managing the country's colonial and postindependence wildlife services.

Just after independence, concern over carefully managing the inevitable process of "Africanization of the game service" led the African Wildlife Leadership Foundation (now known as the African Wildlife Foundation, or AWF) to found the College of African Wildlife Management in Mweka, Tanzania, at the base of Mount Kilimanjaro. This was the first such training school in black Africa, and it remains a unique conservation institution today.[23] "As a result," writes Roderick Neumann, a professor of international relations who specializes in Tanzania, "they helped to create in Tanzania an elite class of conservation bureaucrats, trained in western ideologies and practices of natural resource conservation which essentially replicated the top-down, repressive practices of colonial rule."[24] As Tanzania gazetted dozens of new protected areas over the next three decades, much of the colonial legislation and land-tenure system giving ownership to the central government were maintained, despite the negative effects on surrounding communities. The postindependence policies continued to include mass relocations from new parks, increasingly militarized patrolling and antipoaching techniques, and a bureaucratic structure that concentrated authority and revenue at the top.[25] Conservation practices were generally unsympathetic to the needs of the local communities, whose members were deprived of access to ancestral homelands, grazing land, water, and wildlife, and saw few tangible benefits from either the parks or tourism.[26]

Tanzania's Tourism Policy

The history of Tanzania's national parks and reserves has always been interwoven with tourism. Initially, tourism meant hunting. The gathering spot for hunters was the New Safari, a rambling hotel surrounded by English flower gardens in the center of Arusha, the gateway town to the northern-circuit game parks. In the 1970s, its wood-paneled bar featured signed photographs of Ernest Hemingway and various members of British royalty surrounded by safari gear and African porters. In 1934, the first game park hotel, Ngorongoro Crater Lodge, was built on the oft-misty rim of the caldera. Gradually, hunting was restricted to certain blocks of land, and tourists with cameras began to arrive at the crater and then continue on camping safaris into the Serengeti. The first director of Tanzania National Parks (TANAPA), J. S. Owen, urged that his agency "encourage by every means the growth of a tourist industry."[27] Likewise, Julius Nyerere—the platitudes of the Arusha Manifesto aside—clearly saw the monetary value in this international interest in wildlife. "I do not want," Nyerere said shortly after independence, "to spend my holidays watching crocodiles. Nevertheless, I am entirely in favor of their survival. I believe that after diamonds and sisal, wild animals will provide Tanganyika with its greatest source of income."[28]

However, in reality, Tanzania's tourism policies over the next fifteen years were ambivalent, constrained financially by the country's extreme poverty and lack of infrastructure and politically by the new government's unique brand of socialism. When Tanganyika gained independence in 1961, its annual per-capita income was about fifteen dollars and its population of some 20 million included fewer than one hundred university graduates. As did most other newly independent African countries, Tanzania declared itself a one-party state. Nyerere argued forcefully that a single political party, together with a common language—Swahili—and a carefully balanced tribal and religious composition within the government, the military, and parastatal bodies (semiautonomous government-owned companies), was essential to weld the new country's 120 tribes into a unified nation. Tanzania thus avoided the tribal and ethnic conflicts that have wracked its neighbors (Kenya, Uganda, Rwanda, and Burundi), though its single-party socialism meant that internally, local ethnic rights were suppressed for the sake of nation building and the common good. Maasai leader and former Member of Parliament Moringe Parkipuny complains bitterly that under socialism, the profits from tourism and the national parks first went to the centralized bureaucracy in Dar es Salaam, and then a mere trickle came back to the Maasai. "This is our land, from which we were illegally evicted to create these parks. The profits should have gone first to us for development projects and then we would funnel them upwards, not the other way around," Parkipuny explained in an interview.[29] It wasn't until the political liberalizations began in the early 1990s, when Tanzania agreed to hold multiparty elections, that the Maasai and other rural communities could legally organize to express their views through new organs such as NGOs. During this decade, Parkipuny founded both a secondary school for Maasai on the edge of the Serengeti and KIPOC (Korongoro Integrated Peoples Oriented to Conservation), an organization dedicated to the rights of the Maasai and other pastoralists. KIPOC is a Maasai word meaning "we shall recover," reflecting local attitudes toward the conservation areas bordering them and the rights they had lost over the years.

Although international conservationists were fond of quoting the Arusha Manifesto, it was Julius Nyerere's 1967 Arusha Declaration, delivered in the same city, that set Tanzania apart from other newly independent African states. In this speech, Nyerere laid out the road map for his country's policy of "socialism and self-reliance," declaring that the country should not rely on foreign aid or investment; that political leaders and top civil servants should not be involved in capitalist activities (the so-called Leadership Code); and that the foundation of the country's socialist development should be *ujamaa* (community) villages, where agricultural work and social services were collectively shared.

Tanzania pumped a large proportion of its limited resources into primary education, health care, and provision of potable water. The results were impressive. During the 1970s, 92 percent of Tanzanian children attended primary school, and the country developed one of the best primary health care systems in Africa, with "barefoot doctors" providing basic medical care free of charge to rural communities. Despite Nyerere's warnings about reliance on foreign capital, Tanzania's emphasis on basic human services, its Leadership Code, and its nonaligned foreign policy made the country the darling of foreign aid donors. Tanzania forged politically eclectic trade and aid alliances with China, the Soviet Union, Cuba, Scandinavian countries, and Canada as well as with Britain and the United States.

But while foreign aid flowed in, foreign investment shied away from socialist Tanzania. Following the Arusha Declaration, the government nationalized large sectors of the economy—banks, insurance companies, large trading companies, industries, plantations—that had been owned mainly by British and local Asian (as East Africa's Indian and Pakistani immigrants are collectively known) firms, creating instead a number of new parastatal bodies. Many of these nationalizations were done hastily, without proper planning or trained personnel, and the companies quickly began to operate in the red.[30]

Following the Arusha Declaration, the government created the Tanzania Tourist Corporation (TTC) which owned and operated fifteen luxury hotels and lodges along the Northern Safari Circuit; in Tanzania's capital, Dar es Salaam; in Arusha; and along the Indian Ocean. TTC's broad functions also included travel agencies, publicity and advertising firms, a film company, duty-free shops, ground-handling facilities with more than two hundred vehicles and a phalanx of driver-guides, plus five overseas offices including one in New York. Tanzania's national tourism industry targeted the growing international safari market, was confined to "enclaves"—the Northern Safari Circuit and a few beach hotels outside Dar es Salaam—and was intended to help support health care, education, and other social programs. The government-owned hotels showed architectural sensitivity, incorporating local materials and designs. Interestingly, in this era before ecotourism, "all the hotels and lodges were designed to conform with the environment and culture of this country," according to the TTC's development officer, Phillip Bukuku.[31] I was particularly impressed by Tanzania's game lodges, which were beautiful, innovative, first-class structures positioned to capture spectacular views and to blend into their surroundings. My favorite has always been Lobo Wildlife Lodge, built in the northern Serengeti, just south of Kenya's Masai Mara National Reserve. Completed in 1970, Lobo is a multi-tiered, 150-bed hotel built of East African woods, local stone, and glass, and nestled among a group of ancient granite boulders known as kopjes. It is virtually invisible to tourists approaching on the dirt road from the south, but once inside, guests have a magnificent view of the northern Serengeti.[32]

Tanzania did not nationalize any already existing privately owned hotels or tour operations. However, following the Arusha Declaration, the country didn't attract much foreign investment, and there was very little domestic capital as well. Government and party officials were barred by the Leadership Code from engaging in private enterprise. Local capitalists, most of whom were Arab and Asian immigrants, feared that if they invested, the government might nationalize or simply seize their businesses, as was happening in Kenya and in Uganda. Except for the privately owned Ngorongoro Crater Lodge and a handful of other settler-, Asian-, or foreign-owned hotels in the Northern Safari Circuit, the TTC held a monopoly over accommodations in and near the game parks. During the 1970s, some private local capital did quietly move into smaller tourism enterprises, including taxi services, tour companies, and more modest hotels.

Tanzania's state-run tourism was, however, heavily dependent on foreign expertise, capital, and imports. Initial tourism studies were carried out by the World Bank and the Boston-based consulting firm Arthur D. Little.[33] The TTC's hotels were developed jointly with the British company Hallmark Hotels, and they were designed and built by foreign architectural and construction companies. Because Tanzania's industrial base was very small, an estimated 40 percent of the government's tourism budget went toward importation of construction materials, furniture, cutlery, petroleum, motor vehicles, foodstuffs, liquor, and a whole range of consumer goods.[34] In addition, there were not enough qualified Tanzanians to run these hotels, so the TTC hired Hallmark and an Israeli company to manage its facilities. The Hallmark arrangement, however, ended in 1974, by which time Tanzania had developed a solid cadre of middle- and upper-level tourism professionals.

Building and operating the tourism sector represented an enormous financial investment for the government. Between 1969 and 1974, the TTC budgeted TShs. 194 million (roughly $40 million) for tourism projects including hotels, tour operations, roads, airports, water supplies, and upgrading of existing national parks and creation of new ones.[35] By 1979, the TTC's investment in its hotels and lodges totaled about TShs 250 million (which, due to currency devaluation, equaled about $27 million).[36] Although tourist numbers did rise sharply from 51,000 in 1969, to 63,000 in 1972, to a peak of 167,000 in 1976 (see table 6.1),[37] the investment was so high that Tanzania's government coffers gained little. Reliable statistics are hard to find, but according to Frank Mitchell, a Kenya-based researcher, in the early 1970s, contrary to official figures (table 6.1), Tanzania was actually earning only $1 to $2.5 million per year from tourism, which ranked a lowly eighth among the country's foreign exchange earners.[38]

In the mid-1970s, Tanzania's move into international tourism sparked off lively discussion in the local press and at the national university, becoming the first "serious political debate in print" in postcolonial Tanzania. While some Tanzanian intellectuals and student leaders argued that state-owned tourism was not a sound development strategy, others worried it would bring negative social practices, such as prostitution and corruption.[39] Despite the fears of critics, Tanzania's tourism industry was too tiny and too concentrated in the remote Northern Safari Circuit to do much widespread cultural or social damage. Even though Tanzanians were never barred from visiting the game parks or tourist hotels, the vast majority could not afford to do so and the Tanzanian government did not have the resources to develop a domestic tourism infrastructure for peasants and workers to enjoy. So, as Tanzania's ministry of information argued in an article published in

Table 6.1.
Tanzania's Tourism Growth

	1969	*1972*	*1976*	*1979*	*1985*	*1989*	*1992*	*1995*	*1997*	*2000*	*2002*	*2004*
Arrivals (in thousands)	51	63	167	78	59	138	202	295	359	502	575	582
Gross receipts (in millions of dollars)	—	20	95	—	14	60	120	259	392	739	730	746

Source: Ministry of Natural Resources and Tourism of Tanzania, Tourism Division; I.G. Shivji, ed., *Tourism and Socialist Development* (Dar es Salaam: Tanzania Publishing House, 1975), 95; Estrom Maryogo, "Tourism in National Development," in *Karibu Tanzania: A Decade of TTC's Service to Tourists* (Dar es Salaam: Tanzania Tourist Corporation, 1983), 107. *Note*: Figures are unavailable where there are blanks.

1970, tourism, like diamonds, became an industry designed only for foreign consumption: "We need a socialist discipline to reject the product—tourism—for our own consumption, as much as we do not encourage our women to dangle diamonds."[40]

Conflict with Kenya

In reality, Tanzania's tourism industry during the decade 1967 to 1977 did not fit neatly into either a socialist or a capitalist mold. Whether tourism ultimately could have become profitable without compromising the country's cultural norms or socialist values was never fully tested. Just after the costly capital investments had been made and tourism numbers had begun to rapidly rise, the industry crashed. It fell apart because it carried within it, Tanzanian socialists contended, a fatal flaw: dependence on Kenya. The nub of the problem was that Kenya had the tourists and Tanzania had the best tourist attractions. The vast majority of visitors flew into Nairobi, Kenya, located just a few hours' drive from Tanzania, where they hired a tour van and a guide to take them to the Serengeti and other Tanzanian parks. (Some Nairobi tour agencies went so far as to claim that Mount Kilimanjaro was in Kenya.) The tourists crossed the border, but the tourism dollars did not. Tanzanian Mervin Nunes, who ran the TTC office in Nairobi, said in an interview that although "statistics at that time were not really kept, it would be safe to say 90 percent of the tourism benefits stayed in Kenya."

Efforts to negotiate a more equitable arrangement proved impossible because of the deep animosity between the two countries, which accelerated after independence as the two countries followed radically different economic and political strategies. Whereas Tanzania under Julius Nyerere was pursuing its brand of African socialism, Kenya under Jomo Kenyatta opened its doors wide to international investment in tourism and other fields. Tanzanians accused Kenya of being a "man-eat-man" society; Kenyans countered that Tanzania was a "man-eat-nothing" society. The conflict came to a head in February 1977, when the East African Community—the economic alliance between Kenya, Tanzania, and Uganda—collapsed. Just hours after Kenya announced it was seizing East African Airways planes and other community assets in Nairobi, Nyerere announced he was sealing off all road and air links between Tanzania and Kenya. The border closure caught virtually everyone by surprise. It appeared at the time to be an impulsive retaliatory action, but it took many years to undo, and in the process, it brought down Tanzania's state-run tourism industry.

Right after the border closure, the Tanzanian government launched an ambitious overseas marketing campaign to sell the country as a "self-contained tourist destination." Using such slogans as "Tanzania welcomes the world" and "Tanzania, the land of Kilimanjaro," the TTC "really went on a shopping spree," providing tours to foreign travel agents, tour operators, and filmmakers.[41] It didn't work. By the early 1980s, visits by nonresidents to Tanzania's national parks fell to fewer than fifty thousand per year[42] and tourism ranked just seventh among Tanzania's foreign exchange earners. Most of it was business and conference tourism; holiday tourism had come to almost a complete stop.[43] During this same period, more than 360,000 tourists per year were visiting Kenya, and tourism was that country's second-highest foreign exchange earner.

The situation was further exacerbated by a recession in Europe and the United States and, most important, by Tanzania's war against Idi Amin, the ruthless and erratic dictator of Uganda. In October 1978, Amin's troops invaded and attempted to annex a section of western Tanzania. The Tanzanian army retaliated by invading Uganda and pursuing Amin and his troops across the country, forcing Amin out of office.[44] The toppling of Amin, though hailed as a great moral victory, further hurt tourism and cost Tanzania dearly—including some $608 million in direct costs and a staggering $5.12 billion in forgone production as resources were diverted from economic production and toward military activities.[45] Tanzania's economic situation was further compromised by a fall in the world prices of its principal agricultural exports, a steep rise in the cost of imported oil, and a severe drought at the end of the 1970s.

The state was left holding the bag on an extremely expensive tourism infrastructure, but without foreign exchange for imports, upkeep, and marketing, this infrastructure rapidly fell into disrepair. For years after the border was closed, only a handful of guests were to be found in the government's lovely Ngorongoro and Serengeti hotels. "Lobo would be empty for a week and the government was subsidizing it," Telesphor Mukandara, the lodge's manager, told me in an interview. The TTC needed at least 45 percent occupancy just to break even in the Northern Safari Circuit.[46] Besides guests, these hotels lacked virtually all imported commodities, which had in the past come mainly from Kenya. To this day, one American visitor tells the story of how, during a 1978 visit, he became afflicted with the usual traveler's scourge and, finding no toilet paper in his room, rushed to the front desk. The clerk, noting his desperation, told him reassuringly not to worry—toilet paper from China was expected to arrive within the next two weeks.

Economic and Political Liberalizations

By the mid-1980s Tanzania's economy, like its tourism industry, had ground to nearly a complete halt as a result of external shocks and mismanagement. Nyerere's socialist policies were abandoned in 1986 and a structural adjustment loans package with the International Monetary Fund agreed to that called for more investment-friendly policies. Tourism quickly became a focus of new investment in this "liberalization" period, and since that time the tourism industry has finally begun to realize its potential. By the mid-1990s tourism was becoming a significant part of Tanzania's economy. Everyone seemed to be in on the action—international hotel chains, the World Bank, international conservation organizations, Tanzania National Parks (TANAPA), South Africans, Arab hunters, the Aga Khan, a Congolese importer-exporter, and a burgeoning class of Tanzanian entrepreneurs, including the then-president of the country, Ali Hassan Mwinyi (who was elected to replace Julius Nyerere in 1985). This "mixed grill of investors," as described by Hassan Kibelloh, the director of tourism at the time, was involved in projects running the gamut from conventional five-star city hotels to the refurbishing and upgrading of existing government and private game lodges, construction of new luxury lodges and tented camps inside the parks, creation of the country's first marine park, and a handful of more modest, innovative, ecologically and community-sensitive projects.

These tourism entrepreneurs displayed the energy and confidence of pioneers opening a new frontier. According to one press report in the early 1990s, "National and foreign investment are in the race to capture the free market atmosphere created by the government's liberalization policies, and invest in tourism."[47] As Kenya suffered from internal political turmoil and general government mismanagement under president Daniel arap Moi, Tanzania began to draw an increasing share of East Africa's safari and beach holiday market. "With the restructuring of our tourism sector, Kenya's tourism has to watch it. The new drive is going to turn the pathetic state of tourism in Tanzania into a tourism mecca," proclaimed Paul Lyimo, chairman of Tanzania Hotels Investment (TAHI), a parastatal body charged with attracting private investment, in 1993.[48]

In compliance with the terms of World Bank and IMF loans, Tanzania enacted a new investment code that offered foreign capital broad incentives and declared tourism a "high priority" area for foreign investors.[49] In 1993, Mwinyi dissolved the already-weakened TTC and set up the Tanzania Tourist Board (TTB) to promote tourism. These steps accelerated the influx of foreign capital from private companies in Europe, South Africa, Kenya, and the United States. The government began privatizing its hotels, and by mid-1994, more than sixty foreign investors had applied for tourism projects and forty-three applications had been approved.[50] By 2002 this had risen to 310 approved tourism projects representing about $360 million in investments in the sector.[51]

A major source of investment in Tanzania's burgeoning tourism industry has been South Africa. In 1991, following a decision by the Commonwealth countries to partially lift sanctions against South Africa, Tanzania "announced the scrapping of tourism sanctions against the country, thus opening the Tanzanian industry to the South African market." In 1994, South Africa's huge Protea Hotels chain took over management and acquired 40 percent of the shares of four government hotels.[52] That same year, Conservation Corporation of Africa (CC Africa), South Africa's leading company marketing upscale ecotourism, acquired the Ngorongoro Crater Lodge from Kenya-based Abercrombie & Kent as part of a complex merger scheme. In 1996, CC Africa took over Klein's Camp, a new luxury lodge in Ololosokwan village adjacent to Serengeti National Park.

In 1994, as well, the World Bank and fifteen other donors approved a $900 million transportation and infrastructure project for upgrading and expanding a number of tourism-related roads, bridges, and airports (including Kilimanjaro International Airport). The tourism component of this project also included upgrading personnel, improving government efficiency, and undertaking tourism master plans for both the mainland and Zanzibar with the main purpose of helping to increase numbers of tourists and levels of private investment. Between 2001 and 2003 the road past Lake Manyara was paved all the way to the Ngorongoro Conservation Area entry gate, using funds provided by the Japanese government. The road from Arusha to Ngorongoro is now completely paved, cutting in half the travel time from Arusha to the northern circuit's most popular attraction. While there were fears that this would cause Lake Manyara to become a less attractive stopover destination as tourists rushed to Ngorongoro and Serengeti, this has not occurred.

The combination of a more conducive investment environment and government and donor investments in infrastructure underpinned the tourism boom of the 1990s. From a low of about 50,000 tourists in the early 1980s, tourist numbers grew to 153,000, with gross receipts of $63 million, in 1990. Tanzania projected that it would be attracting five hundred thousand tourists per year by 1995, although it did not surpass this figure until 1999, by which time tourism generated $725 million for the economy.[53] During the 1990s tourism grew between 10 to 20 percent annually, and in 2001 tourism revenues accounted for about 13 percent of the total GDP in the country, with projections of reaching 18 percent of GDP by 2012.[54] "We hope to reach the target of one million tourists by year 2010," the Minister for Natural Resources and Tourism, Zakia Meghji, told an investors' forum in 2002.[55]

With this boom based almost entirely on Tanzania's rich natural resources and cultural heritage, ecotourism has become a major national strategy and is increasingly promoted in government policy documents. The National Tourism Policy emphasizes community participation, environmentally sensitive design and development, and cross-cultural exchange. It also, however, makes clear that the chief aim for tourism is to generate economic growth through increasing revenues and expanding visitor numbers.[56] Policy-makers recognize that it is a fine line between milking the tourism industry to spur growth and controlling tourism development in a way that maintains the resources that sustain the industry. As former President Benjamin Mkapa (1995–2005) once observed, "We have a unique tourism product mix. We must keep it unique by sustaining it. A correct balance has to be established between exploitation and conservation; and between economic interests and the social, environmental, and cultural impact of human activity in tourism."[57] Nowhere has this balancing act between conservation and development, and the different groups trying to control and benefit from this development, proven more difficult than in the country's famous northern safari parks.

Ecotourism in Serengeti and Ngorongoro

The heart of Tanzania's tourism industry is its spectacular national parks on the popular northern circuit. These include Kilimanjaro,

Arusha, Serengeti, Lake Manyara, and Tarangire National Parks, as well as the unique multiple-use Ngorongoro Conservation Area. While tourism to the southern circuit, in areas such as Ruaha National Park and the Selous Game Reserve, is increasingly popular as well, it is the northern circuit that is the bread-and-butter of the country's competitive advantage in the international ecotourism market. There is only one Mount Kilimanjaro, one Serengeti plains, and one Ngorongoro Crater—and northern Tanzania has them all.

During the 1990s, it was these world-renowned attractions that spearheaded Tanzania's tourism boom. By the early 1990s, new lodges were being built in the Northern Safari Circuit, although some conservation organizations and park officials recommended that only temporary camps, not new hotels, be permitted inside these national parks. The largest of these investors was the Aga Khan Fund for Economic Development (AKFED), headquartered in France, which owns Serena Lodges and Hotels. AKFED, together with the World Bank's IFC and Great Britain's Commonwealth Development Corporation (CDC), collectively invested $33 million in three luxury lodges and a tented camp in Ngorongoro Conservation Area and Serengeti and Lake Manyara National Parks.[58]

The other major investment group, Sopa Lodges, owned by the Kenya-based Consolidated Tourist and Hotels Investment Ltd., put up new lodges in Tarangire National Park, Ngorongoro Conservation Area, and Serengeti National Park. The Sopa and Serena lodges roughly doubled the tourist bed occupancy in the Serengeti and Ngorongoro. Serena, Sopa, and the old government-owned safari lodges—now managed and partially owned by a company called Tanzania Hotels and Lodges Ltd.—make up the bulk of the capacity in Ngorongoro and Serengeti. Since the mid-1990s, a range of new lodges have continued to be built inside the parks, although most of these have been smaller, low-volume luxury lodges, such as CC Africa's Crater lodge with thirty luxury suites and Grumeti River camp in the Serengeti, which has ten safari tents.

Visitor numbers to the northern circuit have continued to increase rapidly, dipping after the 9/11 terrorist attacks, but by 2004 and 2005 recovering to the extent that these became lucrative years for Tanzania's tourism industry. As a result of the pressures caused by these increasing numbers of visitors, Tanzania National Parks (TANAPA) instituted a rise in park fees from thirty to fifty dollars per person per day for Serengeti, and from fifty to sixty dollars for Kilimanjaro, starting in 2006.[59] Ngorongoro Conservation Area has also raised fees to thirty dollars for entry, instituted a one-hundred-dollars-per-vehicle fee for Ngorongoro Crater, and restricted visits to the Crater to six hours in order to reduce impacts.

Wildlife in the parks has generally thrived despite the increase in tourism use and the growth of lodges. Elephants in Serengeti and Tarangire have rebounded strongly from the ivory poaching of the 1970s and 1980s. The great herds of wildebeest, zebra, and antelopes in Serengeti and Ngorongoro have been generally stable over the past two decades.[60] Lion numbers have rebounded from a disease outbreak in the early 1990s to reach all-time highs. Tour operators are among the beneficiaries of these healthy wildlife populations. "The wildlife numbers in the Serengeti are as good as they have ever been from a tourism perspective," says Peter Lindstrom of Hoopoe Adventure Tours, one of the main ecotourism ground operators on the northern circuit.[61]

Ecotourism is playing an important role in supporting the conservation of the Serengeti and other northern zone protected areas. Revenues to the parks have increased with the tourism volume; park fees at Tarangire National Park rose from under $40,000 in 1990 to about $1.5 million in 2001, for example.[62] TANAPA's overall revenues increased from about $13 million in 1996/1997 to about $20 million in 2000/2001; Serengeti generates about $6 million of the latter figure.[63] As a parastatal agency, TANAPA pays corporate taxes to the treasury, but retains much of its revenue and puts it back into park management. Revenues from "profitable" parks like Serengeti and Tarangire not only pay for their own management but also for new or remote parks, such as Katavi, Kitulo, or Saadani, without significant visitor numbers or other sources of income.

Some also claim that the increase in lodges and campsites in areas like Serengeti's western corridor has reduced the incidence of poaching because the presence of larger numbers of tourists and guides makes it harder for poachers to operate. This area was a center of illegal wildlife hunting for much of the 1970s and 1980s, with frequent battles between park staff and local hunters. "The security situation in that area has really improved during the last ten years," says Robert Daniel, the general manager of Sopa's operations in Tanzania.[64]

More recently, a major new investment has gone into the heavily poached areas west of Serengeti. Paul Tudor Jones, an American billionaire, Wall Street hedge fund investor, and conservation philanthropist, bought out V.I.P. Safaris, a local hunting outfitter that owned a safari-hunting concession to the west of Serengeti National Park. By buying up the concession, which included a title deed to a five-thousand-acre ranch in the Ikoma area west of Serengeti, as well as exclusive hunting rights in Ikorongo and Grumeti Game Reserves and Ikoma Open Area, Jones's outfit, renamed Grumeti Reserves, aims to invest in the protection of the westernmost portion of the wildebeest migration's annual range, and to develop luxury tourism lodges to earn money for managing the area.[65] Grumeti Reserves offers to its guests the exclusive use of 346,000 acres of land, and in order to eliminate hunting, Grumeti Reserves also claims to have been paying full trophy fees to the government while not killing a single animal for the past four years, as "a goodwill gesture aimed at helping the country realize a natural increase in wildlife numbers."[66] The financial resources that Jones reportedly brings to bear in battling poaching in western Serengeti are virtually unparalleled in the Tanzanian tourism industry.

In 2002, Grumeti Reserves founded the Grumeti Community and Wildlife Conservation Fund, a nonprofit organization that has since dedicated millions of dollars to create community-linked projects, and also plans to reintroduce twenty-five black rhinos into the Grumeti and Ikorongo Game Reserves. The fund has built schools and clinics, and has provided drinking water to communities in the area. In 2006, Grumeti Reserves announced that it was partnering with the well-known South African luxury eco-lodge company Singita, which "offers safari adventures and sophisticated hotel experiences." Paul Tudor Jones explained, "I have personally invested in Singita, to ensure that we continue to fulfill our commitments to the people of Tanzania." He says Grumeti's mission is "to rehabilitate the indigenous biodiversity of the western Serengeti-Mara system to the benefit of local communities and districts, as well as national and international stakeholders, through practices that are financially sustainable, environmentally and culturally responsible, and politically acceptable."[67]

Concerns have, however, been expressed by some conservationists and community leaders as to whether or not this project is really taking local villagers' interests into account. Although the three luxury lodges in Grumeti Reserves employ many local people, they also border the fastest-growing human population anywhere around the Serengeti between the park and Lake Victoria,[68] and as an exclusive reserve, this represents another large chunk of resource-rich land in the Serengeti that is off-limits to the local population. Jones's operation also sought to relocate the entire Robanda village from its lands around Fort Ikoma, and is trying to monopolize control over tourism activities in this area by preventing the village from working with other tour operators, which have been in partnership with the village since the 1990s. In 2005, Robanda village brought its own legal suit against Grumeti Reserves for this interference and intimidation.[69]

While the Serengeti and Ngorongoro are thriving ecologically and financially, their management continues to face complications that revolve around history, local rights, and the division of the spoils of their newfound tourism wealth. As the volume of visitors and the demand for tourism access in Serengeti has increased, so has the impulse for government to set aside more and more land for wildlife conservation—and the tourism dollars that it generates. In 1994, Ikorongo and Grumeti Game Reserves were gazetted along the Serengeti's western border. In the process, local people were, as they have been so many times in the past, evicted from their lands. Although the government paid compensation to the affected people, a number of locals alleged that the compensation was not sufficient in relation to the property they forfeited. This disagreement spawned a long-running feud between the villagers in the area and Serengeti District officials, eventually leading to human rights abuses in the form of over seventy houses razed to the ground by district officials, and legal action by the affected communities in response.[70] By 2003 the case had made its way before the newly formed Tanzania Commission for Human Rights and Good Governance. In 2005, the commission decided in support of the plaintiffs, the communities, but the government has refused to act on the commission's findings and recommendations, which included substantial additional financial compensation for the affected locals. By late 2006, the government had not paid the recommended compensation.[71]

A more complicated controversy along the borders of Serengeti revolves around the creation of Wildlife Management Areas (WMAs) on community lands. The WMAs were proposed in Tanzania's 1998 Wildlife Policy as areas that villages can set aside for wildlife management, and where they would be given control for the wildlife and be able to get revenues from either tourism or hunting carried out therein. However, conservationists and local advocacy groups increasingly question whether or not WMAs are fulfilling their original intended purpose.[72] In the south of the country, around the Selous Game Reserve, more than a decade of investment in developing WMAs has yet to see communities given any new powers over wildlife management (see later section).

Nowhere has the introduction of WMAs proven more controversial than in the Loliondo area lying east of Serengeti National Park and north of Ngorongoro Conservation Area, the same place where, in the 1990s, Moringe Parkipuny founded the land-rights advocacy group KIPOC and the Maasai secondary school. The Maasai living here have a long memory when it comes to wildlife conservation and their land rights. Some of the elders living in the Loliondo villages were among those who agreed to leave Serengeti in 1959 when it was firmly established as a national park where no people would be allowed to live. Since then the Maasai claim that the Serengeti has continually expanded its boundaries onto their land, taking over their cattle-grazing areas.

Klein's Gate, the northeastern entry point to Serengeti National Park, is emblematic of this process. It is actually some distance outside the boundary of the park, built on the lands of Ololosokwan village in the 1980s in what is viewed as an attempted land grab by the park. While local leaders stopped this attempt to expand the park boundary onto their lands, and Klein's Gate has since been recognized to lie outside Serengeti National Park, the outpost is a reminder to the community of the vigilance constantly required to prevent further loss of their lands to wildlife conservation. It is into this context that the government began, in the late 1990s, pushing the communities to set aside large tracts of land for the WMAs. The Maasai in Loliondo responded negatively to this push, alleging that the government and influential conservation interests were simply using a backdoor tactic to take away more of their land for wildlife:

> The German organization, Frankfurt Zoological Society, has pushed the idea of WMA—they are the ones who grabbed Serengeti and Ngorongoro. Now they allege that they want to create a conservation area on behalf of the community. We the community of Ololosokwan reject this agenda and we will never accept it![73]

Similar conflicts over boundaries between national parks and community lands emerged during the same period to the southeast of Tarangire National Park in the village of Kimotorok.[74] This area to the east of Tarangire is also inhabited by Maasai communities, part of the vast Maasai Steppe that covers much of north-central Tanzania. The conflict emerged in 2004 and 2005 because Tarangire park authorities had redemarcated their boundaries, and in doing so had lopped off about half of Kimotorok's land, including numerous farms, homesteads, and grazing areas. "The lesson from Kimotorok is that pastoralist lands continue to be subject to high levels of insecurity and threat from wildlife conservation," says Edward Porokwa, the leader of a local Maasai advocacy coalition that funded a study of the conflicts in Kimotorok.[75]

Because local conflicts over boundaries and resource access have been such a long-running feature of park relations with surrounding communities, TANAPA began in the late 1980s to search for ways of improving these relationships with neighboring villages. Around that time, TANAPA founded the Community Conservation Services (CCS), which is an outreach department with the purpose of supporting local development projects in communities surrounding parks. Spurred by the emerging economic potential of ecotourism, the idea at the time was that the parks would direct a proportion of their gate fee revenues to adjacent communities, which would give local people a share in the conservation and tourism values of the parks and reverse the decades of hostility and resentment. A great deal of TANAPA's revenue has been spent on community development projects over the past decade and a half, with about 7.5 percent of each national park's operating budget being directed to community projects in surrounding lands.[76] For example, around Tarangire National Park from 2000 to 2005, Tarangire National Park's Community Conservation Service (CCS) contributed a total of $329,669 to community development projects in the six districts adjacent to the park, including health facilities, water services, and school construction.[77]

In many cases TANAPA's approach has indeed led to an improved relationship between the park and local villages. The Minister for Natural Resources and Tourism from 1995 to 2005, Zakia Meghji, noted in an interview that these investments have "helped a lot to help make people more aware of the importance of animals and [led to] a reduction of poaching around the park."[78] However, the problem remains one of taking with the left hand what is given with the right. In Kimotorok, for example, the lands that have been reclassified as lying within the park include a school that TANAPA built for the village, which is now apparently within the park's borders. Another basic problem with TANAPA's community projects is that they do not give communities what they really need and want, which is the recovery of access to resources lost when parks were created on former community lands.[79]

If there is a single place in Tanzania that embodies the tensions between wildlife conservation, local rights and development, and tourism investment, it is the Ngorongoro Conservation Area. As mentioned earlier, Ngorongoro was established as a multiple-use area, to be managed for both people and wildlife, in the 1959 agreement between the government and the Maasai that established Serengeti National Park.[80] According to this agreement, it was clear that Ngorongoro would be managed for the development of the Maasai as compensation for the loss of Serengeti. The governor of Tanganyika under the departing British administration famously declared at the time:

> I should like to make it clear to you all that it is the intention of the Government to develop the Crater [Ngorongoro Conservation Area] in the interests of the people who use it. At the same time, the Government intends to protect the game animals in the area, but should there be any conflict between the interests of the game and the human inhabitants, those of the latter must take precedence.[81]

Since then, however, Ngorongoro has progressively moved to erode and reduce the rights of the Maasai living in and around the Crater. In 1975, communities were forcibly evicted from residence on the floor of

Ngorongoro Crater and farming in the conservation area was banned. Restrictions were placed on where locals could graze livestock, and little was done to invest in the villages' development. A Ministerial committee concluded that "NCA's principal conservation values have been well preserved. . . . Little progress has been made in achieving human development objectives."[82] By 1992, the government had made it the unofficial policy that the future of Ngorongoro was to become like a national park, with no people living in it, and the Maasai were to be "convinced to vacate" the conservation area.[83]

Nevertheless, the ecological richness of these famous highlands has made up for some of these difficulties, and the human population of NCA has increased from about ten thousand in 1960 to almost sixty thousand people today as a result of both natural increase and immigration to the area.[84] Wildlife numbers in the conservation area have been generally stable, and during the past forty years Ngorongoro Crater has become the single biggest tourism draw in northern Tanzania, with half of all tourists visiting the legendary caldera. NCA receives over two hundred thousand visitors each year and earns at least $10 million from gate fees alone.[85]

The Maasai in Ngorongoro argue that they have gotten the crumbs and that they have shared very unevenly in the proceeds from tourism. On the one hand, the Pastoralist Council, an organ set up to represent the resident Maasai and manage development funds given to it by NCA, receives about five hundred thousand dollars per year for community development. William Ole Nasha, a Maasai lawyer and activist working for Oxfam and who hails from Ngorongoro, notes that this figure is only about 5 percent of what NCA earns from gate fees. "If one is talking about equitable benefit-sharing, then the situation in Ngorongoro is a travesty of justice."[86]

The Pastoralist Council itself is accused by its critics of being merely an agency of the top-down NCA management, and not able to represent the real issues of land and resource rights that are fundamental to the residents' interests. The Maasai resident in NCA, for example, cannot develop any of their own tourism projects or campsites; everything is controlled by the conservation area authority. Land rights are constantly under threat, as the authority imposes various restrictions on farming and cattle grazing essential to local food security. More profoundly, the effort to coax the Maasai out of Ngorongoro has in recent years taken on a more ominous tone. In 2003, plans were formally announced to evict about two hundred families living in NCA on the grounds that they were illegal immigrants into the conservation area who did not possess customary rights to live there.[87] Pastoralist organizations charged that this decision was merely intended to set a precedent that would lead to the eventual eviction of all the Maasai.[88]

The Maasai and their supporters argue that this insecurity reduces the Maasai in NCA to the status of squatters in their own home. Without any rights to develop tourism agreements with the private sector on their own, the warriors, women, and children are often seen begging for handouts in exchange for tourists taking their pictures by the side of the road. The irony is that while the Maasai are pushed further and further to the margins in Ngorongoro, the government and tour operators continue to trade on the tribe's charismatic culture to market the NCA cash cow. This is a bitter pill for the communities. One Maasai activist ruefully notes, "Watch the advertisements. They say how in Ngorongoro you will see all the wildlife—the elephant, the lion, the buffalo, the rhino, and the Maasai."[89] G.A.P Adventures' description of its Tanzania tour promises "Virtually unlimited wildlife experiences, encounters with indigenous tribes and sleeping under the African stars make this a trip to remember,"[90] while Overseas Adventure Travel says you will "Talk with local residents in a Maasai village and observe them practicing the customs of their ancestors."[91]

Ecotourism in Ngorongoro and Serengeti today is therefore a complex mix of successful funding of conservation and protection of wildlife, practical management of tourism impacts, and historic and escalating conflicts between government and locals over rights and revenues. These conflicts have, occasionally, been brought to the world stage. In November 2004, Martin Saning'o, a Maasai leader from Tanzania, was the only black man in a room packed with environmentalists from around the globe at the IUCN's Third Congress of the World Conservation Union in Thailand. "We were the original conservationists. Now you have made us enemies of conservation," Saning'o told the sea of surprised white faces.[92]

Communities, Hunting, and Local Tourism Projects

Soit Orgoss, Maa for "the boulder pathway,"[93] is one of the most spectacular vantage points and camping sites in the entire Serengeti ecosystem. Nestled among acacias and fig trees at the base of a huge granite kopje (a natural stone outcrop), it is completely secluded yet affords panoramic views of the vast Serengeti savannah. Perhaps best of all for any visitors at Soit Orgoss, the experience is one of total seclusion and exclusivity; there are no other tourists around for miles and miles.

Try to find Soit Orgoss on a map, though, and you will be disappointed. It is a local name known only to the area's resident Maasai living near the eastern border of Serengeti National Park in the Loliondo area, and faint dirt tracks provide the only means of reaching the campsite. When tourists are not there during most of the year, there is nothing at the site—no tents, no buildings, no latrines, no trash, no people—to betray that Soit Orgoss is ever used by more than the local buffalo and lion population.

This site is used by Dorobo Tours and Safaris, a company that is considered by many to be the best ecotourism outfit in the Northern Safari Circuit and that has, via this boulder pathway, paved the way for many of the leading community tourism projects in the region. Dorobo is owned by three brothers, David, Thad, and Mike Peterson, who, as sons of American Lutheran missionaries, grew up among the Maasai. Concerned by rapid and unplanned agricultural expansion, increased cutting of trees and bushes for charcoal production, and the fall in value of cattle (by 1994, it cost about two hundred cattle to buy the same tractor it had cost thirty cattle to buy in 1986), the Peterson brothers came to see ecotourism as one of the few viable alternatives for the Maasai adjacent to the Serengeti. Starting in the late 1980s, they worked with the residents of three villages in Loliondo, who first had to secure legal title deeds to their land, and then tried to convince the Wildlife Division to stop allocating the land for safari hunting concessions. "For the projects to succeed it would be necessary for the Wildlife Division to excise these areas from the hunting concessions as the non-consumptive type of tourism we were proposing directly conflicted with hunting," states a Dorobo background paper written in 1994. Initially the Wildlife Division agreed, and Dorobo then negotiated five-year lease agreements with the three villages. In the legally binding contracts signed by Dorobo and the village governments, the company agrees to pay annual lease payments and visitor night fees "in return for exclusive control of tourist activities in the areas." Dorobo argues that exclusivity, "while controversial, is a critical project component from a marketing perspective," since prospective tourists are seeking "an exclusive wilderness experience with an option of walking." In making payments to the villages, Dorobo says it has "attempted to walk the fine line between ensuring suitable use of funds [and] dictating use." The funds have gone for village priorities, including acquisition of a truck, rehabilitation of boreholes, and construction of an office building.[94]

This model for carrying out small-scale, high-value ecotourism on community lands based on legally binding contractual partnerships between villages and tour companies was a novel type of enterprise when Dorobo first began these formal ventures in Loliondo and Simanjiro

District outside Tarangire National Park in the early 1990s. At that time Tanzania's tourism industry was just gearing up following economic liberalization, and the demand for sites outside the underused national parks was limited. But as the number of tourists increased throughout the 1990s, so did the interest among tour companies in community lands where tourists could have less-crowded and more exclusive and diverse experiences. The model that Dorobo and Oliver's Camp, another high end operator, had together developed for village agreements in Loliondo and Simanjiro was picked up by other companies as they gradually became involved in other communities along the northern circuit.

Like Dorobo, Oliver's Camp is a high-end luxury outfit, which began developing tourism on community lands outside parks as a way of both encouraging conservation on village lands and creating a new exclusive product for its clients in the mid-1990s. Oliver's, which was founded by Paul Oliver, one of the top guides on the northern circuit, initiated a contract with Loiborsoit village adjacent to Tarangire National Park starting in 1994. It was the first permanent camp to bring together wildlife authorities and the local community to build a low-impact, sustainable tourism project. From 1994 to 1998, Oliver's Camp paid the village a total of forty-three thousand dollars in annual and bed night fees, according to the provisions of the contract between the two parties, in exchange for the community's agreement to not farm or settle in the concession area.[95]

More numerous have been the safari operations involved with villages around Loliondo and other areas of the Serengeti. By 2003, the Loliondo area had about a dozen operators working formally in seven different villages, most of them using the formula of bed-night payments to the village in return for an exclusive concession area. The leading venture among these in terms of scale and income is the CC Africa lodge in Ololosokwan village, named Klein's Camp after a hunter who was killed by a buffalo in the area decades ago. CC Africa became involved in Ololosokwan in 1996, when they bought out an existing title deed to twenty-five thousand acres of land in the village's northwestern corner, adjacent to both Serengeti National Park and Masai Mara National Reserve in Kenya to the north. The original granting of title to that land by Ololosokwan village was at the time disputed by the community, so when CC Africa bought the land they also inherited the dispute over the property which was in court at the time. In 1999, to resolve this impasse, CC Africa and Ololosokwan came to a contractual agreement for use of the Klein's property for tourism. The village leased the land to CC Africa for a renewable fifteen-year period, with annual rent of one dollar per acre or twenty-five thousand dollars in total, increasing at 5 percent annually. The village also received payments for each tourist bed night of about three dollars, and additional fees for CC Africa using an airstrip to bring in clients.[96]

These terms have made Ololosokwan the lead village in northern Tanzania in terms of tourism earnings. By 2002 the village was getting about fifty-five thousand dollars in total, much of this from the CC Africa lodge but augmented by payments from other companies for use of a campsite on the village lands just outside the Klein's Gate entrance to Serengeti.[97] The community had used these funds to invest in a refurbished dispensary, a nursery school, and a new village office, and to pay secondary and university school bursaries for numerous students from the village. The money Ololosokwan generated from tourism has given its village government a capacity to invest in the community's own development that has become the envy of Maasai villages throughout the region.

Although local tourism agreements expanded greatly during the 1990s in Loliondo, this growth was not without its obstacles. Dorobo's initial pilot ventures were predicated on government support for operator-village agreements, which it received from the Wildlife Division initially. But in 1992 the government turned around and granted the entire Loliondo area as a hunting concession to Brigadier Abdulrahim al-Ali of the United Arab Emirates, a wealthy member of a Dubai royal family.[98] This hunting lease was granted over the objections of the Loliondo villages, and the so-called Arab concession soon became a national and international controversy dubbed "Loliondogate" by the media, including the *New York Times*.[99]

The Arab hunting parties clashed with the resident villages on a number of occasions, particularly when they tried to stop villagers from grazing cattle near their hunting camps, but the most extended conflict after the granting of the concession in 1992 was between hunting and tourism. The Arabs attempted to exclude companies such as Dorobo, which had been operating in the villages, from the concession area; Dorobo backed off and left the Loliondo area for several years after this initial period of conflict. Other companies that arrived at the area later, such as Hoopoe Adventure Tours, were also subject to intimidation and harassment, such as shooting near their campsites, after they came to Loliondo. "We learned our lesson the hard way," says Peter Lindstrom, the Hoopoe director.[100] Although most tour operators were eventually able to operate and even coexist uneasily with the Arabs to some degree, nearly all of them close down tourism operations in Loliondo during the main July–September hunting season. Since this is also peak season for camera safaris, this compromises the economic viability of these ecotour operations.

While the Loliondo hunting concession garnered widespread attention due to the presence of the Arabs in Maasailand, the problems there simply reflect similar conflicts between hunting concessions and community ecotourism ventures throughout much of the northern circuit. As the earlier case of Kambi ya Tembo and Sinya village illustrates, the main cause of these conflicts was opposing interests among government, villages, and the hunting and tourism companies. Villages and tour operators, on the one hand, benefited from their agreements to use community areas for nonconsumptive ecotourism because the two parties could enter into contracts together for lease of lands by the villages to the operators. In contrast, the system of leasing out hunting concessions was preferable to the Wildlife Division and big game outfitters because the Wildlife Division owns the wildlife and controls the hunting lease system. Communities own the land but not the wildlife, so cannot contract with hunting outfitters. While these conflicts reflected a struggle among these parties to control wildlife and land for their own interests, ultimately they were rooted in a failure on the part of the Tanzanian government to follow its own policies over a period of many years.

Tanzania, like most countries in East and southern Africa with the exception of Kenya, has long permitted trophy hunting in designated "blocks" in game reserves and so-called controlled and open areas, many of which lie on village lands. Historically, sport hunting was conducted by private companies owned by foreigners and white Tanzanian settlers, and colonial Tanganyika developed the first block and quota (designating how many animals can be shot) system in Africa. Just after independence, in the 1960s, the government began giving 25 percent of hunting profits to district councils around game reserves. The scheme was intended to promote rural development and enlist local support for trophy hunting and conservation, but as in Kenya, most of these funds just didn't trickle down to the grass roots.

Then in 1973, Tanzania banned all commercial hunting in an unsuccessful effort to curb poaching. Hunting was reopened in 1978 as a state monopoly run by the Tanzania Wildlife Corporation (TAWICO). (Kenya prohibited hunting in 1977, and it remains banned.) No private companies were permitted to participate, although TAWICO subcontracted a few blocks to private professional hunters. TAWICO's monopoly ended in 1988 "with the liberalization of business under pressure from the IMF and World Bank and also from private hunters." Following liberalization, investment in the tourist hunting industry, like the broader tourism sector, quickly grew, and from TAWICO's monopoly about forty outfitters gained entrance to Tanzania's market by obtaining hunting blocks in different parts of the country. Since the late 1980s the industry has increasingly been dominated by foreign-owned companies, including American, British, and South African, many of which also carry out business in other parts of southern Africa.

Sport hunting is, as one official put it, the ultimate paradox for ecotourism. Although some of those involved in conservation and nature tourism find hunting distasteful, cruel, and ethically reprehensible, many admit that if properly managed, trophy hunting helps curb poaching, does less environmental damage, and brings in much more foreign exchange than do photographic safaris. Conservation advisers with the German aid agency GTZ note that many areas are too remote for photographic tourism, and "without the income generated from tourist hunting, many important wildlife areas would cease to be viable."[101] The advantages of hunting are numerous: less garbage, less pollution, less damage to—or even need for—roads, mobile camp sites instead of game lodges or permanent tented camps, and, ironically, harassment of fewer wild animals. Trophy hunters need to find their target only once; often, photographic safari tourists crave quantity, wanting to bag on film as many elephants, lions, cheetahs, or leopards as possible. Too many camera tourists, hungry for close-ups and action shots, drive off the roads, following very closely as lions and cheetahs stalk their prey. Further, the presence of big game hunters in remote, often poorly patrolled reserves and controlled areas helps deter poaching.

Costa Mlay, who was head of the Wildlife Division in the early 1990s, calculated that a hunter was bringing in a hundred times more revenue than a nonhunting tourist; the Wildlife Conservation Society of Tanzania estimates it is fifty-five times more.[102] Either way, the difference is enormous. A typical twenty-one-day hunting safari costs $50,000 to $150,000, excluding airfare to Tanzania. Following increases in hunting fees instituted in 2007, the price for shooting an elephant is now between $7,500 and $20,000, depending on the size of the animal; a lion, $4,900; a zebra, $1,200. (Giraffes, rhinos, cheetahs, and wild dogs cannot be hunted.) Between 1988 and 1993, the number of hunting safaris in Tanzania rose from some two hundred to around five hundred and the gross income increased from $4.6 million to $13.9 million.[103] More recent estimates claim that the gross income of the industry is worth about $27 million, with the Wildlife Division earning about $10 million directly from fee payments.[104]

Since the late 1980s, Tanzania's Wildlife Division has been developing a community wildlife management program aimed at helping rural villages derive benefits from hunting safaris and also from being able to hunt for their own consumption. The Wildlife Division started working with communities located in buffer zones near national reserves and controlled areas where there was commercial hunting. "We want to create good working relationships between hunters and villagers," explained a Wildlife Division official, Hashim Sariko in an interview in the mid-1990s.

As part of this effort, the government, with German aid and technical advice, undertook an experimental pilot project, the Selous Conservation Program, the country's first major community wildlife management initiative aimed at working with and providing direct benefits to villages in hunting areas. Selous Game Reserve, an enormous, rugged protected area in southern Tanzania that is famed for its large elephant herds, had suffered from two decades of unprecedented levels of poaching carried out by highly organized gangs of as many as fifty men, backed by a network of corrupt government officials. A 1986 aerial count showed that elephants had been reduced from more than one hundred thousand to fewer than half of that number and only a few of the three thousand black rhinos remained.[105] The park is too large, remote, and undeveloped to be adequately supported through photographic tourism alone. The Selous Conservation Program therefore started with an understanding that half of all hunting revenues would be retained by the reserve itself. With these funds, the project began initiating programs with villages in the buffer zone. "Poachers come from the villages surrounding the reserve. To root this out one has to go into the villages and involve the population," wrote German scientist Rolf Baldus, who worked with the Wildlife Division for nearly twenty years in developing the project. Each village elected a Wildlife Management Committee and appointed village game scouts to patrol for poachers and keep wild animals out of villages and cultivated areas.

The project also helped to establish clear boundaries and legal title for farms, villages, and proposed Wildlife Management Areas, where villagers could hunt legally specified quotas of wild game for their own consumption. Although the government was very slow in getting promised resources and revenues to the local communities and in setting up the legal framework to enable villagers to hunt, by 1993 thirty-one villages in three districts were involved in the project. The plan was that eventually, these villages would be able to manage both subsistence hunting and commercial hunting, along the lines of the hunting safaris run by the CAMPFIRE project in Zimbabwe.[106] As Costa Mlay said in the early 1990s, "We hope in the future the total revenue earned by the Selous will be applied for water supply projects, schools, dispensaries. In this way, the Selous will be seen to be contributing meaningfully to the welfare of the people. It will be a catalyst for their rural development efforts."

By the late 1990s Selous's elephant population was increasing, and poaching had decreased significantly. "Now we have a model. We know we need to give guardianship of the resource to those who are closest to it, to the local community," said Hashim Sariko, a Wildlife Division official, in an interview in the mid-1990s. Indeed, this "model" became the center of a new consensus being forged in Tanzania that for wildlife to survive outside the official protected areas, it would have to be owned and managed by local villages.[107]

Tanzania's Wildlife Policy, released in 1998, reflected this new thinking by calling for community management of wildlife outside the core national parks and game reserves. The policy stated its aim "for rural communities and private landholders to manage the wildlife on their land for their own benefit."[108] The mechanism for implementing this goal was for communities to establish Wildlife Management Areas, as has already been discussed in relation to Loliondo, with the aim being to grant locals user rights to wildlife on community lands for both their own consumption and commercial hunting, as the Selous project ultimately hoped to achieve. After the Wildlife Policy was released, a range of pilot projects beyond initial ones like the Selous were developed. The government reaffirmed its commitment to devolving powers to communities on numerous public occasions. At an international conference at Mweka Wildlife College in December 2000, the Director of Wildlife, Emmanuel Severre, presented a speech that concluded, "Suffice it to say that in the new millennium the responsibility for wildlife will be granted to local communities."[109] By the end of 2002, after a long drafting period, new regulations for actually creating WMAs as legal bodies were passed. Pilot projects like the Selous, which had stalled because the legal framework did not enable creation of WMAs, looked forward to finally implementing the long-promised reforms and giving communities fuller control over tourist hunting benefits.

But in the intervening years the government seemed to change course. The major change was reflected in the conflicts between village tourism ventures and safari hunting concessions in places like Sinya and Loliondo. In 1999 and 2000, as conflicts grew between these different activities, particularly on the northern circuit, the ministry came out clearly in favor of the hunters and against the local communities. Through the Tourist Hunting Regulations, released in 2000, the ministry summarily banned all nonconsumptive tourism in any area used for hunting, unless the director of Wildlife had granted express permission.[110] Overnight, all the community tourism ventures that had been developed in places like Loliondo were rendered nominally illegal.

No place has been plagued by conflicts between hunting and wildlife-viewing ecotourism like the village of Sinya in Monduli District discussed in the opening to the chapter. Like in Loliondo, the Sinya camp was located within a larger area—the Longido Game Controlled

Area—that the Wildlife Division leased out as a hunting concession without any participation from the villages in the block. As in Loliondo, the Wildlife Division had initially offered support for ecotourism activities in Sinya and the West Kilimanjaro area so that the villages could earn income and benefit from the wildlife there. At a meeting held in 1997 at the offices of the African Wildlife Foundation in Arusha, Wildlife Division staffers were among the participants recommending tourism as a component of effecting community-based conservation in West Kilimanjaro. But as in Loliondo, as tourism numbers and community benefits increased, so did conflicts with the local hunting outfitters in and around Sinya.[111]

The concession for Longido Game Controlled Area was held by a company called Northern Hunting, owned by a wealthy Tanzanian-Asian entrepreneur, Mohsin Abdallah, known as Sheni. The conflicts that emerged between Kibo and Northern Hunting in 2001 continued for four years and became northern Tanzania's most notorious ecotourism saga. Initially, as in other hunting areas on village lands in the region, the friction consisted of harassment and intimidation.[112] The tour operator and village worked to try to stop hunting in the area, and a number of letters were drafted to ministerial authorities by Sinya to try to, at a minimum, keep Northern Hunting out of the core tourism area in the northern portion of the village.[113] Since this area was within a few kilometers of the Kenyan border, it was questionable as to whether or not hunting was even allowed here according to Tanzanian hunting regulations. But such efforts to limit hunting and mitigate the conflicts were unsuccessful, and from 2001 to 2005 the two companies, village, and Wildlife Division fought in court and in the field over who held the right to control the area and its uses. Eventually, Kibo was thrown out of Sinya by Northern Hunting Company, and today Kibo Safaris no longer operates in Sinya, nor does it have the legal right to enter Sinya Village land.[114] In some respects the villagers in Sinya were their own worst enemy; much of the revenues they received from tourism over those years was mismanaged and reportedly disappeared into the pockets of village leaders when it should have been spent on community projects. Internal village conflicts over these misappropriations led to several village chairmen being kicked out of office, and in a sense tourism helped fuel these internal management problems. But ultimately the situation boiled down to whether the Wildlife Division controlled the land or the village did, and which party could select the commercial investor that it wanted there.[115]

By 2005, community ecotourism in Sinya had, at least temporarily, been closed off and the rights of Northern Hunting to carry out safari hunting at will had triumphed over the rights of the village to benefit from ecotourism. "The government is stealing the people's rights. How can the government say this is a hunting area and the village does not have rights over it when people are living there, with schools, a dispensary, and many homes? This is not the right way," says Mbakuli Nasiyanga, the chairman of Sinya village. "I have come into the chairmanship at a very difficult time for us."[116]

Sinya's experiences are reflective of a move by the Wildlife Division to expand its control over tourism revenues and community lands. In West Kilimanjaro, Loliondo, and areas outside Tarangire National Park like Simanjiro and Lolkisale, government directives continued to support trophy hunting at the expense of local opportunities from game-viewing tourism. After about five years, Oliver's Camp near Tarangire in Loiborsoit village eventually was forced to relocate to a new location inside the park, partly as a result of conflicts with a hunting concession granted over its original area of operation. Despite the release of the WMA regulations, by August 2005, no communities had actually been granted formal WMA status and the rights to manage wildlife that were supposed to come with it.[117] In some of the original community-based conservation pilot areas around the Selous, matters are also regressing quickly. In April 2005, BBC reporter Dan Dickinson described how Ngarambe village, on the border of the Selous, had been selling a quota of wildlife to resident hunters and earning good sums of money under the pilot program, until the Wildlife Division suddenly revoked the quota and allocated it to a safari-hunting concession instead.[118] Like in Sinya, Ngarambe lost their income from wildlife and the developmental benefits that they had been able to invest in. Rolf Baldus says that the original goal of the Selous Conservation Project to give local communities greater control and access to benefits has been largely undermined by the Wildlife Division's refusal to empower communities: "As very little has been achieved after a process of nearly 20 years the conclusion is obvious that the Wildlife Division does not intend to share," Baldus said at a conference in 2006.[119]

The future of community involvement in ecotourism in Tanzania today remains under the cloud of policy conflicts and the clash between government and local rights and interests. While during both Tanzania's colonial and postcolonial socialist eras, local rights and interests were abrogated to the central government, since the mid-1980s, the economic and political liberalizations have held out the promise of more local control. In this atmosphere, ecotourism experiments began to take root. These included, at least initially, the government's commitment to putting a percentage of park fees into community development projects, as well as the pledge that local communities could manage their wildlife—for consumption, commercial hunting, and game-viewing ecotourism. A growing number of tour operators began partnering with local communities to develop high-quality ecotourism that was underwriting a range of community development projects.

But for tour operators who have been pioneering progressive local ventures, the situation is discouraging. "For us the investment in community ecotourism has not been profitable," laments Peter Lindstrom of Hoopoe Tours, which won the Condé Nast Ecotour Operator of the Year award in 2004. He added, "It is a long hard slog to get power in local people's hands, and we're just not there yet." Ironically, a few years earlier, one of Hoopoe's directors was detained into the late hours by the Wildlife Division for practicing ecotourism in village land that fell within the boundaries of hunting blocks. For local communities the situation is discouraging, and confusing because of the conflicting signals the government continues to send, advocating local empowerment with one hand and taking away village ventures with the other. What is most discouraging for all involved is that the present policy seems to represent a roll-back of so many promising ventures established in the mid- and late 1990s.

Ultimately the current situation of contradictory government policies and persecution of local ventures is not sustainable. The parks and community lands in northern Tanzanian ecosystems like the Serengeti are ecologically contiguous across artificial administrative boundaries; all landholders, from villagers to park managers, must benefit if the landscapes are going to survive. And if tourism developments cannot be situated outside the parks through community ventures, then there is little possibility of growing tourism numbers in Tanzania in the way that policy-makers hope. In coming years Tanzania will either become a place where communities are freer to legally develop tourism as a land use and economic option, or wildlife numbers outside the parks will dwindle, the parks will become more congested with tourists, and Tanzania's product will begin to lose the competitive advantage that it now enjoys. The future of ecotourism hangs in this balance.

Tanzania's Ecotourism Scorecard

Tourism in Tanzania has developed rapidly since the mid-1980s. During the 1990s, tourism has become the country's most important foreign exchange earner and one of the drivers of Tanzania's slow recovery from the economic depression of the late 1970s and 1980s. Tourism is now viewed as one of Tanzania's best hopes for development, and ecotourism, loosely defined to include nature tourism, ecotourism lite, and genuine ecotourism, is widely hailed by government and tourism officials as the model Tanzania is pursuing. At the local level an increasing number of villages and rural citizens have become involved in the tourism industry and in benefiting from the nation's rich resources.

Tourism dollars are providing funds to run Tanzania's national parks and support conservation. Tourism development inside the parks has been limited according to TANAPA's general management plans, and park fees have been progressively raised as a way to increase revenue and discourage overcrowding. Wildlife populations in most parks are doing well and tourism infrastructure, such as roads and visitor services, has been improved, such as the new visitor centers at Tarangire and Lake Manyara National Parks and the paved road from Arusha to Ngorongoro. On the other hand, the spiraling levels of government corruption in Tanzania have penetrated the national parks and threaten to undermine their sound management in the near future. Ngorongoro Conservation Area's mismanagement is a violation of its World Heritage Site status.

Some fine examples of private entrepreneurs running tourism projects with sensitivity for the environment and the community have emerged during the past fifteen years, and innovative models for doing business locally have spread, albeit erratically and inconsistently, within Tanzania's tourism community. Ecotourism has made a genuine contribution to local economies in places like Sinya and Loliondo and has also led to community wildlife conservation efforts in these areas. But short-sighted government decisions are turning the tide against these efforts. Local ecotourism initiatives in northern Tanzania have been beset by a series of crises since 2000, when the government issued regulations effectively curtailing village-tourism agreements and setting aside all areas outside the national parks for safari hunting. While safari hunting could potentially be an effective form of ecotourism, the refusal of the government to grant local communities management rights over wildlife outside parks prevents this. Despite government policy calling for communities to manage and benefit from both hunting and tourism, the current legal and political environment is one of continued marginalization of local people.

As Tanzania's international popularity as an ecotourism destination grows, in the country itself there is a widening gap between the official rhetoric and the political realities on the ground. In terms of the definition of real ecotourism, Tanzania stacks up as follows.

Involves Travel to Natural Destinations

Tanzania rates high on this criterion, as natural destinations overwhelmingly drive its tourism industry. Its Northern Safari Circuit continues to provide one of the greatest wildlife spectacles in the world, and tourists are increasingly visiting other, less well-known national parks such as Ruaha, Udzungwa, Mahale, and Katavi. Tanzania's coastal and marine resources are also a popular tourist destination, as are its forests and mountains. Tanzania's tourism industry is fundamentally tied to the condition and management of its natural assets.

Minimizes Impact

To date, damage has been done mainly in the heavily visited destinations, such as Kilimanjaro National Park and Ngorongoro Crater. However, even in these "high impact" areas, the negative environmental effects of nature tourism have been relatively limited. After independence, the Tanzanian government built game lodges that were architecturally respectful, though not very environmentally sensitive in terms of conservation of freshwater, waste disposal, or staff housing. There has periodically been a recognition that no new hotels should be built inside the parks of the Northern Safari Circuit, that hotel staff and park guards must eventually be moved outside the park boundaries, and that only tented camps should be permitted. But these principles continue to be bent and broken. And with a few exceptions, along the coast Tanzania is pushing conventional beach tourism based on overseas package tours, and supports no real community involvement. The fact that Tanzania's extraordinary natural resources are largely unspoiled reflects the reality that tourist numbers are still relatively low, the number of game lodges is still small, and the parks themselves are often vast and difficult to reach. New roads, particularly the new paved road from Arusha to Ngorongoro, may change this, and the government, now locked into tourism as a main source of foreign exchange, shows limited political will or capacity for enforcing many of its own regulations. Although Tanzania's tourism has not resulted in serious problems with prostitution or other social ills—largely because the game parks are fairly isolated from population centers—there is a need to develop more culturally sensitive and educational forms of interaction.

Builds Environmental Awareness

In this category, Tanzania receives reasonably high marks for education of foreign visitors, but not for that of Tanzanians. Since independence, Tanzania has worked to build up a coterie of local, high-quality naturalist guides, park rangers, scientists, and, on Mount Kilimanjaro, mountain guides and porters. In addition, there are now a number of private camps, lodges, and tour companies practicing solid ecotourism and giving their guests highly informative tours. Some tour companies prepare visitors beforehand with articles and lists of books. Despite this, however, the caliber of many Tanzanian tour guides remains low, in particular when it comes to placing tourism and ecology in their historical or social context.

Environmental education is far less widespread among Tanzanians themselves, for whom even a basic secondary education is not always available, particularly in rural areas. Visiting Tanzania's parks is expensive (even with cut-rate prices for those living in the country), so domestic tourism remains low. Although the number of local and international environmental organizations in Tanzania has grown in recent years and there is more popular awareness of environmental issues, for most Tanzanians the national parks are simply a source of foreign exchange and, for the Maasai and many other communities, a source of their own exploitation.

Provides Direct Financial Benefits for Conservation

Conservation is clearly being benefited, but there is a growing divergence in the success of conservation efforts inside the parks and outside on community lands. In the late 1990s, the government made an appropriate decision to raise park entrance fees in the Northern Safari Circuit from twenty to twenty-five dollars per day, while lowering them from twenty to fifteen dollars in the less-visited parks in the Southern Safari Circuit in an effort to better disperse visitors. Recently, fees for the heavily visited Serengeti and Kilimanjaro National Parks have been raised to fifty and sixty dollars per day in order to further increase park revenue and discourage overuse. It addition, it raised to eighty dollars the entry fees to special chimpanzee sites, such as Mahale National Park in western Tanzania, which can accommodate only very limited numbers of visitors. With the increase in tourism numbers and the hike in entry fees, more money is coming into the national parks' coffers. Overall there remains a general perception that the national parks are well-managed and wildlife numbers in most parks are stable. The rise of community ecotourism based on village-operator agreements has produced a major new source of income from wildlife to rural communities and led to land being set aside by these communities for wildlife conservation, but current government efforts to block these projects threaten to undermine wildlife's future outside the national parks.

Provides Financial Benefits and Empowerment for Local People

There has been some significant progress in this area. TANAPA has worked to share revenues with communities around the national parks since the late 1980s. But although benefits have greatly increased from these revenue-sharing schemes, they rarely lead to real empowerment of local people. A more progressive form of community involvement in tourism is through the numerous village-operator agreements that have developed over the past decade based on a few initial pilot efforts—such as those of Dorobo Tours and Oliver's Camp—in the late 1980s and early 1990s. These initiatives have mushroomed as the demand for tourism in village lands outside the parks has increased along with Tanzania's overall tourism boom. Cases such as that of Ololosokwan in Loliondo Division represent the most significant level of locals benefiting from tourism that Tanzania can offer.

Unfortunately, these local arrangements abruptly ceased receiving government support at the end of the 1990s, and the Wildlife Division has carried out a sustained campaign against them since that time. While the government publicly calls for tourism revenues to be captured locally in order to share benefits and reduce poverty, its informal or "real" position is to continuously restrict local opportunities and ensure that money goes to government organs. This explains the conflicts over expanding national park boundaries in places like Serengeti and Tarangire, and the effort to maintain all the areas outside the parks as safari-hunting concessions, which do not benefit local people, and which compromise their land rights.

Respects Local Culture

Tanzania scores poorly in this regard. Despite some efforts, much prejudice remains toward the Maasai and other pastoralists. They continue to be viewed by government officials, tour operators, and visitors as tourist attractions and sources of souvenirs. Little meaningful cultural knowledge is passed between tourists and resident people, and tourists continue to focus on mainly wildlife rather than to learn about the country's people. Although Tanzania's tourism has not resulted in serious social problems in most areas, there is a need to develop more culturally sensitive and educational forms of interaction. Visiting tourists, Tanzanian operators, and government officials bear collective responsibility for redressing this issue.

Supports Human Rights and Democratic Movements

Ecotourism as currently conducted is perversely both a source of support for and repression of human rights in Tanzania. Tanzania is nominally democratic although it remains a de facto one-party state with certain restrictions on freedoms of speech, assembly, and political expression. In recent years there has been an increase in the number of NGOs and independent community and rural organizations and in political activism. The rise of ecotourism is one of the forces giving impetus to these struggles, and local leaders in places like Loliondo look to tourism's economic potential as one of strategies they can use as leverage to secure their rights. But at the same time, tourism provides a relatively authoritarian state with strong incentives to keep on expanding parks and extinguishing local rights and opportunities. Tourism dollars provide the motive behind the recent moves to restrict local tourism agreements and subject these to greater central control. At present, tourism is probably more a source of local land and resource loss to government than a source of support for local rights.

Tanzania has done much to cash in on its great ecotourism potential during the past twenty years. Tourism is the main source of funds for one of the world's largest protected-area networks in one of its most biologically rich countries. Tourism is driving much of the country's economic growth, and local communities have been able to get in on the action through village-level concession agreements developed in collaboration with private sector partners and a few facilitating NGOs. But the government has done disappointingly little to curb corruption or implement a national development strategy that incorporates the principles and practices of ecotourism. Instead, tourism is now the locus of wide-ranging battles over the spoils of "Eden," and conflicts over who will manage and benefit from Tanzania's rich wildlife and land resources.

At present the tide is being pushed back on local opportunities, undermining ecotourism's legitimacy in Tanzania. Regrettably, tourists traveling to Tanzania remain largely ignorant of the demands, desires, and aspirations of those living around the parks and struggling to benefit from wildlife in rural areas. Because Tanzania's political struggles have been largely peaceful and low-key, many tourists are not aware of them, and tour operators and naturalist guides rarely discuss politics unless urged to do so.

Perhaps more than any other country in Africa, Tanzania's natural and cultural assets have made it a true ecotourism Eden today. But the fruits of paradise remain the spoils for relatively few people, and the efforts to bring local communities into this growing industry have repeatedly been met with resistance and conflict. While it is likely that the country's tourism industry will continue to flourish in the near term, its long-term health depends on the ability of these locals to access greater opportunities and successfully struggle for their rights and inclusion.

7

Zanzibar:

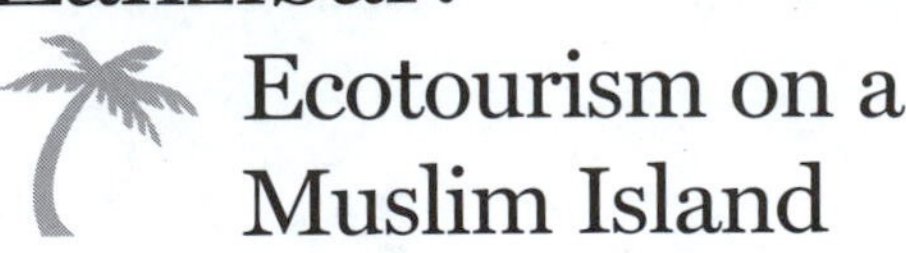

Ecotourism on a Muslim Island

In 2000, Zanzibar's Stone Town was designated a UNESCO World Heritage Site in recognition of its outstanding cultural heritage as one of the most important nineteenth-century Swahili coastal trading centers. The allure of the Stone Town, together with the island's pristine beaches, outstanding reefs, new marine conservation projects, and high-profile international festivals has continued to attract attention and swell tourist numbers. In 2004, *Travel and Leisure* magazine named Zanzibar the "Best Island Destination" in Africa and the Middle East.[1] In July 2005, *The East Africa*, a weekly magazine in Kenya, described Zanzibar's Stone Town as "the Venice of the South," and a visit there as "an adventure of the mind rather than the usual snorkeling expedition in the safe shallows of the tourist circuit."[2] And, two years later, the *New York Times* Sunday Travel Section named Zanzibar one of "24 Destinations of 2007."[3]

However, accolades and honors tell only a small part of the story of Zanzibar's complicated relationship with tourism, and official communiqués gloss over the reality that tourism development has been politically charged and poorly regulated. Despite years of Zanzibar government rhetoric championing ecotourism as a tool for poverty alleviation and environmental conservation, few actions by government or the private sector have reflected a true commitment to these ideals. Just below the surface, Zanzibar's booming tourism industry is rife with stories of corruption, greed, and loss—of land, control, and oppor-

Audrey Davenport carried out research in Zanzibar from August–November 2005 to help update this chapter. Davenport is currently a graduate student at Yale's School of Forestry and Environmental Studies.

tunities. And popular cynicism is widespread, occasionally spilling over into the streets. In the mid-1990s, young Zanzibari demonstrators damaged tourist bureaus and curio shops in the Stone Town, charging that tourism was changing their lives and offering few employment opportunities, while around the island, sporadic acts of suspected sabotage have been carried out against tourist facilities. A decade later, the beautifully renovated House of Wonders, which quickly became a major tourist attraction, featured a display entitled "The Bane of Tourism," where visitors read the following scathing critique:

> Tourism provides limited new employment, mostly to overseas people. Much of the food is imported while the demand from hotels has increased prices for fish and other foodstuffs, which are passed on to locals. Many streets have been blighted by imported tourist junk which is not an expression of Zanzibari culture. Tourism creates enclaves of wealth and development with limited trickle down.[4]

From State-Run to Free-Market Tourism

For centuries, Zanzibar was a cosmopolitan crossroads for ivory, slave, spice, and other types of traders from the East and West, as well as the center of Swahili culture, with an influence penetrating into the heart of the African continent. Although separated by twenty-five miles of emerald blue Indian Ocean, Zanzibar and the Tanzanian mainland, known as Tanganyika, had (along with Kenya and Uganda) been part of Great Britain's East African colonial empire. During the nineteenth century, Zanzibar emerged as the clove-growing capital of the world. Beginning in 1880, Britain ruled Zanzibar nominally through the islands' Arab sultanate. In 1963, when Britain granted independence to Zanzibar, the archipelago was politically divided and had a shaky ruling coalition. Just five weeks later, in January 1964, a brief but bloody populist revolution toppled the government, killed thousands of Arabs and Indians, and sent Sultan Seyyid Jamshid ibn Abdullah and remnants of the British colonial service fleeing by boat.

Zanzibar's postcolonial "revolutionary" government quickly established diplomatic relations with the communist world, including the Soviet Union and eastern Europe, China, and North Vietnam. Horrified, the U.S. government denounced Zanzibar as "the Cuba of Africa" and then, just a few months later in early 1964, breathed a sigh of relief when newly independent Tanganyika and Zanzibar announced they were uniting to form a new country, Tanzania. Dar es Salaam was the capital, and Julius Nyerere, a nonaligned socialist and one of Africa's great statesmen, was the president. Nyerere viewed the union with Zanzibar as a step toward the cause of African unity, a dream that has remained illusory. Under the union's quasi-federal structure, foreign, defense, security, and monetary policy were union matters, while Zanzibar retained authority for most of its internal affairs, with its own president, cabinet, legislature, and judicial system. But it was always an uneasy alliance, with each side suspecting that the other was gaining more advantages.

In the 1970s, the bulk of tourism on Zanzibar was carried out, in a lackluster manner, by the government's Zanzibar Friendship Tourist Bureau (ZFTB) and confined almost exclusively to the main island, Unguja (popularly referred to as Zanzibar). During the decade when I did field research in Zanzibar, from 1973 to 1983, I never saw more than a handful of other foreigners. Most of the tourists were youthful backpackers, aid workers, or diplomats from the mainland. The trickle of tourism was confined to a few badly run government-owned hotels in converted Arab houses, former British colonial hotels in the Stone Town, and the overpriced "modern" Bwawani Hotel, a 114-room, eastern European–style cinder block monstrosity built next to the sewage outlet on the edge of town. The original architectural plans for the hotel, which was designed by Zanzibar's dictator, Abeid Amani Karume, shortly before his assassination in 1972, reportedly included no hallways, the world's largest outdoor swimming pool, and an artificial beach. During construction, someone remembered to add hallways, but the swimming pool, built according to Karume's plan, never functioned and slowly degenerated into a gigantic garbage-filled and mosquito-infested swamp. By the time I left Tanzania and Zanzibar in 1983, tourism, like Karume's pool, had dried up almost completely.

In the mid-1980s, after Nyerere stepped down, Tanzania and Zanzibar shifted gears and gradually began to promote both tourism and manufacturing export zones. The impetus on Zanzibar was twofold: plummeting clove prices (down from nine thousand dollars per ton in the early 1980s to a mere six hundred in the mid-1990s)[5] and pressure from the World Bank, the International Monetary Fund (IMF), and USAID for more liberal trade and investment policies. In 1986, the terms of an IMF structural adjustment loan dictated profound economic "liberalizations" in Zanzibar and on the mainland, including a denationalization of the banks and many other government-owned enterprises; opening of the country to private, including foreign, investment; promotion of new exports; an easing of regulations on repatriation of profits; and abolition of duties and taxes on the import of raw materials for industry.[6]

To facilitate this shift from a state-run to a free-market economy, the Zanzibari government enacted a series of new laws and created new institutions. The 1985 Trade Liberalization Policy advocated diversification of the economy and a greater role for the private sector. That same year, the Stone Town Conservation and Development Authority was established to promote restoration and rehabilitation. In 1987, Zanzibar's Economic Recovery Program stressed, for the first time, that tourism was an important component of Zanzibar's economic development, and in 1989, the Investment Protection Act, designed to attract foreign capital, was amended to include tourism as an export, thereby qualifying it for an array of investment incentives. In 1992, the Zanzibar Investment Promotion Agency (ZIPA) was established to facilitate "one-stop shopping" for both local and foreign investors, and in 1996, the Zanzibar Tourism Commission (ZTC) was created to promote Zanzibar as a tourism destination and to regulate and monitor the tourism industry.[7] As the World Bank's private investment arm, the International Finance Corporation (IFC), summed it up, between 1985 and 1995, Zanzibar moved to facilitate investment "through a generous system of incentives."[8]

In 1994, the World Bank itself began a multimillion-dollar Tourism Infrastructure Project in Tanzania and Zanzibar whose objective was, according to Barbara Koth, the bank's first tourism adviser in Zanzibar, "to 'unstick' private investment through infrastructure improvements,"[9] including roads, electricity, water facilities, and Zanzibar's main airport. The World Bank project also included assistance to upgrade Zanzibar's statistical and data collection capabilities and train local personnel.[10] Taken together, these reforms moved Zanzibar from the socialist camp to the neoliberal USAID–World Bank–IMF camp, with an emphasis on export-oriented, private-sector economic development and multi-party elections.

Over the past decade, tourism has continued to grow, encouraged by a handful of new policies and the formation of new government offices developed to boost tourism investment and revenue. While cloves remain the most important foreign exchange earner, tourism officially ranks second, though real earnings are almost certainly underreported. The national prominence of the tourism industry crystallized in 1996 when the government passed the Promotion of Tourism Act, which laid the legal framework for the creation of the Zanzibar Tourism Commission (ZTC). The Hotel Levy Act passed in 1996, imposing a Value Added Tax (VAT) that rose, over time, from 9 percent to 20 percent. These funds go the treasury, with 5 percent designated for the ZTC, including tourism marketing, training, and issuing of licenses, and another

1 percent for a tourism training school. However, neither the ZTC nor the school has ever received this financial support.[11] In addition, the ZTC was tasked with creating a regulatory and monitoring framework for the tourism industry, which up until that point had been governed by minimal consideration for sociocultural, economic, and ecological issues. A Tourism Policy Statement produced by the ZTC in 1997 outlined the commission's priority to move the market in the direction of culturally and environmentally sensitive tourism and to focus future development on attracting low-volume, high-spending tourists. In policy documents across virtually all branches of the government, the concept of ecotourism has been cited as a valuable tool to achieve sociocultural, environmental, and economic goals.

Simultaneously, the Zanzibar government was completing its first National Land Use Plan, as part of the larger Zanzibar Integrated Environmental Management Project.[12] Due to the rapid and uncoordinated growth in the tourism industry, the National Land Use Planning (NLUP) team undertook a separate land-use plan for the tourism sector. The plan identified six tourism zones that would be assessed for future development, four on the main island of Unguja and two on the sister island of Pemba. The zones included extensive stretches of coastal areas in Zanzibar and allowed for tourism activities to be initiated seaward toward the coral reefs, along the beaches, and inland (although construction was required to be set back thirty meters from the high water mark). Most innovative in the Tourism Zoning Plan was the emphasis placed on the involvement of local villages, giving them the ability to propose changes and ultimately block development they deemed to be detrimental to their collective interests.[13] However, the project lost funding indefinitely because of the political violence and unrest following the 1995 national elections in Zanzibar. As explained below, this aid, from Finland, resumed almost a decade later, but the innovative community tourism projects were never implemented.

Indeed, as donor money and confidence continued to disappear in early 1996, so too did Zanzibar's motivation to follow through on its newly crafted plans for responsible tourism development. The 1997 Tourism Policy Statement was never officially adopted or implemented and the Tourism Zoning Plan was largely ignored, as more and more hotels emerged along the fragile coastlines outside of zoning areas and without local consent or involvement. Issa Mlingoti, the Tourism Commission's director of planning, described the zoning plan as "impossible to implement because tourism had already taken off in the wrong way."[14] The Tourism Commission struggled to rein in the different government departments and private players involved in tourism, but development continued unchecked and tourism training and licensing failed to materialize. Despite the fact that the ZTC is slated to receive 35 percent of the tourism tax collected by the government's Revenue Board each year, the money has rarely been delivered in full. In fact, the ZTC estimates they receive only 40 to 50 percent of their marketing and promotion budget annually, and between 2001 and 2003 they received a mere 25 percent.[15]

By 2001, following another round of political violence in Zanzibar in the wake of election fraud accusations by the opposition Civic United Front (CUF) party, Zanzibar's tourism numbers were falling (see table 7.1), while criticisms of irresponsible development and management mounted. And tourism has been one of the reasons for ongoing political disputes. The ruling CCM party has embraced tourism as an economic development strategy. In contrast, CUF condemns the "negative features" of both socialism and capitalism and focuses on development through agriculture, education, and infrastructure. While some CUF politicians have openly opposed tourism and some suspected sabotage of tourism facilities has occurred in CUF strongholds, the party itself has not officially addressed the issue.

A number of academic studies and internal assessments have revealed that virtually no progress toward sustainable tourism development has been made since 1995. Stefan Gossling, a Swedish scholar who has studied Zanzibar's tourism industry, writes, "Despite the fact that the Zanzibar government has frequently expressed its commitment to ecotourism and even proclaimed it as the national tourism development strategy, social and environmental concerns have largely been ignored."[16] Coupled with this has been the growth of official corruption in tourism projects. Zanzibar is rife with stories about corrupt land-acquisition deals. Almost everyone has a story that tells similarly about "a phone call from a close friend of the President" or "a special request by a businessman" that pushed through a land deal otherwise rejected by ZIPA and the ZTC. Take, for instance, the Zamani Hotel, owned by the German company Kempinski that has hotels and resorts in near two dozen countries around the world, including the refurbished and reopened five-star Kilimanjaro Hotel in Dar es Salaam. As the island's first five-star resort, Zamani Hotel is described on the Web as "designed to harmoniously blend in with its natural surroundings, only materials native to the island have been used in its construction."[17] However, back in 2005, a slough of social and environmental concerns were raised about the construction of massive, gleaming white buildings set behind gates on thirty acres of land. A Chinese contractor was brought in for the construction of the luxury resort, which includes a spa, two outdoor pools, tennis courts, a fitness center, and a handful of restaurants and boutiques. Despite the government's official policy of hiring locally, the majority of construction laborers were migrants from the mainland, who were housed in a virtual shanty town behind the walled-off construction site. Local Zanzibaris accused these workers of causing a rise in crime, drug use, and prostitution along the island's east coast.[18]

The Zanzibar government's 2004 Tourism Policy explicitly discourages "inclusive package tours that hurt the national economy and have no benefits to Zanzibar communities."[19] Yet, they continue to allow construction of large, foreign-owned resorts that will draw package tours and do little to fight the leakage of tourism revenue to foreign tour operators. In addition, the Department of Revenue in Zanzibar does not make tourism revenue numbers available and in September 2005, neither the Ministry of Trade, Industry, Marketing and Tourism nor the Tourism Commission were able to get current figures.[20] This lack of transparency and the fact that infrastructure improvements to the airport, port, and roads never seem to materialize encourages speculation about the government's use of tourism revenue.

In recent years, rhetoric about community involvement in sustainable tourism seems to have gradually returned to Zanzibar. Finnish government assistance has been reinstated to support another round of land-use planning through the Sustainable Management of Land and Environment Program to prepare a strategic plan for 2005 to 2009.[21] In addition, in 2004, Zanzibar's Ministry of Trade, Industry, Marketing, and Tourism produced and adopted a new Tourism Policy based on a 2003 CHL study and replacing the forgotten 1997 Tourism Statement. In an interview, Pereira Silima, principal secretary for the Ministry, emphasized that "local people must understand and receive benefits, empowerment, and ownership from tourism. We [the government] want to use tourism to fight poverty before poverty kills tourism."[22]

In practice, however, these principles are largely ignored. Local people have rarely been consulted and the only financial compensation they are likely to receive for the loss of land is for the sale of their coconut trees to tourism developers. With independence in 1963, all lands became government property, with local communities only retaining rights for what was on the land, which in most coastal areas were coconut trees. The significance of this shift didn't become clear until the advent of tourism in the 1990s. As the government began allotting lands for hotel construction, developers typically received thirty-three-year leases, and in return paid an annual rent to the government of between $1500 and $2000 per hectare and a one-time fee to traditional owners of coconut trees on the land—the only resource with local value. In 1990, payment per tree ranged from $2.50 to $55;

by 2002, the amount had jumped to $410 to $1,545 per tree. "Coastal communities in Zanzibar [are] living in the present," writes Gossling, and they are "unaware of the fact that the seemingly high compensation paid for the trees . . . was extremely low for the foreign investors." In another study, Zanzibar academic M. S. Sulaiman found, "It is common now to hear the lament of villagers who, attracted by the apparently high prices offered for their coconut trees or other assets, rushed to sell them and now regret their decision. The money that they received has been dispersed among their wide, extended family and they are left with nothing—not even the land that previously provided their financial security."[23]

Today Zanzibar's tourism industry continues to be characterized by haphazard development trends. Community-owned lands along the east coast have become private, mostly leased to foreigners, and across the island, most lands of any value for tourism development have already been sold. Zanzibaris remain skeptical that the 2004 Tourism Policy reflects a genuine shift toward local empowerment and benefits, rather than simply a new round of rhetoric. As one Zanzibari elder put it, "The government is not committed to this island. They promise to protect it over and over, but all I see are new hotels every year."[24]

Growth of Tourism

Despite cyclical bouts of political violence in Zanzibar, donor and investor skittishness, and the island's periodic inclusion as an outpost for Islamic terrorists, international tourist arrivals have, over the last two decades, increased more than five-fold (see table 7.1).[25] Italian, British, other European, and American tourists consistently compose the top four categories of nationalities of tourists, making up 65 percent of total arrivals in 2004, with Italians topping the list with 33 percent of arrivals.[26] Americans typically visit the island as an "add-on" to game park safaris in Tanzania or Kenya. Over 43 percent of international tourists who visit Tanzania now include Zanzibar in their itineraries and stay an average of six nights,[27] as compared to one to two nights a decade ago.[28] In 2005, international arrivals rose to 125,500, up 36 percent from 2004. Over one-third—around forty-five thousand—were from Italy, with Britain, Spain, and the United States as the fastest-growing source markets.[29] Approximately three-quarters of international tourists arrive by air from mainland Tanzania or Kenya or aboard charter flights from Europe. Air Tanzania has partnered with South African Airways to run direct flights from Johannesburg to Zanzibar, and with Oman Air to offer packages from Europe to both Oman and Zanzibar. The remainder arrives via ferry from Dar es Salaam. The Zanzibar Tourism Commission (ZTC) predicts that by 2012, the island could receive as many as 220,000 foreign and national tourists a year.[30]

Tourist accommodations have similarly undergone significant growth beginning in the early 1990s. Between 1991 and 1993, for instance, the number of hotel rooms increased by 42 percent. By mid-1993, ZIPA had approved 204 projects totaling a proposed investment of some $265 million. Of these projects, 53.4 percent were for foreign-owned "hotels and tourism," while a mere 1.1 percent were "joint ventures" involving foreign and local capital. Over the next decade, the number of beds increased sixfold, from 1,500 in 1995 to 9,108 beds and 225 hotels and guest houses in 2004.[31] In the early 1990s, government projections called for fifteen thousand beds by 2015,[32] while the 2004 Tourism Plan projected an unrealistic and astronomical increase to 250,000 beds by 2020.[33]

Historically, Zanzibar has been a popular destination for lower-budget backpackers, but the client base is gradually shifting. In 2004, only 14 percent or thirty-one hotels in Zanzibar met international standards, according to the ZTC, and a mere 4 percent (ten hotels) ranked as five-star establishments.[34] Although demand for upscale accommodations is growing, overall occupancy rates are only 40 to 45 percent due to Zanzibar's seasonality (with rainy months from February through June) and political unrest. Most hotels are on the main island of Unguja, either in and around the Stone Town or along the coasts. On the north and east coastlines, the beachfront is dominated by sprawling resorts, mainly owned by Italians or South Africans, which provide nearly half (48 percent) of Zanzibar's beds, despite the fact that they make up only a quarter (23 percent) of all hotels. In contrast Pemba, always a tourism backwater, has seen comparatively little growth. By 2004, it had just seventeen hotels and 129 rooms—mostly small, family-run, guest houses plus three run-down government hostels and a few foreign-owned resorts catering to international visitors.

Tourism's contribution to the national economy in Zanzibar has continued to grow. When the clove industry, long Zanzibar's number-one foreign exchange earner, faltered due to falling global demand and market prices in the 1990s, the government began to actively promote tourism to fill the gap. Exact revenue numbers for tourism earnings in Zanzibar vary and are only intermittently made public by the Department of Revenue. However, most estimates range between $46 and $70 million in tourism receipts for the year 2001, when statistics were last reported.[35] The ZTC predicts that annual tourism revenues could rise to as much as $116 million by the year 2012, and would therefore help to offset Zanzibar's growing trade deficit.[36] Expenditures by inter-

Table 7.1
Zanzibar's Tourism Growth: Number of Visitors (in thousands)

	1986	*1988*	*1990*	*1992*	*1994*	*1996*	*1998*	*2000*	*2001*	*2002*	*2004*	*2005*
Foreigners	22.8	32.1	42.1	59.7	41.4	69.2	86.5	97.2	76.3	87.5	92.1	125.5
Nationals	2	2.4	3.7	4.7	3.2	6.1	7.1	8.2	—	—	—	—
Total	24.8	34.5	45.8	64.4	44.6	75.3	93.6	105.4				

Source: Foreign statistics obtained from the Zanzibar Tourism Commission, September 2005. National statistics obtained from the Zanzibar Ministry of Trade, Industry, Marketing, and Tourism, September 2005. 2005 statistics from www.freesun.be/freesun_news/10_march_2006/freesun_news_303.html. Mainland (national) arrivals were not available for recent years.

national tourists, while still short of government targets, have shown steady growth over the last ten years, and on average, tourists on package tours spend $115 per night, while those traveling independently spend $91 per night.[37]

The personal incomes of some Zanzibaris have also benefited from tourism. In Kiwengwa, a popular tourist area on the east coast of Zanzibar, a recent study found that households involved in tourism averaged 43 percent higher incomes than households not involved in tourism.[38] Farther south, in Jambiani, a small village with glimmering white-sand beaches, Mohammed Kasim, a local man and cultural tour guide, credits tourism with providing badly needed jobs that allow villagers to send their kids to school and build new houses. During a tour of the village, Kasim also observed that the increase in small tourism businesses in his village, predominantly family-run guest houses, was helping to keep younger Zanzibaris from migrating to the Stone Town or the mainland in search of better economic opportunities.[39] The financial benefits to local Zanzibaris from tourism, however, are not widespread or evenly distributed. In fact, overall, tourism contributes only 1.5 percent to per-capita income[40] (assuming the accuracy of official figures) and therefore little, in absolute terms, to poverty reduction. As Gossling concludes, "Tourism may thus be important in terms of foreign exchange earnings, but it contributes little to the livelihoods of most of the local population. Quite the contrary, as local communities remain dependent on agriculture and fisheries, the continued degradation of the environment [from tourism] will instead severely affect their livelihoods."[41]

Although official statistics are not systematically collected on tourism's contribution to employment in Zanzibar, the ZTC estimated that the industry provided about 7,500 direct jobs in 2005[42] (up from just 2,600 in the late 1990s) and more than 36,000 indirect jobs through tourism-related services and activities.[43] This included, for instance, over one hundred licensed tour operators and 325 guides, occupations that only Tanzanian nationals are permitted to fill. The government predicts that by 2020, 50 percent of all jobs in the modern sector will be in tourism.[44] Virtually all managerial positions in the tourism sector are held by foreigners. Poor public education and training for Zanzibaris has kept them from rising to higher positions of employment on the island. Of the 7,500 direct jobs, most are low-paying, lack benefits, and provide little room for growth beyond service-level positions in hotels and guesthouses.

By 2003, the majority of large hotels and resorts in Zanzibar were run by international companies, predominantly Italian and South African companies in the practice of importing their own management.[45] The remainder of Zanzibaris employed directly by tourism work for restaurants and airlines, as tour guides and diver operators, or in the ministry or Tourism Commission.[46] In September 2005, Silima described the lack of public education facilities: "Training [for tourism] is very poor, it is a weak point in Zanzibar now. The tourism school offers three courses in front office, food production and beverage services that enroll about 70 students per year. We are only catering to the lowest segment of the industry and need management and supervisory training for the industry."[47]

Tourism Investment and Aid

In a 2005 interview, Issa Mlingoti, director of planning for the Tourism Commission, observed a stack of new tourism investment proposals that had landed on his desk and lamented, "We are going to be swallowed by globalization. Now, all new development projects are tourism. If we want to keep the island sustainable in terms of tourism we need to stop and evaluate before we continue. We need to develop other subsectors as well."[48] The Zanzibar Investment Promotion Agency (ZIPA), formed in 1992 by the government to streamline and promote investments (ostensibly domestic and foreign), reports that 59 percent of all investment projects they have approved are in the hotel and tourism sector. In all, 162 projects worth $588 million have passed through ZIPA's doors between 1992 and 2005. Between 2000 and 2005, fifty-nine new tourism projects were approved, despite the impact of terrorist attacks and the war on terrorism on the tourism industry. Domestically owned tourism projects account for 35 percent of total investments, while British and Italian investors dominate the foreign presence, composing 13 percent each.[49] In general, domestically owned tourism projects serve the budget traveler in the form of family-run guest houses and hostels, which typically also offer tour and transport services and are concentrated in the Stone Town and along the southeastern coast.

The bulk of construction in the tourism sector occurred in the early 1990s, prior to the government's attempts to establish regulations for the industry, and thus, much of the land with the greatest tourism potential has already been sold. Despite nominal attempts to curb development and enforce zoning laws over the past ten years, the remaining land with tourism appeal appears to have been leased with similar disregard for social and environmental concerns and deals are frequently fraught with allegations of government corruption. Hampered by a lack of resources and poor cooperation among government ministries, ZIPA is often forced to be reactive in approving potential investors' projects, leading to poorly-planned and scattered tourism projects demanding increased infrastructure services. Remarkably, few projects undergo an Environmental Impact Assessment (EIA). According to the Zanzibar government's Environmental Management for Sustainable Development Act of 1996, any person who plans to "undertake an activity which is likely to have a significant impact on the environment" must complete an EIA. However, as late as 2002, consideration of environmentally sustainable measures by hotels was still voluntary, and fewer than ten EIAs had been completed.[50]

In line with the Zanzibar government's desire to attract low-volume, high-paying tourism in the future, ZIPA encourages only four- and five-star developments, restaurants, and tourism-related services. In 2005, the responsibilities of two additional government bodies delineated in the Free Economic Zone Act and the Free Port Act merged to form a newly expanded ZIPA, in an effort to reduce bureaucratic hassle and streamline the investor experience in Zanzibar. ZIPA now offers equal incentives to foreign and domestic investors, such as waiving import duties for capital goods during the construction period. But Mlingoti worries that this streamlining, which altered the approval structure that used to involve representatives from relevant ministries, will lead to a less-thorough approval process for tourism projects. In addition, ZIPA is not a financing body, and no other Zanzibari organization or government body offers loans or technical assistance to Zanzibaris to develop tourism projects.

In the private sector, a group of investors formed the Zanzibar Association of Tourism Investors (ZATI) in November 2003 to liaise with the government and support socioeconomic development of tourism in Zanzibar. ZATI's aim, according to its Web site, "is to ensure a sustainable and professional Tourism industry of the highest standard."[51] By 2005, ZATI represented tourism investments worth over $50 million in Zanzibar and included some thirty hoteliers and tour operators, who meet to work on issues of security and environmental sustainability within the industry. However, to date, ZATI is composed of members from only the upscale establishments in the tourism market because the two-hundred-dollar membership fee is prohibitive for most local Zanzibaris.

While no direct aid money supported Zanzibar's implementation of the 2004 Tourism Policy, renewed interest from the international aid community, which had left in waves following 1995 and 2000 election violence, has stimulated a number of new tourism-related donor projects. In addition to the Finnish government's return to support Zanzibar's land-use planning efforts, the World Bank resumed assistance for infrastructure in Zanzibar via a road fund originally established in 1995. The United Nations Development Programme (UNDP) has also partially renewed its support of tourism development as part of its Poverty Reduction Program in Zanzibar. Between 2000 and 2003, the UNDP provided $745,000 in support of the establishment of Jozani National Park and ecotourism and development initiatives within the park.

The World Bank's private-sector financing arm, the International Finance Corporation (IFC), has also supported the construction of several privately owned beach resorts, as well as a drinking water bottling company in Zanzibar.[52] In 1999, the IFC helped finance the establishment of the Blue Bay Beach Resort, a four-star resort on the east coast of Zanzibar with a $1.5 million dollar loan to Kenyan hotel investors. Approval of the loan was dependent on an environmental review and the requirement that the Kenyan owners adhere to socially and environmentally beneficial regulations in the construction of their resort, including providing water for local villages and building at least thirty meters back from the high water line. The hotel has been praised for its environmental standards during construction and, in 2004, ZIPA gave the hotel its "Responsible Tourism" award for its use of a wastewater treatment plant, a garbage incinerator (the only one in Zanzibar), and organized beach cleanups. However, Blue Bay has angered and inconvenienced neighboring villagers by cutting public access along the road running past the hotel and claiming exclusive beach access for its tourists.[53]

In 2000, the IFC approved a similar loan of seven hundred thousand dollars to assist a Zanzibari businessman, Khamis Khamis, upgrade his hotel, the Zanzibar Safari Club, to international standards. Also located on the east coast of Zanzibar, in the village of Uroa, the loan required that Khamis's project pass an environmental review and implement a series of changes, including providing permanent boat moorings to eliminate impacts on the reef, installing a sewage treatment system, and working with local communities to maintain public access to the beach and tidal flats.[54] The IFC initially praised the project as "developmentally positive" and "a demonstration model to other Zanzibaris as the hotel is one of the very few beach hotels owned by an indigenous Z[anzibari]."[55]

But within a couple of years, this promising model had turned sour when Khamis was forced to sell the Zanzibar Safari Hotel in what was widely viewed as an egregious case of political favoritism. While the reasons behind the forced sale remain unclear, many speculate it was for mismanagement of the terms laid out in the IFC loan. The Smith family, Kenyan owners of the nearby Blue Bay Beach Resort, which had also received IFC financing, stepped up to buy the hotel and were in the final stages of paperwork when the government intervened. The sale to the Smith family was revoked and instead the hotel was sold to GapCo, (Gulf Africa Petroleum Company), a powerful Middle East oil company that serves East Africa and had purchased, through a newly formed Hotels and Lodges subsidiary, four former government-owned game lodges in Tanzania's northern circuit. Many Zanzibaris cite GapCo's alleged close ties to Tanzania's ruling party, the CCM, to explain GapCo's favored treatment. GapCo is also in the process of developing a new resort on Prison Island, a small island frequented by day-trippers from the Stone Town, despite the government's stated desire to halt development on all small islands. The Ministry of Tourism contended that GapCo's plans for the Prison Island resort successfully underwent an Environmental Impact Assessment.[56]

The Search for Ecotourism in Zanzibar

The word ecotourism has been a part of the lexicon of Zanzibar's government officials and tourism promoters since the early 1990s. But today, the word is found mainly in print, not in action. The government's officially proclaimed commitment to ecotourism development in Zanzibar dates back to 1994, when the Department of Environment and the Commission for Tourism held the International Workshop on Ecotourism and Environmental Conservation. The delegates, numbering over one hundred from Zanzibar and abroad, made sixteen recommendations that collectively set forth a dynamic blueprint for implementing sound ecotourism as a national strategy for development. The most innovative of the recommendations was a set of resolutions to increase the involvement of local communities in tourism development in order to benefit the communities' economies and protect their environments.[57] In the wake of this conference, hopes ran high that Zanzibar would play a leading role in Africa in implementing and promoting sound practices of ecotourism.

Today, few people in Zanzibar remember the conference, let alone the recommendations. Tourism officials are quick to explain that while the conference set forth an idealistic framework for tourism, based on the principles of ecotourism, they were never capable of implementing its agenda. At the time, pressure from would-be tourism investors was great and the ZTC had no real legal mandate to act on the community-based or environmental recommendations, so tourism development continued haphazardly.[58] Furthermore, the newly formed ZIPA, tasked with making investment easier and bringing badly needed foreign exchange to Zanzibar, was not in a position to turn away potential investors whose proposals did not embody the recommendations of the conference. As a result, ecotourism projects only materialized when international donor agencies or private individuals provided the motivation and the funding.[59]

Shortly after the conference, the Zanzibar Ecotourism Society was formed by a small group of tourism investors hoping to maintain enthusiasm for socially and environmentally responsible tourism development. But, according to Len Horlin, a cofounder and owner of one of Zanzibar's first ecotourism lodges, the society only operated for three years. Members lost interest, operating funds became scarce, and ecotourism began to loose its luster. As Horlin described it, membership waned when ecotourism came to mean little more than "a green stamp for separating garbage."[60] In 1999, the dissolution of the Ecotourism Society seemed to confirm Zanzibar's move toward individualistic, profit-driven tourism development and the abandonment of ecotourism.

In December 2003, the discussion about ecotourism was half-heartedly revived when the Commission for Tourism in cooperation with the New York–based Africa Travel Association (ATA) cohosted the "7th Cultural and Eco Tourism Symposium" in Zanzibar. In the end, the five-day symposium, with its recycled speeches and stale discussions about the value of ecotourism, seemed to have little impact. One participant and hotel owner described the symposium as "a good show for the media but a disservice to the local people that are still waiting for the government to make good on its promise to bring benefits. Soon, they will stop waiting, and stop listening to anything [the government] says."[61]

Zanzibar's New Offerings: Protection of Natural and Cultural Heritage

Despite the bleak institutional atmosphere and a history of failed attempts to follow a path of sustainable tourism development, Zanzibar's fate is not yet sealed. In the void left by a government with little capacity or funding, enterprising Zanzibaris, NGOs, and foreign investors are implementing innovative ecotourism projects, and contributing substantially to conservation and development efforts. Most notably, ecotourism projects are helping to fund Zanzibar's burgeoning network of marine and terrestrial conservation areas. Unlike virtually every other destination seriously involved in ecotourism, Zanzibar embarked on its ecotourism experiment at a time when it had no credible national park. (The ill-kept Masingini Forest Reserve had been established in the 1950s to conserve the town's groundwater.) In 1996, the government passed the Environmental Management for Sustainable Development Act, legislation designed to bolster the creation of protected areas. The new act created the Zanzibar National Protected Areas Board (ZNPAB) as a replacement for the previous body, the Zanzibar Nature Conservation Trust, which had facilitated the creation of only two nominal Nature Conservation Areas during its ten-year existence. The ZNPAB allows for anyone with a plan and the resources to petition to manage a protected area in Zanzibar, thus opening the door for NGOs, local people, and private investors to play central roles in conservation efforts.[62] As a result, Zanzibar is now home to six protected areas—two forests (the Jozani-Chwaka Bay Conservation Area and the Ngezi Forest on Pemba) and four marine conservation areas (Menai Bay, Misali Island, Chumbe Island, Coral Park, and Mnemba Island)—each based on the initiative and management support of external parties. While each boasts outstanding nature tourism opportunities, it's worth looking in depth at three to get a sense of the potential and pitfalls of these resources.

Zanzibar's First National Park: Jozani-Chwaka Bay Conservation Area

The Jozani-Chwaka Bay Conservation Area (JCBCA), located thirty-five miles southwest of the Stone Town, was formed in 1995 by CARE International, an NGO dedicated to poverty alleviation, in cooperation with Zanzibar's Department of Commercial Crops, Fruits and Forestry (DCCFF). JCBCA encompasses a total of fifty-six square kilometers of protected forest area and eighty additional kilometers of buffer area that includes community forests and cultivated land. Jozani Forest contains the last remaining groundwater forest in Zanzibar and is home to two endemic and threatened species, the red colobus monkey and Ader's duiker, as well as a number of coastal endemic birds, reptiles, invertebrates, and plants. CARE's vision for the JCBCA project was to encourage a new type of conservation in which local people and visitors both played a role in conserving the unique coastal forest and nearby habitats and in raising the standard of living for people in nine surrounding villages. According to Thabit Masoud, a project manager with CARE, they implemented a three-phase project focused on empowering local communities through the development of conservation committees, community development funds, farmer compensation schemes (to account for the damage red colobus monkeys inflict on crops), and credit and savings loan programs.[63] In 1999, CARE helped to establish a community-based NGO, Jozani Environmental Conservation Association (JECA), designed to eventually take over management of the protected area and ecotourism programs.

Today, the ecotourism attractions at Jozani are threefold: visitors are encouraged to take a guided forest walk, view the charismatic red colobus monkeys in their native habitat, and visit a boardwalk that winds through a nearby mangrove forest. Knowledgeable guides are included with the price of admission for the park—five dollars for foreigners and one dollar for locals. Since its inception, Jozani's visitation and revenues have increased significantly, growing from 6,191 visitors and $42,398 in revenue in 1995 to 19,205 visitors and $106,427 in 2002.[64] In 2001, CARE successfully lobbied for a revenue-sharing scheme that required the government to allocate 80 percent of park revenues directly to JECA (up from 30 percent at the park's inception), with only 20 percent going to the government treasury. This change enabled the Conservation Association to implement their Community Development Funds and finance programs to improve health, water supply, and education in the surrounding villages. In 2003, over 20 percent of total tourism entry fee revenues collected at Jozani, $18,491, were allocated by JECA to Community Development Funds.[65] And according to a local guide at Jozani, "People's awareness of conservation issues has improved significantly and now we [the guides] want to start our own project to take tourists fishing."[66]

A New Era of Marine Protection and Tourism in Zanzibar

While coastal tourism development in Zanzibar has certainly contributed to the degradation of the marine environment, ecotourism is now providing a valuable source of finance for marine conservation efforts as well. All of the four marine protected areas in Zanzibar employ ecotourism as a funding mechanism for a range of park management, community development, and educational activities.

Chumbe Island Coral Park Limited (CHICOP)

Chumbe Island, a half-mile-long coral rag island located eight miles and a forty-minute boat ride from the Stone Town, is home to Zanzibar's most celebrated ecotourism destination. Chumbe Island Lodge has won an impressive number of prestigious international and national ecotourism awards, despite the fact that, when Sibylle Riedmiller launched the project in the early 1990s, her purpose was not ecotourism. Riedmiller, a German conservationist and former manager of donor-funded aid projects in Tanzania, recognized qualities in the reef-fringed island that she believed would make Chumbe an ideal site for a small marine park. Riedmiller recalls, "My vision was *not* ecotourism, but marine conservation and environmental education. Tourism income was only meant to be instrumental for that."[67]

In 1991, Riedmiller set out to establish the Chumbe Island Coral Park (CHICOP) as the world's first private marine protected area (MPA). After three years of difficult negotiations and "political struggle" between Riedmiller, several government agencies, and some local fishermen, the government of Zanzibar accepted her investment proposal for the park, and declared the Chumbe Reef Sanctuary in 1994 as Zanzibar's first marine protected area and the island as a forest reserve. They gave CHICOP responsibility for preserving, controlling, and managing the reef and the forest. The Chumbe sanctuary houses exceptional levels of biodiversity, especially on the western side of the island, where two hundred types of coral and over four hundred species of fish can be found in the nearby reef.[68] With her own investment and some additional funding from several European and NGO donors,[69] Riedmiller successfully negotiated a thirty-three-year lease on the island and received approval to build an eco-lodge (opened in 1998) and use its income to manage the protected area and introduce an environmental education program on coral reefs for local schools, the first of its kind in Tanzania. Today, CHICOP includes the Chumbe Reef Sanctuary and the Chumbe Forest Reserve, the seven-room Chumbe Island Lodge, a visitors' center, and an environmental education program for Zanzibaris and other visitors.

But Riedmiller's ambitious vision was not easily achieved, and the project has had a long and, particularly in the early years, somewhat troubled history. By the time construction on the visitors' center began in 1995, CHICOP was already awash in a tangled mess of contradictory stories and grudge-holding among government officials, tourism investors, and disgruntled Zanzibaris. Contentious issues included the government's bureaucratic roadblocks and excessive taxation of CHICOP, disagreements about the boundary of the "no-take" zone around the coral reef, and concerns that leasing Chumbe to a foreigner and creating a private reserve could limit fishermen's access and hurt their livelihoods.[70] Riedmiller acknowledges that "there have been conflicts in the extremely challenging initial phases of this unique and innovative project," adding that "the tenacity required to see CHICOP through this time was unimaginable."[71] From 1995, Riedmiller says that CHICOP established an advisory committee made up of government officials, local academics, and community leaders of the adjacent villages, which met at least yearly to discuss CHICOP's progress reports, management plans, and any problems.[72]

Visitors arriving at Chumbe Island by boat first glimpse the seven whimsically vaulted eco-bungalows and the visitors' center situated in the coral rag forest just beyond the beach. All construction for the ecolodge was carried out with local materials and the daily environmental impact is minimized through the use of photovoltaic energy, rainwater catchments, composting toilets, and grey-water vegetative filtration. Today, conflicts with the community and the government have receded, and CHICOP's conservation and ecotourism activities are thriving—benefiting from a steady stream of rave reviews from guests, the media, and the international travel and conservation communities. Occupancy has increased steadily, from just 13 percent in 1998–1999 (the lodge's first year of operation) to 58 percent from 2004 to 2006, and income from ecotourism grew more than tenfold over the first six years, to $275,819 in 2003–2004.[73] The park management is now fully funded by the income from ecotourism.[74]

CHICOP employs a staff of forty-one, which includes approximately eight park rangers (who also act as guides), an on-site lodge manager, and technical maintenance, cooking, and cleaning staff, all of whom are native Tanzanians. The park rangers, former fishermen from the neighboring villages, have been trained in park management and monitoring techniques for the reef and forest and, since the early 1990s, have collected monitoring data on poaching in the marine park. Their data show that the incidence of illegal fishing has decreased fourfold from 1994 to 2004, while fish size and marine diversity have increased in Chumbe's waters.[75] Some four hundred fishermen in four villages have also attended educational meetings on the ecology of corals and history of Chumbe that CHICOP has held jointly with the Department of Fisheries.[76]

From 2001, CHICOP's environmental education program for schools expanded its operations considerably. Between February 2003 and February 2005 alone, thirty-four different Zanzibari schools and colleges (totaling 1,189 students and 204 teachers) participated in the island field trip and environmental education program.[77] CHICOP, working closely with the Ministry of Education, also initiated the production of environmental education booklets on topics such as marine conservation, coral reefs, and ecotourism for use in secondary schools in Zanzibar, which lack curriculum on environmental issues.[78] In addition, researchers from around the world have studied various aspects of CHICOP. Visits by local researchers and Zanzibari students are free, underwritten by the income from ecotourism and fees of seventy dollars for tourists visiting for a day, and thirty-five dollars for international researchers/students. Chumbe has been the most thoroughly studied, documented, and openly discussed ecotourism experiment in Zanzibar, and this has revealed both its successes and shortcomings. As one 2006 thesis states, despite a range of complaints from local fishermen and others in Zanzibar in the early years, "this situation is starting to change now." This thesis concludes, "Overall, protection of the Chumbe reef and the introduction of ecotourism have had a positive effect on the private sectors, the Government, researchers, students, school children, teachers and tourists. In particular, CHICOP has provided educational, research and conservational benefits to Zanzibar."[79]

Mnemba Island Lodge and Conservation Area

Mnemba Island Marine Conservation Area (MIMCA) comprises the rich coral atoll formation around Mnemba Island, found off the northeastern tip of Unguja. Formed in 2002 as a partnership between Conservation Corporation of Africa (CC Africa), one of South Africa's best-known ecotourism companies (see chapter 9), and Zanzibar's Department of Fisheries, this marine conservation area aims to protect the fragile reefs and provide tangible economic benefits to the local people who rely on the reef for their livelihoods. CC Africa owns and operates the only resort on the island, the exclusive Mnemba Island Lodge, and has been involved in efforts to declare the island a conservation area and develop partnerships with local communities. Mnemba Island Lodge holds a lease on the uninhabited island, and its ten luxurious and pricey beach bandas ($1,200 night/double), built directly on the beach out of indigenous materials, are often fully booked. A stay at Mnemba Island Lodge offers guests the chance to relax in seclusion and swim, snorkel, and scuba dive in the brilliant coral reef that flanks the idyllic (and mosquito-free) island. In 2004, Britain's *Independent* newspaper listed Mnemba Island Lodge as one of the five best private islands in the world.[80] The CC Africa owners carefully designed the lodge to interfere as little as possible with the environment on Mnemba. Solar power is used to heat water, trash is not buried on the island, septic tanks and a desalination system are used, and the physical structures were kept to a minimum. Candlelit dinners are served each night on the beach, eliminating the need for a generator-lit dining room.

But just below the surface, tensions have plagued Mnemba lodge since it first opened in 1988. The original owner was Bruno Brighetti, an Italian entrepreneur whose resorts along the Kenyan coast were associated with rumors of prostitution, money laundering, and even drug trafficking, and these stories have followed Brighetti to Zanzibar. Brighetti was given a ninety-nine-year lease for exclusive use of the island and many suspected that he obtained this sweetheart deal by sweetening the pot of key government functionaries. Perhaps most contentious was the issue of exclusivity: Brighetti's Mnemba Club made it impossible for Zanzibaris to land on Mnemba Island or fish on the reef. Traditionally, fishermen from the nearby coastal villages fished in the waters around the island and dried their fish and nets on the island. Zanzibar's environment director at the time, Abdulrahman Issa, said that the "missing link" in the deal involved failure to consult the fishermen beforehand. In a 1995 interview, Issa conceded that "Fishermen were destroying the reef. We [the government] supported stopping fishermen, but they needed to benefit from what was done on the island and also work out where they would fish instead," he says. Brighetti paid no compensation to the local fishermen or villagers, and the club wouldn't even permit fishermen to make emergency landings on the island during storms. As tempers boiled in mid-1995, fishermen talked of mounting an "armada" of fifty small boats to provoke "an armed confrontation with Mnemba. We want to be able to use the island as in the past."[81]

When CC Africa bought the Mnemba Club in 1996, people expected swift improvements in the community relations. Today, the official creation of the marine park, MIMCA, has brought environmental benefits to the area, but relations between the lodge, government, and local fishermen remain challenging. Peter Siebert, the business-minded general manager of Mnemba Island Lodge, explained in a 2005 interview that he was drafting a code of conduct for MIMCA to officially demarcate the zoning for the marine park, including the no-take and limited-use zones, as well as develop guidelines for fishermen and tourists to follow in the park.[82] He lamented that the lodge was in a difficult spot because the Department of Fisheries was dragging its feet in properly managing the marine protected area. He said the lodge staff often ended up policing the two-hundred-meter coral zone that is part of the island's lease, as well as the outer reef, which is protected only nominally until the marine park is clearly mapped. Siebert stated that Mnemba Island

Lodge is expensive and exclusive, so they have a serious stake in the marine environment's health and should contribute significantly to the conservation of MIMCA. But, he contended, they cannot do it alone. He argued that the Department of Fisheries is well-equipped to manage MIMCA, based on the fee that they collect from the lodge and tour operators who bring tourists to snorkel and dive in the reefs around the island.

In 2005, the MIMCA entrance fee was raised from three to ten dollars per visitor, generating, together with other taxes, sufficient revenue, a World Bank study concluded, to adequately manage the marine reserve.[83] To their credit, the Department of Fisheries did allocate funds and approve a project to distribute forty fishing boats with motors to Zanzibari fishermen to equip them to travel farther out to sea to fish and take pressure off of the near-shore marine protected areas. In addition, four fish-aggregating devices (FADs) were installed out at sea, away from MIMCA, to attract pelagic fish populations.[84] Local fishermen in nearby villages, however, continue to complain about Mnemba's role in creating a marine park that they describe as "really terrible" for excluding them from the resources they use to feed their families and make a living. The most contentious issue for fishermen has been the fact that the marine park excludes them from fishing the safe and reliable waters around the island, where they are protected from strong winds.[85]

Apart from MIMCA, Mnemba Island Lodge's involvement with the local communities has grown considerably since 1996. Siebert described the lodge's engagement as constantly expanding, particularly now that villages have begun approaching Mnemba with project ideas. In 2005, the lodge helped refurbish classrooms in Matemwe village, brought students to the island to teach them about the marine environment, contributed to the education of fishermen, and organized a 1,200-person beach clean-up. The lodge also says over half of its employees are from the nearby villages, although other hoteliers dispute this. Mnemba Lodge has supported the construction of a trash incinerator for the main village to help alleviate trash and pollution problems. However, some other operators who bring tourists to enjoy the waters off Mnemba Island claim that while the lodge has been a catalyst for marine protection in the area, it falls short of delivering substantial benefits to local communities and could make more of an effort to hire from neighboring villages.[86]

Despite significant contributions to marine conservation in Zanzibar, projects like Chumbe Island Coral Park and Mnemba Marine Conservation Area highlight concerns about the ethics of exclusionary conservation models initiated by the private sector. As the number of private conservation area projects increases around the world, most of which require local people to give up partial or full access to valuable natural resources, increasingly careful examination of the benefits and costs of these models is needed. On the one hand, private marine parks may provide a more reliable stream of funding due to better business management of income-generating activities such as ecotourism. However, government- and NGO-managed projects are often more explicitly focused on integrating local communities into the projects, including providing alternative income and livelihood opportunities to local people. In the case of both Mnemba and Chumbe, when the government leased the islands for the development of private ecotourism lodges and marine reserves, fishermen lost access to resources without, many argue, fair and immediate compensation, thus endangering the livelihoods of already poor families. To some Zanzibaris who are struggling to make a living and feed their families, "conservation" remains a dirty word. The sentiments expressed by one fisherman illustrate the enduring complexity of the problem: "The [foreigners] come and pay off my government and steal my livelihood with their projects, and ask me to say okay because they teach my children to use a snorkel. The problem is not so easy to solve."[87]

Freelance Ecotourism: Projects in the Private Sector

Outside of the realm of protected areas, a smattering of private ecotourism projects are also making positive contributions to conservation and community development in Zanzibar, despite an ever-increasing number of challenges.

Matemwe Bungalows

Perhaps the oldest and most authentic ecotourism lodge in Zanzibar, Matemwe Bungalows, is located along an enormous stretch of dazzling white-sand beach on the edge of the village and within eyeshot of Mnemba island. It was built in the early 1990s by Len and Katharina Horlin, two young Swedish sisters, who secured a thirty-three-year lease from the government and then set out to carefully discuss their project with the neighboring village. "We didn't yet know the term ecotourism, but the concept was an old habit because we had grown up in a national park on an island in Sweden where our father worked," recalled Katharina Horlin. "We wanted to build the hotel in the local style, to help the people of the area, and to try not to disturb their way of life."[88] From the outset, the sisters established very positive and mutually beneficial relations with the nearby village. They signed a special agreement not to disturb a local graveyard; educated their guests about local customs and culturally appropriate dress; bought fish, fruit, vegetables, and water locally; helped village women set up a restaurant and a small shop; and hired, trained, taught English, and paid above-normal wages to villagers who filled most jobs in the hotel. Despite many small challenges, Matemwe was an admirable and largely successful ecotourism experiment that won praise from the local community. In a 1995 interview, one villager, who had just rattled off a litany of complaints against the Italian owners of Mnemba Club, told me, "Relations with Matemwe have been very positive. If a boat breaks down, they sail out to rescue it. They use their vehicles to take sick villagers to the hospital. And the employment gives us a way to diversify because we can't all make a living from fishing alone. In turn, we help protect the hotel. Several times, we've helped arrest thieves. So the relationship is mutually beneficial. We've had no problems, no complaints. They help the local people."[89]

In the 1990s, Matemwe also won praise, though no real assistance, from both the Zanzibar government and international financial institutions. A tourism study by the International Finance Corporation (IFC) concluded that "Matemwe is well viewed by the Government as the sort of development it would like to encourage."[90] But in practice, the IFC, the Zanzibari government, and international promoters of ecotourism have done little to help Matemwe. Despite its excellent community involvement programs and architectural and environmental sensitivity, Matemwe Bungalows received no international ecotourism awards (which would have boosted occupancy) and had less favored status with the government than the Mnemba Club. It was given only a thirty-three-year lease for the land and a two-year rather than a three-year reprieve on paying taxes. Zanzibar's Commission for Tourism visitors' guide, published in the mid-1990s, urged tourists traveling to Matemwe to "take a boat and visit Mnemba Island. It is a real Paradise: very clear waters, coral reefs, white sand beaches." It made no pitch for Matemwe Bungalows.[91]

In recent years, Matemwe Bungalows faced new challenges as it underwent an internal reorganization and began to reposition itself from a backpackers' destination to a more upscale beach resort in keeping with the changing tourism market in Zanzibar. When Katharina Horlin left Matemwe, Len Horlin stayed behind to run the lodge with the help of a new assistant manager. She struggled to maintain its positive community relations as villagers became suspicious of the changes taking place. In a 2005 interview, Len stated that lodge operations needed to be streamlined in order to make the lodge more financially viable and to increase standards. She said this was resulting in some hiring changes. "The most difficult thing for the villagers to accept was that we can't just hire them," she explained. "We have had to hire more educated people from the mainland, who are not popular with the villagers, in order to increase standards, including the level of English being spoken. There were unrealistic expectations from the village side."[92] Over the years, Matemwe Bungalows had made significant efforts to increase education levels in the community, including building a four-classroom school in the village and providing staff with English-speaking classes during the tourism season and intensive courses during the off-season.

In 2003, Len decided to upgrade Matemwe Bungalows to keep pace with the growing tourism industry in Zanzibar, and embarked on a project to tastefully renovate and decorate the seafront cottages and add a two-level pool overlooking the ocean. As before, each cottage provides the guests with information on the ecology of the area, appropriate behavior and dress in the villages, and ways that guests can help the lodge reduce its impact on the environment. And although Len has moved to mainland Tanzania, on-site lodge management was turned over to an expatriate couple who have continued to prioritize the cultivation of healthy relationships with the nearby village by holding regular community meetings, purchasing all seafood directly from local fishermen, and hiring a significant number of staff from the neighboring village, Kigomani.[93]

In June 2005, Matemwe Bungalows entered another era of change when Len decided to sell the lodge to a relatively new tourism company she helped found, Asilia Lodges. Asilia (which means "authentic" in Swahili) owns and operates five luxury ecotourism lodges and camps on mainland Tanzania and aims to provide a brand of ecotourism that is intimate and in balance with the local communities and environments.[94] Director Jeroen Harderwijk, originally from the Netherlands, explained that Asilia is an evolving company working to define its own unique style of ecotourism, but is committed to building on the strong community foundations developed by the Horlin sisters. Based on the belief that well-governed communities experience the most development success, Asilia is helping to form a community council in Kigomani village in order to formalize communication with the lodge and provide a forum for issues and disagreements to be discussed.[95] In addition, Asilia plans to allocate a fixed amount of five thousand dollars per year for community projects.

However, in the village, Matemwe Bungalow's recent growth, new ownership, and attempt to control the lodge-community relationship has not been received entirely well. One fisherman commented that the new ownership has everyone worried because everything seems to be changing: "We liked Len and Katharina, we tried to protect them. But now, the new owners are changing everything—ten villagers have lost their jobs and are paid a lower salary than before."[96] Annette Bulman, general manager of Matemwe Bungalows, explained that "Asilia's institutional approach and desire to put things on paper is scaring the locals who had grown to trust Len and Katharina." Of particular concern for Asilia and the local villagers is the issue of employment, and the steady stream of newcomers from mainland Tanzania and other African countries seeking jobs in tourism. Villagers are angry that locals are not being favored for jobs at Matemwe Bungalows; they dislike outsiders, and, like elsewhere in Zanzibar, blame the outsiders for increased crime, prostitution, and drug use in their village. Like CC Africa's managers at Mnemba, Matemwe's managers worry that poor education in Zanzibar leaves them no choice but to hire employees from elsewhere who possess the skills needed in the international tourism industry.

Despite difficult growing pains, Matemwe Bungalows remains a fine example of community-linked ecotourism in Zanzibar. Under Asilia's new management, the lodge and community will be challenged to adapt to a more commercial, up-market type of ecotourism than the small, highly personalized project the Horlin sisters began in the early 1990s.[97] Recently, Len Horlin created a new ecotourism offering, Matemwe Retreat, a small, midmarket lodge consisting of three large split-level beach cottages and set on the beach north of Matemwe Bungalows. She has built on the lessons learned from Matemwe Bungalows and plans to establish the project as a joint venture with 50 percent local ownership.[98]

Fundu Lagoon

Fundu Lagoon, a British-owned and -managed luxury eco-lodge, is one of the few ecotourism projects on Pemba, Zanzibar's sister island to the north. The lodge sits above a breathtaking stretch of white sand on the remote, mangrove-lined Wambaa Peninsula and provides a remarkable example of sensitive tourism development. Opened in 2000, after a protracted struggle with ZIPA to gain approval, the lodge was built with an eye to sustainability as reflected in the lodge's construction and community relations. Like Matemwe, the owners pledged from the outset that their philosophy was "to support the local community" and build "mutual respect and co-operation."[99] Most easily reached by boat,[100] the approach to Fundu Lagoon allows visitors the chance to dock at a long jetty from which they can appreciate the graceful and environmentally sensitive Robinson Crusoe–style tree-house accommodations. Fourteen intimate tented bungalows, along with a restaurant, several bars, and a dive shop, are nestled into the lush hillside above the beach and constructed with local materials by local labor from the neighboring villages. Fundu has also been blessed by positive press coverage. *Condé Nast Traveler* called Fundu Lagoon "a stunning achievement in eco-friendly architecture," while *Vogue* has called it "the epitome in shabby chic."[101]

In 2000, when Fundu was built, the villages were without freshwater, electricity, and a public school close enough for the children to attend. Since then, Fundu has financed the building of a new school, which opened in January 2006, and donated bicycles for the teachers and uniforms for the 170 students, as well as provided medical assistance and the area's first well and water tap. Fundu Lagoon is also the only outside employer for the six rural villages in this remote part of Pemba, and provides the only source of income for villagers whose livelihood has been based on subsistence fishing and farming. Julia Bishop, the Kenyan-born general manager of Fundu Lagoon, is enthusiastically pursuing new projects to expand community involvement and benefit, including helping local women form a cooperative to grow organic vegetables for the lodge to purchase. Bishop has also made 1 million shillings (approximately one thousand dollars), available for loans for her staff to help them pay for school fees, upgrade their homes, and perhaps soon, bring electricity to their villages.[102]

In addition, Fundu Lagoon has been instrumental in bringing together other tourism investors in Pemba and the Zanzibar government to discuss the protection of the Misali Island Conservation Area (MICA). Fundu's guests are responsible for a large percentage of tourism revenues collected at MICA and Bishop has also challenged the government to increase transparency and scientific expertise in its management of MICA. Fundu has also provided uniforms for the rangers at Misali Island and suggested a bonus system whereby they get extra cash every month if the lodge's dive instructors report they are protecting the island from illegal fishing in the no-take zone and checking for proper permits for authorized fishermen.[103]

Critical to Fundu Lagoon's success, and setting it apart from lodges like Chumbe and Mnemba, has been its nonexclusivity—villagers still have access to the beach and waters in front of the hotel—as well as the lodge management's dedicated efforts to provide tangible, consistent benefits to the villages. Bishop describes Fundu's work with the community as "quite time consuming and incredibly rewarding. It is time and energy more than money that makes it [successful community work] happen and keeps it going. We have the will and passion to work with the villagers and fishermen to make changes."[104]

Zanzibar's 2004 Tourism Policy specifically prescribes ecotourism as the way forward for Pemba, and thus far, the government has been successful in controlling development on the island.[105] Recently, the Tourism Commission and the Department of Commercial Crops, Fruits and Forestry rejected a South African company's proposal to build an "eco-lodge" in Ngezi Forest on the basis that the size of the planned lodge would put a strain on Pemba's limited resources and fragile environment.[106] According to Bishop, Suleiman K. Suleiman, the Government of Zanzibar's Tourism Officer in Pemba, expressed his desire for future tourism development in Pemba to be limited to the construction of three to four additional lodges, bringing the total to no more than six (not including the handful of family-run and government guesthouses in Pemba's three small towns).[107] Indeed, if the Zanzibar government is able to stay the course and implement a low-volume ecotourism strategy modeled after Fundu Lagoon, the future of sustainable tourism in Pemba will look very bright.

Grassroots Community Tourism

Despite the fact that the Ministry of Tourism offers little tangible support or encouragement to locals to get involved in the tourism industry, several resourceful Zanzibaris are implementing grassroots projects. While some, such as the aquarium and the zoo, have been plagued with ongoing economic and management problems, others have been successful. One is Eco+Culture, an NGO formed in 1998 in an effort to foster sustainable economic development in Zanzibar. With support from the Austrian government, Eco+Culture seeks to encourage local entrepreneurs to enter into environmentally and culturally friendly income-generating activities that support the growth of the tourism industry. Among its projects are environmental education programs, school partnerships to promote intercultural understanding, and the promotion of environmentally friendly technologies such as solar energy.[108] In 2000, Eco+Culture began to offer a variety of eco-tours and cultural village tours as well. Haji Hamad, director of Eco+Culture, runs a small tourism office in central Stone Town and arranges tours and day trips to see the Stone Town, spice plantations, and several different villages around the island. The tours cost anywhere from ten to fifty dollars and proceeds help support the work of local development projects in agroforestry, seaweed farming, and education.[109]

Kasim Mohamed, a Zanzibari tour guide for Eco+Culture, leads village tours in his home town of Bwejuu, a small village on the southeast coast of Unguja. Mohamed's well-crafted tours provide guests with a glimpse of life in Bwejuu with visits to spice, herb, and coconut plantations, seaweed farms, a local kindergarten (built with money from Eco+Culture), and a traditional medicine man. Mohamed speaks positively of the tourism industry, crediting the jobs and economic development it has brought to his village with keeping young people from migrating to the Stone Town and elsewhere in search of work. Currently, Bwejuu and neighboring villages are experiencing a rapid expansion of tourism, and local people have succeeded in remaining highly involved. They own over 50 percent of the tourism businesses, which include dozens of small guesthouses, several budget tour operators, and a growing cluster of mid-market bungalows, although no four- or five-star hotels as preferred by the government.[110]

Stone Town's Pursuit of Responsible Urban Tourism

Zanzibar's famous Stone Town embodies the island's very contradictory relationship with tourism. On one hand, the influx of tourists has attracted money and attention that are funding rehabilitation and historic preservation projects; on the other hand, uncontrolled tourism threatens the historical integrity of the Arab trading city. The Stone Town Conservation and Development Authority (STCDA), formed in 1987 to manage the preservation of the town, is working to mitigate the negative influences of haphazard tourism development and promote the rehabilitation of historic buildings. With assistance from the Aga Kahn Trust for Culture, a nonprofit philanthropy that supports development in Muslim communities in East Africa and Asia, STCDA has developed building guidelines to preserve the historic character of the Stone Town.[111]

Tourists who travel from Dar es Salaam to Zanzibar by hydrofoil ferry are treated to views of the Stone Town's architectural beauty from the water. The narrow, winding streets and tall stone buildings of the Stone Town, the heart of the old Arab and Asian financial monopoly, still appear much as they did more than a hundred years ago. Zanzibar, together with Lamu (on Lamu Island, off Kenya) and, to a lesser degree, Mombasa, are the only functioning historic stone towns along the East African coast.[112] Since the 1990s, tourism revenues have helped to spur restoration of some of the elegant stone homes with ornate wooden balconies and carved wooden doors, as well as several of the main cobblestone streets. Between 1989 and early 1994, about half of the hotel projects approved by the government involved the conversion of the Stone Town homes into guest houses. Today, rehabilitated buildings are not only converted into hotels and guest houses, but also into government offices, museums, private homes, and businesses. In a 2005 interview, Pereira Silima, permanent secretary at the Ministry of Tourism, credited the STCDA with doing a good job and developing sound policies, but explains that its effectiveness was compromised by an uncoordinated government that follows its own guidelines only sporadically. As a result, more than 85 percent of Stone Town houses are in various stages of decay and some have collapsed already; in addition, 40 percent of the structures have been inappropriately repaired over the past two decades. Thankfully, in 2005, the Commission for Tourism put a halt to hotel and guesthouse construction by refusing to license more businesses in the Stone Town, which already has too much accommodation for its market size.[113]

Despite UNESCO's designation of the Stone Town as a World Heritage Site with "outstanding universal value," the government has done very little to improve conditions in the city or increase its tourism appeal. The narrow streets are littered with trash and the air is thick with exhaust from the taxis and tour vans that roar through town, forcing pedestrians to jump out of the way. The winding alleys and public spaces in the Stone Town are also crowded with souvenir hawkers and youth selling sunglasses, water, and other sundries. Many hoteliers are disgusted by the prevalence of what they describe as "mainland junk." John Babtist da Silva, a native Zanzibari artist and historian, explains that the souvenirs being sold in Zanzibar are the same generic souvenirs that can be produced anywhere in East Africa: "Zanzibari artists work in shops, they do not sit on the street,"[114] says da Silva. "The bright, flat colors of Tinga Tinga painting, this is not Zanzibari. Our art is more ornate, more influenced by the Arab world."[115] Emerson Skeens, whose popular hotel, Emerson + Green, is located on a street clogged with souvenir stalls, expressed similar dismay over the transformation of Zanzibar into a "giant craft market with souvenirs from Kenya." He blames the Tourism Commission for not developing a method or "branding" tool to help guests identify Zanzibari-made handicrafts and goods. In addition, Stone Town souvenir stalls sell a surprising number of endangered and illegally traded animal products, such as corals, triton shells, and shark products.[116]

Nowhere is the clash between Western culture and conservative Muslim culture more apparent than in the streets of the Stone Town. Each evening, sun-worshiping, scantily clad tourists crowd into the many bars for sundowners while Zanzibari men head to mosque for prayer. Despite efforts to mitigate the effects of a more liberal Western tourist clientele, Zanzibar is still home to one bar or pub for every ten homes, and many Zanzibaris are concerned about the effect this is having on local youth. While most of the hoteliers in the Stone Town conscientiously inform guests about appropriate dress and etiquette in a Muslim society, the east coast resorts and many tour operators who escort day visitors from cruise ships make no effort. In one particularly insensitive incident, the U.S. television "reality" show *The Amazing Race* sent teams of contestants to Zanzibar, where they literally raced across the island following a set of clues. More surreal than reality, the show filmed scantily outfitted women contestants in short shorts and tank tops throwing traditional wooden clubs (*rungu*) with Maasai (there is no Maasai village in Zanzibar), smiling next to a *kanzu*-clad Muslim elder, and racing through the Stone Town to their final destination in the old fort.[117]

Although the *Amazing Race* contestants had no time to notice, Zanzibar's Stone Town is not without merits, and beneath its grimy surface, a fascinating and vibrant town emerges. Since 2000, two museums have opened in Zanzibar: the National Museum, which showcases relics from the days when Omani Sultanates ruled from the Stone Town, and the House of Wonders in the old Omani Sultanate's Palace facing the seafront, with extensive displays on Zanzibar's rich culture and history. Renovations to the House of Wonders, also known as the Beit al-Ajaib Museum, were completed with support from the Dutch government, and it quickly became a major tourist attraction. Its exhibits, including the critical display on the history and impact of tourism in Zanzibar (mentioned at the beginning of the chapter), are all in English and Swahili, and tourists often share the museum with schoolchildren and other Zanzibaris.[118]

One of the highlights for visitors to the Stone Town is a meal at the lively food stalls that operate each evening at Forodhani Gardens, the seafront center of historic Stone Town. For several years, the Aga Khan Trust for Culture and the government worked collaboratively on plans to renovate and upgrade the gardens, sea wall, and eating area. Just before construction was to begin in 2005, however, the project fell apart over a dispute between Aga Khan Trust and the government and, sadly, the gardens remain decrepit.[119] Historian and former museum curator Abdul Sheriff laments that the Stone Town has been abandoned by a government that claims to be committed to tourism development. "Other than museums, what else is there for tourists in the Stone Town?" he asks. "The city is not clean, security is bad, [public spaces] have not been beautified. Surprisingly little effort has been put forth by the government."[120]

The private sector and NGOs have, however, played a key role in recent years in an extraordinary growth in cultural festivals in Zanzibar. The largest is the annual Zanzibar International Film Festival (ZIFF), begun in 1997 to celebrate the "unique cultural heritage of Africa and the Dhow countries of the Indian Ocean region and their global diaspora,"[121] which draws thousands of visitors from around the world. Another popular event is the Sauti za Busara, a Swahili festival organized every February by a local NGO to showcase theater, music, and dance.

Several of the upscale hotels in the Stone Town do strive to inform their guests about how to be more culturally and environmentally sensitive. The most luxurious hotel accommodations in the Stone Town can be found at The Zanzibar Serena Inn, The Tembo House Hotel, and Emerson + Green, three foreign-owned hotels that make efforts to educate their guests about appropriate behavior and customs in the Stone Town. All hotels provide guests with written information about covering their shoulders and knees as a sign of respect in Zanzibar's conservative Muslim society. The fifty-two-room Zanzibar Serena Inn comprises two blocks of beautifully restored buildings near the ocean. The multimillion-dollar Serena Inn, which received funding from the International Finance Corporation (IFC) and a generous ninety-nine-year lease from the government, is one of ten East African hotels and lodges owned by the Switzerland-based Aga Khan Fund for Economic Development (AKFED). (It has also been leased land for a beach hotel at Mangapwani, eight miles north of town.) The Fund is one of several development agencies and charities set up by Karim al-Hussain Shah, the Aga Khan IV, leader of the Ismailis, a Muslim sect with followers in Zanzibar and elsewhere in East Africa.

Another hotel practicing some ecotourism principles is Emerson + Green Hotel, an elegant restored merchant's mansion decorated with fine Zanzibari antiques and a rooftop restaurant lined with cushions, long, low dining tables, billowing scarves, spicy curries, and a panoramic view of the town and nearby Indian Ocean. The owners are dancer-turned-innkeeper Thomas Green and New York psychologist-turned-innkeeper Emerson Skeens—known simply as Emerson—who arrived in 1989 and opened the hotel in 1994. While Green is reserved, Emerson likes the spotlight and projects himself as the unofficial spokesman for the Stone Town.[122] Emerson is a superb host and master at marketing through the media, and his clientele has included a steady stream of travel writers.

Emerson + Green Hotel is active in promoting Zanzibari culture and educating its guests. The hotel hosts weekly performances of local music, such as Taarab ensembles, and supports a handful of projects showcasing Zanzibari culture, including the Zanzibar film and Dhow musical festivals. Emerson also founded Mgu Mitatu, a project designed to provide employment opportunities to disabled people in the Stone Town by offering rides aboard a *mitatu*, or rickshaws, to locals and tourists.

Emerson says that "tourism has a lot of positive and a lot of negative effects on the Stone Town." Among the positives, he ticked off "jobs, education, opening toward the world, a decrease in Islamic fundamentalism, and sociological changes that are healthy."[123] At the same time, the island's conservative Muslim society and election violence over the last decade make navigating the political and cultural shoals difficult and often uncertain. Emerson, who is openly gay, has managed to run a successful hotel while walking a fine line. He promotes cultural understanding and respects Muslim restrictions on dress and public displays of affection. Yet he remains true to his personal lifestyle and markets the hotel in part to gay travelers. Zanzibar has long had a relatively tolerant, laissez-faire, "don't' ask, don't tell" official attitude toward homosexuality. In recent years it has become the favorite gay tourist destination in East Africa,[124] with Emerson + Green being one of the most popular stops.[125]

Then, in April of 2004, under pressure from conservative Islamic groups with ties to Saudi Arabia, Zanzibar's Parliament passed a law making homosexuality and lesbianism illegal on the islands. The law imposed a twenty-five-year jail term for men found to be in gay relationships and a seven-year jail term for lesbian relationships. However, a scathing international response and calls for tourism boycotts from activist groups around the world have kept the government from attempting to prosecute more than a handful of offenders.

Curator and historian Abdul Sheriff, who has written widely on the Stone Town's history and commercial importance as a crossroads of trade between Arab, Indian, and African cultures during its peak in the nineteenth century, has deep concerns about the long-term impacts of tourism. He worries about further disintegration of the cultural and social fabric of his home, now that foreigners dominate the tourism industry. As he puts it, "For centuries, Zanzibar was a commercial capital. Why are we a renter class now? What has happened to the entrepreneurship and mercantilism of the old days? Zanzibaris are missing out."

Zanzibar's Ecotourism Scorecard

As the decade of the 1990s opened, Zanzibar was still a sort of *tabula rasa* on which ecotourism could be built. In the early and mid-1990s, promises and prospects were high: there was a national conference and good deal of government, industry, international donor, media, and NGO attention to developing Zanzibar as an ecotourism destination. Despite these good intentions, in Zanzibar today there is, sadly, no national strategy or vibrant popular movement for ecotourism. Rather, ecotourism is found in only a handful of hotels, community projects, and protected areas. In contrast, uncontrolled tourism development and political instability and ineptness have stifled ecotourism while Islamic conservatism helped to fuel concerns among Zanzibaris about the growth of Western-dominated tourism.

Here's the scorecard:

Involves Travel to Natural Destinations

Unlike most other countries, ecotourism in Zanzibar did not begin on the foundation of a strong national park system. Rather, the archipelago has had its own unique attractions—the Stone Town and Arab ruins, pristine beaches, tiny offshore islands, and coral reefs—that have been successfully marketed as complements to eco-safaris in Tanzania and Kenya. Protected areas followed, rather than served as the basis for, ecotourism. Over the last decade, one of the positive developments has been the successful designation of a number of national parks and marine reserves. But despite these important achievements, the growth of tourism has led, outside the protected areas, to environmental damage, the undermining of social and cultural mores, and the very uneven distribution of economic impacts.

Minimizes Impact

Several of the beach hotels, including Matemwe Bungalows, Fundu Lagoon, Blue Bay Beach Resort, Chumbe Island, and the Mnemba Island, have used local building materials and architectural styles and have made attempts to adopt other environmentally sensitive practices. But beyond this handful of notable exceptions, the government has permitted construction of far too many typical cement block hotels that are heavy on imports and use of energy and water. As a result, Zanzibar is blighted by irresponsible tourism development in coastal zones, where poor sewage and waste treatment are polluting both freshwater supplies and marine ecosystems.[126] By the end of 2006, a UN report warned that "Zanzibar is now one of the world's most endangered islands because of increased destruction of water sources as well as the disposal of untreated liquid waste directly into the Indian Ocean."[127] In addition, Swedish scholar Stefan Gossling found that tourists "directly affect coral reefs by trampling, breaking, picking and buying reef species. Tourism is also responsible for an increasing demand in seafood, which has to be seen in view of the fact that the reefs around Zanzibar already show signs of overfishing. . . . These threats add to other external stresses like climate change, which are partly a result of tourist activities themselves."[128]

Zanzibar's east and north coasts are home to the island's most severe environmental problems, due in large part to the ever-growing number of larger resorts that dominate coastlines and access to resources. (In global terms, the resorts are still fairly modest: most are well under a hundred rooms and not more than two stories high.) Rainfall on the east coast is low, and it is lowest during peak tourist season, when unsustainable quantities of groundwater are used by the tourist resorts.[129] Hotel construction in Zanzibar has also led to the unnecessary removal of trees and vegetation, causing sedimentation and erosion that negatively affects the nearshore marine environment.[130]

In the Stone Town, however, the effects of tourism, at least on the surface, appear be far more positive. Most construction involves the repair of existing historic buildings, and again, although environmental impact has not been rigorously assessed or monitored, these urban hotels are clearly an improvement over the unsanitary conditions that were the norm for many decades. The rise of tourism and increased environmental awareness have stimulated other basic rehabilitations in the Stone Town, including repair and paving of the streets, an overhaul and modernization of the sewage system, and remodeling and preservation of historically important sites.

While the international media still continues to praise the allure of both Zanzibar's Stone Town and white-sand beaches, government policies these days promote ecotourism primarily in the economic backwater of Pemba. So far Pemba has avoided many of the environmental and social tourism-related ills that plague the main island, Unguja. However, whether the official pledge to control development in Pemba reflects a true commitment to responsible tourism or a punishment to an island that is viewed as a stronghold of the political opposition, the CUF party, is unclear.

Builds Environmental Awareness

Despite the fact that the major economic activities in Zanzibar—tourism, fishing, and farming—all rely on a healthy environment, a lack of accountability and a focus on short-term profits have kept environmental protection from becoming an integral part of tourism development. Of further concern is the fact that natural resources are, as Gossling notes, increasingly "subject to transactions operating outside the pre-existing tradition-based systems and local legislation fails to control and manage their exploitation."[131]

Together with Kenya, Zanzibar had the first ecotourism society in Africa. However, this and some other tourism-related NGOs in Zanzibar were built on weak foundations, in part because the political climate in Zanzibar remained unstable and inhospitable, and in part because the NGOs were dominated by foreigners. They did manage to mount some campaigns, such as one in the 1990s against purchase of endangered and illegally traded animal products. Ultimately, however, they remained small and isolated, and eventually ceased to exist. Some of the foreign-owned hotels provide visitor education and a few—most actively Chumbe Island and Fundu Lagoon—have educational programs for schoolchildren. However, Zanzibari historian and museum curator Abdul Sheriff, questions the effectiveness of these initiatives, arguing they "ultimately become ineffective because they are made up of foreigners and expats . . . who lack a deep understanding of Swahili culture."[132] According to a UN report, "To date, Zanzibar does not have environmental activist groups, nor does it have journalists specialized in environmental reporting."[133]

Provides Direct Financial Benefits for Conservation

The growth of both environmentalism and ecotourism has given impetus to the designation, for the first time, of national parks and marine reserves in Zanzibar. International conservation organizations pledged funds to help in these efforts, but these donations, along with bilateral and multilateral aid, were suspended when political tensions and repression escalated following the 1995 and 2000 elections. In 2005, the World Bank began a major $51-million project on marine and coastal environmental management.[134] Ecotourism has been an important component in financing these protected areas. While largely positive, the creation of marine protected areas has led to controversy and hostility, with local fisherman charging they were not adequately consulted. They have also protested the loss of rich fishing grounds and questioned the creation of private parks.

Provides Financial Benefits and Empowerment for Local People

Here, the record is poor. Despite the laudable recommendations resulting from the 1994 ecotourism workshop, villagers and townspeople have continued to be enticed into selling their property to tourism investors who do not guarantee any profit sharing, joint ownership, or other form of sustained benefit. Land speculation has forced up prices and competition for government-issued leases along the coasts and on the tiny islands around Unguja and Pemba.

Virtually all government-based efforts to incorporate local people in tourism development and benefit-sharing in Zanzibar have failed.

Villagers have lost access to land and the resources found on that land, such as coconut trees, fish, and seaweed. In some cases, open conflict has resulted from disagreements between locals and hotel owners about access to and use of resources. In 2002, angry villagers in Kendwa, a village on the north coast of Zanzibar, tore down the jetty of a luxury hotel because they believed it would harm the coral reef. In addition, a series of hotel fires plagued the nearby village of Nungwi around the same time, and many people believed these were intentional retaliations against the tourism industry.[135]

Zanzibaris are poor, and as education has deteriorated in the postrevolutionary and politically volatile climate on the island, unemployment has risen to almost 25 percent.[136] Years of high-volume tourism seem to have made little difference in the economy. As Sheriff argues, "Tourism is not solving the problems [of development and unemployment] for Zanzibaris. It is providing employment for people from the outside and benefits mostly to hotel owners and restaurateurs, very few benefits after that."[137] In April 2005, the Zanzibar government passed a bill barring foreigners, including mainland Tanzanians, from being hired for jobs that Zanzibari can perform. Despite the fact that the bill was passed unanimously, with pledges that it would help reduce unemployment in Zanzibar by prioritizing islanders in the job market, it has yet to be enforced.[138]

For those Zanzibaris involved in tourism, it can constitute a sizeable portion of a family's income. According to Gossling, for families in Kiwengwa on Zanzibar's east coast, fishing contributes 22 percent of total annual incomes, while tourism contributes 41 percent.[139]

While a few lodges—Matemwe and Fundu Lagoon—have developed social and economic programs to benefit village women, many Zanzibari women have experienced negative impacts associated with tourism development. The only tourism training center in Zanzibar, the Maruhubi College, is academically very poor according to the Tourism Commission and only offers two-month training courses in housekeeping, laundry, reception, and food and beverage production.[140] Approximately seventy-two students take the course each year and receive no managerial or financial training to allow them to advance to upper-level positions in the industry. Poor English language instruction in Zanzibar schools contributes to Zanzibaris being out-competed for jobs in tourism.

Tourism has also greatly increased the demand for seafood, which is the number-one source of protein for Zanzibari families. While some fishermen have benefited from sales to hotels, overfishing due to the tourism industry is leading to smaller average catches by local fishermen. One local fisherman explains that the booming tourism industry means that he and his family have had to change their habits: "Fresh fish is no longer available to us. Before we were eating bluefish, ball fish, and octopus but now we have to eat sardines. We also used to observe the breeding season but because of the hotels' demand for fish, we no longer do that."[141]

Respects Local Culture

Whereas elsewhere, increased tourism has frequently led to liberalization of social mores and strengthening of social movements of women, gays and lesbians, and other oppressed groups, Zanzibar's tourism boom coincides with a rise in conservative Muslim practices, particularly among religious leaders and some politicians. This marks a shift from the island's tradition of religious moderation and tolerance stemming from its location as a cultural, commercial, and intellectual crossroads.

In recent years, Islamist groups in Zanzibar have officially proclaimed their disapproval for public displays of affection, homosexuality, and Western-style dress. In response to what is viewed as increasingly inappropriate behavior by Western tourists, groups like the Society for Islamic Awareness and the Zanzibar Imams' Association have spoken out about the need to regulate tourists' behavior. However, in recognition of the valuable foreign exchange earned from the tourism industry, the Zanzibari courts have tended to side with the tourist industry's argument that applying Islamic laws to visitors will be bad for business.

Often the cultural debates have centered on a dress code for women. The debate has, however, led several leading hoteliers to distribute rules of acceptable behavior to their guests and to negotiate specifically designated beaches where tourists can sunbathe. The relationship between Zanzibari women and tourism is complicated by the traditional Islamic cultural mores and religious beliefs. Women in Nungwi reported that men in their village were reluctant to let them leave the confines of the homes and enter the formal workforce. As one woman explained, "The problem is with our husbands and brothers. Our husbands will not allow us to go work in the hotels."

Youth in Zanzibar also report negative experiences with the growing tourism industry. According to a 2002 Ford Foundation study, 78 percent of participants agreed that tourism has a negative influence in their communities. Among the social issues cited were an increasing dropout rate among teenage students, a disappearing sense of traditional "Zanzibar hospitality," and culturally inappropriate imitation of Western dress and behavior.[142] A rise in alcohol and drug use, prostitution, and theft among Zanzibar youth has occurred simultaneously with the growth of the tourism industry and the social disintegration, intentional or not, has put a strain on many Zanzibari families.

Supports Human Rights and Democratic Movements

In Zanzibar, like elsewhere, there is a delicate balance between sensitivity to cultural and religious practices and protection of basic human rights. While sound ecotourism must help to educate tourists to respect local cultural and religious practices, it also must stand firm against human rights abuses. The unpopular and undemocratic Zanzibari government lacks a clear moral and political compass and has opportunistically used hot-button cultural issues in seeking political control. In April 2004, under pressure from conservative Islamic groups, Zanzibar's Parliament passed a law making homosexuality and lesbianism illegal on the islands. While not enforced, this law both hurt Zanzibar's international reputation and signaled a move away from its historically more tolerant and cosmopolitan cultural practices.

Ecotourism could help to moderate this opportunism, but currently has little effect. In late 2005, the political instability and general sense of lawlessness on the island led one foreign tourism investor to question doing business in Zanzibar: "For several years, I have been drawing up plans to try and upgrade and 'green' my facilities, but in the absence of any law or order here, I have to be prepared to pick up and leave at any moment. As poverty and desperation on the island increase, it becomes a less and less desirable place to do business."[143] In this unstable atmosphere, corruption has also taken hold and helps to dictate the winners and the losers in Zanzibar's tourism industry. The archipelago is awash in suspicious transactions. One of the oldest foreign hoteliers explains that a prospective hotel investor has only to "say the right things, pay the right people and he gets the land."[144] The Zanzibar archipelago cannot afford to let haphazard tourism development continue any longer. Along with creating more stability, transparency, and order for investors, it must also, most urgently and fundamentally, work to ensure that tourism becomes a tool for poverty alleviation, sustainable development, and local empowerment. Today, ecotourism offers a development model that can benefit the environment and local communities. But this cannot happen in Zanzibar without the active involvement of its citizenry. As Gossling writes, "Tourism development thus needs to become a public debate to raise awareness of the environmental and social changes caused by this activity, and to exert pressure on the government to seriously address negative developments."[145]

8

Kenya: The Ups and Downs of Africa's Ecotourism "Mzee"

The horrible state of the road into the reserve was the first tip-off that all was not well. As early as 1990, a World Bank study of ecotourism in Africa had concluded that Kenya's Masai Mara National Reserve "is arguably Africa's most sustained success in incorporating local communities in conservation."[1] What makes the Mara exceptional, in comparison to most famous wildlife parks and reserves in Africa, is that the local community, through their elected County Council, actually owns and manages the reserve instead of the central government. I had expected to find the area around Masai Mara dotted with small development projects—primary schools, clinics, water pumps, cattle dips—and, I naively thought, good roads.

Every July and August over a million wildebeest, gazelles, and zebras pour into the 1,700-square-kilometer (656-square-mile) Masai Mara from the Serengeti to the south. Together these areas form a natural ecosystem containing the largest concentration of wildlife anywhere in Africa and accommodating the greatest land migration of animals anywhere in the world. The Mara has been the chief attraction in a country that has done perhaps the most to launch Africa's rapidly growing ecotourism industry. But today the Mara has become a symbol of misman-

I am grateful to a number of people who assisted with the revisions of this chapter. Fred Nelson, an American consultant based in Tanzania, did an excellent job with pulling together the final research and polishing the writing. Judy Kepher-Gona, who has worked for many years at Ecotourism Kenya, provided a great amount of information and personal insights. Kamweti Mutu, a Kenyan studying in the United States, also provided valuable documents. David (Jonah) Western generously shared his views, and Kenya architect Hitesh Mehta provided information, particularly on the community-based ecotourism section.

agement, overdevelopment, and public graft. While the reserve earns millions of dollars annually that should go to the local communities, most of this is siphoned off by a few avaricious leaders. There is limited evidence of development projects and the area's wildlife populations are in a serious decline. When we finally reached our hotel, I learned that most tourists at the upscale lodges fly into Masai Mara and then rent vehicles for game viewing. When I left, I flew out.

The Rise of Nature Tourism in the Land of the Safari

Kenya is the *mzee*, or elder statesman, of nature tourism and ecotourism in Africa. From the end of British colonialism (in 1963) onward, Kenya's vibrant, wide-open capitalism helped turn the country into Africa's most popular wildlife tourism destination. By 1987, tourism had become Kenya's number-one foreign exchange earner, surpassing both tea and coffee. By the early 1990s, no other African country was earning as much as Kenya from wildlife tourism,[2] and Kenya was being hailed as "the world's foremost ecotourist attraction."[3] Under David ("Jonah") Western, the Kenya Wildlife Service pioneered the concept of "parks beyond parks," which helped to propel the growth of ecotourism in Kenya with new community and private sector initiatives, even as the country's overall tourism industry declined as a result of internal political conflicts in the late 1990s and security problems linked to terrorist attacks in 1998 and 2002. But by 2007, Kenya had reemerged as a leader in ecotourism, with the continent's first certification program, the oldest and most successful national ecotourism society, and a growing array of innovative community-run ecotourism developments. These initiatives were, however, driven more by local communities, innovative NGOs, and private-sector entrepreneurs than any cohesive national strategy.

As in Tanzania, nature tourism and ecotourism in Kenya have been built on a foundation of famous national parks and the legacy of big game hunting safaris. "The era of big game hunting in East Africa coincided with the establishment of colonial rule," and hunting safaris became "a symbol of Western dominance over nature" and European racial and class domination over black Africans, writes John Akama, a Kenyan university professor and tourism scholar.[4] The scale of slaughter by these early hunting safaris was astounding. Theodore Roosevelt, for instance, who, together with two hundred trackers, porters, skinners, and gun bearers, went on a year-long hunting spree through East

Africa following his presidency in 1909, shipped back to Washington, D.C., three thousand specimens of African game.[5]

The earliest Kenyan wildlife legislation dates from 1898, when regulations were enacted to try to control indiscriminate hunting. In 1907, the colonial government created a game department to oversee hunting. The National Parks Ordinance of 1945 marked "a shift in conservation policy from protection through hunting legislation to preservation through land protection"[6] and eviction of local people from newly established national parks. Gradually, about 8 percent of Kenya's territory was set aside for protection in thirty parks (including four marine parks) and thirty-eight reserves (including six marine reserves).[7] With the exception of Tsavo East and Tsavo West National Parks, most are relatively small areas that are part of much larger ecosystems. Wildlife inevitably migrates into surrounding areas, where the animals interact with both people and cattle.

Following independence, nature tourism in Kenya took off, increasing at the extraordinary rate of more than 300 percent between 1960 and 1972.[8] By the early 1970s, writes Western, wildlife was viewed as "a golden egg, a gift needing little promotion or management," and tourists seemed to arrive spontaneously,[9] drawn by wildlife films, good airline connections, and package tours. However, by the mid-1970s, this laissez-faire attitude was shattered: poaching was on the rise, and the quality of wildlife viewing began to decline.[10] In 1977, partly out of concern for rising levels of poaching in the country, Kenya banned sport hunting.

Between 1978 and 1983, tourism stagnated due to these internal problems and international factors including the 1979 oil crisis, the border closure with Tanzania, and the regional consequences of Tanzania's war against Ugandan dictator Idi Amin. Then, in 1984, tourism once again began to pick up sharply, both because the international climate improved and because Kenya's economic liberalizations, promoted by international donors such as the World Bank, provided new incentives and tax breaks for private investment. The Foreign Investments Act, for instance, guaranteed repatriation of capital and profits. International airlines were offered tax exemptions on capital investments and property to encourage them to invest in game lodge and hotel development. As a result, a number of airlines promoted package tours combining airfare with stays in particular hotels.[11] Kenya also received technical assistance and funds for tourism projects from British, German, Swiss, and Italian development agencies, as well as USAID. And in 1987, boosted by the Oscar-winning Hollywood film *Out of Africa*, tourism became Kenya's number-one foreign exchange earner, bringing in some $350 million annually. By 1990, tourism was earning $443 million per year, or about 40 percent of Kenya's total foreign exchange.[12]

Parallel with this, increasing numbers of Kenyan entrepreneurs and politicians moved into the tourism business. According to Perez Olindo, former director of Kenya's Wildlife Conservation and Management Department (WCMD), Kenya's 1977 ban on commercial hunting inadvertently provided an impetus for a number of former hunters, guides, and trackers to move into nature tourism under the slogan "Come shooting in Kenya with your camera." Sport hunting had been dominated by whites, who were the tour operators and guides while Africans served as porters, gun bearers, and skinners. Various colonial regulations had made it virtually impossible for Africans to cross this color line. Olindo says the shift from hunting to photographic safaris helped to break the white monopoly, allowing "the more enterprising" (or politically influential) black Kenyans to start their own companies or move into management positions in tour companies, hotels, and ground transportation.[13] The Kenya Tourist Development Corporation (KTDC), established by the Jomo Kenyatta government in 1966, became primarily a vehicle for using public funds to help handpicked private capitalists get pieces of the tourism pie. Kenyan law requires that all businesses be at least partly owned by Kenyans. Foreign investors, in turn, found it advantageous to form partnerships with powerful politicians and businessmen who could help them cut through red tape and provide a shield against expropriation or expulsion.

Kenya's tourism grew rapidly in the early 1980s (see table 8.1), helping to finance, together with foreign aid receipts, Kenya's growing export receipts.[14] However, despite the growing importance of tourism, conditions in national parks and reserves continued to deteriorate: poaching of elephants and rhinos spiraled out of control by the 1980s, and, in 1989, armed gangs attacked tourists several times while they were on game drives.[15]

In addition to world-famous game parks, Kenya has a wealth of coastal attractions that include several marine parks and reserves, white coral sand beaches, and the historic settlement of Lamu in the northeast. Since the late 1970s, beach resort tourism, based north and south of the main coastal city of Mombasa, has grown enormously. The majority (about 60 percent) of holiday visitors spend time at Kenya's coast. The bulk of the beach tourism consists of relatively cheap conventional package tours for Europeans, particularly Italians and Germans. But despite the growth of sun-and-sand tourism, wildlife still accounts for about 70 percent of Kenya's tourism industry.[16] Furthermore, Kenya earns more from wildlife tourism than from beach

Table 8.1.
Kenya's Tourism Growth

	1955	*1980*	*1985*	*1990*	*1995*	*1997*	*2000*	*2003*	*2005*
Arrivals (in thousands)	36	362	541	814	937	1001	1037	1146	1479
Gross receipts (in millions of shillings or U.S. dollars)	80	$24.7	$249	$443	$486	$502	$283	$347	$579

Source: Correspondent, "Tourist Arrivals Worse in Kenya," *Nairobi Daily Nation*, August 5, 1998; Steve Shelley, "Marketing Strategies for Ecotourism in Africa," in C. G. Gakahu and B. E. Goode, eds., *Ecotourism and Sustainable Development in Kenya*, proceedings of the Kenya Ecotourism Workshop, held at Lake Nakuru National Park, September 13–17, 1992 (Nairobi: Wildlife Conservation International, 1992), 133–137; David Western, "Handling the Wildlife Time-Bomb That Is KWS," The Eastern African, November 17–23, 1997; Economist Intelligence Unit, Kenya: EIU Country Report, 3rd quarter 1997, 23; Economist Intelligence Unit, *Kenya: EIU Country Report*, 1st quarter 1998, 6; World Tourism Organization (WTO), *Africa: Trends of Tourism Receipts by Country, 1989–1993* (Madrid: WTO, 1994), 32; World Tourism Organization (WTO), Yearbook of Tourism Statistics, vols. 1 and 2 (Madrid: WTO, 1995); Government of Kenya, *Economic Survey*, 2000, 2002, 2003, 2004, 2005; "Draft Tourism Policy," 2003, 7; *KWS Strategic Plan—2006*, 15; WTO, "Tourism Market Trends" 2006 Edition; Republic of Kenya, "Statistical Analysis of Tourism Trends (Globally and Locally)," Ministry of Tourism and Wildlife, Central Planning Unit, 2006

tourism. According to the Kenya Tourist Board, in 2006 the average tourist spent approximately 1,500 Euros (around $1,875) at the coast, as opposed to 3,500 Euros (around $4,375) for tourists visiting lodges in wildlife areas. Since 2002, coastal tourism has accounted for about 60 percent of all bed nights but only 40 percent of total tourism earnings.[17]

Troubled Times in the New Millennium

Overall, however, from the early 1990s onward, Kenya's tourism industry has been buffeted by internal and external catastrophes, both natural and man-made. Domestic travails included deteriorating infrastructure, a rise in crime as Nairobi has cemented its reputation as one of the world's most dangerous cities, the 1997 El Niño floods followed by one of the worst droughts in recent history, and a rise in politically linked ethnic clashes and killings. These latter political tensions escalated in the years after 1992, when Kenya became a multi-party state. Kenya also began to face stiff competition from South Africa in 1994—the year of majority rule—when that economic powerhouse became Africa's leading tourism destination. Tanzania's economic reforms and rapidly growing tourism industry provided a strong new competitor next door, which lacked Kenya's infrastructure but could match and even surpass its wildlife-and-beach product.

The year 1997 marked the beginning of a deepening crisis for Kenya's tourism industry. The elections in December, which international as well as Kenyan observers charged were riddled with fraud, gave President Daniel arap Moi his fifth consecutive term. At the coast, politically motivated ethnic violence erupted in the Likoni clashes, which left over one hundred people dead and soon led to the loss of thousands of resort jobs over the course of the next six months as tourism virtually shut down.[18] By mid-1998, about 50 percent of Kenya's tourist hotels—most along the coast—had closed down or reduced their staffs, and about fifty thousand workers, or 30 percent of the total tourism sector workforce, had been laid off.[19]

Things moved from bad to worse on August 7, 1998, when a terrorist bomb ripped apart the U.S. Embassy and neighboring buildings in downtown Nairobi, killing over two hundred people and wounding thousands more, mostly Kenyans. The U.S. State Department immediately issued a travel warning, advising Americans against traveling to both Kenya and Tanzania, where another bomb had exploded simultaneously at the American Embassy in Dar es Salaam. The Kenyan government, business leaders, and even the Council of [Muslim] Imams called on the United States to rescind the advisory, arguing that, as Mike Kirkland of the Kenya Association of Tour Operators, Coast branch, put it, there were "absolutely no danger or anti-U.S. feelings in Kenya and no reason for any tourist to cancel their holiday." Several weeks later, the State Department did withdraw the warning, but many Kenyans foresaw, as the *Daily Nation* predicted, that these events would plunge their "country's tourism industry into greater problems."[20] By 2000, Tanzania surpassed Kenya in tourism earnings, and internally, coffee and tea regained their position atop tourism as Kenya's largest foreign exchange earner. That year Kenya earned a paltry $283 million from tourism—about 40 percent less than a decade earlier.[21] With the global recession in 2000 and 2001 following the stock market crash, the 9/11 attacks in the United States, and war in Afghanistan, the opening years of the new millennium were a despondent time for Kenya's already battered tourism industry. Then, in November 2002, geopolitical violence struck again when terrorist operatives, reportedly crossing into Kenya from Somalia, bombed an Israeli-owned beach resort in Kikambala, north of Mombasa, and fired surface-to-air missiles at an Israeli charter airplane.[22] In May 2003, the government in London banned flights by British planes to Nairobi and

Mombasa due to security concerns, severely curtailing access to Kenya for the entire European market.[23]

For Kenya, these events exposed the vulnerability of the sector to its dependence on foreign capital, governments, and infrastructure, and also highlighted the lack of government policy and planning. In 1996, Kenya finally created a national tourism board, but failed to give it an adequate budget, especially for overseas marketing. In 2003, the first comprehensive national tourism policy was finally drafted, but it proceeded to languish in parliament without formal sanction. In terms of the market, one quarter of Kenya's foreign tourists are from the United Kingdom and another 13 percent are from the United States; similarly, many investors in safari tourism are white Kenyans of British decent.[24] Many of the black Kenyans who have invested in tourism are beneficiaries of long-standing government strategies to spread tourism benefits to nationals. The Kenya Tourist Development Corporation (KTDC) became primarily a vehicle for using public funds to help handpicked private capitalists get pieces of the tourism pie. They were also beneficiaries of a new law requiring that all businesses be at least partly owned by Kenyans. The KTDC's mission of buying shares in foreign-owned tour companies, travel agencies, hotels, and lodges and then selling these shares "to promising Kenyan entrepreneurs on special terms,"[25] served to subsidize the business activities of the rich, powerful, and politically well-connected. Foreign investors, in turn, found it advantageous to form partnerships with powerful politicians and businessmen who could help them cut through red tape and provide a shield against expropriation or expulsion. Thus the tourism industry has become part and parcel of the larger webs of informal relationships, patronage, and corruption that characterize the Kenyan state. With the sector dominated by a relatively small local and foreign elite, most Kenyans associate tourism with high prices, immoral behavior, discrimination against locals, and generally an "us" versus "them" attitude, according to a Kenya Tourist Board study.[26]

The two terrorist attacks, in 1998 in Nairobi and on the coast in 2002, that so damaged Kenya's tourism industry also highlighted some of the security problems that result from the anarchy prevailing in neighboring Somalia since its disintegration in the early 1990s. Both incidents were linked in part to al Qaeda operatives working out of Somalia's disorder and chaos.[27] The Somalia connection also harkens back to the 1970s and 1980s, when the defining security challenge for Kenya was not Islamic fundamentalist terrorism but an epidemic of ivory and rhino horn poaching—some of it carried out by armed Somali bandits—that devastated the country's wildlife and endangered its growing tourism industry.[28] In confronting the poaching problem, the country's wildlife and tourism management strategies were remolded and reformed, and debates emerged that, while yet to be resolved, play a central role in ecotourism's future in Kenya.

Parks, Wildlife, and Communities: Good Theory, Poor Performance

By the mid-1970s, it was clear to many wildlife experts in Kenya that uncontrolled tourism could be harmful to wildlife conservation and that communities around parks could not continue to be excluded from tourism's benefits. In an effort to better address tourism and conservation issues, the Kenyan government amalgamated several agencies and established the Wildlife Conservation and Management Department (WCMD). In 1975, the government approved a broad, bold national strategy that encompassed many of the principles of ecotourism and attempted to expand the concept beyond the Masai Mara and Amboseli National Park experiments (discussed in detail in the following sections). This wildlife management policy for national parks as well as game reserves was "based on local participation in all forms of wildlife utilization . . . including tourism, hunting, cropping for meat and trophies, game ranching, live animal captures for restocking or export, and the associated value-added processing of animal products." The policy stated that wildlife must "pay its way"; that the vigor of wildlife depended on access to larger ecosystems, which included private and communal lands around protected areas; and that wildlife officials should be "facilitators, advisors and assessors working with landowners rather than 'policemen' working against them."[29]

The following year, Kenya secured a $37.5 million loan package from the World Bank to help implement this policy, including strengthening antipoaching activities, preparing the country's first tourism development plans, and devising programs to involve local communities around the parks. In 1977, as a condition for continued World Bank funding,[30] Kenya banned hunting and outlawed commercial trade in wildlife trophies and products. From this date forward, all forms of consumptive utilization of wildlife ceased, except for limited game cropping in national parks and reserves and, under a quota, on some private ranches. But the wave of poaching continued, fueled by the WCMD's incompetence, corruption among top government officials and their family members, and the rising world price of ivory and rhino horn. After Daniel arap Moi succeeded founding President Jomo Kenyatta, who died in 1978, cronyism and corruption continued to characterize Kenya's economic and political life. Between 1975 and 1990,

Kenya's elephant population dropped by 85 percent, from over two hundred thousand to approximately twenty thousand, and its rhino population fell by 97 percent, down to fewer than five hundred.[31]

In addition, the broader objectives of the government's policy and the World Bank project were never implemented, and according to one critique, the WCMD continued to deal with conflicts between people and parks "through its role as a 'policeman.'"[32] Even the World Bank's own 1990 evaluation report was devastatingly critical. Despite the massive influx of aid, the bank's evaluation found that "park and reserve infrastructure [had] deteriorated badly and maintenance of roads, vehicles, plants, and equipment virtually ceased. The WCMD was unable to guarantee the safety of tourists and unable to address their growing dissatisfaction with poor facilities. . . . Unregulated tourism was seriously damaging numerous wildlife habitats." Further, the bank's evaluation found, the project failed to deal with the growing conflict between wildlife and increasing agricultural activities around parks and reserves. "The conversion of range to agricultural lands has not only permanently destroyed certain wildlife habitat zones, but has also changed the symbiotic relationship between nomadic pastoralists and wildlife to one of continual conflict between the sedentary farmer/herder and wildlife, as wildlife has become a major pest," the report stated.[33]

Under pressure from international conservation organizations and the U.S. Embassy, the Moi government finally took action. In April 1989, it scrapped the inept WCMD and replaced it with a new parastatal body, the Kenya Wildlife Service (KWS), headed by Richard Leakey, a museum director and son of the world-renowned paleontologists Louis and Mary Leakey. As a semiautonomous institution, the KWS had its own board of trustees, managed its affairs internally, and was financially independent from the government. Income from user fees and donations was retained for park management. The KWS was given, at least in theory, presidential backing and wide authority to clean up corruption, remove officials involved in poaching and skimming of gate fees, implement the integrated tourism and wildlife management plans, initiate new programs involving local participation, and "tackle the thorny issues of improved distribution of benefits derived from tourism."[34] The national parks and two reserves are directly under KWS management; the other reserves, including Masai Mara and Samburu Game Reserves, continue to be owned and managed by the county councils.

In late 1989, Leakey won international acclaim when he endorsed the campaign to have elephants listed as an endangered (or Appendix I) species under CITES (the Convention on International Trade in

Endangered Species of Wild Fauna and Flora), thereby imposing a worldwide trade ban on ivory and other elephant parts. As Ray Bonner details, the lobby that led to a total ban on sale of ivory and other elephant products was orchestrated by a handful of Western environmentalist and animal rights groups, which portrayed elephants as near extinction throughout Africa when in reality poaching was rampant only in East Africa, not southern Africa.[35] They succeeded in convincing the United States, Great Britain, Canada, and other Western governments to endorse the ivory ban, and at the October 1989 CITES meeting they had African elephants declared an endangered species.

Earlier that year, Leakey had proposed selling Kenya's ivory to raise money for the KWS's antipoaching operations. However, when the CITES Ivory Trade Review Group reached the conclusion that although "sustainable utilization" (controlled hunting) was an ideal goal, poaching had so decimated the elephant and rhino populations in East Africa that nothing but a complete ban would prevent the slaughter, Leakey revised his views. He says that he came to realize "we were never going to stop the ivory trade in time if we didn't do something very dramatic, and I was heavily influenced by the mortal blow Bridget Bardot's burning of fur coats in Paris and London had dealt to the spotted cat trade."[36] Just a few months before the CITES meeting, Leakey staged his own dramatic demonstration to prove Kenya's commitment to elephant and rhino protection. Although Kenya had banned hunting since 1977, the park service had ivory stocks from culling operations, confiscations from poachers, and animals that had died of natural causes. With the flair of a theater director, Leakey orchestrated a public burning of the country's entire ivory stock. In Nairobi National Park, twelve tons of ivory were piled into a gigantic twenty-foot-high tepee, and as the cameras rolled, President Moi lit the pyre. To the dismay of many Africans and the cheers of Western animal rights activists, $3 million worth of ivory went up in smoke. Leakey's calculation was shrewd: the publicity stunt improved Kenya's conservation and wildlife tourism image, served to legitimize Moi as an "environmental leader," and contributed to Leakey's success in landing foreign aid.

Further, the ivory ban and ivory burning did achieve their immediate goals. The international price of ivory plummeted, and so, too, did poaching in both Kenya and Tanzania. As Leakey put it in a 1996 interview, "The ivory burning had an enormous impact on people's attitudes and permanently affected the use of ivory in the West. Before the ban we were losing 4,000 to 5,000 elephants a year, and afterwards, up to this moment, we are losing less than 100 a year."[37] Parallel with the ban, Leakey treated his mandate to protect wildlife in the parks as sacrosanct, equipping rangers in his new KWS "army" with automatic rifles and orders to shoot to kill poachers.[38]

Following the 1989 ivory debate, Leakey quickly set about reorganizing the wildlife service, retiring a lot of the dead wood, weeding out corrupt elements, and implementing sounder revenue-collection methods. Within the first year, the KWS doubled its income from gate fees simply by use of stricter collection practices. Leakey and his staff also drew up a new set of goals, captured in the service's "Zebra Book," for developing a sound and integrated national conservation and ecotourism strategy. The Zebra Book pledged, for instance, that the KWS would minimize the environmental impacts of tourism, contribute to the national economy, train and license guides and drivers, monitor visitor impact, require environmental assessment studies of lodging units, and provide better visitor information. The Zebra Book also stressed that the KWS must "forge an effective partnership with communities living adjacent to parks and reserves,"[39] including protecting people and their property from wildlife damage. To this end, in 1992 Leakey announced the formation of the Community Wildlife Service (CWS) to assist communities outside the parks and reserves with funds and development projects. And Leakey made an ambitious pledge: that the KWS would give 25 percent of gate revenues from all parks to the surrounding communities. It was a promise he quickly discovered he could not fully deliver on.

At the time, however, international lending and conservation organizations enthusiastically welcomed these pronouncements and reforms. USAID proclaimed that the KWS "marks a radical departure from the previous conservation approach under the WCMD."[40] Donors lined up with checkbooks and in-kind contributions, including eighty vehicles and seven airplanes. By 1992, Leakey had landed a hefty $153 million, five-year World Bank loan package and a pledge for a second loan package if the first program were successfully carried out.[41] Other donors, including the U.S., Dutch, British, and Japanese governments, quickly joined up to support the KWS, even as the Kenyan government's overall reputation with aid agencies and foreign governments deteriorated as a result of entrenched corruption. The goal, Leakey explained, was to rehabilitate the national parks and reserves, increase their revenue-generating capacity, and make the KWS self-supporting within five years, by the end of 1996. This was a second promise that Leakey soon discovered he could not fulfill.

USAID, through a program (1993–1999) branded with a typically colorful donor acronym—COBRA (Conservation of Biodiverse Resource Areas)—aimed to assist the KWS Community Wildlife Service "to implement its new community conservation approach in order to demonstrate that it is in people's financial and social interest to promote and protect wildlife."[42] While much of the World Bank funding and early KWS priorities focused on national parks, COBRA's "core objective" was the "development of income-generating activities for local landholders and communities," and its mandate included helping the KWS to develop a system for "sharing revenue from gate receipts directly with communities."[43] However, a COBRA evaluation was sobering regarding the enterprises open to rural communities at the time. It found that "the most lucrative opportunities have already been seized by the private sector" and "the management requirements are usually considerable, generally beyond the means of communities."[44]

COBRA's community projects were to be financed partly from USAID's Development Fund for Africa[45] and partly from the 25 percent Leakey pledged from the KWS's gate receipts. USAID projected that over the course of five years, the KWS would distribute $8.3 million in revenue sharing to communities in selected areas. This didn't happen. A government inquiry concluded that between 1991 and 1994, the KWS spent only 2 percent of gate fees on communities surrounding parks.[46] In the 1990s, the KWS's earned income was simply too meager to turn over one-quarter to local communities. Despite these early shortcomings, there were some promising projects. The KWS supported, for instance, creation of the Mwaluganje-Golini Community Wildlife Reserve on Kenya's southern coast, which by 2002 had one of the highest concentrations of elephants in the country. A coalition of local subsistence farmers, NGOs, tour operators, and government agencies worked to protect and use for tourism a vital corridor for elephants and other wildlife, with its income going to the local community. But, as often happens with small projects, its marketing was extremely poor and it failed to make a profit. According to the head of one international NGO, beach resorts only twenty miles away were unaware of the reserve and so were not sending guests there.[47]

Leakey's failure to fulfill his pledge to contribute the 25 percent of gate revenue to local communities became one of the issues raised by President Moi, and this led to Leakey's resignation under pressure in January 1994. By then, Leakey himself had doubts about the program. "I don't believe community-based conservation has a hope in hell," he told the press.[48] At the 2003 World Parks Congress in Durban, South Africa, Leakey once again stirred controversy by declaring that conservation comes before indigenous rights and that protected areas are too important to be "subjugated" to "people complaining of eviction from ancestral lands."[49]

Despite Leakey's successes in reorganizing and strengthening Kenya's wildlife department and his support in international conservation and donor circles, he made other strategic errors and some powerful enemies. In late 1993, Leakey's lightplane mysteriously crashed: the KWS's director lost both of his legs and nearly lost his life. Although

Leakey, fitted with artificial limbs, continued to work, by January 1994 he had had enough. Telling the press that "the stress and pain of being vilified by senior politicians and others is more than I think is good for my health," he resigned. Once out of office, he also hinted that his plane had been sabotaged, although this suspicion was never verified.[50]

Leakey was a hard act to follow. The World Bank and other foreign donors were not pleased to see him driven from office. President Moi's choice of another white, David "Jonah" Western, for the top conservationist slot helped ease their fears. Although Western lacked Leakey's international reputation, charisma, and management experience, he was a highly respected scientist who had directed the Kenya program of the New York Zoological Society (Wildlife Conservation Society) and had accrued decades of hands-on field experience. Western had grown up in Tanzania, where his father was a part-time hunter and honorary game warden, and in the late 1960s he had begun research in Amboseli National Park, where he pioneered conservation projects with the Maasai. He spent much of the next two decades in Amboseli, developed a deep respect for the Maasai, and became a naturalized Kenyan citizen.

Western was particularly committed to the concept that sound conservation and ecotourism depended on involving and benefiting local people. To be a positive force for conservation, he argued, "ecotourism had to pump billions of dollars into the economies of cash-strapped developing countries to compete against loggers, farmers, and herders."[51] He argued that this was especially necessary in Kenya, where 70 percent of the wildlife migrated or lived outside the national parks and reserves, on land occupied by farmers and herders. In this way Western articulated the basic conservation challenge—to make wildlife a locally valuable resource and form of land use—in a way that few East African park directors, before or after, have been able or willing to.

Recognizing that Leakey's pledge to turn over one-quarter of park revenue to local communities was too ambitious, Western quickly announced that the KWS would strive to reach 10 percent. Western viewed his job as deepening the mandate of the KWS's ecotourism initiatives and restructured the organization to reflect three principal goals: (1) conserving biodiversity; (2) linking conservation and tourism; and (3) creating partners among local, national, and international interests. The KWS began decentralizing its administration away from Nairobi to ecologically determined regional units and, via the COBRA project, accelerated its funding of income-generating activities for local landholders and communities in the dispersal areas.

By the end of 1995, KSh 80 million (some $1.6 million) had been disbursed to communities, local associations, and local governments, and almost three hundred projects had been approved and financed.

About one-third of these projects involved either school construction or bursaries (school scholarships); however, emphasis was also placed on productive community investments, capacity building, and the development of income-generating activities linked to wildlife and conservation. These included provision of funds and training to start locally owned and managed tourist enterprises and encouraging lodge designs that incorporated local materials and culture. A 1996 evaluation of the COBRA project perceptively notes, "While social investments such as schools, bursaries, clinics, and social infrastructure represent genuine community priorities, they are not overtly tied to conservation practices. Furthermore, in some cases they appear to be creating a sense of entitlement based simply on living in proximity to protected areas rather than being tied to positive measures taken by the community to improve wildlife conservation and management."[52] Overall, however, the evaluation's conclusions were positive. It stated, "Significant progress has been made toward attaining the stated purpose of the COBRA project" and "Benefits have been generated for communities, primarily through revenue sharing and to a more limited extent from enterprise development. Perhaps more important," the report concluded, "community attitudes toward KWS and toward the possibility of deriving meaningful economic and other benefits from community-based conservation have changed radically, especially in the focal areas of the COBRA project."[53] Western also worked to help local communities and landowners organize themselves into district-level bodies, called wildlife forums, that could serve to represent local management interests and facilitate better communication with government. In 1997, Kenya's national parks system celebrated its fiftieth anniversary with the theme "Parks Beyond Parks" to signify the aim of conserving wildlife and creating diversified tourist destinations in dispersal areas for the benefit of local communities.

However, all was not well: tourism was in a three-year slump, and with 95 percent of the KWS's revenue coming from tourism, the agency's deficit was mounting. Western toyed with another hot-button income-generating idea: reopening limited commercial hunting for certain species as part of his aim to "reverse the dependency on park profits . . . and make wildlife profitable outside the parks."[54] Western envisioned permitting not only certain private ranches but also communities in the dispersal areas to offer hunting safaris on an experimental basis, similar to the CAMPFIRE program in Zimbabwe, to see whether this could generate significant income. A joint study by the KWS and the African Wildlife Foundation in 1995 and the draft Wildlife Policy of 1996 both recommended lifting the hunting ban and permitting "wildlife utilization" in dispersal areas and on private ranches, including hunting of certain animals (other than elephants) as well as bird shooting, game farming, and live animal trade.[55] Part of the rationale for reintroducing hunting, at least from the conservationist's perspective, stems from the fact that tourism revenue from wildlife is limited to only about 5 percent of the total area in Kenya where wildlife populations occur.[56] Some private, largely white ranchers and some local communities weighed in to endorse the resumption of controlled hunting. Ultimately these reforms were unable to gain sufficient traction at the national parliamentary level during Western's tenure as the KWS director, but the debate over hunting would simmer, and reemerge with a new intensity in subsequent years.

On the world stage, Western played a nuanced role in the ivory and hunting debates. As the 1997 CITES meeting neared, the ivory-ban consensus was weakening, with both international organizations and African countries divided, and pressure was mounting to lift the ban in southern Africa. Powerful hunting advocacy groups joined with southern African countries to argue for ending the ban. At the 1997 meeting, Kenya (led by Western) and South Africa ended up playing a key role in brokering the unusual compromise that partially altered the 1989 ban. CITES voted to downgrade the large elephant populations in Namibia, Botswana, and Zimbabwe to Appendix II (designating "protected" but not "endangered" species), allowing these countries to sell their stockpiled ivory to one country, Japan, in 1999, subject to certain conditions. The elephant populations in Kenya, Tanzania, and elsewhere remain classified as Appendix I (endangered). This compromise has endured for the past decade, with limited sales allowed from southern African countries, although Kenya has continued its general opposition to the ivory trade in these international negotiations.

By late 1997, both Western's personal reputation and the promising community conservation projects were becoming tarnished as the KWS was buffeted by both internal weaknesses and external troubles. While Western tirelessly promoted the KWS and ecotourism across the United States and in Europe and the KWS hosted an international ecotourism conference in Nairobi, the local press began lobbing criticisms. Citing a host of statistics, a Kenyan newspaper, *The People*, charged that KWS was continuing to pay "inflated salaries to a well-connected circle of cronies," including a hefty $148,000 annual salary for the director himself.[57] There were, as well, accusations that Western was a poor administrator, that the organization was adrift, and that institutional decentralization was likely to weaken the KWS's financial position and ability to carry out its core mandate. One local paper claimed the KWS was verging on "operational and financial breakdown," another called it "a facade held together by a demoralized field staff," and a third contended that foreign donors had "given up on KWS."[58] Western countered that he had eliminated all expatriate positions at the KWS, was implementing other cost-saving and income-generating measures, and had convinced USAID to extend the COBRA project into 1998.[59]

More fundamentally, some donors and conservationists voiced concern that Western was concentrating too heavily on community projects in the buffer zones and neglecting conservation, protection, infrastructure improvement, and income-generation priorities within the KWS's parks and reserves. Agi Kiss, principal ecologist for the World Bank's African Environmental Group, told *Science* magazine, "We've been increasingly concerned and dissatisfied about how the KWS manages its resources and sets priorities."[60] Consultant Robert Hall, who assessed the COBRA project, had somewhat different concerns. He worried that Western's very active role in community conservation would "pull KWS further into land management conflicts in areas outside the parks—as the KWS tries to solve problems in its external environment, it is likely to be seen as an interloper and the source of problems."[61]

Then, in May 1998, President Moi weighed in, announcing that he was removing Western, just months after extending his contract as the KWS director for another two years. Moi gave no reason for the decision, but Western contended that it had nothing to do with the KWS's financial or other problems. Rather, Western asserted, he was fired because he had rebuffed efforts by cabinet ministers to open new gemstone mines in Tsavo West National Park and grab other land owned by the KWS.[62]

Through it all, Western held his ground, arguing that although there were inevitably problems in implementing community-based conservation projects, it was the only viable course for Kenya. "Protecting parks alone, as the World Bank would have the KWS do, carries a high cost," Western wrote in answer to one critical article. "Although still the KWS's top priority, protected areas cover less than 8% of the land surface and simply don't give adequate biodiversity coverage. Furthermore," he contended, "few if any are ecologically viable. Difficult or not, the human-wildlife conflict must be tackled if Kenya's wealth of species and migratory herds is to be preserved."[63]

As debate over these management issues intensified and donors threatened to withhold millions of dollars if Western were not reinstated, Moi reversed his decision, and Western returned to the helm of the beleaguered KWS.[64] But the battle was not over. In September 1998, following the U.S. Embassy bombings and fears of further drops in tourism numbers, Moi again forced Western to resign. And, to the surprise of many, Moi replaced Western with his old rival, Richard Leakey—despite Leakey's own acrimonious exit as the KWS chief in 1994. Leakey's second tenure at the KWS would be far less memorable than his initial directorship; after a little more than a year, he was transferred by Moi to a position as head of Kenya's civil service. Although Leakey was placed in one of the most powerful positions in Moi's government, ostensibly with a mandate to reform Kenya's increasingly dysfunctional and corrupt governing institutions, Leakey soon found the task impossible and stepped down in March 2001.[65]

Since then Leakey has gradually receded from Kenyan public life, and Western has focused primarily on continuing to promote community-based conservation and ecotourism through the Kenyan NGO he helped found in 1995, the African Conservation Centre. One thing that both former directors and occasional rivals agree on is that the KWS has become a shadow of the institution that it was in the early 1990s. Since 2002, it has had a revolving door of unmemorable directors, few lasting more than a year and several leaving under cloud of scandal. "KWS has ceased to function effectively," Leakey told a conference in 2006, characterizing the organization as one that "is in debt, is totally corrupt, has created a very bad political relationship between itself and the communities it is supposed to serve, and which is going nowhere."[66] Western concedes that the KWS "has ceased to be an independent body" and has lacked both direction and leadership since 1999.[67] While Leakey and Western's personalities no longer dominate Kenyan conservation like they did a decade ago, the debates over management policy that they fostered have taken on an increasing urgency for Kenya's wildlife and tourism industry. By the late 1990s, as data from long-term monitoring studies became available, it was becoming increasingly clear that Kenya's wildlife had undergone serious declines during the previous twenty years. Since 1977—the year that monitoring began and also coinciding with the hunting ban—Kenya has lost about 40 percent of its wildlife.[68] What is particularly notable, as Western and two coauthors recently pointed out in a paper examining these trends, is that wildlife has declined almost as substantially inside national parks as in the broader landscape.[69]

Unlike the ivory and rhino-horn poaching crisis of the 1970s and 1980s, the causes of this broader loss of wildlife are harder to pinpoint. Poaching, mainly for bushmeat, continues to play a major role. Equally important are land-use changes, particularly the conversion of rangelands to agriculture as human populations grow. The driving forces behind the depletion of Kenya's wildlife populations, says Mike Norton-Griffiths, one of Kenya's most prominent conservationists, are economic in nature. "For most [small scale African] landowners, returns from agriculture are vastly greater than are those from livestock, while wildlife returns are so meager as to be uncompetitive with either," he writes, "so to the great majority of landowners, wildlife is simply a cost that Government expects them to bear."

As the scale of Kenya's wildlife population declines have become more widely known, and their causes researched, against a backdrop of deteriorating capacity in the KWS and declining tourism revenues, the movement to revive sport hunting has gained momentum. Norton-Griffiths argues that "if Kenya wishes to maintain significant wildlife populations outside its protected areas, then it has to ensure that landowners can gain an income from wildlife that is competitive with what they can earn from agriculture and livestock," and that controlled sport hunting is perhaps the most important way of doing this.[70] The local wildlife forums that Western supported when he was the director of the KWS have played a lead role, along with national conservation groups like the East African Wildlife Society, in pushing for a repeal of the 1977 hunting ban. In 2004, these reformers had a major breakthrough, working closely with veteran Member of Parliament, G. G. Kariuki, to draft a private bill for revising Kenya's 1975 wildlife legislation. The bill provided for decentralizing aspects of management to the district level, reintroducing hunting, placing local representatives on the KWS board of directors, and increasing levels of compensation for damages caused by wildlife. These populist provisions quickly garnered support in Parliament across party lines, but after a public debate the president, Mwai Kibaki, who took over the office in 2002, decided to veto the bill.

The bill's downfall at the hand of the presidential veto was engineered mainly by several influential animal rights organizations active in Kenya, who Mike Norton-Griffiths accuses of "deliberately misleading" the president through an aggressive lobbying campaign.[71] These groups have acquired substantial political influence in Kenya largely by directing money to the KWS and other local organizations. Kenya remains the only country from South Africa to Ethiopia with significant wildlife populations but no legal hunting. In 2005, for example, the International Fund for Animal Welfare, a group with over a million members, mostly in the United States and Europe, disbursed grants in Kenya of $684,098, of which over half a million dollars went directly to the KWS.[72]

The influence of these foreign organizations, which seem more concerned with an antihunting ideology than sustaining Kenya's natural resources, has led to growing frustration among the reformists within Kenya. Omara Kalasingha, the chairman of the Kenya Wildlife Working Group and one of the leading reform advocates, calls the influence of these groups "destructive and selfish."[73] A Kenyan policy analyst, James Shikwati, editorializes, "A business approach to sustaining wildlife populations in Kenya is long overdue. The situation as it is now: NGO's are raking in millions of dollars in the name of protecting animal rights while violating human rights by sustaining people in poverty."[74] Ironically, although the tourism industry's health and future are threatened by current wildlife trends in Kenya, the industry is not a main proponent of reform and is generally seen as opposing the return of hunting.

These debates over the future role of utilization, communities, and parks continued through 2007, with a new draft wildlife policy and bill developed after a long and unprecedented process of national consultations. The bill nevertheless continued to face stiff resistance from the animal welfare groups, who Norton-Griffiths charges have "managed to highjack this entire process" by using their financial clout.[75] Ali Kaka, the director of the East African Wildlife Society, a former KWS deputy director, and leading proponent of reform, called the campaign against the new wildlife policy a "huge disappointment," adding that he and others would continue to work for "long overdue changes that would make a real difference to the lives of people sharing land with wildlife."[76] Without a new policy, they argued, a cloud continues to hang over the future of Kenya's declining wildlife populations.

Community Conservation and Early Ecotourism: Experiments in Amboseli and Masai Mara

While Kenya's conservation policy debates have continued for the past two decades, efforts to develop ecotourism successfully at the local level have emerged in ways that reflect both entrenched challenges and new opportunities. Over forty years ago, long before ecotourism or community-based conservation had entered the popular lexicon, two areas—the Masai Mara Game Reserve and Amboseli Game Reserve—took important steps toward putting into action the principles of local community participation in wildlife conservation and tourism. These are often considered the earliest ecotourism programs in Africa, and represent Kenya's initial experiments with revenue sharing of park fees and tourism in several of its most famous protected areas.

Masai Mara and Amboseli are both located on land historically used by Maasai pastoralists for grazing and watering their herds of cattle, goats, and sheep. Traditionally, the Maasai have not hunted; their domestic herds share land with wildlife, but, as in Tanzania (see chapter

6), the Maasai derived little financial benefit from it. Under the treaties of 1904 and 1911 between the British colonial administrators and the Maasai's leader at the time, pastoralists in the Southern Reserve encompassing these two areas were to be left unmolested "for as long as the Maasai shall exist as a race."[77]

This, of course, was not to be. It was challenged by the 1945 National Parks Ordinance, which marked the start of efforts to curb Maasai access to both Amboseli and Masai Mara.[78] In the late 1940s, both areas were declared national reserves within the Royal National Parks of Kenya, and the Maasai pastoralists were allowed only limited entry and use of the reserves. The Maasai rightly saw this as yet another step toward taking away their remaining grazing, water, and spiritual sites. They began to call the reserves *shamba la bibi*, literally "the old lady's garden," a reference to the British queen.[79]

Then, in the late 1950s, as independence neared, a new plan was proposed. The Maasai, along with the Game Department and the wildlife adviser to the Kenyan government, opposed efforts to turn these reserves into full-blown national parks. "Their rationale, very innovative for the time," wrote Lee Talbot and Perez Olindo, "was that if the areas were to be conserved for the benefit of the country and posterity, they would have to be supported by the people who lived near them. To accomplish this, those people would have to receive a share of the tangible benefits of the areas and, ideally, they should participate fully in their creation and management."[80] The reality was that as much as 70 percent of the wildlife either migrated or lived permanently in so-called dispersal areas, which were inhabited by pastoralists and their livestock. It was imperative that these people come to see wildlife as a positive economic benefit, worth protecting. Under the agreement reached in 1961, Amboseli, Masai Mara, and a few other Kenyan reserves were to be managed by the local district or county councils rather than the central government.

Masai Mara Game Reserve

Today, Masai Mara receives more visitors than any other wildlife area in East Africa, and about 50 percent of tourists visiting Kenya go to this reserve. Even though it is twelve times smaller than Serengeti National Park, Masai Mara National Reserve still receives slightly more visitors than its equally famous Tanzanian counterpart.[81] As much as anywhere in Africa, Masai Mara reveals how struggles over land, wildlife, and tourism revenues can undermine ecotourism's underlying aspirations.

Back in 1961, under a plan proposed by Masai Mara's longtime colonial-era game warden, Major Lynn Temple-Boreham, management of the reserve was granted to the Narok County Council (NCC),[82] with the central portion of the game reserve set aside solely for wildlife-viewing tourism. The NCC was responsible for developing tourism facilities, establishing and maintaining roads, appointing the warden, rangers, and other staff, and collecting entrance and other fees. The Game Department provided training for the staff. In 1962, the NCC built the first permanent tourist facility, which included a number of self-catering *bandas* (thatched-roof bungalows) at a lovely location near freshwater. Three years later, these were replaced with a private hotel, Keekorok Lodge. All subsequent lodges and tented camps in the reserve have been built by private developers, who lease the land from the NCC.

In addition, the dispersal area surrounding the reserve, which is more than twice the reserve's size, was divided into hunting and photographic concession areas. The NCC set and collected the fees for visitor entry, camping, trophy collection, and vehicle use in these blocks. It was supposed to use the funds derived from these various tourism sources within and on the periphery of Masai Mara to do upkeep of the reserve and to benefit the group ranches in the surrounding area. Most of the Maasai living around the reserve are members of group ranches that hold land communally, with elected committees responsible for group ranch management.

By the end of the first decade, the reserve was being hailed as "a complete success" in terms of both conservation and community involvement.[83] Neither poaching nor livestock grazing was a serious problem within the reserve and tourist numbers increased steadily, making the Masai Mara the mainstay of Kenya's nature tourism industry. The NCC used its revenue for a variety of community projects, including mobile and fixed dispensaries and schools, water pumps, cattle dips, and road maintenance. In terms of equitable distribution of the Narok County Council's revenue, these early years were by far the most successful.

With the 1977 border closure between Tanzania and Kenya, Masai Mara suddenly became the terminus of what had been a popular circuit through the Serengeti to Ngorongoro Crater. This caused a sharp rise in visitor numbers in Masai Mara, "triggering inadequately planned development of ecotourism infrastructures," according to biologist and founder of the Ecotourism Society of Kenya (ESOK) Chris Gakahu, who worked in the reserve.[84] That same year, Kenya imposed its hunting ban, eliminating the income the Maasai group ranches had been receiving from the leasing of hunting blocks. Some of this loss was offset by an increase in entrance fees to the reserve and construction of new lodges and tented camps on communal lands as many hunters shifted over to wildlife-viewing tourism. By 1987, about half of the tourism development was in the dispersal areas, and Maasai landowners were found to "have a positive attitude toward tourism."[85] With tourism proving so lucrative, both poaching and the cost of antipoaching efforts had dropped to almost nothing. Contrary to the situation in most of the rest of Kenya, numbers of elephants and rhinos were increasing. In 1990, Masai Mara recorded only five elephant deaths (three from natural causes) and the killing of only one rhino—the first in six years.[86]

But despite its high income and low incidence of poaching, Masai Mara faced some serious troubles. "The problems have always centered around money, and how the money is being spent," says one dissident Maasai leader. There are a number of intertwined issues regarding use and management of funds. One is that as income from the Mara soared, the Narok County Council began using its tourism revenues to support projects throughout the entire district, not just for upkeep within the reserve and development programs in the dispersal area surrounding it. As elsewhere in East and southern Africa, deciding what constitutes the community living around a protected area is a delicate political issue. The Maasai in the dispersal areas nearest the reserve compellingly argue that they are the ones barred from grazing and watering their livestock in the reserve and on whose lands wildlife live or migrate. Historically, these Maasai have borne the costs of wildlife that kill their cattle, compete for grazing land, transmit diseases, and destroy property.[87] They wanted fair compensation, but the NCC's disbursements have typically been minimal and spread thinly among all NCC's constituents, not just those living near the park. According to a 2002 study, only about 20 percent of the $3.5 million in revenues from the reserve were being distributed back to the group ranches bordering the Mara; the rest was going into the general NCC coffers.[88] Prior to the mid-1990s, fees paid by tourism developments located outside the reserve, on the group ranches themselves, also accrued to NCC.

But in 1994 the Olchoro Oiroua wildlife association was formed by a group of private landowning families owning a total of twenty-two thousand acres.[89] Led by a white Kenyan, Willie Roberts, who had leased land in the area for wheat farming, Olchoro Oiroua sued NCC for the right to collect the fees from developments on their land. Not only was it given permission, but the court also ruled that the Narok County Council had to pay the association KSh 14 million ($467,000) in back revenue. The association began collecting entrance fees—$20 from foreigners and KSh 100 ($3.30) from Kenyans—plus land rent from the Paradise Lodge and three other luxury tourism lodges located on association land, all of which resulted in an average income of KSh 10 million ($333,333) per month by the mid-1990s. By 2002, a study found, tourism payments for facilities on the group ranches were being made directly to the private landowners controlling a given area.[90]

A fundamental issue shaping tourism in the Mara is corruption, with powerful politicians on the NCC or within the central government simply pocketing large sums of the tourism money or using their power to get both permits for hotels and other concessions and land for farming. Tourism experts report that rip-offs are routine of revenues from gate fees, hotel levies, and various other concessions. Game-viewing balloon rides, for instance, cost around three hundred dollars per hour. Of this, the company retains only a small fraction; the rest is paid to local officials as "administrative fees." William Ole Ntimama, the long-standing government minister, parliamentary representative for Narok, and former chair of the Narok County Council, is widely reputed to be one of Kenya's most corrupt politicians. Ntimama owns two luxury lodges in Masai Mara. One of his classmates referred to him as "half Maasai," noting that he dons the traditional dress and behavior "only when he comes to see us, and quickly forgets who we are once his car is turned toward Nairobi."[91] Those I interviewed said that Ntimama and several other Maasai officials had also been behind many of the illegal transactions to get tracts of land for tourism projects or wheat farms in Masai Mara. Reflecting the general prevalence of "land-grabbing" throughout Kenya, increasing numbers of non-Maasai have moved in and managed to get title to lands around the Mara. "People who want land go through these big bosses," said Maasai group-ranch leader and game driver James Morinte. "They then go to the Lands Office in Nairobi, take out a map and say they want such and such a piece and they are given the title."

As a result, much of the tourism now occurring on the group ranches does not return revenue to the overall community, but occurs on lands now owned by connected elites. The wealthiest and most powerful individuals within the Maasai community have effectively seized the best lands for tourism, with the majority of the community left out in the cold. Research by Michael Thompson of the University College London carried out in the group ranches around the Mara found that, on one group ranch, 25 percent of the entire annual budget was spent on sitting allowances for committee members, which amounted to four thousand dollars annually, while individual group ranch members received a dividend of only seventy dollars from the year's tourism earnings.[92] "The councilors are the major and sometimes the only beneficiaries" of the Mara's considerable tourism earnings, notes East African Wildlife Society director Ali Kaka.[93]

On the group ranches around the Mara, as throughout southern Kenya, communal land has increasingly given way to individualized landholdings. As the scramble for land continues in Kenya amid rising human populations, communal ownership has been replaced by individual parcels, even if this makes little ecological sense in these semi-arid rangelands.[94] This change in land-ownership patterns has meant that more and more tourism is controlled by those who are better-off and that more land is being converted to farming as pastoralism becomes less viable. Wheat farming, in particular, has spread rapidly around the Mara since the 1980s, fueled by investment from outside the area. While there were about 12,500 acres of farmed lands in the area in 1975, some twenty-five years later this had increased to 125,000 acres.[95]

These changing land-use patterns have been disastrous for wildlife populations. The Loita plains wildebeest population, which migrates from the Mara east toward Narok during the wet season, has declined by over 80 percent, from about 120,000 to only 22,000 animals. Overall resident game populations in and around the Mara declined by nearly 60 percent from 1977 to 1997.[96] Only the migratory populations that spend most of the year in Tanzania, on the Serengeti, have remained stable during this period.

Thus the past two decades have witnessed building evidence that the reserve, local people, and tourism are all suffering from the corruption, land grabbing, and general mismanagement. A 1991 survey of Masai Mara Game Reserve found a deterioration of the tourism experience, infrastructure, and visitor facilities as well as wildlife protection. A 1995 article in the Kenyan magazine *Wajibu* concluded, "Measures to preserve the unique environment in the Mara are long overdue if we wish to continue to attract visitors to this area. As things stand now, the visitors' perception of 'wild Africa' as viewed through the eyes of discerning tourists has gone; instead they see hordes of vehicles surrounding animals, and their anticipated experience of enjoyment in the wild is replaced with something more akin to a mobile visit to a zoo."[97]

The two dozen lodges and permanent tented camps were clustered into two main areas in the northwestern and southeastern parts of the reserve, causing problems with waste disposal and shortages of firewood for cooking and heating water. With the poor distribution and condition of the roads, this has meant overuse of the parts of the reserve nearest the lodges. Drivers prefer to stay in these areas because they know where the game animals are likely to be found and they want to reduce gasoline costs and wear and tear on the vehicles. Off-track driving is illegal but very common, and this causes deep ruts and destroys grasses and shrubs eaten by the animals. Vehicles often crowd and harass the animals; research has found that regulations controlling the number of vehicles and distance from animals were broken in over 90 percent of lion and cheetah viewings.[98] In 2006, Kenyan journalist Storm Stanley described the situation in terms that had changed little since the 1980s: "Too many vehicles are harassing the wildlife . . . too many trails are being blazed off-road, and the Reserve's natural resources—with 40 permanent lodges, as well as many 'mobile camps'—are under strain as never before."[99]

The Mara has become Kenya's poster child for tourism overdevelopment, and it is tourism revenue that largely fuels the corruption and land-grabbing within NCC and the group ranches. For Maasai women, cultural centers and handicrafts have long been the most important legitimate sources of income from tourism, and are particularly valued in a society where ownership of land and livestock is almost exclusively restricted to men. There are numerous cultural villages, known as *bomas*, scattered around both Masai Mara and Amboseli, where Maasai dance, sing, and sell their famous beaded jewelry. Visitors pay an admission fee in return for being allowed to see and photograph "traditional" activities. However, most *bomas* are not professionally run, and many concentrate solely on hustling sales rather than educating tourists about Maasai traditions and culture. One Maasai leader called these cultural centers "black holes of exploitation," since a lion's share of the entrance fees goes to a few big businessmen and to the safari drivers, who get commissions for bringing in tourists.[100] Research carried out around the Mara's Sekenani gate found that of $11,859 paid by 566 visitors at cultural *bomas* in four villages between June 2005 and July 2006, only $813 went to the residents and over 90 percent was taken as commission by drivers.[101]

The problems experienced by these tourist *bomas* are emblematic of the broader exploitation that passes for cultural education in Kenya's tourism industry. "Maasai" dancers perform at many of the hotels, although they are often hotel employees who are asked by management to dance for the guests for a very minimal fee. Although Masai Mara's antipoaching and other reserve staff have long been largely Maasai, in 1987, only 39 percent of the tourism workforce (hotel and campsite operators and drivers) were Maasai, and most upper-level managers were non-Maasai.[102] Crude forms of cultural exploitation reached a new height when *Sports Illustrated* used the Iltilal Maasai village in Kajiado District as a setting for its winter 1998 swimsuit edition. The magazine paid "the chief" one thousand dollars, and he delivered the village's young men. "The idea was to capture the raw, unspoiled beauty of this place and people," writes Walter Chin. "We [arrived] with models. A camera crew. TV people. A whole international, multimedia traveling circus. 'Oh,' we said, 'we won't bother anyone, and besides it'll be fun!' When the first model dropped her sarong, leaving her only in a bikini and high heels, the "warriors pressed forward to touch her."[103] The Kenyan press related a different story—that "the Massai women screamed" and hid in their houses, "elders herded their children away," while "the young warriors stayed put as the cameramen went wild with their flashes."

If tourism has become something of a curse to the Mara, culturally and economically it is also ultimately the hope for its salvation, in terms of both local development and wildlife conservation. After all, no matter how mismanaged, it is tourism revenues that must provide the incentive for conserving wildlife, most critically on the group ranch dispersal areas around the Mara.

A trend toward more controlled, small-scale tourism development is emerging. The Kenyan government, through its National Environmental Management Authority, recently put on hold thirty-six applications for new tourism facilities in the Mara area, pending development of a comprehensive management plan.[104] Judy Kepher-Gona, the executive officer of Ecotourism Kenya, says that many of the new camps being developed around the Mara, most of which are on group ranches and dispersal areas, are more oriented toward ecotourism principles. "Ecotourism and the concept of sustainable tourism is fast catching up in the Mara, on community land," she says.

One of the leading examples of this new trend is the Basecamp Masai Mara, located on thirty thousand hectares (seventy-four thousand acres) on the Talek River outside the reserve and part of an eclectic set of global Basecamp Explorer destinations, which are backed by Swedish and Norwegian management and also include Spitsbergen in the Arctic and Dharamsala in India.[105] The Masai Mara development is limited to fifteen tents with thatched roofs, employs about thirty local Maasai as guides and staff, uses solar power for all lighting and heating, and promotes cultural interaction that "engages the visitor intellectually and emotionally."[106] Executive Chairman Lars Lindkvist describes the "holistic model" of Basecamp Masai Mara as "creating a conservation area together with the community" and targeting "the Big Five of ecotourism: education, health, energy, water and biodiversity conservation."[107] The camp won the World Travel Market's Responsible Tourism Award in 2005, and is one of only three "Gold" eco-rated facilities in Kenya according to Ecotourism Kenya's rating scheme (see later section on this program).

While operators like Basecamp Explorer pioneer new environmentally sensitive forms of tourism development, an even more profound experiment has been undertaken within the reserve itself. In 1994, the southwestern section of the reserve, to the west of the Mara River (this area is known as the Mara Triangle), was included in the territory of the newly formed Transmara County when it broke away from Narok County. In 2001, Transmara County contracted out the management of the Mara Triangle to a nonprofit private firm known as the Mara Conservancy. As a result of resorting to professional private-sector management, this part of the Mara now has the best infrastructure, security, and antipoaching in the reserve. "The council is happy, the community is happy—those who aren't happy are the politicians who can't dip their hand in the pot anymore," comments Ali Kaka about the Mara Conservancy's success.[108]

Some of these recent developments provide reason for guarded optimism about the future. But the Mara remains emblematic of the challenges facing community ecotourism ventures in rural Africa. The problem in the Mara, unlike many other parts of Africa, is not that wildlife does not generate sufficient revenue for locals—millions of dollars flow through the hands of the Narok and Transmara County Councils, group ranches, and private landowners in the area every year. Rather, the overwhelming problem in the Mara is finding ways to equitably and transparently manage that income. The challenge is one of developing functional democratic institutions to replace the corrupt and often parasitic ones that control these resources today. This is a challenge not only for the Mara, but for Kenya as a whole.

Amboseli National Park

In the 1930s, Ernest Hemingway and, before him, Teddy Roosevelt, trekked to Amboseli Game Reserve (later to become Amboseli National Park) on big-game safaris, hunting lions and elephants against the backdrop of snow-capped Mount Kilimanjaro. Although it is generally held to be more successful in terms of conservation and developmental outcomes than Masai Mara, Amboseli has also suffered from decades of conflicts that have shaped local community tourism ventures.

In 1961, the colonial government handed control of the Amboseli reserve to the Kajiado County Council, the local authority for a 20,000-square-kilometer (7,722-square-mile) district that included the 600-square-kilometer Amboseli basin. The council secured agreement from the local Maasai group ranches to set aside a seventy-eight-square-kilometer area within the basin solely for wildlife. Tourism in Amboseli, which is located just a few hours' drive south of Nairobi and near the Tanzanian border, grew quickly. By 1968 the council was getting 75 percent of its annual income from the reserve.

From the outset, however, serious conflicts emerged between the council and the local Maasai and their traditional leaders over how the reserve and the revenue were being used. Out of necessity, the Maasai continued to move their cattle into the basin for water and grazing, leading to complaints that they were interfering with tourism. As in Masai Mara, development projects built with tourism profits were widely scattered, and those in the settlements closest to the reserve complained that they were not receiving sufficient benefits. In addition, the council had little expertise or training in finances, and there was a series of incidents involving mismanagement.[109]

By the late 1960s, the conflict had intensified, with the local Maasai demanding that they be given title to the entire region and conservationists urging that Amboseli be declared a national park from which the Maasai would be totally excluded. In 1971, Kenya's president, Jomo Kenyatta, precipitously decreed that the government was taking over a large area within the basin and that the Maasai would be compensated with alternative water sources. The Maasai retaliated by spearing rhinos, lions, leopards, and elephants. Their message was clear: take the land and the Maasai would take the animals.

At this point, David Western, who had been studying Amboseli for his doctoral dissertation, became deeply involved in negotiating a settlement that would protect much of the original Maasai-based ecotourism experiment, integrate the livestock and wildlife economies, and focus primarily on providing the Maasai nearest the reserve with benefits from tourism and wildlife utilization.[110] For the first time, there were public meetings between local leaders and Ministry of Tourism and Wildlife officials, a development Western calls the "most enduring impact" of this crisis. They sought to create, Western says, a "Maasai park rather than a national park, and that was accepted—begrudgingly—by the government, but was overturned in the late 1960s during the general elections. It was only later, when the government unilaterally took over Amboseli, that we tried to negotiate some compromise between the state and local participation."[111] Finally, in 1974, a compromise was struck by which Amboseli became a national park under central government control and administered by the newly created Wildlife Conservation and Management Department (WCMD). The agreement contained, however, a number of innovative provisos to encourage local support: (1) the government would construct boreholes and a pipeline to pump water from the swamp to surrounding communal lands; (2) the Kajiado County Council would be guaranteed income from land surrounding tourist lodges located inside the park as well as a portion of the gate entrance fees; (3) the government would use its share of the entrance fees for park maintenance and development; (4)

the government would retain all local staff members as rangers, scouts, and lodge employees; and (5) the Maasai group ranches would receive title to the remainder of the land. In addition, nearly $6 million of a $37.5-million World Bank Tourism and Wildlife Project was allocated for Amboseli.[112]

Problems, however, continued, and so did power- and revenue-sharing negotiations between the central government, the county council, group ranches, and park authorities. The plan was that the four group ranches outside the park would get increasing revenues from tourist lodges and campsites, game cropping, and safari hunting, as well as a "wildlife utilization fee" or rent to compensate for the loss of grazing lands to wildlife. In addition, a school, dispensary, and community center were built on the edge of the park, and roads inside the park were improved. Western recounts that at a meeting held to distribute to the group ranches the first payments from hunting concessions—KSh 1.9 million ($271,000)—the Maasai responded, once again, that they considered wildlife to be valuable. As the elders told the government officials, "The national park has gained two thousand extra pairs of eyes to help watch out for poachers."[113] Feeling confident that this deal would hold, the Maasai agreed to vacate the park completely by 1977.

But conflicts soon arose again, in part because there was no written agreement and the terms of the oral understanding were never fully implemented. The WCMD was severely underfunded and plagued with ineptitude, corruption, and nepotism. The agency proved to be, Western wrote, "disastrous not just for Amboseli, but for the locally based approach and Kenya's wildlife generally."[114]

However, by the mid-1980s, the situation began to improve slightly as tourist numbers increased and Amboseli's group ranches began, for the first time, to take the initiative in implementing wildlife and tourism projects. By this time, the Maasai around Amboseli, as elsewhere, were in the process of making a rapid transition from pastoralism to a more mixed economy of farming, salaried employment, and—as beef prices rose—commercial livestock ranching. A new generation of Maasai leaders emerged and began to devise novel ways of relating to wildlife and tourism.

In one notable project, each of two hundred families on one group ranch contributed three hundred Kenyan shillings to build a 9.7-kilometer (6-mile) solar-powered electric fence to keep out wildlife.[115] Another group of Maasai opened a campsite, which by 1987 was earning more than three hundred thousand Kenyan shillings (eighteen thousand dollars) per year. The four group ranches all contracted with safari operators to bring in tourists. For instance, in 1991, the Olalarashi Group Ranch negotiated a twenty-thousand-dollar-per-year deal with two big tour operators, Abercrombie & Kent and Ker and Downey, for eight campsites.[116] These self-initiated and profitable ecotourism schemes contributed to keeping poaching out of the Amboseli ecosystem during the "ivory wars" of the 1980s. As Western wrote, "Despite the failure of the government program, WCMD's contribution to the collapse of park infrastructure, and a much-publicized poaching scandal . . . the Maasai's own wildlife programs sustained and improved their development activities as well as wildlife numbers."[117]

By 1989, Amboseli National Park ranked, with Masai Mara Game Reserve and Nairobi National Park, among Kenya's top tourist attractions. It was receiving some one hundred thousand visitors and bringing in an estimated KSh 3 million (about $67,000) from gate earnings per year. By 1984, the numbers had risen sharply, and gate earnings were an estimated KSh 12 million ($268,000), giving it an enviable revenue base to share with the local communities, county council, and central government.[118] But those living closest to the park, and suffering the most from wildlife eating crops and killing livestock and sometimes people, continued to benefit little. In early 1990, after the Kenya Wildlife Service (KWS) replaced the WCMD, government officials and the Amboseli group ranches reached several broad agreements, including one to resume revenue disbursements and another to create a team of local Maasai scouts to protect wildlife. As part of KWS director Richard Leakey's pledge to distribute 25 percent of gate revenues to local communities, the Amboseli group ranches became, in 1991, the first to receive payment. The ranches used part of this KSh 4 million (more than $100,000) to build four schools and several cattle dips and to hire twenty Maasai game scouts to protect wildlife.

But when the KWS failed to follow through and systematically implement the 25 percent revenue-sharing scheme, several Amboseli group ranches set up their own wildlife association to undertake conservation programs and tourist concessions.[119] In 1996, the Kimana Group Ranch opened its own 40-square-kilometer (15.4-square-mile) wildlife sanctuary in a stretch of swampy land east of Amboseli.[120] The ranch's chairman, Paul Ole Nangoro, admitted that the sanctuary was a gamble because many Maasai feared it was simply a device to turn more of their land over to wildlife protection. In subsequent years, the Kimana model spread throughout the Amboseli area, including to nearby Selengei group ranch, which created Eselenkei Conservation Area on about twelve thousand acres. The conservation area was set up following the signing of a contract between the group ranch and Porini Ecotourism Ltd., a company run by Jake Grieves-Cook, a leading figure in the Kenyan tourism industry.[121] Although the Eselenkei Conservation Area represents a promising model of community-based ecotourism and the Porini Camp is an eco-rated facility (one of only five at the Silver level), this project has also been plagued by conflicts within the community and between the community and operator. One researcher found, in a 2002 study, that the core problem was that "there was no genuine motivation by the tour operator to develop the sanctuary for the benefit of the local people," and that financial benefits to the community have neither met expectations nor been presented transparently.[122]

A more recently acclaimed community venture is Campi ya Kanzi, a joint venture between a group ranch and an Italian safari company, Luca Safari, which is owned and managed by Luca Belpietro and Antonella Bonomi. Campi ya Kanzi, which means Camp of the Hidden Treasure, is situated in the Kuku group ranch, which lies between Amboseli, Tsavo West, and Chyulu National Parks. The camp, like Basecamp Mara, has earned the top eco-rating as an Ecotourism Kenya Gold-certified facility, and has won a number of international awards including the Skål International Ecotourism Award in 2005 and the WTTC's Tourism for Tomorrow Conservation Award in 2006.[123] It employs over seventy local Maasai as staff and as workers with an array of tourism-related projects, including Maasai-led walking safaris and traditional craft making by Maasai women. Seven exclusive guest cottages, with views of Mount Kilimanjaro to the south, employ state-of-the-art solar power, rainwater collection, and local construction materials. The camp collects a twenty-dollar-per-day conservation fee that is directed toward local development projects, and also pays an additional fee to the group ranch.[124]

Despite the growth of these community ventures, Amboseli faces many of the same challenges as the Mara. Land-use patterns have changed from communal to individual, with more fences and more agriculture, although the Amboseli area is generally too dry to support the kind of large-scale commercial farming that occurs outside Masai Mara. The recent growth of community conservancies around Amboseli is largely driven by recognition that much of the land will gradually be individualized and fenced off if active efforts are not made to retain areas under group ownership. But unlike the Mara, wildlife populations around Amboseli have proven remarkably stable during the past thirty years, and the renowned elephant population has continued to increase to over 1,300 animals, with animals now spreading south into Tanzania for much of the year.[125] The stability of these wildlife populations is partially attributed to the long-term involvement of communities in benefiting from wildlife and tourism around Amboseli, and bodes well for the future of many local ventures.

Amboseli itself continues to be a mainstay of the national tourism industry. But in 2005 controversy once again broke out over the area, as the Kibaki government announced a plan to "degazette" the national park and return control of it to the Kajiado County Council. This move was widely viewed as an attempt to buy Maasai support for a contentious national constitutional referendum that the government was lobbying support for, and although conservationists around Kenya objected, the degazettement was carried out. Given the low regard that the KWS is now afforded, most objections centered around the way the change in status was carried out rather than its results, although there are clearly fears that Amboseli will now become another Mara, fueling increased conflicts and corruption within the County Council. "There has to be a very clear framework on what the community will do for their people so we don't have a repeat of the Mara," cautions the East African Wildlife Society's Ali Kaka.[126] Today Amboseli is, as it was in the 1960s, under the authority of Kajiado County Council, although the KWS maintains a presence as the reserve's managers and court battles continue over the legality of the de-gazettement process. Whether Amboseli will become a model of decentralized, district-level management, or repeat the troubles of the Mara, is an open question.

Facing Mount Kenya: Private Ranches and Community Lodges in Laikipia

The Laikipia Plateau lies to the north of Mount Kenya, an expanse of rolling savannah stretching toward Kenya's endless arid north beyond. In the early twentieth century, Laikipia became notorious in the colonial history of dispossession in Kenya when most of the resident Maasai were relocated and forced to move into the designated reserve to the south. Most of the best lands on the plateau closer to Mount Kenya were taken over as settler properties, with indigenous pastoralists (Maasai, Samburu, and Turkana) remaining to the north in drier and less-productive areas. Today, Laikipia remains a center of disproportionate white land ownership, and simmering—occasionally boiling—tensions over land rights. It is here that Kenya's ecotourism industry has developed two very different faces: one built on illusion and nostalgia, looking back to the early twentieth century, and the other, decidedly modern, rooted in the realities the twenty-first century.

Out of Africa: Private Ranches and Reserves

During the late 1980s and 1990s, with the overcrowding and deteriorating conditions within the national parks and council-run reserves, international visitors with sufficient funds began seeking "wild Africa" elsewhere, in Kenya's growing number of private estates and ranches that were converted to exclusive conservation and wildlife-viewing areas. Most are owned by white Kenyans from settler families who stayed on after independence and, in many cases, obtained citizenship. Some began using their large tracts of land as conservation sanctuaries, protecting and raising endangered species such as black rhinos, Rothchild's giraffes, and Grevy's zebras. Others care for orphaned or wounded wild animals, specialize in bird-watching or fishing, or have fenced off their estates to make wildlife parks. These white-owned estates quickly became the darlings of documentary filmmakers, wildlife photographers, and travel magazine writers, who traded close-up access to wildlife for enormously valuable and nearly free advertising.

The atmosphere on many of these private ranches remains distinctly colonial, reflecting the area's heritage. In terms of ecotourism, this amounts to, as David Western says, "the old fashioned Kenya safari, the 1920 safari."[127] Most accommodate no more than two dozen guests. They offer game-viewing drives in open jeeps (à la South Africa) as well as walking tours, night rides, game viewing via horseback and camel, picnics beside water holes, and sundowners on the savanna, often accompanied by the owner of the estate. They permit, even encourage, off-road driving, and when leopards or cheetahs are sighted, there are never more than a handful of other vehicles around. But this sense of being on safari in the wild is carefully orchestrated. Whereas the national parks are unfenced, large, and lightly patrolled by comparison, these private sanctuaries are comparatively small, fenced, meticulously managed, well groomed, and heavily guarded. Game-viewing vehicles are connected by radio, and scouts are sent ahead to spot the animals. The owners have named many of the animals, some of which are so accustomed to humans that they come right up to the vehicles or living quarters. Little is left to chance. Visitors who pay the price are virtually guaranteed close encounters with the "Big Five"[128]—or whatever else these luxury zoos have to offer.

Studies done of private reserves have found that those in Africa are, on average, much larger than those in Latin America. Seventy-three percent exceed 2,500 hectares (6,177 acres) and, according to the study, a majority (53.3 percent) of these reserves in Africa (Kenya, South Africa, Zimbabwe, and Madagascar) combined tourism and farming, a quarter (26.7 percent) were only for tourism, and 20 percent did research, conservation, and education, with or without tourism.[129] Although these ranches may provide sanctuary for endangered species and intimate and educative game-viewing experiences for tourists, on other ecotourism fronts they are sadly wanting: they preserve sizable tracts of privately owned land and resources in a few privileged hands;

generally offer only menial employment for local people; provide little financial benefit to the central government; and transmit to visitors a distorted, frequently racist view of modern-day Kenya. Fundamentally, these private reserves are an attempt to maintain family wealth and a lifestyle from a bygone colonial era "under the guise of conservation and ecotourism," said Maasai activist Meitamei Ole Dapash in a 2004 interview.

The magnitude of these imbalances was pointed out to me during sundowners at Delamere's Camp at Lake Elementaita. This tranquil tented camp, where I was the only guest one weekend in the late 1990s, is a bird and wildlife sanctuary, with a wide green lawn shaded by yellow-barked acacia trees and sprinkled with dozens of bird feeders. The air was filled with a symphony of chirping, and the pink hue of flamingos colored a distant edge of the lake. At dusk, the staff took me via jeep up to a cliff overlooking the lake for drinks and marinated Thomson's gazelle shish kebobs grilled over a charcoal stove. Standing on the windy edge of the cliff, the chief guide, a young Kamba man with a knack for bird calls, talked about the Delameres, the most famous of Kenya's colonial families. With an outstretched arm, he drew almost a complete circle around the lake, pointing out the extent of their property in this part of Kenya. Sixty-four thousand acres, the whole horizon save one narrow slice, belongs to Thomas Cholmondeley, the great-great-grandson of the original Lord Delamere. Much of this estate, where beef cattle were raised before the prices plummeted, had been sheltered in a nature conservancy.

"Yes, we see this as part of ecotourism," explained the camp's Kenyan manager as we sat beside the large fireplace in the open-sided lounge. "We keep everything as natural as possible. There are no nonindigenous plants or wildlife, except for giraffes that we've brought in." The wildlife sanctuary, which has no elephants or predators (except leopards), is a 6,475-hectare (16,000-acre) fenced "peaceable kingdom" of gazelles, impalas, zebras, elands, and buffalo. But the fences were also intended to keep people, especially local people, out. Even though the camp is located just off a main highway, no day visitors or drop-ins were allowed. All bookings had to be made ahead of time in Nairobi. "We don't want the wrong kind of guests," said the manager. "We're near Nakuru and Naivasha [two popular lakes frequented by both Kenyans and foreigners], and it could easily turn into a carnival. We don't allow school tours for locals. It's not a public stomping ground." The manager went on to explain that turning the land into a wildlife conservancy "was a business proposition. The Delameres realized that with the presence of game, they could make money from tourism." He added that because the sanctuary was private, none of the revenue went to the government, although the government, which technically owns the wildlife, must approve all culling—including that of the gazelles served at sundowners.

In his Nairobi office, Steve Turner, who built the lodge at Delamere's Camp and was bringing in most of its guests through his Ornithological Safaris, talked openly with me about the motivation behind establishing private reserves. Turner, who is also from a settler family, explained, "These private landowners are under incredible pressure to share their land. Africa is no place for whites to be owning huge tracts of land and seeming to do nothing with it. The Delameres are under pressure from locals to utilize the land." He said that in the 1960s and 1970s, vast amounts of land were taken from whites and sold off cheaply. The remaining whites continued to fear they would lose their land if it seemed to be underutilized. So, as the director of one Western NGO caustically put it, "They slap on a rhino and say it's a reserve."

Although the private reserves have helped protect and breed endangered species such as rhinos, few other benefits pass from the private reserves to the public parks or national coffers. At one point, the Kenyan government attempted to impose a tax on private lands used for wildlife that was several times greater than the tax for livestock. This caused "extreme consternation, and so it was reversed," explained one top NGO official. "The major problem with settler-owned or corporate-owned game farms," said environmental consultant Robert Hall in a 1998 interview, is what they "return to the government/national economy. They are not properly taxed." He continued, "These owners cry about their huge expenses to maintain their fences and protect their pet rhinos, but the truth is more complex. These guys have their own air strips, and no one, and I mean no one, knows how many people come and go during a year. Their charges are generally at least $250 to $600 per person per night. And what does the Treasury receive? Nada."

As Steve Turner recognized, local resentment toward these large landholdings has been growing. In 2004, Laikipia landed in the headlines of newspapers around the world when Maasai herders invaded a number of white-owned ranches, cutting fences, moving in their livestock, and claiming that the lands should legally be returned to them. Driven by drought conditions and a need for pasture and water for their cattle, the pastoralists also had a century-old legal claim. In 1904 and 1911, the Maasai had signed two treaties with the British colonial government leasing huge swathes of land to British settlers for ninety-nine years. Arguing that the lease was now up and demanding restitution, the Maasai community proposed either they get back their ancestral lands or receive KSh 10 billion (nearly $130 million) as compensation. Although they had the support of the powerful Maasai cabinet minister William Ole Ntimama, the Kenyan government, insisting that the treaty was valid for 999 (not 99) years, refused to support this uprising, and it soon died away.[130]

These smoldering tensions surfaced again in 2005 and 2006 when the Delamere heir, Thomas Cholmondeley, owner of Delamere's Camp, was arrested not just once, but twice, for shooting and killing Africans he suspected of illegally intruding on his vast estate. Despite public outcries, the court acquitted him of the first murder—an undercover ranger (and father of eight) who Cholmondeley said he mistook for a robber. Then, a year later, the landowner shot and killed an African stonemason who had poached a gazelle for meat. As Maasai villagers demanded that he "not be allowed to get away with it a second time," Cholmondeley again pleaded self-defense.[131] The legal process dragged on without resolution, but the second murder and arrest proved too much for Delamere's Camp. No longer able to maintain its peaceable kingdom image, the camp was, according to a Web posting, "temporarily closed"—for renovations.[132]

A far more positive conservation and ecotourism project that has emerged, via some bizarre twists, from the Delamere heritage is the Ol Pejeta Conservancy. This ninety-thousand-acre expanse of land in Laikipia was owned during the colonial era by Lord Delamere, and used mainly for cattle ranching.[133] Part of the property later passed into the hands of Adnan Khasshogi, a Saudi tycoon, arms trader, and financier who was involved in the Iran-contra scandal in the 1980s, and more recently with terrorist Osama bin Laden.[134] The Ol Pejeta area was subsequently managed by Lonrho Africa as Sweetwaters Game Sanctuary, which included a substantial population of reintroduced black rhinos (including one highly tame rhino named Morani, who lets tourists pet his massive horns) and a rather out-of-place chimpanzee orphanage. In 2004 the entire property was purchased by Fauna and Flora International, a well-respected, British-based conservation organization, and the conservancy established over the entire ninety thousand acres. Today Ol Pejeta is one of Laikipia's leading efforts to try and integrate wildlife conservation, ecotourism, livestock ranching, and local community development in a holistic way.

Community-owned Ranches and Conservancies

This *Out of Africa* lifestyle clung to by old settler families like the Delameres, and sometimes marketed as ecotourism, is out of place in present-day Kenya. The reality is that the fate of Kenya's wildlife depends on the future of the national reserves and their surrounding dispersal areas, not on this handful of white-owned farms. It also depends on the "other face" of tourism, the growing number of community-owned and -run lodges and sanctuaries, many in the Laikipia area. Over the last decade, Laikipia has undertaken some innovative experiments in community-run ecotourism, ultimately creating an entirely new tourism destination and product. These developments have been driven by an unusual—and sometimes seemingly incompatible—mixture of local pastoralist communities, white ranchers, foreign donors, and conservation organizations.

In contrast with the Delameres, a handful of other white ranchers have been at the forefront of pioneering community tourism ventures in this part of Kenya, and ultimately creating models that have pushed ecotourism into a new phase throughout Kenya. The key player in these developments has been Lewa Wildlife Conservancy, a 24,686-hectare (61,000-acre) wildlife reserve headed by Ian Craig.[135] The Craig family came to Kenya in 1922 and ran Lewa as a cattle ranch for over fifty years. Starting in the late 1970s, the Craigs began using part of their property for wildlife tourism, offering walking safaris—something unheard of at that time in East Africa. They started with four tents and gradually expanded to fifteen double tents and a permanent camp. Lewa has gradually built up its tourism operations, capitalizing on the overcrowding and the deteriorating conditions within the national parks and council-run reserves, and on the local presence of rare or unusual species found in northern Kenya such Grevy's zebras, reticulated giraffes, Somali ostrich, and oryx. The Craigs set up the Lewa Wildlife Conservancy to protect their property by means of a conservation trust, and started a rhino sanctuary—Lewa now has about 10 percent of all the black rhinos in Kenya, and has introduced nonnative white rhinos onto the property as well.[136] They also built three beautiful double cottages, using cut lava stone, wooden pillars, and thatch roofs, in a style similar to that of their main ranch house. A room there now costs $578 per night, including meals and game drives.

By the late 1990s, Lewa was "the furthest along in the country as a private conservancy," according to one leading tour operator, and the success of their conversion encouraged many of the other Laikipia ranches to do likewise. As the wildlife business grew, the landowners organized the Laikipia Wildlife Forum in 1992, which has become one of Kenya's leading conservation organizations and the first forum with the capacity to foster development and conservation on a district-wide level. By 2000, its membership included thirty-one large-scale ranches, thirty community groups, and twelve tour operators. It succeeded in stopping commercial poaching and began developing and marketing what USAID describes as "world class community-owned tourism projects."[137] In addition, on a ranch adjacent to Lewa, the Mpala Research Centre was formed, and as a result the Laikipia area has become a locus for some of the best long-term wildlife research in East Africa.

In the 1990s, Lewa began reaching beyond its borders to create a product that is distinctly twenty-first century and that has created ripples throughout Kenyan ecotourism world. To the north of Lewa lies the Il Ng'wesi Group Ranch, and wildlife traditionally moved between the private and group ranches and the Samburu Game Reserve to the north. In order to spread the benefits of wildlife among the broader landholding community, as well develop a new tourism product, Lewa began working with Il Ng'wesi to create its own wildlife sanctuary and eco-lodge. With support from the Kenya Wildlife Service, as well as conservation organizations like African Conservation Centre and donors including USAID, a lodge was constructed that opened for business in 1996.

Several things set Il Ng'wesi apart from earlier Kenyan ecotourism initiatives. The most fundamental is that the community owns and manages the property. This difference is immediately visible upon arrival at Il Ng'wesi, where guests are met by the dozen or so local Maasai who run the lodge, not only portering luggage—as Maasai are relegated to at most tourist facilities—but handling all operational aspects of the property. David Western considers this Il Ng'wesi's most important achievement: they have shown "that a community can own and effectively run a lodge. They gave enormous encouragement to lots of other communities to come in and do the same thing."[138] The Il Ng'wesi group ranch is also the owner of the property, although a number of outsiders, including the Craigs, sit on the board of the trust. The second major innovation that Il Ng'wesi has brought is one of design, which is simply revolutionary. The lodge has been built solely with local materials, and the eight rooms are sprawling, wide-open units, organically built into the landscape, around rocks and trees, in a way that few other lodges at the time had tried.

As a result of these characteristics, Il Ng'wesi has become "the showcase of ecotourism in Kenya," according to Judy Kepher-Gona of Ecotourism Kenya (formerly ESOK). Its numerous accolades include the United Nations Development Programme (UNDP) Equator Initiative Award, given during the 2002 World Summit on Sustainable Development in Johannesburg to six outstanding projects around the world that integrate biodiversity conservation with local livelihoods.

Il Ng'wesi's global fame and marketing has been largely generated by Lewa and some of the conservation organizations that have been involved. "II Ng'wesi was known abroad before the local tourism industry had heard of it," says Kepher-Gona. And while Lewa's role in setting up

Il Ng'wesi and developing its business have been critical, this has led many to question how much of an active role the community itself is playing. Ian Craig of Lewa remains the managing director of Il Ng'wesi lodge, and all marketing and booking are handled by Lewa and associated travel agents. "Il Ng'wesi does not have its own website or postal address," notes Kepher-Gona, who adds that Il Ng'wesi's experiences have led many ecotourism proponents in Kenya to question whether community ecotourism initiatives can survive "without a 'big brother.'" Western adds that "if you took Lewa away [Il Ng'wesi] would not stand on its own and it's really got to move through the next stage" of becoming a more independent, community-run facility.[139] As in the Masai Mara and around Amboseli, concerns about transparent management are also an issue. Initially Il Ng'wesi was managed by the group ranch committee, but, Kepher-Gona explains, in order to prevent a few people from dominating, a trust was established in 2003.

Even as Il Ng'wesi works to ensure that the benefits from tourism are dispersed in a transparent manner and to prevent the "elite capture" that has characterized many local tourism projects in Kenya, others are copying the model of organic design and local ownership. Initially, the Il Ng'wesi model spread to the surrounding area—Laikipia and on into Samburu and Northern Frontier Districts. Tassia Lodge, for example, has been constructed just to the north of Il Ng'wesi on sixty thousand acres set aside by the Lekurruki group ranch. Tassia is similar to Il Ng'wesi, but with minor improvements and modifications to the lodge's design made along the way. Most spectacular is the swimming pool, nestled amongst the huge boulders—*kopjes*—on which it is built. Returns from ecotourism are split, with 60 percent going back to the lodge and 40 percent paid to the community. The group ranch has used profits to build a dispensary, send children to secondary school, provide cattle dips, and purchase a vehicle.[140] Another example is the Ol Gaboli Community Lodge, built on the Il Motiok group ranch with support from Mpala Conservancy and the European Union. It proudly boasts of being "the only known tourism facility owned by an all-women's pastoralist group in sub-Saharan Africa."[141] Farther to the north in Samburu District's Mathews Range, the Namunyak Wildlife Conservation Trust has established the Sarara tented camp and a seventy-five thousand acre conservancy.[142] In total, a profusion of new lodges and tented camps of various stripes have been built on community lands and under community management over the past decade in Laikipia, Samburu, and adjacent districts.[143]

The impacts of these ecotourism experiments on the broader conservation and community landscape are manifold. First, it has greatly increased the area conserved for wildlife, well beyond the land contained in private ranches. Second, it has spread the benefits from wildlife tourism beyond the confines of privileged white landowners to increasing numbers of local communities. Third, the growth of these lodges and recovery of local wildlife populations have created an entirely new tourism destination and ecotourism product in central Kenya, which is offering an increasingly diversified range of products. Lastly, it has given the Laikipia region political lobbying clout as communities have become more involved in international tourism and wildlife conservation. For example, the 2004 wildlife bill that (as explained earlier) president Kibaki ultimately vetoed was introduced by the Laikipia member of parliament. In addition, Speaker of Parliament Francis Ole Kaparo represented a neighboring constituency and has been closely linked to several community lodges.

Community eco-lodges, all generally fashioned along the line of Il Ng'wesi, are now spreading far beyond Laikipia and Samburu. Hundreds of miles to the south, on the border with Tanzania, the Shompole Group Ranch occupies about 150,000 acres between Lake Magadi and Lake Natron, the breeding site of the Rift Valley's 2 million flamingos. In 2001, the Shompole Group Ranch, with support from the African Conservation Centre (ACC), formed a joint venture with Anthony Russell, a safari guide and conservationist with decades of experience in Kenya. They set up a partnership to build an "upmarket" ($330 per day) eco-lodge and set aside one-sixth of the ranch (twenty-five thousand acres) for conservation and wildlife, not cattle. The joint venture secured funding from the European Union through the Biodiversity Conservation Project (BCP) and private investors to construct six tented rooms using local white quartz stone, pale thatch, and other natural materials. The Shompole Maasai own 30 percent of the lodge, and plans call for increasing their share to 80 percent in fifteen years. The Shompole lodge opened in 2002 to rave reviews for its architectural style, its community ownership, and its spectacular location on the side of the escarpment overlooking the Great Rift Valley.[144] Since then Shompole has been featured in *Vogue* magazine (February 2004) and has captured various awards including the UNDP's prestigious Equator Prize (in 2006).[145]

According to a Web site featuring Shompole, "The 4-Cs: Community, Conservation, Commerce and Capacity-building, are the watchwords of this project."[146] Yet while Shompole's national and international popularity has grown, locally its reputation is more blemished. During its first five years in operation, the community, which had anticipated receiving 30 percent of revenue from all bed-night charges at the lodge, received very little financial benefit. Despite reasonably high occupancy rates, income has not lived up to forecasts. The African Conservation Centre is now working to take things a step further in the communities around Shompole by creating links among adjacent group ranches through the creation of a Southern Rift Landowners Association. The goal, according to David Western, is that "through the community linkage we will have a wildlife connection all the way from Tsavo to the west side of Masai Mara."[147] By coordinating adjacent community developments, the hope is to create entirely new community ecotourism destinations, as has been achieved in Laikipia. Another organization with a similar mission is the KECOBAT Network, which was launched in 2003 as "a membership umbrella organization representing the interest of Community Based Tourism (BT) in Kenya." While Ecotourism Kenya tends to represent larger tourism businesses, KECOBAT was created as a trade association to represent "the poorest sections of the tourism sector" and "open up opportunities for rural communities to enhance their participation in the tourism industry especially in planning and running of enterprises on their land."[148]

In the last few years, community eco-lodges catering to the international market have become an important part of Kenya's tourism industry. However, a central challenge for these community-based businesses and their trade associations is how to achieve market access. Today, a growing number of tour operators and safari companies are involved in either marketing community eco-lodges and/or supporting social service or conservation projects in communities around Kenya. For instance, Let's Go Travel,[149] one of Kenya's leading travel agencies and a founding member of Ecotourism Kenya, has begun to promote community lodges. "This company has brought community products to the market place," says Kepher-Gona. Among the international operators, Seattle-based Wildland Adventures (see chapter 3) has been working for a number of years with the Maasai Environmental Resource Coalition (MERC) and the Maasai Association to develop a model community-based ecotourism program in Maasailand in Kenya and Tanzania. Wildland runs, for instance, a Maasailand Safari in partnership with MERC, described by *Outside* magazine as a "safari-with-a-conscience" and selected as the "Best Africa Trip of the Year 2005." Its newer "Living Among the Maasai Safari" is designed to promote cross-cultural understanding through a stay in a Maasai community. Wildland and its guests have also donated more than twenty-five thousand dollars to MERC. Wildland President Kurt Kutay says, "By involving local communities, indigenous people can share in the economic benefits of tourism including better health, education and overall living conditions." He adds, "As a result they have an alternative model to the destructive social and environmental impacts of conventional safari tourism on their lands."[150] Another leading tour operator, Micato Safaris, has created a nonprofit arm called America Share that provides financial and material assistance to children in East Africa, many of whom are AIDS orphans. With offices in New York and Nairobi, Micato offers high-end game-viewing safaris and has been selected four times (2003–2006) by *Travel & Leisure* magazine as the "world's best tour operator and safari outfitter." Micato is owned by the Pinto family, Kenyans of Indian (Goan) descent who created this foundation more than fifteen years ago as a "personal project" to help the "youngest and neediest" in East Africa. It gradually grew into a large project through which guests can visit schools and AIDS orphanages in East Africa and make material and financial donations. The company covers all administrative costs so that 100 percent of guest contributions can go to the local communities. Micato director Dennis Pinto says that the company has been surprised to discover that many of their guests say their visit to a community project was the most meaningful part of their safari.[151]

The Resurgent Mzee

The spread of community eco-lodges has provided a powerful source of innovation and led to new destinations such as Laikipia and Shompole becoming increasingly established parts of Kenya's tourism map. What is perhaps most interesting about initiatives like Il Ng'wesi and Shompole is that they emerged at a time when the rest of Kenya's tourism industry was in a severe slump, providing a growing subsector in an otherwise depressed industry. In 2004 and 2005, the rest of the tourism industry awoke from its long recession and began to recover. In 2006, tourism generated over $800 million, and once again surpassed tea and horticulture as the top foreign exchange earner.[152] During 2007, Kenya was speculatively forecast to reach $1 billion in tourism revenue for the first time. Even as the KWS continued to cope with widespread wildlife declines and the debate over wildlife policy, the agency was on a more solid financial footing and had embarked on initiatives to rebrand its parks and open up new tourism circuits in western Kenya. Then, following the disputed presidential election results in late 2007, Kenya was once again thrown into political turmoil, and tourism dropped during what should have been a record high season. At this writing in early 2008, a historic power-sharing agreement has been worked out between presidential contenders Rwai Kibaki and Raila Kibaki, and tourism appears to be bouncing back.

Kenya's surprising recovery from the severe slump of a decade ago is due to a wide range of factors. In part it is a reflection of the general economic rebound Kenya has undergone since 2002, when the Moi regime was finally routed from office in a remarkably peaceful general election, and the new president, Mwai Kibaki, and the opposition

NARC alliance took over the government. Although the Kibaki administration failed miserably to stem the pervasive corruption in Kenya's public institutions—Kenya remains near the bottom of Transparency International's annual corruption perceptions index, ranked 142 out of 163 places—the economy has awakened.[153] In 2006, GDP grew over 8 percent, compared to several years of negative growth toward the end of the Moi era.[154] The Kibaki government played a role in reviving tourism, with the government and the European Union partnering in a Tourism Marketing Recovery Program initiated in the wake of the terrorist attacks on the coast in 2003.[155] This marketing under the banner of "Magical Kenya," led by a rejuvenated Kenya Tourist Board,[156] helped Kenya recapture its mainstay European markets.

Key private companies and NGOs have also played key roles in leading this revival. Founded in 1993 and officially registered in 1996 shortly after David Western became director of the KWS, Ecotourism Kenya (formerly known as the Ecotourism Society of Kenya or ESOK) was the first national ecotourism society in Africa. It is a nonprofit organization aiming at "bringing together commerce, conservation and communities," and composed of tour operators, hoteliers, travel agents, educational institutions, tourism professionals, tourism and conservation organizations, and community and district associations.

Ecotourism Kenya's original ambitious and somewhat conflicting mission, as described by Chris Gakahu, the organization's founding director, included setting standards and helping to certify the training of guides and tour drivers, lobbying the government to give economic incentives to hotels to adopt environmentally friendly practices and systems, "flagging environmentally friendly destinations for potential investors," promoting Kenya's diverse ecotourism options overseas, and providing expertise to local communities wanting to develop tented camps or other ecotourism projects. Gakahu said that Ecotourism Kenya struggled to live up to its pledge to be "a professional society" unrelated to "any particular special interest group." Rather, David Western's recollection is somewhat different: he recalls that "at an early stage, there was a clear effort by various people from the industry to make it an industry tool"[157] of a small but powerful group of largely white-settler-owned companies. Controversy emerged in these formative years over "The Ecotourism Partnership," an initiative designed, according to Ecotourism Kenya literature, as "the commercial implementing agency for projects which meet the aims of the Ecotourism Society of Kenya and to provide an impetus to the promotion of community-based wildlife tourism projects" by bringing "together a team of tourism industry professionals who will provide investment and management and marketing skills to such projects."[158]

These contradictory goals raised eyebrows among some community organizers and ecotourism experts early on, and membership of Ecotourism Kenya dwindled to less than ten companies by 1999. David Western claimed at the time that Ecotourism Kenya was "invaded, taken over by white tour operators who set up Ecotourism Partnership to try to promote ecotourism for their own benefit." By 1999–2000, the original founding members were forced out and a new group led by Chris Gakahu, Helen Gichohi, and Alan Dixson of Let's Go Travel attempted to revive the organization and its battered image.[159] Judy Kepher-Gona became the competent CEO of the organization and by mid-2007, Ecotourism Kenya had clearly rebounded, with some 175 businesses listed on its Web site as members.[160]

Other private-sector associations have also emerged to create coherence and provide leadership within Kenya's tourism industry, both in terms of internal organization and to try and influence government policy. In 1999, the Kenya Tourism Federation (KTF), an umbrella organization representing various tourism associations, was formed. The KTF soon became the tourism industry's mouthpiece, led by Jake Grieves-Cook, a charismatic Kenyan citizen of British decent and KTF's first chairman.[161]

With support from KTF, Ecotourism Kenya launched Africa's first green tourism certification program in 2003. The so-called Eco-rating scheme was developed through industry-wide consultations, and garnered government support. "The aim was to provide the industry with a scale against which to measure performance . . . and introduce standards to the business of ecotourism," says Judy Kepher-Gona, who as Ecotourism Kenya's executive officer has led the development of the scheme. She had attended the Mohonk conference in 2002, the first-ever meeting of "green" tourism certification programs from around the world (see chapter 3). The Eco-rating certification program receives applications from companies, carries out detailed audits using a range of environmental, social, and economic criteria, and then awards rankings of Bronze, Silver, or Gold, based on actual performance. The certification is valid for two years, after which properties can upgrade or reapply for their current rating.

The Eco-rating scheme has received mixed scores since its inception. Within its first year, more than a hundred facilities had requested copies of the assessment tool designed to evaluate lodge performance. But few applications were forthcoming, and by the end of that year fewer than twenty facilities had completed and returned the assessment tool. Fewer still, only six facilities in total, had been eco-rated that year. "The reluctance of lodges to participate became of concern to ESOK and many in the industry," says Kepher-Gona. However, by 2006, more than thirty lodges had received Eco-rating certification, including community lodges such as Il Ng'wesi, Shompole, and Tassia.[162] Three properties had received Gold ratings, including Basecamp Masai Mara and Campi ya Kanzi, while the Amboseli Porini Camp in Selekei conservancy was one of five Silver-rated facilities. Although the turnout is still relatively low, Kepher-Gona remains optimistic. "The eco-rating tool has created tremendous awareness among the property owners and many are working towards meeting the criteria," she notes. Although many within the industry remain skeptical as to the value of certification programs, Kepher-Gona asserts that "the future of the industry is in sustainable practices and if the scheme contributes to this future, Ecotourism Kenya will have played its role."

Other certification efforts have emerged in Kenya as well in order to improve the quality of the tourism industry's products and services. The Kenya Professional Safari Guide Association (KPSGA) operates a voluntary accreditation program for tour guides. Aspiring members of the association undergo examinations, earning accreditation at Bronze, Silver, or Gold grades. Like the Ecotourism Kenya Eco-rating scheme, this program faced initial hurdles. After many years of rejection, the government finally agreed to recognize and work with KPSGA, and is now planning to incorporate the KPSGA standards into a national curriculum of tour guide training. KECOBAT also is working to develop a certification program for the community-based eco-lodges.[163]

Kenya's Ecotourism Scorecard

Kenya has been a trailblazer in ecotourism. It gave birth to some of Africa's earliest experiments in community-based conservation using park and tourism revenues and began the first efforts to systematically adopt ecotourism principles and practices in its national park system. The director of its park service was the first head of The International Ecotourism Society (TIES) in the United States, and Africa's first nongovernmental ecotourism society was established in Kenya. However, Kenya's increasingly corrupt and violent political environment, a lack of planning, and an array of unfortunate external shocks all brought about a serious downturn in the tourism industry by the mid-1990s. And the political upheaval following the December 2007 elections threatened to cause a new downturn if not quickly resolved.

In the opening address of a 1997 international workshop held in Kenya titled "Ecotourism at the Crossroads," David Western was candid in his assessment of Kenya's progress and problems. "Kenya personifies the best and worst of nature tourism," he told the gathering.[164] Recent appraisals of areas such as the Masai Mara reflect this continuing Jekyl and Hyde nature of Kenya's ecotourism industry. With the spread of many leading community ventures since the late 1990s and the surprising resurgence of the national tourism industry in 2007, helped by both private-sector and government leadership, it would appear that Kenya is ready to resume its place of leadership in Africa's ecotourism experiments—if it can avoid prolonged political unrest. While this experiment is among the world's longest running, its record remains very mixed.

Travel to Natural Destinations

Since the 1960s, Kenya has been Africa's most popular wildlife tourism destination. Despite the growth of beach tourism, more than 90 percent of tourists visiting Kenya go "on safari" to a game park, even if only for a day, and nearly 80 percent of those interviewed cited nature and wildlife as their major reasons for coming to Kenya.[165]

Minimizes Impact

On this criterion, Kenya's record is fairly poor, particularly in the most popular game-viewing areas. Since the 1970s, the quality of Kenya's national parks and reserves has declined as a result of poorly controlled and, in the half-dozen most populated locations, excessive tourism. Protected areas have suffered from the presence of too many lodges, which consume water, wood, and electricity and produce large amounts of waste; off-road driving, which scars the land and disturbs the wildlife; poaching, which has ebbed and flowed over the years and from park to park; and competition from a rapidly expanding human population and both large- and small-scale farming.

Ten years ago David Western asked, "Why does Kenya, a pioneer in ecotourism, today lag far behind Latin America and Southern Africa?" He went on to lament that, "Kenya is better known for its tourism gone wrong, conjuring up visions of minibus congestion around lions, harassment of cheetahs, mindless destruction of habitat due to unregulated off-road driving, lodge congestion in parks, and coral reef destruction by rapacious tourists. As a result, Kenya today has the unenviable reputation of being the Costa del Sol of the wildlife world—overcrowded, overrated, and badly abused—with visitors decamping for greener pastures."[166]

Although this description remains all too applicable to Kenya's most famous national parks and reserves, an alternative model has emerged in the privately controlled community ventures, eco-lodges, and private ranches—some in partnership with or with assistance from white Kenyan landowners and operators. In addition, the green certification programs led by Ecotourism Kenya promise to hold industry to a higher standard if they can gain sufficiently wide adoption. Until 1999, Kenya did not have a consolidated environmental law to regulate developments, which generally took place without due regard for environmental and social impacts. With the coming of a new law in 1999 called the Environmental Management and Coordination Act, all new developments, including tourist camps and lodges, must undertake Environmental Impact Assessments and existing developments must perform Environmental Audits and present them to the government.

Builds Environmental Awareness

Here, the record is mixed. While Kenya has excellent tour companies and naturalist guides, one of the most common complaints from tourists has been that their guides have poor interpretive skills, lessening the overall quality of the nature tourism experience. The cultural *bomas* in areas like the Masai Mara represent one of the few mainstream efforts to integrate a cultural component into wildlife safaris, but these facilities tend to be outrageously exploitative, with operator drivers taking up to 90 percent of the proceeds.

Kenya has wildlife clubs for schoolchildren and some of its leading environmental activists are products of these clubs, but most Kenyans are never able to visit parks and reserves. Ecotourism Kenya was begun with high hope that it would be an industry watchdog, but initially suffered from low visibility and government suspicion, and was manipulated by powerful white ranchers and tour operators. Today its membership and its functions have expanded. Efforts by Ecotourism Kenya to develop certification on a more widespread basis and by the Kenya Professional Safari Guide Association to develop parallel standards for guides may lead to significant improvements in environmental awareness.

Provides Direct Financial Benefits for Conservation

Until the 1990s, Kenya faced little competition from elsewhere in Africa, and tourism became the country's top dollar-earner with little overseas promotion, investment in infrastructure, or national planning and regulation. Similarly, millions of dollars' worth of foreign aid has, since the 1970s, been given to support programs in Kenya's parks and reserves. But through corruption, mismanagement, and ill-conceived projects, little of this money has gone for environmental protection and improvement in the national or county council–controlled parks and reserves. The Masai Mara is clearly the worst example of this wasted economic potential. Despite (or, according to some conservationists, because of) the bans on hunting and trade in ivory, wildlife numbers continue to decline in many of Kenya's parks and reserves. The only exceptions are the Amboseli and Laikipia areas, where the local people are seeing the most direct benefits from camera safari tourism and wildlife. Kenya's policy of prohibiting tourist hunting as a revenue-earning option for wildlife in remote areas has not been successful, and despite long and contentious debates about reintroducing hunting under local control, changes have yet to be made.

Tourism revenues have provided the incentive for the growth of private and community wildlife conservancies in places like Amboseli and Laikipia, which contain an increasing proportion of Kenya's wildlife populations. The spread of ecotourism ventures in Laikipia and Samburu Districts has led to the rapid growth of these conservancies and an expansion of land set aside for wildlife. In the seemingly intractable Masai Mara, the formation of a private management company to run part of the reserve, the Mara Conservancy, has led to new hope that alternative systems to the heavily politicized County Council management can be found.

Provides Financial Benefits and Empowerment for Local People

Despite the growth of both private reserves and beach tourism, the heart of Kenya's nature tourism and ecotourism industry remains its national parks and reserves and their surrounding buffer zones. It is in these areas that Kenya has conducted its most innovative and long-term ecotourism experiments. Over the course of three decades, the community conservation schemes in Amboseli and Masai Mara followed somewhat different paths but produced some common lessons. These experiments are significant because they were large, government-backed initiatives involving the country's foremost tourist attractions, sizable populations, and, at times, international conservation and lending agencies. They represent the most concerted, long-term efforts in Africa to apply ecotourism principles on a national scale.

Both international and national economic and political conditions have undermined and limited these efforts to develop ecotourism. During the 1990s, the KWS's numerous community conservation projects aimed to apply ecotourism principles and practices more broadly throughout the park system. There is a need to better tie revenue sharing with positive community programs to improve wildlife conservation and management. Although there are many local ecotourism ventures, usually labeled as "joint ventures" or "community-based" and situated on community lands, little is known about the real economic returns from these projects. Some of Kenya's most famous community lodges do not appear to have generated significant revenue for the local community despite advertisements to the contrary. "Overall, tourism in Kenya has failed to improve the livelihoods of rural populations," said Ecotourism Kenya's Judy Kepher-Gona in a 2007 interview.

In terms of employment within the tourism industry, the county councils' deep involvement in Masai Mara and Amboseli has meant that significant numbers of Maasai have long been hired as guides, drivers, hotel staff, artisans, and cultural performers. Production of traditional handicrafts "has been an integral feature of Kenya's tourism development" and capital requirements have been low, permitting small entrepreneurs, including women, to enter this field.[167] In terms of ownership, although at the national level much of Kenya's tourism industry is in the hands of local whites or international corporations, the country does have a well-established and powerful black elite who are involved in tourism enterprises. The spread of local community ecolodges, although still evolving in terms of their structure, promises to lead to progressively greater local ownership of many tourism ventures over time.

Respects Local Culture

On this point, the record is poor. From the outset, Kenya's conservation and tourism policies have been tied to big game hunting, colonial control, and Western social and environmental values that are often at odds with the values and needs of Kenya's rural farmers and pastoralists. In his study of Kenya's environmental values and nature-based tourism, John Akama contends that "the socioeconomic conditions which led to increasing public support of wildlife conservation and the appreciation of the aesthetic and ethical values of wildlife are, most often, non-existent in rural Kenya."[168] Although more controlled environments at new small-scale, more socially conscious developments provide a growing alternative to these mainstream problems, Kenya's nature tourism continues to suffer all the negative cultural abuses of conventional mass tourism. The government and tourist industry, fixated on capturing dollars, have not addressed this problem with determination and imagination.

Supports Human Rights and Democratic Movements

Political conflicts in Kenya have intensified since the 1990s, and rural struggles have frequently centered on the use of land, including the question of who should control the parks and reserves and the profits from nature-based tourism. Although some of the community-based ecotourism projects have explicitly challenged the political status quo, most have been rather narrowly focused on income generation and social welfare. The spread of organized local wildlife forums, supported by David Western and other conservation organizations such as the East African Wildlife Society and Laikipia Wildlife Forum, have provided an important new form of community-based mobilization for policy reform.

In 2004, Wangari Maathai won the environmental Nobel Peace Prize for her work as a forest conservation advocate and campaigner in Kenya. Maathai, leader of the Greenbelt Movement, had for years courageously battled the Kenyan government's efforts to parcel out thousands of acres of Kenya's remaining forests for political purposes; her award symbolizes the way that environmental issues have emerged as a central component of debates over Kenya's sociopolitical development. Wildlife, tourism, land, and human rights continue to be the subject of national debates and will continue to be front and center as the coalition government that took office in April 2008 strives to restore peace, unity, and economic growth.

9

South Africa: People and Parks under Majority Rule

The haunting beauty of the melody disguises the sadness of a song that recalls how in 1969, soldiers arrived and forced—at gun point—women, children, and old people to burn their own homes. The Makuleke villagers were then loaded into the back of the trucks, transported twenty kilometers (twelve miles), and deposited on a barren piece of land. The men from this village of three thousand, who were off working in the gold mines and white-owned farms of apartheid-run South Africa, returned to find smoking ruins; they were told that their land had been incorporated into Kruger National Park. "Don't be deceived," the song says. "Our hearts are sore because of poverty. Don't be deceived because many of us are dying. Even if you take us back, only a few will be able to return. Because the rest will be dead."[1]

Today, the ruins still litter parts of the present-day Pafuri region of Kruger, but this ballad about forced removals intermingles with newer, happier melodies. At the Makuleke's cultural center, visitors can hear a choir singing about the way the villagers are developing their own game lodges and tourism projects in what is today known as the Makuleke Region of the Kruger National Park (KNP).

The turnabout began in 1997 with a landmark legal case that returned the Pafuri area to the Makuleke people. Under this farsighted court decision, the post-apartheid government of Nelson Mandela ruled that the Makuleke would be allowed to return to the area but that

I am indebted to Anna Spenceley (www.anna.spenceley.co.uk) and Duan Biggs in South Africa who supplied the updated information for the revisions to this chapter. In addition, I am grateful to Zoe Chafe, CESD coordinator in Washington, D.C., who did many interviews and site visits to help update the chapter during three months in South Africa in late 2004.

the land would be retained for conservation purposes as a contractual national park. The only economic activity permitted would be ecotourism—which, to the consternation of some, was deemed to include trophy hunting. The Makuleke initially opted for commercial hunting because it was able to deliver quick revenues and "venison" to the entire community with low levels of capital investment. However, hunting was strongly opposed by KNP management, who argued it should not take place in a national park.

The first hunt in 2000 earned the Makuleke Communal Property Association (CPA) about rand (R)520,000 ($70,000) which was used for a variety of village development projects and to purchase a car for the chief, P. J. Makuleke.[2] In addition, the meat from the elephants and buffalos was equally distributed among people in the villages. Subsequent hunts in the following years earned between $100,000 and $235,000, and these funds were used for additional community projects, including to help build a cultural interpretation center, operate the office and purchase a vehicle for the CPA, upgrade the schools, award student scholarships, construct boreholes, and provide food for the poorest families in the villages. By 2003, however, the Makuleke decided that although hunting had been a great source of income, they would downscale it significantly because photographic tourism could not operate together with hunting in this small area with a limited road network.

In 2005, the Makuleke community signed a forty-five-year mutually beneficial lease with Wilderness Safaris, one of southern Africa's top nature tourism companies, bringing an internationally recognized brand of sensitive and authentic ecotourism to the region. Wilderness Safaris has invested some R26 million ($3.3 million)[3] to develop the new twenty-room Pafuri lodge on the land, located in perhaps the most remote, pristine, and diverse area in Kruger. The Makuleke, in turn, benefit from direct cash, skills transfer, job creation, training, and community development projects.

While on the surface this looked like a "win-win" for ecotourism, the community, and the park, the reality was more complex. As one workshop revealed, "The contract with Wilderness Safaris stated that the Makuleke would have to stop hunting, although lots of money was generated from the hunts. [T]here would be less from [photographic safari] tourism than hunting because of the way the contract was structured, and . . . this had effectively disempowered [the] community in terms of their benefits."[4] Clearly, at least in the short term, it is difficult for a small eco-lodge with considerable overhead to earn as much profit and provide benefits as quickly to the community as big game hunting. As Wilderness Safaris' Chris Roche explained in a 2007 interview, "At this stage, we do not benefit the community in the same financial terms that hunting did, but combining straight revenue payments with wages (to local people), money invested in their assets, etc., I think it is clear that this has been a beneficial move for the sustainability of the concession." Roche added, "Interestingly enough, since hunting [was banned] and the introduction of ecotourism, during which we have spent considerable amounts of money on removing snares, shoring up cross-border security, etc., game numbers have apparently increased, particularly of small and medium-sized ungulates and also the local eland population (which was hunted)."[5]

Despite the debate over hunting, the Makuleke case was precedent-setting in terms of the basic land claim rights it upheld. The Makuleke were one of the first tribes to get their land back in a formally protected area, and the case has been cited across South Africa and around the world.[6] Some old-timers proclaimed that it marked an end to conservation in South Africa. As one senior conservation official predicted, "If the Makuleke claim is upheld in respect of land within the Kruger Park, all conservation areas will be under threat. Conservation status will not be worth the paper it is written on."[7] Such dire prognoses have not materialized; instead the Makuleke people and Wilderness Safaris have made this area a showpiece of what communities, park authorities, and ethical private-sector partners can achieve when they work together for the benefit of all stakeholders and the long-term conservation of the area.

Kruger National Park, located in South Africa's Limpopo and Mpumalanga Provinces, lies along the national borders with Mozambique and Zimbabwe, and is the flagship of the country's world-renowned national park system. Covering a staggering 19,425 square kilometers (7,500 square miles or the size of New Jersey) Kruger now forms part of the Greater Limpopo Transfrontier Park, which encompasses parts of South Africa, Mozambique, and Zimbabwe, and covers 35,000 square kilometers (13,500 square miles). Kruger has two dozen rest camps, including meticulously remodeled whitewashed wattle-and-daub guest houses dating from the 1930s; secluded cottages built of rough stone, wood, and thatching grass; and a modern conference facility with theaters, lecture hall, and boardroom. It accounts for over 75 percent of the bed nights sold by the South African National Parks (SANParks).[8] As one of South Africa's most heavily visited parks, Kruger not only pays for itself but also has helped finance other, less well-known parks. By 2004, Kruger was receiving around 1.3 million visitors per year; only the newly established Table Mountain National Park, incorporating Table Mountain and the picturesque Cape Peninsula, and situated within the tourist mecca of Cape Town, superseded this with 1.5 million visitors in 2004.[9]

The drawing card, of course, is the game, including, according to Kruger's official count for 2004: 12,177 zebras, 1,126 warthogs, 2,517 waterbuck, 4,533 white rhinos, 4,614 kudu, 9,574 wildebeests, 4,140 giraffes, 61,433 impalas, and 11,454 elephants. Predators are not included in the standard census because of the difficulty of counting them, but they are plentiful; the estimates are that Kruger has about 1,500 lion, 1,000 leopard, 250 cheetah, and 200 wild dogs.[10] The park offers multiple ways to view the game: self-guided tours, with tourists driving their own cars; bush drives with a ranger; night drives; guided walking tours; and one- to five-day hikes conducted by armed rangers. In contrast with the rough, vast, and untended wildness of East Africa's game parks, Kruger's paved roads and meticulous planning and grooming make it feel more like a tasteful, tranquil, upscale theme park.

Indeed, over the past century, South Africa has built some of the world's top scientifically managed, best-policed, most luxurious, least expensive, and most exclusive national parks. Subsidized with millions of rand per year in government funding, South Africa's park system was built under apartheid to serve a certain vision of conservation and the pleasures of the white elite. Like South Africa's other game parks, Kruger was, as one environmentalist explained, run by an "old white boys' network": a small community of managers, conservationists, and scientists that was 99 percent white and very ingrown, with a pecking order and an "us-versus-them" mentality. The "them" are the sprawling, impoverished rural communities ringing Kruger and other parks where unemployment can be as high as 40 percent and political expectations are soaring. In first visiting Kruger and other South African parks in 1995, a few years after president Nelson Mandela took office, I found them, on the surface, surprisingly unchanged by South Africa's transition to majority rule: their senior and midlevel staff and clientele were still overwhelmingly white.

But behind its facade of business-as-usual, Kruger National Park, like nearly every institution in what everyone terms "the new South Africa," was under tremendous pressure to change. By 1998, when Kruger celebrated its centennial, there was a black African director and the board had instituted a transformation program to remedy past imbalances in hiring and bring in more black visitors.

The Creation of Apartheid's Parks

When apartheid ended in 1994, 5.52 percent (about 67,340 square kilometers, or 26,000 square miles) of South Africa's total land area was under state-run wildlife protection.[11] In addition to provincial parks, this included sixteen national parks (with six more in the process of formation) totaling 3,394 square kilometers or 1,310 square miles, and more than a hundred provincial or homeland nature conservation areas. A somewhat larger amount (some 80,290 square kilometers, or 31,000 square miles) was protected in 9,000 privately owned game farms and nature reserves that offered upscale hunting safaris and lodges. In addition, there were small protected areas controlled by urban municipalities or regional governments as well as forests and mountain catchments protected by the country's conservation laws.[12] The expanse and tranquility of these public and private parks and reserves masks the reality that they were all created by evicting tens of thousands of Africans from their homes and lands. Built through forced relocations of the Makuleke and scores of other groups, protected by military force, financed through heavy government subsidies, and run with political and social blinders, South Africa's parks became some of the most luxurious and racially exclusive playgrounds in the world.

The creation of Kruger, South Africa's first park and the second oldest in Africa, began in the 1890s, when Boer farmers trekked into what they called the Transvaal (today the Northern and Mpumalanga Provinces), forcibly evicting an estimated three thousand Tsonga people from land between the Sabie and Crocodile Rivers. In an act signed by the president of the Transvaal, Paul Kruger, this vast area was proclaimed a game reserve. Like other settlers in the Transvaal, Kruger made a fortune through ivory hunting. Then, however, he became concerned that if the slaughter continued, the elephants and other game would be wiped out within a generation, as had already happened in South Africa's Cape Colony.

South Africa's parks and reserves were created as an emergency response to the decimation of wildlife that began as European settlers cleared and fenced land for ranches, agriculture, mines, and towns. Until the late nineteenth century, whites hunted wild game indiscriminately, sometimes for food, sometimes for trade, and increasingly for pleasure and trophies. Following the Anglo-Boer War at the turn of the century, the British seized control of the Transvaal, created more reserves, and, in 1926, passed the National Parks Act and merged the reserves into Kruger National Park.

From the outset, park authorities had two mandates: to conserve wildlife and to promote tourism. Finding the park largely denuded of game, the first ranger, Major James Stevenson-Hamilton, set about restocking the park and establishing a system of armed patrols and fences that is still in use. Between 1926 and 1969, Kruger's borders remained substantially the same and Africans within its boundaries continued to be forcibly removed.[13] In 1969, the 19,840-hectare Pafuri Game Reserve, which had been a reserve since 1903,[14] was incorporated into

Kruger National Park, at which time the Makuleke community was evicted from their lands. In the precolonial era, traditional hunting practices and, often, a conservation ethic that reserved rare species for royalty and ceremonial functions ensured that Africans and wildlife coexisted in relative equilibrium. It was only with the advent of colonial game reserves that indigenous Africans began to view wildlife with hostility. Not only were Africans forcibly moved to overcrowded and marginal agricultural lands on the periphery of these new reserves, colonial laws also denied them hunting and fishing licenses and the right to use firearms or hunting dogs. They were also forbidden to kill wildlife that wandered outside the reserves and destroyed their crops and domestic animals, and they were banned from collecting any wood or grasses within the reserves. Invariably, the colonial state chose to protect wildlife instead of the local Africans. In times of drought or when water was scarce, Africans were forced to move out. "From 1948 [the year apartheid officially began]," recounted villager James Maluleke, "the park started bringing in lots of elephants. They [the authorities] said people are coming to see the animals so it is better that you move."[15]

Couched in terms of conservation protection and tourism, these harsh policies also helped turn some rural farmers and herders into an impoverished black proletariat. Through forced labor and prison labor, Africans on the periphery of the parks and reserves were compelled to build roads and clear bush while others provided labor for South Africa's mines and industries. Historically, South Africa's parks have been closely linked to military and paramilitary personnel and operations. Parks have been used as staging areas, rear bases, and smuggling routes for the region's anticolonial and civil wars. As well as elsewhere in southern Africa, the park service includes many former military officers and its tactics mirror military operations. In the 1980s and early 1990s, for instance, Kruger was patrolled by a military unit trained by South African Defense Force instructors, and the border Kruger shared with Mozambique was one of the most strategically sensitive in southern Africa. Close to Kruger's headquarters at Skukuza, a secret rest camp called Jakkalsbessie was built for clandestine ministerial and military meetings with apartheid's allies. Just on the park's edge at Phalaborwa there was a clandestine support base for the right-wing Mozambique rebel army, the Mozambican National Resistance, known as Renamo.

Although South Africa's national park system was a product of and instrument for white rule, it managed to maintain a benevolent image under apartheid. In the eyes of most white South Africans and much of the Western world, wildlife protection was viewed as "a righteous cause," implemented with scientific and technical professionalism and unsullied by the country's policies. While apartheid South Africa was officially shunned by the rest of the world, its park system and conservation efforts continued to receive international accolades.

Ecotourism in South Africa

Despite the practices and policies of the apartheid old guard, the new South Africa widely and innovatively embraced ecotourism, based largely around the game parks. Today, ecotourism is being promoted by the central government; the ruling African National Congress (ANC); the government's South African Tourism agency; national and provincial conservation agencies; NGOs; academic institutions; and many other groups. In South Africa, more than elsewhere, ecotourism is defined as synonymous with local community involvement, profit sharing, and empowerment through tourism projects and conservation programs.

From the outset, the post-apartheid government was under enormous pressure to change the status quo in and around the park system. One of the first issues was whether the game parks would continue to exist at all. Throughout the country, marginalized and impoverished communities on the edges of the parks demanded that parkland from which they had been evicted be returned to them; that they be given access to firewood, plants, grazing pasture, water, and other resources inside the parks; and that they get real economic benefits from tourism. Quickly, the new government decided that the parks would not be dismantled, and president Mandela went further, pledging that the ANC would increase the amount of land under protection to 10 percent as recommended by the IUCN.[16] Although the IUCN's 5th World Parks Congress was held in Durban in 2003, South Africa did not achieve its goal of having 10 percent under protection. However, the extent of protected areas in South Africa has increased since then. Between March 2004 and March 2005, a total of 27,698 hectares (107 square miles) of land was acquired for inclusion in the national parks system. This cost a total of R53.34 million ($9.17 million), and funds were obtained from government grants, the SANParks Park Development Fund (PDF), and donor money.[17]

At the end of apartheid, the new government committed itself to reorganizing park operations, carrying out substantial land redistribution, and developing programs so that people on the periphery would begin to benefit from the parks and from tourism. Since then, the South African government undertook its land restitution program to provide a legal mechanism for equitably redistributing land to those who lost access to it through expropriation of land for parks, commercial agriculture, and other purposes during apartheid. By August 2004, ten years after the end of apartheid, the 48,825 restitution claims had resulted in 3,457,662 hectares (about 8.5 million acres) being returned through the various land-reform programs. More than 6.6 million people had benefited from this process.[18]

In the Makuleke restitution case, numerous factors were critical to making it largely successful, and can be considered important elements of any restitution project regarding protected areas and tourism joint ventures. Winning back formal and secure title has given the Makuleke considerable power to participate on a relatively equal basis with SANParks and their private partners to enforce their interests. The Makuleke demonstrated the importance of setting up "hard" legal structures capable of engaging with the commercial world and conservation agencies. They have also been successful in terms of merging traditional and new democratic organizations. And the Makuleke leadership has engaged with experts and agencies from outside their villages and focused on partnerships with the private sector in order to create their nature tourism enterprises.

There is some tension between pursuing pro-poor objectives and ensuring private investment. Although not insurmountable, this tension can never be completely avoided and must be addressed through numerous mechanisms. The Makuleke leadership ran open and transparent bids to attract and finalize deals with the private sector. The Makuleke Communal Property Association (CPA) received extensive technical and financial support from a range of outside agencies, and this has proven to be a critical factor for success. The facilitation given by outsiders was sensitive, skilled, and helped the community to pursue its vision over a period long enough to approach the set goals. The Makuleke leadership initiated extensive programs in leadership training, conservation management, hospitality and tourism training, and commercial skills. They also managed the conflicts that always arise in the course of implementing integrated conservation and development programs. In many cases, this mediation has been provided by some of the outside agencies. Finally, the Makuleke leadership has always recognized that theirs is a "living" program that requires constant change and adaptive management.

The State of South African Tourism

Along with the land restitution policy, the new government also embraced international tourism, including ecotourism, as a leading economic activity by which the country could jumpstart its economy and move from isolation into full integration in the world economy. Tourism was hailed as the "new gold," holding the potential to be "one of the largest contributors to the country's gross domestic product, without many of the negative environmental impacts of other industries."[19] The blueprint for building the new South Africa was, initially, the Reconstruction and Development Program (RDP), the ANC's election campaign platform. The RDP's basic strategy included "participation of communities in management and decision making in wildlife conservation and the related tourism benefits." Although the RDP has since become subsumed by other policies, its fundamental approach to dealing with wildlife conservation and related tourism benefits remains the same.

The task is enormous because during apartheid South Africa had been an international pariah. An ANC-led boycott called on multilateral institutions and foreign countries, companies, and individuals to withdraw businesses and investments from white-ruled South Africa; to stop sports, cultural, and educational contacts; and to forgo travel to South Africa. The impact was clearly seen in tourism. Although statistics from the World Tourism Organization purport that even at the height of apartheid, South Africa had more foreign visitors than did any other sub-Saharan African country, these figures are deceptive because they include visitors from other African countries, many of whom came for shopping, business, or work-related activities. For instance, of South Africa's 3 million foreign visitors in 1993, 2.4 million were from other African countries and only 618,508 were from non-African countries, primarily England and Germany. In fact, according to one study, "South Africa was a net exporter of tourism during the apartheid years. Earnings from foreign tourists were some 40 percent less than the amount spent by South Africans abroad."[20] Between 1980 and 1987, tourist arrivals in South Africa fluctuated between a low of 645,000 and peak of 792,000; with the end of apartheid, arrivals jumped 30 percent in 1994 and 42 percent in 1995. By 1996, arrivals totaled over 4.9 million (see table 9.1). South Africa was transformed almost overnight from an international outcast to a fascinating "rainbow nation."[21] Between 2001 and 2005, tourism grew an average of 6.2 percent a year; between 2004 and 2005, it jumped over 10 percent, exceeding the global average of 5.5 percent. Direct and indirect expenditures from tourism totaled R124 billion ($22 billion) or 8.15 percent of GDP, and the number of direct and indirect jobs from tourism was just over one million.[22]

Following the elimination of apartheid, South Africa's tourism attractions, including the nature-based facilities, have been opened and

Table 9.1.
South Africa's Tourism Growth

	1976	*1981*	*1984*	*1988*	*1990*	*1992*	*1994*	*1996*	*1997*	*2000*	*2005*
Arrivals from outside Africa (millions)	0.340	0.450	0.455	0.400	0.500	0.550	0.700	—	—	1.8	1.9
Total foreign arrivals (millions)	—	0.709	0.792	0.805	1.7	2.7	3.7	4.9	5.1	5.87	7.37
Earnings (in billions of U.S. Dollars)	—	0.658	0.610	0.673	0.992	1.3	1.42	1.74	2.2	2.5	8.4*

Sources: David Grossman and Eddie Koch, *Ecotourism Report—Nature Tourism in South Africa: Links with the Reconstruction and Development Program*, report prepared for SATOUR, August 1995, 16; Somerset Waters, *Travel Industry World Yearbook: The Big Picture, 1996–1997* (New York: Child & Waters, 1997), 139, 146; UN World Tourism Organization, *Yearbook of Tourism Statistics* (Madrid, Spain: UNWTO, 1995), 12, 13, 26, 27; UNWTO, *Yearbook of Tourism Statistics* (Madrid, Spain: UNWTO, 1986), 18; UNWTO, *Yearbook of Tourism Statistics* (Madrid, Spain: UNWTO, 1988), 19; for 2000 and 2005 statistics see South Africa Tourism website at www.southafrica.net/satourism/index.cfm (news releases, research & annual reports). * = Total foreign direct spending excluding capital expenditures. *Note*: Figures are unavailable where there are blanks.

diversified in terms of race, national origin, and, to a degree, class. South Africa's parks were officially opened to all races in the 1980s, but non-whites were accommodated in separate facilities from whites, to avoid, park officials contended, "incidents." A 1989 study found that even low-income blacks were entering the market, often as day visitors. A subsequent study found that following the April 1994 elections and declaration of affirmative action, "a black executive class, and with it a new leisure traveler, [was] being created overnight."[23] According to its 2005 annual report, SANParks has three primary tourism marketing objectives: to maintain its current market; to capture the disinterested market; and to attract the previously disallowed communities. In 2003, only 4 percent of the 3.4 million people who visited South Africa's National Parks were black. In 2005, this figure had leaped to 19.7 percent.[24] One innovative project has been to use a popular South African television soap opera, *Isidingo*, to promote national parks. Some scenes of the soap opera are being filmed in South Africa's National Parks, as part of a SANParks marketing strategy to showcase what the parks have to offer to all South Africans.[25]

Since 1996, the South Africa government has had a policy to promote "responsible tourism," which, put simply, is about providing better holiday experiences for guests and good business opportunities for tourism enterprises. Responsible tourism also strives to enable local communities to enjoy a better quality of life through increased socioeconomic benefits and improved natural resource management. As such, "responsible tourism" is compatible with the basic tenets of ecotourism. Jennifer Seif, executive director of Fair Trade in Tourism South Africa (FTTSA), an innovative certification program for tourism businesses in South Africa, contends that the responsible tourism sector is growing faster than the overall economy in South Africa. She worries, however, that the principles that should guide South Africa's tourism are not well known. "Everyone endorses responsible tourism, but not many groups understand it," says Seif. "The government just doesn't have the resources to fund it, and most of the private sector just doesn't get it."[26]

In the promotion of responsible tourism, as in all spheres of government, an important goal is black economic empowerment (BEE).[27] The Black Economic Empowerment Charter for the tourism industry (the Tourism Charter), issued in 2006, aims to address two main challenges: to become more globally competitive and to include black people in the tourism sector. The Tourism Charter has set a number of targets, including increasing the overall level of participation of black people among total staff and in management. The 2009 milestone is to have blacks represent 53 percent of total staff and 35 percent of management; and by 2014, the Charter aims to have blacks represent 75 percent of total staff and 50 percent of management.[28] The successful implementation of BEE principles and policies is key to building a less racially divided and more equitable South Africa.

Tourism Growth and Change in South African National Parks

Tourism to national parks in South Africa is over three-quarters of a century old and has long been regarded as a mechanism to ensure the continued existence of these conservation areas. Back in 1925, the warden of the Sabi Game Reserve (the southern portion of the area proclaimed as Kruger National Park in 1926), James Stevenson-Hamilton, noted that "without public support and revenue from visitors, the Park's future was severely limited, if not doomed." Since the Kruger National Park was opened to the public in 1927 when twenty-seven guests in three vehicles entered the gates, tourism figures have gone through various stages of growth. They reached a significant milestone between March 2002 and March 2003, when for the first time, over one million visitors were recorded within a twelve-month period.

Operation Prevail

Beginning in 2001, the South African National Parks began implementing an extensive restructuring plan, code-named "Operation Prevail" and designed to make it a more efficient and cost-effective organization. Its most obvious result was a downsizing of the workforce. In Kruger, for instance, Operation Prevail started with wide consultations among supervisory staff, senior managers, and the unions, and culminated in a comprehensive restructuring plan that declared "redundant" 663 positions in all sectors of the park administration. Overall, the restructuring led to a 26 percent reduction in SANPark's human resources cost.[29] By March 2005, the race and gender complexion of SANParks was dramatically transformed: 40.5 percent of employees at the top two occupational levels were nonwhite and 24 percent were female. Another objective was to transform SANParks into a learning organization that encourages employees to acquire new skills. In 2005, SANParks was offering professional training to 95 employees and 142 unemployed people from neighboring communities adjacent to the national parks.

Operation Prevail had its detractors. It was attacked by the white-dominated opposition party, the Democratic Alliance, which charged that there were gross irregularities in the management of Kruger. Criticism also came from many old conservation stalwarts, who felt that Operation Prevail was simply a mechanism to get rid of the white employees. However, most of the cutbacks were among lower and less-skilled employees and over 90 percent of those retrenched were black.[30]

Commercialization: Granting Concessions within the Parks

Until 2000, tourism infrastructure inside most of the country's national parks was developed, owned, and operated by South African National Parks (SANParks). At this time SANParks and some regional parks boards, including Gauteng, Limpopo, and Greater St. Lucia Wetland, embarked on a commercialization process that allowed park authorities to grant concessionaires rights for the use of defined areas of land and infrastructure within parks, coupled with the opportunity to build and operate tourism facilities over specific time periods.[31] Under this program, a wide range of nature-based tourism operations—including hotels, lodges, self-catering resorts, camping and caravan, and other accommodations, restaurants, museums, exhibition centers, and activities such as hiking trails, hot-air ballooning, water transport, and aerial walkways[32]—were to be sold to private operators. According to Annemie Van Jaarsveld, a SANParks official involved in the commercialization process, "A typical concession allows a private operator to construct and operate tourism facilities within a national park on the basis of a 20-year contract. Investors have either taken over or are upgrading specified existing lodge facilities, or they are in the process of building new ones. In most cases the concessionaire is granted exclusive commercial use rights to a defined area of land, typically between 5,000 hectares and 15,000 hectares within a national park in return for payment of concession fees. At the end of the contract term, all facilities revert to SANParks."[33] She adds that "the processes were designed to encourage partnerships that exhibited the correct mix of financial strength, requisite experience, and strong empowerment credentials. For the purpose of the concessioning program, economic empowerment comprised three principal elements: shareholding, affirmative action and training, and the economic empowerment of communities through the development of small, medium and micro-enterprises (SMMEs)."[34]

The major objectives of this program were to "invigorate the tourism sector"[35] through these public-private partnerships (PPPs), promote economic empowerment of the formerly disadvantaged, provide business opportunities to emerging entrepreneurs (in particular, local communities adjacent to national parks), and apply SANPark's environmental regulations and global parameters to all concessions.[36] In December 2000, seven accommodation concession contracts were negotiated in Kruger that guaranteed SANParks a minimum income of R202 million (about $26 million) over a twenty-year period. Three of the concessionaires were black-controlled consortia; and all of the others had significant percentages—on average 53 percent—of shareholding by historically disadvantaged individuals (HDIs).[37] By early 2005, the commercialization program had attracted over R250 million of capital investment in a network of new game lodges in Kruger and other national parks. Overall, the government had signed contracts for concessions valued at R8 billion 7 (about $1.2 billion) and "more than 50 further deals [were] in the pipeline."[38] According to one government study, South Africa's commercialization initiative was "one of the most advanced programmes in the world for using PPPs as a tool for economic growth and reconstruction."[39] Given the success of the program, the National Treasury appointed a taskforce in September 2004 to create a "Tourism Public Private Partnerships Toolkit" with practical guidelines "to make it easier for the private sector to enter into partnerships with government agencies in the area of nature tourism."[40]

Not all commercialization schemes proved successful. In some cases, there was little market interest, and some investors miscalculated demand while others were overly ambitious in their investments. In addition, although one aim of the program was to provide economic benefits to historically disadvantaged entrepreneurs, particularly those from local communities living adjacent to the parks, by the end of 2006, there were still no thorough studies analyzing if this had happened. The Toolkit study did identify "a number of cases where rural residents have been included as partners in the tourism enterprises" created through the commercialization process, and it found these "to be highly empowering models making a significant contribution to poverty alleviation and effectively allowing for the incorporation of the rural poor as active players in the nature tourism sector." While encouraging, the study also noted a number of problems including "a lack of clarity over who owns the land" in many rural areas, the need for communities to have access to "independent legal and technical support" in all stages of tourism partnerships, and the inability of local entrepreneurs to make any equity contributions and therefore the critical need for grant funding as "critical to these processes."[41]

Transfrontier Conservation Areas

In November 2000, the governments of South Africa, Mozambique, and Zimbabwe signed an agreement establishing the 99,800-square-kilometer Gaza-Kruger-Gonarezhou Transfrontier Conservation Area. This historic cross-border conservation area, popularly dubbed a "peace park," became the world's largest wildlife reserve. In South Africa, the press, major environmental organizations, development agencies, and private consultants and investors have enthusiastically welcomed cross-border parks as among the most promising experiments for protecting biodiversity, improving the quality of life for rural people by providing employment, and expanding nature-based tourism.

Following an end to the Renamo insurgency in the early 1990s and the country's first multiparty elections in late 1994, Mozambique, like

South Africa, begun to rebuild its war-torn economy. The advent of peace in southern Africa, together with economic collaboration between the region's countries via the Southern African Development Community (SADC), has stimulated moves to encourage cross-border tourism, including a proposal to introduce a single tourist visa for overseas visitors. Creating the cross-border park involved significant challenges, including the dismantling of an 80.5-kilometer (50-mile) electrified fence put up in the 1980s to stop Mozambicans from fleeing to South Africa. (The infamous "fence of fire" electrocuted and killed at least a hundred Mozambican refugees.) More fundamentally, the project involves building cooperation between once-hostile neighboring countries and between rural communities and park authorities.

Transfrontier Conservation Areas (TFCAs) or peace parks are relatively large areas, encompassing one or more protected areas, that straddle frontiers between two or more countries. In comparison to national parks, TFCAs have the potential to conserve a greater diversity of species within larger geographical areas and to promote cooperative wildlife management between nations. TFCAs may also improve tourism, allowing visitors to disperse over greater areas, obtain better-quality experiences, and view more diverse attractions.

Other peace parks have followed, yet despite their name, peace parks have stirred up their share of controversies and challenges. Unequal levels of tourist infrastructure and access to resources, as well as unequal power relations between South Africa and its lesser-developed neighbors make negotiations and agreements regarding revenue sharing and the functioning of TFCAs a tricky business. Other challenges include local community institutions that are too weak to successfully engage in negotiations and tourism development; overly optimistic expectations by communities; the perception that TFCAs are top-down creations driven by elites and dominated by South Africa; governance and security issues, such as social and political instability and corruption; the volatility of the international tourism market; and the impact on rural peoples who become dependent on tourism.[42]

Still, park officials and governments in southern Africa are optimistic that such international parks will bring benefits. South African president Thabo Mbeki, in reference to the establishment of the Great Limpopo Transfrontier Park, stated, "It serves to encourage us further to deepen the co-operation and partnership among our three countries. . . . This park is a tangible symbol that we can and must use sustainable development to confront the legacy of colonialism and apartheid, to eradicate poverty and underdevelopment and build a better world for all our people."[43]

The Seeds of Change within the Homelands

While the innovations in and around Kruger have been well documented, similar experiences are being played out all across South Africa, and the country today is a mosaic of ecotourism experimentation. According to many, the earliest experiments occurred, ironically, inside one of apartheid's most odious institutions: the Bantustans. Created in the 1960s and 1970s, South Africa's ten so-called independent tribal homelands were formed through the forced relocation of all Africans deemed, according to historian Allister Sparks, "surplus to the white man's needs in the city." [44] In all, some 17 million people—44 percent of South Africa's total population—were stripped of their South African citizenship and relocated in ethnic groupings on just 17 percent of the country's total land. The so-called independent government of each ethnic group received "foreign aid" from South Africa and was run by handpicked African collaborators. They were loathed by their African occupants and ridiculed by the world community. The homelands were a political charade and an economic disaster, constituting, as Eddie Koch put it, "overcrowded rural ghettos."[45] One of the Mandela government's first moves was to abolish the homelands and reintegrate these territories into the new South Africa.

It was, however, in two of these homelands—Bophuthatswana (commonly called "Bop"), a fragmented collection of seven impoverished Tswana territories near the border with Botswana, and KaNgwane, on the southern edge of Kruger—that South Africa's ecotourism formed its roots. In 1979, two years after the Bophuthatswana homeland was formed, its repressive figurehead president, Chief Lucas Mangope, announced that his "country" would promote conservation and tourism by establishing a 549-square-kilometer (212-square-mile) Pilanesberg National Park, a compact, biologically diverse stretch of volcanic hills and lush valleys. It was a massive operation for a poor state, and initially it followed South Africa's repressive formula for park creation. Thousands of subsistence cattle farmers, mostly BaKgatla people, members of a Tswana clan who opposed both the homeland and Chief Mangope, were moved out. Their homesteads were razed; alien plants were removed; water was brought in; camps, picnic sites, roads, and an educational center were constructed; and the boundary was fenced. With funding from WWF–South Africa, private companies, and the government, the park was restocked with indigenous wildlife. Only lions were not reintroduced at this time.

Today, the Bop park board's headquarters (its official post-apartheid name is the North West Park Board) in Pilanesberg National Park looks much like Kruger's—an attractive complex of offices located close to public recreational facilities, including restaurants and a bar, swimming pools, game rooms, chalets, a bird sanctuary, and beautifully planted and manicured lawns. In 1995, the official behind the large wooden park director's desk was Hector Magome, the park system's energetic and sharp-minded acting director, who has since moved high up the bureaucratic ladder to become the Director for Conservation Services for SANParks as a whole.[46]

Although Pilanesberg was one of the youngest of South Africa's parks, under Magome and his predecessors, it quickly gained a reputation as the most innovative and community-sensitive in the country. "The significance of the Pilanesberg project," wrote ecological consultant David Grossman and journalist Eddie Koch, "lies in the fact that it was the first attempt, at least in greater South Africa, at integrating protected area conservation and community development."[47] The reasons are several. Pilanesberg offered better salary packages and thus attracted better people. By the early 1980s, Pilanesberg's management included a handful of black officials as well as some renegade whites from the national park system who were chafing under its apartheid-driven rigidity. They found Pilanesberg smaller, more intimate, and more flexible, in part because it was set up as an autonomous homeland institution rather than as part of South Africa's civil service structure. From the outset, Pilanesberg instituted revenue-generating projects, including hunting safaris, something that infuriated the national park's old guard. One ethically dubious but lucrative scheme permitted big game hunters to shoot endangered white rhinos with tranquilizer dart guns and then have their photographs taken next to their sleeping "trophies."[48] The park also began promoting outdoor rock music concerts at one of its campsites. In a joint venture with a private company, the Pilanesberg board built two luxury lodges and formed its own commercial subsidiary to establish other park facilities. This venture in the early 1980s marked the first commercialization scheme in a park in South Africa.[49]

Although it was a pioneer in income-generating schemes, Pilanesberg, like South Africa's other parks, was running at a deficit, which was being covered by a government grant.[50] Now, like all parks in the new South Africa, Pilanesberg is under pressure to become increasingly self-supporting. Under the homeland government, the staff at Pilanesberg set low entrance fees, built a day-visitors' complex, set up programs for scholars, students, and teachers, and organized almost two hundred youth conservation clubs in the surrounding black communities, all of which made the park more accessible to the mass market and helped build a constituency supporting its survival. "The Parks Board was the only agent of the government from which people could get friendly services," says David Grossman. Pilanesberg's first director, Roger Collinson, moved over from the Natal Parks Board with, Magome says, "a personal vision long before the rest of the country that parks would do well if local blacks were involved." In the early 1980s, Collinson hired a British social anthropologist, Jeremy Keenan, to survey the surrounding communities to gauge their opinion of the park. Magome explains, Keenan found that "the BaKgatla people were pissed off with the park," just as park officials found a dozen years later was the case at Kruger. [51]

Over the next few years, Collinson and his successor, Levy "Rams" Rammutla (who, like Magome, is a Tswana speaker), instituted a variety of projects and, Magome says, "put us on the map in terms of progressive community projects." These included granting permission for local people to harvest firewood and medicinal plants and to visit ancestral grave sites in the park. By the mid-1990s, several hundred local people were working in the park or its hotels, and many senior positions were filled by Tswana people. (Most of the white employees held technical or scientific positions.) The park also trained local game guards and hunters, and several villages conducted commercial hunting on their own land. In addition, the Bop Park Board began dividing work projects, such as chalet construction, brick making, and road construction, into what Magome termed "chewable chunks" so that small local contractors, rather than big (white) firms, could get contracts. For each project, the park board hired a professional engineer to oversee the contract bidding and construction processes.

Most ambitious was the park's effort to address the BaKgatla's central and long-standing grievance: the fact that they had not received compensation for the loss of their land. In 1992, with the help of Alan Mountain, an environmental consultant hired by the park board, the BaKgatla set up a Community Development Organization (CDO), a legally constituted and democratically elected body to oversee community projects. The park board agreed to contribute to the CDO fund 10 percent of gate revenues, or about R50,000 (some $12,500 in 1998) annually, and to pay retroactively for all years since the forced removals. The CDO fund also began receiving a percentage of proceeds from concerts and hunting.

Although there was some grumbling that the community should be more directly involved in running it, Pilanesberg National Park has been solidly supported by those who live around it. Several surveys of the local communities and scientific studies in the early 1990s concluded that conservation, parks, and ecotourism were the most profitable use for this land. According to one survey, using 751 square kilometers (290 square miles) for cattle ranching would provide about eighty jobs at a cost of R150,000 ($37,500) per job, whereas wildlife-based tourism would create 1,200 jobs at a cost of R25,000 ($6,250) each. Although a Keenan survey in the 1980s revealed some hostility toward the park, in a 1993 survey of Pilanesberg's neighbors, more than 70 percent of those interviewed favored the continued existence of "their park." As Magome explained in the mid-1990s, "Two-thirds of the money generated by wildlife now goes directly to the community." Poaching, a bellwether of local attitudes toward parks, is very low at Pilanesberg.[52]

Sun City

Pilanesberg National Park's success and popularity are due not only to management foresight and community involvement but also to its strategic location relatively near to the Johannesburg-Pretoria axis and, most important, very close to another tourist magnet. Sun City (and the newer theme park, Lost City) is a vast and garish gambling and entertainment complex rising, Oz-like, out of the arid plain. It was built in the late 1970s by Sol Kerzner, owner of the South African resort chain Sun International (and later the hugely successful Atlantis pleasure palace in the Bahamas), in alliance with Chief Mangope, and has been marketed as a fantasy world next to a "real" African experience, the game park. Sun City is the first and most financially successful of a string of pleasure palaces put up in the homelands to circumvent the international cultural boycott against South Africa, as well as apartheid's own Calvinist restrictions on gambling and racial intermingling. It was christened by Frank Sinatra, and over the years a number of U.S. entertainers performed here under the fiction that Bophuthatswana was an independent country. Writer Allister Sparks describes how, during apartheid, South Africans flocked to Bop and the other "casino-state" homelands for "weekends of sensual permissiveness [including] roulette wheel and blackjack, porn movies, nude stage shows, and the opportunity for cross-colour dalliance."[53] Sun City's doors were always open to white and black, rich and poor. As one guidebook describes, with commendable honesty: "A common sight on the gaming machines is a poor black gambler throwing hard-earned money into the great Moloch with the fixed intensity of one who cannot afford to lose."[54]

As did Pilanesberg, Sun City began with the forced eviction of BaKgatla farmers, and from the outset relations between the community and this tinsel-and-glitz monstrosity were tense. Surrounded by water-starved, impoverished shanties, Sun City pipes in water for its golf courses, swimming pools, lawns, giant wave pool, and artificial rain forest. "It's a huge user of water, and in this area water is a huge issue. Bop's repressive government stilled protests," explains David Fig. Other than offering menial jobs, it wasn't until the twilight of apartheid that

Sun City began to make some overtures to the community. The issue was lions. Sun City's owners urged Pilanesberg's management to introduce lions—which had once lived in the area—into the park so Pilanesberg could be marketed as a Big Five park, in turn enhancing its draw and that of Sun City. Before making a decision, the park board insisted on canvassing the surrounding communities, since lions presented a threat to their livestock. After lengthy discussions, the board agreed to bring in lions if the area was securely fenced. Sun City's owners agreed to pay R10 million ($2.5 million) to obtain the lions, put up fencing, and finance their upkeep. The lion project has gone smoothly, and Sun City has subsequently assisted in several community projects including supplying the CDO with sewing machines and buying tablecloths and other linens from the women's cooperative. By 2001, it was estimated that 66 percent of permanent staff (2,012 employees) came from within twenty kilometers of the complex, representing 35 percent of Sun City's total wage bill of R234 million (about $23 million). Sun City was also purchasing 5.6 percent of its goods from within fifty kilometers, and 12.1 percent of services were being sourced from within fifty kilometers, with the bulk of expenditures on laundry and cleaning.[55]

Though many see Sun City as anathema to ecotourism, tourism expert Alan Mountain argues that there can be a "symbiosis" between the gambling casinos, the parks, and rural communities: the casinos are the magnet to attract masses of tourists, some of whom visit the park and help make ecotourism financially viable. "Although I personally find it repugnant," he said, "Sun City is the key to ecotourism. My analysis is that Sun City was by accident conceptually right, but its design was wrong because it does not interface with the community." He contends that if casinos are designed so that they are near game parks and are, for example, co-owned by the tribal authority or local community, they can provide revenues for both conservation and community development. And, Mountain proposed, casinos combined with conservation and ecotourism might offer a viable economic alternative to mining or other financially attractive but environmentally destructive industries: "You have to have ecotourism projects which match other forms of development. For conservation to survive, you have to fight fire with fire."

The Battle for St. Lucia: "Conservation Fight of the Century"

Nowhere has the contest between ecotourism and other forms of development been more evident than at St. Lucia Game Reserve, an extensive wetlands system that includes an 11.3-kilometer (7-mile) stretch of sand dunes along South Africa's northeastern coast, which has been the scene of the country's longest and biggest environmental protest. The dunes, 241.4 kilometers (150 miles) north of the port city of Durban in politically turbulent KwaZulu-Natal Province, form a vital barrier between the Indian Ocean and a beautiful and biologically unique estuary. This is the largest estuarine lake system in Africa and one of the world's great breeding grounds for birds and fish, as well as home of the largest concentration of hippos in southern Africa. Daily, this long body of water is criss-crossed by double-decker tour boats filled with camera-carrying vacationers out to spot hippos, crocodiles, and dozens of species of waterfowl. When I first visited St. Lucia in the mid-1990s, the tour guide standing beside me pointed to rolling green dunes in the distance, covered with some of the world's last remaining sand forests. He explained that these dunes are crucial to the life of the estuary, which depends on the shifting balance between seawater and freshwater, and, the guide said, they were endangered: a mining conglomerate, Richards Bay Minerals (RBM), had plans to strip-mine these dunes for titanium and other heavy metals, estimated to be worth about $1.5 to $3 billion.[56]

The dunes and estuary are part of a nature reserve, one of many parks and protected areas in Maputaland, as this coastal section of KwaZulu-Natal Province is known in the tourism trade. Under apartheid, the KwaZulu portions were a separate homeland, led by Chief Mangosuthu Buthelezi, head of the Inkatha Freedom Party and a leading rival of Nelson Mandela and the African National Congress (ANC). After Mandela's election, Buthelezi, a conservative tribalist, became the main holdout in reintegrating his Zulu homeland into the new South Africa.[57] Under apartheid, this region was a conservation patchwork, with two park authorities—the Natal Parks Board (NPB), created in 1895, and the KwaZulu Bureau of Natural Resources (later named the KwaZulu Department of Nature Conservation, or KDNC), established in 1982—dividing control of the protected areas and natural resources. The divisions followed apartheid's racial dictates, with the game parks in the white-ruled areas staying under the NPB's control and the Zulu, Thonga, and other African areas given to the KDNC. As a result, the two authorities were separate and unequal: the KDNC, the young stepchild of the NPB, was given the smaller, more remote, and less well-funded parks.[58] The Mandela government ordered that the two boards be merged into one park authority, a move welcomed in principle but disputed in its details.

The NPB's spectacular parks contain a wide range of facilities—bush lodges, rest camps, safari camps, resorts—with more rooms than any other park system in South Africa. Its annual budget for 1995 was R128 million ($32 million), of which only R50 million ($12.5 million) was earned through sales and culling of wildlife, entrance fees, accommodations, and its designer line of souvenirs. Government subsidies covered the bulk of expenses, some R80 million ($20 million), and despite pressure from the post-apartheid government to earn more, the NPB's chief executive, George Hughes, balked: "There's a bizarre belief that parks and tourism should pay for themselves and solve the problems of poverty. Tourism cannot be sold as a panacea for all ills. And we [the Natal Parks Board] should never become self-sufficient."[59]

Although Hughes claimed in a 1995 interview that "75 percent to 80 percent" of Natal Parks staff were black and further contended that "one-third of the money going into black communities adjacent to the parks is from ecotourism," he admitted that no blacks were holding top management positions: "We have no black executives and are unlikely to get any for many years. They need a lot of training and education." Hughes retired in about 2000, and by 2006 the picture had changed considerably: 80 percent of the top managers and 41 percent of the professionals in the KwaZulu-Natal parks system were black.[60]

The St. Lucia Game Reserve, on KwaZulu-Natal Province's northern coast, has long been, along with Kruger National Park, Cape Town, Sun City, and Durban, one of South Africa's most popular holiday destinations. The town of St. Lucia depends entirely on tourism. St. Lucia Game Reserve was set up in 1895 as part of the Natal Parks system and further expanded in 1939 to protect both the land and the water. However, in the 1950s, large swaths of coastal land on the edge of the park, including stretches of dune, were planted with nonindigenous pine, Australian eucalyptus, and casuarinas trees as part of an ill-conceived reforestation project by the state-owned pulp company. It was believed that this would stabilize the dunes, but instead the exotic species displaced other vegetation, wildlife, and birds. More of St. Lucia's conservation area was lost when the South African Defense Force took over a sizable chunk of land for a rocket-firing and testing range.

Then, beginning in the 1970s, South Africa's government granted prospecting leases for heavy-metal mining in the dunes and processing at the port town of Richards Bay, 24.1 kilometers (15 miles) south of St. Lucia. Even though in 1986 the St. Lucia system, including the eastern shore, was declared an internationally important wetland under the Ramsar Convention, the powerful conglomerate Richards Bay Minerals (a subsidiary of Rio Tinto Zinc and South Africa's Gencor) was, three years later, given rights to prospect (but not yet to mine) in these dunes. A year later, the Natal Parks Board formed the Greater St. Lucia Wetland Park, encompassing 2,800 square kilometers (1,081 square miles), including the dunes. It also announced plans to propose that this area be declared a United Nations World Heritage Site, something that could happen only if St. Lucia became a national rather than a provincial park. A mining operation would destroy any chance of having St. Lucia designated a World Heritage Site. Clearly, different government departments were working at cross-purposes, headed on a collision course in what was soon to be dubbed "the conservation fight of the century."[61]

Prior to this tug-of-war between mining and conservation interests, the local people had been forcibly removed from St. Lucia. Between 1950 and 1970, two large communities were evicted from the dunes. In the late 1970s, another 3,400 people were moved out so that the South African army could build a missile-testing site. (This area has since been turned into a game reserve.) Those displaced were forced to live as squatters in already-overcrowded KwaZulu townships. In response, some invaded Dukuduku State Forest, on the outskirts of the town of St. Lucia, where with the end of apartheid they began negotiating with the Natal Parks Board for the right to stay. These communities subsequently filed claims under the restitution program, demanding title to the land and its resources[62]—an option the mining company and the parks board both opposed.

But as apartheid neared its end, both Richards Bay Minerals (RBM) and the conservationists, feeling the winds of change, began wooing the local community. RBM spokesman Barry Clements claimed that if it was permitted to expand into St. Lucia, the company would create "at least 2,500 high-paying jobs" and would replant and rehabilitate the sand dunes, thereby benefiting both the local communities and conservation. RBM began donating to rural development projects and providing start-up money to some 1,500 small entrepreneurs. According to Clements, "This 'battle for St. Lucia' is the greatest hoax in the annals of conservation."[63]

Flanked against RBM was the Campaign to Save St. Lucia, a coalition of some two hundred largely white, middle-class environmental and conservation organizations that, together with the Natal Parks Board, argued that nature-based tourism was the more sustainable form of development for this delicate and beautiful area.[64] The coalition estimated that RBM mining in St. Lucia would create a mere 159 new jobs, and it pointed to the abysmal track record of RBM's multinational parent company, Rio Tinto Zinc, in other countries, where the company has been accused of engaging in price-fixing and union busting, buying politicians, and plundering the environment. It had not lived up to its promise to rehabilitate dunes at Richards Bay, where it was currently mining. Further, in St. Lucia, mining would disrupt water flows, and this could kill Lake St. Lucia and its surroundings. Opponents claimed that RBM could mine titanium elsewhere than the environmentally sensitive and unique St. Lucia dunes. In 1993, the Campaign to Save St. Lucia collected some three hundred thousand signatures, including Nelson Mandela's, on petitions to stop the mining.

Then, in December 1993, on the eve of the demise of apartheid, the conservation coalition won a stunning victory: a review panel, headed by a distinguished judge, concluded that mining would permanently damage the dunes. The panel ruled that the dislocated communities should be compensated for their lost land and that the Natal Parks Board should implement ecotourism schemes to both protect the ecology of St. Lucia and directly improve the livelihood of those who had lost their land. The review panel's ruling was based on the findings of a four-year environmental impact assessment by an independent parastatal research council. Although it was financed by RBM and other prodevelopment interests, the assessment was the most extensive ever undertaken in South Africa, and it concluded that "mining would cause unacceptable damage. The Greater St. Lucia area is a very special asset for the nation." The assessment also urged that the area be designated a World Heritage Site. Subsequently, experts contracted by the Ministry of Land Affairs to do a series of six studies also weighed in, even more convincingly, against mining and for ecotourism. As one argued, "The foregone tourist potential of St. Lucia . . . would have effects on the economy because fewer overseas tourists would come to South Africa."[65] These rulings placed the ball in the Natal Parks Board's (which changed its name in 1994 to Ezemvelo KZN Wildlife) court to prove that ecotourism could be an economically viable alternative to mining and could benefit the local communities.

Dukuduku One and Two

In March 1996, residents of the two communities in the forest outside St. Lucia, known as Dukuduku One and Two, were threatening to blockade the town over the Easter holiday to protest the government's failure to consult them before deciding against mining.[66] Both communities claimed to be the legitimate owners of the eastern shores, from which they were evicted in the 1950s when the area was declared a state forest. The traditional chief of one displaced group filed a land claim favoring mining, whereas a rival group demanded that its land be returned first before a decision was made about how it should be used.[67] Dukuduku One, an Inkatha Freedom Party stronghold, was made up of the poorest of the poor, who subsisted in the forest by growing bananas and sweet potatoes through slash-and-burn farming and "illegal" fishing in the St. Lucia estuary. Community members were skeptical of arguments that they should leave the forest so that it could be utilized for ecotourism. "The nature people are *izigebengu* [criminals]. They arrest us and they destroy our homes. They have destroyed the forest . . . to build their big homes. Now they say we are the ones who are destroying it. Yet we stay here because we like trees. We live in limbo. That is why we build with planks. We have no money and we may have to move at any time. But at least here we are independent," Dukuduku One elders told the *Weekly Mail & Guardian*.[68]

In contrast, residents of the other community, Dukuduku Two, had begun in small but concrete ways to see some tangible benefits from conservation and ecotourism and to receive some modest assistance from the government. The sprawling settlement was located along the paved road leading out of the honky-tonk resort town of St. Lucia. At the intersection of two muddy tracks stood a tiny wooden shack that served as headquarters of the Dukuduku Development and Tourism Association. The association's only staff member was Leslie Walters, a journalist-turned-community-organizer who had lived in the area for sixteen years and spoke Zulu. In a 1995 interview, Walters said she had first encountered the Dukuduku settlement eighteen months earlier when a massive fire drove the residents off parkland where they had been squatting. "I became part of the group looking for an alternative site, and when they were given a new site across the road, I moved across with them. I realized their need for a community-based organization."[69] She said that 95 percent of the estimated seven thousand Dukuduku residents were unemployed and 80 percent were illiterate, but they were fortunate in not being embroiled in the ANC-Inkatha conflicts and in being united under one capable *nduna* (headman), Caiphus Mkhwanazi. Walters, whose husband had been a ranger with the Natal Parks Board until his death in 1994, was working largely on a volunteer basis, assisting Mkhwanazi and the community in setting up income-generating, health, and educational projects and in negotiating with the NPB, the government, and the private sector. "From the beginning, they have talked about getting involved in ecotourism because this is such a popular tourist area," Walters said, adding that with majority rule this was becoming a reality. The Mandela government had promised the Dukuduku residents they would not be moved again and had begun providing proper housing sites and services such as electricity, roads, and water.

One of the Natal Parks Board's first concessions was to permit the Dukuduku residents and members of other local communities into the park to gather *incema* grass, used for making traditional Zulu baskets and sleeping mats. In late 1995, sales to tourists expanded greatly with the opening of a modern handicrafts center at the wharf on the estuary where tour boats dock. The park raised close to R90,000 ($22,500) to build the center, which was to be owned and run by Dukuduku women. Walters explained that not only was the center providing employment and income, but it was also helping to revive dying crafts such as carving, beadwork, and basketry. However, when I revisited St. Lucia in 2003, I found this lovely craft center closed, and it had apparently ceased to function. Dukuduku residents who attended a 2004 workshop on ecotourism reported that "markets in the area where women had previously sold their products were closed due to the conservation projects and now Dukuduku women don't have a place to sell their goods."[70]

In the mid-1995s, a number of Dukuduku men found employment in another project, making charcoal from exotic wood "harvested" from the sand dunes. The project involved the park, the community, and a local businessman, Mr. Sithole. The Dukuduku community had also requested permission to collect firewood inside the park. The park, in turn, wanted to get rid of the nonindigenous pines planted on the dunes. A scheme was worked out for Sithole to hire about thirty local men, who cut down the unwanted pine trees inside the park and turned them into charcoal. By the mid-1990s, the sound of a buzz saw led inside the park boundary to a dozen rubber-booted men felling pine trees.[71] The logs were hauled from the park to a large field, where a dozen or so old metal container boxes, left by ships in the port of Durban and donated to this project, sat in a row. When I visited the project site in 1995, gray smoke curled from basketball-sized holes cut in the sides and tops of the containers. The end of one container was open and a group of men was carefully loading it with tree trunks. Off to the side, several women were sorting, bagging, and weighing the finished charcoal, which was of exceptionally high grade and suitable for export. The workers received a salary, the community got free charcoal, and Sithole, who handled the charcoal sales, paid an additional R1,000 (US$250) per month into a community development fund.

In Dukuduku Two itself, Walters had helped start other projects, using funds she raised from the Natal Parks Board and private businesses. These included a preschool, a nutrition and growth monitoring program, sewing classes, community skills and tour-guide training courses, and a scheme to provide every household with a toilet. Next to the clinic, a small nursery grew medicinal plants. The Natal Parks Board had sent the local *nyanga* (medicine man) to Durban for training so that the clinic could offer patients both traditional and Western herbal treatments. There were plans to offer school groups and tourists guided tours in the park and the village to learn about medicinal plants. Walters was preparing three booklets for these tours, on Zulu culture, the fauna and flora of St. Lucia, and ecotourism, which, she explained, would "put across the principle that ecotourism can uplift the quality of life of the local people and the economy of the area."[72]

However, the battle for St. Lucia was not over. In late 1997, after most conservationists had retired from the fight, believing it had been won, the South African government announced it had withdrawn its application to make St. Lucia a World Heritage Site. The decision was prompted by officials of the UNESCO World Heritage Center, who believed that two other South African sites, Table Mountain and Robben Island, had better chances of approval. An ANC leader in KwaZulu-Natal Province declared that if tourism did not soon become a major force in job creation in the area, the option of mining might be reexamined, and rumors spread that RBM was dusting off its files in preparation for a new mining application. While the South African government had repeatedly stated that local communities must be part of this decision-making process, this setback raised suspicions among residents of both Dukuduku One and Two that they would never receive land, jobs, or other economic and social benefits from either the government or the tourist industry. As the *Weekly Mail & Guardian* warned, "Unless the strident calls for tourism job creation in the area are heeded, perhaps the only option, sadly, will be [the] short-term, vote-getting quick-fix of revenue and jobs from mining."[73]

Fortunately, the winds of change continued to blow over St. Lucia. In 1999, UNESCO did finally declare the Greater St. Lucia Wetland Park (GSLWP) as a World Heritage Site. The park is the largest estuarine system in Africa, consisting of thirteen contiguous protected areas, and it includes the southernmost extension of coral reefs on the continent. Tourism development is viewed as a mechanism for poverty alleviation of the region's 160,000 historically disadvantaged people. In addition to building eleven key access roads, creating a malaria-control program, and settling land claims on the eastern shores and in the Sodwana State Forest, the government began a crafts program to support two thousand artisans. The program began as a partnership between twenty-four small producer groups and a private retailer, Price Home, which was committed to eliminating middlemen and paying a fair price for high-quality woven baskets and other handicrafts. The GSLWP Authority has also helped incubate small tourism businesses.[74]

But despite these initiatives, some local concerns persist. In 2003, for instance, Dukuduku community members declared that while supporting the creation of the World Heritage Site, they continue to feel marginalized "in negotiations for benefits and decisions for the continued use of our land within the Greater St. Lucia Wetland Park."[75] A year later, an assessment of community conservation and ecotourism found a "lack of an inclusive consultative process involving adjacent and affected communities in the development and implementation of the World Heritage site submission" and a lack of involvement "in conservation and eco-tourism initiatives . . . in accordance with the principles of the World Heritage Convention. . . . " Further, while some residents were victorious in their restitution cases, other claims dragged on for years. In addition, the study found that the approach and strategy of the Commission on Restitution of Land Rights did not comply "with the restitution legislation, policy or implementation principles." This study concluded that despite the "high profile" battle to protect St. Lucia's wetlands and empower the Dukuduku forest communities through ecotourism, "there is a need to ensure that real economic opportunities are developed and implemented which are supportive of and sensitive to the livelihood strategies and needs of the residents of the forest."[76]

Tourism, only a portion of which qualifies as ecotourism, continues to be the main economic activity in St. Lucia. Currently, the area attracts approximately a half-million tourists per year, and has 11,200 beds, either privately or government owned. By 2010, projections are for an increase in tourist numbers to 1.4 million, the bed capacity reaching 18,700, and foreign currency earnings to R850 million (about $115 million) a year. With careful conservation and resource management, it is predicted that nine thousand temporary jobs will be created during the infrastructure development phase, and four thousand permanent jobs in the long term. Nonetheless, Steve Kotze, an academic who has worked with the GSLWP, worries about the "unrealized expectations" of communities surrounding the Park and wonders whether "the environmental lobby has harmed the credibility of ecotourism by opposing the mining option, but then failing to mobilize active support for sustainable development in the area with the same degree of passion and commitment. As a result," Kotze contends, "there is an argument to be made that local people might have been better off with the immediate financial benefits of mining."[77]

KwaZulu-Natal Province: Pioneering Joint Ventures with the Private Sector and Local Communities

Elsewhere in KwaZulu-Natal Province, a variety of ecotourism experiments involving rural villages and private investors have sprouted up. The KwaZulu Department of Nature Conservation (KDNC) was first set up in 1982 as the KwaZulu Homeland's Bureau of Natural Resources. In its first dozen years, it increased the amount of land under its control from a mere 0.5 percent to 2.5 percent of KwaZulu-Natal Province, including twelve parks, reserves, and protected areas. By 2007, KwaZulu-Natal had ninety-seven parks and reserves,[78] many of which are in the remote, inaccessible, heavily forested border region, and until recently they had little or no tourist facilities. As elsewhere in South Africa, these conservation areas were formed under apartheid through forced removals, so the KDNC has been deeply resented by the communities on the parks' peripheries. Just before the all-races elections in 1994, the KDNC announced it would no longer move people without obtaining their consent and providing compensation.[79]

In addition to the forced removals, the KDNC has been viewed with suspicion for another reason: many former Rhodesian military and intelligence officers joined its ranks, and the KDNC's longtime head, Nick Steele, was himself a former Rhodesian soldier (Steele died in 1996). In 1991, the *Weekly Mail & Guardian* reported that KwaZulu conservation authorities had operated a "secret services" division that spied on local political activists as well as ivory and rhino-horn smugglers.[80] On the other hand, the KDNC, unlike the Natal Parks Board, had from its outset a "policy of sharing" that included community profit-sharing programs and several ecotourism ventures. As Chief Mangosuthu Buthelezi stated in 1989, the Zulu homeland, like Bophuthatswana and other homelands, "has clearly understood that people must be the cornerstone of any conservation effort and that unless conservation is made relevant to ordinary people, it has no hope of gaining their support."[81] Since its inception, the KDNC has admitted local people into protected areas to collect, using traditional methods, wood, bark, reeds, and grasses; to visit ancestral graves; to fish in the Kosi Bay estuary; and to purchase low-priced meat from culling operations. The KDNC has also helped set up several community conservation areas on marginal land no longer suitable for cattle or agriculture as well as to start community game farms that raise wildlife for sale to zoos or other parks and run hunting safaris. As early as 1986, the KDNC included elected representatives of local communities or community liaison officers on their management committees. The department also initiated a scheme to give the three KwaZulu regional tribal authorities 25 percent of all the profits from culling, sale of wildlife, park entrance fees, and tourism-related facilities and services to use for "social upliftment" projects.

As the end of apartheid neared, it became clear that government funds for parks would be cut and the KDNC would have to raise more of its own budget through tourism-related projects. Unlike the Natal Parks Board, the younger and poorer KDNC had built only campsites and other self-catering facilities in its parks. It responded with an innovative scheme to bolster its tourism infrastructure by building hotels and lodges in partnership with private developers and the local community. It created a nonprofit tourism development trust company called Isivuno (Harvest), through which the department channels some of the revenue received from park entrance fees, culling, sale of wildlife, and tourism-related activities. Normally, these funds would be turned over to the general provincial coffers, but under this new plan, Isivuno, as the KDNC's commercial arm, was to invest a portion in new revenue-generating projects. The department identified thirty-five sites inside game parks and reserves on which tourist facilities—ranging in size from a 120-bed lodge to 8-bed luxury camps—would be developed.[82] This marks the first time in South Africa that local communities have been involved as partners with both the private sector and the parks in the ownership and management of hotels. After 1994, the KDNC and Natal Parks Board merged and officially became Ezemvelo KwaZulu-Natal Wildlife.

Wilderness Safaris

Isivuno's first two projects were in partnership with Wilderness Safaris, a South African company with a solid track record in nature tourism throughout southern Africa. (As discussed earlier, Wilderness Safaris subsequently partnered with the Makuleke in Kruger.) One of its early projects in KwaZulu-Natal Province was the Rocktail Bay Lodge, which consists of eleven wood-and-thatch A-frame chalets built on stilts under a forest canopy in the Maputaland Coastal Forest Reserve, adjacent to the Maputaland Marine Reserve and within the St. Lucia World Heritage Site.[83] A wooden walkway runs from the rustic, solar-powered lodge and over the tree-covered dunes to a magnificent, secluded stretch of the Indian Ocean, part of forty kilometers of unspoiled, undeveloped and pristine coastline. *Outside* magazine voted this one of the best beaches in the world and in 2005, rated a stay at Rocktail Lodge as one of the world's "best trips."[84] Due to its protected status, tourists need permits to enter, making this one of the most private beaches in South Africa where, during the summer months, loggerhead and leatherback turtles lay their eggs.

The second project was the Ndumo Wilderness Camp, built in a small reserve in northern KwaZulu Province, right on the border with Mozambique. First established in 1924 and acquired by the Natal Parks Board in 1954, the Ndumo Game Reserve was viewed with hostility by the surrounding Thonga people, who were moved out when the reserve was fenced. During Mozambique's long civil war, Ndumo and the tiny neighboring Tembe Game Reserve had been abused by poachers, refugees, Renamo rebels, and smugglers. In 1989, Ndumo and many other areas were taken over by the KDNC. Conservation authorities long wanted to consolidate the two reserves so that elephants from Tembe could have access to the abundant water in Ndumo's twin rivers. But the 150 families living in the corridor resisted, resenting the fact that they had been forcibly removed from Ndumo and denied access to water within the reserve. In the mid-1990s, the villagers, with the assistance of rural development workers, struck a deal whereby they agreed to move farther south in return for access to a corner of Ndumo, where the Pongolo River flows.

With the 1990 Mozambique peace accord, tourism in this border region again became possible. Ndumo was considered by many to be South Africa's finest bird-watching location, containing more than four hundred species, or 60 percent of South Africa's birds, and the reserve's two wide, shallow rivers (known as pans) and its floodplains attract waterfowl, hippos, and crocodiles. Browsing among the acacia, wild fig, and fever tree forest were black and white rhinos, blue wildebeests, red duikers, giraffes, suni antelopes, and other wildlife.

As apartheid ended, Isivuno obtained a ninety-nine-year lease from the government for the Ndumo and Rocktail Bay lodge sites. Isivuno then subleased the sites to a lodge operating company for an initial twenty-year period. Rocktail Bay Lodge opened in February 1992 with a complex legal structure in which Wilderness Safaris apparently has no ownership[85] but a controlling interest in management, while the community has a minority interest in ownership and management.[86] In March 1995, Ndumo Wilderness Camp opened, with joint ownership by Isivuno and Wilderness Safaris and joint management by these two plus the local community. The camp's eight luxurious, solar-powered tents were built on raised wooden decks interlinked with walkways made from old railroad ties and overlooking a bend in the broad Banzi Pan.

In both projects, a trust was formed to represent the community interests, and profits were to be distributed by the trustees. A study of these two ecotourism experiments concluded that they were "implicitly pro-poor" and as such were "quite different from standard practice," which was to build a private lodge on private land or within a game reserve.[87] While the legal arrangements ensured the community received a portion of profits through its ownership and management shares, by 2001, neither lodge had produced a profit. Instead, the community benefits came through employment, job training, purchase of local goods and services, and a gradual increase in community shares in the partnership.

At Ndumo, for instance, the community opened a caravan park on the edge of the reserve and rented the lodge space for a laundry and parking lot. But despite its promising start, the lodge at Ndumo struggled. It was remote, did not receive cooperation from the conservation authority, and was not aggressively marketed within the Wilderness Safaris portfolio. In 2004, after operating irregularly, it finally closed permanently. Its demise was due to a combination of factors including low occupancy, competition from more accessible and better-marketed properties like Phinda, and its specialized "product"—bird life and lagoons—rather than the more popular Big Five game.[88] In an interview, Wilderness Safaris officials lamented "Everything that could go wrong, went wrong." They said that Wilderness Safaris lost R5 million (about $860,000) on the Ndumo project, and the staff lost their employment.[89] Ndumo's neighbor, the Tembe Elephant National Park, which is part of the KwaZulu-Natal National Parks, has, fortunately, fared better. Its attractions—the largest African elephants in the world—and a well-run private luxury tented camp with strong local leadership and effective community outreach programs have made Tembe a popular destination for both national and international visitors.

The results at Wilderness Safaris' other community experiment, Rocktail Bay, have also been better. The 1,500 members of the Mqobela community live on communal land adjacent to the lodge in a traditional authority ward administered by the Tembe Tribal Authority. The salaries of the 32 Mqobela employed directly by Rocktail Bay Lodge are estimated to support some 170 people indirectly. Communal income is supposed to be generated through the lodge owning company (in which the community owns a 14.5 percent share) and the lodge management company (in which the community owns a 12.5 percent share). The community participates in decision-making through the trust, which elects two rotating members to serve as directors in the development company. The community receives R2500 (about $35) per month in rent, plus 5 percent of the turnover of the lodge, and a percentage of the profit based on its ownership share. However, given the cost of running Rocktail, a profit dividend has rarely if ever been paid.[90] Instead, benefits come from other tourism-related goods and services including community cultural tours, choirs and dance troupes, traditional cuisine, and a local taxi company. Wilderness Safaris and the community also work together on mitigating environmental impacts, including a beach-cleaning initiative and providing beach access to local villagers.

Many community and conservation projects are financed through the Wilderness Safaris Wildlife Trust, which was created in the early 1990s as an independent trust fund. As its Web site explains, "A portion of each Wilderness Safaris guest's fare is allocated to the Trust, and 100 percent of these funds go to Trust-approved projects. The projects deal with the needs of existing wildlife populations, seek solutions to save endangered species and provide education and training for local people and their communities,"[91] including schools, scholarships and training, and wildlife protection of leatherback turtles and other endangered animals. Wilderness Safaris has learned that this type of Travelers' Philanthropy must be controlled and regularized. In the past, lodge guests would sometimes give money or gifts to community members they met, and this caused imbalances in terms of who was benefiting. Now the lodge has a collection box so that guests can make donations that go to the trust for equitable and transparent distribution. Sometimes guests send books or school supplies, which are distributed at the school. However, the partnership with Wilderness had not, as of 2005, brought the Mqobela community what it said it wanted most: electricity.[92]

The considerable success of Rocktail Bay is linked to Wilderness Safaris' extensive community development programs, its partnership model, the widespread recognition and number of awards Rocktail Bay has received,[93] and its generally high occupancy.[94] Wilderness Safaris is developing, in partnership with the nearby Mpukane community, a new diving lodge near Rocktail, and has plans to expand to other sites in the Greater St. Lucia Wetlands Park, where it plans to replicate the community involvement model.[95] James Ramsay, Managing Director of Wilderness Safaris' South African lodges, explained that Rocktail Bay has been successful in part because it involved the community from the beginning, invested in well-trained local guides (a hallmark of the Wilderness Safaris model elsewhere in southern Africa), and secured longer-than-usual tenure terms for the land, making it possible to invest more capital in projects. "We've evolved our own model of low-volume, high-value tourism. We're a business at the end of the day and must respond to market forces. However, the senior management is very conservation focused, even if they won't admit it. Still, the business needs to be successful to accomplish the conservation goals they have. It needs to be innovative," stated Ramsay.[96]

Conservation Corporation of Africa

It is Conservation Corporation of Africa (also known as Concord or CC Africa) that has earned the mantle as the best-known early example of Travelers' Philanthropy in South Africa. A visit to Londolozi and Phinda, two of CC Africa's five lodges in South Africa, shows how the company combines luxury ecotourism with a range of programs to benefit its employees and the wider community. Londolozi is one of a handful of private resorts located in Sabi Sands, which is 646 square kilometers (250 square miles) of bushveld (arid scrub brush) private reserves and is situated between two rivers on the western border of Kruger. Londolozi is aesthetically beautiful and bucolic, with whitewashed rondavels, brick-lined walkways, lush green shrubs, arching trees, and splashes of colorful hibiscus and bougainvillea. The dining area is on a wide wooden deck overlooking trees and bushes alive with baboons, elephants, buffalo, and other wildlife.

A short distance behind this restful setting, tucked out of view of the guests, is a small town of 230 people, 150 of whom work for Londolozi. This is Londolozi's most important contribution to ecotourism. Here, the whitewashed rondavels where staff members and some of their families live are painted with bright pictures signifying the occupants' work—a car for a driver, wine bottles and glasses for a bartender, animals for a tracker. There is an open-sided community center with a large television set and games, a restaurant selling hamburgers and other fast-food items as well as traditional African dishes, a store, a laundry, a library, a health clinic, a preschool, an adult literacy program, skill training classes, and an interracial primary school, all begun before apartheid ended. There are also workshops where people weave grass mats; sew napkins, tablecloths, and uniforms; and make paper, bricks, clay pots, and drums. Paper, cans, and glass are recycled, food scraps are composted and used on vegetable gardens, and water is recycled. Beginning in the early 1990s, Londolozi also employed a full-time community liaison person to work with Gazankulu, a sprawling city of 250,000 on the edge of this private reserve, where other family members live.

"Our motto," said Londolozi's managing director, Ronnie McKilvey, in an interview in the mid-1990s, "is care of the land, care of the wildlife, care of the people. We encourage training and small-business development and we provide seed capital and low-interest loans. Our philosophy is 'don't give a man a fish; teach him to fish.' We don't believe in aid: it's a black hole, and patronizing," he contended.[97] People pay (modestly) for services, including health care and literacy and training courses; they also receive dividends from the communally owned village store. Employees can take out small personal loans but must pay them back by the end of the month, with 10 percent interest. The profits on these loans go to the community and have been used, for instance, to build the preschool. The Londolozi "experiment," begun in 1987, was the company's first, and McKilvey candidly admitted, "We've developed with a lot of trial and error. There's not a blueprint, and we've made mistakes."

When Londolozi began, the term ecotourism was unknown in apartheid South Africa. In the late 1970s, two brothers, David and John Varty, decided to turn their family hunting and vacation lodge into a wildlife tourism lodge. David Varty, who was director of CC Africa until 2001, explained that, "From the outset, we have described ourselves as conservation developers. We use international tourism, primarily low-density, high-priced tourism, to attract the discerning international traveler to remote parts of Africa. In so doing, we create an economic 'exciter' in the region and bring in investment for self-funding conservation efforts and small businesses." He added, "We created Londolozi as a model not because we're good guys. We know if we want to stay in tourism, we have to have friendly neighbors."[98]

In 1989, Varty teamed up with Alan Bernstein, a wealthy white South African who was managing director of a company focused on attracting international investment to sub-Saharan Africa. They set up CC Africa and began seeking "international investors and more land." Bernstein displayed a tremendous talent for attracting financing, even into white-ruled South Africa. By 1990–1991, CC Africa had secured the first substantial new international investment in wildlife tourism in rural South Africa in some eight years, despite the intense civil war and international economic boycott against apartheid.

With the end of apartheid, CC Africa rapidly expanded. By 2007, it had grown from five properties in South Africa to over forty safari camps and wilderness lodges, and operates in sixteen African countries.[99] Its latest expansion is a joint venture with Taj Hotels Resorts and Palaces to offer high-end wildlife safaris in India. Ecotourism expert Costas Christ, who has worked for CC Africa, describes the company's mercurial rise as "a Ben & Jerry kind of story. The Vartys were not rolling in dough. But they and their partners were enlightened whites, all guys in the progressive political and business circles under apartheid. They were young idealists who wanted to do good for the world, and they thought they could do it through business." When Nelson Mandela was released from prison, he went to Londolozi to recoup, praising the village as an example of the type of rural development the new South Africa must pursue.

In southern Africa, CC Africa has been the pioneer in financing its community outreach through a separate trust fund. It does not earmark a portion of its tourism profits for its community projects, other than to pay the salaries of its community liaison workers. Instead, it set out to raise community development funds separately, mainly from international donations and to some extent through contributions from its guests. In their ecotourism study, David Grossman and Eddie Koch explain that in the initial period, "[CC Africa's] main vehicle for promoting development [was] the Rural Investment Fund [now the Africa Foundation]. This was established to channel capital, obtained from outside funding and donor agencies, into community development programmes that surround the core tourism projects. This institution is designed to spread the benefits of the tourism enterprise, primarily through the mobilization of external funds rather than the redistribution of company profits."[100] A flowchart of CC Africa's "model of conservation development" designed by David Varty graphically illustrates the financial flow. It shows no funds flowing from the corporation's tourism profits into community projects. Rather, the Rural Investment Fund is the source, with its funds flowing first into "sustained resource utilization," "employment and training," "education and health," and "small business opportunities," then upward into "maintenance of biodiversity," "development of local economies," and so forth, all of which ultimately flow into and support "game reserve and tourism facilities." In essence, CC Africa envisions rural development projects bolstering its core tourism enterprises, not vice versa.

Whereas at Londolozi the emphasis has been on improving the lot of the African staff members and their families, at Phinda, another of CC Africa's five South African lodges, social programs are primarily geared toward the surrounding communities. Located in KwaZulu-Natal Province on more than 22,000 hectares (54,500 acres) of agriculturally denuded land bought from ten white farmers, Phinda, which opened in 1994, has six stunning and distinct lodges, including the Rock Lodge consisting of six stone and adobe rondavel suites and the Forest Lodge, comprising sixteen luxury suites raised on stilts and encased in glass.[101] CC Africa "really cut its teeth on Phinda. It's the company's most cherished baby," says Costas Christ. "With time and care, it has become a model of ecotourism." Environmentally, Phinda represents the largest land restoration project in South Africa. The reserve has been restocked with wildlife and the bush has been thinned to restore open woodland and enhance game viewing. This has also provided opportunities, as in St. Lucia, for small local entrepreneurs to manufacture and sell charcoal from the cleared wood. Phinda's lodges make extensive (although not exclusive) use of solar power, recycle bottles and cans, and compost organic waste.

But it is in the three extremely poor communities surrounding Phinda—Mnqobokazi, Mduku, and Nibela, with a combined population of about forty thousand—where the corporation's community effects have been the most extensive. In 1992, the Rural Investment Fund received a sizable anonymous donation to set up the Phinda Community Development Trust Fund, and by 1995, some $625,000 had been raised. CC Africa committed two staff members to engage in community development and also provided vehicles, a telephone, fax machines, and other office equipment. "Part of the challenge is [finding] how to link First World funding agencies with Third World communities. In that process, we operate like an NGO," explained Les Carlisle, then regional development manager for Phinda and currently CC Africa Group Conservation Manager. He explained that at Phinda, the CC Africa's investment in staff housing has been far less than at Londolozi. The company's investment in the lodges and the reserve has been "incredibly high," said Carlisle, and what got "cut" was staff housing.[102] Phinda does employ several hundred staff from the surrounding community and runs a three-month training course for prospective employees.

In 1994, CC Africa hired Issac Tembe, who has a background in community development and comes from Kwa Zulu Natal province, to oversee its projects in the three neighboring communities. By 2003, the trust funds had raised R6 million (about $690,000) over the previous decade, which had been used to build forty-six classrooms and three libraries at a half dozen schools; set up eighteen preschools, a health clinic, and an environmental education center; and provide skills training and adult literacy classes.[103] They have also paid for boreholes, water pumps, and fences and helped to finance small industries such as brick making. The villagers in turn provide the labor for projects, and parents pay about one dollar per month to send a child to preschools supported by Phinda. In 2004, CC Africa hired Bheki Ntuli, a passionate and energetic young man, to work with Tembe on community outreach and to take guests to see the schools, clinics, and other projects. Ntuli said that most funds from guests are earmarked for specific projects, such as sponsoring a child's education or building a classroom.[104]

In a December 2004 interview, Magdelle Dempers, the general manager of Phinda's lodges, reflected, "What Phinda does is simply give these guys a chance. That's all they need, is a chance." She recounted how several of the employees moved up in the ranks within Phinda, including one who went from mending game fences to becoming a tracker to eventually becoming the executive chef at Mountain Lodge. Around 80 percent of Phinda's permanent staff come from local communities, and they receive over 70 percent of the entire wage bill.

Dempers also spoke about the often taboo topic of AIDS. She recalled that at the hotel she had worked at in Cape Town, there was not even a poster about AIDS prevention. In contrast, at Phinda and other CC Africa properties, CC Africa is supporting programs within the local schools targeting the children. "It is too late for many of the adults," she says, "but we can still educate the children." According to Les Carlisle, this AIDS prevention work has been very challenging. "CC Africa has put years and years of training and money into AIDS prevention, only to discover that many of the trained educators have AIDS themselves, and often die, thus taking years of training along with them," he recounted.[105] By 2007, Phinda was readying for a new community-based tourism enterprise. Under an amicable land claims agreement, sixteen thousand hectares (sixty-one square miles) of the reserve will be transferred to the local community, and then CC Africa will lease the land back from them. This will provide a significant and reliable source of income for the community that will help, Carlisle said, to reduce poverty in the area.[106]

In 1992, CC Africa created the Africa Foundation, which includes the Phinda Community Trust Fund and the RIF, and today serves as the umbrella organization for community projects at all the company's lodges in southern and eastern Africa. Each lodge has a development officer responsible for community programs under the Africa Foundation. The foundation's mission is to help empower communities through conservation, and it focuses on three main projects areas: education, income generation, and health. Under education, the foundation provides infrastructural support to schools, conducts conservation lessons for rural children, and gives educational scholarships. Its health projects include building primary health care facilities, providing access to water, assisting development of vegetable gardens, and conducting HIV/AIDS training courses and awareness, with a focus on children. Its income-generation activities include small business training courses, support for women's markets, and assistance with training and production centers. Community groups can apply for funds by writing a proposal outlining their needs. After a project has been implemented, Africa Foundation writes up a report, and sends it back to the donor to show how the money was spent. African Foundation partners with a wide variety of South African corporations and with the South African government. However, so far no other tourism companies use the Africa Foundation to channel donations from tourists back to communities. Africa Foundation's annual budget is about $1 million, and it takes 10 percent for overhead costs.[107] Since its inception, the Africa Foundation has raised and committed approximately $5.5 million to consultative community development projects in six African countries.[108]

Although Les Carlisle contends that CC Africa has "developed a model that's exportable," the corporation has in fact had difficulties reproducing its Phinda model in eastern Africa and Zimbabwe. At a number of its properties outside South Africa, CC Africa opted, at least initially, for luxury nature tourism without significant community outreach or a consistent commitment to environmentally sensitive practices (see chapters 6, 7, and 8). The corporation has been constrained by a number of factors. In some cases, it has bought existing properties; in others, it leases rather than owns the land; some of the staff it has hired are not imbued with CC Africa's commitment to community development; and it is operating on foreign and unfamiliar turf, where it may have little political clout or know-how.

Growth of Travelers' Philanthropy

While Wilderness Safaris and CC Africa were among South Africa's ecotourism pioneers in providing tangible benefits to host communities, today a growing number of South African tourism companies are involved in what is known globally as the Travelers' Philanthropy movement. They include other high-end lodges such as Sabi Sabi and Bushman's Kloof (see below), as well as more moderately priced companies. One is Calabash Lodge and Tours in Port Elizabeth, which has a small three-star guest house and runs "Real City" and "Shebeen" tours where visitors get an overview of the city's social history, meet local people, and enjoy African music and dance. It is a founding member of the Calabash Trust, an NGO founded in 1999 to make tourism work for disadvantaged communities within Port Elizabeth. The Trust is run by two permanent staff and a host of volunteers who implement projects funded by donations from Calabash clients. Much of this money is raised through child sponsorship programs or donations from individuals and companies. The trust has focused on supporting primary education (school fees, furniture, and books for schools), youth development, and community health and nutrition schemes in townships visited by Calabash tours, including New Brighton and Red Location.[109] Calabash works closely with Thompsons, a large tour operator in South Africa. When Thompsons sends their passengers on Calabash's township tours, they pay the trust a percentage, or a price per head.[110] The Calabash Trust supports many programs in nearby townships that benefit children and youth, including an education trust, food provision and a nutritional scheme, youth groups, cultural exchange, HIV/AIDS home-based care, and school furniture provision.[111]

The Grootbos Private Nature Reserve[112] is an example of a project that links poor communities to conservation. The reserve conserves 1,700 hectares of pristine fynbos, milkwood trees, and ancient tropical rain forests, plus more than 650 protean species of indigenous plants and abundant bird life. Activities include viewing tidal pools and coastal caves, horse riding, wild-herb spotting, and whale, shark, and

Cape fur seal viewing. Grootbos has two distinct lodges, one catering to families and the other, more contemporary and modern, appealing to the cosmopolitan travelers. Grootbos also runs Green Futures College,[113] a unique-skills development school that provides training to unemployed youths from nearby communities. The program gives young people knowledge and practical skills around conservation, fynbos landscaping, horticulture, and ecotourism. Linked to the college is an indigenous plant nursery and fynbos landscaping business that generates income for the foundation. In this way, each year students are growing plants and working in landscaping projects that will help to pay for the next year's students' tuition. Grootbos has demonstrated that fairness, ethical business practices, and environmental respect form the basis for sustainable tourism.[114]

Certification: Fair Trade in Tourism South Africa

In the new South Africa, a number of factors and actors have combined to support creative experiments in ecotourism. These include cohesive and vocal rural communities with clear sets of demands, strong leadership, and political skills learned through the struggle against apartheid. The local press has helped to expose the conditions of rural poverty on the perimeters of game parks and reserves and has brought these struggles to national attention. Many environmental groups and activists, as well as policy groups and private consultants, have lent their expertise to assist rural communities and promote ecotourism projects as alternatives to both protectionist conservation practices and more destructive economic activities. Since 1994, successive South African governments have strongly endorsed ecotourism as fitting with development strategies and have devoted government resources and personnel to facilitate ecotourism experiments and promote South Africa internationally.

Yet in South Africa, as elsewhere, some entrepreneurs, conservation organizations, and consultants are using the "ecotourism" label to promote ventures that are not environmentally sustainable, culturally sensitive, or economically beneficial to local communities. As elsewhere, one of the challenges in South Africa has been how to set criteria for ensuring that ecotourism adheres to certain standards, including meeting the standards set by the government. Voluntary, third-party certification programs can provide an answer, and South Africa now has two major tourism certification programs. South Africa's Tourism Grading Council (TGCSA) is a quality-assurance certification program awarding one to five stars based on internationally accepted criteria regarding facilities, amenities, and service. In an effort to measure the social impacts of tourism businesses, a new certification program, Fair Trade in Tourism South Africa (FTTSA) was launched in 2002 as an initiative of IUCN (the World Conservation Union). "In contrast with TGCSA, FTTSA's criteria have a socio-economic focus. The two systems thus provide complementary information for guests" and most FTTSA certified businesses are also star-graded, according to the FTTSA Web site.[115]

FTTSA is an independent NGO aligned with the international fair trade movement, whose mission "is to facilitate the integration of Fair Trade in Tourism principles and criteria into South African tourism so that the industry is more sustainable."[116] FTTSA is the world's first fair trade program developed for tourism. It builds on the success of fair trade initiatives for other commodities such as tea, coffee, wine, and chocolate. By January 2007, FTTSA had certified twenty-one tourism enterprises in South Africa, including accommodations (game lodges, bush camps, guest houses, hotels, and homestays), tourism attractions (museums and places of interest), and tourism activities (adventure tourism, whale-watching, golf products, and township tours). By comparison, TGCSA, which was launched in 2000 and is compatible with other five-star programs around the world, has been far more successful, certifying an estimated three-quarters of South Africa's "accommodation rooms," according to its Web site.[117]

FTTSA assesses tourism businesses based on criteria that fall under six broad principles: fair share, democracy, respect, reliability, transparency, and sustainability. Under these principles are some 363 quantifiable criteria that emphasize fair wages and working conditions, including profit sharing, transparency in contracts, fair distribution of benefits, ethical business practices, protection of children and young workers, gender equality, understanding and tolerating sociocultural norms, and HIV/AIDS awareness. The criteria also seek to ensure that both hosts and visitors respect human rights, culture, and the environment, and that the tourism products and services are reliable, operate safely and securely, and provide good value for money. In addition, all businesses must be compliant with the Employment Equity Act, which promotes affirmative action in training and hiring. Unlike other ecotourism and sustainable tourism certification programs elsewhere, FTTSA is not heavily focused on criteria to measure environmental performance and impact. In addition, it is a single-level pass-fail system, rather than a graded or tiered program that can encourage continual improvement as businesses seek recertification in order to earn a higher rating. FTTSA does, however, provide confidential feedback to all applicants and works with them to identify areas where improvements are needed in order to qualify for recertification.

The FTTSA certification process takes about three months. Applicants first complete a questionnaire that is reviewed by an independent panel. Then a trained consultant conducts an on-site evaluation, which takes from one to three days, depending on the size and complexity of the business. The assessor's report is reviewed by a three-person panel that decides whether or not the company has passed. The exact standards used to award certification are, however, a "closely guarded secret."[118] Successful applicants can use the FTTSA logo and receive various marketing and promotional benefits. They must submit a new paper audit after twelve months and then undergo another on-site inspection after twenty-four months. All applicants receive feedback, and those that are certified also agree to certain targets designed to improve performance. Applicants pay an annual user's fee, calculated on a sliding scale linked to a business's size and rates.[119]

FTTSA monitors its own performance by collecting monthly M&E (monitoring and evaluation) information, conducting bi-annual client satisfaction surveys, commissioning independent research, and undertaking an annual brand awareness survey at the Tourism Indaba. FTTSA executive director Jennifer Seif says that the certification program's "major obstacle to success is funding," most of which comes from grants from international organizations. FTTSA's operating budget is about R3 million (about $400,000) a year, "but we could do a lot more if we had some more money," says Seif. The FTTSA Web site lists other challenges, including the fact that FTTSA is "working with pioneering concepts and systems" that are unfamiliar to many South Africans and that the application and assessment process requires companies to commit considerable time and resources. The national Tourism Enterprise Program can provide a 50 percent subsidy to small businesses.[120] Another challenge is that several of the best-known ecotourism companies, including Wilderness Safaris and CC Africa, have been unwilling to be certified by FTTSA because they already have a strong brand and a solid portfolio of exclusive properties. They fear their reputation could be watered down if they are ranked together with a range of other accommodations.[121]

Sabi Sabi: Shoring up Its Ecotourism Principles and Practices

Sabi Sabi Game Lodge, a luxury safari lodge located in Sabi Sand reserve on the western boarder of Kruger, is among those certified by

FTTSA. In the 1990s, the lodge had somewhat fallen from grace in terms of its ecotourism reputation.[122] Established in 1980, Sabi Sabi is owned by Hilton Loon, a self-made businessman, and a group of other white South Africans, including several of the country's leading environmentalists. During the tumultuous years of international sanctions and internal resistance to apartheid, Loon recalls that "a game lodge was not a profitable enterprise so we became involved only as a result of our love of the bushveld. During the entire 1980s my other successful commercial business subsidised the losses of Sabi Sabi." He adds, "Only after apartheid ended in 1994 did game lodges become a thriving business."[123]

To the casual observer, Sabi Sabi seems a fine example of competent and carefully run ecotourism. The setting is lovely, the attention to guests beyond compare, and the game viewing, including walking safaris, night rides, and off-the-road drives to track the Big Five, wild dogs, and cheetahs, is superb. In the late 1990s, when I took a close look at Sabi Sabi, I encountered a range of complaints about management's relations with both staff and the neighboring community. I had concluded then that it was an example of ecotourism lite because it fell short in several key areas of the principles and practices of sound ecotourism. This might not have mattered except that Sabi Sabi representatives had been taking part in ecotourism conferences worldwide and portraying the lodge as South Africa's premier upmarket ecotourism destination.

However, since 1999, new management has worked hard to turn around its reputation and, more importantly, its practices. So now, fortunately, a different story can be told. In recent years, Sabi Sabi has received a number of sustainable tourism awards including the Imvelo Responsible Tourism Award in 2002 and designation as one of fifty international "hot spots" by *Condé Nast Traveler* in 2003.[124] But its FTTSA certification in 2004 has provided the most rigorous, independent confirmation of significant change, "a new wave" as general manager Patrick Shorten puts it. That year, Sabi Sabi became the first game lodge in South Africa to be certified by the FTTSA. Shorten explained that the FTTSA auditors "came on-site for several days to do a comprehensive audit. They focused on aspects such as the treatment of staff and community involvement." He added, "We believed we were doing things right," but since FTTSA is "a very sought-after certification, we thought it might give us an edge over the competition, especially for 'eco-minded' people."[125] The FTTSA report based on the audit states that "Sabi Sabi game rangers and Shangaan trackers are acknowledged as the best and most highly trained in the region. Under their guidance, game viewing has earned the reserve worldwide acclaim." It states further that Sabi Sabi's "management actively promotes a workplace culture that is based on respect, participation, and performance excellence. There are 150 staff at Sabi Sabi, all of whom enjoy the benefit of programs that include adult literacy, English proficiency, business orientation, and HIV/AIDS awareness." It adds that Sabi Sabi also supports the community through an educational center and "other pioneering natural resource management schemes."[126]

In an interview, Shorten elaborated on the changes at Sabi Sabi, as well as on his own management philosophy.[127] Shorten, who studied at Cornell University's hotel school, worked at Sabi Sabi in the 1980s and then left in the 1990s. When he was hired back as managing director in 1989, Shorten says he approached the job with "a new broom sweeping out the old dirt." Asked what has changed, he said, "There was a total transformation which included the attitudes within the company, as well as the standards of operation, from guest relations, to safaris, to habitat operations and community involvement."

In terms of staff relations and community projects, Shorten acknowledges that "some community involvement projects have not gone very well." However, others are functioning well, including a preschool where Sabi Sabi helps pay the teacher's salary and an educational center that Sabi Sabi helped to set up and stock with reference books and computers, some donated by guests. A major goal is to reduce financial leakage through buying and employing locally and "gaining back the trust of the locals," which has been repeatedly destroyed through colonialism, apartheid, and failed social programs. Owner Hilton Loon has also created a foundation, called "Swi ta Lunga" ("Things shall come right") to enhance, he says, "the commercial knowledge of community leaders in order to stimulate and develop a sustainable local economy and attract investment."[128]

Shorten said that Sabi Sabi pays higher wages to its staff than any lodge in the area and has purchased a bus and provides free transport for workers to and from the village. In addition, employees are unionized, which "creates an open line of consultation between staff and management. We support the union," Shorten affirmed.[129] In 1983, eleven years before the end of apartheid, Sabi Sabi became the first lodge in South Africa to have a black ranger[130] and it continues to work to train and promote black trackers to move up to rangers, and other workers to advance into skilled and management positions. Less successful, explained Shorten, has been has been the HIV/AIDS awareness program. "We hit a brick wall. There is a state of denial among the staff members," who refused plans to provided a confidential testing program. Management wanted simply to know the total number of cases and scope of the problem, but test results would only be made available to individual staff members. Shorten said that "AIDS education is still a big challenge."

The turnabout at Sabi Sabi illustrates both the role of effective management in improving social and environmental performance and of certification programs such as FTTSA in providing objective, third-party assessments of the business that can help to reverse a less-than-stellar reputation. FTTSA is in the process of reviewing its criteria, a process all good certification programs go through every several years. In addition, as ecotourism expert Eddie Koch has observed, the standard of luxury at Londolozi, Phinda, Sabi Sabi and other high-end lodges "makes it hard to be truly ecologically responsible." He predicts that the next generation of safari lodges "will be towards a more rustic style" and will be "more proactive in their conservation of the land."[131]

Other FTTSA-Certified Businesses

Other businesses that have earned the FTTSA label include the Djuma Game Reserve, also located in the Sabi Sands Game Reserve; Singita, which comprises five luxury safari lodges in two game reserves; Spier, a winery, resort and conference center in Stellenbosch; and Grootbos Private Nature Reserve near Capetown (described above). Not all certified businesses are high-end; some are community-based tourism enterprises catering to or owned by black South Africans. As mentioned above, Calabash Tours has a small three-star guesthouse and runs "reality" city tours in Port Elizabeth. While FTTSA gave Calabash high marks on their community activities, it recommended that, by the next audit, they improve internal recycling and educate staff about conserving water and energy.[132] Another is Phumulani Lodge, located near the Numbi Gate of Kruger. The four-star lodge is 100 percent owned by the Mdluli Trust, and is committed to the social, economic, and environmental well-being of its staff and community. Guests can arrange for bush walks and game drives in the Mdluli Reserve and in Kruger National Park, as well as cultural tours with local guides.

Phumulani Lodge and Calabash Tours are part of another initiative as well. They are among hundreds of community-based tourism enterprises (CBTE) across southern Africa that are now included on a searchable Internet-based tourism directory. The initiative, from the United Nations World Tourism Organization (UNWTO), the Regional Tourism Organization for Southern Africa (RETOSA), and the Dutch development organization SNV, aims to improve the market access and marketing capacity of community operators. To be included in the directory, tourism enterprises have to be located within a community (i.e., on communal rather than private land), be owned by one or more community members, or be managed by community members who can influence decisions regarding the business. The directory is creating a process of identifying community businesses and assessing them against predetermined criteria, independent assessments, and audits. In effect this means that all community-based tourism businesses included on the RETOSA Web site have passed an integrated certification process.[133] The directory allows tourists and tour operators across the world to access information about nearly two hundred of these small tourism businesses in South Africa (and southern Africa) from RETOSA's Web site.[134] The objective is ultimately to give the community-based tourism businesses better access to more customers, and to help with income generation and poverty reduction in their host communities.

South Africa's Ecotourism Scorecard

Ecotourism is playing a dual role in the new South Africa: helping to reintegrate South Africa into the world economy and helping to redress grievances and redistribute wealth to the country's rural poor. Under apartheid, South Africa was an international pariah, boycotted by both foreign tourists and investors. Most tourism within South Africa was domestic, predominantly run by the white minority; South Africa was a net exporter of tourists; and most investment in tourism was with national capital. The commitment to genuine ecotourism, often termed "responsible" or "pro-poor" tourism, is one of the outgrowths of the anti-apartheid struggle. Whereas elsewhere, ecotourism evolved out of environmental movements, in South Africa it has deep roots in the struggle against white minority rule and for a broad-based democracy committed to economic and racial equality and social justice. Ecotourism is seen as a tool for social change, and its principles fit the objectives of the Reconstruction and Development Program (RDP), Nelson Mandela's first blueprint for development. Today, a broad swath of South African society, including government and park officials, the national tourism agency, dozens of NGOs, academics, consultants, environmentalists, journalists, community organizers, rural activists, and private tour operators, developers, and investors are all involved in ecotourism experiments and initiatives. All this adds up to giving South Africa a high rating on the ecotourism scorecard. However, the country continues to face substantial challenges in implementing ecotourism so that it meets black economic empowerment goals and brings real benefits to larger numbers of historically disadvantaged communities.

Weak government capacity in some departments is inhibiting successful ecotourism development. In addition, while the number of foreign visitors grew by 7 percent—to about 2 million—in 2006, fear of crime was reportedly scaring off many international travelers. According to one survey, foreign tour operators said they would send 50 percent more people to South Africa if crime were not a factor. This translated to a loss of 125,000 jobs that could be created by overseas tourists.[135] Despite these challenges, South Africa continues to rate well on the ecotourism scorecard.

Involves Travel to Natural Destinations

South Africa is a large and enormously diverse country, offering a wide range of tourism attractions. Its wildlife and game parks and reserves, both public and private, are among the finest in the world. Since 1994, ecotourism has been diversifying, moving beyond the Big Five safari viewing to other attractions, with flower-, bird-, and whale-watching; winery, cultural and "heritage" tourism; and township tours all growing rapidly. Today, ecotourism is playing an increasingly important role in the economy.

Minimizes Impact

South Africa's system of national, provincial, and homeland parks has long been considered among the world's best protected and most carefully tended. Visitor numbers are well regulated, poaching is minimal, accommodations are well dispersed, and architecture fits the landscape and often utilizes local materials. But this facade of environmental responsibility conceals a great deal of social engineering, and since the fall of apartheid, conservationists have begun to reexamine these practices with a more critical eye. South Africa's parks were created by evicting tens of thousands of rural Africans, who were forced to live in overcrowded communities on the parks' perimeters and were denied access to land, water, wood, and other resources inside the parks. But in contrast with the situation in East Africa, South Africa's protectionist school of conservation and park management did not stop there. For decades, apartheid-era scientists and park officials aggressively rearranged the landscape and wildlife—importing the Big Five animal species into parks, culling elephants and other species, putting up electric fences, planting alien trees and shrubs, clearing brush, and cutting (and sometimes paving) roads, all to make the parks more pleasurable for the country's white minority. In some sections of the game parks, there has been even greater impact: golf courses, conference centers, flowered lawns, and so forth.

Now a realization has emerged that some of these practices were not grounded in good science, and as part of a fundamental restructuring and overhaul of the national parks, they are being reassessed. Since 1994, focus has grown on both land "restitution" for evicted groups and community participation and benefits from conservation. Some projects and initiatives have been more successful than others, but the broad national commitment to using tourism to benefit historically disadvantaged communities is impressive and unprecedented. In addition, new ecotourism projects typically strive for low-impact construction and practices, including use of solar power, raised walkways, recycling of water and waste, use of local materials, and incorporation of indigenous designs.

Builds Environmental Awareness

Even under apartheid, South Africa's national park system managed to maintain a carefully groomed international image of apolitical excellence and outstanding conservation practices. Today, the principles and practices of ecotourism are being used to help challenge the old order, which narrowly promoted environmental protection at a cost of human exploitation. Environmentalists and social activists who cut their teeth on the struggle against apartheid are today committed to a more holistic and integrated view, one that links conservation to community development. Now that tourism is expanding beyond a tiny racial and economic elite, it can offer leisure activities and build support for conservation among a broad cross-section of the population.

Provides Direct Financial Benefits for Conservation

Under apartheid, South Africa's parks were heavily financed by the government. When apartheid ended, there was a strong movement among the rural poor to dismantle the parks and turn over the land and resources to the original occupants. The post-apartheid governments made it clear that the park system would continue and in fact would be expanded. But at the same time, the new government declared that the existing level of government subsidies could not be maintained. Park budgets have been cut, and the national and provincial protected areas have embarked on a variety of income-generating projects under the banner of privatization and commercialization to ensure that they can continue functioning in an era of decreasing financial support from government. Ecotourism's contribution to conservation in South Africa is not only in direct financial flows to protected areas but also in the provision of a new model for operating that is helping the national parks make the transition from white rule to non-racially oriented democratic rule.

Provides Financial Benefits and Empowerment for Local People

More than in the other countries examined in this book, ecotourism in South Africa is grounded in the principle that it must involve and benefit local communities. Ironically, the earliest experiments in the country's community-based conservation and ecotourism were in parks within the Bantustans or black homelands, one of the most hated institutions of apartheid. Today, ecotourism is being used or proposed as a development tool and an alternative to more destructive forms of income generation in many areas of the country. Ecotourism has proved most successful in overgrazed or parched regions, where wildlife can survive better than cattle. It remains to be seen whether ecotourism can be developed as a viable alternative to more lucrative (at least in the short run) alternatives such as mining for diamonds or metals.

In South Africa today, local communities are involved in ecotourism in a wide variety of ways. These range from entitlement to empowerment models and from passive to more active engagement. They include rent or bed-night payments made by an eco-lodge or private reserve to the local communities; employment; training and education programs; co-management or co-ownership arrangements between communities and private companies; provision of social services (schools, clinics, wells) and infrastructure (roads, electricity, pumped water); and the purchase of local produce, charcoal, and handicrafts. Some of what is marketed as ecotourism is dubious, but overall there is a level of experimentation and cross-fertilization of ideas that is deepening the definition of real ecotourism. Nevertheless, unequal power relations between communities, tourism developers, and conservation agencies remain a key challenge to ensuring real empowerment for local people.

Respects local culture

Under apartheid, South Africa's tourism industry either ignored or crudely exploited the country's non-European cultures. Tourism brochures, for instance, showed only white tourists while picturing Africans dancing or selling crafts. Ecotourism, as interpreted in the new South Africa, includes respecting and learning about local cultures and customs and paying a fair price for handicrafts. In KwaZulu-Natal Province, for instance, Kwabhe Kithunga, located on Stewarts Farm, is a cultural village run as a cooperative where artisans demonstrate how they make their round traditional houses, bead jewelry, and women's clothing.[136] And ecotourism, together with cultural and "heritage" tourism, are the fastest-growing markets in South Africa. Typically, ecotours or cultural tours include visits to Robben Island, Soweto, rural communities, and game parks. Although exploitation, particularly of the San (Bushmen), continues in some parks and tourism establishments, the government's commitment to ecotourism as a tool for both conservation and community development provides a platform from which to expose and oppose these practices.

Supports Human Rights and Democratic Movements

The international trade, travel, and investment boycott of apartheid South Africa helped end white rule. This represents the best example to date of how tourists can play a constructive role in assisting popular democratic struggles. Today, the anti-apartheid boycott is cited by those struggling for democratic change in Nigeria, Tibet, Burma, and elsewhere. Given South Africa's history, it is not surprising that the link between human rights and tourism is a central piece of the country's unique "fair trade" certification program, the FTTSA. And today, the South African government is promoting ecotourism and cultural tourism as its passport to international acceptance and respectability.

10

Ecotourism in the United States

In 1851, gold miner Lafayette Bunnell and the Mariposa Battalion, one of the West's most aggressive militias, rode into and "discovered" the Yosemite Valley.[1] The militia, commanded by the appropriately named James Savage, set about to forcibly remove the local residents, Ahwahneechee Indians from a small band known as Miwoks, who had lived in the valley for some four thousand years. In 1864, President Abraham Lincoln signed the Yosemite Act, giving the state of California the valley "for public use, resort and recreation"[2] and empowering the U.S. Army to protect it from "illegal" settlement. In the coming years, most Indians who tried to return were either killed or relocated to a reservation; because of a scarcity of labor, some Miwoks were allowed to return to the park to guide tourists, supply fishing parties, chop wood, harvest hay, and provide "amusement" for the tourists. By the 1880s, Miwoks were weaving baskets, dancing, and charging visitors for the privilege of taking their photos. They became, as one writer puts it, the first Native Americans "to experience the mixed blessings of park tourism."[3] In 1890, Yosemite was declared a national park and, over the coming decades, "park service policy toward Indians in Yosemite vacillated wildly from accommodation to expulsion." In 1969, the last of the Miwoks were evicted from Yosemite.[4]

As elsewhere around the world, the origins of ecotourism in the United States can be most concretely traced back to the growth of the National Parks System. Ecotourism grows in part out of the debates

I am grateful to Emy Rodriquez, Katrina Shum, and Molly Chapman for pulling together much of the research for this chapter. Katrina deserves special thanks for compiling and organizing the research materials.

over which philosophy should dictate the formation and underpin the governance of parks and protected areas. In the United States, as in many other countries, military force was often used to clear the land of its local human inhabitants and then patrol the parks with the notion of protecting them as "forever wild." As Berkeley professor Mark Dowie writes, "The fortress model of wildland conservation is largely an American invention," and, "like most other American inventions, was being aggressively exported."[5] Over the course of the next century (as earlier chapters in this volume depict), country after country around the world copied both the physical model and the philosophical rationale behind the U.S. parks service.

One of the realities is that while in the United States and elsewhere around the world, many local communities are turning to ecotourism as a cleaner and "greener" alternative to more extractive and exploitative economic activities, many also hold a fundamental distrust that ecotourism is being used as a tool for further exploitation, penetration of native lands, and abuse of cultural values. This ambiguity toward ecotourism was articulated, for instance, in 2004 in a report by the Alaska Native Science Commission (ANSC):

> When the spring came, the snow melted, the whales came north and the geese flew over our lands. We knew there would come a scientist or two to dig around and ask us questions. They would stay about as long as the geese did. The only difference was, we hated to see the geese leave.
>
> In the Native community, we sort of feel the same way about ecotourism. We walk that fine line of navigating between the ideals of development (which would lead one to advocate rural tourism), and the ideals of cultural tradition and integrity (which might lead one to reject rural tourism).[6]

This ambivalence toward ecotourism—its promise and its realities—continues to be felt most poignantly by Native Americans across much of the United States. Ecotourism is still a relatively new phenomenon on the American landscape, and has yet to prove that it is qualitatively different from conventional tourism. Ecotourism has still to demonstrate that it is not simply further exploitation under a new name, but rather that it can offer host communities opportunities for tangible financial benefits and empowerment, while respecting their culture.

The ecotourism movement in the United States is building on American institutions and intellectual movements, most importantly the National Parks System and conservation activists and environmentalists. It also draws from ecotourism experiences around the world. A number of the pioneers in U.S. ecotourism first learned about it while traveling abroad; for others, ecotourism endeavors evolved from local issues and popular movements centered on control of land, resources, and culture. Unlike the Galapagos or East Africa, where ecotourism is confined to particular geographic areas or activities, ecotourism in the United States spans the coasts, the cities, and the countryside. It also involves a wide array of businesses, academics, NGOs, government officials, the media, and community groups. It is therefore difficult to fully capture in one chapter the arc of ecotourism in the United States. Instead, we will trace the history, growth, and trends as well as the most important institutions involved in ecotourism, and will sample some of the rich array of ecotourism experiments found across this vast country.

The U.S. Tourism Industry and the Growth of Ecotourism

The United States is a tourism superpower: it is the number-one country in the world in tourism receipts and the third-highest in international tourist arrivals (behind France and Spain). However, unlike other destinations included in this book, tourism by U.S. nationals, both within this country and overseas, is very significant. In 2006, 30.1 million Americans traveled internationally, an all-time high. Within the U.S. economy, travel is the nation's largest export industry, the third-largest retail sales industry (after auto and food store sales), and one of the largest U.S. employers.[7] For domestic tourists, outdoor activities rank third in importance, after shopping and "attend[ing] a social/family event." The top states for domestic tourism are California, Florida, Texas, New York, and Pennsylvania.[8] According to a recent government assessment, "The U.S. benefits from perhaps the widest, richest array of tourism attractions in the world, as well as a world class level of service, infrastructure and hospitality facilities."[9]

In a 1997 study, direct spending on leisure activities (tourism, recreation, and business travel) in the United States was calculated to be between $436 billion and $512 billion (see table 10.1). From 1992 to 1997, tourism spending grew at an average annual rate of 6.9 percent, faster than the Gross Domestic Product (GDP), which grew at a rate of 5.6 percent a year.[10] The 9/11 terrorist attacks caused a decline in the U.S. vacation and leisure travel market, and by the end of 2005, North America was the only subregion in the world to have recorded a decline in arrivals since 2000.[11] The fallout from the terrorist attacks and U.S. war on terrorism continued to hurt the tourism industry: the United States has fallen from first to sixth among "dream destinations for

Table 10.1.
United States Tourism

	1976	*1982*	*1985*	*1990*	*1995*	*2000*	*2001*	*2005*	*2006*
International arrivals (millions)	17.3	21.5	25	39.4	43.5	51.3	47	49.2	51
Domestic tourism (millions)	n.a.	n.a.	n.a.	n.a.	1,770	1,892.1	1,869.2	1,992.4	2,000.6
U.S. overseas tourism (millions)	6.8	n.a.	12.7	16	19	26.9	25.2	28.8	30.1
Domestic spending in U.S. ($ billions)	n.a.	n.a.	n.a.	n.a.	n.a.	503	484	572	614
International spending in U.S. ($ billions)	6	12	18	43	63	82	72	82	86
% of foreign exchange	5	6	8	11	10	10	9	8	7

Sources: Ron Erdmann, Office of Travel and Tourism Industries, U.S. Department of Commerce, correspondence, September–December, 2007; Tien X. Tian, vice president and chief economist, Travel Industry Association of America correspondence, 2007; ITA, Office of Travel and Tourism Industries, see www.tinet.ita.doc.gov/outreachpages/inbound.general_information.inbound_overview.html; www.tinet.ita.doc.gov/view/f-1998-06-001/index.html; www.tinet.ita.doc.gov/outreachpages/inbound.exports_2001-2006.html; Travel Industry Association of America, see www.tia.org/uploads/research/doc/NationalSummary1006.doc; www.census.gov/compendia/statab/tables/07s1243.xls; www.tia.org/researchpubs/us_overview _volumes_trends.html.

international travelers," and 77 percent of travelers believe "the U.S. is more difficult to visit than other destinations." Overall, the U.S. market share of international travel has fallen 35 percent since 1992.[12] However, by 2006, international arrivals to the United States had regained their pre-9/11 level and travel industry spending in the United States was valued at $700 billion—largely because of the strength of the domestic tourism market.[13]

Size of the Ecotourism Market

Measuring the importance of ecotourism is more difficult. Since surveys rarely ask either travelers or businesses specifically about ecotourism, precise statistics are difficult to determine. A 2002 U.S. State Department report stated, "While there are no consolidated data on all ecotourism activities taking place in the U.S., it is estimated that Americans spend billions of dollars annually."[14] That same year, the U.S. Commerce Department estimated that about 13 percent of the 18.6 million U.S. outbound leisure travelers (approximately 2.4 million Americans) could be regarded as ecotourists.[15]

There have been some useful nongovernmental surveys as well. A 2003 survey by *National Geographic Travelers* and the Travel Industry Association of America (TIA) found that 55.1 percent of U.S. travelers can be classified as "geotourists" or interested in nature, culture, and heritage tourism. It also found that more than three-quarters of U.S. travelers "feel it is important their visits not damage the environment," according to a 2003 study. This study estimates that 17 million U.S. travelers consider environmental factors when deciding which travel companies to patronize.[16] In 2005, LOHAS ("Lifestyles of Health and Sustainability") estimated that ecotourism, including eco-travel networks, "green" tourism, eco-volunteering trips, and environmentally responsible tourism, are among the fastest-growing travel trends, and are estimated to be a $77 billion market. In addition, 75 percent in the LOHAS survey said they are interested in environmentally responsible travel.[17] One interesting survey, done in 2002, found that U.S. travelers are more likely to select hotels with a "responsible environmental attitude"; however, only 14 percent actually ask hotels if they have an environmental policy.[18] What this indicates is that while there is broad interest in responsible travel—in ecotourism—U.S. consumers are fairly passive in carrying out their views.

One indication of the strength of ecotourism is to assess how much tourism takes place within parks and protected areas—federal, state, and private. A 2002 TIA survey found that national parks enjoy "high awareness and satisfaction among American travelers." The survey found that nearly 40 percent of all U.S. adults had visited a national park at least once in the past five years, and that, in 2002 alone, 20 percent of international visitors visited a national or state park while in the United States. The great majority of those visiting parks (93 percent) said they were "highly satisfied" with their park experience. They said they were drawn to visit parks in order to experience nature (92 percent), for educational benefit (90 percent), to experience culture and history (89 percent), and to spend time with their family (80 percent). Further, 75 percent reported staying overnight in or within ten miles of the parks.[19]

Ecotourism can be measured in relation to other categories of U.S. protected areas. The State Department found that "on federal lands alone, there are an estimated 900 million visits a year to national forests, parks, monuments, historic sites, recreation areas, protected areas and wildlife refuges, reserves and management areas—most of these visits include sightseeing, hiking, wildlife observation, swimming, snorkeling or other forms of ecotourism."[20] A recent Department of Interior study indicated that almost 37 million people visited national wildlife refuges in one year, creating almost twenty-four thousand private-sector jobs, and producing about $454 million in employment income and $151 million in state, local, and federal taxes.[21] And, according to the 2001 National Survey of Fishing, Hunting, and Wildlife-Associated Recreation, 39 percent of all American adults participate in some form of wildlife-related recreation. Wildlife watchers alone spent $38 billion in the United States in 2001.[22]

U.S. Government Policies and Administration of Tourism

Although the United States is the world's leader in tourism earnings and a top-tier tourism destination, travel, and tourism currently hold a rather lowly position in the federal government's bureaucratic pecking order. While other countries where tourism is a significant foreign exchange earner have full tourism ministries headed by a cabinet-level official, in Washington, what passes for the national tourism office is buried deep within the Commerce Department—the smallest of the government's fifty departments. And, counterintuitively, as more Americans have engaged in tourism at home and abroad, over the last decade this Commerce Department tourism office has been demoted and downsized, through rare bipartisan congressional and executive action. In 1996, under the Clinton administration, Congress voted to cease funding for the U.S. National Tourism Organization and dissolve the U.S. Travel and Tourism Administration (USTTA). In its place, they created the Office of Travel and Tourism Industries (OTTI), a smaller and weaker unit located within the Commerce Department's International Trade Administration (ITA).

Ron Erdmann, who has worked as a federal tourism functionary since the 1980s, recalls that he and the handful of other tourism officials who survived the cuts in 1996 saw their office moved down three rungs on the bureaucratic ladder. He says the USTTA became one of the sacrificial lambs, slaughtered as part of the budget standoff between the Bill Clinton White House and a clique of right-wing House Republicans, led by Congressman Newt Gingrich, who were demanding downsizing of the federal government. Erdmann says the reason tourism was targeted was that it had "no constituency" lobbying to protect it and that in Congress, the view was that "the tourism industry was big enough and healthy enough to be handled by the private sector."[23]

With these changes, the United States resigned as a member of the UN's World Tourism Organization (UNWTO)[24] and the slimmed-down OTTI lost much of its overseas marketing function and budget,[25] foreign tourism offices, and all but thirteen staff. Although the OTTI Web site describes it as "the National Tourism Office for tourism policy coordination," including research and representation abroad and international travel statistics in the United States,[26] its role is in reality far more limited than tourism offices in many other countries.

Also within the Commerce Department's ITA is the Commercial Service, with scores of domestic and overseas offices geared to promoting U.S. exports, including tourism. Its staff in this country offers export counseling to U.S. businesses and destinations trying to increase their presence internationally. Overseas, it has some eighty offices carrying out sales promotion in U.S. Embassies and Consulates.[27] According to Erdmann, "A number of these export counselors do travel and tourism, but it is very low key."[28] Today, the real locus of tourism power, at least in terms of marketing and lobbying, is found in state governments and private industry organizations, most importantly, the Tourism Industry Association of America (TIA). According to a 2005 Mintel study, "Two of the top advertisers for inbound U.S. travel are TIA and individual state tourism agencies."[29] In the last few years, pressure has mounted from various quarters for the United States to rejoin the UNWTO and other international bodies and increase the national budgets for marketing and branding so that the United States can compete more effectively with other countries.[30]

Ecotourism shows up only marginally in the OTTI's data collection, via airport surveys of international visitors to the United States. (Excluded are visitors from the two biggest markets, Mexico and Canada, because so many tourists travel by land.) It also does not collect data on Americans who vacation within the United States. In airport surveys of visitors arriving in the United States and Americans leaving for overseas, one of the questions asks if the vacation includes "ecological/environmental excursions." (Again, travelers to and from Mexico and Canada are not included since so many go overland.) For international travelers these surveys are conducted as they are leaving the United States and therefore reflect actual activities; for American vacationers traveling abroad, the questionnaires are done as they depart, and therefore their answers reflect intent, not actual activities. Therefore, as stated above, the survey results showing higher interest in ecotourism among Americans traveling abroad than among foreigners coming to the United States *may* be skewed because one measures intent, and the other actual behavior.

Other Government Agencies Involved in Ecotourism

The OTTI has one other function worth noting: it serves as the secretariat for the Tourism Policy Council (TPC), an interagency committee representing seventeen federal agencies and departments to ensure, as its Web site states, "that the national tourism interests are considered in Federal decision-making."[31] First created in 1981 and reauthorized in 1996, the TPC has been far from a vigorous tourism advocate. Its first meeting wasn't held until after 1996, and it last met in 2001, following the 9/11 terrorist attacks.[32] The TPC members do include, however, the other federal agencies involved in tourism. Many of these, together with a wide range of states, counties, and cities, promote tourism and ecotourism on public lands and waterways in the United States. Finding a sustainable balance between recreation and conservation has been, for all these agencies, an ongoing challenge. As former NPS Deputy Director Denis Galvin writes, "There is no credible debate over whether parks should be used by the American people; the debate centers on how the use occurs, or sometimes when and where." Galvin notes that national parks "do not have to sustain all recreation; that is why we have various other federal, state, local and private recreation providers."[33] All have helped to encourage travel to natural and cultural destinations within the country, and all have had some programs and policies explicitly supporting ecotourism. One of the few studies of ecotourism in the United States notes that the collection of public lands provide "ideal tourism destinations for many different travel experiences including ecotourism."[34] And a State Department report lists a variety of "sustainable ecotourism" activities and programs run by an alphabet soup of government agencies.[35]

The largest is the U.S. Forest Service (USFS), located in the Department of Agriculture, which manages 700 million acres of national forests and wilderness areas across all fifty states. The Forest Service is "committed to providing quality recreation opportunities consistent with sustainable ecosystem management principles through programs, service, conservation education and interpretation, and community partnerships."[36] More than 208 million people visit national forests and 258 million travel on forest roads to view scenery and wildlife each year. The USFS works with over six thousand private tourism guides and outfitters on federal land, sets policy for a majority of the country's ski slopes, and sponsors, together with local communities, a portion of the National Scenic Byways designated by the Department of Transportation. It manages a variety of ecotourism programs, including grassroots projects in the Ozark Mountains, upper Michigan Peninsula, Tennessee, and elsewhere to foster ecotourism experiences.

Another agency involved in tourism, and ecotourism, is the National Oceanic and Atmospheric Administration (NOAA), which administers the National Marine Sanctuary Programs. This latter serves as "trustee" of thirteen underwater parks and Great Lakes waters with a mission of balancing recreation and long-term conservation. "Ecotourism is very popular at many sites and visitation is increasing." NOAA, works closely with other agencies and local businesses in a range of public education and outreach, scientific research, and monitoring programs "to help ensure that ecotourism operations do not harm habitat or wildlife," according to the State Department report.[37] These include, for example, the National Marine Fisheries Services which works to educate the public about safe and respectful viewing of marine wildlife via public brochures and posters at coastal recreational sites, public service announcements, and the Internet. It participates in the National Watchable Wildlife Program, a consortium of federal and state wildlife agencies and conservation and outdoor groups, to promote wildlife viewing from a safe and appropriate distance. The National Sea Grant Program, a partnership between NOAA and U.S. universities, has developed several "thematic specialties related to sustainable tourism," including one focused on ecotourism development in the Carolinas; another to promote "Public Education and Eco-tourism" around birdwatching and to build and maintain trails, boardwalks, wildlife-viewing platforms, and nature center exhibits; and a third, a *Guide to Coastal Ecotourism* in New Jersey.[38]

The Department of Interior houses, in addition to the NPS, three other federal agencies involved in tourism and ecotourism. One, the U.S. Fish and Wildlife Service (USFWS), manages over five hundred wildlife refuges covering more acreage than all the national parks put together. Some 30 million visitors make use of the refuges a year, and the FWS is involved in a variety of ecotourism programs. One is the National Wildlife Refuge System, where visitors enjoy wildlife observation, photography, interpretation, fishing and hunting, and other activities that generate millions of dollars for communities surrounding the refuges. In another program, FWS partners with municipalities to conserve migratory birds through education and habitat improvement. Every year, over 18 million Americans take bird-watching trips, an activity often described as the original ecotourism activity. As a *New York Times* article put it, "Managers of the nation's wildlife refuges are dealing with the complexities of bringing ecotourism to their far-flung empire,"[39] but the problem is that "there is no coherent policy, nor even a comprehensive law, directing the agency's decisions at a time when pressures from people using the refuges are growing steadily."[40]

A second agency, the Bureau of Land Management (BLM), manages over 264 million acres of public lands used by over 60 million visitors annually. Its ecotourism programs have included a partnership with the National Watchable Wildlife Program to develop some three hundred wildlife-viewing areas on BLM land from Alaska to Florida. The BLM has also collaborated with the U.S. Forest Service in two nationally recognized environmental programs, "Leave No Trace," which teaches visitors techniques to minimize outdoor recreation impacts, and "Tread Lightly," designed to protect natural areas through education.

The third agency is the Bureau of Reclamation (BOR), which provides water-based recreation activities on 8.5 million acres of land and water to about 80 million visitors a year. Its ecotourism programs are focused on the nearly three hundred lakes BOR administers in seventeen western states and include flora, fauna, and geological observations and scientific research studies as well as organized adventure travel trips conducted by conservation organizations and commercial outfitters and guides.

Tourism—and ecotourism—is also handled by other federal agencies that are not involved in management of public land. One is the Environmental Protection Agency (EPA), established in 1970 to foster "governmental action on behalf of the environment" and "to serve as the public's advocate for a livable environment." It seeks to "control pollution systematically" through integrating a variety of "research, monitoring, standard setting, and enforcement activities" and to coordinate with state and local governments, private and public groups, and educational institutions.[41] EPA has a wide variety of programs that assist environmental tourism and operations of the tourism industry, including data, case studies, technical assistance, and free software. The EPA has developed an impressive model for assessing the economic and environmental impacts of U.S. recreation and tourism industries. The model quantifies environmental impacts of ten leading "leisure activities," including skiing, fishing, hunting, boating, golfing, historic places and museums, and waterside recreation, and measures these against nine environmental indicators, including water use, energy use, air pollution, and greenhouse gas emissions. "Though the model covers tourism broadly, the theory and methodology can be applied at the local level as a tool to assess ecotourism impacts and develop plans to improve ecotourism efficiency and resource management."[42]

In addition, the EPA, together with Purdue University, developed an online toolkit, "Environmental Enrichment for the Lodging Industry," to help hotel and restaurant owners implement more sustainable practices, improve their day-to-day operations, and understand the principles of ecotourism.[43] The EPA has also developed other technical assistance manuals to "enable flexible, collaborative, market-driven solutions that can deliver measurable environmental results"[44] in a number of fields, including water, waste management, transportation, pollution prevention, air quality, and energy efficiency and global climate change. While not designed specifically for the tourism industry, these online programs contain information relevant to implementing sound ecotourism practices. In recent years, as discussed below, EPA offices at the state level have also been involved in creating and running a number of hotel certification programs.

Ecotourism Roots: National Parks and "Fortress Conservation"

Yellowstone, located mostly in modern day Wyoming, holds the mantle as the United States'—and the world's—first legally authorized national park.[45] In 1872, Congress set aside more than 800,000 hectares (2 million acres) at the headwaters of the Yellowstone River "as a public park or pleasuring ground for the benefit and enjoyment of the people." National parks historian Richard Sellars writes, "Vast and spectacularly beautiful, Yellowstone provided . . . the most enduring image of a national park: a romantic landscape of mountains, canyons, abundant wildlife, and fantastic natural phenomena."[46] In 1866, the federal government dispatched the U.S. Army to manage the park and "protect natural features and arrest poachers."[47]

From the beginning, the U.S. parks were formed, through purchase and conquest, with the twin goals of conserving "the last remnants of free land" for future generations[48] and promoting enjoyment through tourism. The forces inside the nation pushing for parks "reflected a complex intermingling of corporate, governmental and altruistic motivations."[49] As Rachel Cox notes in her comprehensive article on ecotourism, "Private tourism promoters also played a large role in the creation and expansion of the National Park System, with the Northern Pacific Railroad urging the creation of Yellowstone as a draw for its passengers." In the late nineteenth century, railroads played a large part in the creation of other parks in the West, including Sequoia and Yosemite, Mount Rainier, and Glacier.[50] Cox notes that "the creation and promotion of the parks" gave railroads "an enticing marketing device. Tourism became a powerful new economic engine shaping the face of the West."[51]

The number and range of protected areas grew rapidly. In the first decade of the twentieth century, President Theodore Roosevelt, an avid outdoorsman, doubled the nation's park acreage and extended federal protection to cover as "national monuments" threatened lands deemed to be of historic, prehistoric, and scientific value. In 1916, President Woodrow Wilson signed the Organic Act, creating the National Parks Service (NPS) for the purpose of conserving natural and historic areas and their wildlife and providing for public enjoyment "by such means as will leave them unimpaired for the enjoyment of future generations"[52]—language that echoes that of the Bruntland Commission some seventy years later. The NPS brought together thirty-six different parks under one roof, the Department of the Interior, which also housed the Bureau of Indian Affairs.

The parks system also expanded beyond the West, with the creation in 1919 of Acadia in Maine and the Great Smoky Mountains in Tennessee and North Carolina in 1926. In the 1930s, President Franklin Roosevelt matched his relative's earlier accomplishment by again doubling the park system. Of the fifty-six sites he added, many were historic battlefields, colonial settlements, and national shrines and parks in Washington, D.C. and other parts of the East coast. Since the 1930s, the majority of areas added to the NPS have been selected primarily for their cultural significance.

In 1964, a century after Yosemite was set aside, Congress passed the U.S. Wilderness Act, protecting wild landscapes in national parks and on public lands around national parks as areas "where the earth and its community of life are untrammeled by man, where man himself is a visitor who does not remain."[53] In 1980, President Jimmy Carter signed into law the landmark Alaska Lands bill, a massive piece of legislation that restricted development on over 100 million acres of land, created ten new national parks, and expanded three existing parks in Alaska. Hailed by environmentalists as the "conservation vote of the century," the law more than doubled the size of the U.S. national park and wildlife refuge system and nearly tripled the amount of land designated as wilderness.[54]

Today, the United States includes twelve major ecological regions has the highest number of legally protected areas (1.615 billion hectares or 3.989 billion acres) in the world. The National Parks System is made up of 390 "units" in twenty different categories including parks, monuments, battlefields, and trails. They cover more than 84 million acres in every state (except Delaware), the District of Columbia, and four U.S.

territories (American Samoa, Guam, Puerto Rico, and the Virgin Islands).[55] These cover a dozen major ecological regions, from deserts to tropical humid forests, providing a "broad backdrop to the ecological mosaic of the country." The variety and vastness of the United States' natural areas gives the country great potential to develop a broad range of ecotourism activities.[56]

National Parks and Organized Nature Tours

The U.S. National Parks System has become the country's leading recreation attraction. The link between parks and tourism in the United States dates back to at least 1855. That year what has been described as the first recreational trek into a protected wilderness area occurred when James Mason Hutchins led a "tourist expedition" to Yosemite.[57] Organized nature expeditions date from 1901, when the Sierra Club started its annual High Trips into the Sierra Nevada Mountains (see chapter 1). In recent years, the rapid growth of nature tourism to U.S. parks and protected areas has been facilitated by the expansion and accessibility of modern transport: first trains, then cars, and most recently airplanes. From the beginning of the twentieth century, the automobile industry lobbied for the expansion of the country's highway system, linking it to the marketing of family vacations by car. With the economic boom after World War II, many young families owned cars, and spurred by the American Automobile Association (AAA) guidebooks and American Express traveler checks, the summer holiday by road became a national tradition. Visitors to the National Parks System in the United States rose by 20 percent in the decade from 1980 to 1990, from about 190 million to more than 250 million. At present, nearly 300 million people visit parks annually, the equivalent of about one visit to a national park per U.S. resident each year.

Balancing Recreation, Development, and Conservation

The National Parks Service is one of the most widely respected government agencies, and the U.S. park system is the envy of countries around the world. "Like the Declaration of Independence," writes Rachel Cox, "America's national parks . . . conjure images of freedom and integrity, of an enduring, priceless patrimony to be protected for the common good and enjoyed by all people."[58] The national parks' positive public image was reaffirmed, for instance, by the 2002 TIA survey cited above, which found parks enjoy "high awareness and satisfaction among American travelers."

But despite such popularity, most experts agree that the National Parks System is troubled by a range of both external and internal pressures. "All around the country," writes Tom Arrandale, "America's beloved national parks are falling on hard times."[59] The issues most often raised by people, businesses, the media, and civic organizations in gateway communities, as well as by ranchers and other private property owners next to the parks, include pressures from outside development, particularly for vacation homes; the rising cost of living; real estate speculation; displacement of local residents; pressure from recreational businesses for more access to park lands; and damage caused by spillovers of elk, bears, wolves, and other wildlife.

Among the most pressing concerns inside the national parks are inadequate budgets, expanded responsibilities and numbers of parks, vastly increased visitation, aging infrastructure, disposal of garbage, conflicts over wildlife management, controlling introduced species, declining biodiversity and wildlife habitat, inappropriate commercialization, and recreational activities such as snowmobiles and Jet Skis inside the parks. A central dilemma has been around "the question of exactly what in the park should be preserved," writes Richard Sellars. He asks, is it the "scenic façade of nature" for the public's enjoyment or "is it the integrity of each park's entire natural system?" Debate has also been generated about whether the U.S needs more national parks. And, at the most extreme, some property rights advocates oppose the very concept of national parks, arguing that the government should divest and privatize the parks system.[60]

As is the case elsewhere around the world, park entrance fees have long been contentious. Visitors have paid to enter parks since Mount Rainier National Park began charging fees in 1908, and when the Parks Service was created in 1916, seven of the fourteen units were already charging entrance fees to drive an automobile into the park. However, in recent years national parks have brought in, through entrance fees and other charges, less than 10 percent of their total budget.[61] When funding programs plagued the parks service in the 1990s, Congress created, in 1996, a fee program, and in 2000, began selling fifty-dollar-a-year passes, allowing access to all units.[62] Environmentalists and other national parks advocates argue that the government's funding priorities are skewed, with the United States spending nearly three times more on the federal prison system than the NPS and an equal amount on cotton subsidies.[63]

As a way to solidify public support for national parks, the first two NPS directors worked to encourage tourism by building roads, campgrounds, rustic lodges, and restaurants.[64] The tourism industry and philanthropists were also important in publicizing the national parks.[65] During World War II, park funding was inadequate, leaving many facilities in disrepair just as tourism took off with the postwar economic boom. In the 1950s, NPS Director Conrad Wirth launched "Mission 66" to make the parks more accessible to visitors by 1966, the fiftieth anniversary of the founding of the park service. This ambitious campaign built or improved three thousand kilometers (two thousand miles) of roads and constructed 114 visitor centers, many including restaurants, gift shops, and auditoriums.[66]

In addition, the parks have struggled with issues of how to control visitor numbers and behavior. Crowds have become such a problem that the national parks maintain long waiting lists for campgrounds and cabins. In Yellowstone in the 1950s, park officials allowed tourists to feed black bears begging for handouts along the roads. They also erected viewing stands so that tourists could watch grizzlies foraging in open garbage dumps. However, in the 1960s, a reassessment by park management led rangers to close the dumps and begin fining tourists caught feeding bears.[68]

One of the longest-running, most controversial and complex issues has surrounded the reintroduction of wolves. In keeping with prevailing attitudes toward wildlife, park officials in Yellowstone had promoted the "picturesque" wildlife—elk, bison, and deer—while eliminating their predators—wolves and mountain lions. With natural predators exterminated, the elk population exploded, threatening to strip bare the park's northern range. But public objections forced park rangers to stop a program for culling elk and bison in order to maintain sustainable numbers. Gradually, beginning in the early 1960s, park management philosophy began to tilt more strongly to conservation, and in 1995, the Clinton administration bucked the rancher lobby and approved transplanting fourteen wolves from Canada into Yellowstone in order to keep the elk and bison in check. This was one of a number of controversial moves by Clinton's Interior Secretary Bruce Babbitt aimed at restricting recreational activities in order to conserve parks as unimpaired and natural as possible.[69] Many of the decisions were strongly opposed by the recreation industry, gateway community, and rancher lobbyists, who again gained an upper hand during the second Bush administration. And as the wolf population has grown and moved onto private lands around Yellowstone, even those ranchers most supportive of the reintroduction policy continue to grapple with the conundrum of balancing livestock and wildlife. (See the Lodge at Sun Ranch discussion below.)

National Parks and Ecotourism Today

In 2005, *National Geographic Traveler* magazine published the results of an innovative survey designed to assess the impacts of recreation and other pressures on national parks. The magazine surveyed fifty-five U.S. and Canadian parks and their gateway communities. Each park was chosen in part because of the importance of its gateway community—the nearby town or region—where visitors also spend considerable time. As *Traveler* wrote, "A park and its gateway are really a single destination, with similar history, scenery, and climate. The way park and gateway interact can make all the difference in the quality of your trip and in the sustainability of the destination."[70] Some three hundred experts in sustainable tourism, destination quality, and park management were asked to rate the parks based on a one-to-one-hundred Sustainable Index scale. The scores found no park rated above ninety ("unspoiled and likely to remain so") or fell below twenty ("catastrophic") and, overall, Canada's parks fared better than those in the United States. Top-ranked was Gwaii Haanas National Park Reserve in British Columbia, Canada (score: eighty-eight), while the top U.S. parks included Apostle Islands National Lakeshore in Wisconsin, Great Basin National Park in Nevada, Wrangell–St. Elias National Park in Alaska, Hawaii Volcanoes National Park on Big Island, Chaco Culture National Historical Park in New Mexico, Crater Lake National Park in Oregon, and Point Reyes National Seashore in California, with scores between seventy-eight and seventy-two. Most of these parks have light visitor traffic and tasteful, restrained gateway towns.

On the survey, three U.S. parks ranked "rock bottom" because of "destructive external pressures and major internal difficulties." These were Florida's Everglades National Park/Big Cypress National Preserve (score: thirty-four), Tennessee's Great Smoky Mountains National Park (forty) and Virginia's Shenandoah National Park (forty-eight). The much-loved Great Smokies topped all others for negative adjectives of its three gateway communities. Those surveyed described Gatlinburg, Pigeon Forge, and Cherokee as "appalling," "distasteful," and "horrible." Similarly, the Everglades were also decried for an "unpleasant, unattractive gateway to one of the planet's unique places."[71]

The Grand Canyon, a crown jewel in the National Parks System and one of the most spectacular natural wonders in the world, was rated by the *National Geographic Traveler* survey as "facing trouble" (score:

fifty-three). Nearly 5 million visitors come here each year, making this Arizona's premier tourism attraction and the second-most-visited National Park, as well as a UNESCO designated World Heritage Site. Although park officials have successfully addressed a number of problems (such as tourists feeding the deer), the experts polled by *Traveler* reported that at the NPS's main tourist hub on the South Rim, the visitor experience is disturbed by "throngs" of other tourists, air pollution, noisy helicopter overflights, and too many cars, among other problems.[72] And this is all on the South Rim, *the better side* of the canyon.

Even more troubled is the tourist destination some 400 kilometers (250 miles) away, on the Canyon's West Rim, which is on the Hualapai Indian reservation and outside the boundary—and the restrictions—of the national park. "Our tribe started in these canyons," says Hualapai tribal chairman Charlie Vaughn, "We've always been here, and we'll always be here."[73] The Hualapai were moved to the four-hundred-thousand-hectare (1-million-acre) reservation in 1883, the national park was created in 1919, and the Hualapai have languished in poverty, despite various efforts to tap into tourism. When a new interstate opened in 1979, making it easier for tour buses and cars from Flagstaff to get to the park's South Rim entrance, the West Rim lost visitors. While no less spectacular and beautiful, the West Rim lacks amenities—paved roads, hotels, restaurants, visitors' centers, even running water—and so receives only one-twentieth the number of tourists (about 250,000 in 2006) as the national park.

In March 2007, the Hualapai ignited public debate with the opening of the Skywalk, a twenty-one-meter-wide (seventy-foot), horseshoe-shaped observation platform that juts out from the lip of the Canyon's West Rim. Tribal leaders partnered with a Las Vegas entrepreneur, who financed construction of the $30-million, four-inch-thick glass platform that weighs some five hundred tons, but has no visible supports from above or below. Dubbed "one of the greatest engineering marvels of our times," the platform is harnessed into the Canyon's wall with giant steel bolts driven 46 feet into the bedrock. Because it's not on government land, it was not subject to environmental impact reviews, water assessments, or other bureaucratic checks. Unnerved by possible failure, the first contractor quit.[74]

The platform allows visitors who pay twenty-five dollars to gaze down the four thousand feet to the canyon's floor and "simulate a sensation of floating over the abyss."[75] Tribal leaders say the Skywalk is also intended to jump-start West Rim tourism and with it, the Hualapai's ascent out of poverty. "When we have so much poverty and so much unemployment, we had to do something," explained Sheri Yellowhawk, the Hualapai official overseeing the project.[76] The hope is to attract visitors from Las Vegas, a short day trip (some 120 miles) away; the business plan projects doubling the number of visitors in the first year and pumping revenues into other West Rim tourism facilities.

The fear, however, is that the Skywalk and the Canyon itself will become just another Vegas attraction—"a place where tourists can come, be amazed, and lose as much of the contents of their wallets as can be pried out of them."[77] Indeed critics, including some Hualapai Indians, slam the Skywalk as "tacky," "an abomination," a "travesty," and a "horrific blight" on sacred land. "Our people died right there. It's spiritual ground," said one Hualapai elder. Nonetheless, at the opening ceremony, the Hualapai burned sage and blew into gourds, and a spiritual leader blessed the structure, which he termed "the white man's idea."[78]

So where do proponents of ecotourism line up in this debate? Both nature tourism and ecotourism have grown upon the foundation of the National Parks System. Proponents of nature tourism have often embraced a "forever wild" attitude toward parks and the "fortress conservation" philosophy that guided the gazetting and much of the governance of the parks. Ecotourism, with its core principles of benefits to conservation *and to host communities*, rejects the notion that, when created, many parks were devoid of all human settlement, and it seeks strategies that will create harmony, rather than hostility, with the park's historic occupants. Ecotourism thereby promotes a "stakeholders theory" that holds that people will protect what they receive value from, and it endorses policies to involve communities in park management and ecotourism businesses and, in some cases, in sustainable use of resources within the parks.[79] However, in part because ecotourism has not been seen as a critical tool for economic development in the United States and because it has not been discussed at a national level, this country has been slow to develop a consensus on the importance of ecotourism and what it really means. In 2005, a national dialogue did, finally, begin when The International Ecotourism Society (TIES) organized, for the first time, a national conference on ecotourism in the United States.

National Ecotourism Summit: Bar Harbor, Maine

With fog clinging to the coastline of Bar Harbor, Maine, the first national conference on ecotourism in the United States opened in mid-September in 2005. Some three hundred delegates from about half the states gathered in the historic Bar Harbor Club for an opening ceremony featuring local organic foods and the state's top brass. Just beyond view of the conferees, in the harbor dotted with lobster buoys, fishing craft, sailboats, and pleasure yachts, an enormous cruise ship pulled in, dropped anchor, and began unloading several thousand passengers for an afternoon of shopping and bus rides through the nearby Acadia National Park. Here on one early autumn day, the two faces of tourism—mass and eco—shared this storybook New England town, surrounded by bucolic dairy farms, rugged coastland, and one of the country's most popular national parks.[80]

Often described as tourism's polar opposites, cruise tourism and ecotourism had simultaneously fixed their sites on Bar Harbor. Massive cruise vessels had recently expanded beyond Florida to new ports of call up the U.S. East Coast and down through Central America, plying their reputation for safe and inexpensive getaways in the wake of the 9/11 terrorist attacks. Ecotourism had also only recently begun to be identified as a growing trend within the U.S. market.[81] And, in a number of places, from Bar Harbor to Belize and beyond, ecotourism and cruise tourism are competing over the same pieces of paradise.

I was at the time of the U.S. conference the executive director of TIES, but like many others in the field, my focus had always been elsewhere, on other places around the globe where the imperative of ecotourism seemed greatest for biodiversity protection, poverty alleviation, and cultural survival.[82] Within the global mix of exotic and alluring hot spots, the United States always looked a little plain, tame, and frankly, boring. Although TIES had been founded in the United States in 1990 and more than half its members live in this country, the society had rarely worked on projects on its home turf. Now that I've taken some time to look more closely at my home country, I've come to see that ecotourism has been growing quietly in many places across this land, often below the radar screen, and under a variety of names. But, as indicated above, the principles and practices that are playing out around the world are also informing ecotourism developments in the United States. Many of the struggles and tensions are similar, and involve a mix of its citizens—from the private sector, government, NGOs, local communities, and academia—who are working to curb the excesses of mass tourism and other forms of destructive "development" and put in place tourism that truly benefits host communities and conservation, while offering visitors a richer and rewarding vacation experience.

At the end of the conference, which was jointly organized by TIES and the local Chamber of Commerce, the delegates adopted, through a consultative and participatory project, The Bar Harbor Declaration, which called on the U.S. "government, at the federal, state and local levels, to adopt a series of policies to promote socially and environmentally responsible tourism." It continued, "We believe that, done well, ecotourism has the potential to transform the travel industry to be a positive force in safeguarding our natural and cultural heritage upon which tourism's future depends."[83]

The Bar Harbor meeting marked the start of a national dialogue around ecotourism, one that is to continue every two years. The next conference on ecotourism in North America occurred in September 2007 in Madison, Wisconsin, and this time included Canada as well as the United States. While these are small steps on the path toward elevating ecotourism to a national level, the real centers of activity have been, since the 1990s, at the state, local, and regional levels.

Ecotourism at the State Level: Policies and Ecotourism Societies

Tourism, including ecotourism, is heavily concentrated at the state level in terms of parks systems, government agencies, private-sector associations, and tourism attractions, activities, facilities, and marketing. State agencies, from their tourism, environmental, recreation, natural resources, waste management, and other departments to their convention and visitor bureaus, have been involved in an array of programs that may or may not carry the ecotourism label but do adhere to its principles and practices. Often these programs are run together with environmental organizations or private tourism businesses. For instance, as discussed below, a growing number of states are creating and running "green" lodging certification programs. Many of these state programs are geared to ensuring that tourists and tour operators properly use natural resources. The Virginia Ecotour Guide Certification course, for instance, is run by the Virginia Institute of Marine Science and designed "to encourage more responsible kayaking and boating tours" on the Eastern Shore. As the Web site explains, "Promoting ecotourism is a way of creating an economic reason to protect natural areas, in addition to increasing awareness of the value of our natural resources. By providing ecotour training to guides, we can reduce potential conflicts over use of resources and the inadvertent damage to animals, plants and natural areas often associated with tourism."[84] Some two dozen guides are listed as certified instructors.

Across the country, in Washington State, the state Department of Fish and Wildlife, several U.S. and Canadian federal agencies, the Whale Museum, and others have worked with the Whale Watch Operators Association–Northwest (WWOA-NW) to develop best-practices guidelines for all member boat operators. Whale-watching tours around the San Juan Islands have become a $10-million industry catering to more than a half-million visitors a year. This is said to represent the largest concentration of whale-watching operations in the world. The voluntary guidelines assist boaters in viewing Orcas and other marine wildlife with minimal impact to the animals. Since 1993, the Whale Museum has run the Southwatch Boater Education Program through, which volunteers monitor boater activity near whales.[85] Similar types of programs geared at educating tourism businesses and the public about protecting natural and cultural resources are found in virtually every state and reflect a broad commitment to the values of ecotourism.

Yet those values are still not fully embraced in the United States. Over the last two decades, for example, no one in the United States has done more to popularize ecotourism with the public and the press or within the tourism industry and government circles than Stanley Selengut, owner of Maho Bay Camps and three other resorts in St. Johns, in the U.S. Virgin Islands (see chapter 3). The tented camp, his best-known facility, was first built in 1976 with eco-sensitive construction on a private holding within the national park. As the concept of ecotourism took hold, Maho Bay quickly took on the mantle as the leading U.S. ecotourism resort and Selengut, an engaging and affable New Yorker with a signature white golf cap, became ecotourism's most high-profile spokesperson.[86] But Selengut focuses on sustainable design, "green" building techniques, and his own eco-innovations; less attention is given to ecotourism's other leg: relations with and benefits to host communities.[87]

While Stanley Selengut has been a major promoter of ecotourism in the Caribbean, it was in Alaska and Hawaii that the first successful ecotourism societies were formed, spearheaded by ecotourism operators and lodge owners and local environmental NGOs who were concerned with protecting both the natural and cultural resources in the United States' most far-flung states. In both states, tourism centers around the richness of both the natural and cultural attractions, and both rank among the top states in traveler satisfaction polls.[88]

Ecotourism in Alaska

Alaska has nineteen federally designated parks, historical sites, and wild rivers, including the country's largest park (Wrangell–St. Elias), tallest mountain (Mount McKinley), and breathtakingly beautiful Glacier Bay. Tourism dates back to 1880, when the Pacific Steamship Company began cruises to Glacier Bay, but until World War II, the numbers of tourists were small—thirty thousand or fewer per year—because travel to Alaska was expensive and inconvenient, and the season very short. In recent years, about 1 million people visit Alaska each year and spend almost $1 billion a year; tourism has become the state's second-largest primary employer, after commercial fishing.

The first state-based ecotourism was the Alaska Wilderness Recreation and Tourism Association (AWRTA), "a member-driven trade association formed to be a collective voice for wilderness-dependent businesses." Today AWRTA has over three hundred members. In 1994, it began holding annual state ecotourism conferences in Alaska, and in 1995, it adopted a comprehensive set of eight Ecotourism Guidelines. The guidelines, which demonstrate a holistic understanding of ecotourism, state that businesses should "seek environmentally sustainable economic growth while minimizing visitor impacts on wildlands, wildlife, Native cultures, and local communities" and should "provide direct benefits to the local economy and local inhabitants." Guideline Seven proposes that AWRTA member companies have "a formula for the business and guests to contribute to local non-profit efforts for environmental protection." Based on this, AWRTA launched the Dollars a Day for Conservation program, an innovative funding mechanism to collect donations for three designated conservation organizations in Alaska. In this early and fine example of Travelers' Philanthropy, participating businesses ask their guests to voluntarily contribute one dollar for each day of their trip, and then the company matches these contributions and passes the donations to the three organizations. In 2001, for instance, the thirty-five participating companies raised over twenty-five thousand dollars for these conservation organizations. "It's not only been successful in raising funds for environmental organizations," says Kirk Hoessle, owner of Alaska Wildland Adventures, "but it's been good for business, too. People like the opportunity to get involved."

Hoessle runs one of Alaska's most respected tour companies. For over thirty years, Alaska Wildland Adventures has organized tours and vacation packages featuring wilderness lodges and small groups. A 2005 winner of *Condé Nast Traveler*'s Green List award, the company focuses on visiting remote and relatively unaltered natural areas, puts an emphasis on educating guests about the natural and cultural history of the places they visit, and seeks to adopt low-impact and sustainable technologies. This includes the successful transition from diesel to an ultra-quiet and clean hydroelectric system to provide lights and hot water at its remote backcountry lodge in the Kenai National Wildlife Refuge. In another innovation, Hoessle developed "Greenworks," a program for monitoring all the company's activities and identifying ways to lessen their environmental impact.[89]

Over the years AWRTA and its members such as Hoessle have been involved in a number of the key environmental and social issues in Alaska that impact sustainable tourism. These have included how to best manage and control the growth of mass tourism via cruise ships, what, if any, types of hunting and fishing should be permitted as part of ecotourism, and how to deal with global warming. As AWRTA's Web site states, "Alaska is the first to feel the ecological implications of global climate change, as well as its effect on the tourism industry."

One of the most complex issues in Alaska and around the world involves the interaction between ecotourism and indigenous people. Cultural tourism is a central component of ecotourism, and AWRTA's Web site includes information about Alaska Natives, who represent some 16 percent of Alaska's population and "are a significant segment of the population in over 200 rural villages and communities. Many Alaska Natives," the Web site goes on to say, "have retained their customs, language, hunting and fishing practices and ways of living since 'the creation of times.'"[90] AWRTA describes five main cultural groupings, based on information from the Alaska Native Heritage Center in Anchorage. Since opening in 1999 the center has been "a gathering place that celebrates, perpetuates and preserves the unique Alaska Native Cultures, languages, traditions and values through celebration and education."[91] But, as the Alaska Native Science Commission study quoted above shows, many Alaska Natives remain skeptical about the benefits of ecotourism.

Ecotourism in Hawaii

Hawaii's tourism industry took off in the 1950s and early 1960s, as faster, long-range aircraft and U.S. statehood (in 1959) led to "a political and economic revolution" on the islands and a decision to embrace "a wholehearted strategy to develop mass tourism." By the mid-1970s, tourism was producing twice the jobs and revenue as the military, pineapple, and sugar industries combined. Today, tourism is Hawaii's main export, representing the single largest economic activity and accounting directly and indirectly for 22 percent of jobs in the state. In 2005, Hawaii had nearly 7.5 million visitors (65 percent from the mainland United States and 21 percent from Japan) who spent about $11.6 billion. A 2006 government study indicated "tourism in Hawaii is a mature industry" and is "more advanced, stable, and unlikely to see massive expansion."[92]

The dominant tourism model in Hawaii is characterized, according to tourism consultant John Knox, by a concentration of tourism development into "resort nodes ranging from 'tourist towns' such as Waikiki to self-contained 'planned resorts' like Ka'anapali on Maui and North Kahala on the Big Island." Knox observes that for many years "the prevailing paradigm of Hawaii tourism involved the idea that the great majority of visitors would spend most of their time in these resorts, venturing only occasionally in tour buses and rental cars to visit specific scenic or commercial attractions." About half the state's tourism inventory is concentrated in Waikiki, a tourism town that attracts a range of visitors, from high-spending Japanese to budget-conscious Canadians. Over the last several decades, much tourism growth has been through master-planned resorts built on huge tracts of rural and agricultural land. These low-density developments include a handful of all-inclusive hotels, together with golf courses, recreational activities, retail complexes, and condos and home lots. Knox notes that the "real estate component is central to understanding master-planned resorts" where "hotels may have been developed (at least initially) as loss leaders, to attract buyers for the resort's real estate products."[93]

One of the most vibrant areas for ecotourism has been agritourism, with a range of activities involving 187 Hawaiian farms and valued at $33.9 million in 2003; another 145 farms have reported intentions to start agritourism businesses. The main activities include sales of farm produce, products, and souvenirs, outdoor recreation, accommodations, and entertainment.[94]

But ecotourism per se has remained relatively small-scale, low-key, and on the fringes. As in Alaska, ecotourism initiatives date from 1994 when Hawaii environmentalists, nature tourism operators, academics, and Native Hawaiian activists held the first statewide ecotourism conference. In 1995, the conference planning committee went on to form the Hawaii Ecotourism Association (HEA), a nonprofit membership organization "committed to diversifying Hawaii's travel industry through advocacy for ecotourism to protect Hawaii's unique natural environment and cultures." By 1999, HEA had over one hundred members including ecotour and lodging operators, travel agents, community and environmental organizations, travel writers, government officials, and academics. Over the years, HEA's activities have included publishing *The Ecotourism Manual*, drafting a certification program (which has not been launched), and developing a set of brochures and a Web site for the windward Oahu communities of Koolaupoko.[95]

HEA has been only one of the players promoting socially and environmentally responsible tourism in Hawaii. While HEA has focused largely on small-scale, community-based nature, rural, and cultural tourism, other NGOs, civic groups, academics, private consultants, and various government departments and special commissions have looked at the impacts of mass tourism and proposed alternatives. On occasion, concerns over mass tourism led to public protests. In 2002, as international cruise lines were expanding their ports of call in Hawaii, residents on the island of Molokai mounted a beachfront protest that successfully stopped a Holland America ship from disembarking its passengers.

One of the most innovative civic actions was instigated by the local Sierra Club, which, in 2000, filed a lawsuit against the Hawaii Tourism Authority (HTA). The legal action sought to require that a statewide environmental assessment be conducted before the HTA could award a $114-million contract to expand Hawaii's international marketing. The Sierra Club suit argued that the current level of visitors was eroding the state's environment, culture, and public infrastructure and demanded a full review of the impact of tourism. While the Supreme Court dismissed the lawsuit in 2002, it helped fuel public concern over mass tourism, which led the legislature to commission a study of "the carrying capacity of Hawaii for tourism." The multi-faceted study involved teams of researchers and advisers as well as a series of statewide public meetings organized by Knox's team that gave participants a chance to make wide-ranging comments about tourism issues.[96] A special advisory panel for the study examined Native Hawaiian perspectives on Hawaii's tourism industry and found that many said it had "eroded their rights and culture," including devaluing sacred places, compromising their cultural integrity, and diminishing the Native Hawaiian "sense of place" in Waikiki and other tourism towns.[97]

Four years and $1.2 million later, the 2,560-page *Planning for Sustainable Tourism* report was finally released in April 2006. The study sidestepped its mandate from the legislature that it calculate the islands' "carrying capacity" for tourism, arguing that it was impossible to come up with a precise number given varied geography, infrastructure, and social composition of the islands.[98] The study did, however, propose for the first time a system of new economic models called the "Hawaii Sustainable Tourism Modeling System" to determine how much fuel, water, and lodging would be used by a given number of visitors.[99] The study also noted a series of "emerging tourism issues" in the twenty-first century involving cruise tourism, recreational real estate, and the growth of individual vacation rentals. How these and other issues will be addressed in the future remains to be seen. While the study is exhaustive, some faulted it for failing to break new ground in terms of solutions or for failing to recognize that, in some areas, the limits of sustainability have already been passed.[100]

Ecotourism in the Lower Forty-eight

While the early experiments with ecotourism businesses, the first successful state ecotourism societies, and debates over how to control and tame mass tourism began in the most remote U.S. states, they quickly began to be mirrored, with local variations, across much of the lower forty-eight. Over the last decade or so, there have been ecotourism conferences and symposia in a number of states, efforts to form additional statewide ecotourism organizations, experiments with a wide range of ecotourism businesses, and a proliferation of "green" tourism certification programs.

And again and again, ecotourism has been put forward as at least a piece of the "solution" to particular problems. Here are just a few of the scores of examples. Delaware, the only state without any national parks, set out early on to position itself as a nature tourism destination. In 1994, it held a statewide ecotourism workshop, and in Sussex County, the Convention and Tourism Commission worked with the University of Delaware and the state park system to develop and market ecotourism activities and to produce *Delaware Eco-Discoveries*, a nature-based tourism guide.[101]

Perhaps more than any other state, Vermont has used ecotourism, if not in name, then in practice, to protect its rural farms and small towns. In 1936, long before ecotourism was born as a concept, Vermont voted down an interstate parkway "that would have broken the state wide open to tourists, millions of dollars, and potentially wrenching change."[102] This strategic decision positioned the Green Mountain State to promote locally owned and small-scale tourism, based on family farms, bed and breakfasts, locally owned inns and lodges, small towns, and year-round nature-based activities. In 2000, Johnson State College professor Todd Comen organized a regional ecotourism conference followed by week-long, field-based workshops in four different parts of the state that brought together practitioners from throughout the region.[103] One of the central themes was agritourism, or how to use ecotourism to help protect Vermont's family-owned farms. A 2002 survey found that earnings from agritourism totaled $10.5 million. One-third (2,200 farms) of all Vermont farms received an average of $8,900 in income from agritourism. A greater percentage of smaller farms (under fifty acres) were involved in agritourism activities, with income generated from on-farm sales of commodities, accommodation, outdoor recreation, education, and entertainment.[104]

In Moss Point, Mississippi, and on the Pascagoula River, the Audubon Society has been helping to rebuild livelihoods in coastal communities devastated by Hurricane Katrina. They have done so, in part, through a mosaic of ecotourism activities, including a new nature and educational center, guide-training courses, birding and kayaking tours, bed and breakfasts, tree planting, and a boat tour company.[105] In Florida, Kerri Post and handful of other state tourism officials were convinced that Florida had more to offer than theme parks and beaches. Beginning in 1995, an Ecotourism/Heritage Tourism Advisory Committee was formed as part of the state's Visit Florida program to promote nature and cultural tourism in rural communities. The plan included taking an inventory of the tourism assets, ensuring protection of the sites and ecosystems, and marketing these "new" products, including "off-the-beaten path, self-driving tours."[106]

In West Virginia, one of the nation's poorest and most beautiful states, government officials, university professors, local tourism businesses, community activists, and NGOs have worked for a number of years to create an ecotourism society and a range of government programs, as well as to hold several ecotourism conferences.[107] They have viewed ecotourism as a way to help protect the state's rivers, streams, mountains, and wildlife habitats and to provide an alternative to the state's declining and destructive extractive industries, coal mining and logging. In 2001, the Department of Environmental Protection and the Division of Tourism signed a Memorandum of Agreement to promote ecotourism "in order to create a sustainable ecotourism economy for the State of West Virginia, thus improving the quality of life for its citizens."[108] That same year, the West Virginia Eco-Tourism Association, "a collection of businesses united under eco-friendly tenets and the urge to bring more visitors to their state," was formed and began operating out of the Natural Seasons Bed & Breakfast, in the tiny town of Westin. By 2005, the association had teamed up with Solimar Marketing, a Washington, D.C.–based eco-travel agency, to promote the state's "green" offerings including white-water rafting, hiking, biking, hot springs, family farms, wineries, inns and bed and breakfasts, and a rich range of crafts, culture, and local festivals, as well as skiing and other winter sports. Several historic towns, including Berkeley Springs, are collectively marketing their ecotourism accommodations and activities and are seeking to promote the state as a leading ecotourism destination.[109] "A large majority of our market—D.C. metro area folks—are looking for this kind of tourism," said Ben Isenberg, of Solimar Marketing.[110] In 2005, the *Washington Post* pronounced that "In West Virginia, Eco-Tourism is Becoming Second Nature."

In Iowa, H. Peter Jorgensen runs Silos & Smokestacks National Heritage Area, comprising thirty-seven counties in the northeast part of the state. This nonprofit organization was created to support development of regional heritage tourism and share the story of American agriculture through tourism. And from his vantage point, Jorgensen has a clear-eyed sense that ecotourism does have roots here in the American heartland.[111] "[P]eople think ecotourism is for diehard environmentalists and tree huggers who can afford to travel to far-flung exotic places," he tells journalist Frances Figart. "But they don't realize that when they took the kids to Yellowstone Park, they were participating in ecotourism. Or when they visited Uncle Merle and Aunt Betty on their Iowa farm and saw how the environment on that farm was managed sustainably, they were ecotourists."[112]

Varieties of Ecotourism in the Lower Forty-eight

As the above indicates, ecotourism is deeply tied to the land and to rural communities. Two of the most common forms of ecotourism in the lower forty-eight are agritourism and eco-ranching, both of which are efforts to preserve family-owned businesses and the land, local crops, cultural traditions, and ways of life from outside encroachment by, for instance, developers, industrial agriculture, resort complexes, and gated vacation-home communities.

Protecting Farmlands, Ranchlands, and Rural Lifestyles

Of all the types of ecotourism, agritourism[113] is one of the fastest-growing sectors in the United States, just as it has been in Europe, Australia, Canada, Argentina, and elsewhere. Generally defined as activities that include visiting a working farm or any agricultural, horticultural, or agribusiness operations, it has traditionally involved farm tours for families or schoolchildren, hands-on chores, self-harvesting, purchase of farm products or handicrafts, hay and sleigh rides, and overnight stays. In recent years, U.S. agritourism has also been propelled by the growing interest in more "designer" agriculture, including organics, "slow" or local foods, heirloom crops, and wineries. Today there is a wide range of agritourism offerings, from inexpensive day visits to exclusive gourmet goods and wine getaways.

According to a TIA study, nearly two-thirds of U.S. adults, or 87 million people, have taken a trip to a rural destination in the last three years, and nine out of ten of these did so for "leisure purposes." While nationwide statistics aren't available, there is some information on individual states. In addition to Vermont and Hawaii (described above), and Montana (below), California is an increasingly important state for agritourism, and is the leading state for wine tourism. Family-owned wineries are popular attractions, hosting visitors for educational tours and wine tastings. California has 2,275 wineries, concentrated in Napa and Sonoma counties, while there are more than 4,900 wineries in the United States. California accounts for 90 percent of all U.S. wine production, and wine is the state's number-one agricultural product, generating $17.8 billion in retail sales in the United States alone. Wine tourism in California accounts for 19.7 million visitors and expenditures of $2 billion annually. A growing number of these wineries have become organic and are also working to "green" their operations and their buildings.[114]

From Dude Ranch to Eco-Ranch and Green Cowboys

Tourism grew up in the West both around and within the national parks, on the Indian reservations, and on private lands. For the last two decades there have been a handful of ranches and tour operators in the western mountain states who have experimented with ecotourism. According to Bill Bryan, owner of the ecotourism outfitter company Off the Beaten Path and a sort of unofficial historian of ecotourism in the West, "In the Rockies, the states, the stakes, and the estates are all enormous." Montana, for instance, had 10.3 million nonresidents visit the state in 2006, spending $2.9 billion. Yellowstone and Glacier Parks are the most visited sites, overall, while fishing, wildlife-watching, hiking, and shopping are primary Montana tourist activities.[115] As has been the case in other countries, there has been a growing amount of private land in the United States put under conservancy and used for ecotourism activities. A 1997 survey found, for instance, that 47 percent of rural landowners permitted recreational use of their land by non–family members, and that this totaled 60 percent of U.S. privately owned land.[116]

In the western states, "dude" ranches have over the last century offered guests horseback riding, camping, fishing, hunting, hiking, and other outdoor activities. One of the first dude ranches was the partnership between Marshall Cunningham and Carl Biering who had vast acreage in the Gallatin and Madison Valleys in southwestern Montana, which included the Nine Quarters Circle ranches and some ten-thousand cattle. During the summer months from 1907 to 1913, they hosted about thirty guests who each paid $150 a week. They suspended operations during World War I, and then opened up again in 1928. As the Depression and drought hit in the 1930s, other ranches in the area also began hospitality operations to supplement their income from stock raising. "In a pattern that has continued today, many people who first came to the Madison Valley on vacation at these dude ranches later bought property here themselves,"[117] some setting up their own dude ranches, others buying ranches as vacation homes.

The first ranch or farm "hospitality operation" in Wyoming to be described as doing ecotourism was the twelve-thousand-acre Z Bar O Ranch, set along the Tongue River at the foot of the spectacular Big Horn Mountains. Owned by Dick and Jean Masters, this working ranch had been in the family for a century. In the early 1980s, an economic crisis forced the Masters to diversify beyond cattle and crops. They opened a bed and breakfast using several guesthouses already on their property. Their start-up costs were almost nil and by 1990, they were hosting about one hundred guests during the summer season, and earning about 25 percent of their total income from visitors. Described by Bryan as "an example of an entirely new form of ecotourism in the West," the Masters combined sustainable agriculture—including cattle rotation, using natural alternatives to pesticides and chemical fertilizers, and keeping riparian habitat and wetlands untouched—with "sustainable ecotourism"—educating their guests about farm life, western wildlife, and the environment.[118]

Other farms and ranches followed suit. Between 1985 and 1990, the number of farms and ranches involved in tourism in the tri-state region of Wyoming, Montana, and Idaho rapidly grew from a handful to between seventy and ninety. "This phenomenon," writes Bryan 1991, "has its roots in the fact that the western family farm and ranch is experiencing troubled times, and that many Americans are looking for ways to 'get back to the land.'" The economic difficulties in the agricultural industry forced many small farmers and ranchers out of business and off the land; ecotourism helped save some of these. Bryan estimates that this type of ranch ecotourism was generating "at least $750 million" a year and was offering the potential to "contribute to the sustainable development of rural communities, and offset pressure toward less environmentally sensitive alternatives such as agribusiness."[119]

Sadly, the Z Bar O Ranch didn't survive, brought down by a combination of inadequate capital and marketing and declining health of the owners. Bryan cautions that ecotourism is not an easy "quick economic fix" and "can dash just as many hopes and dreams in implementation as it creates in concept."[120] Today, he says that there's no inventory of good eco-lodges in the West. "I don't know of many." One of the "very very few eco-lodges in the West is the Lodge at Sun Ranch, formerly Papoose Creek," located in Cameron, Montana.

The Lodge at Sun Ranch

In 1998, Roger and Cindy Lang bought the twenty-six-thousand-acre Sun Ranch in southwestern Montana's upper Madison River Valley, forty miles from Yellowstone. Sun Ranch had been a working ranch for some fifty years and given its enormity (it's three-quarters the size of San Francisco) and proximity to Yellowstone, biologists consider it one of the most important wildlife corridors in the Rockies. To locals, however, the Langs' purchase appeared to be just another instance of the 1990s "gold rush"—deep-pocketed Californians buying up ranches in the West for vacation homes. But, as Roger Lang explains, "I'm not into jet planes or Ferraris. We thought: let's do something meaningful that will last. I can't think of a better way to spend the money."

In their early forties with two young sons, the Langs were both graduates of Stanford University. Roger, who holds a Masters in anthropology and speaks five languages, had seen ecotourism firsthand while studying and traveling abroad. Unable to find employment as an anthropologist in the 1980s, he went instead into various high-tech industries in Silicon Valley and Wall Street. The Langs came to Montana with resources to invest and a commitment to conserve both the natural environment and the local ranching culture and community through a multidimensional "eco-enterprise."[121]

As Roger Lang tells a group of guests, "This business model has to work because we're in a race against time: according to regional surveys, 70 percent of the traditionally owned ranches in the greater Rocky Mountains will turn over ownership in the next five years."[122] And the consequences are enormous. Farmers and ranchers own two-thirds of private property in the United States, and, according to the U.S. Fish and Wildlife Service, about 70 percent of endangered species are found on private land. So parceling out ranches for resort developments, with trophy homes, swimming pools, golf courses, ski lifts, and fences, destroys the corridors for elk, deer, bears, and other wildlife.

Roger Lang knew what he wanted to avoid, but he had not, at first, a clear road map for what he wanted to achieve. With no ranching experience, Lang says there's been a lot of trial and error, experimentation and mistakes, but that he, unlike many Montana ranchers, has had the resources to permit recalibrations. An attempt to raise cashmere goats, for instance, failed. "I came up here with the Sierra Club ethos, thinking 'Cows are bad,'" recalls Lang. "I was a classic, detached-from-the-land suburbanite. But," he says he came to learn, "if you manage for wildlife, there's a win-win. For the next twenty to thirty years, cows and other sustainable forms of agriculture are what will preserve open spaces."

Like Dan Janzen, who used cattle to rejuvenate the Guanacaste National Park in Costa Rica, Lang has come to see that "cows are the rough proximity to the bison that used to be here." Today Sun Ranch has about 1,800 grass-fed beef cattle, many of which are raised without growth-inducing hormones or antibiotics and kept healthy by rotating them across the ranch's pastures. Their meat has commanded a higher price; on the menus in Yellowstone National Park's restaurants it has been listed as "conservation beef."[123] Sun Ranch follows a philosophy of "holistic resource management," which seeks to create a healthy balance between cattle, grass, and wildlife. The ranch has replaced over forty miles of barbed-wire fencing with barb-less, moveable fencing that is taken down to allow free movement of elk and other wildlife through the property. Over 30 percent of Sun Ranch has been put under a conservation easement to ensure that open space and habitat are protected for future generations and, Lang says, more than 95 percent of the total acreage will shortly be added under conservation easement.

Initially, ecotourism was also not part of the Langs' vision. Bill Bryan recalls that they planned to open a restaurant on the ranch, but he convinced them to do an eco-lodge instead. They transformed the existing log home, built three cabins set among spruce and aspen trees, and in 2001, opened the sixteen-guest Papoose Creek Lodge. They began marketing upscale, all-inclusive eco-packages starting at $1,440 per person for three days and offering fly-fishing, hiking, horseback riding, birding, canoeing, white-water rafting, and wildlife-watching. In the winter, they offer high-end hunting packages (upwards of $3,500 for food, accommodation and a guide) that permit controlled shooting of elk on the ranch—something that doesn't sit well with some ecotourism proponents.[124]

Almost immediately, Papoose Creek (now renamed Lodge at Sun Ranch) captured media attention. Within a few years, Papoose Creek had been named as one of the top eco-lodges in the world by *Condé Nast Traveler*'s Green List, *Men's Journal*, and *USA Today*. Its own website describes Papoose Creek as "the premier ecolodge in the continental U.S."[125] But while the eco-lodge has brought publicity and accolades, it is just one piece of the sustainable ranch management model. As Lang explains his big vision, "Our philosophy is to do sustainable recreation, sustainable agriculture, and sustainable real estate, all anchored with an NGO carrying out good empirical science and social science and all blended under the proposition of involving the community."

In 2006, Roger Lang started the Sun Ranch Institute, a nonprofit organization dedicated to carrying out good science and social research and education for the benefit of the ranch, conservation, and the surrounding community. Headed by a young Stanford MBA Josh Spitzer, the institute's mission is to find innovative and sustainable solutions to the real-life issues. One of the biggest, most complex challenge has been determining how cattle can coexist with wolves. Since they were first reintroduced to Yellowstone in 1995, the original fourteen wolves had increased to over 1,200 by 2007 and, in following the elk migrations, they have spread onto neighboring ranches.

"I'm a new rancher living with wolves on a daily basis," Lang tells his guests. "When I bought Sun Ranch, my first inclination was to support them. I hung up beautiful calendars of wolves. I said its okay if I lose a few cows." For nearly two years, the ranch's "predator management program" permitted cattle and a pack of wolves to coexist by carefully moving the cattle and using nonlethal techniques to keep the wolves at bay. Then, in August 2006, cattle started being killed in larger numbers, and ranch staff and federal authorities responded by killing several wolves. Lang says "all hell broke lose," with environmentalists denouncing the killing of the wolves while ranchers called for their complete elimination. Lang, with a foot in both the rancher and the conservationist camps, sought outside help: "We invited Maasai cattle herders from East Africa to come here and teach us how to live with wildlife. The Maasai said, 'It's easy. You just have to sleep with your cattle.'" So in 2007, Sun Ranch/Papoose Creek launched its "Sleeping with Cattle and Wolves" program, offering guests the opportunity to serve as "a human-presence deterrent to the wolves" by spending a night, African-safari style, in luxury tents surrounding the cattle.[126] While this innovative response has been popular with guests, it hasn't, unfortunately, kept out the wolves. Sun Ranch has lost several more cattle and the institute has gone back to the drawing board in search of solutions. "We're committed to coexistence with wolves," says Lang. "But we now know that there are no easy solutions."

The institute also devotes one-third of its time and resources to community outreach. In 2007 this included the launch of one of the first Travelers' Philanthropy programs in the United States. Based on an investigation by a Stanford researcher, the institute selected a half-dozen community organizations involved in protecting wildlife, fisheries, open space, and the community spirit of the Madison Valley. Sun Ranch guests are encouraged to learn about and support these organizations through voluntary donations. The lodge's handbook suggests guests make a tax-deductible donation equivalent to 5 percent of their bill, but, it stresses, "no gift is too small."

Roger Lang says he hopes that the Sun Ranch mix of cattle, recreation, and real estate offers "a blended model between pure conservation and pure development" that can be "intelligently exported." In late 2007, he purchased another nearby ranch and hopes, he says, to eventually conserve 1 million acres using the Sun Ranch model. He also sold the Papoose Creek Lodge to a private family and laid plans to build, over the next two years, a new, "very green" eco-lodge on another section of the property, away from wildlife migration routes. In less than a decade, Papoose Creek and Sun Ranch have demonstrated that sustainable tourism, farming, and real estate, backed by financial resources and good science, can protect large tracks of land for both cattle and wildlife. This experiment in integrated "eco-development" has deepened the concept of ecotourism and provided an alternative to the gated luxury communities and resort developments that are so rapidly subdividing the West's ranching lands. However, the Sun Ranch/Papoose Creek Lodge experiment also raises the question of whether this type of sustainable development, at least in the context of the United States, can only be done by the very rich for the very rich. Roger Lang says he's contemplating, for instance, building some lower-cost housing for employees on his ranch. But Lang recognizes that, like living with wolves, finding the right model for sustainable *and affordable* eco-development is a challenge.

Ecotour Operators

U.S. tour operators or outfitters who organize customized and small-group tours are an essential component of the ecotourism chain linking the traveler with the destination (see chapter 3). While in the United States several dozen "outbound" nature and adventure tour operators organize trips to other countries, only a handful have specialized in ecotourism within the United States. One of the oldest is Off the Beaten Path, headquartered in Bozeman, Montana, and founded and owned, since 1986, by Bill and Pam Bryan. "We started in three states—Montana, Idaho, and Wyoming doing customized trips with individual clients and working with them to really learn about the place. We had a passionate commitment around the environment and the Rocky Mountain West. We wanted to drill down more than anyone else. This was our signature," says Bill Bryan. They pioneered the concept of designing itineraries from scratch to fit the desires of their clients and using the best guides, accommodations, and other vendors, based on the long personal experience in the West. Early on *Condé Nast Traveler* dubbed Off the Beaten Path "the travel shrinks of the West" because, says Bryan, "We listen. That's a hallmark. And we offer in-depth information and advice. We had to create experiences that people couldn't get on their own, including connections with local people."[127]

Off the Beaten Path built up a client base through word-of-mouth referrals, strategic advertising in a few upscale magazines like the *New*

Yorker and *Smithsonian*, and a small, understated but elegant catalog. Their clients are typically "traveled" people who have seen the globe but have spent very little time traveling in their own backyard. Gradually, the Bryans began to expand beyond their home turf in the Rockies, in part because they acquired loyal "repeat" clients who wanted new destinations. In 1991, they began offering trips to the Canadian Rockies, and in 1998, they expanded to Patagonia, at the tip of both Chile and Argentina. Why Patagonia? "The topography and the type of people are very similar to the Rockies," says Bryan. "And because it's the opposite season, it helped alleviate our problem of a short summer season in the West." Most recently, Off the Beaten Path has started organizing trips to Peru and Ecuador. They also gradually began to handle some fixed-itinerary small-group tours, and today, Bryan says, they do 55 percent customized itineraries and 45 percent group trips, totaling 2,200 individuals. The company has grown from three employees to twenty, and is grossing $5.6 million in 2007, their best year yet.[128]

Off the Beaten Path is a member of the Adventure Collection, an exclusive "club" comprising ten of the finest ecotourism operators in the United States and Canada (see chapter 3).[129] The Adventure Collection was the brainchild of Sven Lindblad, owner of Lindblad Expeditions,[130] which specializes in small boat trips to Alaska and the Pacific Northwest, as well as the Galapagos, Sea of Cortés (Mexico), and other overseas destinations. "Sven's idea," recalls Bryan, "was to bundle together the best tour operators and to share what we were doing." Collectively, they have won a long list of eco-awards and, under the Adventure Collection umbrella, they undertake some common advertising, exchange client lists, and have agreed upon five "responsibility principles" that each company is working to implement.[131] In addition to Off the Beaten Path, only two other Adventure Collection members began by offering high-quality ecotourism within the United States: O.A.R.S.,[132] a thirty-five-year-old rafting and sea kayaking company specializing in rivers of the West, and NOLS (National Outdoor Leadership School),[133] which was created in 1965 by legendary mountaineer Paul Petzoldt to train outdoor leaders in mountaineering, rock climbing, white-water expeditions, wilderness horse-packing, skiing, and backpacking.

From Green to Eco-Certified Hotels

While ecotour operators play a crucial role in packaging socially and environmentally responsible trips, it is the hotels that often form the centerpiece of a holiday. In the United States, the $114-billion lodging industry includes more than fifty-four thousand hotels (of fifteen rooms or more). As in other countries, central efforts to create "green" practices and standards within the tourism industry have focused on accommodations. This makes sense: hotels are the second-largest employers in the United States; contribute to environmental, social, and economic impacts; and are sensitive about their reputations with the public and media. The U.S. Travel Data Center estimates that 43 million U.S. travelers are "ecologically concerned,"[134] and a 2007 survey found that three of four hotel guests in North America say they take part in hotel conservation programs "when they know about those efforts."[135] But this survey and others have found that often hotels do not adequately inform guests about "green" practices or sufficiently educate their staffs about how to implement such efforts.

Green Hotels and Ecotourism Lite

In 1993, Patricia Griffin founded the Green Hotels Association (GHA), based in Houston, Texas, and launched a campaign for accommodations across the United States to give guests the "option" not to change their sheets and towels every day (see chapter 2). The campaign caught on, and today it is commonplace to find cards in hotel bathrooms or on the bed with bold headlines such as "Save Our Planet!," "One Person Can Make All the Difference in the World," "Project Planet," and "Save Mother Earth!"[136] Griffin says GHA has sold "hundreds of thousands of towel-rack hangers and sheet-changing cards" and nowadays "virtually no guest is surprised to learn of such a program during a hotel stay."[137] While billed to guests as saving the environment, this highly successful initiative offers significant bottom-line savings for hotels. GHA says hotels save an estimated $6.50 a day per occupied room and a total of 5 percent on utilities. For larger hotels this adds up to many thousands of dollars a year.[138] "Hotels have benefited enormously via reducing use of water, detergent, energy, labor, [and] wear and tear on linens and equipment," says Griffin.

In addition to the towel-and-sheets campaign, GHA has provided hotels with scores of other ideas and techniques "that save water, save energy, and reduce solid waste—while saving money." As one press release puts it, "GHA has presented enough money-saving ideas to hoteliers to prove that conservation saves money." For as little as a hundred dollars a year, any hotel can join GHA and receive not only publications "packed with smart, practical ideas," but also "heavy media publicity, an Internet listing and public identification as a 'Green' Hotel' via pole and front desk flags." GHA has over three hundred members, in every state, and ranging from small bed and breakfasts to large hotel chains.

While its eco-suggestions are sensible, some are concerned that the scope of GHA's program is narrow, hotels too often make exaggerated claims of benefits, and the public may get a false impression that the association verifies the "green" practices of member hotels. As the towel-and-sheet cards illustrate, the hype around these eco-efficiency programs often overstates their true environmental impacts. Further, GHA's promotion of member hotels on its Web site and with its Green Hotels flag and certificate can make it appear that the association has examined the environmental practices of member hotels. In fact, GHA simply supplies information; it sets no criteria for membership and does no on-site inspections. And because GHA only promotes cost-saving environmental reforms, it may miss other necessary practices that cost rather than save money. GHA is ecotourism lite: it falls short of far broader environmental, social, and economic principles and good practices that underpin genuine ecotourism.

But GHA has played an important role in building an environmental consciousness among both hoteliers and the traveling public.[139] Today there are a number of "copycat" programs, with similar names, programs, missions, and Web sites,[140] including CERES' Green Hotel Initiative (see chapter 2). In addition, in recent years, an increasing number of hotel chains have developed company-wide environmental policies. Leaders among the hotel chains are, among others, the Saunders Hotel Group, whose properties include The Lenox, an historic and very "green" hotel in Boston; the San Francisco–based Kimpton Hotels, with dozens of small hotels across the country; Fairmont Hotels and Resorts, the largest luxury hotel company in North America and one of the very first to develop detailed and company-wide environmental policies; and the New York–based Starwood Hotels and Resorts.

The Greening of Historic Hotels

Still, until recently, finding a genuine eco-accommodation wasn't that easy. In 2000, a colleague and I organized the first international conference on "green" tourism certification. We brought together some eighty people who had created and were running tourism certification programs around the world. Since these were, in essence, among the world's leading experts in deciding what are the most important criteria to ensure that hotels are environmentally and socially responsible, it was clear that we needed to hold the conference in a sustainable hotel—one that had more than a towel and sheet reuse program. After checking out the short list of possibilities in the greater Washington area (including the Airlie House Conference Center in Virginia, where the first Earth Day meeting took place), we cast our net farther afield. We found the Mohonk Mountain House,[141] a magnificent, 265-room Victorian castle and one of the country's oldest family-owned resorts, located in the heart of New York's Hudson Valley. When Amos Bien arrived from Costa Rica, he was thrilled: he said that, being originally from

New York, he had long heard of Mohonk, which he called "the U.S.'s first and oldest eco-lodge." Since Amos's eco-lodge, Rara Avis, holds a similar distinction in Costa Rica, I took this as gospel, breathed a sigh of relief, and we all settled into this grand old resort for what turned out to be an historic conference within the esoteric annals of ecotourism certification. Over the coming years, I gradually learned that Mohonk Mountain House is part of a longer tradition of upscale, nature-based resort tourism in the eastern United States, the equivalent of the nineteenth-century European Grand Tour (see chapter 1). Set among spectacular natural beauty and catering to healthy lifestyles, these old-time resorts are one of the origins of U.S. ecotourism today.

The roots of ecotourism can be found, in part, in some of these old hotels, including, for instance, The Colony Hotels in Delray Beach, Florida and Kennebunkport, Maine. Jestena Boughton, whose family has owned these two historic resorts for more than seventy years, says her father was a conservationist committed to repairing and reusing, rather than discarding and replacing. Since she became owner in 1994, Boughton has systematically worked to "green" the resorts' operations using what are today considered best practices within the field of sustainable tourism. "It's like being on a diet. Every day you have to think about it. It doesn't just happen," says Boughton. "We have to continually educate our staff, but we don't want to be too preachy with the guests."[142]

At the height of the summer season, The Colony in Kennebunkport is full, mainly with multi-generational families. While many have been coming for decades, general manager Donna Kabay says, "We are getting a lot of people who call and say they want to stay here because we're 'green'." She says it's driven by two trends: "Baby Boomers who have more money to travel and care about the environment" and "the growing number of people with allergies. There seem to be more people who are sensitive to chemicals, smoke, dust, and so on. They chose us because we are smoke-free, very careful about our cleaning products, and so on." The Colony also permits pets, and Kabay says staff totally strip bedrooms, cleaning the rugs, curtains, and all the bedding, after a dog or other pet has departed.

Boughton says she did not intend to make a career in the hotel world. She holds advanced degrees in landscape architecture and taught at the University of Massachusetts, Amherst. But she was the only heir and, in 1994, after both her parents had died, she quit teaching and took over. "It was harder to imagine selling than running the hotels," she explained. In both locations, the hotels strive to purchase goods and services from the local community. They also make regular donations to a range of civic organizations, from historic and land-trust societies, to the arts, animal shelters, and environmental organizations.

Today, The Colony's three-page list of ecological improvements reads like the pretty standard fare of "reduce, reuse, and recycle." While Boughton says that "there were some easy decisions"—composting, recycling, fluorescents, bulk buying, biodegradable soaps—other reforms have been more challenging, both because of the hotels' age and because she extended the seasons. The hotels were therefore consuming more electricity and water, and didn't show a lot of improvement on the audits. And staff education and training has been another ongoing challenge, given the high turnover and entrenched attitudes among some of the older workers. Cleaning staff often ignores customers' desires not to have sheets and towels changed daily—as my family found during our stay at The Colony in Maine.[143]

Overall, Boughton says she has found synergy between being historic and being "green": "My father grew up in the Depression and he was very thrifty and never threw anything out. I think there's overlap in keeping the traditions, in repairing rather than replacing. This can also mean being environmentally responsible because it keeps a sense of place and time, and doesn't create waste."

"I feel we're at the tipping point," Boughton says. "The media used to feature us as an historic hotel. Now we're featured as a 'green' hotel. It's hip to be 'green.'"

From Green Hotels to Eco-Certification

Back in 2000, at the Mohonk Mountain House certification conference, we had delegates from around the world, but none from a certification program in the United States. Seven years later, several national certification programs and more than a dozen state-based eco-labeling programs in the United States measure the environmental performance of hotels. Most of these programs are geared to larger resort, urban, and chain hotels rather than eco-lodges, and most have only environmental—not social or economic—criteria. What sets them apart from the "green" hotels programs that are membership organizations is that these certification programs have "third-party verification" by independent auditors. Most often this is done by a review of the paper forms submitted by the hotel, but some programs do have independent, onsite inspection, which is clearly the best option. Fortunately, all go well beyond "those ubiquitous towel reuse cards"[144] and encompass a rather broad range of environmental criteria. This growing number of certified hotels, while still small, is beginning to capture media attention. As *USA Weekend* magazine notes, "Travelers in most U.S. cities now can choose to stay in 'green' hotels whose Earth-friendly practices minimize their environmental impact."[145] *SmartMoney* is even more emphatic: "The eco-revolution has officially hit the hotel industry, with everyone from staid business chains to hipper-than-thou boutiques now billing themselves as green."[146]

At least five nationwide "green" hotel certification programs exist within the United States, all very small. The oldest program in the United States is ECOTEL, started in 1994 by HVS Eco Services, a division of a hospitality industry association. ECOTEL's rigorous environmental criteria and onsite inspection system was designed by experts from the EPA and the Rocky Mountain Institute, a Colorado-based environmental think tank. However, for a variety of reasons, ECOTEL floundered,[147] and by 2007, ECOTEL's Web site showed only five certified hotels in the United States (and a mere thirteen worldwide, down from thirty-six in 2001).[148] Another national program, Audubon's Green Leaf, based in Canada, emphasizes cost savings through more efficient use of water and energy. By 2007, it had only thirteen certified hotels in the United States, including the two Colony resorts.[149] The most widely recognized U.S. certification program is LEED (Leadership in Energy and Environmental Design), which is run by the U.S. Green Building Council. It certifies all types of new and existing buildings and awards four levels of plaques "as proof that a building is environmentally responsible, profitable, and a healthy place to live and work." The Gaia Napa Valley Hotel & Spa, in California's bucolic wine country, was the first LEED hotel in the world to receive a Gold plaque; none have yet been awarded the top, Platinum plaque. In 2007, there were five LEED-certified hotels in the United States and dozens more in process.[150] The fourth and newest national program, Sustainable Tourism Eco-Certification Program (STEP), is being developed by the Colorado-based nonprofit organization STI (Sustainable Tourism International) and NSF International, a company that specializes in certification. Unlike the other purely environmental programs, STEP includes sociocultural and economic criteria, requires onsite audits, and incorporates features and lessons learned from other eco-certification programs around the world. By 2007, the program was being piloted with a small number of U.S. businesses, but none had been certified.[151]

The most successful of the national hotel certification programs is Green Seal. Since 1989, Green Seal, a Washington, D.C.–based nonprofit, has been creating "science-based environmental certification standards" and "encouraging the purchase and production of products and services that work well and have less impact on the environment." It has developed certification programs for a number of products (paints, cleaners, floor care products, etc.) and encouraged hotels to adopt environmentally sensitive purchasing policies. In 1999, it began certifying "lodging properties" under its environmental standard

GS-33 program, and by 2007, it listed forty-three certified hotels in ten states (including Washington, D.C.), with the largest number in Pennsylvania.[152] Green Seal also works with the American Hotel & Lodging Association (AH&LA), the U.S. EPA, and several state "green" lodging programs, including initiatives to require that state and EPA employees use "green" hotels for business travel.[153]

In fact, it is at the state level that "green" tourism certification programs have been most successful. While several early eco-certification efforts in Hawaii, West Virginia, Maine, and elsewhere didn't get off the ground, a rough count shows that by late 2007, at least thirteen states had "green" lodging-certification programs.[154] These programs were all developed separately, but they have many similar features. They all are free or low-cost, voluntary, and focused solely on environmental criteria, offer technical advice and assistance in "green" strategies, provide third-party assessments (and some have onsite audits), and have government support, through either the environmental protection department, waste management or energy offices, or tourism and visitors bureaus. "The bottom line is that someone in each state needs to champion the idea, gather other interested parties and come up with a plan," writes *Green Lodging News*.[155] It is this state support, with staff, resources, marketing, and benefits, that appears crucial to the rapid growth and growing popularity of these programs.

One of the oldest is Vermont's Green Hotels in the Green Mountain State, run by the state EPA and Agency of Natural Resources, with a very modest operating budget of only five thousand dollars a year and no resources for onsite audits. However, by 2007, it had forty certified hotels.[156] Among the most impressive of the state programs is Florida Green Lodging, which was created in 2004 by the Department of Environmental Protection (DEP). It covers all types of accommodations "from the quaint bed & breakfast to the large resort complex," including some of the state's most well-known properties.[157] By late 2007, there were thirty-three certified hotels and nearly a hundred more applicants. While impressive, it is just a tiny fraction of Florida's lodging sector, which has some 4,700 hotels and motels accommodating over 40 million visitors a year. According to State Secretary Michael Sole, "The lodging industry plays an important role in protecting our environment," and therefore the government is stepping up incentives for those that become certified. The governor directed that, beginning in 2008, all state agencies use only Green Lodging–certified hotels for conferences, meetings, and travel. The hotel industry media took immediate notice. "That sounds like a Category 5 incentive to us," wrote *Hotel Chatter*, while *Green Lodging News* predicted that "you can be sure that even more hotels will be signing up for the program soon."[158]

The Florida Green Lodging certification program offers three levels of logo—one, two, or three palm trees—and is designed to reinforce sustainable practices, promote continual improvements, and "encourage hotels to understand and improve their environmental performance rather than simply implement a few green practices." Obtaining One Palm certification takes up to a year and requires a hotel to form an employees' Green Team to oversee the process, including conducting a self-assessment to establish baseline utility data, set short- and long-term goals and benchmarks, and monitor a set of best management practices. An outside auditor then conducts a short, onsite inspection and, if the criteria are met, One Palm is given. Two Palm certification is awarded to hotels that maintain their One Palm status for at least a year, demonstrate additional improvements in environmental performance, and pass another onsite audit. By late 2007, only one hotel had achieved Two Palm status[159] and none had achieved Three Palm status, which requires continual improvements for three consecutive years. Certified hotels receive a range of benefits, including listings on various Web sites and the state's list of preferred hotels, as well as a Green Lodging flag to fly on their property. The Florida Green Lodging program is gaining support. Rick Hawkins, a director at The Breakers, says, "If we don't do things to save the planet, our lovely historic hotel is going to be a dive site one day," he told the *South Florida Sun Sentinel*. "And everything we've done boosts profitability. The return on investment long-term is huge."[160]

While these eco-certification programs are a significant step beyond the "green" hotels programs because they involve third-party verification and common standards, there are limitations and challenges. One is that these state programs, unlike many sustainable tourism certification programs in other countries, do not cover sociocultural or economic criteria. This means that areas critical to good ecotourism, such as hiring policies, workers' rights and wages, buying locally, and support for community projects, are not measured. With plans proceeding under the direction of the Rainforest Alliance to create a global accreditation body, the Sustainable Tourism Stewardship Council (STSC), it is vital that these U.S. programs expand their criteria or they will not conform with the new global standard.[161]

Another reality is that they still cover only a tiny fraction of the lodging sector. Green Seal's Mark Petruzzi estimates that "less than 2% of U.S. properties [are] participating in green lodging [certification and affiliation] programs."[162] However, the number of "green" lodging programs and certified hotels is likely to continue to increase. In 2007, the EPA announced that it would only use hotels that have an environmental program in place. Even more significant, the General Services Administration directed that all government travel should "screen for green"—that is, seek to use eco-certified hotels.[163] In addition, it seems clear that ultimately a national certification program is needed, to which the state programs must conform. Because "there's no agreed upon national standard," notes Glenn Hasek, editor of *Green Lodging News*, it is difficult "for even the most environmentally savvy traveler to tell the green from the 'greenwashed' hotels that claim to be more 'eco-friendly' than they are."[164] Jestena Boughton, owner of The Colony hotels, agrees. She has personally tested several certification programs and now says, "I think we need a national certification system, but one that recognizes the differences among different types of hotels and different areas of the country."

The New Green Revolution

The growth of the "green" hotels and "green" certification programs is just one of the signs of the rise and mainstreaming of environmentalism in the United States. In 2008, for instance, the American Hotel & Lodging Association, the hotel industry's leading trade organization, announced that its annual conference would focus on "educating the industry's leaders on best practices and the importance of environmentally friendly green hotels." As the conference chair, Jim Burba, put it, "While a small number of people in the hotel industry have been promoting the logic and merits of 'green'/sustainable development and operations for decades, the interest in the past few years has shot up like a rocket." He added, "Green is now being embraced by developers and owners and is being discussed in the boardrooms of the largest companies in the travel industry."[165]

Indeed, many observers see a new "green" revolution in the making. While in the 1970s, the global environmental revolution led to the birth of scores of NGOs focused on influencing government policies, the "green" revolution at the opening of this millennium is driven once again by NGOs as well as by consumers, particularly the Baby Boomers. And while some focus is on governments, a central theme is voluntary corporate social responsibility by the industry. The new environmentalism is being driven as well by genuine end-of-the-world-as-we-know-it fears of global warming. One response has been a dramatic upswing in volunteer carbon-offset programs for airline travel, as well as efforts to get the major airlines to offer such programs to their passengers.

The growth of the new "green" consumer movement that includes ecotourism was documented as early as 2002. According to the State Department report, "Trends in the U.S. ecotourism industry indicate growing numbers of educated ecotourists with average or above average annual family incomes, increases in the number of nature education and conservation programs, and increasing concern among the population about the degradation of resources due to poor management or overuse of ecotourism destinations."[166]

By 2007, ecotourism was indeed chic. Take, for instance, the *Knoxville News Sentinel*'s feature December 31, 2006. It begins, "Ecotourism—once a tiny niche in the travel industry—has grown into a worldwide multi-million dollar business." After ticking off a list of benefits that come from tourism done right, the writer proposes: "With 2007 approaching in a few hours, perhaps it's wise to make a New Year's resolution to uphold guidelines for responsible travel. Whether a destination is in the United States or abroad, the environment and cultural heritage need protection from harmful outside elements."[167]

The United States' Ecotourism Scorecard

While the growing interest in ecotourism within the United States is exhilarating, a closer look at the scorecard offers a more sobering portrait.

Involves Travel to Natural Destination

Ecotourism in the United States has been built, as in many other countries, on the foundation of the national parks system. Visits to national parks and visitor satisfaction with these parks both remain high. However, today U.S. ecotourism encompasses a broad array of activities and terrain beyond parks. Increasingly, as well, we are seeing ecotourism reaching urban areas—as Madison, Wisconsin, demonstrated in hosting the North American Ecotourism Conference 2007. Therefore, the current mosaic of ecotourism in the United States is more complex and diverse than in many other countries. In addition, the United States is an important outbound market for ecotourists traveling to other countries, and with both the growth of a new environmentalism and the Baby Boomers entering retirement, even more Americans are likely to be involved in ecotourism at home and abroad. In 2002, the State Department forecast, "As urban populations, income levels and free time in the U.S. continue to grow, demand and spending on leisure activities in general, and ecotourism in particular, is expected to grow as well."[168]

Minimizes Impact

Despite the continuing strength of nature-based tourism and the emergence of ecotourism, conventional and mass tourism, much of it unsustainable, dominate the U.S. market. Even national parks have suffered from lack of controls, inadequate funding, and a range of political assaults. Sound and robust ecotourism takes national planning and government leadership, and this does not yet exist in the United States. As the 2002 State Department report concludes, "Despite our wealth of marine and terrestrial areas still available for potential development of ecotourism operations, appropriate planning, regulation, promotion of education and best practices, and monitoring will be needed to ensure that demand for nature tourism and other forms of outdoor recreation does not degrade the resources and ecosystems on which they depend."[169]

Ecotourism has developed only in pockets, at a state or regional level, and while it has helped to minimize environmental impacts in some instances, the successes are relatively minor. One of the more hopeful signs has been the growth of eco-certification for hotels, which now appears to be rather rapidly expanding among the states. In addition, a growing number of environmental certification programs have sprouted up for beaches, ski slopes, golf courses, and other parts of the tourism industry. In many cases, these need to be strengthened with third-party, on-site audits and with the addition of criteria to measure social and economic impacts.

Builds Environmental Awareness

In the United States today, there is a reemergence of a new environmentalism, and ecotourism is one of its components. The growth of state ecotourism societies and initiatives and, most recently, the holding of regular national ecotourism conferences, are helping to build press interest and public awareness. Within the industry, ecotourism operators and outfitters, along with naturalist guides, are also extremely important in building environmental consciousness among travelers. In addition, beginning over a century ago with the Sierra Club, a number of environmental organizations have conducted nature-based tourism and, over the last two decades, several have opened ecotourism programs. In addition, there are a growing number of university departments offering courses on ecotourism. But despite progress, knowledge of ecotourism as part of the wider environmental movement remains fairly limited.

Provides Direct Financial Benefits for Conservation

The record is mixed. Visitor fees to national parks—one of the barometers of ecotourism's financial support for conservation—remain modest. Despite the increase in numbers of visitors to the national parks, entrance fees still cover only about 10 percent of operating costs. Ecotourism has been important as one of the components contributing to the growth of private conservancies, with a number of these lands supporting agri- and eco-ranch tourism. As the concept of corporate social responsibility grows in the United States, under the umbrella of the Travelers' Philanthropy project, more companies and travelers will contribute to both conservation and community projects in tourism destinations. So, overall, ecotourism is providing modest benefits to conservation, particularly through the private sector, rather than through national government programs or gate fees.

Provides Financial Benefits and Empowerment for Local People

In state after state, ecotourism is serving as an alternative or supplementary source of income for people trying to save their family farm or ranch, to protect the old homes and character of historic towns, to move out of extractive industries like logging and coal mining, and to build healthier lifestyles with organic farming, wineries, bed and breakfasts, and nature-based tourism companies. Some are driven to ecotourism by economic necessity; others have the financial luxury to make lifestyle changes into ecotourism. Tangible financial benefits are being recorded, particularly from various types of rural tourism.

However, within the "green" hotels and eco-certification programs, the emphasis has been on environmental reforms, not on labor conditions or workers' or host-community rights. Clearly, genuine ecotourism requires the delivery of social and economic benefits. While scattered empirical and much anecdotal evidence exists that ecotourism businesses offer better employment, there is a need to collect such data regularly and consistently in order to be able to measure the social and economic sides of ecotourism against conventional tourism businesses.

Respect Local Culture

The picture here is very mixed. Ecotourism is clearly helping to promote local crafts, music, festivals, farm products, and traditions in many parts of the United States. One relatively new development has been the growth of civil rights tourism tracing, particularly across the South, the struggles of Black Americans. In addition, there are scattered efforts by African-American communities to use tourism as a way to protect their culture and their communities and keep real-estate developers at bay. But there remains, particularly among Native Americans, a deep suspicion that ecotourism is just another form of exploitation and expropriation. With a few fine exceptions, there has been surprisingly little interconnection between those involved in ecotourism and Native American–run tourism. Clearly there is a need for more organized engagement between Native American communities and ecotourism organizations, and it may be that experiences from other parts of the world—South Africa's "restitution" movement, for instance—could be instructive.

Supports Human Rights and Democratic Movements

Again, much needs to be done. As has been argued for other countries, real ecotourism requires political stability and democracy, as well as national leadership and planning. The United States has historically been viewed, both by its own citizens and by much of the world, as a country that welcomes immigrants and promotes democracy and liberty. Tragically, this reputation has been shredded by the Bush administration's abuses of human rights and civil liberties abroad and at home. This is reflected in America's declining image as a travel destination. According to a recent study, "The U.S. has fallen from 1st to 6th among dream destinations for international travelers."[170] It will take years and dramatically different government policies to rebuild our reputation as the world's leading democracy and defender of human rights. Proponents of ecotourism need to add their voices to those advocating a return to our democratic principles and adherence to civil liberties. At present, this broader, more holistic view of ecotourism is largely absent within the United States. Proponents and practitioners of ecotourism in this country have not been organically situated within the popular struggles for human rights and democracy, either at home or abroad. While an undercurrent of some of the ecotourism initiatives, particularly in Hawaii and Alaska, has been around protection of cultural customs and Native American/Hawaiian rights, these have generally not been framed in human-rights terms. In addition, most visitors to national parks are unaware that many protected areas were created by forcibly expelling their Native American inhabitants, and that many of their descendants continue to view tourism, including ecotourism, as another form of exploitation. A core tenet of ecotourism is that it should be educational as well as enjoyable for the visitor. One step toward rebuilding our democracy would be to incorporate into ecotourism a full and holistic discussion of the political and social landscape, both its history and its present realities.

Conclusion

The Road Less Traveled

As we move through the first decade of the new millennium, ecotourism is charting a bold new direction in how we explore the world. Ecotourism has become one of the most rapidly growing and most dynamic sector of the tourism market. Yet it still remains, to paraphrase Robert Frost's poem, the less-traveled road. Hundreds of millions of tourists still go on conventional cruises, sun-and-sea beach holidays, or mass tourism vacations during which distortions of nature are viewed at palm-fringed poolsides, theme parks, and overcrowded campgrounds. Much of what is marketed as ecotourism amounts to only ecotourism lite, which offers tidbits of nature or minor environmental reforms such as not changing the sheets daily. Even worse, "greenwashing" scams use environmentally friendly images but follow none of the principles and practices of sound ecotourism. Growing numbers of travelers, however, are walking the path of socially responsible and environmentally respectful tourism.

Even more significant than the increased numbers of ecotourists is the shift over the last three decades in the paradigm and in the discourse on both protected area management and on nature tourism. Effective conservation now includes involving and benefiting the people living nearest the protected areas—finding harmony between people and parks—and nature tourism has come to mean not just wilderness experiences, but also activities that minimize visitor impact and benefit both protected areas and surrounding human populations. This shift in consciousness and understanding has led to a great deal of experimentation and creativity, most often at the local level—of a project or park—occasionally at the national level, and, more rarely, at the international level.

At the local level, ecotourism principles have become part of many rural struggles over control of land, resources, and tourism profits. Wherever people in the world are in conflict over parks and tourism—whether the gold miners in Costa Rica's Corcovado National Park; the Galapagos Islands settlers; the Maasai in East Africa; or the displaced communities around Kruger National Park, St. Lucia Nature Reserve, and elsewhere in South Africa—ecotourism is part of the demand and part of the solution. In the most fragile ecosystems, like the Galapagos, well-run ecotourism is the only option, the only foreign exchange-earning activity that, if done with care and controls, does not lead to irreparable damage to the environment. In other instances, ecotourism is clearly more profitable than the alternative economic activities: for example, studies in three Central American countries found that a stay-over ecotourist puts eighteen to twenty-eight times more money into the local economy than a cruise passenger, while a study of game farming in Kenya found that wildlife tourism was fifty times more lucrative than cattle grazing. Other research calculated that a lion is worth $575,000, and a single free-flying macaw in Peru is estimated to generate as much as $4,700 per year in tourism dollars. In the old Bophuthatswana homeland in South Africa, cattle farming could generate only 80 jobs, whereas six new luxury lodges planned for a game reserve were projected to create 1,200 jobs, and ecotourism was estimated to be sixty times more profitable than cattle ranching. Even when pitted against the seemingly lucrative industry of mining in St. Lucia, South Africa, ecotourism is calculated to have the potential to provide more jobs for a longer period of time without destroying the sand dunes and the estuary.[1]

At the local or village level, there is a wide range of models for involvement of communities in ecotourism. A study by the International Institute for Environment and Development describes a "typology of participation," moving from "passive" to "self-mobilization/active" participation, that is, from local people simply being told what is going to happen or has already happened to communities taking initiatives independently of and sometimes in conflict with external institutions (either government or private).[2] Similarly, there is a range of models for the distribution of profits, from rent for use of land to co-ownership to full community ownership of the park or tourism facilities.

Most common is the distribution of revenue in the form of cash payments or tangible benefits (a road, a clinic, a grinding mill, a classroom, electricity, a truck, etc.) to the local community based on rent for use of land, a set fee per visitor-night, a percentage of park entrance fees, or guest and company donations via Travelers' Philanthropy projects. Although such compensation can significantly improve daily life in poor rural communities, it may do little to equip local communities with the educational and technical skills and political know-how they will need to assume an active role in ecotourism projects and park management and in negotiations with private-sector participants and government authorities.

The ideal is active community participation in the management and distribution of revenues that gives local residents, in the words of David Grossman and Eddie Koch, "the will, power and skills to improve their standard of living through the wise use of wildlife and natural resources."[3] But in reality, many community-based tourism and conservation programs are "relational" rather than participatory: they seek to improve relationships between the community and either the state or the private enterprise through trade-offs, rather than to devolve ownership and management of the protected area or tourism project to the local community. "Without proprietorship," write Grossman and Koch, "most forms of participation become co-optive, cooperative or collaborative arrangements."[4] Frequently, local communities strengthen their skills and political influence through alliances with national and international environment, development, and human rights organizations, scientists, journalists, and academics, who help them build a counterweight to the power of outside private corporations or negotiate terms with the national government. These external alliances can also help community-owned ecotourism projects develop internationally acceptable standards of accommodation and effective overseas marketing. In recent years, for instance, Kenya has emerged as a leader in community-owned eco-lodges, a number of which have been supported by NGOs as well as white-owned ranches, while Costa Rica has built a network of small-scale local and indigenous ecotourism businesses that have been assisted by local NGOs and the United Nations Development Program (UNDP).

Although alliances with NGOs and experts can provide skills, funds, and political clout, it is difficult for community-based ecotourism to take hold and expand without strong government support. As John Akama observes in discussing Kenya, "For local community participation to succeed, local people need sanctioned authority to enable them to implement programme responsibilities." As seen in Kenya, Tanzania, and Zanzibar, national governments frequently stifle rural initiatives, hand out lucrative contracts to politically or economically powerful elites, and cede to the private sector or local park officials development responsibilities—construction of roads, wells, schools, and the like—traditionally carried by the state.

Although nearly every developing country is nowadays promoting ecotourism, in reality much of the implementation has been left to the private sector, with little overall planning or control exerted by national governments. Over the past several decades, economic globalization, free trade, and structural adjustment policies have undercut the capacity of governments in developing countries to provide basic social services or implement sound governmental guidelines. A number of governments have devised revenue-sharing schemes with people living around national parks, or undertaken international advertising campaigns promoting ecotourism (South Africa and Costa Rica), but none has fully embraced the principles and practices of community-based ecotourism as a national development strategy. As Akama says, "Probably, the main reason why community-based wildlife tourism programmes fail is the lack of coherent policies and legislation which delegate responsibility and authority for tourism development and wildlife conservation from powerful stakeholders (the state, conservation organizations, tourism groups and local elites) to rural peasants."[5]

The concept of ecotourism has brought new principles and altered practices to a stratum of the private sector through, for instance, voluntary "green" certification programs, Travelers' Philanthropy projects, and eco-awards. Over the past several decades, a number of entrepreneurs, many with backgrounds in environmental or political movements, have embarked on ecotourism with the conviction that they can do so in a socially and environmentally responsible manner. These enterprises include, as the case studies in this book show, outbound tour operators (Wildland Adventures, Tamu Safaris, G.A.P. Adventures), inbound operators (Horizontes, Unique Safaris, Micato Safaris, Wilderness Safaris, Off the Beaten Path), rustic and rugged projects (Rara Avis), tented camps (Dorobo Tours and Safaris), family-run lodges (La Quinta, Selva Verde), community-run lodges (Il Ng'wesi, Basecamp Masai Mara, Tassia Lodge), eco-beach resorts (Punta Islita, Rocktail Bay, Chumbe Eco-lodge, Matemwe Bungalows, Fundu Lagoon), scientific centers (La Selva Biological Station, Monteverde Cloud Forest Reserve), "soft" ecotourism (Rain Forest Aerial Tram, Villablanca Hotel, Lindblad Expeditions, and many other floating hotels in the Galapagos), moderate- to high-end eco-lodges (Lapa Rios, Oliver's Camp, Campi ya Kanzi), and high-end luxury (CC Africa's Phinda and Klein's Camp; Sabi Sabi, Finca Rosa Blanca, the Lodge at Sun Ranch). These are among the finest examples of innovative ecoprojects that benefit, to various degrees, both conservation and local communities.

In all developing countries, there is movement away from government-owned and government-run tourism projects. With the end of the cold war and the collapse of the Soviet Union, foreign investment and free trade have become the mantras for economic development, and the private sector vigorously argues for self-regulation, low or no taxation, and a bevy of government incentives to stimulate investment. However, the ample examples of ecotourism shams; the growth of private parks, which despite their appeal and benefits are undercutting tourism revenues to national park systems; and the continuing leakage of profits away from ecotourism projects all highlight a continuing need for governments to develop and enforce clear standards, guidelines, and monitoring procedures, more equitable taxing policies, and investment and promotional strategies that support sound national, particularly community-based, ecotourism enterprises.

Over the last decade, it has been encouraging to see the application of the principles and good practices of ecotourism to more mainstream sectors of the tourism industry. Usually termed "sustainable tourism," these initiatives include efforts to create "greener" practices in the construction of golf courses, ski slopes, larger resorts, and hotel chains. While both sustainable tourism and ecotourism continue to grow rapidly, they are still far from transforming the way in which modern, mass tourism is conducted. At its core, ecotourism is about power relationships and on-the-ground struggles. It will take much stronger grassroots movements, combined with alliances among activists, experts, and NGOs and carefully planned and implemented national ecotourism strategies, to curb the power of the conventional tourism industry. Although this appears unlikely to happen soon, it is still worth the struggle. Along the way, some excellent models are being built; some local communities are being empowered and their members' lives improved; national parks and other fragile ecosystems are receiving more support; and awareness is growing that we cannot continue to play in other people's lands as we have in the past. Despite the constraints, today's traveler does, as Robert Frost suggests, have a choice about which road to take.

Notes

Chapter 1: In Search of the Golden Toad

1. Sandra Blakeslee, "New Culprit in Deaths of Frogs." *New York Times*, September 16, 1997, F1.

2. Brenda Goodman, "To Stem Widespread Extinction, Scientists Airlift Frogs in Carry-On Bags." *New York Times*, June 6, 2006, F3.

3. Twan Leenders from Yale University and the Peabody Museum of Natural History rediscovered the harlequin frog, which was also thought to be extinct, at the Rainmaker Rainforest Reserve near Quepos, Costa Rica. Correspondence with Ann Gutierrez, Rainmaker Conservation Project, July 24, 2006.

4. Blakeslee, "New Culprit in Deaths of Frogs," F1.

5. Nearly 100,000 more acres in the Monteverde area have been acquired for conservation purposes by other scientific organizations; some of this land is also used for ecotourism (see chapter 5). Interview with John and Sue Trostle and Ree Sheck; Ree Strange Sheck, *Costa Rica: A Natural Destination* (Santa Fe, NM: John Muir Publications, 1990), 232.

6. José Luis Vargas Leiton, "Principales aspectos del desarrollo de Monteverde, 1920–1995," paper presented at El Foro Internacional Sobre Ecoalojamiento: Principales Aspectos del Desarrollo de Monteverde (International Forum on Eco-Lodging: Principal Aspects of Development in Monteverde), October 1995; John Burnett, "Ecotourism in Costa Rica," *All Things Considered*, National Public Radio, September 3, 1997; Tropical Science Center, "Monteverde Cloud Forest Biological Reserve," see www.cct.or.cr/english/; "Monteverde Info," see www.monte verdeinfo.com.

7. The UN World Tourism Organization (UNWTO) has declared that tourism has the potential to be "a great and sustaining force for peace in the world," and the International Institute for Peace through Tourism (IIPT) seeks to demonstrate "the potential of the travel tourism industry to contribute to a sustainable and peaceful world—peace within the global family, and peace with nature." Tourism industry giant Hilton Hotels Corporation has sought to capitalize on this theme, adopting as its motto "World peace through world travel." Conference program, "Building a Sustainable World through Tourism," IIPT Second Global Conference, Montreal, September 12–14, 1994, 2; David Nicholson-Lord, "The Politics of Travel: Is Tourism Just Colonialism in Another Guise?" *The Nation*, October 6, 1997, 12, and "Exploring Tourism," *The Nation*, October 6, 1997, 3.

8. Emma Stewart. "Achieving Sustainable Development through Corporate Sustainability: An Assessment of Environmental and Social Performance in the Caribbean Tourism Industry (Cuba, Dominican Republic)," Ph.D. dissertation, Stanford University, October 2005.

9. See www.ecotourism.org for a report of this conference. In addition, a CD with conference proceedings is available through the TIES Store.

10. Originally called The Ecotourism Society, in 2000 its name was changed to The International Ecotourism Society (TIES) in preparation for the UN's International Year of Ecotourism in 2002.

11. The Ecotourism Society's original definition was somewhat longer, but was quickly honed down to this succinct version. *The Ecotourism Society Newsletter* 1, no. 1 (spring 1991), 1, cited in Katrina Brandon, "Ecotourism and Conservation: A Review of Key Issues," *Environment Department Papers*, Biodiversity Series, No. 033 (Washington, D.C.: World Bank, April 1996), 1; The Ecotourism Society, membership brochure, "Uniting Conservation & Travel Worldwide" (North Bennington, VT: The Ecotourism Society, 1992); Sylvie Blangy and Megan Epler Wood, "Developing and Implementing Ecotourism Guidelines for Wildlands and Neighboring Communities" (North Bennington, VT: The Ecotourism Society, 1992).

12. Barbara Crossette, "Surprises in the Global Tourism Boom," *New York Times*, April 12, 1998, 6.

13. Kurt Kutay, "Brave New Role: Ecotour Operators Take Center Stage in the Era of Green Travel," *Going Green: The Ecotourism Resource for Travel Agents*, Supplement to *Tour & Travel News*, October 25, 1993, 80.

14. Lisa Mastny, *Treading Lightly: New Paths for International Tourism*, Worldwatch Paper 159 (Washington, D.C.: Worldwatch Institute, December 2001), 37.

15. Christopher Solomon, "Where the High Life Comes Naturally," *New York Times*, May 1, 2005.

16. The Tourism Network, April 2005 newsletter, www.tourismknowledge.com/Newsletters/Issue6.pdf.

17. UNWTO, "Global Forecasts and Profiles of Market Segments," *Tourism 2020 Vision*, vol. 7 (Madrid: UNWTO, 2001).

18. "The Quebec Declaration on Ecotourism," see www.world-tour ism.org/sustainable/IYE/quebec/anglais/declaration.html.

19. George Washington University, International Institute of Tourism Studies. Taken from Development Assistance Network for Tourism Enhancement and Investment Database, 2005, see www.dantei.org.

20. These include the World Travel & Tourism Council (WTTC), Africa Travel Association, and Pacific Asia Travel Association (PATA).

21. Among these are British Airways, Virgin Atlantic Airlines, Lufthansa Airlines, Fairmont Hotels & Resorts, and Scandic Hotels.

22. For a list of the national and regional associations, see www.ecotourism.org. TIES, which serves as the umbrella organization, organized (together with Ecotourism Norway) the first-ever conference for these associations, held in Oslo, Norway in May 2007.

23. Héctor Ceballos-Lascuráin, *Tourism, Ecotourism, and Protected Areas*, (Gland, Switzerland: IUCN, 1996), 1–5; Nicholson-Lord, "Politics of Travel," 11–18.

24. Anita Pleumarom, "The Political Economy of Tourism," *The Ecologist* 24, no. 4 (July–August 1994): 142; Anita Pleumarom, "Ecotourism: A New 'Green Revolution' in the Third World," draft of article obtained from author, 1996, 2;

Paula DiPerna, "Caution Must Be Exercised in Eco-tourism Growth," *Earth Times*, July 7, 1997; Ceballos-Lascuráin, *Tourism*, 1–5; Nicholson-Lord, "Politics of Travel," 11–18; Center on Ecotourism and Sustainable Development (CESD), "Ecotourism Fact Sheet: Global," September 2005, see www.ecotourismcesd.org; Brandon, *Ecotourism and Conservation*, 1.

25. UNWTO, *Tourism 2020 Vision*.

26. International Labor Organization, *International Labor Standards: A Workers' Education Manual* (Geneva, Switzerland: International Labor Organization, 1990), 52–54.

27. Helene Jorgensen, "Give Me a Break: The Extent of Paid Holidays and Vacation," *Center for Economic and Policy Research*, September 3, 2002.

28. UNWTO, *Tourism Highlights*, 2006 edition, see www.bmwa.gv.at/NR/rdonlyres/11944AC0-DA9D-478B-98F2-A0D303E7E8E8/0/Highlights2007.pdf; Mintel Report, *Eco and Ethical Tourism-UK*, (UK: Mintel International Group, October 2003), 1.

29. Nicholson-Lord, "Politics of Travel," 14; Ceballos-Lascuráin, *Tourism*, 9; Crossette, "Surprises," 5.

30. Ceballos-Lascuráin, *Tourism*, 23.

31. Nicholson-Lord, "Politics of Travel," 12. A subsequent conference in 1989 resulted in The Hague Declaration on Tourism, which reflects growing sensitivity to sustainable and community-based development. It calls on "states to strike a harmonious balance between economic and ecological consideration" and to give "priority attention to selective and controlled development of tourist infrastructure, facilities, demand, and overall tourist capacity, in order to protect the environment, and local population." Although such agreements are nonbinding, they do bring social and environmental considerations to the attention of both government and the tourism industry. Ceballos-Lascuráin, *Tourism*, 100.

32. Ceballos-Lascuráin, *Tourism*, 19.

33. Bruskin Goldring Research, *Nature-Based Activities and the Florida Tourist*, New Jersey, 1999. Conducted for the Visit Florida: Research Office.

34. H. Stewart Kimball, *History of the Sierra Club Outing Committee, 1901–1972* (San Francisco: Sierra Club, 1990), 7–20; Charles Hardy, director of the Sierra Club Outing program, interview, 1996.

35. Hardy, interview.

36. National Park Service Visitation Statistics, see www2.nature.nps.gov/stats/visitbody.htm.

37. Ibid.

38. Associated Press, "Rangers Killing Deer Addicted to Snacks," *New York Times*, January 7, 1995.

39. In the wake of this crisis, park officials began using "pretty blatant and graphic [educational] material" in order to "affect the visitors' behavior," explained Grand Canyon National Park biologist Elaine Lesley in a July 1997 telephone interview. She said they were seeing positive results: "The last deer was put down over a year ago, and the deer are in pretty good health now."

40. Malcolm Lillywhite claims to have coined the term low-impact tourism (LIT) in 1985. He defines LIT as establishing natural resource management through private investment in rural village–based tourism. In a study for USAID,

he argues that LIT is distinct from ecotourism because it puts control and regulation of tourism development in the hands of the destination country and local communities, not in the hands of foreign travel agents and tour operators. However, Lillywhite's definition in fact fits within the definition of ecotourism used in this book. Malcolm Lillywhite, *Low Impact Tourism as a Strategy for Sustaining Natural and Cultural Resources in Sub Saharan Africa,* Mid Term Report (Washington, D.C.: U.S. Agency for International Development, Bureau of Africa, June 1990).

41. The concept of "pro-poor tourism" is focused on increased benefits to poor people, while "geotourism," promoted by the National Geographic Society, emphasizes the geographical character of a place, including its environment, heritage, and aesthetics, as well as the culture and well-being of its residents. Both terms have Web sites, see www.propoortourism.org.uk/ and www.nationalgeographic .com/travel/sustainable/.

42. Ceballos-Lascuráin, *Tourism*, 35–39.

43. The World Conservation Union: World Commission on Protected Areas, "Outputs on the United Nations List and State of the World's Protected Areas," 2003, see www.iucn.org/themes/wcpa/wpc2003/english/outputs/un.htm.

44. Ibid. Nearly half of these (43,000 protected areas) are found within Europe, while North Eurasia boasts 18,000. There are 13,000 in North America, 9,000 in Australia and New Zealand, and a meager 7,000 for the entire African continent. Another 1.8 million square kilometers, or 695,000 square miles, were under protection in marine parks.

45. G. E. Machlis and D. L. Tichnell, *The State of the World's Parks: An International Assessment for Resources Management, Policy and Research* (Boulder, CO: Westview Press, 1985), 96, quoted in Michael Wells and Katrina Brandon, *People and Parks: Linking Protected Area Management with Local Communities* (Washington, D.C.: World Bank, World Wildlife Fund, and U.S. Agency for International Development, 1992), 1.

46. David Western, "Ecotourism: The Kenya Challenge," in C. G. Gakahu and B. E. Goode, *Ecotourism and Sustainable Development in Kenya,* Proceedings of the Kenya Ecotourism Workshop, Lake Nakuru National Park, Kenya, September 13–17, 1992 (Nairobi: Wildlife Conservation International, 1992), 15.

47. Gerardo Budowski, "Tourism and Environmental Conservation: Conflict, Coexistence, or Symbiosis?" *Environmental Conservation* 3, no. 1 (1976): 27–31.

48. Ceballos-Lascuráin, "The Future of Ecotourism," *Mexico Journal,* January 17, 1988, cited in International Resources Group, *Ecotourism: A Viable Alternative for Sustainable Management of Natural Resources in Africa* (Washington, D.C.: U.S. Agency for International Development, June 1992), 5.

49. Jean Hopfensperger, "Wilderness Adventures Spice Up Local Travel," *Tico Times,* October 10, 1980, 12.

50. Caballos-Lascuráin, *Tourism,* 21; Kenton Miller, *Planning National Parks for Ecodevelopment: Methods and Cases from Latin America* (Ann Arbor: University of Michigan, Center for Strategic Wildland Management Studies, 1978); Ray Ashton and Patricia Ashton, "An Introduction to Sustainable Tourism (Ecotourism) in Central America," unpublished paper prepared for Paseo Pantera: Regional Wetlands Management in Central America project Gainesville, FL:

Wildlife Conservation International, 1993, 18; Paul Eagles et al., eds., *Ecotourism: Annotated Bibliography for Planners and Managers*, 3rd ed. (North Bennington, VT: The Ecotourism Society, 1995), 41.

51. Author's personal correspondences with Hector Ceballos-Lascuráin; www.planeta.com/ecotravel/weaving/hectorceballos.html.

52. Ibid.; Ceballos-Lascuráin, *Tourism,* 213. The IUCN brings together some 5,000 experts in governments, government agencies, and NGOs from more than 130 countries, with a central secretariat in Geneva.

53. Wells and Brandon, *People and Parks,* 2.

54. Ceballos-Lascuráin, *Tourism,* 226.

55. Author attended the conference and heard Mandela's address. For details on the 5th World Parks Congress and its Task Force on Tourism and Protected Areas see Paul F. J. Eagles and Robyn Bushell, *Tourism and Protected Areas: Benefits beyond Boundaries* (England: CABI, 2007) and www.iucn.org/themes/wcpa/wpc2003/english/outputs/tourism.htm. For the ongoing struggles between indigenous people and parks see Mark Dowie, "The Hidden Cost of Paradise: Indigenous people are being displaced to create wilderness areas, to the detriment of all," *Stanford Social Innovation Review*, Spring 2006: 31–38.

56. Donald E. Hawkins and Shaun Mann, "The World Bank's Role in Tourism Development," *Annals of Tourism Research* 34, no. 2 (2007): 353–354. The United Nations had declared 1967 the Year of the Tourist, an indication that tourism was increasingly viewed by multilateral institutions as an avenue for economic development in nonindustrialized countries.

57. International Finance Corporation, World Bank Group, see www.ifc.org/; Multilateral Investment Guarantee Agency, World Bank Group, see www.miga.org/. The fourth and final arm of the World Bank Group is the International Center for the Settlement of Investment Disputes (ICSID), see http://icsid.worldbank.org/ICSID/Index.jsp.

58. This included huge resort complexes in Bali, Turkey, Tunisia, Mexico, and the Caribbean. Total investment in these projects was approximately $1.5 billion. In addition, the bank extended another $250 million in loans and credits for airport projects, for a total of about $2 billion.

59. Hawkins and Mann, "World Bank's Role in Tourism"; Correspondence by Marcus Lenzen and author with various World Bank officials; Thanh-Dam Truong, "The Political Economy of International Tourism," in *Sex, Money, and Morality: Prostitution and Tourism in Southeast Asia* (London: Zed Books, 1990), 122; Pleumarom, "Political Economy of Tourism," 143; International Resources Group, *Ecotourism*, 44.

60. A. Cynthia Enloe, *Bananas, Beaches, and Bases: Making Feminist Sense of International Politics* (Berkeley: University of California Press, 1990), 32.

61. World Bank, "Lending Policies: Sectoral, OP4.04," in *World Bank Operational Manual* (Washington, D.C.: World Bank, September 1995); Wells and Brandon, *People and Parks*, 3; Telephone interview by Marcus Lenzen with Lou Scura, senior natural resource economist, Environment Department, World Bank, July 1997.

62. From the late 1960s onward, a variety of United Nations agencies, most importantly UNEP and the UNDP, financed and assisted international mass

tourism through research, feasibility studies, master plans, education and training programs, and historic preservation projects.

63. Global Environment Facility, *Operational Strategy* (Washington, D.C.: Global Environment Facility, February 1996), vii–viii, 18–19; International Resources Group, *Ecotourism*, 44.

64. International Finance Corporation, *IFC Tourism Sector Review* (Washington, D.C.: International Finance Corporation, Tourism Unit, February 1995), 12.

65. Correspondence with Iain Christie, a World Bank tourism expert, August 2006; *World Bank Annual Report, Operational Summary,* Fiscal 2005, see http://web.worldbank.org/WBSITE/EXTERNAL/EXTABOUTUS/EXTANNREP/EXTANNREP2K5/0,,contentMDK:20635316~menuPK:1512365~pagePK:64168445~piPK:64168309~theSitePK:1397343,00.html.

66. Correspondence with Christie.

67. George Washington University, International Institute of Tourism Studies. Taken from Development Assistance Network for Tourism Enhancement and Investment Database, 2005, www.dantei.org.

68. Wells and Brandon, *People and Parks*, 3.

69. U.S. Agency for International Development (USAID), *Parks in Peril,* Project Paper, Project No. 598-0782 (Washington, D.C.: USAID, 1990).

70. International Resources Group, *Ecotourism*, iii.

71. "Table of USAID Environmental Projects with Ecotourism Components," mimeographed seven-page document compiled by Molly Davis, research associate, PPC/CDIE/DI Research and References Services Project, USAID, 1995.

72. "USAID's Sustainable Tourism Portfolio," Section 3, *USAID and Sustainable Tourism: Meeting Development Objectives,* Washington, DC: (United States Agency for International Development, June 2005), 26, See www.nric.net/tourism/Sustain ableTourismObjectives.pdf.

73. Ibid., 9.

74. Ibid.

75. "USAID's Sustainable Tourism Portfolio," Section 3.

76. Interviews with USAID contract official, who asked to remain anonymous, March–April 1996.

77. USAID, "The Global Develoment Alliance: Public-Private Alliances for Transformational Development," January 2006, see http://www.usaid.gov/our_work/global_partnerships/gda/pdf/GDA_Report_Jan2006_Full.pdf; author's correspondence with several USAID officials and consultants and review of documents, 2005–2007.

78. Author's interviews with IDB officials, 2005–2007.

79. Altes, Carmen, "El Turismo en América Latina y el Caribe y la Experiencia del BID," (Washington, D.C., Inter-American Development Bank, July 2006), 21–24.

80. Ibid. This report concluded that numerous lessons have been learned: that infrastructural investments need to also prepare local institutions to better handle increases in tourist numbers while minimizing any detrimental environmental or social impacts, and that ecotourism projects need to be integrated into comprehensive regional development plans. The IDB outlined a range of other strategies that are to be incorporated into tourism development projects, including promot-

ing sustainable environmental practices, revitalizing historical centers, consulting both local populations and large industries, devising simple monitoring strategies, and incorporating tourism specialists as part of the team of experts.

81. Author interviews with various IDB officials and participation in several IDB tourism seminars, 2005–2007.

82. Santiago Soler and Carmen Altes, "Cluster Action Plan: Sustainable Tourism as a Development Strategy," Inter-American Development Bank, Washington, D.C., June 2004.

83. Ibid.

84. IDB/IMF, "International Partnership to Market Sustainable Tourism Services," RG-M113, Donors Memorandum, June 5, 2007; Ronald Sanabria, Rainforest Alliance, personal correspondence, September 2007.

85. David Grossman and Eddie Koch, *Ecotourism Report: Nature Tourism in South Africa: Links with the Reconstruction and Development Program* (Pretoria, South Africa: SATOUR, August 1995), 8; Price Waterhouse, a 1994 study discussed in Kreg Lindberg, "Economic Aspects of Ecotourism," draft of article obtained from author, November 1997, 2.

86. Nicholson-Lord, "Politics of Travel," 16.

87. Murray A. Rudd, "The non-extractive economic value of spiny lobster *Panuliris argus*, in the Turks and Caicos," *Environmental Conservation* 28, 2001, 226–234. Published online by Cambridge University Press, May 10, 2002, see http://journals.cambridge.org/action/displayAbstract;jsessionid=E00B9EAAD96A3E54BA6134095F44A570.tomcat1?fromPage=online&aid=88155.

88. John H. Cushman, "Whale Watching Grows Into a $1 Billion Industry," *New York Times*, September 9, 2001, see http://query.nytimes.com/gst/fullpage.html?res=9B01E1DE1030F93AA3575AC0A9679C8B63&partner=rssnyt&emc=rss.

89. Republic of Namibia, *Constitution* (Windhoek: Rossing Uranium Ltd., 1990), 52.

90. Commonwealth Department of Tourism, Australia, *National Ecotourism Strategy* (Sydney: Australian Government Publishing Service, 1994), iii, 1–6; Barbara Jones and Tanya Tear, "Australia's National Ecotourism Strategy," *Tourism Focus*, no. 1 (Paris, France: United National Environment Program, January–March 1995).

91. "Program for the Development of Ecotourism in the Legal Amazon Region: Project Abstract," see www.world-tourism.org/sustainable/IYE/quebec/cd/statmnts/pdfs/sobrae.pdf#search=%22proecotur%22; The Technical Cooperation Program for the Development of Ecotourism in the Legal Amazon Region (PROECOTUR) has been established with the Brazilian Ministry for the Environment. The Inter-American Development Bank (IDB) provided a total of $13.8 million in order to enable the nine Brazilian Amazonian states (Acre, Amapá, Amazonas, Maranhão, Mato Grosso, Pará, Rondônia, Roraima, and Tocantins) to prepare themselves for sound and responsible management of selected ecotourism areas.

92. Charles Mkoka, "Malawi Plans to Jumpstart Economy with Ecotourism," *Environment News Service*, January 9, 2003, see www.ens-newswire.com/ens/jan2003/2003-01-09-02.asp.

93. Ramesh Jaura, "Tourism: Developing Nations Expect Big Cut from Tourism Income," Inter-Press Service, March 11, 1998.

94. On Croatia, for instance, International Special Reports, 2001, see www.internationalspecialreports.com/europe/01/croatia/privatized.html.

95. Martha Honey, "Cuba: Tourism/Ecotourism During the 'Special Period,'" in *Ecotourism and Sustainable Development: Who Owns Paradise* (Washington, D.C.: Island Press, 1999); Stewart, "Achieving Sustainable Development."

96. John Pomfret, "Privatizing China's Parks: As Firms Take Over Scenic Treasures, Government Officials Occupy Executive Suites," *Washington Post*, July 5, 2001, A08.

97. U.S. Library of Congress, see http://countrystudies.us/bhutan/44.htm.

98. National Tourism Office, "Welcome to Bhutan," see http://designindia.com/dotbhutan/.

99. Bhutan Tourism Corporation, see www.kingdomofbhutan.com/visitor/visitor_.html.

100. Marti Ann Reinfeld, "Tourism and the Politics of Cultural Preservation: A Case Study of Bhutan," *Journal of Public and International Affairs* 14, Spring 2003.

101. Zoe Chafe, "Vital Signs 2005," World Watch Institute.

102. Zoe Chafe, "Consumer Demand and Operator Support for Socially and Environmentally Responsible Tourism," Center on Ecotourism and Sustainable Development, Working Paper No. 104.

103. Quoted in U.S. Travel Data Center, *Discover America*, 15; Grossman and Koch, *Ecotourism Report*, 11.

104. See www.wttc.org/.

105. See www.tia.org/index.html.

106. Travel Industry Association of America (TIA) and *National Geographic Traveler* (NGT) magazine, "Geotourism: The New Trend in Travel," 2003, see www.tia.org/travel/geo03_es.pdf.

107. See www.unwto.org/frameset/frame_sustainable.html.

108. See www.uneptie.org/pc/tourism/home.htm.

109. See www.astanet.com/.

110. Frederic Dimanche, "Greening Traditional Hotels," *Tour and Travel News*, August 29, 1994, G28.

111. Interviews with Marie Walters, ASTA, 1994; Correspondence with ASTA representative Fred Bursch, July 2006; telephone communication with ASTA representative Haley Jones, August 2006.

112. United Nations, *Agenda 21: The United Nations Program of Action from Rio* (New York: United Nations, 1992). Even though travel and tourism may constitute the world's largest industry, the Earth Summit's *Agenda 21* mentioned it in only a few sections. Chapter 11, for example, advocates that governments "promote and support the management of wildlife [and] . . . ecotourism," and chapter 36 calls for countries to "promote, as appropriate, environmentally sound leisure and tourism activities." Quoted in WTTC, UNWTO, and Earth Council, *Agenda 21 for the Travel and Tourism Industry*, 34.

113. WTTC, UNWTO, and Earth Council, *Agenda 21 for the Travel and Tourism Industry*, 34.

114. Ibid., 1.

115. Kutay, "Brave New Role," 40.

116. Western, "Ecotourism: The Kenya Challenge," 15–16 (italics added).

117. Some other organizations posit similar definitions. The Canadian Environmental Advisory Council, for instance, states, "Ecotourism is an enlightening nature travel experience that contributes to conservation of the ecosystem, while respecting the integrity of host communities." However, although this definition speaks of respecting local communities, it does not state that the communities must benefit from ecotourism. Quoted by Pamela A. Wight, "North American Ecotourists: Market Profile and Trip Characteristics," Spring 1996.

118. Trade Environment Database (TED) Case Study, see www.american.edu/TED/campfire.htm.

119. Correspondence with Lara Goepferd, operations manager for Papoose Creek Lodge, August 2006. See www.papoosecreek.com.

120. The Ecotourism Society, *Ecotourism Guidelines for Nature Tour Operators* (North Bennington, VT: The Ecotourism Society, 1993), 3.

121. "The Tourist Trap: Who's Getting Caught?" *Cultural Survival Quarterly* 2, no. 3, Summer 1982: 3.

122. Telephone interview with Bruno Coulombe, USA Cuba Travel, August 28, 2006, see www.usacubatravel.com/.

123. William Schulz, "Conscientious Projectors: Tourists with an Eye on Human Rights Can Make a Difference," *The Nation*, October 6, 1997, 31.

124. Martha Honey, "Burma: Visit or Boycott?" *The International Ecotourism Society Newsletter*, Washington, D.C., 4th Quarter 2003.

Chapter 2: The World Travel Industry

1. World Travel & Tourism Council (WTTC), UN World Tourism Organization (UNWTO) Earth Council, *Agenda 21 for the Travel and Tourism Industry: Towards Environmentally Sustainable Development* (London: WTTC, 1995), 34.

2. UNWTO enforces more than 100 agreements and regulations, the latest of which are in the current Doha Round, see http://en.wikipedia.org/wiki/Doha_round.

3. Remarks at the United Nations Conference on Trade and Development, October 8, 1996.

4. After passage of the Trade Act of 2002, President George W. Bush negotiated free trade agreements with some dozen countries; a number, however, awaited legislative approval, either by the foreign country or the U.S. Congress, see www.uschamber.com/issues/index/international/default.

5. Barton H. Thompson, Jr. and Jennifer Coyle, "Trade Issues in Sustainable Tourism," draft, Stanford University: Center on Ecotourism and Sustainable Development, January 2005, 17, see under publications at www.ecotourismcesd.org.

6. Anita Pleumarom, "Ecotourism: A New 'Green Revolution' in the Third World," (Thialand: Third World Network, Tourism Investigation & Monitoring Team, undated), see www.twnside.org.sg/title/eco2.htm.

7. Faxed copy of the World Travel & Tourism Council's "Environmental Guidelines," 1997.

8. Tourism Investigation & Monitoring Team, "2002: International Year of Reviewing Ecotourism," copy in possession of author.

9. "The Quebec Declaration on Ecotourism" can be found at www.world-tourism.org/sustainable/IYE/quebec/anglais/declaration.html.

10. World Travel & Tourism Council, *Blueprint for New Tourism* (London: WTTC, 2003), see http://www.tourismfortomorrow.com/images/WTTCBlue printFinal.pdf.

11. Kreg Lindberg, "Economic Aspects of Ecotourism," draft of article obtained from author, November 1997, 12.

12. Thanh-Dam Truong, *Sex, Money, and Morality: Prostitution and Tourism in Southeast Asia* (London: Zed Books, 1990), 116.

13. "History: Pan American Heritage," see www.panam.org/newhist1.asp.

14. Truong, *Sex, Money, and Morality*, 110–111.

15. Andrey Shlevkov, "Tourism on the Threshold of the Third Millennium," Prague, the Czech Republic, March 29, 2004.

16. American Express Company, Annual Report 2004, see www.onlineproxy .com/amex/2005/nonvote/ar/AXP_annual04.pdf.

17. Somerset R. Waters, *Travel Industry World Yearbook: The Big Picture—1996–97*, vol. 40 (New York: Child & Waters, 1997), 150; International Resources Group, *Ecotourism: A Viable Alternative for Sustainable Management of Natural Resources in Africa* (Washington, D.C.: U.S. Agency for International Development, June 1992), 63; Lindberg, "Economic Aspects of Ecotourism," 12.

18. ASTA, "Agency Profile," see www.astanet.com/about/agencyprofile.asp.

19. Travel Industry of America, press release, "Online Travel Booking Jumps in 2002, Despite Plateau in Online Travel Planning," December 9, 2002.

20. Peter Yesawich, CEO, Yesawich, Pepperdine, Brown & Russel, Keynote speech at the Vermont Travel Industry Conference, Stowe, VT, November 29, 2006.

21. Truong, *Sex, Money, and Morality*, 109.

22. Ibid., 104–105.

23. Waters, *Travel Industry World Yearbook*, 77.

24. Star Alliance, see www.staralliance.com/star_alliance/star/frame/main _10.html; Waters, *Travel Industry World Yearbook*, 6.

25. BBC News, "Group Misses Varig Money Deadline," June 23, 2006, see http: //news.bbc.co.uk/1/hi/business/5111690.stm.

26. Ian Katz, "Shakeout in the Latin Skies," *Business Week*, February 28, 2000, see www.businessweek.com/2000/00_09/b3670216.htm; "US Accused of Unjustly Taxing Brazilian and Latin American Crews," *Brazil Magazine*, March 22, 2005, see www.brazzilmag.com/content/view/1755; David Grossman, "Column," *USA Today*, June 13, 2005, see www.usatoday.com/travel/columnist/grossman/ 2005-06-10-grossman_x.htm.

27. Japan Airlines, "Environmental Report," chapter 2, 2004, see www.jal.com /en/environment/report/2004/pdf/all.pdf.

28. "Environmental Auditing: A Tool for Assessing the Environmental Performance of Tourism Firms," *Geographical Journal* 1, no. 161, 1995: 29–37, cited in Pleumarom, "Ecotourism: A New 'Green Revolution,'" 7.

29. G.E. Ecoimagination, see http://ge.ecomagination.com/@v=312005 _0548@/index.html.

30. International Air Transportation Association (IATA), "IATA at the Air Transport Industry Side," see www.iata.org/about/.

31. "IATA Fuel Conservation," see www.iata.org/whatwedo/aircraft_operations/fuel/fuelaction/fuel_conservation.htm.

32. FAA, see www.faa.gov/airports_airtraffic/air_traffic/drvsm/.

33. European Commission, "The Framework Regulation, EC 550/2004," "The Service Provision Regulation, EC 551.2004," "The Airspace Regulation, EC 552/2004," and "The Interoperability Regulation," see www.dft.gov.uk/pgr/aviation/atm/ses/impactassessmentsingleeurope2858.

34. Wolfgang Strasdas, "Voluntary Offsetting of Flight Emissions: An Effective Way to Mitigate the Environmental Impacts on Long-Haul Tourism," February 2007, see www.ecotourismcesd.org.

35. Joanna Walters, "Save the planet . . . stay on the ground", *The Observer*, May 12, 2002, see http://observer.guardian.co.uk/travel/story/0,6903,713881,00.html. In addition, according to IATA, the already high technological and operational standards within the air transport industry make additional improvements increasingly difficult and costly to achieve. See International Air Transport Association, "Local Air Quality: Challenges," 2007 at www.iata.org/whatwedo/environment/laq.htm.

36. Walters, "Save the planet . . . stay on the ground."

37. Green Futures, "Golden Opportunity," see http://www.forumforthefuture.org.uk/greenfutures/articles/602411.

38. Closer examination of Virgin Atlantic's practices did raise some eyebrows. According to *The Guardian* (London), "In March this year, environmentalists accused Virgin Atlantic of double standards over an initiative to plant trees to compensate for the carbon emissions from limousines used to drive its upper class customers to airports. Sustainable transport activists said the step to make the limousine service carbon neutral would be tiny compared with the amount of harmful pollution caused by the airline's fleet of 33 aircraft. According to the government's formula, each kilometre traveled by an airline passenger on a long-haul flight accounts for 0.11 kg of carbon dioxide. *The Guardian* calculated that offsetting Virgin Atlantic's entire annual flight operation would involve planting 59m trees." Mark Oliver, "Virgin pledges $3bn to Combat Global Warming," *The Guardian Unlimited*, September 21, 2006, see http://environment.guardian.co.uk/climatechange/story/0,,1878131,00.html.

39. Adventure Travel Media Service (ATMS), "World's only green airline expands its efforts with alternative fuels," August 14, 2006, see www.atmstravelnews.com/viewpressreleases.asp?ClientID=381&RID=1355.

40. Michelle Higgins, "Carbon Neutral: Raising the Ante on Ecotourism," *New York Times*, December 10, 2006, see www.nytimes.com/2006/12/10/travel/10carbon.html?ex=1169269200&en=748409296d4a830f&ei=5070.

41. Correspondence with Jill Zanger, CR Communications Manager, Nike Inc., November 2006. Zanger said that Nike was using three offset companies—The Climate Trust, NatSource, and the Oregon Office of Energy's Business Energy Tax Credit program—and that in 2005, 45 percent of the total CO_2 emissions from Nike business travel were offset through these programs.

42. Waters, *Travel Industry World Yearbook*, 153. The leaders include U.S.-owned ITT Sheraton Corporation, Holiday Inn, Hyatt Hotels and Resorts, and Marriott International, as well as Inter-Continental Hotels and Hilton International (United Kingdom), Accor (France), and Grupo Sol Meliá (Spain).

43. Mintel Travel & Tourism Intelligence, *Mintel Hotel Industry Report*, 2003, accessed by Emy Rodriguez through University of Maryland library system.

44. Stephanie Thullen, "Ecotourism and Sustainability: The Problematic Role of Transnational Corporations in Ecotourism," master's thesis, American University, 1997; Truong, *Sex, Money, and Morality*, 109–116.

45. The Tourism Partnership, see www.tourismpartnership.org/.

46. Ceres, "Green Hotel Initiative," see www.ceres.org/NETCOMMUNITY/Page.aspx?pid=761&srcid=563; "Meeting Planners Send Wake-Up Call to Hotel Industry," *GreenMoneyJournal.com*, Fall 2007, see http://greenmoneyjournal.com/article.mpl?newsletterid=1&articleid=50.

47. Advertisement in *Going Green: The Ecotourism Resource for Travel Agents*, supplement to *Tour & Travel News*, October 25, 1993, 11; interviews with a representative of DHC Hotels; brochures from DHC Hotels; Thullen, "Ecotourism and Sustainability," 53–57.

48. Martha Honey, ed., *Ecotourism and Certification: Setting Standards in Practice* (Washington, D.C.: Island Press, 2002).

49. Michelin Travel Publications, see www.michelintravel.com/products/product_list_2006.html#5.

50. American Automobile Association (AAA), see www.aaa.com/AAA_Travel/Travel/travel.htm.

51. International Organization for Standardization (ISO), see www.iso.org/iso/en/ISOOnline.frontpage.

52. European Flower, "The EU Eco Label," see www.eco-label.com/default.htm.

53. Blue Swallow, "Vertraglich Reisen: Blaue Schwalbe—Gastgeber von Verträglich Reisen," see www.vertraeglich-reisen.de.

54. Nordic Swan Ecolabelling, see www.wiserearth.org/resource/view/e42b5fe7e8594413700c7cb86dbbdeba.

55. Rainforest Alliance, Sustainable Tourism Stewardship Council documents, see http://www.rainforest-alliance.org/tourism.cfm?id=council/.

56. CESD and INCAE, *Cruise Tourism Impacts in Costa Rica & Honduras: Policy Recommendations for Decision Makers,* January 2007, 9, see www.ecotourismcesd.org under "Publications"; Ross Klein, *Cruise Ship Blues: The Underside of the Cruise Industry* (Gabriola Island, BC, Canada: New Society Publishers, 2002), 2; Conservation International CELB (Center for Environmental Leadership in Business), "Travel & Leisure: Cruises," see www.celb.org/xp/CELB/programs/travel-leisure/cruises.xml.

57. Ross Klein, "Executive Summary," *Cruising—Out of Control: The Cruise Industry, the Environment, Workers* (Halifax, Canada: Canadian Centre for Policy Alternatives–Nova Scotia, March 2003), *1*. For this and many other resources, see www.cruisejunkie.com/.

58. The International Ecotourism Society, "Facts about the Cruise Industry," *Eco Currents*, Second/Third Quarter 2004, 7, see Resources: Newsletters at www.ecotourism.org.

59. International Council of Cruise Lines, "The Contribution of the North American Cruise Industry to the US Economy in 2002," August 2003, see www.iccl.org/resources/economicstudies.cfm; Mintel Marketing Intelligence,

Cruises: North America and the Caribbean, June 2004 and *Cruises: US*, April 2005, accessed through University of Maryland library system.

60. Ross Klein, *Charting a Course: The Cruise Industry, the Government of Canada and Purposeful Development* (Ottawa, Canada: Canadian Centre for Policy Alternatives, September 2004), see www.cruisejunkie.com/ccpa2.pdf.

61. General Session Remarks of ASTA President and CEO Joe Galloway at "ASTA's 69th World Travel Congress," Strasbourg, France, November 11, 1999. Copy in possession of author. Only available to ASTA members on ASTA Web site, see www.asta.org/News/SpeechArchive.cfm?navItemNumber=541#1999.

62. "Agent Highlights: Still Solo, Small and Selling Hard," *Travel Weekly*, 2005, see www.travelweekly.com/multimedia/TWSURVEY2005/agent_hl.htm.

63. Cruise Lines International Association, "Summary of Travel Agency Membership Benefits for 2006," 2006, see www.cruising.org/travelagents/public/index.cfm.

64. Marc Lacey, "Amid the Woe, a Haitian Paradise Beckons," *New York Times*, February 16, 2007.

65. Mintel, *Cruises*, April 2005.

66. James Anderson, "No Fun in the Sun," Associated Press, 2000.

67. Sierra Club, "Turning on Cruise Control," see www.sierraclub.org/sierra/200407/lol.asp; Klein, *Cruise Ship Blues*, 7, 84–85.

68. Teri Shore, "Cruise Ships—Polluting for Fun & Profit," *Eco Currents*, Washington, D.C.: The International Ecotourism Society, Second/Third Quarter, 2004, 5, see Resources: Newsletters at www.ecotourism.org.

69. Michael Crye, President, International Council of Cruise Lines and Jamie Sweeting, Diretor, Travel & Leisure, Center for Environmental Leadership in Business, Conservation International, "Cruise Lines as Responsible Environmental Partners," *Eco Currents*, Second/Third Quarter 2004, see Resources: Newsletters at www.ecotourism.org; Michael Crye, executive vice president, CLIA, "Cruise Port and Tourism," powerpoint presentation to IAPH World Ports Conference, Houston, Texas, May 2, 2007, see www.iaph2007.com/Presentations/IAPH 2007-Crye.pdf.

70. "The Contribution of the North American Cruise Industry to the US Economy in 2002," prepared for the International Council of Cruise Lines, August 2003 by Business & Economic Advisors, see www.iccl.org/resources/economic-studies.cfm. The International Council of Cruise Lines, "Cruise Industry Generates $20 Billion in Economic Benefit to the U.S. Economy in 2001," see www.iccl.org/clc; Crye, "Cruise Port and Tourism." For Ross Klein's critical analysis of the cruise association figures, see *Cruise Ship Squeeze*, (British Columbia, Canada: New Society Publishers, 2005).

71. Blaine Harden, "Tourism Buoys Economy of Tiny Alaskan Village," *Washington Post*, August 7, 2004.

72. Craig Welch, "Rush of Cruise Ships to Alaska Delivers Dollars—and Doubts," *Seattle Times*, February 24, 2004, see http://seattletimes.nwsource.com/html/localnews/2001682132_yakutat31m.html.

73. Karen Gorecki and Bruce Wallace, *Ripple Effects: The Need to Assess the Impacts of Cruise Ships in Victoria B.C.*, Vancouver Island Public Interest Research Group, 2003, 27, see www.vipirg.ca/publications/pubs/research_reports/0305_ripple_effects.pdf.

74. "Campaign to Safeguard America's Waters," *Earth Island Journal* 21, no. 2 (Summer 2006), see www.earthisland.org/eijournal/new_articles.cfm?articleID=1049&journalID=87.

75. The Associated Press, "Cruise Ship Companies form a New Alaska Association, Group Seeks Better Relations with State," Anchorage, February 7, 2007, see www.juneauempire.com/stories/020707/sta_20070207022.shtml.

76. Fifteen million reflects the total number of port visits by cruise passengers. Since cruise itineraries include visits to a number of ports, the 15 million represents the total number of passengers arriving at all ports. Some 6 million discrete cruise passengers go to the Caribbean each year. In contrast, stayover passengers usually visit only one country or island, therefore the 15 million represents close to the total number of persons currently vacationing in the Caribbean each year.

77. The UNWTO's January 2006 *World Tourism Barometer* reported that "the cruise sector shows a continued robust performance." UNWTO, *World Tourism Barometer* 4, no. 1, January 2006, 3.

78. World Travel & Tourism Council (WTTC), *The Caribbean: The Impact of Travel and Tourism on Jobs and the Economy*, June 2004, see www.hospitalitynet.org/file/152001490.pdf.

79.CESD and INCAE, *Cruise Tourism Impacts,* 10.

80. Ibid.

81. CESD, *Cruise Tourism in Belize: Perceptions of Economic, Social, and Environmental Impacts,* November 2006, 9, www.ecotownsmcesd.org, under "Publications"; Belize Tourism Board, "Strategic Vision for Belize Tourism in the New Millennium," 2004.

82. CESD, Executive Summary, *Cruise Tourism in Belize.*

83. WTTC, *The Caribbean*; CESD and INCAE, *Cruise Tourism Impacts.*

84. Although travel agents are categorized as both corporate and leisure agencies, the focus here is on leisure. International Resources Group, *Ecotourism*, 23.

85. Interview with Sue DiCicco from Circle Travel, Laurel Springs, NJ, August 2006.

86. Interview with Chris Seek from Solimar Travel, Washington D.C., August 2006.

87. Interviews with Seek, DiCicco, and others; Karen Ziffer, *Ecotourism: The Uneasy Alliance* (Washington, D.C.: Conservation International, 1989), 21.

88. Interviews with ASTA officials in Alexandria, Virginia, in September 1998, and with Yvonne Rodgers, International Ecotourism Education Foundation, Falls Church, Virginia, in May 1996; Barbara Crossette, "Surprises in the Global Tourism Boom," *New York Times*, April 12, 1998, 5.

89. Peter Yesawich, keynote address at the Vermont Travel Industry conference, Stowe, Vermont, November 29, 2006.

90. Interview, Seek.

91. CESD, "Executive Summary," *Cruise Tourism in Belize.*

92. E. Weiner, "Ecotourism: Can it Protect the Planet?" *New York Times*, May 19, 1991, cited in Pleumarom, "Political Economy of Tourism," 144, n. 21. Another expert estimates that "there are 50,000 travel agencies with over 300,000 travel agents selling travel in the U.S. alone." M. J. Kietzke, "The Role of Travel Agents in Ecotourism," *Earth Ways*, January 1996, EW4; Interviews with ASTA officials, September 1998.

93. "Travel Agents and Their Specialties," *Washington Post*, September 28, 1997, E6; Green Earth Travel, see www.vegtravel.com; Solimar Travel, see www.solimartravel.com/index.html.

94. American Society of Travel Agents (ASTA), see www.astanet.com/about/faq.asp#2.

95. International Resources Group, *Ecotourism*, 23–25; The Ecotourism Society (TES, now TIES), training course packet (Burlington, Vermont, 1996).

96. International Resources Group, *Ecotourism*, 27–28; USTOA, see www.ustoa.com/fastfacts.cfm.

97. Gabor Vereczi, program officer, Sustainable Development of Tourism, UNWTO, "Preliminary Results of the WTO Research Programme on Ecotourism Generating Markets," presented at the Conference on Sustainable Development & Management of Ecotourism in Small Island Developing States and Other Islands, Seychelles, December 2001, see www.world-tourism.org/sustain able/IYE/Regional_Activites/Seychelles/Vereczi-Eco-market.htm.

98. Bryan Higgins, "The Global Structure of the Nature Tourism Industry: Ecotourists, Tour Operators, and Local Business," *Journal of Travel Research* 35, no. 2, (fall 1996), 13.

99. I was very surprised when I first learned about fam trips. As a news reporter, I had always adhered to a creed of never taking favors from those I was covering. However, in the course of researching this book, I took three fam trips organized by public relations firms—one to Chile's Patagonia and two to the Virgin Islands of the United States. I also negotiated discounted or free hotel accommodations and airline tickets for some of my travels to Costa Rica, the Galapagos, Cuba, and Africa. My motivation was partly to learn how the travel press operates, but the reality is that I couldn't have covered the expenses involved in writing this book without fam trips (and several generous foundation grants).

100. Deborah Cooper, "Turning Press Trips into Client Trips," *Adventure Travel Business*, October 1997, 22.

101. Author's interviews; Tom McNicol, "Misguided," *Washington Post*, April 19, 1998, E6.

102. Quoted in McNicol, "Misguided," E6–E8.

103. I found myself torn emotionally and ethically by these fam trips. I went, with three other writers, on a fam trip to Chile's Patagonia that was billed by the public relations firm as ecotourism. We were fed the story with a silver spoon: everything was covered but tips; we were accompanied by guides, flown in business class, and even had a day of sightseeing in Santiago en route to Patagonia. There, we were taken to an amazing new luxury hotel, Explora Salto Chico, at the time the only hotel in Torres del Paine National Park open year-round. The architect himself arrived to explain his marvelous creation. I was thrilled to hike through the windswept park, with its bonsai-like shrubs in tones of blue-green and burnt orange; jagged, snow-dusted Andean peaks; and dazzling blue-and-white icebergs floating across dark, choppy lakes. I never would have been able to visit this end of the earth otherwise. But in reality, we were experiencing luxury nature travel, not ecotourism. The hotel, owned by one of Chile's wealthiest families, which also owns the airline on which we flew, has no program for benefiting the park, scientific research, or the scattered homesteaders in the region. The guides working for the hotel are young, hip, bilingual college kids from Santiago

without deep knowledge of Patagonia's unique ecosystem and history. The local park rangers I met on my own were far more informative. Salto Chico, though a beautiful, architecturally sensitive resort, does not qualify as an exemplary ecotourism project.

104. Interview with Kim Lisagor, August 2005.

105. McNicol, "Misguided," E6, E8.

106. Interviews with several *Condé Nast Traveler* editors and writers.

107. Interview with Brook Wilkinson, *Condé Nast Traveler*, July 2005.

108. Interviews with travel writers and editors; McNicol, "Misguided," E6–E8.

109. McNicol, "Misguided," E6.

110. Interviews by the author with some dozen travel writers between 1996 and 2006.

111. Society of American Travel Writers (SATW), "Membership Guidelines"; interviews with SATW officials and travel writers.

112. SATW, "Code of Ethics", see www.satw.org/satw/index.asp?SId=81.

113. Telephone interview, Ed Malone, past president, Society of American Travel Writers, Raleigh, NC, August 2006. For more information on the Society of American Travel Writers see www.satw.org.

114. Steve Hendrix, "Burma in the Balance: Should you go? The politics of travel to Asia's most controversial destination," *Washington Post*, Travel Section, Sunday, May 25, 2003.

115. Steve Hendrix, "I Went To Burma. Bad Move. A Place Where Tourism Carries Political Baggage by Steve Hendrix," *Washington Post*, Opinion Section, Sunday, June 15, 2003.

116. Martha Honey, "Burma: Visit or Boycott?" *The International Ecotourism Society Newsletter*, Fourth Quarter 2003, see Resources: Newsletters at www.ecotourism.org.

117. Jennifer Saranow, "Getting Travel Advice From a Stranger; Online Blogs Emerge As Popular Resource; How to Find Useful Ones," *Wall Street Journal*, Eastern Edition, September 28, 2004.

118. "The Thorn Tree," Lonely Planet 2005, see http://thorntree.lonelyplanet.com.

119. Ziffer, *Uneasy Alliance*, 22.

120. International Resources Group, *Ecotourism*, 26.

121. Ronnie Casella, "Dinosaurs in Paradise: Off the Path with the Time-Traveling Tourist," in "The Educated Traveler," Ph.D. dissertation, Syracuse University, 1996.

122. Brochures quoted are from Casella, "The Educated Traveler," or in author's files.

123. News from British Airways, "Keep Your Towels—and Help Save the World!" press release, 1999, in possession of author; British Airways, *Social and Environmental Report 2000*, see www.britishairways.com/cms/masterEN/content/company_information/community_and_environmental/supplementary_data2000.pdf.

124. Arthur Frommer, "Frommer's World: Writing Reasonable Rules for Real Ecotourism," *Travel Holiday*, February 1994, 25.

125. Denise Ingram and Patrick Durst, *Nature-Oriented Travel to Developing Countries,* FPEI Working Paper No. 28 (Research Triangle Park, NC: Southeastern Center for Forest Economics Research, October 1987), 6.

126. Correspondence with Kimberly Beck, Marketing & Sales, Mountain Travel Sobek, September 2006.

127. Correspondence with Karen Hansen, Media Relations, Grand Circle Corporation, Overseas Adventure Travel, September 2006.

128. Marla Pleyte, "Online Undercover Marketing," *Business Law Journal*, University of California, Davis, School of Law, May 1, 2006, see http://blj.ucdavis.edu/article.asp?id=637.

129. Richard Ord, "The Blog Marketing Explosion," *iEntry Inc*, October 5, 2004, see www.webpronews.com/insiderreports/searchinsider/wpn-49-20041005TheBlogMarketingExplosion.html.

130. I visited Mahenye and interviewed Clive Stckil and others in the mid-1990s and was impressed with the contributions this small eco-lodge had made to the neighboring village as part of the CAMPFIRE project. The Shangaan village received an average of 10 percent of the profits from the Mahenye Safari Lodge and the neighboring Chilo Gorge Safari Lodge and also received a percentage from a trophy-hunting concession. These funds were distributed annually to family households and used for village projects including to build school classrooms, buy a grinding mill, and put in electricity, telephones, and water pumps. Through being involved in both photographic and hunting safaris, the Shangaan were being transformed from poachers into protectors of the local wildlife. During the 1990s, Mahenye was one of the most successful projects within CAMPFIRE. However, since then ecotourism at Mahenye and in all of Zimbabwe has been going through difficult times because of the country's ongoing political and economic crisis. This has been compounded at the village level by corruption, clan patronage, and a decline in community participation, but the lodge continues to be marketed in the portfolio of leading ecotourism lodges in southern Africa. Author's visit to Mahenye and interviews with Clive Stockil and others; Marisa Milanese, "Africa's Ghost in the Machine: Clive Stockil's CAMPFIRE Project Generates Tourism, Jobs—and Controversy," *Condé Nast Traveler*, June 1997, 24–31; Judith Mashinya, "The decline of a model community-based conservation project: Governance, capacity, and devolution in Mahenye, Zimbabwe," Ph.D. dissertation, University of Maryland, College Park, 2007, see www.sciencedirect.com/science?_ob=ArticleURL&_udi=B6V68-4JCBM27-1&_user=10&_rdoc=1&_fmt=&_orig=search&_sort=d&view=c&_acct=C000050221&_version=1&_urlVersion=0&_userid=10&md5=dddf7c3b72a9aab4a1ab39e676275c83#cor1.

131. American Society of Travel Agents (ASTA), Environment Committee, "Destination Earth—Save It, Share It," ASTA newsletter, September 1993; ASTA/*Smithsonian Magazine* Environmental Awards for 1991–1996; "Princess wins prestigious environmental award; first cruise line to receive top recognition for 'green' efforts," The Free Library, see www.thefreelibrary.com/Princess+wins+prestigious+environmental+award%3B+first+cruise+line+to...-a018736289.

132. ASTA, "ASTA Announces Call for 2005 Travel Industry Awards Nominations," press release, 2005, see www.astanet.com/news/releasearchive05/04220.asp; Martha Honey, "The 'Oscars of Tourism': Raising the Bar on Eco-Award Programs," *The International Ecotourism Society Newsletter*, Washington, D.C., Second Quarter 2003.

133. Brook Wilkinson, "Condé Nast Traveler Presents the 12th Annual Green

List," *Condé Nast Traveler*, September 2006, see www.concierge.com/cntraveler/articles/detail?articleId=10419&pageNumber=1; Honey, "The 'Oscars of Tourism.'"

134. Correspondence with Brook Wilkinson, February 2007.

135. Responsibletravel.com, "Responsible Tourism Award Competition Rules," see www.responsibletravel.com/Copy/Copy900273.htm and "The First Choice Responsible Tourism Awards 2006," see www.responsibletravel.com/Copy/Copy102214.htm.

136. The author attended the November 2, 2005 ceremony at the U.S. State Department, Washington, D.C.; Lapa Rios Rainforest Ecolodge, "US State Department Corporate Excellence Award 2005," see www.laparios.com/articles/lapa_rios_state_dept_award_2005.htm.

137. "Ecotourism Case by Case: Conservation Travel," *Travel World News: The Monthly Review for Travel Agent* no. 72, June 1994, 126.

138. Tourism Concern, "Press statement and briefing: Why Tourism Concern is cautious about the International Year of Ecotourism," 2001.

139. Mireya Navarro, "New Disney Kingdom Comes with Real-Life Obstacles," *New York Times*, April 16, 1998; Jon Nordheimer, "Disney Goes Live with Its Newest Park," *New York Times*, April 26, 1998, 8–9, 25.

140. Walt Disney World Theme Parks, "Animal Kingdom," see www.wdwinfo.com/wdwinfo/guides/animalkingdom/ak-overview.htm; "Disney's Animal Kingdom," see http://pixiedust-travel.com/DisneysAnimalKingdom.html.

141. David Western, "Ecotourism: The Kenya Challenge," in C. G. Gakahu and B. E. Goode, *Ecotourism and Sustainable Development in Kenya*, proceedings of the Kenya Ecotourism Workshop held at Nakuru National Park, Kenya, September 13–17, 1992 (Nairobi: Wildlife Conservation International, 1992), 16.

142. World Resources Institute, "Ecotourism: Rising Interest in Nature Vacations Has Mixed Results for Host Countries and the Resources They Promote," in *Environmental Almanac* (Boston: Houghton Mifflin, 1993), 150; Jim Motavalli, "Transforming Travel: Eco-tourism Is More Than a Buzzword; It's a Seismic Shift in a Trillion-Dollar Industry," Motavalli, "Africa Wakes," and John Ivanko, "Far-Flung Fantasies," all in *The Environmental Magazine*, April 1995, 38–45; CESD, "Fact Sheet: Global."

143. "Nepal: How to Kill," InterPress Service, June 3, 1995.

144. Imtiaz Muqbil, "German Tourism Activist Sounds Warning on Bogus 'Ecotourism,'" *Bangkok Post*, tourism supplement, April 7, 1994, 3.

145. "Ecotourism Case by Case," 126.

Chapter 3: Ecotourism Today

1. U.S. Department of the Interior, National Park Service, *Guiding Principles of Sustainable Design* (Denver, Colorado: National Park Service, Denver Service Center, September 1993).

2. Suzanne Oliver, "Eco-profitable," *Forbes*, 153, no. 13, June 20, 1994.

3. "Clipboard," *Travel Weekly*, June 6, 1994.

4. Ann Kalosh, "The Travel Industry's Green Guru: An Interview with Stanley Selengut," *Hemispheres*, United Airlines flight magazine, April 1994.

5. Stanley Selengut, interviews, Maho Bay, St. John, December 1994 and January 1995; "Ecotourism Investigation," *Agenda 21* series, Worldwide Television News, London, March 1995, produced by author.

6. Correspondence with Adrian Davis, resident manager, Maho Bay Camps, September 2006.

7. Correspondence with Barbara Richman, September 2006.

8. *U.S. Virgin Islands*, U.S. Department of Labor, Bureau of Statistics, see www.bls.gov/eag/eag.vi.htm.

9. Author's interviews on St. John, including with Ray Ashton, Joshua Reichert, and others; with Stanley Selengut, various occasions, 1994–2007; telephone interview with Jossette Pacquin, Employment and Training Office, Department of Labor, St. Thomas Island, June 1998; Davis, 2006.

10. Ray Ashton, interview, Maho Bay, St. John, October 1994.

11. "Trash for Treasure's Art Center," see www.maho.org/TTAC.cfm.

12. Interviews and correspondence with Bernard Kemp, 1995.

13. Colette Bachand-Wood, "Commentary: Pioneer Eco-resort's Fate Still Unknown," *Travel New England*, February 2006.

14. ITA, Office of Travel & Tourism Industries, U.S. Dept of Commerce, "2002 Profile of U.S. Resident Traveler Visiting Overseas Destinations," report from *Survey of International Air Travelers,* posted July 2003, see http://tinet .ita.doc.gov/view/f-2002-101-001/index.html.

15. UNWTO, press release, June 2004, cited in Center on Ecotourism and Sustainable Development (CESD), "Fact Sheet: Ecotourism in the U.S.," see www .ecotourismcesd.org.

16. Pamela Wight, "Ecotourists: Not a Homogenous Market Segment," chapter 3 in *The Encyclopedia of Ecotourism,* David Weaver, ed. (New York: CABI Publishing, 2001).

17. CESD,"Fact Sheet: Ecotourism in the U.S."

18. Caroline Wild, Toronto-based ecotourism consultant, interview, Montreal, September 1994.

19. Kurt Kutay, "Brave New Role: Ecotour Operators Take Center Stage in the Era of Green Travel," in *Going Green: The Ecotourism Resource for Travel Agents,* supplement to *Tour & Travel News,* October 25, 1993, 40–41; author's interviews with Kutay between 1995–1997 and in 2006.

20. David Grossman and Eddie Koch, *Ecotourism Report: Nature Tourism in South Africa: Links with the Reconstruction and Development Program* (Pretoria, South Africa: SATOUR, August 1995), 11.

21. Correspondence with Kurt Kutay, August 2006.

22. Correspondence with Pamela Wight, August 2006; Wight, "Ecotourists". Wight defined experienced ecotourists as those who had taken an out-of-state vacation in the past three years or planned to do so.

23. CESD, "Fact Sheet: Ecotourism in the U.S."

24. Correspondence with Herbert Hamale, Ecotrans, Germany. Statistics are from a 2002 survey.

25. Tearfund, "Tourism—an Ethical Issue: Market Research Report," Tearfund, London, January 2000.

26. MORI, *Package Holidays*, Survey of U.K. consumers commissioned by the

Association of British Travel Agents (ABTA), September 2002, cited in Pro Poor Tourism Pilots (Southern Africa) Programme, *Business Implementation of Pro Poor Tourism: Case Study Briefs,* No. 7, "Ethical Consumerism and Tourism," see www.pptpilot.org.za.

27. Pamela Wight, "North American Ecotourism Markets: Motivations, Preferences and Destinations," *Journal of Travel Research* 35, Issue 1, Summer 1996.

28. Pamela Wight, "Appealing and Marketing to the North American Ecotourist," paper presented at Shaping Tomorrow's North: The Role of Tourism and Recreation, conference held at Lakehead Centre for Northern Studies, Lakehead University, Thunder Bay, Ontario, October 12–15, 1995.

29. Ibid.

30. Denise Ingram and Patrick Durst, "Nature-Oriented Travel to Developing Countries," FPEI Working Paper No. 28, (Research Triangle Park, NC: Southeastern Center for Forest Economics Research, October 1987), 8.

31. Herbert Hamele, Ecotrans, Germany, 2004.

32. The Ecotourism Society (TES) training course packet, Burlington, VT, 1996.

33. Peter Frank and Jon Bowermaster, "Can Ecotourism Save the Planet?" and "Seven Golden Rules . . . and the People Who Stick to Them," *Condé Nast Traveler,* December 1994, 138–139, 161–162.

34. Interviews with Marie Walters and Carolyn Wild, September, International Peace Through Tourism (IPTT) conference, 1994, Montreal, Canada.

35. Brian Higgins, "Global Structure of the Nature Tourism Industry: Ecotourists, Tour Operators, and Local Businesses," *Journal of Travel Research* 35, no. 2, 1996: 15.

36. *Specialty Travel Index* (STI) publication and interview. According to STI publisher Steen Hansen, some 550 tour operators, or about half the specialty companies in the United States, advertise in the STI, which is distributed to all travel agents. There are 11,000–12,000 tour operators and travel agents in the United States.

37. Correspondence with Steen Hansen, The Specialty Travel Index, September 2006.

38. Karen Ziffer, *Ecotourism: The Uneasy Alliance,* (Washington, D.C.: Conservation International, 1989) 19–20.

39. Author's correspondence with Kurt Kutay, August 2006.

40. Numerous interviews with Sally and Costas Christ, 1995–2007, see also Tamu Safari's Web site at www.tamusafaris.com.

41. G.A.P Adventures, see www.gapadventures.com/.

42. G.A.P Adventures Media Kit, 2006, see www.gapadventures.com/docs/MediaKit.pdf.

43. G.A.P Adventures Mission Statement, see www.gapadventures.com/about_us/mission_statement.

44. G.A.P Adventures Media Kit, 2006.

45. Kali Pearson "10 Trailblazers: Entrepreneurs Who Have Rocked Their Industries," *Profit,* Issue 3, May 1, 2002, Toronto, 28.

46. Planeta.com; see www.planeterra.org.

47. Ibid.; the three charities they support are Plan International, Charles Darwin Foundation, and Youth Challenge International.

48. G.A.P Adventures: Awards and Recognition, see www.gapadventures.com/about_us/awards_and_recognition.

49. Correspondence with Kutay; "Adventure Travel Companies Rated," *National Geographic Adventure*, November 2007, see http://atr.nationalgeographic.com/outfitters/searchMain.action.

50. Tour Operators' Initiative for Sustainable Tourism Development, see www.toinitiative.org.

51. Adventure Collection, see www.adventurecollection.com/members. The ten members are: Backroads, Bushtracks Expeditions, Canadian Mountain Holidays, Geographic Expeditions, Lindblad Expeditions, Micato Safaris, Natural Habitat Adventures, National Outdoor Leadership School (NOLS), Outdoor Adventure River Specialists (OARS), and Off the Beaten Path, see www.adventurecollection.com/ac_html/htdocs/whatsnew.html#no26.

52. Adventure Collection, "Our Travel Ethic," see www.adventurecollection.com/about/ethic.

53. Correspondence with Sandra Townsend, Larry Mogelonsky, and Bill Bryan, Adventure Collection, 2005–2007; see also Adventure Collection at www.adventurecollection.com/home.

54. International Resources Group, *Ecotourism: A Viable Alternative for Sustainable Management of Natural Resources in Africa* (Washington, D.C.: U.S. Agency for International Development, June 1992), 34–40.

55. Correspondence with William Durham, Stanford University, 2007. Durham is also the Stanford director of the Center on Ecotourism and Sustainable Development (CESD).

56. These trips were only advertised in their magazine and through a direct mail brochure to a list from their member database; correspondence with Jill Bernier, TNC Conservation Journeys Program, December 2006.

57. Correspondence with Rebecca Goodstein and Jill Bernier, TNC Conservation Journeys Program, August and October 2006; See also the TNC travel Web site at www.nature.org/aboutus/travel/travel/.

58. Telephone interviews with Karen Ferrante, WWF Membership Travel Program, August 2006. See also the WWF travel Web site at www.worldwildlife.org/travel.

59. Natural Habitat Adventures, see www.nathab.com/app/cda/nha_cda.php.

60. For details of the annual conference, which is usually held in the Washington, D.C./Baltimore area, see www.travelearning.com.

61. Jan Laarman, Timothy Stewart, and Jeffrey Prestermon, "International Travel by U.S. Conservation Groups and Professional Societies," *Journal of Travel Research*, Summer 1989, 12–17.

62. E. A. Halpenny, "Ecotourism-related Organizations" in *Encyclopedia of Ecotourism*, Weaver, ed.

63. Correspondence with Jill Bernier, October 2006.

64. Héctor Ceballos-Lascuráin, *Tourism, Ecotourism, and Protected Areas*, (Gland, Switzerland: IUCN, 1996), 6, 9.

65. UNWTO, *Tourism Highlights*, 2005 Edition.

66. This figure excludes arrivals from Hong Kong, Macau, and Taiwan, which constitute the majority of foreign arrivals into China. These international arrivals

generated nearly $30 *billion* in receipts and marked a 19 percent increase in arrival numbers over 2004; the growth of domestic tourism has been even more astounding, generating $67 billion in 2005. China National Tourist Office: *China Tourism Statistics,* see www.cnto.org/chinastats.asp#Stats.

67. *The China Daily*, May 13, 2004, see www.chinadaily.com.cn/english/doc/2004-05/13/content_330514.htm.

68. Erlet A. Cater, "Tourism in the Yunnan Great Rivers National Parks System Project: Prospects for Sustainability," *Tourism Geographies* 2(4), 2000, 472–489; Julie Jie Wen and Clement A. Tisdell, *Tourism and China's Development: Policies, Regional Economic Growth and Ecotourism* (River Edge, NJ: World Scientific Publishing Co., 2001).

69. In January 2007, for instance, Machik, a Washington, D.C.–based NGO, brought a group of Tibetan leaders involved in community-based tourism to meet with TIES experts and learn more about ecotourism, fair trade in handicrafts, and "geotourism."

70. Frances Figart, "China's First Planned Ecolodge Takes a Metaphysical Approach," TIES, *EcoCurrents*, 3rd quarter 2006, see Resources: Newsletters at www.ecotourism.org.

71. Among the tour operators promoting ecotourism trips in China are: Wild China Company, see www.wildchina.com; China Adventure Travel, see www.c-adventure.com, and Khampa Caravan, see www.khampacaravan.com.

72. In 2006, during China's traditional Golden Week holiday, domestic travelers within China numbered 146 million, an increase of 20 percent over 2005, and tourism earnings grew by 25 percent, some $7.3 billion. "Asia: Golden Years; China and Tourism," *The Economist* 379, no. 847, May 11, 2006, 72, available by subscription at www.economist.com/world/asia/displaystory.cfm?story_id=E1_GJNRRRR.

73. Slow Food is a nonprofit, member-supported organization, see www.slowfood.com. For its U.S. member organization, Slow Food USA, see www.slowfoodusa.org/. Agritourism World, an Internet directory for agritourism, provides links to agritourism projects and destinations around the world, see www.agritourismworld.com/.

74. Caroline J. Stem, et al., "How 'Eco' is Ecotourism? A Comparative Case Study of Ecotourism in Costa Rica," *Journal of Sustainable Tourism* 11, no. 4 2003.

75. Horizontes Nature Tours, see www.horizontes.com/en/horizontes-earns-highest-5-leaf-certification-for-sustainable-prac-2.html; correspondence with Amos Bien, consultant for CESD and TIES International Programs director, December 13, 2006.

76. Interviews with Costas Christ, 1995–2006.

77. Correspondence with Meg Katzman, the exclusive direct U.S. agent for Unique Safaris, August 2006; see also Unique Safari Web site at www.uniquesafaris.com.

78. By 2006, bank loan rates in Tanzania had fallen to between 10 and 20 percent due to the privatization of the banking system and increasing numbers of banking options. With free-market policies, competition for loans increased and lowered interest rates. Correspondence with Katzman, Unique Safaris, 2006.

79. Ibid.; For the Overseas Development Institute's program for Pro Poor Tourism Programme, see www.odi.org.uk.

80. Michele Zebich-Knos, "A Good Neighbor Policy? Ecotourism, Park Systems and Environmental Justice in Latin America," working paper presented at the Latin American Studies Association, San Juan, Puerto Rico, March 15–18, 2006, 4, 37.

81. George Washington University, International Institute of Tourism Studies. Taken from Development Assistance Network for Tourism Enhancement and Investment Database, 2005, see www.dantei.org; Mac Chapin, "A Challenge to Conservationists," *Worldwatch*, Nov/Dec 2004.

82. Anita Pleumarom, "The Political Economy of Tourism," *The Ecologist* 24, no. 4, July–August 1994, 144.

83. World Wildlife Fund (WWF), The Nature Conservancy (TNC), and World Resources Institute (WRI), "Biodiversity Conservation Network: Getting Down to Business, 1997 Annual Report," 1997, iii.

84. Correspondence with Iain Thornton Christie, Tourism Adviser, World Bank, Washington, D.C., August 16, 2006.

85. Michael Wells and Katrina Brandon, *People and Parks: Linking Protected Area Management with Local Communities* (Washington, D.C.: World Bank, World Wildlife Fund, and U.S. Agency for International Development, 1992), 3.

86. Jonathan Adams, "Ecotourism: Conservation Tool or Threat?" *Conservation Issues* 2, no. 3, June 1995.

87. Correspondence with Mingma Sherpa, World Wildlife Fund, August 2006. (Sherpa was tragically killed in a helicopter crash shortly after this correspondence.) Nepal Tourism Board, "Visitor Arrivals in Nepal Show Strong Growth in 2007," January 7, 2008, see www.traveldailynews.com/pages/show_page/24013.

88. In 2007, CESD was commissioned to undertake a study, "Global Trends in Coastal Tourism," as part of WWF's internal initiative to decide if they should start a tourism program. See Publications, www.ecotourismcesd.org. Elizabeth Boo, *Ecotourism: The Potentials and Pitfalls*, vols. 1 and 2 (Washington, D.C.: World Wildlife Fund, 1990); This seminal study was financed by USAID.

89. See www.coralreefalliance.org/.

90. Information provided by Gina DeFerrari, WWF, December 2006.

91. PAN Parks, see www.panparks.org/.

92. TNC Ecotourism, see www.nature.org/ecotourism/; correspondence with John Terborgh, ecotourism specialist, The Nature Conservancy, August 2006; correspondence with Andrew Drumm, director, TNC Ecotourism Program, December 2006.

93. Correspondence with Eileen Gutierrez, ecotourism advisor, Conservation International, December 2006. (She subsequently left CI.) For CI's ecotourism program, see www.ecotour.org.

94. This program is part of CI's Center for Environmental Leadership in Business, see www.celb.org/xp/CELB/.

95. CELB's Travel & Leisure program, see www.celb.org/xp/CELB/programs/travel-leisure.

96. "Cruise Industry Campaign Splits Environmental Community," *Environment News Service,* March 16, 2004, see www.ens-newswire.com/ens/mar2004/2004-03-16-03.asp.

97. World Bank, "Greening of the World Bank: Notable Shift Since Rio Signals Billions for the Environment," press release no. 96/S/13, September 1995.

98. A. Hamilton, et al., "Conservation in a Region of Political Instability: Bwindi Impenetrable Forest, Uganda," *Conservation Biology* 14, no. 6 (December 2000): 1722–1725.

99. Sam Keller, International Finance Corporation Projects Officer, "Ecotourism, What does IFC look for?" presented at Ecotourism Symposium, February 2003, in Rosslyn, Virginia, see www.state.gov/g/oes/rls/rm/2003/26092.htm.

100. Shaun Mann, "MIGA: Tourism and the World Bank," Washington D.C., 2006; Correspondence with Christie; Ken Kwaku, Global Program Manager, MIGA, "Challenges and Opportunities for Supporting Ecotourism Projects," speech delivered at International Ecolodge Development Forum and Field Seminar, Maho Bay, St. John Island, October 1994; Various other IFC and MEGA (IFC) documents and interviews officials, 1997 and 2003–2006.

101. Interviews with Maurice Desthuis-Francis, International Finance Corporation, Tourism Unit, IFC, Washington, D.C., April 1996 and Christie, August 2006.

102. Interviews with Kwaku, Desthuis-Francis, and Carolyn Cain, IFC, 2006; literature and various reports from the World Bank, the Global Environment Facility and the International Finance Corporation.

103. Correspondence with Christie.

104. The two-part study was carried out in 2003 by TIES and EplerWood International, see www.ifc.org/ifcext/enviro.nsf/Content/EBFP_Ecolodge.

105. Through its Industry and Environment Program, UNEP "works in cooperation with industry associations, international organizations and NGOs to provide decision-makers in government and industry with information and tools to achieve environmentally sound tourism development and management." United Nations Environment Programme, Tourism Section, "UNEP Industry and Environment: 1996 Achievements," see www.unep.org; various UNEP briefing papers and documents.

106. Correspondence with Stefanos Fotiou, tourism programme officer, UNEP, December 2006. For more information about UNEP's tourism program, see www.uneptie.org/pc/tourism/.

107. Brook Wilkinson, "Condé Nast Traveler Presents the 12th Annual Green List," *Condé Nast Traveler*, September 2006, see www.concierge.com/cntraveler/articles/detail?articleId=10419.

108. Address by former President Nelson Mandela during the opening of the World's Parks Congress, September 8, 2003, copy obtained from the Nelson Mandela Foundation, Houghton, South Africa. See also the WPC Web site at www.iucn.org/themes/wcpa/wpc2003/english/daybyday/m8.htm.

109. Mark Dowie, "The Hidden Cost of Paradise: Indigenous people are being displaced to create wilderness areas, to the detriment of all," *Stanford Social Innovation Review*, Spring 2006, 34.

110. Ibid. Numerous studies have been carried out on how the creation of protected areas has resulted in the evictions of human communities in Africa and worldwide. See, for example, Michael Cernea and Kai Schmidt-Soltau, "Poverty Risks and National Parks: Policy Issues in Conservation and Resettlement," *World Development* 34, no. 10, 2006, 1808–1830; and Charles Geisler, "A new kind of

trouble: evictions in Eden," *International Social Science Journal* 55, Issue 175, March 2003, 69–78.

111. Ian McIntosh, "Ecotourism: A Boon for Indigenous People?" editorial, *Cultural Survival*, Summer 1999.

112. Zebich-Knos, "A Good Neighbor Policy?" 5.

113. The BINGOs include five U.S.-based international conservation organizations—The Nature Conservancy, Conservation International, World Wide Fund for Nature, Wildlife Conservation Society, and African Wildlife Foundation—which collectively capture over 40 percent of all moneys donated to conservation and have a combined annual revenue of over $1 billion. Dowie, "The Hidden Cost of Paradise," 36.

114. Mac Chapin, "A Challenge to Conservationists," *Worldwatch*, Nov/Dec 2004, 30.

115. Cynthia Enloe, *Bananas, Beaches, and Bases: Making Feminist Sense of International Politics* (Berkeley: University of California Press, 1990), 40.

116. Numerous case studies have been done on the CAMPFIRE program. See, for instance, either of the following: www.globaleye.org.uk/archive/summer2k/focuson/mars_pt1.html or www.american.edu/TED/campfire.htm.

117. Wells and Brandon, *People and Parks*, 34.

118. Miguel Hilario, "Going Beyond Window Dressing for the Indigenous Rights of Consultation, Participation, and Engagement," in *CESD, Rights and Responsibilities: A Compilation of Codes of Conduct for Tourism and Indigenous & Local Communities* (Washington, D.C.: CESD, new edition forthcoming 2008), see www.ecotourismcesd.org. Zebich-Knos makes a similar point in noting, "Environmental impact does not fall equally on everyone" and greater concern needs to be given to "what is placed in one's 'backyard,'" Zebich-Knos, "A Good Neighbor Policy?" 5.

119. Médico Internacional, "Project Dossier about Maputaland," Obermainanlage 2, D-60314, Frankfurt am Main, Germany, quoted in Pleumarom, "Political Economy of Tourism," 144–146.

120. CESD, *Rights and Responsibilties.*

121. Dowie, "The Hidden Cost of Paradise," 37.

122. BBC News, "Botswana bushmen win land ruling," December 13, 2006; and "Bitter dispute over bushmen lands," November 24, 2005, see http://news.bbc.co.uk/2/hi/africa.

123. Pleumarom, "Political Economy of Tourism," 143. For a discussion of these issues, see Deborah McLaren, *Rethinking Tourism and Ecotravel: The Paving of Paradise and What You Can Do to Stop It* (West Hartford, CN: Kumarian Press, 1997).

124. Michael Behar, "The Selling of the Last Savage," *Outside*, February 2005, see http://outside.away.com/outside/destinations/200502/fist-contact_1.html; Papua Adventures, see www.papua-adventures.com/.

125. Zebich-Knos, "A Good Neighbor Policy?" 1.

126. Elizabeth Becker, "A Pact on Central America Trade Zone, Minus One," *New York Times*, Dec. 18, 2003, C1; Alternet, "CAFTA Wins in Razor-Close Costa Rica Vote," October 8, 2007, see www.citizenstrade.org/caftanews.php.

127. Stephanie Garrett, "Poppies and Mangoes," *Women & Environments International Magazine*, Toronto, Issue 64/65, Fall 2004/Winter 2005, 23–25.

128. See, for instance, World Wide Fund for Nature, "Preliminary Assessment of

the Environmental & Social Effects of Trade in Tourism," WWF International Discussion Paper, Gland, Switzerland, May 2001, see www.wwf.org.uk/filelibrary/pdf/trade_and_tourism.pdf; Barton H. Thompson, Jr. and Jennifer Coyle, "Trade Issues in Sustainable Tourism," draft, Stanford University, Center on Ecotourism and Sustainable Development, January 2005, see www.ecotourism-cesd.org; "Literature Review: Trade & Environment in North America," 4th North American Symposium on Assessing the Environmental Effects of Trade: Services and the Environment," see www.cec.org/files/pdf/ECONOMY/T-E-Literature Review_en.pdf.

129. David Diaz Benavides, chief, Trade in Services Section, Division of International Trade in Goods and Services, and Commodities, UNCTAD, "International Symposium on Liberalization and Trade in Tourism Services: A Think Tank to Show a Way Forward," Madrid, Spain, March 23–23, 2004, 4, obtained from author. Anita Pleumarom provides a similar analysis, "[M]ost of the profits are made by foreign airlines, tourist operators, and developers who repatriate them to their own economically more advanced countries. With increasing privatization and deregulation of the global economy, there are now great and justifiable concerns that Southern countries will lose out even more. More liberalization will lead to more foreign-owned tourist facilities and tour operations, and as a result, less income from tourism will remain in the local economy." Pleumarom, "Ecotourism: A New 'Green Revolution,'" 10.

130. Interview with Bob Davis, president, The Mountain Institute, Washington, D.C., December 2006.

131. Zebich-Knos, "A Good Neighbor Policy."

132. Kathrin Forstner, "Community Ventures and Access to Markets: The Role of Intermediaries in Marketing Rural Tourism Products," *Development Policy Review* 22, 5 (2004), 497–514. For abstract and to purchase full paper, see http://papers.ssrn.com/sol3/papers.cfm?abstract_id=584044.

133. Mafisa Research and Planning Agency, see www.mafisa.co.za/.

134. Natasha Singer, "The Word's Ten Best Eco-lodges: Posada Amazonas, The Amazon through the eyes of the true people," *Outside Online*, March 2003, see http://outside.away.com/outside/destinations/200303/200303_resort_virtue_1.html; see also Rainforest Expeditions at www.perunature.com/pages/index.htm.

135. United Nations Development Programme, Global Environment Facilities' (GEF) Small Grants Programme (SGP) was launched in 1992 to support activities of nongovernmental and community-based organizations by providing financial and technical support to projects in developing countries that conserve and restore the natural world while enhancing well-being and livelihoods. The SGP demonstrates that community action can maintain the fine balance between human needs and environmental imperatives, see www.undp.org/gef/undp-gef_small_grants_programme/undp-gef_small_grants_programme.html.

136. Cooprena stands for the Consorcio Cooperativo Red Ecoturística Nacional or the National Consortium of Ecotourism Cooperatives.

137. NGO MOST, see www.ngo-most.org/opsirnije_eng.php?id=150&cat=home_page_english.

138. Mesoamerican Ecotourism Alliance (MEA) is a nonprofit composed of local organizations committed to the development and promotion of sustainable

tourism as a means for supporting conservation efforts in Mesoamerica (Southern Mexico, Belize, Guatemala, Honduras, El Salvador, Nicaragua, and Panama). See MesoAmerican Ecotourism Alliance Web site at www.travelwithmea.com/.

139. World Hotel Link, see www.whl.travel/.

140. Brandon, *Ecotourism and Conservation*, 32.

141. Joe Peter, "Sharing National Park Entrance Fees: Forging New Partnerships in Madagascar," *Society & Natural Resources* 1, Issue 5 (July/August 1998): 517–530.

142. Interview with Phil Church, official with Center for Development Information and Evaluation, U.S. Agency for International Development, March 1995.

143. David Diaz Benavides, "The Viability and Sustainability of International Tourism in Developing Countries," presented at the Symposium on Tourism Services, World Trade Organization, Geneva, February 2001.

144. Ibid.

145. Katrina Brandon, *Bellagio Conference on Ecotourism: Briefing Book* (New York: Rockefeller Foundation, 1993), 32.

146. W. G. Meijer, "Rucksacks and Dollars: Organized and Unorganized Tourism in Bolivia," 1989, referenced in Ceballos-Lascuráin, *Tourism,* 11.

147. Ceballos-Lascuráin, *Tourism*, 10–11.

148. For a discussion of carrying capacity, see Robert E. Manning, *Parks and Carrying Capacity: Commons Without Tragedy* (Washington, D.C.: Island Press, 2007).

149. Interview with Craig MacFarland, November 1997. Ceballos-Lascuráin discusses several modifications of the traditional methods for measuring carrying capacity. One, the Limits of Acceptable Change (LAC) technique, focuses on identifying what management strategies are necessary to maintain or restore desired conditions. Another, Visitor Impact Management (VIM), seeks to measure the social impacts of increasing recreational use. Ceballos-Lascuráin, *Tourism*, 133–146.

150. "The LAC process consists of four major components: (1) the specification of acceptable and achievable resource and social conditions, defined by a series of measurable parameters; (2) an analysis of the relationship between existing conditions and those judged acceptable; (3) identification of management actions necessary to achieve these conditions; and (4) a program of monitoring and evaluation of management effectiveness. These four are broken down into nine steps to facilitate application." George Stankey, Lucas Robert, and Frissell Sidney, "Limits of Acceptable Change (LAC) System for Wilderness Planning," United States Department of Agriculture, January 1985, see http://72.14.209.104/search?q=cache:EgqF3ugB-7YJ:www.fs.fed.us/r8/boone/documents/lac/lacsummary.pdf+roots+of+Limits+of+Acceptable+Change+theories+of+Protected+area+managment&hl=en&gl=us&ct=clnk&cd=1.

151. John Shores, online conference on Tourism and Biodiversity, session title "Limits of Acceptable Change," November 17, 2004, see www.edinburgh.ceh.ac.uk/biota/Archive_researchmatters/6337.htm.

152. Alexandra Mexa and Harry Coccossis, *Challenge of Tourism Carrying Capacity Assessment: Theory and Practice* (Burlington, VT: Ashgate Publishing, Ltd., 2004), 44.

153. Ceballos-Lascuráin, *Tourism*, 9. He writes, "This may not have secured

much income for the government, but doubtless considerable national interest in and support for protected areas were created."

154. Ministry of the Environment Government of Japan, *Launch of Ecotourism in Ramsar Sites*, May 2006, see www.env.go.jp/en/headline/headline.php?serial=83. Ramsar sites are wetlands of international importance, designated under the Ramsar Convention. The Convention on Wetlands, signed in Ramsar, Iran, in 1971, is an intergovernmental treaty that provides the framework for national action and international cooperation for the conservation and wise use of wetlands and their resources. For more information see www.ramsar.org/. As of 2005, Japan had designated 33 Ramsar Sites that were protected under the national law for nature and conservation and wildlife protection, see www.ramsar.org/wn/w.n.japan_20sites.htm.

155. AFP, "9/11 costs US billion in tourism revenue," *The Sydney Morning Herald*, January 24, 2007.

156. Suchat Sritama, "Post-Tsunami Tourism: Phuket Struggles to Reverse Slump," *The Nation*, June 27, 2005, see www.thaiWebsites.com/tourism.asp.

157. Ceballos-Lascuráin, *Tourism*, 9.

158. Lisa Mastny, *Treading Lightly: New Paths for International Tourism*, Worldwatch Paper 159 (Washington, D.C.: Worldwatch Institute, December 2001), 15.

159. An early study done in Britain uses this term: Richard Denman and Peter Ashcroft, *Visitor Payback: Encouraging Visitors to Give Money Voluntarily to Conserve the Places They Visit*, The Tourism Company, U.K., 1997, see www.ecotourismcesd.org/webarticles/articlefiles/visitorpayback.pdf.

160. The Intrepid Foundation, see www.intrepidtravel.com/about/foundation/.

161. Micato Safaris has won "Best Tour Operator 2004", *Travel Agent*, "Best African Safari Company," *Porthole*, and the prestigious "World's Best Tour Operator/Safari Outfitter" award from *Travel + Leisure* from 1995–2006. Micato Safaris, see www.micato.com/.

162. America Share, see www.americashare.org/.

163. "Lend a Helping Hand on Safari" brochure, see www.micato.com/2006brochurepdfs/LendaHelpingHand.pdf.

164. Travel Industry of Association of America (TIA) and National Geographic Traveler (NGT). "Geotourism: The New Trend in Travel," press release, October 8, 2003. This refers to the second portion of a two-part survey.

165. See Abernethy's paper and other 2004 conference proceedings as well as other details on the 2008 conference at the Travelers' Philanthropy Web site, www.travelersphilanthropy.org.

166. Sustainable Travel International, see www.sustainabletravelinternational.org/documents/op_tp_voluntourism.html.

167. VolunTourism, see www.voluntourism.org/.

168. Gary Gereffi, Ronie Garcia-Johnson, and Erika Sasser, "The NGO-Industrial Complex," *Foreign Affairs*, July–August 2001, 64–65.

169. Michael E. Conroy, *Branded! How the 'Certification Revolution' is Transforming Global Corporations* (Gabriola Island, BC: New Society Publishers, 2007), 287.

170. "Quebec Declaration on Ecotourism," Quebec City, Canada, May 22, 2002, see www.world-tourism.org/sustainable/IYE/quebec/anglais/declaration.html.

171. Rainforest Alliance, *Sustainable Tourism Stewardship Council: Raising the*

Standards and Benefits for Sustainable Tourism and Ecotourism Certification, final report to the Ford Foundation, December 2002, version 8.4., see www.rainforest-alliance.org/tourism.cfm?id=council.

172. "Mohonk Agreement" and "Minutes of Mohonk Meeting," and report based on the meeting, see www.ecotourismcesd.org. This conference, organized by the author and Abigail Rome, was the first effort to bring together tourism certification programs from around the world.

173. Rainforest Alliance, see Sustainable Tourism Stewardship Council documents at www.rainforest-alliance.org/. Author's correspondence regarding the STSC with Ronald Sanabria and Michael Conroy, February 2008.

174. Quoted in "Tourism, Environment, and Culture," *Wajibu* 10, no. 1, 1995, 7.

175. UNWTO *Tourism Highlights,* 2004 ed.

Chapter 4: The Galapagos Islands

1. In 1535, the archipelago's first recorded visitor, the bishop of Panama, Tomás de Berlanga, landed here and dubbed the hunks of lava rock the Enchanted Isles. The name stuck for nearly half a millennium before being replaced with Galapagos, Spanish for "giant tortoise." Edward J. Larson, *Evolutions Workshop, God and Science on the Galapagos Islands* (New York: Basic Books, 2002), 23; Herman Melville, *The Encantadas* (New York: G. P. Putnam & Co. ,1854), 143.

2. David Pearson and David Middleton, *The New Key to Ecuador and the Galapagos* (Berkeley, CA: Ulysses Press, 1996), 9.

3. Bruce Epler, *An Economic and Social Analysis of Tourism in the Galapagos Islands* (Providence: University of Rhode Island, Coastal Resource Center, 1993), preface.

4. Bi-institutional video CDF/GNPS, 2003.

5. Robert Bensted-Smith, et al., *The Strategy for Conservation of Terrestrial Biodiversity in Galapagos,* (Puerto Ayora, Galapagos: Charles Darwin Research Station, 1999–2000).

6. Charles Darwin, *The Voyage of the Beagle* (New York: Penguin Books, 1988), 340–343.

7. Kurt Vonnegut, *Galapagos* (New York: Delacorte Press, Seymour Lawrence, 1985), 16.

8. José Enrique Machuca Mestanza, *Cronología Histórica de Galápagos 1535–2000* (Guayaquil: privately printed, 2006), 87.

9. Larson, *Evolutions Workshop,* 185.

10. Consuelo Albornoz Tinajero, "Galapagos Threatened by Invasion," Inter-Press Service, June 13, 1995.

11. E. Danulat and G. J. Edgar, eds., "Reserva Marina de Galápagos, Linea Base de la Biodiversidad," Charles Darwin Foundation and Galapagos National Park Service, Galapagos, Ecuador, 2002, 10, see www.darwinfoundation.org/down loads/RMG-Linea-Base-Bio.pdf.

12. UNESCO, "World Heritage in Danger List," see http://whc.unesco.org/en/danger/.

13. During World War II, the United States constructed a military base at Baltra and stationed several thousand people there. Godfrey Merlen, "Use and Mis-

use of the Seas around the Galapagos Archipelago," April 1995, unpublished paper obtained from author.

14. Silvia P. Benitez, "Visitor Use Fees and Concession Systems in Protected Areas, Galapagos National Park Case Study," Ecotourism Program Technical Report Series Number 3, April 2001, cited in D. Southgate and M. Whitaker, *Development and the Environment: Ecuador's Policy Crisis* (Quito, Ecuador: Instituto de Estrategias Agropecuarias, 1992).

15. Epler, *Tourism in the Galapagos Islands*, 1.

16. Jennifer Conlin, "Can Darwin's Lab Survive Success," *New York Times*, travel section, January 27, 2008, 6.

17. Correspondence with Scott Henderson, regional marine coordinator for the Andes and Eastern Tropical Pacific, Conservation International, August 2005.

18. Epler, *Tourism in the Galapagos Islands*, 4–5.

19. Emma Stewart, "SmartVoyager: Environmental and Social Certification Program for Tour Boat Operators in the Galapagos," Stanford University, Graduate School of Business case study, August 28, 2002, see www.rainforest-alliance.org/tourism/documents/smartvoyager.pdf.

20. Bruce Epler and Maria Eugenia Proano, "Cuantas plazas y cuantos cupos hay en Galapagos?", in GNPS, Charles Darwin Foundation, and INGALA, *Informe Galapagos 2006–2007*, Puerto Ayora, 2007, 36–41, copy obtained by author; Galapagos National Park Service, "Unidad de Uso Público," 2005 spreadsheet.

21. Barry Boyce, *A Traveler's Guide to the Galapagos Islands*, 2nd ed. (San Juan Bautista, CA: Galapagos Travel, 1994), 78.

22. IGTOA, see "About Us" at www.igtoa.org.

23. "Tanker Spills 185,000 Gallons in Fragile Galápagos," *American Maritime Officer*, see www.amo-union.org/newspaper/Morgue/2-2001/Sections/News/Galapagos.htm.

24. Ibid.; *Galapagos Report 2000–2001*, (Quito, Ecuador, Fundación Natura and WWF, 2001), 9–15; CNN.com, "Tanker spills remaining fuel near Galapagos as captain detained," January 24, 2001, see http://archives.cnn.com/2001/NATURE/01/24/galapagos.spill.02/index.html.

25. At the time of the spill, the *Explorer II* did have permission to be using bunker oil. However, by October 2001, the vessel had changed its propulsion system to be able to use diesel fuel. Correspondence with Mauricio Ferro, Conservación y Desarrollo, Quito, Ecuador, October 2006.

26. Kapawi Ecolodge was started in 1993 as a $2 million copartnership experiment between the Achuar, an indigenous group in Ecuador's remote Amazon region, and Canodros, a private ecotourism company. "Kapawi: The Outer Limits of Soft Adventure," see www.romartraveler.com/RomarPages/Kapawi.html; "Kapawi: The Story of an Ecuadorian Ecolodge," see www.planeta.com/planeta/00/0006 eckapawi.html; and Kapawi's Web site, see www.kapawi.com/html/en/home/aboutus.htm.

27. "Galápagos *Explorer II* Canodros," see www.traveltrade.com/academy_detail.jsp?academyMaster ID=7590&articleID=7594.

28. Smart Voyager criteria does state: "Gas used in the boat must be lead-free. The type of gas to be used must be above 85 octane, that which is known in Ecuador as 'super' gas; if diesel is used it must be filtered," see http://rainforest-alliance.org/programs/tourism/smartvoyager/standards.pdf.

29. CNN.com, "Tanker spills," various stories, January 18–24, 2001. The Spe-

cial Law for Galapagos, Chapter 5, paragraph 1, art. 16, "Area Marina De Protección Especial," 1998, a zone of protection of 60 nautical miles in order to regulate the transport of toxic or dangerous products.

30. "Galapagos National Park enhances 'top ten' competitiveness with ISO 9001:2000," *ISO Management Systems*, July–August 2004.

31. Special Law for Galapagos, Title 10 of the General and Transitory Dispositions, Chapter 1, General Disposition, 1998, 12.

32. Epler and Proano, "Cuantas plazas," 39.

33. Airfares on the Ecuadorian government airline TAME (Transporte Aereo Militar Ecuatoriano) are scaled. In 2005, they were as follows: for permanent and temporary Galapagos residents, $113 round trip from Quito and $93 from Guayaquil; for Ecuadorian nationals, $220 from Quito and $180 from Guayaquil; and for international visitors, $390 from Quito and $345 from Guayaquil. See TAME Web site at www.tame.com.ec/tame/english/tarifas/default.asp.

34. Epler and Proano, "Cuantas plazas," 37; E-mail correspondence with Bruce Epler, December 1997.

35. An example of this is the Royal Palm Hotel, which offers weekend packages and day excursions to numerous sites around the Galapagos Islands. See www .royalpalmgalapagos.com/tour_en.htm.

36. J. Willen and M. Stewart, "Economic Analysis of the Galapagos Marine Reserve Resources Management Plan," March 2000, cited in *Galapagos Report 2000–2001*, 65.

37. Epler, *Tourism in the Galapagos Islands,* 8.

38. CAPTURGAL see www.galapagostour.org/. All hotels must be registered with CAPTURGAL in order to be legal.

39. Correspondence with Bruce Epler, October 2006.

40. *Galapagos Report 2000–2001,* 65–70; Epler and Proano, "Cuantas plazas," 37.

41. Epler, *Tourism in the Galapagos Islands,* 18.

42. Robert Bensted-Smith, ed., *A Biodiversity Vision for the Galapagos Islands.* (Puerto Ayora, Galapagos: Charles Darwin Foundation and WWF, 2002), 6–7.

43. Interviews with David Blanton, executive director, IGTOA, 2005–2006.

44. "Balanza de pagos del Ecuador," table, Central Bank, 2001, Galapagos Report 2001–2002, 87; J. Edward Taylor, Jared Hardner, Micki Stewart, "The Economics of Ecotourism: A Galapagos Islands Economy-wide Perspective," *Economic Development and Cultural Change,* Department of Agricultural and Resource Economics, University of California, Davis, Working Paper No. 06-001, August 2006, Table 6, 25, see http:/repositories.cdlib.org/are/arcrop/06-001.

45. Epler, *Tourism in the Galapagos Islands,* pp. 12–17.

46. Correspondence, Henderson.

47. William H. Durham, "Fishing for Solutions: Ecotourism and Conservation in Galapagos," draft chapter 5 in Amanda Stronzo and William Durham, eds., *Putting Ecotourism to Work in the Americas,* (Wallingford, UK: CABI publishing, forthcoming 2008).

48. Michael Lemonick, "Can the Galapagos Survive?" *Time,* October 30, 1995.

49. Craig MacFarland, *Case Study: Biodiversity Conservation and Human Population Impacts in the Galapagos Islands, Ecuador* (Falls Church, VA: Charles Darwin Foundation, 1995), 22.

50. Charles Darwin Foundation, *Galapagos Bulletin*, special issue, fall 1995.

51. Martha Honey, "Galapagos under Threat," *Living on Earth*, July 22, 2004, see transcript of this radio documentary at www.loe.org/shows/shows.htm?programID=94-P13-00029#feature1.

52. L. Cayot and Ed Lewis, "Recent Increase in Killings of Giant Tortoises on Isabela Island," *Noticias de Galapagos*, Charles Darwin Foundation, vol. 54, November 1994, 6.

53. Ibid.

54. C. Marquez, G. Gordillo, and A. Tupiza, "The Fire of 1994 and Herpetofauna of Southern Isabela," *Noticias de Galapagos*, Charles Darwin Foundation, vol. 54, November 1994, 8.

55. Ibid.; Interviews and correspondence with Johannah Barry, executive director, Galapagos Conservancy (previously Charles Darwin Foundation), 1994–2005; Linda Cayot, "Recent Increase in Killings of Giant Tortoises on Isabela Island, Galapagos Archipelago" (Puerto Ayora: Charles Darwin Research Station, n.d.).

56. Lemonick, "Can the Galapagos Survive?" 82.

57. "Galapagos Crisis," *News from Conservation Network International*, January 31, 1995, see www.bio.net/bionet/mm/plantbio/1995-February/005195.html.

58. Johannah Barry, "Memorandum: Seizure of Galapagos National Park and Charles Darwin Research Station, Charles Darwin Foundation, Inc., September 5, 1995, see http://mailman.nhm.ku.edu/pipermail/taxacom/1995-September/016980.html.

59. Correspondence with Andrew Drumm, Ecotourism Program, The Nature Conservancy, December 2006.

60. Charles Darwin Foundation, *Noticias de Galapagos*, no. 58, May 1997, 2–3.

61. Mario González, "Stoppage in Galapagos Urges Passage of Law," InterPress Service, November 20, 1997.

62. Ibid.; Galapagos National Park, "The Future of the Galapagos Marine Reserve," memo obtained from the Charles Darwin Foundation, November 7, 1997.

63. Mario González, "New Galapagos Protection Law in Force," InterPress Service, March 9, 1998.

64. *Galapagos Report 2000–2001*, 21.

65. Robert Bensted-Smith, "The Special Law for Galapagos," Charles Darwin Foundation, n.d., see www.darwinfoundation.org/en/library/pubs/gal-research/n5900049816.

66. Johannah Barry, "The Special Law for Galapagos: Comments by the Charles Darwin Foundation," Charles Darwin Foundation, document received via e-mail, March 24, 1998.

67. *Resumen Ejecutivo* Repartición del Tributo desde Mayo 1998–Mayo 2005"; Galapagos National Park Service, *Gestión Financiera*, May 2005.

68. Durham, "Fishing for Solutions."

69. Ibid.; Barry, "Special Law for Galapagos"; González, "New Galapagos Protection Law."

70. Barry, "Special Law for Galapagos."

71. *Galapagos Report 2001–2002*, 87.

72. *Resumen Ejecutivo Repartición del Tributo.*

73. Interview with Ivonne Torres, director, Dirección de Turismo Municipal, Gobierno Municipal de Santa Cruz, Galapagos, August 2005.

74. Craig MacFarland, "An Analysis of Nature Tourism in the Galapagos Islands," 2000, see www.darwinfoundation.org/en/library/pubs/journals/brl5049801.

75. Interview, MacFarland.

76. Diego Andrade Ubidia, "The Legal Framework of Ecotourism in Ecuador," www.planeta.com/planeta/02/0203ecuadorb.html. Andrade was the executive director of the Ecuadorian Ecotourism Association.

77. Correspondence with Aldo F. Salvador-Hidalgo, executive director, ASOGAL, September 2005.

78. Interview with Rocio Malo, president, Asociación de Armadores Turísticos (ADATUR), August 2005.

79. IGTOA see www.igtoa.org/about_us/.

80. CAPTURGAL, Galapagos Chamber of Tourism, Galapagostour.org Web site, see www.galapagostour.org.

81. "Documento del Banco Interamericano de Desarrollo Fondo Multilateral de Inversiones, Proyecto Desarrollo Sostenible de Los Sectores Productivos de Galapagos (EC-M1010)", Donors' memorandum, 2005.

82. Martha Honey and Emma Stewart, "The Evolution of 'Green' Standards for Tourism," in Martha Honey, ed., *Ecotourism and Certification: Setting Standards in Practice* (Washington, D.C.: Island Press, 2002), 53–58.

83. Conservacion y Desarrollo, "SmartVoyager Galapagos," see www.ccd.org.ec/pages/smart_voyager_galapagos_en.htm; Rainforest Alliance, "Sustainable Tourism: SmartVoyager Program," see www.rainforest-alliance.org/programs/tourism/smartvoyager/; Stewart, "SmartVoyager."

84. Santiago Dunn, EcoVentura owner, see Profiles in Sustainable Development Partnerships at www.rainforestalliance.com.

85. Correspondence with Hugo Andrade Serrano, owner of *Angelito* tourism boat, Puerto Ayora, Galapagos, August 25, 2002, cited in Stewart, "'SmartVoyager' Environmental and Social Certification Program."

86. Interview with Rocio Malo, owner of Daphne Cruises, Puerto Ayora, Galapagos, September 2005.

87. "Smart Voyager," Conservación y Desarrollo Web site, see www.ccd.org.ec/pages/turismo_en.htm.

88. Interviews, Blanton; IGTOA Web site, see www.igtoa.org/.

89. Various interviews with Sven Lindblad and Mary Jo Viederman, Lindblad Expeditions, 2003–2007; "The Galapagos Conservation Fund" Web site, see www.solutions-site.org/cat1_sol116.htm; "Can tourism save the planet," Lindblad Expeditions press release, New York, September 12, 2005.

90. The GNPS regularly checks sites for signs of impact and closes them if necessary. Animals that nest directly on the paths are the only ones that would likely to be affected if the tourists are following park rules. For more information on park monitoring, see the GNPS Web site www.galapagospark.org.

91. Various interviews, 1994–2007; Bruce Epler found that 99 percent of tourists surveyed were "very satisfied or satisfied with the nature they observed in the islands." *Tourism in the Galapagos Islands*, 24.

92. I. R. Grimwood and D. W. Snow, "Recommendations on the Administra-

tion of the Proposed Galapagos National Park and the Development of Its Tourist Potential," June 1966, 1, in Edward Larson, "Evolution's Workshop," 226, footnote 16; Vertical file 333–783, "Parque Nacional," Charles Darwin Research Station library, Puerto Ayora , Galapagos Islands.

93. At this time, the GNPS and Charles Darwin Research Center began to train guides.

94. MacFarland, "An Analysis of Nature Tourism."

95. *Galapagos Report 2000–2001,* 74; Indira Medina, "Elaboración de un sistema de monitoreo de impactos por visitación para los sitios de visita terrestre del PNG," master's thesis, 2000.

96. Interview, MacFarland.

97. "El Cuido de los Ecosistemas," *Galapagos Report 1996–1997,* Chapter 2, 19–32; interviews, David Balfour, Metropolitan Tourism and Marta Lucia Burneo, Permanent Galapagos Commission, 1996.

98. "Enter the Cruise Industry," IGTOA Newsletter, October 2005, see www.igtoa.org/newsletter/2005/october/. RETANP (Regulación Especial para Turismo en Areas Naturales Protegidas—Special Regulation for Tourism in Natural Protected Areas) created a special regulation to allow for twelve 500-passenger cruise ships to visit San Cristobal Island each year.

99. Voyages of Discovery, see www.voyagesofdiscovery.com.

100. Legislación Ambiental, Galapagos Tomo VI, Libro VII, titulo II Capítulo VI, 2003, 180.

101. Telephone interview with Mark Flager, October 3, 2006.

102. "Galapagos Face Destruction By Tourism," *UK News,* October 12, 2006, see www.lse.co.uk/ShowStory.asp?story=QO1230000I&news_headline=galapa.

103. Ibid; Conlin, "Can Darwin's Lab Survive Success?".

104. ROW International, see www.rowinternational.com/galapagos_kayak.htm.

105. Telephone interview with Laurie Deans, ROW International, September 29, 2006.

106. Julian Smith, "Galapagos Now," *Washington Post,* April 2, 2006.

107. Correspondence with ROW International and CDRS, February 2008.

108. Reforms to the Ecuadorian Tourism Law, Executive Decree 244, Registro Oficial No. 304, March 2004.

109. Interviews, Blanton.

110. Boyce, *Traveler's Guide,* 122; inteviews with tour operator Georgina Martin de Cruz, guides, and tourists, 1996, 2004.

111. Interviews, Blanton.

112. Interview with Ivonne Torres, Galapagos naturalist guide, Puerto Ayora, August 2005.

113. Galapagos National Park Service, standard letter to tour operators for license renewal, 2004.

114. Personal conversation with Galapagos National Park Service Public Use Department staff, 2005.

115. "Entrevista Alberto Granja," *La Garua* 9, May 2005.

116. Interview with Alberto Granja, who runs the RELUGAL program, October 2006.

117. Jack Grove, *Fishes of the Galapagos* (Stanford, CA: Stanford University

Press, 1997); Telephone interviews with Jack Grove, November 1997 and October 2006.

118. "Artisanal fishing as a cultural experience, a novel alternative," Charles Darwin Foundation press release, August 2005.

119. Durham, "Fishing for Solutions."

120. George Wallace, *Visitor Management in Galapagos National Park*, draft, (Ft. Collins, CO: College of Natural Resources, Colorado State University, January 1992), 4.

121. "Galapagos invasive species: The 'Invasive Species in Galapagos' Project," Project ECU/00/G31, Galapagos Invasive Species, 2001–2007, see www.hear.org/galapagos/invasives/features/gef.htm.

122. "Isabela Achieves the Impossible," Charles Darwin Foundation press release, July 5, 2006, see www.darwinfoundation.org/en/newsroom/news-releases/2006-07-05_isabela_achieves.

123. Various Charles Darwin Foundation publications; Richard Harris, "Galapagos Islands at the Crossroads," *All Things Considered*, National Public Radio, December 18, 1995.

124. Craig MacFarland, a biologist who was president of the Charles Darwin Foundation for more than a decade, pointed out in an interview, the source of the trouble isn't tourism itself but the economic boom: "If the economic boom were goldmining or petroleum or fishing we might have had the same thing as tourism has brought. So it really isn't a function of tourism, per se. It's just because tourism has become the boom."

125. *Galapagos Report 2000–2001*, 24.

126. *Las Regulaciones Migratorias de Galapagos: Manual de información para el residente insular* (Quito, Ecuador: Fundación Natura/Ingala, July 2002), 56.

127. Pablo Ospina and Fernando Carrasco, "The Economy of the Family in Galapagos: Poverty levels in Galapagos," *Galapagos Report 2000–2001*, 34.

128. Durham, "Fishing for Solutions." Some observers put the size at 30,000. For official population estimates for Ecuadorian provinces, see www.supertel.gov.ec/telecomunicaciones/poblacion.htm.

129. An indication of the magnitude of the problem is the number of deportations. During 2000, for instance, close to 100 people per month were ordered to leave the islands for overstaying their visas.

130. *Galapagos Report 2000–2001*, 21.

131. *Galapagos Report 2001–2002*, table 1, 10.

132. Interview, Lyjia Ayove, 1994.

133. *Las Regulaciones Migratorias*, 9.

134. Interview, Martin de Cruz.

135. Graham Watkins and Felipe Cruz, *Galapagos at Risk: A Socioeconomic Analysis of the Situation in the Archipelago* (Puerto Ayora: Charles Darwin Foundation, 2007), 2, see www.darwinfoundation.org/files/library/pdf/2007/Galapagos_at_Risk_7-4-07-EN.pdf.

136. "Sustainable Fisheries: A Goal for all Users of the Galapagos Marine Reserve," Charles Darwin Foundation press release, June 5, 2005, Galapagos Conservation Trust, see www.gct.org/jun05_1.html.

137. IUCN, "Galapagos Islands added to the World Heritage Danger List," press

release, June 28, 2007, see www.iucn.org/en/news/archive/2007/06/28_pr_galapagos.htm.

138. "UNESCO adds Galapagos to World Heritage Site in Danger List," News detail, Ecoventura—Tours and Cruises to Galapagos, see www.ecoventura.com/news_detail.aspx?a=126.

139. Durham, "Fishing for Solutions."

140. Taylor et al., "The Economics of Ecotourism," 1, 3, 14–15.

141. Bensted-Smith, *Biodiversity Vision for the Galapagos Islands,* 7.

142. IGTOA Web site, see www.igtoa.org/info_for_travelers/issues_facing_galapagos.php.

143. Charles Darwin Foundation (CDF) Newsletter, November, 2005, see http://darwinfoundation.org/newsletter/english/archives/november05-full.htm.

144. Jonathan B. Tourtellot, "Destination Scorecard," *National Geographic Traveler* 21, Issue 2, March 2004, 64; Personal correspondence with Jonathan Tourtellot, *National Geographic Traveler* Geotourism editor, September–October 2006.

145. Correspondence, Tourtellot.

146. Quoted in William Stolzenburg, "Collision at the Galapagos," *Nature Conservancy,* November/December 1996, 16.

147. Inter-American Development Bank press release, September 23, 2005, see www.iadb.org/news/articledetail.cfm?font=1&artid=887&language=English.

148. Marc Miller and Donald Kennedy, "Saving the Galapagos," *New York Times,* op. ed., October 12, 1995, A23.

149. Wallace, "Visitor Management," 16–17.

Chapter 5: Costa Rica

1. Martha Honey, *Hostile Acts: U.S. Policy in Costa Rica in the 1980s* (Gainesville: University Press of Florida, 1994).

2. "What's Wrong with Mass Ecotourism?" *Contours* Bangkok 6, nos. 3–4, November 1993, 16; Costa Rica Tourism Board (ICT) statistics cited in Polly Jo Morrison, "The Monteverde Area of Costa Rica: A Case Study of Ecotourism Development," master's thesis, University of Texas, Austin, 1994, 31.

3. Gustavo Segura, "Comentarios acerca de la Campaña de Promoción Turística de Costa Rica en los Estados Unidos, 1996–1997," INCAE publication CEN 652, October 1998, see www.incae.ac.cr/EN/clacds/nuestras-investigaciones/pdf/cen652.pdf.

4. Author spoke at the symposium to launch the Peace with Nature Initiative, San José, Costa Rica, July 5, 2007; David Sherwood, "Ceremony Inaugurates Peace with Nature Initiative," *Tico Times Online,* July 9, 2007, see www.ticotimes.net/dailyarchive/2007_07/070907.htm; Revolution Places, "Revolution Launches New Luxury Resort Development Company," press release, August 3, 2007, see www.prnewswire.com/cgi-bin/stories.pl?ACCT=104&STORY=/www/story/08-03-2007/0004639030&EDATE=.

5. Instituto Costarricense de Turismo (ICT), "Airport exit surveys, high season," 2005.

6. ICT, "Anuario estadístico," 2005.

7. Costa Rica set up its first tourism board in 1931, and in 1955 it became the Costa Rican Tourism Board (ICT), which continues to the present. Somerset R. Waters, *Travel Industry World Yearbook: The Big Picture—1996–97*, vol. 40 (New York: Child & Waters, 1997), 89.

8. Honey, *Hostile Acts*, 51–196.

9. Carole Hill, "The Paradox of Tourism in Costa Rica," *Cultural Survival Quarterly* 14, no. 1 (1990): 17.

10. Somerset R. Waters, *Travel Industry World Yearbook*, 89 and "Anuario estadístico", 2005, Instituto Costarricense de Turismo (ICT).

11. The 1985 Law 6990 for Tourism Incentives was modified in 1992 by Law 7293 and in 2001 by Law 8114. The original tax holiday on income and real estate taxes for 12 years, as well as on import duties and other taxes on all capital purchases, was eliminated. Also eliminated was an income tax deduction for 50 percent of the value of investment in new tourist projects.

12. In the late 1990s, INTEL opened a plant in Costa Rica that became, for a few years, the largest source of foreign exchange. "Anuario estadístico," 2005, Instituto Costarricense de Turismo (ICT).

13. Honey, *Hostile Acts*, 179–180; Hill, "Paradox of Tourism in Costa Rica," 17.

14. Dave Sherwood, "Park Debate Rages as Turtles Vanish," *Tico Times*, San José, April 15, 2007, see www.tortugamarina.org/index2.php?option=com_content&do_pdf=1&id=200. For a full account of the "green luxury" development scam and the early struggles on Playa Grande, see the first edition of this book, 165–169.

15. Revolution Places, "Revolution Launches New Luxury Resort Development Company," San José, Costa Rica, August 3, 2007, see www.prnewswire.com/cgi-bin/stories.pl?ACCT=109&STORY=/www/story/08-03-2007/0004639030&EDATE=.; Kendra Marr, "Steve Case's Eco-Getaway," *Washington Post*, August 3, 2007, see www.washingtonpost.com/wp-dyn/content/article/2007/08/02/AR2007080202316.html.

16. Anne Becher, correspondence with author, including Becher's notes on hotel ownership on selected Pacific Coast beaches, which she used in compiling the Sustainable Tourism Rating Survey for *The New Key to Costa Rica*, 1995–1996.

17. Beatrice Blake, correspondence with author, 2002–2007.

18. "Sector creció 59% en últimos 12 meses," *La Nación*, March 22, 2007.

19. The 18th edition of *The New Key to Costa Rica*, the country's oldest guidebook, lists some 600 accommodations, most of which fall under the ecotourism umbrella, and editor Beatrice Blake estimates that this is only half the true number of eco-lodges. Beatrice Blake, personal correspondence with author, August 2007.

20. Eduardo Villafranca, interview with author during tour of hotel and community projects, September 2006.

21. Ibid.

22. "Hotel Punta Islita: Responsible Tourism," PowerPoint obtained from Eduardo Villafranca.

23. Villafranca interview.

24. The story is actually a bit more complicated. Columbus did indeed claim that this area was rich in gold, as he said that he obtained a large quantity of it when he landed in Cariay (Limón) in 1502. He named the territory Veragua, com-

prising land from Panama to Honduras. The name "Costa Rica," however, came about because of a lawsuit by the Columbus family claiming all of Veragua, as well as conflicting territorial claims by Spaniards in both Panama and Nicaragua. Spain quickly renamed most of the territory in 1539, calling one portion "Costarica," and left a small district of Panama with the original name. This was awarded to the Columbus family as a dukedom, and it remains one of the least developed areas of Panama. See Carlos Meléndez Chavarría, *Conquistadores y pobladores: orígenes histórico-sociales de los costarricenses* (San José, Costa Rica: EUNED press, 1982), 16–27.

25. Katrina Brandon and Alvaro Umaña, "Rooting for Costa Rica's Megaparks," *Américas*, August 1991.

26. Sistema Nacional de Areas Protegidas, Número y tamaño de ASPs terrestres y marinas, legalmente declaradas, see www.sinaccr.net/planificacionasp.php.

27. Gerencia de Áreas Silvestres, Protegidas del SINAC, 2006.

28. Inter-American Development Bank, "IDB Approved $20 Million Loan to Costa Rica for Sustainable Tourism in Protected Wilderness Areas," December 18, 2006, see www.iadb.org/news/articledetail.cfm?language=English&ARTID=3541&FONT=1.

29. ProParques, see www.proparques.org/boletines.

30. Corcovado Osa, see www.osacampaign.org.

31. "Costa Rica's Megaparks," 29; "Unique Debt Swap to Protect Forest," *The Canopy*, published by the Rainforest Alliance, Spring 1991, 1–2.

32. See Lisa Chase et al., "Economic demand and differential pricing of national park access in Costa Rica," *Land Economics* 74, 4, 466, for a detailed economic study of the Costa Rican example and the elasticity of park entrance fees in tourist markets.

33. The pricing preference for local residents is used for state universities in the United States, access to municipal beaches in New York and New Jersey, entrance to Colonial Williamsburg, the entertainment parks in Orlando, Florida, and so on.

34. MINAE Decreto Ejecutivo No. 30355.

35. Pro Parques, see www.proparques.org/index2.html.

36. A 2003 study of the net change in forest cover for 15 ecological corridors found much greater deforestation rates from 1979 to 1986 than for 1986 to 1997. G. Sanchez-Azofeifa, et al., "Integrity and Isolation of Costa Rica's National Parks and Biological Reserves: Examining the Dynamics of Land-Cover Change," *Biological Conservation* 109, 123–135.

37. Angelica Almeyda Zambrano, Eben Broadbent, and William Durham, "Social and Environmental Effects of Ecotourism on the Osa Peninsula of Costa Rica: The Lapa Rios Case," Center on Ecotourism and Sustainable Development, June 2007, 15.

38. David Rains Wallace, *The Quetzal and the Macaw: The Story of Costa Rica's National Parks* (San Francisco: Sierra Club Books, 1992), 128.

39. Ibid., 134–136.

40. Eduardo Alvarado, "Gobierno plantea pago a nuevo grupo de exoreros," *La Nación*, September 18, 2005, see www.nacion.com/ln_ee/2005/enero/05/pais4.html.

41. Corcovado Foundation, see http://fundacioncorcovado.org/threatwearefacing.html.

42. Vanessa Loaiza, "Aeropuerto de zona sur se construirá en valle de Sierpe," *La Nación*, April 15, 2006, see www.nacion.com/ln_ee/2006/abril/15/pais2.html.

43. Japan International Cooperation Agency (JICA) and Instituto Costarricense De Turismo (ICT), "Estudio Para el Plan de Uso de la Tierra en las Zonas Costeras de las Unidades de Planeamiento Turístico en la Republica de Costa Rica, Reporte Final," 2001.

44. ICT, "Plan General de Desarrollo Turístico Sostenible 2002–2012," 2002, Anexo 1, 93.

45. Lapa Rios, see www.laparios.com.

46. The November 2, 2005 ceremony, attended by the author and a handful of others invited by Lewis Karen, was held simultaneously in the State Department's ornate, top-floor Benjamin Franklin Room and at the U.S. Embassy in Costa Rica. Secretary Condoleezza Rice, U.S. Department of State, "2005 Award for Corporate Excellence Ceremony," see www.state.gov/secretary/rm/2005/55964.htm.

47. Lapa Rios, "The Carbonera School and Community," see www.laparios.com/lapscho.htm.

48. Almeyda, Broadbent, and Durham, "The Lapa Rios Case," 22, 23.

49. Ibid., 22. This study found that slightly more than 24 percent of Lapa Rios's expenditures, not counting salaries, were being made locally. Given the region's lack of development, many supplies for the hotel must be imported from San José or from overseas.

50. The two partners, Hans Pfister and Andrea Bonilla, are both Cornell University Hotel School graduates (hence the name), and Bonilla worked as the manager of Lapa Rios for five years.

51. This section is based upon the author's several visits to Lapa Rios and numerous interviews with Karen Lewis, as well as in-depth interviews with John Lewis and Andrea Bonilla and correspondence with Hans Pfister, 2000–2007.

52. Blake and Becher, *New Key to Costa Rica*, 202–203; Susan Place "Nature Tourism and Rural Development in Tortuguero," *Annals of Tourism Research*, 18, no. 2, 1991, 186–201.

53. Caribbean Conservation Corporation (CCC), see www.cccturtle.org.

54. Eliot Wajskol, "Abstract: Ecotourism-Based Entrepreneurship and Wealth in Tortuguero, Costa Rica: Patterns in a Noncohesive Community with Ill-Defined Land Rights," proposal for master's thesis, Duke University, 1994.

55. In the mid- to late 1990s, Anne Becher, Susan Place, and Beatrice Blake all conducted ownership surveys. As of 1995, of Tortuguero's seventeen hotels and lodges, six of the eight very modest ones in town were mostly locally owned; the two less expensive package-tour lodges were owned by nonresident Costa Ricans from the Central Valley; and seven higher-priced package tour lodges were owned by either nonlocal Costa Ricans or foreigners. Two of the three foreign owners, including Michael Kaye, live permanently in Costa Rica. Most of these bigger lodges bring in managers, leaving only the menial jobs for local people. Five simple restaurants, two souvenir shops, and two small grocery stores are owned by Tortuguero residents. Most of the canal boat owners are from Limón; some live in San José.

56. Place, "Nature Tourism," 186–201.

57. Susan Place, "Ecotourism for Sustainable Development: Oxymoron or Plausible Strategy?" *GeoJournal* 35, no. 2, 1995, 170–171.

58. Red Costarricense de Reservas Naturales, see www.reservasprivadascr.org/paginas/ubicacion02.html#cuadro3.

59. In contrast, Costa Rica's 25 national parks are much larger, comprising over 12 percent of the national territory. Red Costarricense de Reservas Naturales Privadas, see www.reservasprivadascr.org.

60. "Unique Debt Swap," *The Canopy*.

61. "Santa Elena Cloud Forest Reserve," see www.monteverdeinfo.com/reserve.htm. For a critical analysis of the Santa Elena Reserve and the role of NGOs and ecotourism in Monteverde, based on research in the late 1990s, see Luis Antonio Vivanco, *Green Encounters: Shaping and Contesting Environmentalism in Rural Costa Rica* (Oxford, England: Berghahn Books, 2006).

62. Elizabeth Boo, *Ecotourism: The Potentials and Pitfalls*, vol. 2 (Washington, D.C.: World Wildlife Fund), 44.

63. According to the municipal government of Puntarenas; Tropical Science Center statistics.

64. Morrison, "Monteverde Area of Costa Rica," 42; author's interviews and correspondence, 1995–2007.

65. Interview with Richard LaVal, April 2007.

66. Interviews with Nery Gomez and Jim Wolf, November 2006.

67. John Burnett, "Ecotourism in Costa Rica," *All Things Considered*, National Public Radio, September 3, 1997. See Eco Verde, www.infoturistica.com/hospedajes/ecoverde_eng.html and Guanacaste Costa Rica Real Estate, www .guanacastecostaricanrealestate.com/index.php?action=listingview&listing ID=186.

68. Interview with Sue Trostle; Ilse Abshagen Leitinger, "Survival of a Women's Organization over the Long Term: Growing Sophistication of Institutional Strategies and Responses at CASEM, the Artisans' Cooperative in the Santa Elena-Monteverde Region of Costa Rica, and New Challenges," paper presented at the Nineteenth International Congress of the Latin American Studies Association, Washington, D.C., September 1995; "Monteverde Info", see CASEM Web site, www.monteverdeinfo.com/casem.

69. Women of the Cloud Forest, see www.womenofthecloudforest.com/

70. Villablanca, see www.villablanca-costarica.com.

71. Si Como No Resort Spa, see www.sicomono.com.

72. Interview with Jim Damalas, June 2007.

73. The author visited Villablanca at least three times between 1995 and 2006.

74. José Luis Vargas, Jon Kohl, "No Reserve Is an Island," *Education*, September–October 1993, 77.

75. "OTS Palo Verde Lodge," Costa Rican Guide, Toucan Guides, see http://costa-rica-guide.com/travel/index.php?option=com_content&task=view&id=261&Itemid=460.

76. Jan G. Laarman and Richard R. Perdue. "A Survey of Return Visits to Costa Rica by OTS Participants and Associates," Southeastern Center for Forest Economics Research, Research Triangle Park, NC. FPEI Working Paper No. 29, 1987; Laarman, Jan G. and Richard R. Perdue, "Tropical Science as Economic Activity: OTS in Costa Rica," Southeastern Center for Forest Economics Research, Research Triangle Park, NC. FPEI Working Paper No. 33, 1987.

77. Selva Verde Lodge and Rainforest Reserve, see www.holbrooktravel.com/SelvaVerdeLodge/Sustainability.aspx.

78. Yanina Rovinski, "Private Reserves, Parks, and Ecotourism in Costa Rica," in Tensie Whelan, ed., *Nature Tourism: Managing for the Environment* (Washington, D.C.: Island Press, 1991), 49; Amos Bien, interview.

79. Interview with Beatriz Gomez, La Quinta, September 2006. Beatriz explained that recently she had to move back to San José to provide their children with more educational options, but Leonardo stays on site. Together they continue to share responsibilities for management, marketing, and different levels of the project's development.

80. "Special Attractions," La Quinta Sarapiqui, see www.laquintasarapiqui.com/activities_special.shtml.

81. Other fine examples of ecotourism on private reserves include the 486-hectare (1,200-acre) Marenco Biological Station, which is dedicated to "conservation, education, tourism, and adventure" and located on a hilltop overlooking the Pacific Ocean and adjacent to Corcovado; El Mirador de San Gerardo, a 300-hectare (741-acre) primary forest located on a working Costa Rican–owned dairy farm with a simple lodge overlooking Arenal Volcano; the Chacón family's Albergue de Montaña Río Savegre, a 300-hectare forest and finca with cabins, quetzals, trout fishing, home cooking, and mountain walks; the Dúrika Biological Reserve, which combines primary and secondary growth and is owned by a community aspiring to self-sufficiency, has impressive terraced gardens with sixty-six crops, and is using its ecotourism profits for purchase of a corridor to La Amistad International Park; and Costa Rican agronomist Peter Aspinall's idyllic Tiskita Lodge, featuring fruit trees, hiking trails, a twenty-meter (sixty-five-foot) waterfall, and a view of the Pacific. Blake and Becher, *New Key to Costa Rica*, 354, 392–393, 423, 439, 446–447. Nicki Solloway, "Back to Nature: Costa Rican Commune Opens Its Doors to Ecotourism," *Costa Rica Today*, March 2, 1995.

82. Claudia Alderman, Environment Division, Latin America and the Caribbean, World Bank, "The Economics and the Role of Privately Owned Lands Used for Nature Tourism, Education, and Conservation," paper presented at the Fourth World Parks Congress of National Parks and Protected Areas, Caracas, Venezuela, February 1992; Jeff Langholz, "Economics, Objectives, and Success of Private Nature Reserves in Sub-Saharan Africa and Latin America," *Conservation Biology* 10, no. 1, February 1996.

83. Costa Ricans benignly refer to squatters as *precaristas*, a reference to their precarious existence, rather than the common Spanish term, *paracaidistas*, meaning "parachutists."

84. Anne Becher and Beatrice Blake, "Reflections on 'Green Ratings,'" August 1998, see www.planeta.com/planeta/98/0898rating.html.

85. By 1990, the tenth edition of the *New Key* was number one on the *Publisher's Weekly* List of "Guidebooks to Warm Weather Destinations." At that point, the publication of guidebooks mushroomed, and by the late 1990s, *New Key* had been muscled aside by the larger companies. In late 2002, *Lonely Planet*'s Costa Rica guidebook (5th edition) was listed as the first-place best-selling travel guidebook to Latin America at Amazon.com, and *New Key* had fallen behind all the major guidebook chains.

86. Interviews with Blake, Becher, and various lodge owners and managers in Costa Rica, 1995–2007; "Costa Rica ecotourism green rating," see www.keyto costarica.com/green-rating.htm.

87. Amos Bien, "Environmental Certification for Sustainable Tourism and Ecotourism: Can They Transform Social and Environmental Practices," in Honey, *Ecotourism and Certification*, 147.

88. In parallel with the development of CST, the Costa Rican water board (Acueductos y Alcantarillados—AyA) developed a certification program for beaches, modeled loosely on a highly respected and successful Blue Flag certification program first begun in Europe to certify beaches and marinas. The Costa Rican Ecological Blue Flag Program (BAE or Bandera Azul Ecológica), which was launched in 1996 as part of an effort to greatly improve health and safety conditions on beaches, had by 2007 certified 58 beaches in Costa Rica, including the main tourism sites. Amos Bien, "The Costa Rican Ecological Blue Flag Program," unpublished manuscript, 2002; Xaviar Font and Tanja Mihalic, "Beyond Hotels: Nature-Based Certification in Europe," in Honey, *Ecotourism & Certification*, 214–222; Programa Bandera Azul Ecologica, see www.guiascostarica .com/bazul /; Blake, Rodolfo Lizano, Amos Bien, Chris Spilsbury, and others, interviews with author, 2002–2007.

89. Author's telephone interviews with Rodolfo Lizano and Lawrence Pratt, July 2000.

90. Rodolfo Lizano, "CST—Towards a New Competitive Advantage," draft paper, ICT, 1997, 7 pages.

91. Robert Toth, "Enhancing Credibility of Costa Rica's Sustainable Tourism Certification System" R.B. Toth Associates, Alexandria, VA, 1998, 8.

92. Toth, "Enhancing Credibility," 6.

93. Rodolfo Lizano, interview with author, August 2002.

94. Andrea Bonilla, General Manager, Lapa Rios, interview with author, August 2002. Bonilla subsequently joined Cayuga Sustainable Hospitality, a Costa Rican–based company that manages Lapa Rios and other hotels based on sustainability principles.

95. Beatrice Blake, correspondence with author, September, 2002.

96. Glenn Jampol, numerous interviews with author, August 2002–2007. Lizano concurs, contending that the process is more important than the score: "Sustainable tourism is a synonym for responsible tourism. What's important is not arriving at the goal but the work towards getting there. Along the way, you're changing the mentality of businessmen. The goal is never entirely reached. It's a learning process." Lizano, interview, 2002.

97. "'Sustainable Tourism' Can Work, CR Shows the World," *Tico Times*, January 28, 2000; Jampol, interview, 2002.

98. CST, see www.turismo-sostenible.co.cr and www.turismo-sostenible.co.cr/ EN/home.shtml.

99. Jorge Rivera, "Institutional pressures and voluntary environmental behavior in developing countries: Evidence from Costa Rica," *Society and Natural Resources* 17, 2004, 779–797, see http://papers.ssrn.com/sol3/papers.cfm?ab stract_id=904374.

100. The International Ecotourism Society (TIES), "Marketing Strategy for Sus-

tainable Tourism Certification," for Rainforest Alliance's project for the IDB-IMF, Activity 3.1, 2005, see http://ecotourismcesd.org/webarticles/articlefiles/53-3.1.4.5_marketing%20plan%20_final_20-Feb-05.pdf.

101. Jampol, interview, August 2002.

102. Zoe Chafe, "Consumer Demand and Operator Support for Socially and Environmentally Responsible Tourism," Center on Ecotourism and Sustainable Development, 2005, see www.ecotourismcesd.org/webarticles/articlefiles/15-Consumer%20Demand%20April%202005.pdf.

103. ICT, "Airport Exit Surveys," 2005, 2006.

104. Key to Costa Rica, see www.keytocostarica.com.

105. Rainforest Alliance, see www.rainforest-alliance.org/locations/costa-rica/tourism.html.

106. Amos Bien, personal correspondence, 2007.

107. Simbiosis Tours, see www.turismoruralcr.com/ingles/ingles.htm.

108. Ibid.

109. Paraphrased from Leyla Solano, 2003, "Simbiosis Tours, COOPRENA: Community-based rural tourism Network in Costa Rica, see www.turismoruralcr.com/ingles/ingles.htm.

110. Leyla Solano, "Turismo Rural Comunitario en Costa Rica. La experiencia del Consorcio Cooperativo Red Ecoturística Nacional—COOPRENA R.L. y el Proyecto INFOCOOP-BID/FOMIN," COOPRENA, 2005.

111. SURCO, see www.acepesa.org/surco/english.html.

112. Correspondence with Yorlenny Fontana, 2007.

113. Actuar, Community-Based Rural Tourism in Costa Rica, see www.actuarcostarica.com/ingles/pulperia.php.

114. Ibid.

115. Edited by Cooprena and UNDP, *The Real Costa Rica* is available through Actuar's Eco Shop, see www.actuarcostarica.com/ingles/pulperia.php.

116. CANAECO, see www.canaeco.com.

117. Amos Bien, correspondence, 2007.

118. Glenn Jampol of Finca Rosa Blanca and Karen Lewis of Lapa Rios became TIES board members, while Amos Bien worked as TIES' internacional director from 2003 to 2006. CANAECO was one of the most active national associations in the Global Ecotourism Conference, held in Oslo, Norway in April 2007. In the 1990s, Geraldo Budowski, a leading scientist in Costa Rica, served as TIES board chair and his daughter, Tamara Budowski, owner of Horizontes Nature Tours, was one of a number of Costa Ricans actively involved in ecotourism at an international level.

119. Finca Rosa Blanca, see www.finca-rblanca.co.cr.

120. Nature Air, see www.natureair.com/; The Alternative Consumer, "Nature Air: Carbon Neutral in Costa Rica," August 6, 2007, see www.alternativeconsumer.com/2007/08/06/nature-air-carbon-neutral-in-costa-rica/.

121. From 435,037 to 1,659,167, ICT, "Anuario estadístico", 1998, 2000, 2005.

122. Guillermo Escofet, "Mega-Resorts the Trend in C.R.," *Tico Times*, special Expotur supplement, May 23, 1997.

123. Boo, *Ecotourism: Potentials and Pitfalls*, vol. 1, 27–28.

124. David Petritz, "Cruise Covers Caribbean," *Tico Times*, Weekend section, January 3, 1997.

125. Information supplied by Anne Becher; Ana Báez, "Binomio turismo-conservación: Una alternativa desarrollo," *Technitur: Costa Rica International Magazine*, published by the Professional Tourism Association of Costa Rica, no. 46, June 1993, 48–53.

126. Barbara Ras, ed., *Costa Rica: A Traveler's Literary Companion* (San Francisco: Whereabout Press, 1994).

Chapter 6: Tanzania

1. Kibo Safaris, see www.kibosafaris.com, was founded by a Tanzanian, Willy Chambulo.

2. Interview at Kambi ya Tembo with staff, December 8, 2004.

3. J. Teigell, Tanganyika Wilderness Camps; correspondence with Fred Nelson, 2005–2006.

4. Fred Nelson, "The Evolution and Impacts of Community-based Ecotourism in Northern Tanzania," IIED Drylands Issue Paper, No. 131, 2004.

5. *The Wildlife Policy of Tanzania*, Ministry of Natural Resources and Tourism (Dar es Salaam: Government Printer, 1998).

6. Benjamin William Mkapa, "Prudent Exploitation of Tourism Potential for Wealth Creation and Poverty Reduction," keynote address by the President of the United Republic of Tanzania, at the Tanzania Tourism Investment Forum, 2002.

7. Author's interview with Hassan Kibelloh, director of tourism, Dar es Salaam, August 1995.

8. Africatravelresource, see www.africatravelresource.com/T1/africa/tanzania/0/intro.

9. I am grateful to Roderick Neumann for the phrase "conservation without representation" to describe this style of management, as well as many of the other insights and analysis I have found in his writings: Roderick Neumann, "Local Challenges to Global Agendas: Conservation, Economic Liberalization, and the Pastoralists' Rights Movement in Tanzania," *Antipode* 27, no. 4, October 1995, 364; see also Roderick Neumann, *Imposing Wilderness: Struggles over Livelihoods and Nature Preservation in Africa* (Berkeley, University of California Press, 1998).

10. Raymond Bonner, *At the Hand of Man: Peril and Hope for Africa's Wildlife* (New York: Vintage Books, 1993), 39–41.

11. Ibid., 42–43.

12. International Institute for Environment and Development (IIED), *Whose Eden? An Overview of Community Approaches to Wildlife Management* (London: Overseas Development Administration, July 1994), 11–12.

13. From the 1880s through World War I, the colonial name for Tanzania was German East Africa. Then it became Tanganyika until 1964, when the postcolonial government merged with Zanzibar to form Tanzania.

14. Bonner, *At the Hand of Man*, 174.

15. Ibid., 174–175; B. Grzimek and M. Grzimek, *Serengeti Shall not Die* (New York: E. P. Dutton & Co., Inc., 1960).

16. Neumann, "Local Challenges," 365.

17. This is frequently cited as an example of enlightened conservation policy, although until very recently the cash-strapped and top-down management of the

NCA did virtually nothing to assist the Maasai. See K. M. Homewood and W. A. Rodgers, *Maasailand Ecology: Pastoralist Development and Wildlife Conservation in Ngorongoro, Tanzania* (Cambridge: Cambridge University Press, 1991).

18. Quoted in Bonner, *At the Hand of Man*, 178.

19. Roderick Neumann, "Ways of Seeing Africa: Colonial Recasting of African Society and Landscape in Serengeti National Park," *Ecumene* 2, no. 2, 1995, 163.

20. Bonner, *At the Hand of Man*, 178.

21. Neumann, "Local Challenges," 366; Bonner, *At the Hand of Man*, 65.

22. Bonner, *At the Hand of Man*, 64.

23. Ibid., 58.

24. Neumann, "Local Challenges," 366.

25. Neumann, *Imposing Wilderness.*

26. IIED, *Whose Eden?* 11–12.

27. Neumann, "Local Challenges," 367.

28. Ibid., 361.

29. Author's interviews with Moringe Parkipuny, Washington, D.C., August 2005 and August 1995.

30. For instance, a 1962 study found that Tanganyika had proportionately "amongst the lowest figures of high-level manpower encountered in any country, even the least industrially developed." Cranford Pratt, *The Critical Phase in Tanzania, 1945–1968: Nyerere and the Emergence of a Socialist Strategy* (Cambridge: Cambridge University Press, 1976), 21.

31. Phillip Bukuku, "Tanzania Tourist Corporation Development Decade," in *Karibu Tanzania: A Decade of TTC's Service to Tourists* (Dar es Salaam: Tanzania Tourist Corporation, 1983), 139.

32. Unfortunately, following decades of mismanagement and a long and erratic privatization process, Lobo is currently in a state of decay and badly in need of upgrade and renovation.

33. Issa Shivji, ed., *Tourism and Socialist Development* (Dar es Salaam: Tanzania Publishing House, 1975), 36, 90–94.

34. Ibid., 37.

35. United Republic of Tanzania, *Second Five Year Plan for Economic and Social Development*, vol. 1 (Dar es Salaam: Government Printer, 1969), cited in Mohan Ranjit Wikramanayake, "The Development of Tourism in Tanzania," master's thesis, George Washington University, 1970, 63–64.

36. Bukuku, "Tanzania Tourist Corporation," 139.

37. Shivji, *Tourism and Socialist Development*, 95; Estrom Maryogo, "Tourism in National Development," in *Karibu Tanzania*, 107.

38. Shivji, *Tourism and Socialist Development*, 50, 32, 45.

39. Reflecting the views of many socialists, the youth wing of Tanzania's ruling TANU party argued "[T]ourism reinforced the existing colonial and neo-colonial social, cultural and economic relationships" and argued that Tanzania should concentrate on more socially beneficial and stable activities such as food production, manufacturing of textiles and other basic goods largely for domestic consumption, and processing of agricultural exports. Shivji, *Tourism and Socialist Development*, vii.

40. Ibid., 87.

41. Author's interviews with tour operator and former TTC official Nervin

Nunes, Arusha, August 1995; Esrom Maryogo, "The Tanzania Tourist Corporation Reintroduced," in *Karibu Tanzania*, 4.

42. United Republic of Tanzania, "The Changing Face of Tanzania: Business Prospects: Tourism Potential and Investment Opportunities in Tanzania," Dar es Salaam, Investment Promotion Center, paper presented at Investment Promotion Seminar, London, May 21–22, 1992, 4.

43. Esrom Maryogo, "Tanzania Tourist Corporation," 4–5.

44. Tony Avirgan and Martha Honey, *War in Uganda: The Legacy of Idi Amin* (Westport, CT: Lawrence Hill Books, 1982).

45. Joyce Francis, *War as a Social Trap: The Case of Tanzania*, Ph.D. dissertation, American University, Washington, D.C. (1994) 128, 146–155, 222.

46. Maryogo, "Tourism in National Development," 109.

47. Lugano Mbwina, "Tanzania Tourism Begins to Attract Foreign Investment," InterPress Service, April 28, 1993.

48. Ibid.

49. Maryogo, "Tourism in National Development"; Interviews with World Bank officials who asked not to be named, Washington, D.C., 1998.

50. Paul Chintowa, "You Are Safe, Visitors Assured," InterPress Service, June 10, 1994.

51. United Republic of Tanzania, *The Tourism Investment Giant of Sub-Saharan Africa*, (Dar es Salaam: Tourism Division, no date).

52. Interviews by author and Marcus Lenzen with various World Bank officials, Washington, D.C., 1998; Author's correspondence with Dr. Julius Nyerere, November 1998.

53. Z. Meghji, "Tourism Development Policy and Strategy in Tanzania," Paper presented to the Tanzania Tourism Investment Forum, October 22–24, 2002.

54. CHL Consulting Group, "Tourism Master Plan: Strategy & Actions, Final Summary Update," prepared for the United Republic of Tanzania, Ministry of Natural Resources and Tourism, Dublin, Ireland, 2002..

55. Meghji, "Tourism Development Policy and Strategy," n.p., Washington, D.C., 2002. Copy of speech obtained by author.

56. Ministry of Natural Resources and Tourism, The United Republic of Tanzania, *National Tourism Policy* (Dar es Salaam: MNRT, 1999).

57. Mkapa, "Prudent Exploitation," 2002, 8.

58. Neumann, "Local Challenges," 369; Anver Versi, "Dawn of a New Age?" *African Business*, November 1994, 40.

59. See www.tanzaniaparks.com.

60. This stands in contrast to the situation across the border in Kenya's Masai Mara, where wildlife numbers have dropped by about 50 percent since the 1970s.

61. Interview with Peter Lindstrom, Hoopoe Tours, July 7, 2005.

62. Alan Rodgers, Lota Melamari, and Fred Nelson, "Wildlife Conservation in Northern Tanzanian Rangelands," paper presented to the symposium: Conservation in Crisis: Experiences and Prospects for Saving Africa's Natural Resources, held at Mweka, Tanzania, December 10–12, 2003.

63. Tanzania National Parks, *2000/2001 Annual Report*, Arusha, 2002.

64. Interview with Robert Daniel, July, 2005.

65. Robert M. Poole, "Heartbreak on the Serengeti," *National Geographic*, February 2006, see www7.nationalgeographic.com/ngm/0602/feature1/index.html.

66. Richard Graham, "Funds for Wildlife: Concession Pays Not To Hunt," *Sports Afield*, April–May 2006, 16.

67. Singita News, "Singita to Manage and Market Grumeti Reserves in Tanzania's Serengeti," see www.singita.com/site/about/news.asp; Graham, "Funds for Wildlife," 16; Verlyn Klinkenborg, "Your Own Private Africa," *New York Times Style Magazine: Travel*, September 24, 2006.

68. Graham, "Funds for Wildlife," 16.

69. Lawi Joel, "Land Wrangle Threatens Serengeti Village with loss of Millions," *The Guardian*, October 10, 2005, see www.ippmedia.com/ipp/guardian/2005/10/10/51527.html.

70. Legal and Human Rights Centre, *The Serengeti Killings: Wildlife Conservation and Human Rights in the Balance Sheet* (Dar es Salaam: Legal and Human Rights Centre, 2003).

71. Francis Stolla correspondence with Fred Nelson, December 2006.

72. Fred Nelson and Sinandei Ole Makko, "Communities, conservation and conflict in the Tanzanian Serengeti," in Brian Child and Martha West Lyman, eds., *Natural Resources as Community Assets: Lessons from Two Continents* (Madison, WI: Sand County Foundation and the Aspen Institute, 2005) .

73. KIHACHA, *Food is Politics: Struggles over Food, Land, and Democracy* (Dar es Salaam: E & D Limited, 2002).

74. Y. B. Masara, "Wildlife Areas Expansion and Local Land Rights: The Case of Kimotorok Village, Simanjiro District," report prepared for Pastoralists, Indigenous, Non Governmental Organization's Forum, Arusha, 2005.

75. E. Porokwa, interview with Fred Nelson, Arusha July 8, 2005.

76. Emmanuel Greta, "Community Conservation Services for Serengeti National Park's Surrounding Communities," 107–114, in A. Wondrak Biel, ed., *Beyond the Arch: Community and Conservation in Greater Yellowstone and East Africa,* proceedings of the 7th Biennial Scientific Conference on the Greater Yellowstone Ecosystem, Mammoth Hotsprings Hotel, Yellowstone National Park, October 6–8, 2003.

77. Hassan Sachedina, "Conservation, Land Rights, and Livelihoods in the Tarangire Ecosystem of Tanzania: Increasing Incentives for Non-conservation Compatible Land Use Change through Conservation Policy," paper presented to Pastoralism and Poverty Reduction in East Africa: A Policy Research Conference, held in Nairobi June 27–28, 2006.

78. Zakia Meghji, Minister of Natural Resources and Tourism, interviewed by researcher Audrey Davenport, August 30, 2005, Dar es Salaam. Meghji became Minister for Finance in the next Tanzanian administration.

79. James Igoe, *Conservation and Globalization: A Study of National Parks and Indigenous Communities from East Africa to South Dakota* (Belmont, CA: Wadsworth/Thomson Learning, 2004).

80. Homewood and Rodgers, *Maasailand Ecology.*

81. Quoted in C. Lane, "Ngorongoro Voices: Indigenous Maasai residents of the Ngorongoro Conservation Area in Tanzania give their views on the proposed General Management Plan," Forest, Trees and People Working People, FAO, 1996.

82. Ibid., 4.

83. L. Mayeta, "Land Use conflicts in Ngorongoro Conservation Area and the

Proposed Eviction of Maasai Pastoralists," a consultancy report submitted to PINGOs Forum-Arusha, Tanzania, 2004.

84. Ibid.

85. Ibid.

86. W. Ole Nasha, correspondence, July 7, 2005.

87. Mayeta, "Land Use Conflicts in Ngorongoro."

88. E. Porokwa, interview, Arusha, July, 2005.

89. C. K. Ole Memantoki, interview, July, 2005.

90. G.A.P Adventures, see www.gapadventures.com/tour/DCA.

91. Overseas Adventure Travel, see www.oattravel.com/gcc/general/default.aspx?oid=119073.

92. Mark Dowie, "The Hidden Cost of Paradise: Indigenous people are being displaced to create wilderness areas, to the detriment of all," *Stanford Social Innovation Review*, Spring 2006, 31.

93. Maa is the Maasai language.

94. Correspondence with David Peterson, directors, Dorobo Tours and Safaris; "Community Centered Conservation," paper presented to Tanzania Community Conservation Workshop, Arusha, Tanzania, February 1994.

95. African Wildlife Foundation (AWF). *The Impact of Wildlife-Based Enterprises on Local Livelihoods and Conservation in Tanzania*, (Nairobi: AWF Wildlife Enterprise for Local Development Project, 2001); Bailey Robinson, "Oliver's Camp," see www.rbrww.com/safari/381.

96. Nelson and Makko, "Communities, Conservation and Conflict."

97. Ibid.

98. Maasai Environmental Resource Coalition, "The Killing Fields of Loliondo: The Hunting Operations of Ortello Business Company and their Impact on Maasai Rights, Wildlife, and the Environment," a report by the Maasai Environmental Resource Coalition, Washington, D.C., 2002.

99. "Loliondogate," editorial, *Miombo*, newsletter of the Wildlife Conservation Society of Tanzania, no. 10, July 1993, 2, 17–18; Caroline Alexander, "The Brigadier's Shooting Party," *New York Times*, November 13, 1993.

100. Peter Lindstrom, interview, December 2006.

101. Rolf Baldus and Andrew Cauldwell, "Tourist hunting and its role in development of Wildlife Management Areas in Tanzania," paper presented to the sixth International Game Ranching Symposium, Paris, July 6–9, 2004.

102. Bonner, *At the Hand of Man*, 244; "The Hunting Industry in Tanzania: From World Leadership to National Concern," *Miombo* 12, January 1995, 2.

103. "Hunting Industry in Tanzania," 1–2.

104. Baldus and Cauldwell, "Tourist Hunting," 11.

105. Rolf Baldus, "The Selous Project: Saving Many By Killing a Few," *Miombo*, January 1995, 8.

106. Baldus, "Selous Project," 8; IIED, *Whose Eden?* 41; Werner Rohs, "The Environmental Impact of Tourism in the Northern Selous Game Reserve," SCP Discussion Paper No. 9, Selous Conservation Programme, Dar es Salaam, 1991. In Zimbabwe, some CAMPFIRE projects continued to operate despite the political repression and unrest. In fact, as tourism dried up almost completely because of the turmoil, CAMPFIRE has become more important because hunters are less

sensitive to political disturbances. Hunting safaris have continued to earn significant revenue for those districts involved in CAMPFIRE.

107. N. Leader-Williams, J. Kayera, and G. Overton, "Community-based Conservation in Tanzania," occasional paper of the IUCN Species Survival Commission No. 15, 1996.

108. Ministry of Natural Resources and Tourism, *The Wildlife Policy of Tanzania* (Dar es Salaam: Government Printer, 1998).

109. E. L. M. Severre, "Conservation of wildlife outside core wildlife protected areas in the new millennium," paper presented to the conference African Wildlife Management in the New Millennium, College of African Wildlife Management, Mweka, Tanzania, 13–15 December, 2000.

110. Fred Nelson, *The Evolution and Impacts of Ecotourism in Northern Tanzania,* (London: IIED, October 2004).

111. Ibid.

112. Y. B. Masara, "The Conflict of Legislation and Collision of Jurisdictions: An Impediment to the Realization of Community-based Conservation in Tanzania," report prepared for the African Wildlife Foundation, 2000.

113. Wildlife Working Group, "West Kilimanjaro-Longido: A Case Study of Wildlife Management in Northern Tanzania," unpublished report, 2002.

114. Correspondence with Andy Harris, Kibo Safaris, September 2006.

115. Based on extensive field interviews by Fred Nelson, 2005–2006.

116. Interview in Arusha on July 25, 2005.

117. Rolf Baldus, David Kaggi, and Philbert Ngoti, "Community Based Conservation (CBC): Where are we now? Where are we going?" *Miombo* 27, 2004, 3, 7, 10–11.

118. Dan Dickinson, "Anger Over Tanzanian Hunting Rights," *BBC News 24*, April 14, 2005. see http://news.bbc.co.uk/1/hi/world/africa/4440375.stm.

119. Rolf Baldus, "Case Study: The Crucial Role of Governance in Ecosystem Management—Results and Conclusions of the Selous Conservation Programme, 1987–2003," paper presented to the Serengeti Conference, 2006.

Chapter 7: Zanzibar

1. "Zanzibar Named Best Island Destination in Africa and the Middle East by Travel and Leisure Magazine Readers," Africa Travel Association, see www.africa-ata.org/zz_award.htm.

2. Dana Seidenberg, "Zanzibar: Smile of the Spice Isles," *The East African*, Nairobi, Kenya, July 11–17, 2005.

3. "Zanzibar: Among Americans' Top Destinations," *Travel Daily News*, see http://home.globalfrontiers.com/zanzibar/2006_news.htm.

4. Research notes from Audrey Davenport, November 2005.

5. Moyiga Nduru, "Turning to Services as Clove Prices Fall," InterPress Service, April 19, 1996.

6. Office of East African Affairs, U.S. Department of State, *Investment Climate Report: Tanzania* (Washington, D.C.: U.S. Department of State, Office of East African Affairs, February 1995).

7. Proceedings of the International Workshop on Ecotourism and Environ-

mental Conservation in Zanzibar, held at Inn By The Sea, March 21–24, 1994 (Zanzibar: Commission for Lands and Environment of the Department of Environment, 1994), 14.

8. International Finance Corporation (IFC), *Zanzibar Tourism Investment Study* (Washington, D.C.: IFC, March 1995), 9.

9. Barbara Koth, "Zanzibar Tourism Policy," speech in *Proceedings of Tourism Infrastructure Workshop*, Commission for Tourism held at Bwawani Hotel, Zanzibar, January 18, 1995, n.p.; interviews with Koth and World Bank officials., 1995–2003.

10. Ahmada Khatib, Commission for Tourism, Zanzibar, "The Present State of Tourism Development in Zanzibar," in *Proceedings of Workshop on Ecotourism*, March 1994, annex 3, 5; Nduru, "Turning to Services."

11. Ibid., 187.

12. A. Hamzah and Kari Londfors, eds., "Sustainable Management of Land and Environment in Zanzibar," Zanzibar Ministry of Water Construction, Energy and Land and Finnish Ministry of Foreign Affairs, December 2002, 2.

13. Muhammed Haji Ali and Muhammad Salim Sualiman, "The Makings and Contents of Zanzibar National Land Use Plan: A brief account of a donor funded project," FIG XXII International Congress, Washington, D.C., April 19–26, 2002, 7.

14. Issa Mlingoti, director of Planning, Zanzibar Tourism Commission, interview by Audrey Davenport, September 2005.

15. URT, "Indicative," 39. Audrey Davenport said that it was unclear from government documents and interviews whether the funds were unavailable because they were used for other government projects or if they disappeared through corruption. In 2005, Davenport found that the Commission for Tourism maintained 61 staff in Unguja and 19 staff in Pemba, as well as four information offices scattered around the Stone Town, though none of them, when they are open, have maps or printed information to offer visitors.

16. Stefan Gossling, "The Political Ecology of Tourism in Zanzibar," in Gossling, ed., *Tourism and Development in Tropical Islands: Political Ecology Perspectives* (Cheltenham UK: Edward Elgar Publisher, 2003), 179–180, 186, 192.

17. Overview of Zamani Zanzibar Kempinski Tanzania, see www.nextag.com/zamani-zanzibar-kempinski-deals/search-html.

18. Benjamin Bayo, assistant manager and Jonathan Cox, general manager, Bluebay Beach Resort, Zanzibar, interviewed by Audrey Davenport, September 2005, plus Davenport's personal observations. The hotel has since opened. See www.kempinski-zanzibar.com/en/home/index.htm. In "Political Ecology," Gossling reports on similar problems with other hotel projects.

19. Revolutionary Government of Zanzibar (GoZ), Zanzibar Ministry of Trade, Industry, Marketing and Tourism, "Zanzibar Tourism Policy," January 2004.

20. Pereira Silima, principal secretary, Ministry of Trade, Industry, Marketing and Tourism, Revolutionary Government of Zanzibar, interview with Audrey Davenport, September 2005; Mlingoti, interview, 2005.

21. GoZ, Zanzibar Ministry of Water, Energy, Construction, Lands and Environment, "Report on the Sustainable Management of Land and Environment (SMOLE) Programme," August 21, 2004.

22. Silima, interview, September 2005.

23. Gossling, "Political Ecology," 189–190; M. S. Sulaiman, "Islands within Islands: Exclusive Tourism and Sustainable Utilization of Coastal Resources in Zanzibar," in L. Briguglio, R. Butlet, D. Harrison and W. Leal Filho, eds., *Sustainable Tourism in Islands and Small States: Case Studies* (London and New York: Pinter, 1996), 23–49.

24. Off-the-record interview with Audrey Davenport, September 2005.

25. Ramadhan Mwinyi, director of Tourism, speech in *Proceedings of Tourism Infrastructure Workshop*; Khatib, "Present State of Tourism Development," 4. A study by the IFC, however, warns that official statistics on Zanzibar's tourism arrivals and earnings are notoriously unreliable, both because of "deficient data collection methods" and because they are based solely on occupancy in hotels whose owners underestimate visitor numbers in order to avoid taxes. The IFC estimates that "the figures probably underestimate Zanzibar's visitation by 25% to 30%." IFC, "Zanzibar Tourist Investment," 9, 13.

26. Mlingoti, interview, September 2005.

27. United Republic of Tanzania (URT), Tanzania Ministry of Natural Resources and Tourism, "Tanzania Tourism Sector Survey 2003," 2003, 28. Copy obtained from Ministry by Davenport.

28. Mlingoti, interview, September 2005.

29. Zanzibar Tourism Commission, see www.freesun.be/freesun_news/10_march_2006/freesun_news_303.html.

30. URT, "Indicative," 51.

31. Statistics obtained from Mlingoti, September 2005.

32. Gossling, "Political Ecology," 182.

33. GoZ, "Tourism Policy," 2004.

34. Statistics obtained from Mlingoti, September 2005.

35. URT, "Indicative," 48. As stated earlier, the government's official figure for 2000 of $3.1 million is clearly a gross underestimation.

36. Ibid.

37. URT, "Sector Survey," 28.

38. Stefan Gossling, "Market Integration and Ecosystem Degradation: Is sustainable tourism development in rural communities a contradiction in terms?" *Environment, Development and Sustainability*, 2003; v. 5, no. 3–4: 383.

39. Mohammed Kasim, guide for Eco+Culture Tours in Jambiani Village, interviewed by Davenport, September 2005.

40. Gossling, "Political Ecology," 197.

41. Ibid.

42. Mlingoti, interview, September 2005.

43. Mlingoti, interview, September 2005. In his speech to the 2003 ATA conference, Mohamed Aboud, Zanzibar's Minister of Trade, Industry, Marketing and Tourism, said that directly and indirectly, tourism "could presently produce about 37,000 jobs." Untitled speech, 4. Copy obtained by Davenport.

44. GoZ, *Zanzibar Vision 2020,* Zanzibar Revolutionary Government, 2002.

45. Gossling, "Political Ecology," 183.

46. Birgit La Cour Madsen, "Islands of Development: What Do Poor Women in Zanzibar Get Out of Tourism Liberalization?" Prepared for World Tourism Day, September 27, 2003, Action Aid, Dar es Salaam, Tanzania, 3.

47. Silima, interview, September 2005.

48. Mlingoti, interview, September 2005.

49. Data provided by Zanzibar Investment Promotion Agency (ZIPA), July 2005.

50. Gossling, "Political Ecology," 183.

51. ZATI Opening Doors, see www.zati.org.

52. Also in support of the tourism industry, in 1998, the IFC financed a $400,000 loan for a private mineral-water bottling company run by a joint Italian, Zanzibari, and Liberian team of shareholders. Drop of Zanzibar, the water bottling company, has made safe drinking water more available to tourists, and the bottled water is for sale on every street corner. Sadly, the IFC's loan stipulations did not require Drop of Zanzibar to build a recycling facility for the plastic bottles, which now contribute substantially to litter in towns and beaches across Zanzibar. International Finance Corporation Project Summary, project number 8101, see www.ifc.org/projects; Len Horlin, founder and former coowner, Matemwe Bungalows, interview with Davenport, September 2005.

53. Jonathan Cox, general manager of Blue Bay Beach Resort, interview with Audrey Davenport, September 2005; Gossling, correspondence with author, August 2007.

54. IFC, see www.ifc.org/projects, project number 10074.

55. IFC, "Summary of Project Information: AEF Zanzibar Safari Club," February 18, 2000, see http://www.ifc.org/IFCExt/spiwebsite1.nsf/0/5e9edeb2e1e9e8ed8525688e007c4a07?OpenDocument.

56. Silima, interview, September 2005; IFC, "Summary of Project Information: AEF Zanzibar Safari Club"; "Zanzibar Fuel Supply: Gapco Steps In," *The East African*, September 29, 2003, see www.nationaudio.com/News?EastAfrican/29092003/Regional.

57. Executive Summary with Key Resolutions, *Proceedings of Workshop on Ecotourism*, 5–8. See first edition of this book for complete listing of the resolutions.

58. Mlingoti, interview, September 2005.

59. Gossling, "Market Integration," 396.

60. Horlin, interview, September 2005.

61. Anonymous interview with Davenport, August 2005.

62. URT, "Indicative," 48.

63. Thabit Masoud, Program Manager for CARE International, Zanzibar, Tanzania, interview with Audrey Davenport, August 2005.

64. Global Environmental Facility (GEF), *The Nature and Role of Local Benefits in GEF Programme Areas, Case Study: Tanzania – Zanzibar. Jozani-Chwaka Bay Conservation Area* (Washington D.C.: GEF Office of Monitoring and Evaluation, November 2004), 24.

65. Ibid.

66. Unnamed guide, interview with Audrey Davenport, September 2005.

67. Riedmiller writes that "I had no interest in ecotourism as such, but marine conservation and environmental education, after living for decades in a country where rampant dynamite fishing was the norm—one reason being that people believe corals are 'rocks and stones'." Sibylle Riedmiller, correspondence with Audrey Davenport, September 2005 and with author, March 2007; Sibylle Ried-

miller, "Private Sector Investment in Marine Protected Areas: Experiences of the Chumbe Island Coral Park in Zanzibar/Tanzania," presented at Sustainable Finance Stream, 5th World Parks Congress, Durban, South Africa, 2003; Sibylle Riedmiller, "Tourism and Communities: How the Culture of the Coast is Kept Intact through Sustainable Tourism Activities," presented at ATA Symposium, Zanzibar Beach Resort and Conference Center, December 2004.

68. CHICOP, *Management Plan 2006-2016*, Zanzibar, 2006.

69. The overall investment has been about $1.2 million, of which about two-thirds was financed by Riedmiller and the rest by a variety of international, mainly German, donors. Sibylle Riedmiller, "Private Sector Investment in Marine Protected Areas: Experiences of the Chumbe Island Coral Park in Zanzibar/Tanzania," presented at Sustainable Finance Stream, 5th World Parks Congress, Durban, South Africa, 2003.

70. As I wrote in the first edition of this book, in the mid-1990s, a number of NGOs, government officials, fishermen, and other hoteliers and tour operators whom I interviewed expressed reservations about the Chumbe project. While this is partly attributable to mistrust of foreign-owned ventures, it appeared exacerbated by the brusque management style of the director and a lack of close and regular interactions with the local fishing communities that, for instance, characterized Matemwe Bungalows during its formative years. In 2005, when Audrey Davenport conducted field research, she found that while many of these old grudges and concerns about Chumbe remained just below the surface, the project had clearly achieved both international recognition and improvements in its local relations. Thorkidsen's 2006 thesis assesses "20 acknowledged stakeholder groups' rights, responsibilities, returns and relationships ['4R's'] . . . in order to understand the distribution of costs and benefits and thereby conflicts of interests." She concludes that "CHICOP has provided educational, research and conservational benefits to Zanzibar. However, some of the objectives in the management plan and promises made by the proprietor have not been fulfilled. The major underlying cause for conflicts was the poor information flow that existed between and within the various stakeholder groups, which reduces transparency of the project and creates mistrust." Kjersti Thorkildsen, "Socio-Economic and Ecological Analysis of a Privately Managed Marine Protected Area: Chumbe Island Coral Park, Zanzibar," master's thesis, Norwegian University of Life Sciences, Department of International Environment and Development Studies, Oslo, Norway, May 2006, vii.

71. Riedmiller, correspondence.

72. Ibid.

73. *Management Plan 2006–2016.*

74. Ibid. Riedmiller provided a document detailing the social benefits being provided by Chumbe Island Coral Park (CHICOP) Ltd.

75. Ibid.

76. CHICOP Manager, Helen Peeks, interview with Audrey Davenport, September 2005.

77. Lisa Baum, "Chumbe Island Environmental Education, Phase 3 Report: 2003–2004," provided by Mikala Peters, Conservation and Education Coordinator, Chumbe Island.

78. In terms of community education for Zanzibari fisherman and schoolchildren, Davenport concluded that it took Chumbe some time to go large-scale with the education program, but since 2001 the education coordinators have produced a series of impressive materials, including marine conservation and ecology teaching curriculum, and worked hard to increase the number of Zanzibari students who have visited the island.

79. Thorkilsen, "Chumbe Island Coral Park, Zanzibar," 57.

80. Mnemba Island Lodge, see www.mnemba-island.com.

81. Author's interviews with Department of Environment director Abdulrahman Issa and local fishermen in August 1995.

82. Peter Seibert, general manager of Mnemba Island Lodge, interview with Audrey Davenport, September 2005.

83. "Tanzania: Marine and Coastal Environmental Management Project. Submission for Final CEO Endorsement," Official Memorandum, Global Environmental Fund (GEF), The World Bank, April 21, 2005, 113, see www.gefweb.org/Documents/Project_Proposals_for_Endorsem/Tanzania_-_Marine___Coastal-MACEMP.pdf.

84. Horlin, interview, September 2005.

85. Vuai Ali, Dive Center staff at Matemwe Bungalows, interview with Audrey Davenport, September 2005.

86. Anonymous interview with Audrey Davenport, August 2005.

87. Local fishermen in Kigomani Village, interviews with Audrey Davenport, September 2005.

88. Author's interview with Katherina Horlin, August 1995. They had grown up on an island off the Swedish coast where their father managed the national park. In 1989, they set off on a round-the-world trip, fell in love with Zanzibar, and decided to start a small hotel committed to living in harmony with nature and the community.

89. Author's interviews with local villagers, August 1995.

90. IFC, "Zanzibar, Tourism Investment," 51.

91. Commission for Tourism, *A Tale of Two Islands* (Zanzibar: Commission for Tourism, n.d.), E28. Copy in possession of author.

92. Len Horlin, interview, September 2005.

93. Annette Bulman, manager of Matemwe Bungalows, interview with Audrey Davenport, September 2005.

94. Asilia lodges, see www.asilialodges.com/index.php?id=6.

95. Jeroen Harderwijk, interview at Matemwe with Audrey Davenport, September 2005.

96. Local fishermen in Kigomani Village, interviews, September 2005.

97. The demands and expectations of the neighboring village can be difficult to meet. The manager of Matemwe Bungalows told Gossling that "managing this place is more like political bargaining. Half of my time goes to this." Gossling perceptively writes, "From the locals' point of view, tourism may often be understood as a superior industry with infinite financial resources, potentially able to solve any problem. From a socio-cultural perspective, donations and jobs 'given' to locals have turned formerly self-sufficient villagers into passive beneficiaries." Gossling, "Political Ecology," 194.

98. Matemwe Retreat, Expert Africa Web Site, see www.expertafrica.com/lodge/Matemwe_Retreat.htm; Len Horlin, interview, September 2005.

99. Fundu Lagoon Community Projects, see www.fundulagoon.com/pdf/community/community2006.pdf?unique=1411.

100. Visitors fly to Pemba's only airport, Chake Chake, in the center of the island, and are then transported to Makoani Port where a private boat service takes them to Fundu Lagoon, see www.fundulagoon.com/pdf/latestinfo/airlineschedule.pdf?unique=2602.

101. "Press," Fundu Lagoon, see www.fundulagoon.com.

102. Audrey Davenport's correspondence with Julia Bishop, general manager of Fundu Lagoon, November 21, 2005.

103. Ibid.

104. Ibid.

105. GoZ, "Tourism Policy," 2004.

106. Mlingoti, interview, September 2005.

107. Julia Bishop, manager, Fundu Lagoon, interview with Audrey Davenport, September 2005.

108. Eco+Culture brochure, obtained from Eco+Culture office in the Stone Town, Zanzibar, September 2005.

109. Ibid.; "Tourist Attractions: Eco-Culture," *Tanzania Holidays.com* Web Site, see www.tanzaniaholidays.com/ZnzEco.html.

110. Stefan Gossling and Narriman Jiddawi, "Proceeding from the Regional Workshop on Planning for Sustainable Tourism," held in Zanzibar, Institute of Marine Sciences, October 22–30, 2003, 43.

111. Silima, interview, September 2005.

112. Ulrich Malisius, *The Stone Town of Zanzibar* (Zanzibar: Ministry of Water, Construction, and Energy, 1985). Lamu is classified as the only "living pre-industrial" stone town (i.e., no cars), in sub-Saharan Africa.

113. Silima, interview, September 2005.

114. This is a reference to Makonde wood carvings and Tinga Tinga paintings, two of the best-known forms of art from Tanzania's mainland, who typically work in outside stalls.

115. John Babtist da Silva, interview with Audrey Davenport, September 2005.

116. Audrey Davenport, personal observations, September–October 2005; Gossling, "Political Ecology," 193.

117. "Episode 6: Pitstop Zanzibar, Tanzania," *The Amazing Race*, CBS television, March 25, 2007.

118. The curator of these two museums was Abdul Sheriff, a former professor of history at the University of Dar es Salaam, who since 1992 has played a crucial role in preserving Zanzibar's cultural heritage. Sheriff, who was my Ph.D. advisor at the University of Dar es Salaam, is author of a number of books and articles on Zanzibar, the Swahili coast, and the dhow trade and recipient, in 2005, of the prestigious Prince Claus Fund award for his "profound knowledge, curiosity and dedication to academic standards." Abdul Sheriff, interview with Audrey Davenport, September 2005, and correspondence with author, 2005–2007; Beit al-Ajaib Museum Exhibit on Tourism, viewed by Davenport, September 2005.

119. Off-the-record interviews with Audrey Davenport, September 2005.

120. Sheriff, interview, October 2005.

121. ZIFF: The Zanzibar International Film Festival, see www.ziff.or.tz.

122. Darren Frei, "East African Eden?" *The Advocate*, October 26, 2004, see http://findarticles.com/p/articles/mi_m1589/is_2004_Oct_26/ai_n7579852.

123. Skeens, interview, September 2005.

124. "Zanzibar threatened with tourism boycott," *Afrol News*, April 27, 2004, see www.afrol.com/articles/12126.

125. Emerson + Green is advertised, for instance, on Purple Roofs, a Web site for gay and lesbian travelers, see www.purpleroofs.com/africa/tanzania.html.

126. URT, "Indicative," 48.

127. "Tanzania: New Drive for the Environment in Zanzibar," UN Integrated Regional Information Networks, December 18, 2006, see http://home.global-frontiers.com/zanzibar/2006_news.htm.

128. Stefan Gossling, "The Consequences of Tourism for Sustainable Water Use on a Tropical Island: Zanzibar, Tanzania," *Journal of Environmental Management* 61, 2001, 188.

129. Gossling, "Political Ecology," 182.

130. URT, "Indicative," 48.

131. Gossling, "Political Ecology," 197.

132. Sheriff, interview, September 16, 2005.

133. "Tanzania: New Drive."

134. "Tanzania Marine and Coastal Environmental Management Project," World Bank, see http://web.worldbank.org/WBSITE/EXTERNAL/COUNTRIES/AFRICAEXT/TANZANIAEXTN/0,,contentMDK:20992192~menuPK:287367~pagePK:1497618~piPK:217854~theSitePK:258799,00.html.

135. Gossling, "Political Ecology," 192, 193.

136. Sheriff, interview, September 2005.

137. Ibid. Sheriff speculates that the bill may just have been designed to "pacify" unemployed Zanzibaris, angry about jobs being taken by mainlanders.

138. Ibid. The bill is controversial in mainland Tanzania where Zanzibaris do not require work permits.

139. Gossling, "Political Ecology," 195.

140. Mlingoti, interview, September 2005.

141. Madsen, "Islands of Development," 4.

142. *Sustainable Advancement of Zanzibar: A Study on the Status of Youth in Zanzibar*, with funding from the Ford Foundation of East Africa: February 2002.

143. Off-the-record interview with Audrey Davenport, September 2005.

144. Off-the-record interview with Audrey Davenport, September 2005.

145. Gossling, "Political Ecology," 199.

Chapter 8: Kenya

1. L. Talbot and P. Olindo, "Kenya: The Maasai Mara and Amboseli Reserves," in Agnes Kiss, ed., *Living with Wildlife: Wildlife Resource Management with Lo-*

cal Participation in Africa, World Bank Technical Paper No. 130, Africa Technical Department Series (Washington, D.C.: World Bank, 1990), 67.

2. Joseph Carvahlo, *COBRA Project: Financial and Economic Analysis* (Nairobi: U.S. Agency for International Development, Bureau for Africa, Regional Economic Development Services Office, East and Southern Africa, September 1991), 1.

3. Perez Olindo, "The Old Man of Nature Tourism: Kenya," in Tensie Whelan, ed., *Nature Tourism: Managing for the Environment* (Washington, D.C.: Island Press, 1991), 23.

4. John S. Akama, "Western Environmental Values and Nature-Based Tourism in Kenya," *Tourism Management* 17, no. 8, 1996, 568.

5. Ibid.

6. Grace Lusiola, "The Role of the COBRA Project in Economic Development of Local Communities," in C. G. Gakahu and B. E. Goode, *Ecotourism and Sustainable Development in Kenya,* proceedings of the Kenya Ecotourism Workshop, Lake Nakuru National Park, September 13–17, 1992 (Nairobi: Wildlife Conservation International, 1992), 125; David Western, "Ecosystem Conservation and Rural Development: The Case of Amboseli," in David Western and R. Michael Wright, eds., *Natural Connections: Perspectives in Community-Based Conservation* (Washington, D.C.: Island Press, 1994), 15.

7. Kenya Wildlife Service, (KWS), National Parks, Reserves and Sanctuaries Data. Electronic Media, Nairobi, 2004, see www.kws.org/parks.html.

8. P. F. J. Eagles, J. L. Ballantine, and D. A. Fennell, "Marketing to the Ecotourist: Case Studies from Kenya and Costa Rica" paper presented at the IVth World Congress on National Parks and Protected Areas, Caracas, Venezuela, 1992.

9. Western, "Ecotourism: The Kenya Challenge," 17.

10. Ibid., 18.

11. Olindo, "Old Man," 29.

12. UN World Tourism Organisation, *Tourism Market Trends,* 2006 Edition-Annex, see www.unwto.org/facts/eng/pdf/indicators/new/ITR05_africa_US$.pdf.

13. Olindo, "Old Man," 25.

14. Carvahlo, *COBRA Project,* 2–3.

15. Raymond Bonner, *At the Hand of Man: Peril and Hope for Africa's Wildlife* (New York: Vintage Books, 1994), 130–131.

16. Institute of Policy Analysis and Research, "Policy Dimensions in Human-Wildlife Conflict in Kenya: Laikipia and Nyandarua Districts," *Policy Brief* 11, No. 3, 2005.

17. Kennedy Manyalla, Kenya Tourism Bureau (KTB), interview, July, 2006; Ministry of Natural Resources and Tourism (MNRT) statistics, obtained from Manyalla.

18. Human Rights Watch, "Case Study: Armed Political Violence at the Coast," see www.hrw.org/reports/2002/kenya/Kenya0502-06.htm. Donald Mombo, Kenya Community Based Tourism Network, Nairobi, interview, May, 2007.

19. David Western, "Handling the Wildlife Time-Bomb That Is KWS," *The East African,* November 17–23, 1997; "Travel Warnings Issued," *Nairobi Sunday Nation,* August 9, 1998.

20. Various other articles regarding the embassy bombings and their impact on tourism.

21. UNWTO, *Tourism Market Trends,* 2006.

22. Kamau Ngotho, "The Terrorist Next Door," *The Standard,* July 31, 2005, see www.eastandard.net/archives/cl/hm_news/news.php?articleid=26470.

23. Tourism Marketing Recovery Programme/Tourism Trust Fund, "The Tourism Marketing Recovery Programme," see www.ttfkenya.org/?q=tmrp.

24. Kenya Tourism Bureau (KTB), *Annual Marketing Plan,* 2005, 4.

25. Olindo, "Old Man," 29.

26. KTB, "Strategic Direction," *Annual Marketing Plan,* 2006, 15.

27. Ngotho, "The Terrorist Next Door"; Combating Terrorism Center at West Point, "Al-Qua'ida's (mis)Adventures in the Horn of Africa: Case Study: Kenya," see www.ctc.usma.edu/aq_kenyaII.asp.

28. Bonner, *At the Hand of Man.*

29. Kenya Wildlife Service (KWS), "Wildlife Policy 1996," draft, January 15, 1996, 1–2.

30. Western, "Ecosystem Conservation and Rural Development," 37.

31. "Executive Summary," untitled 1991 USAID document on the COBRA project, 4. Copy in possession of author.

32. Lusiola, "Role of the COBRA Project," 125.

33. "Executive Summary," untitled 1991 USAID document, 4–6. Several USAID reports also panned the Kenyan government's performance and the World Bank project. Although wildlife-based tourism was bringing in around $200 million a year, "most of those who border Kenya's parks and reserves received few, if any, tangible benefits from tourism-based utilization," concluded one report. Carvahlo, *COBRA Project,* 2.

34. Ibid.

35. Bonner, *At the Hand of Man,* 130–159.

36. Richard Leakey, interview, Washington, D.C., April 1996; Correspondence with David Western, June 1998. Western said that by June 1989, well before the CITES meeting, the Ivory Trade Review Group had convinced the United States, Europe, Japan, Hong Kong, and other countries to impose domestic bans on ivory, and this made CITES's international ban inevitable.

37. Leakey, interview, April 1996.

38. Kevin Fedarko, "When Elephants Collide: Two Legends of Conservation Vie for the Soul of Kenya's Hallowed National Parks," *Outside,* June 1998, 25.

39. "Executive Summary," untitled 1991 USAID document, 1.

40. Ibid., 6

41. Bonner, *At the Hand of Man,* 132; Leakey, interview, 1996.

42. "Executive Summary," untitled 1991 USAID document, 1.

43. Ibid., 13; Lusiola, "Role of the COBRA Project," 127; *Mid-Term Evaluation of the COBRA Project Synthesis of Findings and Recommendations* (Washington, D.C.: U.S. Agency for International Development, May 1996), 8–9.

44. Carvahlo, *COBRA Project,* 6, 13.

45. Lusiola, "Role of the COBRA Project," 126.

46. "After the Investigation, a Damning Report," *Nairobi Daily Nation,* April 2, 1994.

47. Costas Christ, "Kenya Makes Revenue Sharing Top Priority," *The Ecotourism Society Newsletter*, 4, no. 1, winter 1994, 1–2; Mark Stanley Price, Africa director, African Wildlife Foundation, interview April 1996; IUCN, *Pachyderm*, no. 32, January–June 2002.

48. Fedarko, "When Elephants Collide," 26. In his interview with the author, Leakey explained, "By the time I left, it was very clear that the 25 percent made no sense. The ability for many of the communities to absorb some of that money simply wasn't there. We were beginning to see problems of accountability, all sorts of political shenanigans as to who should receive and control the money."

49. Rory Carrol, "Land First: Conservationist Angers Indigenous Groups," *The Guardian*, September 13, 2003, see www.smh.com.au/articles/2003/09/12/1063341771125.html.

50. Donatella Lorch, "Noted Kenya Conservationist Resigning in a Political Storm," *New York Times*, January 15, 1994, 3; "Richard Leakey: His Early Life, Careers, and Presidential Aspirations," *60 Minutes* (CBS), February 4, 1996.

51. David Western, "Ecotourism at the Crossroads in Kenya," *The Ecotourism Society*, 3rd quarter 1997, 1.

52. USAID, *Mid-Term Evaluation,* 8–9.

53. Ibid., ii.

54. David Western, quoted in Yvonne Baskin, "There's a New Wildlife Policy in Kenya: Use It or Lose It," *Science* 265, 1994, 733.

55. Kenya Wildlife Service and African Wildlife Foundation, "Summaries and Conclusions from Five Components of the Wildlife Utilisation Study," draft, September 1995; USAID, *Mid-Term Evaluation,* 16–17.

56. Mike Norton-Griffiths, "Kenya's Conservation Crisis Set to Continue?" Langata, Kenya, December 2006, 3, see www.mng5.com/papers/consCrisisCont.pdf.

57. By contrast, the director of Tanzania's national park service was earning a mere one-fifth of the salary of Western's personal assistant. Economist Intelligence Unit, *Kenya: EIU Country Report,* 1st quarter 1998, 19.

58. Reported in Michael McRae, "Survival Test for Kenya's Wildlife," *Science* 280, April 24, 1998, 510–512.

59. Knowledgeable experts say that despite the problems with the COBRA project, USAID was, in reality, reluctant to shut it down because it fit into one of the agency's priority areas and it justified the size of its mission in Nairobi.

60. Michael McRae, "Crisis Management," *Science* 280, April 24, 1998, 512; World Bank officials who asked not to be identified, interviews, June 1998.

61. Correspondence with Robert Hall, June 1998.

62. Kipkoech Tanui and Esther Im, "David Western Replaced at KWS," *Nairobi Daily Nation*, May 22, 1998; Kipkoech Tanui and Esther Im, "Why I've Lost My KWS Job—Western," *Nairobi Daily Nation,* May 23, 1998; Njeri Rugene and Kenya News Agency (KNA), "Moi Criticises Western," *Nairobi Sunday Nation*, May 24, 1998; Agence France Press (AFP), untitled story, May 23, 1998; David Western, "Press Statement on Termination of My Contract," press release, May 22, 1998.

63. David Western, letter, and Kurt Benirschke et al., letter, "Wildlife Conservation in Kenya," both appeared in *Science*, 280, June 5, 1998, 1507–1510.

64. Interviews with officials at international conservation organizations based in Washington, D.C., May–June 1998.

65. BBC News, "Profile: Dr. Richard Leakey," see http://news.bbc.co.uk/2/hi/africa/1330228.stm.

66. Richard Leakey, "The way forward—as I see it", *Swara* 301: 67–69.

67. David Western, interview, CESD office, Washington, D.C., May 2005.

68. David Western, Samantha Russell, and Kamweti Mutu, "The Status of Wildlife in Kenya's Protected and Non-protected Areas," paper commissioned by Kenya's Wildlife Policy Review Team, 2006, see www.conservationafrica.org/conservation-publications/wildlife_poicy_review_paper.pdf.

69. Ibid.

70. Mike Norton-Griffiths, "Whose Wildlife Is It Anyway?", *New Scientist*, March 24, 2007, 24.

71. Norton-Griffiths, "Whose Wildlife Is It Anyway?"; Norton-Griffiths, "Kenya's Conservation Crisis," p. 2. Norton-Griffiths identifies the Humane Society and the International Fund for Animal Welfare as the principal organizations involved in opposing and lobbying against the bill.

72. International Fund for Animal Welfare, Inc., 2005 Income Tax Return, Form 990, see http://dynamodata.fdncenter.org/990_pdf_archive/311/311594197/311594197_200606_990.pdf.

73. Omara Kalasingha, chair, Kenya Wildlife Working Group, interview, Arusha, Tanzania, June, 2007.

74. James Shikwati, "Ignore Profiteers and Make Use of Wildlife,'" *Business Daily*, April 18, 2007, 23.

75. Norton Griffiths, "Kenya's Conservation Crisis," 2.

76. Ali A. Kaka. "Society Notes—From the Director's Desk," *Swara* 30, 1, 72.

77. Western, "Ecosystem Conservation and Rural Development," 15.

78. Ibid., 15–17.

79. Ibid., 18.

80. Talbot and Olindo, "Kenya," 69.

81. Government of Kenya, *Economic Survey 2005*, Central Bureau of Statistics, Ministry of Planning, Nairobi, Kenya, 2006.

82. It was originally called the Narok District Council, but to minimize confusion I have referred to it as the Narok County Council, the postcolonial name, throughout this book.

83. Talbot and Olindo, "Kenya," 70.

84. C. G. Gakahu, "Visitor Dispersal Strategies in Ecotourism Management," paper presented at Fourth World Congress of National Parks and Protected Areas, Caracas, Venezuela, February 1992, 11.

85. W. Henry, J. Waithaka, and C. G. Gakahu, "Visitor Attitudes, Perceptions, Norms, and Use Patterns Influencing Visitor Carrying Capacity," 57 and J. Sindiyo, "Management Proposal for the Mara Dispersal Areas," 77, in C. G. Gakahu, ed., *Tourist Attitudes and Use Impacts in Masai Mara National Reserve*, proceedings of workshop organized by Wildlife Conservation International, Masai Mara Game Reserve, March 1991 (Nairobi: English Press, 1992).

86. M. K. Koikai, "Why Masai Mara Is the Most Visited Reserve in East Africa," 8–9, in Gakahu, *Tourist Attitudes*.

87. Christ, "Kenya Makes Revenue Sharing Top Priority," 1.

88. Michael Thompson and Katherine Homewood, "Entrepreneurs, Elites and Exclusion in Maasailand: Trends in Wildlife Conservation and Pastoralist Development," *Human Ecology* 30, 1, 2002, 126.

89. Correspondence with David Western and Robert Hall, June 1998.

90. Thompson and Homewood, "Entrepreneurs, elites, and exclusion," 127.

91. Quote contained in correspondence from Robert Hall, a consultant who evaluates international development projects in Africa, with a specialization in environmental, community-based, and institutional issues, June 1998.

92. Ibid., 127.

93. Ali Kaka, former KWS Director, interview, Arusha, Tanzania, June, 2007.

94. Thompson and Homewood, "Entrepreneurs, Elites, and Exclusion," 127.

95. Wilber Khasilwa Ottichilo, "Wildlife Dynamics: An Analysis of Change in the Masai Mara Ecosystem of Kenya," dissertation n. 2766, Wageningen University, Enshcede, The Netherlands, 2000, 8.

96. Ottichilo, "Wildlife Dynamics," 163–4.

97. David Drummond, "Impacts of Tourism on the Ecology of Masai Mara," *Wajibu* 10, no. 1, 1995, 9–11.

98. Geoffrey Karanja, "Tourism Impacts in Masai Mara National Reserve," 5–16, in Matt Walpole, Geoffrey Karanja, Noah Sitati, and Nigel Leader-Williams, eds., *Wildlife and People: Conflict and Conservation in Masai Mara, Kenya* (London: IIED Wildlife and Development Series, No. 14, 2001).

99. Storm Stanley, "Uncertain Future?" *Swara* 29, 4, 2006, 49.

100. Interviews in Kenya, July 1995; Carvahlo, *COBRA Project,* 11; John Ole Kisimir, "Who Is Exploiting the Other?" *Nairobi Daily Nation*, July 1, 1998.

101. Stanley, "Uncertain Future?" 54.

102. Sindiyo, "Management Proposal," 77.

103. Walter Chin, "Kenya: The Maasai," *Sports Illustrated*, February 20, 1998, 66.

104. Stanley, "Uncertain Future?," 50.

105. Basecamp Explorer: Our History, see www.basecampexplorer.com/About/History/en.

106. Justin Francis. "Walking with the Maasai," see www.responsibletravel .com /Copy/Copy100782.htm.

107. Lars Lindkvist, Basecamp Masai Mara, speech at the Global Ecotourism Conference, May 15, 2007, Oslo, Norway.

108. Ali Kaka, interview.

109. Talbot and Olindo, "Kenya," 70.

110. Western, "Ecosystem Conservation and Rural Development," 30.

111. Ibid., 34; correspondence with Western, June 1998.

112. Western, "Ecosystem Conservation and Rural Development," 35.

113. Ibid., 36.

114. Ibid., 35.

115. Bonner, *At the Hand of Man*, 229.

116. Ibid., 230.

117. Western, "Ecosystem Conservation and Rural Development," 42.

118. Marcel Rutten, *Linking Western Tour Operators with Community-Based Protected Areas in Kenya: Globalising Paradise for Whom?* (Leiden, Nether-

lands: African Studies Centre, 2002), 18, see http://dlc.dlib.indiana.edu/archive/00000914.

119. Western, "Ecosystem Conservation and Rural Development," 42–43; "Executive Summary," untitled USAID document, 18; Bonner, *At the Hand of Man*, 230.

120. Western, "Ecotourism at the Crossroads," 2.

121. Marcel Rutten, *Parks beyond Parks: Genuine Community-based Ecotourism or Just Another Loss of Maasai Land?* IIED Drylands Issue Paper No. 111 (London: IIED, 2002), 14–21; Rutten, *Linking Western Tour Operators.*

122. Rutten, *Parks beyond Parks*, 23–24; Amboseli Porini Camp, see www.porini.com/amboseli_porini_camp.html.

123. Campi ya Kanzi, see www.maasai.com/98.asp.

124. "Campi ya Kanzi, Kenya, Ecolodge Footprint Case Study 2," TIES Ecolodge Footprint Study, Washington, D.C.: International Finance Corporation, 2003.

125. Western et al., "The Status of Wildlife."

126. Ali Kaka, interview, Arusha, Tanzania, June 2007.

127. Western, interview, May 2005.

128. Traditionally the "Big Five" were the preferred hunting trophies—lions, buffalos, elephants, leopards, rhinos—although nowadays camera safaris often substitute cheetahs for buffalos.

129. Claudia Alderman, "The Economics and the Role of Privately Owned Lands Used for Nature Tourism, Education, and Conservation," paper presented at Fourth World Congress of National Parks and Protected Areas, Caracas, Venezuela, February 1992.

130. Stephen Faris. "The Land is Ours," *Time*, see www.time.com/time/maga zine/article/0,9171,699336,00.html; "Property Issues: General: Both victims and perpetrators of displacements seek compensation from the government," *Profile of Internal Displacement: Kenya*, compilation of the information available in the Global IDP Database of the Norwegian Refugee Council, see www.ecoi.net/file_up load/625_1161673415_2004-11-30-4914-ken.pdf.

131. Among the numerous press reports are: "The End of a Dynasty? Aristocrat Faces Second Murder Trial in Kenya," *The Guardian* (London), September 22, 2006, see www.guardian.co.uk/world/2006/sep/23/kenya.chrismcgreal; Daniel Howden, "Kenya set to drop murder case against aristocrat," *The Independent* (London), May 18, 2005, see http://findarticles.com/p/articles/mi_qn4158/is_20050518/ai_n14631613.

132. Delamere's Camp, The Great Rift Valley, see www.savannahcamps.com/scl/greatrift.html.

133. Ol Pejeta Conservancy, "What is Ol Pejeta?" see www.olpejetaconservancy.org/sub-news.php?spageID=1.

134. On Adnan Khasshoggi's checkered career, see, for instance, "US Arms Group Heads for Lisbon," *The News*, Portugal's English language weekly, April 4, 2003, see www.globalresearch.ca/articles/NEW304A.html.

135. In the first edition of this book, I wrote critically of the colonial-style tourism I had seen at the Craig's Lewa Downs ranch and rhino sanctuary. However, since then Ian Craig's work with Il Ng'wesi has been pioneering, paving the way for Kenya's new style of community-based ecotourism.

136. Lewa Wildlife Conservancy, see www.lewa.org.

137. USAID/Kenya, "Natural Resources Management, Success Story: Laikipia Wildlife Forum: Showcasing District-Wide Conservation through Capacity Building," n.d., see www.usaidkenya.org/ke.naremgnt/success_laikipia.htm.

138. Western, interview, May 2005.

139. Ibid.

140. USAID/Kenya, "Natural Resources Management."

141. "Ol Gaboli Community Lodge," *Mpala News,* Issue 3, November 2006, 2.

142. Ralph Johnstone, "Talking ecotourism," *Swara* 22, 4, 2000, 5–9.

143. Laikipia Wildlife Forum, see www.laikipia.org/laikipia-safari.htm; Northern Rangelands Trust, see www.nrt-kenya.org/conservancies.html.

144. See www.choiceswild.com/holidays/shompole.htm.

145. Enhanced Online News Business Wire, "A Dialogue for the Future: Aveda and its Partners Discuss the Opportunities and Challenges of Indigenous Entrepreneurship," press release, May 31, 2007, see http://eon.businesswire.com/releases/aveda/indigenous/prweb530248.htm.

146. "Shampole—Great Rift Valley," Africa Mecca, see www.africanmeccasafaris.com/kenya/safaris/lodges/shompole.asp.

147. Western, interview, May 2005.

148. Correspondence with Ole Taiko Lemayian, executive director, Kecobat Network, Nairobi, June 2007; "KECOBAT Profile" obtained from Lemayian; see www.kecobat.org.

149. See www.lets-go-travel.net.

150. Correspondence with Kurt Kutay, June 28, 2007; "How Are Our Maasailand Safaris Different?," "Living Among the Maasai," and "Wildland Adventures Awarded 'Best Africa Trip of the Year 2005'," see www.wildland.com.

151. Micato Safaris, www.micato.com; Various interviews with Dennis Pinto, managing director, Micato Safaris, New York, 2002–2007.

152. Reuters, "Kenya Tourism on Crest of Wave," *The Citizen,* May 15, 2007, 22.

153. Transparency International, "Corruption Perceptions Index 2006," see www.transparency.org/policy_research/surveys_indices/cpi/2006.

154. Reuters, "Kenya Tourism on Crest of Wave."

155. Tourism Marketing Recovery Programme (TMRP), see www.ttfkenya .org/?q=tmrp.

156. Kenya Tourist Board, see www.magicalkenya.com.

157. Western, interview, May 2005.

158. Interviews with Chris Gakahu, Costas Christ, and Meitimei Ole Dapash, 1996–2004; documents from the Ecotourism Society of Kenya (ESOK), including "Mission and Values," and "The Ecotourism Partnership."

159. Judy Kepher-Gona, correspondence, 2005–2007.

160. "Ecotourism Kenya: Promoting Responsible and Sustainable Tourism," see www.ecotourismkenya.org.

161. Judy Kepher-Gona, correspondence.

162. ESOK, *Ecotourism Kenya, 1996–2006: The First Decade,* (Nairobi: ESOK, 2006).

163. Lemayian, correspondence, June 2007.

164. Program for Ecotourism at the Crossroads conference, October 31–

November 3, 1997, Nairobi; Western, "Ecotourism at the Crossroads," 4; Fedarko, "When Elephants Collide," 26.

165. Nigel Carpenter, Kenya Wildlife Service, "Revenue Generation for the Management and Conservation of Protected Areas," paper presented at The Ecotourism Society workshop, Costa Rica, October 1995, 6.

166. Western, "Ecotourism at the Crossroads," 2.

167. Carvahlo, *COBRA Project,* 10–11.

168. Akama, "Western Environmental Values," 567.

Chapter 9: South Africa

1. Words to the Makuleke ballad as quoted in C. Thornill and D. M. Mello, "Community-based Natural Resource Management: A Case Study of the Makuleke Community," *Journal of Public Administration,* South Africa, vol. 42, no. 3, August 2007, 293.

2. Ford Foundation, "The Displaced Makulekes Recover Community Land and Wildlife Assets, Sustainable Solutions," 2002, 46–51, cited in Anna Spenceley, "Tourism Investment in the Greater Limpopo Transfrontier Conservation Area: A Scoping Report," Report to the Transboundary Protected Areas Research Initiative, University of the Wittwatersrand, Johannesburg, March 2005, see www.anna.spenceley.co.uk. Previously the chief had borrowed cars. The fact that the chief now owns a car is a source of pride to the entire community because it demonstrates that it is successfully building its assets.

3. Chris Roche, Trustee, Wilderness Safaris, personal correspondence with Spenceley, January 2007. The value of the rand to the dollar fluctuates dramatically, therefore the conversion represents a figure as close as possible to the rate at each particular date.

4. Anna Spenceley, ed., "Tourism in the Great Limpopo Transfrontier Conservation Area: Relating Strategic Visions to Local Activities that Promote Sustainable Tourism Development," workshop proceedings, April 14–16, 2005, Wits Rural Facility, Kruger National Park, South Africa, 14–15.

5. Roche correspondence, January 2007.

6. In September 2003, I was fortunate to attend, at the invitation of Eddie Koch of Mafisa Research and Planning, a historic meeting of nine South African communities involved in the restitution process, together with leading social and natural scientists. At this "People and Parks: Processes of Change" community workshop, the Makuleke were viewed as the most successful of the claimants. The workshop wrote "The Cape Vidal Memorandum" outlining their ongoing concerns with South Africa's parks system and management, which they presented at the 5th World Parks Congress held that same month in Durban, South Africa. "The Cape Vidal Memorandum," Statement to the 5th World Parks Congress: Outcome of the People and Park Processes of Change community workshop, Cape Vidal, Greater St. Lucia Wetland Park, September 5–7, 2003, see www.iucnsa.org.za/documents/key_issues_vidal.pdf.

7. Wilderness Safaris, see www.wilderness-safaris.com.

8. J. G. Castley, C. Patton and H. Magome, "Parks for People. The Performance

of South African National Parks," in B. Child, B. Jones, M. Murphree, A. Spenceley, and H. Suich, eds., *Evolution of Innovation in Wildlife Conservation in Southern Africa*, IUCN-Southern African Sustainable Use Specialist Group, in preparation.

9. Ibid.

10. Rina Grant, Scientific Services, Kruger National Park, personal correspondence with Anna Spenceley, 2006.

11. M. Wahl and K. Naude, *National Register of Protected Areas* (Pretoria: Department of Environmental Affairs and Tourism, 1994), 21.

12. Eddie Koch, *Reality or Rhetoric? Ecotourism and Rural Reconstruction in South Africa* (Geneva: United Nations Research Institute for Social Development, August 1994), 10.

13. Rupert Isaacson, *South Africa: Swaziland and Lesotho* (London: Cadogan Books, 1995), 550–551; Eddie Koch, "Dead Cows, a Long Bicycle Ride, the Fence of Fire, and a Man on the Run," report prepared by the United Nations Research Institute for Social Development and Group for Environmental Monitoring, second draft, January 1995, 6–17.

14. "Pafuri Gate Fact Sheet," 2004, see www.sanparks.org/about/media/2004/pafuri_gate_fact_sheet.pdf.

15. Koch, "Dead Cows," 147.

16. Koch, *Reality or Rhetoric?*, 12.

17. Although the government grant made up the largest single financial contribution, it only accounted for 9,400 hectares (36 square miles), owing to the high price paid for land in the Mapungubwe National Park. South African National Parks *Annual Report 2004/5,* see www.sanparks.org/about/acts/info_act.php.

18. "Land Reform Update," July 1, 2005, see www.senwes.co.za/afr/media/artikels/2005/2005-07-01_Land_Reform_update.asp; "South Africa: Deadline for land transfer negotiations set," August 15, 2006, see www.irinnews.org/report.asp?ReportID=55132.

19. "Private Public Partnerships in the Tourism Sector, Report 1: An Analytical review of South African Public Private Partnerships to date," Tourism PPP Toolkit, South African National Treasury, February 2005.

20. Study by the Board of Trade and Industries, cited in David Grossman and Eddie Koch, *Ecotourism Report—Nature Tourism in South Africa: Links with the Reconstruction and Development Programme*, report prepared for SATOUR, August 1995, 4.

21. Ibid.

22. "Indaba 2006 Fact Sheet: Tourism arrivals 2005," South African Tourism, May 2006, see www.southafrica.net/satourism.

23. Paul Olivier, "Backpacking Isn't Just for Impoverished Students," *Capetown Saturday Star*, January 3, 1998, 15.

24. See www.sanparks.org/about/annual/2005.pdf.

25. For example, in June 2006, an episode of *Isidingo* was filmed in South Africa's Addo Elephant National Park, see www.sanparks.org/about/news/2006/july/isidingo.php?PHPSESSID=09inp2h61f9gj6ii7lf153kpr1.

26. Jennifer Seif, Fair Trade in Tourism South Africa, interview, November 2004.

27. Black people are defined as Africans, Coloreds (mixed race), and Indians who are South African citizens.

28. Department of Environmental Affairs and Tourism, "Tourism BEE Charter and Scorecard," 2006, see www.dti.gov.za/bee/BEEManualInside.pdf.

29. "Operation Prevail Moves to Kruger National Park," Media Release, May 23, 2001, see http://celtis.sanparks.org/about/media/2001/knpoperationprevail.pdf.

30. "Operation Prevail—Kruger National Park," television broadcast, Sunday, November 25, 2000. For transcript see www.5050.co.za/inserts.asp?ID=2362.

31. Spenceley, "Tourism Investment"; SANParks, "Prequalification Memorandum for the Second Phase of the Concession Programme," South African National Parks, 2001. Commercialization—like many other innovations—was first tried in the 1980s by the Pilanesberg Parks Board (subsequently the North West Parks Board).

32. "Private Public Partnership in Tourism," 11.

33. A. van Jaarsveld, Application in terms of Regulation 16.8 of the Public Finance Management Act ("PFMA"), 1999, dealing with Public Private Partnerships, for approval of amendment and variation of agreements for the concession contracts, South African National Parks, 2004, 7.

34. Ibid.

35. "Private Public Partnership in Tourism," 1.

36. SANParks, Bidding memorandum for the tender of concession sites, 2nd Draft, September 25, 2000.

37. SANParks, "Prequalification memorandum."

38. "Private Public Partnership in Tourism," 1.

39. Ibid.

40. Ibid.

41. Ibid., 11.

42. Spenceley, "Tourism."

43. Thabo Mbeki gave this statement at a ceremony in Giriyondo, South Africa, in August 2006, in the presence of the presidents of Zimbabwe and Mozambique. See Planet Ark World Environment News at www.planetark.com/avantgo/daily newsstory.cfm?newsid=37691.

44. Allister Sparks, *The Mind of South Africa* (London: Mandarin, 1991), 138.

45. Koch, "Dead Cows," 142, 151.

46. Hector Magome, interview at Pilanesberg National Park, August 1995. In the middle of our conversation, Magome suddenly propped his leg up on the desk and rolled up his trousers, revealing dark scars up and down his shins. "I come from one of the poorest families in South Africa," Magome explained. "My body is covered with scars from sores caused by malnutrition. My mother died when I was seven, but shortly beforehand, she took me aside and said she was giving me a new name, 'Hector.' She said it's the name of a bully, of someone who would persevere. She told me I had to learn to be strong." Magome took his mother's words to heart: "In terms of my makeup, I fight. I don't run away." He received a scholarship to study in the U.S. from the Endangered Wildlife Trust, one of South Africa's largest and most mainstream environmental organizations, and came back with two master's degrees (and later earned a Ph.D.). In 1986, he joined the Bop Parks as an assistant ecologist and began moving up through the ranks. In 1997, Magome became the general manager for planning at the South African National

Parks in Pretoria. Despite his high-ranking position within SANParks, Magome continued to be trusted by the local communities involved in land claims against the parks. He was, for instance, the only SANParks official invited by the communities to attend the September 2003 community workshop at Cape Vidal that involved a frank exchange about the successes and challenges of the restitution process.

47. Grossman and Koch, *Ecotourism Report*, 42.

48. A much more palatable rhino revenue-generating scheme goes on today at Phinda, a private reserve owned by CC Africa, which sells its surplus white rhinos to other parks and zoos. Phinda permits tourists to participate in rhino-darting excursions in preparation for transporting the rhinos to their new homes. The tourist income from these rhino-darting safaris are used to finance the process of inserting identification chips into the rhino horns. Between 1999 and 2004, Phinda took 132 people on 28 "rhino darting safaris" for a cost of between $1,555 for two and $6,685 for a group of twelve. These safaris cumulatively netted a total profit of $435,300. Anna Spenceley and Jon Barnes, "Economic Analysis of Rhino Conservation in a Land-Use Context within the SADC region," SADC Regional Programme for Rhino Conservation, SADC RPRC Task 6.3-1.2 (Phase II), September 2005, 3,21.

49. "Private Public Partnership in Tourism," 1.

50. Magome, interview, August 1995 and subsequent interviews and communications, 2003–2007. See the opening section of the South Africa chapter in the first edition of this book for the story of how journalists and parks officials discovered, as apartheid was ending, that people living on the edge of Kruger deeply resented this world icon of wildlife conservation.

51. Grossman and Koch., *Ecotourism Report*, 38–41.

52. Ibid., 42–43; Hector Magome, correspondence with Spenceley, January 2007.

53. Sparks, *Mind of South Africa*, 36.

54. Isaacson, *South Africa*, 605.

55. A. Spenceley and J. Seif, "Strategies, Impacts and Costs of Pro-poor tourism approaches in South Africa," Pro-Poor Tourism, Working Paper, Number 11, January 2003.

56. Interviews at St. Lucia, August 1995; Koch, *Reality or Rhetoric?*, 2; Douglas Chadwick, "A Place for Parks," *National Geographic*, July 1996, 41.

57. Following the 1994 national elections, Buthelezi was appointed minister of home affairs by Nelson Mandela, a post that he held until 2004. In 2004, the Inkatha Freedom Party joined the Democratic Alliance, the major opposition party to the currently dominant ANC party.

58. The Natal Parks Board (NPB) was South Africa's most wealthy, powerful, and independent provincial parks board and, internationally, it was garnered more acclaim than any other parks board in the country. In 1994, the NPB received the prestigious ASTA (American Society of Travel Agents)/*Smithsonian* Magazine Environmental Award for its work in both conservation and tourism. In 1995, NPB's Hilltop Camp, a spectacular mountain lodge in the Hluhluwe-Umfolozi Park, received a British Airways' "Tourism for Tomorrow" award for its environmental sensitivity, quality, and community outreach. When the NPB was

founded at the end of the nineteenth century, there were only fourteen white rhinos left in the world—all in the Umfolozi area of Natal. Today, the NPB is the world's sole supplier of white rhinos and chief supplier of black rhinos to parks, reserves, sanctuaries, and zoos in other parts of Africa, the United States, Europe, Asia, and even Cuba.

59. George Hughes, interview, August 1995.

60. KwaZulu-Natal Nature Conservation Board, "Summary by Race Group and Occupational Category for the Year Ended 31 March 2006," *Annual Report 2005–2006*, Pietermaritzburg, Ezembelo KwaZulu-Natal Wildlife: 2006, 26; speech by Narend Singh, KwaZulu-Natal Minister of Agriculture and Environmental Affairs, March 8, 2002, see http://agriculture.kzntl.gov.za/speeches/2002/8_mar.asp.

61. Nicky Barker, "The Battle for St. Lucia Is Far from Over," *Weekly Mail & Guardian*, Johannesburg, November 14, 1997.

62. Koch, *Reality or Rhetoric?*, 22–23.

63. Telephone interview with Barry Clements, August 1995; Victor Munnik, "St. Lucia: The Impact on Conservationists, Miners, Scientists, and Mr. Mkhize," *New Ground*, winter 1993, 6–9; Chadwick, "Parks," 41.

64. Endangered Wildlife Trust, *Vision of Wildlife, Ecotourism and the Environment in Southern Africa*, 1993–1994 (Johannesburg: Endangered Wildlife Trust, 1995), 80–90. Only the conservative Endangered Wildlife Trust, which has close ties to business, came out in favor of mining, arguing that RBM has developed "a highly specialized technique . . . for mining coastal dunes." RBM advertises in the Endangered Wildlife Trust's publications, and the trust in turn lists RBM as an "environmentally responsible business in Southern Africa. Munnik, "St. Lucia," 6–9; Koch, *Reality or Rhetoric?*, 1–22; J. D. F. Jones, "The Price of a Great African Wilderness," *Financial Times*, January 20–21, 1996; Chadwick, "Parks," 41.

65. Jones, "Price of a Great African Wilderness"; Barker, "Battle for St. Lucia."

66. Eddie Koch, "'Nature People, Leave Us Alone!'" and "St. Lucia's Villagers Snubbed," *Weekly Mail & Guardian*, Johannesburg, South Africa, March 22, 1996.

67. Various community representatives, interviews with author, August 1995; Koch, *Reality or Rhetoric?*, 3.

68. Koch, "St. Lucia's Villagers Snubbed."

69. Leslie Walters, interview, August 1995.

70. Author's visit to Greater St. Lucia Wetlands Park in September 2003; Association for Rural Advancement, "Communities, Conservation, Eco-tourism and Tenure Security Workshop," African Enterprise Conference Center, Pietermaritzburg, KwaZulu-Natal, July 2004, 13.

71. Author's visit to the project; Annette Gerber, KNP official, interview, August 1995.

72. Several years later, I learned that Waters died of an illness, but I was unable to find out details of what happened to her project work.

73. Barker, "Battle for St. Lucia."

74. Meeting with Jane Porter, KwaZulu-Natal Wildlife, St. Lucia, September 2003; information from Roland Vorwerk, media and communications coordina-

tor, The Greater St Lucia Wetland Park World Heritage Site, personal correspondence with Anna Spenceley, February 2007.

75. "Cape Vidal Memorandum."

76. "Communities, Conservation, Eco-tourism and Tenure Security Workshop, 2, 3, 7 13–14, 19.

77. Barker, "Battle for St. Lucia;" Steve Kotze, a historian who has worked with the GSLWP and Gina Thompson, consultant with EnvironDev, correspondence with Anna Spenceley, January 2007. Thompson wrote, "The situation is a very thorny and complex one. Different sections of the community have been moved and relocated at different times" and new groups have moved in. She added that "the forest itself has been extremely badly impacted by ongoing construction of dwellings, cultivation, stock, and use of indigenous trees for various products and fuel. In my view, it will be very difficult to rehabilitate even if they do manage to persuade all those living in the actual Dukuduku forest to move out."

78. Jeff Gaisford, KZN Wildlife, correspondence with Spenceley, January 2007.

79. Koch, *Reality or Rhetoric?*, 22.

80. Anonymous interviews in South Africa and United States, 1995–1998; Stephen Ellis, "Of Elephants and Men: Politics and Nature Conservation in South Africa," *Journal of Southern African Studies* 20, no. 1, March 1994, 66. This division had placed under surveillance anthropologist David Webster who worked near Kosi Bay and was murdered in Johannesburg in 1989. Investigators found that Webster was probably murdered by a death squad set up by South Africa's Special Forces, perhaps because he stumbled on evidence of ivory smuggling. There is suspicion as well that KwaZulu park officials may have been involved in the death of Claire Stewart, another researcher and activist mysteriously murdered in 1993 in the same area.

81. Quoted in Koch, *Reality or Rhetoric?*, 33.

82. Department of Nature Conservation, KwaZulu-Natal Province, "Policies," n.d.

83. The author visited and conducted interviews at Rocktail Bay in August 1995 and Zoe Chafe did the same in November 2004; Anna Spenceley provided additional information in 2007.

84. "2005 Best Trips," *Outside*, February 2005, see http://outside.away.com/outside/toc/200502.html. Numerous articles and Web sites refer to *Outside*'s designation of Rocktail's beach as one of the best in the world. See, for instance: Taga Safaris, Rocktail Bay Lodge, at www.tagasafaris.co.za/rocktail-bay-lodge.htm.

85. The Wilderness Safaris Web site states, "Rocktail Bay has a complicated ownership structure that successfully integrates our neighbouring community, the Parks, Wilderness Safaris and our partners. There is a lodge owning company that is owned by the local community and by the KwaZulu-Natal parks through a section 21 company (i.e., a nonprofit company) called Isivuno. The rights to operate the lodge are then ceded to Wilderness Safaris and we pay the lodge owning company a fixed monthly rental and a percentage of our turnover. The community shareholders are the Nqobela villagers who live closest to Rocktail Bay's park boundary. Like Ndumo, as the community has direct shares and significant own-

ership in the lodge, barriers have fallen and we enjoy a stimulating, invigorating and enriching relationship with our community partners." See www.wilderness-safaris.com.

86. The lodge-owning company includes Isivuno with a 43.5 percent share, a local bank with 42 percent, and the local community with 14.5 percent. Rocktail's operating company is 50 percent controlled by Wilderness Safaris, 37.5 percent by Isivuno and 12.5 percent by the community. Clive Poultney and Anna Spenceley, "Practical Strategies for Pro-Poor Tourism, Wilderness Safaris South Africa: Rocktail Bay and Ndumu Lodge," Pro-Poor Tourism Working Paper No. 1, April 2001, 3, 4, see www.propoortourism.org.uk/safrica_cs1.pdf.

87. Ibid., 5.

88. Murray Simpson, research scientist, Centre for the Environment, Oxford University, correspondence with Spenceley, January 2007.

89. James Ramsay, Russel Friedman, and Malcolm Mcullogh, Wilderness Safaris, interviewed by Zoe Chafe, November 2004.

90. Simpson, correspondence, January 2007.

91. Wilderness Safaris Wildlife Trust, see www.wildernesstrust.com/trust/main.jsp.

92. Simpson, correspondence, January 2007; Zoe Chafe, CESD, memo based on her field work in South Africa, October–December 2004.

93. Rocktail has won several other national and international awards including the Imvelo Award for Best Community Tourism Partnership in 2003 and the World Legacy Award in 2002/3. Wilderness Safaris won a total of 15 ecoawards between 2002 and 2006. See Awards, Wilderness Safaris, www.eyesonafrica.net/south-african-safari/rocktail-bay.htm.

94. Roche, correspondence, January 2007.

95. PPT in Practice, "Pro Poor Tourism Pilots in South Africa: Wilderness Safaris, Rocktail Bay Lodge," see www.pptpilot.org.za/Wilderness.html.

96. Ramsay, interview with Chafe, November 2004.

97. Ronnie McKilvey, interview with author, Londolozi, South Africa, August 1995. McKilvey has since left Londolozi and in 2007 the managing director was Stof Kane-Berman. Spenceley correspondence with CC Africa.

98. David Varty, interview with author, Londolozi, South Africa, August 2005.

99. In 2006, CC Africa moved for the first time outside Africa, forming a joint venture with Taj Hotels and Palaces to offer wildlife-viewing ecotourism at five lodges in India. CC Africa, see www.ccafrica.com.

100. Grossman and Koch, *Ecotourism Report*, 29.

101. See www.ccafrica.com/reserve-1-id-2-1; A. Spenceley, "Ecotourism: Benefits for conservation and local people?" *African Wildlife* 60, 3, 2006, 16–18.

102. Isaac Tembe, community development liaison, and Les Carlisle, regional development manager, interviews with Chafe, Phinda, December 2004, and author, 1995–2007.

103. Spencely and Seif, "Strategies, Impacts and Costs," 14.

104. Bheki Ntuli, interview with Chafe, Phinda, December 2004.

105. Zoe Chafe, research notes from Phinda, December 2004.

106. Spenceley, "Ecotourism: Benefits."

107. Correspondence with Wendy Wood, executive director, Friends of Africa Foundation, which raises funds for the foundation in the United States, January 2007; interview with Ntul, December 2004.

108. Information obtained from the Africa Foundation, see www.africafoundation.org/about/default.php. See also CC Africa's Responsible Safaris Web site, which describes their community outreach and conservation projects at Phinda and other lodges, at www.responsiblesafaris.com/south_africa/phinda_private_game_reserve/2/default.php.

109. FTTSA, "Case Study 1: Calabash Lodge & Tours," undated. Copy obtained by Anna Spenceley.

110. Jennifer Seif, Fair Trade in Tourism South Africa (FTTSA), interview, November 2004.

111. See www.fairtourismsa.org.za and www.calabashtours.co.za.

112. Gootbos Private Nature Reserve, Eye on Africa, see www.eyesonafrica.net/south-african-safari/grootbos.htm.

113. Green Futures, see www.greenfutures.co.za/supporters.htm.

114. Gootbos is an FTTSA certified business, see www.fairtourismsa.org.za/temp/grootbos.html.

115. Anna Spenceley, "Certification in Africa," draft of article submitted to *Tourism Management*; J. Seif, *Trademark Users' Guide*, (Pretoria: FTTSA and IUCN, 2002), various interviews with Jennifer Seif, executive director, FTTSA, 2004–2006; FTTSA, "Tourism Certification Programme," see www.fairtourismsa.org.za/trademark/Tourism.pdf. In addition to FTTSA, several other green experiments were tried in South Africa to set and measure environmental and social standards. These include a short-lived branding experiment by CC Africa and the National Geographic Society; a Heritage Ecotourism Rating Program run by Qualitour, a private company and the international certification program Green Globe; and the Department of Environment Affairs and Tourism's National Guidelines for Sustainable Tourism released for the 2002 International Year of Ecotourism.

116. FTTSA, see www.fairtourismsa.org.za/aboutus/index.html.

117. Tourism Grading Council, "Our History," see www.tourismgrading.co.za/tgcsa/view/tgcsa/en/page20.

118. Correspondence with Spenceley, January 2007.

119. J. Seif and K. Gordon, *FTTSA Trademark Users' Guide*, 2nd ed. (Pretoria: FTTSA and IUCN, 2003), see www.fairtourismsa.org.za.

120. See www.fairtourismsa.org.za/trademark/Tourism.pdf.

121. Zoe Chafe's interviews with CC Africa and Wilderness Safaris officials, November–December 2004.

122. In the original edition of this book, I quoted a number experts, including staff and former managers, who listed a number of complaints. Honey, *Who Owns Paradise*, 377–39.

123. Hilton Loon, correspondence with author, February 2007.

124. Fair Trade in Tourism South Africa (FTTSA), "Sabi Sabi," see www.fairtourismsa.org.za/fttsa/display.php?id=125. In fact, Sabi Sabi had received eco-awards in the 1990s, but, as described in chapter 2, at that time these awards were

usually based on self-nomination with no on-site inspection. With the advent of certification, a number of these awards have become more rigorous, and therefore more valuable to the recipient and the public.

125. Patrick Shorten, general manager, Sabi Sabi, interview with Zoe Chafe, Johannesburg, December 2004.

126. FTTSA, "Sabi Sabi."

127. Shorten, interview, December 2004.

128. Loon, correspondence, February 2007.

129. Among the complaints I heard from staff in the mid-1990s: the staff committee was handpicked by the owner rather than elected by the workers, transport for workers on their days off was not provided, and management had stopped offering literacy classes and skill-training projects.

130. Sabi Sabi is recognized throughout South Africa for what was seen as a courageous step in appointing a black ranger to what was then an all-white profession. In correspondence, Hilton Loon recalled, "This may not seem remarkable to you in a free America but we recall that at the time every hotel in South Africa, in terms of apartheid laws required that in order to admit a nonwhite guest, including visitors from abroad, we were compelled to telephone a government agency in Pretoria in order to obtain permission to admit that guest!" Loon, correspondence, February 2007.

131. Eddie Koch, director of Mafisa Research and Planning, interview with Zoe Chafe, Johannesburg, December, 2004.

132. Jennifer Seif, FTTSA, interviews with Zoe Chafe, Pretoria, November 2004.

133. Information on products that did not meet these criteria is retained within the database, but is not publicly available on the RETOSA Web site, www.retosa.org. A. Spenceley and Z. Rozga, *UNWTO/STEP-ESA/RETOSA (Regional Tourism Organization of Southern Africa)/SNV Tourism Practice Areas (East and South Africa), Technical Assistance to RETOSA for Update of Database and Marketing Support for Community-based Tourism Products in Southern Africa*, final report to UNWTO, November 3, 2006.

134. RETOSA, see www.retosa.org.

135. Stephanie Saville, "Crime weights down SA tourism figures," *Cape Times*, February 7, 2007.

136. Author's visit to Kwabhe Kithunga and Stewarts Farm, August 2005.

Chapter 10: Ecotourism in the United States

1. Rachel S. Cox, "Protecting the National Parks," *CQ Researcher* 10, no. 23, June 16, 2000, 532; Mark Dowie, "The Hidden Cost of Paradise: Indigenous People are Being Displaced to Create Wilderness Areas, to the Detriment of All," *Stanford Social Innovation Review*, Spring 2006, 33.

2. Philip Burnham, *Indian Country, God's Country: Native Americans and the National Parks* (Washington, D.C.: Island Press, 2000), 20.

3. Dowie, "The Hidden Cost of Paradise," 33.

4. Ibid., 32–34.

5. Alaska Native Science Commission (ANSC), "Impacts of Eco-Tourism:

Alaska Native Perspective," 2004; personal correspondence with Patricia Cochran, ANSC executive director who wrote the report, September 2007.

6. ProQuest, "United States' Travel and Tourism Policy," see http://proquest.umi.com.proxygw.wrlc.org/pqdweb?index=30?sid+4&srchmode=1&vins.

7. The next five states are Illinois, Ohio, North Carolina, Georgia, and Virginia. Malinda Geisler, content specialist, AgMRC, Iowa State University, "Agritourism Profile," August 2007, AgMRC, see www.agmrc.org/agmrc/commodity/agri tourism/agritourism/agritourismprofile.htm.

8. U.S. Travel and Tourism Advisory Board, Restoring America's Travel Brand: National Strategy to Compete for International Visitors, Recommendations to the U.S. Secretary of Commerce, September 5, 2006, 6. See www.commerce.gov/opa/pressSecretary_Gutierrez/2006_Releases/September/TTAB%20National %20Tourism%20Strategy.pdf.

9. U.S. State Department, "Overview of Sustainable Ecotourism in the United States of America," April 8, 2002, ten pages submitted to the World Ecotourism Summit, May 2002, 8, see www.state.gov/g/oes/rls/or/19412.htm.

10. U.N. World Tourism Organization (UNWTO), *World Tourism Barometer*, January 2006, cited in *Restoring America's Travel Brand*, 4.

11. Cited in *Restoring America's Travel Brand*, 5, 6.

12. Tien X. Tian, vice president and chief economist, Travel Industry Association of America, interview with author, September, 2007.

13. State Department, "Overview," 1.

14. U.S. Dept of Commerce, "2002 Survey of US Resident Travelers to Overseas Destinations," cited in *CESD*, "Fact Sheet: Ecotourism in the U.S.," September 2005, see www.ecotourismcesd.org.

15. Travel Industry Association of America (TIA) and *National Geographic Traveler* (NGT), "Geotourism: The New Trend in Travel. Overview of American Travelers," 2003. This refers to the second portion of a two-part study. Cited in "Fact Sheet: Ecotourism in the U.S."

16. National Marketing Institute's 2005 LOHAS study, LOHAS Consumer Trends Database, www.lohas8.com/market, cited in "Fact Sheet: Ecotourism in the U.S."

17. International Hotels Environment Initiative (IHEI), "Consumer Attitudes Towards the Role of Hotels in International Environmental Sustainability," Press release of report commissioned by Small Luxury Hotels of the World, July 23, 2002, see www.hotel-online.com/Neo/News/PR2002_3rd/Jul02_IHEI.html.

18. TIA, press release, "U.S. National Parks Enjoy High Awareness and Satisfaction Among American Travelers," February 25, 2004, see www.tia.org/researchpubs/ra_aug1704.html. TIA is a nonprofit organization representing the whole of the U.S. travel industry, whose mission is to promote and facilitate increased travel to and within the United States. It partnered with the National Parks Service and the National Park Foundation to launch a "See America's National Parks" campaign, see www.SeeAmerica.org.

19. State Department, "Overview."

20. Cited in Linda Lange, "Growth of ecotourism reflects travelers' desires for responsibility," *Knoxville News Sentinel*, December 31, 2006.

21. Defenders of Wildlife, "Incentives for Ecosystem Restoration in Wisconsin: A Public-Private Partnership in Agricultural Stewardship," n.d., see www.defend

ers.org/resources/publications/programs_and_policy/science_and_economics/conservation_economics/fact_sheet_wolf_ecotourism.pdf.

22. Erdmann adds, "We don't agree. The U.S. needs a high-level tourism office to effectively promote our country and provide services to tourism businesses." Ron Erdmann, OTTI, U.S. Department of Commerce, Washington, D.C., telephone interview and email correspondence with author, September–October, 2007.

23. OTTI is a member of some regional trade associations, including the APEC (Asia Pacific Economic Cooperation) Tourism Working Group and the OCED (Organization for Economic Cooperation and Development) Tourism Committee.

24. In recent years, the OTTI and TIA have collaborated in tourism-promotion campaigns in the U.K. and Japan, both top sender markets, and in 2008, expanded to target the five top markets. As Erdmann put it, "We're fishing where the fish are."

25. International Trade Administration (ITA), Office of Travel and Tourism Industry, Department of Commerce, "Travel and Tourism and the U.S. Department of Commerce," see http://tinet.ita.doc.gov/outreachpages/commerce_team.html.

26. ITA et al., "Travel and Tourism and the U.S. Department of Commerce."

27. Erdmann, interview.

28. Mintel, *Inbound Tourism - US - May 2005, Advertising and Promotion* (UK: Mintel International Group, 2005), 1.

29. For instance, the 2005 Bar Harbor Declaration (see endnote 82) that came out of the national ecotourism conference urged that the government "Reinstate official U.S. membership in the World Tourism Organization, and endorse the WTO's 'Global Code of Ethics in Tourism'." The 2006 study, *Restoring America's Travel Brand,* presented the U.S. Secretary of Commerce a broad set of reforms for increasing tourism marketing and strengthening federal agencies.

30. ITA, OTTI, Department of Commerce, "Tourism Policy," see http://tinet.ita.doc.gov/about/tourism_policy.html.

31. Department of Commerce, "Secretary Evans Convenes Meeting of Cabinet Secretaries to address Travel and Tourism Industry Recovery Efforts," press release, October 29, 2001, see www.commerce.gov/opa/press/Secretary_Evans/2001_Releases/Oct_29_Evans_Tourism_Cabinet.html.

32. Denis Galvin, Deputy Director, National Park Service (Retired) on Behalf of National Parks Conservation Association, tesimony before the U.S. Senate Subcommittee on National Parks, November 1, 2005, see www.npca.org/media_center/testimonies/testimony110105.html. Galvin notes that taken together, "all these agencies provide for many forms of public recreation—but not all forms of recreation are appropriate in national parks."

33. Alicia Pinto, *Ecotourism Case Studies in the United States* (Burlington, VT: TIES, 2000), 6.

34. State Department, "Overview."

35. Ibid., 4–5.

36. Ibid., 7.

37. Ibid., 7; NOAA, Sea Grant National, "Sea Grant's 2006 4th Quarter Highlights," see www.seagrant.noaa.gov/aboutsg/archive_sg_highlights/sghighlights_4qtr_2006.html; and "Sea Grant Communications Fact Book: Mid-Atlantic Region," see www.seagrant.noaa.gov/communicators/midatlantic.html.

38. John H. Cushman Jr., "Wildlife Bureau Weighs Eco-tourism Policy," *New York Times*, January 19, 1997.

39. Cushman, "Wildlife Bureau Weighs Eco-tourism"; Cushman, "Tourism Venture Ends on Midway Atoll Refuge," *New York Times*, March 31, 2002. Another article concluded that the "promising experiment" in ecotourism turned into "a model of the kinds of problems that can go wrong in managing wildlands through a public-private partnership." Pamela Frierson, "How Paradise Lost a Radical Public-Private Venture," *The Christian Science Monitor*, June 26, 2002, see www.csmonitor.com/2002/0626/p02s01-usgn.html.

40. U.S. Environmental Protection Agency, "Agency Overview," see www.epa.gov/history/org/origins/overview.htm.

41. State Department, "Overview," 8.

42. U.S. Environmental Protection Agency, Software for Environmental Awareness, "Environmental Enrichment for the Lodging Industry: A Toolkit," see www.epa.gov/seahome/hotels.html.

43. U.S. Environmental Protection Agency, "Partnership Programs," see www.epa.gov/partners.

44. Actually, the first effort by any government to set aside protected lands was in 1832 when President Andrew Jackson signed legislation authorizing creation of the Hot Springs Reservation in Arkansas. However, federal control over these thermal springs and surrounding mountains was not clearly established until 1877.

45. Richard West Sellars, *Preserving Nature in the National Parks* (New Haven: Yale University Press, 1997), 4, quoted in Cox, "Protecting the National Parks," 532.

46. Tom Arrandale, "National Parks Under Pressure," *CQ Researcher* 16, no. 35, October 6, 2006, 827.

47. William Cronon, "The Trouble with Wilderness," in William Cronon, ed., *Uncommon Ground: Rethinking the Human Place in Nature* (New York: W.W. Norton & Company, 1996), cited in Emy Rodriguez, "Ecotourism in the United States: A Vehicle for Sustainable Development," submitted to Graduate Program in Sustainable Development and Conservation Biology, University of Maryland, November 2005, 10. Burnham's *Indian Country, God's Country* is a thoroughly researched and devastating account of the abuses of Native Americans in creating the U.S. National Parks System.

48. Cox, "Protecting the National Parks," 532.

49. Rachel S. Cox, "Ecotourism," *CQ Researcher* 16, no. 37, Oct. 20, 2006, 877.

50. Cox, "Protecting the National Parks," 532.

51. Arrandale, "National Parks Under Pressure," 828.

52. Quoted in Dowie, "The Hidden Cost of Paradise," 32.

53. Arrandale, "National Parks Under Pressure," 830.

54. Cox, "Protecting the National Parks," 523.

55. Commission for Environmental Cooperation (CEC), "The Development of Sustainable Tourism in Natural Areas of North America: Background, Issues and Opportunities." Discussion paper prepared for CEC workshop, A Dialogue on Sustainable Tourism in Natural Areas in North America, Playa del Carmen, Mexico, 1999. Author attended this conference. Also cited in Rodriguez, "Ecotourism in the United States," 30.

56. Cox, "Protecting the National Parks," 532.

57. Ibid., 523.

58. Arrandale, "National Parks Under Pressure," 819.

59. This list is compiled mainly from two excellent CQ Researcher articles, Cox, "Protecting the National Parks" and Arrandale, "National Parks Under Pressure."

60. James Ridenour, "Confronting the Crisis in our National Parks," *USA Today*, Society for the Advancement of Education, September 1997, see http://findarticles.com/p/articles/mi_m1272/is_n2628_v126/ai_19782183.

61. Arrandale, "National Parks Under Pressure," 831.

62. Cox, "Protecting the National Parks," 525.

63. Arrandale, "National Parks Under Pressure," 828–829.

64. Ibid., 830. The Rockefellers were particularly important: John D., Jr. donated $25 million plus land in Grand Teton, Great Smoky Mountains, Shenandoah, and Yosemite, while Laurence donated land in the U.S. Virgin Islands. The Rockefeller family helped the National Parks Service acquire lands for Big Bend, Glacier, Grand Canyon, Lassen Volcanic, Olympic, and Rocky Mountain national parks; Antietam, Big Hole, and Fort Donelson national battlefields; and Capulin Volcano National Monument. "National Park Stewardship: Vermont Law School Honors the Legacy of Laurence S. Rockefeller," press release, Vermont Law School, November 2, 2004, see www.vermontlaw.edu/media/emp_medpre_template.cfm?doc_id=969.

65. Arrandale, "National Parks Under Pressure," 829.

66. For an excellent account of the changing views on how to use science to manage parks see Robert Manning, *Parks and Carrying Capacity: Commons Without Tragedy* (Washington, D.C.: Island Press, 2007).

67. Arrandale, "National Parks Under Pressure," 830.

68. Ibid., 830–832.

69. "Destination Scorecard: The List," *National Geographic Traveler*, July/August 2005, 82.

70. Ibid., 92. The Everglades has long been on a downward spiral. When the Everglades became a national park in 1947, it was a vast, unspoiled marshland ecosystem. By the early 1990s, rampant development in South Florida had reduced the wetlands to half their original size and the bird population had declined 70 percent. Cox, "Protecting the National Parks," 523.

71. "Destination Scorecard," 91, 92.

72. "Great Divide: The Fight for America's Heritage," *The Independent* (London), March 9, 2007.

73. "Great Divide," *The Independent*.

74. Ibid.; Another report notes that the platform offers "a vantage point more than twice as high as the world's tallest buildings." Devika Bhat, "Glass Platform Opens up Grand Canyon Chasm," *Times Online* (London), March 20, 2007.

75. "In the News," *The Scout Report*, March 23, 2007, see http://scout.wisc.edu/Reports/ScoutReport/2007/scout-070323-inthenews.php.

76. "Great Divide," *The Independent*.

77. References in this paragraph are from the various newspaper reports of the opening ceremony, cited above.

78. These issues are discussed as well in chapters 1 and 3.

79. The U.S. National Parks Service ranks Acadia the tenth most visited national park. Cited in Arrandale, "National Parks Under Pressure," 820.

80. Todd Gabe, "Economic Impact of Cruise Ship Passengers in Bar Harbor, Maine," REP Staff Paper 518, Department of Resource Economics and Policy, University of Maine, March 2003, see www.umext.maine.edu/topics/cruise.pdf; CESD, "Cruise Tourism in Belize: Perceptions of Economic, Social & Environmental Impact," November 2006, see www.ecotourismcesd.org.

81. In the minds of much of the traveling public, ecotourism is perceived as rooted most strongly in developing countries. In fact, a number of developed countries have active and, in some cases, high-profile ecotourism sectors. These include Australia, New Zealand, Canada, Sweden, Norway, Germany, and Italy.

82. "Bar Harbor Declaration on Ecotourism in the U.S.: A Road Map for Responsible Tourism Development," drafted by Martha Honey, executive director, TIES and Costas Christ, executive director, Bar Harbor Chamber of Commerce and approved by conference participants, September 2005, see www.ecotourism.org/webmodules/webarticlesnet/articlefiles/36-bar%20harbor%20de claration.pdf.

83. "Virginia Ecotour Guide Certification Program," Virginia Department of Environmental Quality, see www.deq.state.va.us/coastal/seasidewatertrail/tour guides.html.

84. Among the various Web sites are Whale Watch Operators Association Northwest, see www.nwwhalewatchers.org/ and The Whale Museum, see www.whale-museum.org/education/library/whalewatch/watchmain.html.

85. In 1994, United Airlines' in-flight magazine dubbed Selengut "the travel industry's green guru." Since then he's garnered a string of accolades and honors, including, in 2008, the American Hotel & Lodging Association (AH&LA) "Pioneer Award" as one of the "fathers of 'ecotourism.'" Ann Kalosh, "The Travel Industry's Green Guru: An Interview with Stanley Selengut," *Hemispheres*, United Airlines flight magazine, April 1994; "ALIS Programming Goes Green," AH&LA News Release, August 22, 2007, see www.ahla.com/news_view_reease.asp?mstr=602.

86. Stanley Selengut, interview, Maho Bay, St. John, December 1994 and January 1995; "Ecotourism Investigation," *Agenda 21*, Worldwide Television News, London, March 1995, produced by author and Tony Avirgan.

87. Cited by Ginny Fay, director, DCED Division of Tourism, "Marketing and Guiding Alaska Tourism—Defining Our Roles," AWRTA, 7th Annual Ecotourism in Alaska Conference, Anchorage, Alaska, February 3, 2000.

88. Alaska Wildland Adventures, see www.alaskawildland.com.

89. "Overview," Alaska Wilderness, Ecotourism, & Cultural Trip Planning Information, AWRTA, see www.awrta.org/index.cfm?section=native.

90. Alaska Native Heritage Center, see www.alaskanative.net.

91. Department of Business, Economic Development & Tourism (DBED&T), State of Hawaii, *Planning for Sustainable Tourism*, April 2006, 21–26. Copy in author's possession.

92. DBED&T, *Planning for Sustainable Tourism*, 25.

93. Geisler, "Agritourism Profile," 2007.

94. Hawaii Ecotourism Association, see http://hawaiiecotourism.org.

95. In 2003, I was invited to give presentations at one of these lively and well-attended public meetings, organized by John Knox, as well as to attend some

community meetings organized by the Sierra Club to discuss cruise tourism. Both HEA and the Sierra Club, along with several dozen other tourism experts, were part of the study's advisory group.

96. DBED&T, *Planning for Sustainable Tourism*, 50.

97. While the commission was publicly criticized for its failure to come up with a precise figure for the acceptable carrying capacity for tourism in Hawaii, I would agree with the report's assessment that "it has been very difficult to apply the notion of 'carrying capacity' developed for specific environmental areas, to the level of regional tourism." DBED&T, *Planning for Sustainable Tourism*, 12. The notion of carrying capacity has evolved over the last several decades, as Manning outlines in his book, *Parks and Carrying Capacity*.

98. One of the conclusions of the report is that "residents have a larger overall impact on key infrastructure and resources than do tourists," which would imply that sustainable long-term development will involve looking at consumption by the permanent residents and not simply the tourist population. DBED&T, *Planning for Sustainable Tourism*; "Sustainable tourism study breaks little new ground," *Pacific Business News*, April 28, 2006, see www.bizjournals.com/pacific/stories/2006/05/01/story1.html.

99. "Sustainable tourism study breaks little new ground."

100. "Sussex County, Delaware – Embraces Ecotourism," in Pinto, *Ecotourism Case Studies*, 30–34.

101. "About Vermont: The Green Mountain Character," see www.visit-vermont.com/about_vt.html.

102. Program, "Ecotourism and Regional Sustainability: Foundations for Tourism Development," July 2000, Johnson State College, Johnson, Vermont. I was privileged to be one of the keynote speakers.

103. Geisler, "Agritourism Profile," 2007.

104. In April 2006, I was invited by Audubon to participate in a workshop on ecotourism in Vicksburg, Mississippi. Subsequent correspondence with Bruce Reid, Lower Mississippi River programs director, National Audubon Society.

105. "Florida – Rethinking Tourism," in Pinto, *Ecotourism Case Studies*, 20–28.

106. I took part in several statewide conferences, as did a number of other international ecotourism experts. Ron Mader, "Exploring Ecotourism: What West Virginia can learn from ecotourism in the Americas," Planeta.com, see www.planeta.com/planeta/99/1299wv.html.

107. West Virginia Department of Environmental Protection and West Virginia Division of Tourism, "Memorandum of Agreement: Growing the WV Ecotourism Industry," 2001, cited in "Fact Sheet: Ecotourism in the U.S."

108. "Berkeley Springs: What is Ecotourism in Morgan Country, West Virginia?" see www.berkeleysprings.com/ecotourism/econotes.htm.

109. Christina Talcott, "In West Virginia, Eco-Tourism is Becoming Second Nature," *Washington Post*, August 26, 2005, see www.washingtonpost.com/wp-dyn/content/article/2005/08/25/AR2005082500706.html; Tara Tuckwiller, "States Aim to Attract Ecotourists," *The Charleston Gazette*, July 19, 2005, Environmental News Network, see www.enn.com/top_stories/article/2088?PHPSESSID=00aadd909b9226aa340bd8d19df517d0/print/print.

110. Silos & Smokestacks National Heritage Area, see www.silosandsmokestacks.org.

111. Frances Figart, "Goodness Sells: A Modest Proposal for the Rebranding of Ecotourism in the United States," Planeta Forum, updated October 12, 2006, see www.planeta.com/planeta/05/0509goodness.html.

112. Sometimes the even clumsier term "agriecotourism" is used.

113. Geisler, "Agritourism Profile," 2007.

114. Ibid.

115. State Department, "Overview," 1.

116. Sun Ranch, Papoose Creek Lodge, "Guest Directory," 2007, 25.

117. Bill Bryan, "Ecotourism on Family Farms and Ranches in the American West," in Tensie Whelan, ed., *Nature Tourism: Managing for the Environment* (Washington, D.C.: Island Press, 1991), 75–78.

118. Bryan, "Ecotourism," 77–82.

119. Ibid., 82.

120. Paul Rogers, "Betting the Ranch," *Stanford Magazine*, November/December 2004, see www.stanfordalumni.org/news/magazine/2004/novdec/features/ranch.html. Roger and Cindy Lang have since divorced, but both retain a financial and personal interest in Papoose Creek Lodge and Sun Ranch.

121. Roger Lang, discussions with author and other guests, Papoose Creek Lodge, August 2007, January 2008.

122. Rogers, "Betting the Ranch."

123. Hitesh Mehta, a TIES board member, argues that no forms of hunting and fishing (even catch-and-release) can be considered ecotourism. Roger Lang, in turn, defends sustainable hunting and fishing as part of keeping a balanced wildlife.

124. Sun Ranch, Papoose Creek, "Guest Directory," 27.

125. Sun Ranch press release, "Two Wolves Killed on Sun Ranch," August 2, 2006; Press release, "Sleeping with Cattle—and Wolves," n.d., see www.papoosecreek.com/news/releases/releases.asp.

126. Bill Bryan, interviews via telephone and e-mail, September 2007; "Interview: Bill and Pam Bryan: The Intricate Balance," August 22, 2007, Adventure Collection, see http://donsplace.adventurecollection.com/interview.php; Off the Beaten Path, see www.offthebeatenpath.com/about-obp/company-history.

127. Bill Bryan, interview.

128. Adventure Collection, see www.adventurecollection.com/about/timeline.

129. Lindblad Expeditions, see www.expeditions.com.

130. "Our Travel Ethic," Adventure Collection, see www.adventurecollection.com/about/ethic.

131. "Our Member Companies: O.A.R.S.," Adventure Collection, see www.adventurecollection.com/members/oars.

132. "Our Member Companies: NOLS," Adventure Collection, see www.adventurecollection.com/members/nols.

133. Green Hotel Association, "Green Travel: How Green are Your Travels?" see www.greenhotels.com/grntrav.htm.

134. Doreen Hemlock, "South Florida Hotels Find Going Green Helps Bottom Line and the Planet," South Florida Sun-Sentinel, August 26, 2007, see www.hotel-online.com/News/PR2007_3rd/Aug07_FlaGreen.html.

135. From samples of cards collected by the author from various hotels.

136. Patricia Griffin, "'Green' Hotels Association Impacts Entire Hospitality Industry," press release, "Green" Hotel Association, www.greenhotels.com.

137. "Green" Hotels Association, various sections and press releases; Kristen Bellstrom, "Eco-Lodging," *SmartMoney*, September 14, 2007, see www.smartmoney.com/mag/index.cfm?story=september2007-eco.

138. A quick Internet search turns up dozens of "green" or "environmentally friendly" sites, all listing hotels. In 2002, for instance, Griffin was given ASTA's Environmental Award for "elevating environmentalism in the hospitality industry." "Green" Hotels Association, press release.

139. In 2004, for instance, the American Hotel and Lodging Association (AHLA) created the Good Earthkeeping Alliance in partnership with the EPA, to help hoteliers assess energy performance. Marge O'Conner, "Sustainable Travel: Bright Ideas—Saving Energy Improves Guest Comfort and Bottom Line," see http://blog.sustainabletravel.com/bright_ideas_saving_energy_imp.html.

140. See www.mohonk.com.

141. Jestena Boughton, telephone interview with author, September 7, 2007. Both hotels were founding members of the national Green Hotels Association (1995) and have been certified under the Audubon Green Leaf Eco-Rating (2004). The Colony in Delray Beach is among the first hotels certified under the Florida EPA's Green Lodging Certification Program (2006), and the Maine resort was voted one of the 50 best hotels in the world (1998), and lays claim to being Maine's first environmental hotel.

142. In the interview, Boughton said that while there are often "no easy answers" to various problems, on the whole, the various "green" certification programs have been beneficial. "The good thing," she notes, "about audits is that they give a framework for measuring performance and an incentive to do better." But, she suggests, certification programs should have a special category for historic hotels: "We should get points for conserving and preserving, for fixing up, not knocking down."

143. "Eco-lodging," *SmartMoney*.

144. Kimberly Lisagor, "TravelSmart: Tap a 'green' hotel," *USA Weekend Magazine*, July 24, 2005.

145. "Eco-Lodging," *SmartMoney*.

146. Martha Honey and Emma Stewart, "The Evolution of 'Green' Standards for Tourism," in Honey, *Ecotourism and Certification: Settings Standards in Practice* (Washington, D.C.: Island Press, 2002), 61–62.

147. ECOTEL, see www.concepthospitality.com/ecotel/ECOTEL.htm; Correspondence with Harinakshi Nair, senior associate, HVS Eco Services - Mumbai, September 2007. Nair wrote that Ecotel is still "very much active."

148. Audubon International, "Green Leaf Eco-Rating Program," see www.terrachoice.ca/hotelWeb site/indexcanada.htm. The Colony owner Boughton described the Green Leaf criteria as "very very difficult." Boughton interview.

149. U.S. Green Building Council, "LEED," see www.usgbc.org/DisplayPage.aspx?CMSPageID=64&; Hotel Chatter, "Taking the Eco-Lead: Hotels Jump on Green LEED Certification Bandwagon," July 16, 2007, see www.hotelchatter.com/story/2007/7/16/141131/304/hotels/Taking_the_Eco_Lead_Hotels_Jump_On_Green_LEED_Certification_Bandwagon_; Bellstrom, "Eco-Lodging."

150. "Eco-Certification," Sustainable Travel International, see www.sustainabletravelinternational.org/documents/op_ecocertification.html.

151. Green Seal, see www.greenseal.org/certification/standards/lodgingproperties.cfm.

152. In late 2006, The AH&LA, the voice of the lodging industry, announced that it was going to "increase the volume of conversation about the environment" because of growing interest among its member hotels. Mark Petruzzi, Green Seal VP of Certification, "Achieving Certification: Greening the Hospitality Industry," February 6–8, 2007, powerpoint, see www.greenmeetings.info/presentations/2007/AchievingCertification_GHIC2007.pdf.

153. The states include Florida, Maine, Michigan, Virginia, California, North Carolina, Vermont, Pennsylvania, Maryland, Georgia, New Hampshire, Wisconsin, and the District of Columbia.

154. Glenn Hasek, "More States Should Develop Green Lodging Certification Programs," Green Lodging News, July 29, 2007, see www.greenlodgingnews.com/Content.aspx?=1258.

155. Laura McLendon and Abigail Rome, CESD, "Marketing Strategies for Tourism Certification Programs and Lessons Learned for Sustainable Tourism Certification: Programs in North America," September 29, 2004, 10–11, see www.ecotourismcesd.org; Green Hotels in the Green Mountain State, see www.vtgreenhotels.org.

156. Florida Department of Environmental Protection, "About Green Lodging," see www.dep.state.fl.us/greenlodging/about.htm.

157. "Two Key West Resorts Get Florida 'Green Lodging' Approval," *Hotel Chatter*, August 23, 2007, see www.hotelchatter.com/tag/Green%20Hotels; Hasek, "More States."

158. In March 2006, the Hyatt Regency Coconut Point Resort and Spa in Bonita Springs was awarded Two Palm Certification status. Press Office, Florida Department of Environmental Protection, "Florida Resort Achieves the State's First Two Palm Green Lodging Certification," March 9, 2006, see www.dep.state .fl.us/secretary/news/2006/03/0309/_02.htm.

159. Hemlock, "South Florida Hotels."

160. Rainforest Alliance, "Sustainable Tourism: Sustainable Tourism Stewardship Council," see www.rainforest-alliance.org/tourism.cfm?id=network; Michael E. Conroy, "Can Tourism be Tamed: Toward a Sustainable Tourism Stewardship Council," in *Branded: How the 'Certification Revolution' is Transforming Global Corporations* (Gabriola Island, BC, Canada: New Society Publishers, 2007), 149–168.

161. Petruzzi, "Achieving Certification."

162. Hasek, "More States."

163. Bellstram, "Eco-lodging," *SmartMoney*.

164. AH&LA News Release, August 22, 2007.

165. State Department, "Overview," 1.

166. Lange, "Growth of ecotourism."

167. State Department, "Overview," 4.

168. Ibid.

169. The Anholt-GMIK Nation Brands Index, quoted in *Restoring America's Travel Brand*, 6.

Conclusion

1. CESD and INCAE, *Cruise Tourism Impacts in Costa Rica and Honduras: Policy Recommendations for Decision Makers,* January 2007, see http://eco

tourismcesd.org/webarticles/articlefiles / 42-Cruise_Tourism_Impacts_in _Costa_Rica_Honduras.pdf; CESD, "Cruise Tourism in Belize: Perceptions of Economic, Social & Environmental Impact," November 2006, see www.eco tourismcesd.org; Eddie Koch, *Reality or Rhetoric? Ecotourism and Rural Reconstruction in South Africa* (Geneva: United Nations Research Institute for Social Development, August 1994), 6, 10, 2.

2. International Institute for Environment and Development (IIED), *Whose Eden? An Overview of Community Approaches to Wildlife Management* (London: Overseas Development Administration, July 1994), 19.

3. David Grossman and Eddie Koch, *Ecotourism Report—Nature Tourism in South Africa: Links with the Reconstruction and Development Program,* (Pretoria, South Africa: SATOUR, August 1995), 22.

4. Ibid., 22; Marshall Murphree, "The Role of Institutions in Community-based Conservation," in David Western and R. Michael Wright, eds., *Natural Connections: Perspectives in Community-Based Conservation* (Washington, D.C.: Island Press, 1994), 403–427.

5. John S. Akama, "Western Environmental Values and Nature-Based Tourism in Kenya," *Tourism Management* 17, no. 8, 1996, 573.

Index

Island Press | Board of Directors